Let Us Prove Strong

Brandeis Series in American Jewish History, Culture, and Life

Jonathan D. Sarna, Editor
Sylvia Barack Fishman, Associate Editor

For a complete list of books in the series, visit www.upne.com and www.upne.com/series/BSAJ.html

Marianne R. Sanua
Let Us Prove Strong: The American Jewish Committee, 1945–2006

Hollace Ava Weiner and Kenneth D. Roseman, editors
Lone Stars of David: The Jews of Texas

Jack Wertheimer, editor
Jewish Education in an Age of Choice

Edward S. Shapiro
Crown Heights: Blacks, Jews, and the 1991 Brooklyn Riot

Kirsten Fermaglich
American Dreams and Nazi Nightmares: Early Holocaust Consciousness and Liberal America, 1957–1965

Andrea Greenbaum, editor
Jews of South Florida

Sylvia Barack Fishman
Double or Nothing? Jewish Families and Mixed Marriage

George M. Goodwin and Ellen Smith, editors
The Jews of Rhode Island

Shulamit Reinharz and Mark A. Raider, editors
American Jewish Women and the Zionist Enterprise

Michael E. Staub, editor
The Jewish 1960s: An American Sourcebook

Judah M. Cohen
Through the Sands of Time: A History of the Jewish Community of St. Thomas, U.S. Virgin Islands

Naomi W. Cohen
The Americanization of Zionism, 1897–1948

Seth Farber
An American Orthodox Dreamer: Rabbi Joseph B. Soloveitchik and Boston's Maimonides School

Ava F. Kahn and Marc Dollinger, editors
California Jews

Amy L. Sales and Leonard Saxe
"How Goodly Are Thy Tents": Summer Camps as Jewish Socializing Experiences

Ori Z. Soltes
Fixing the World: Jewish American Painters in the Twentieth Century

Gary P. Zola, editor
The Dynamics of American Jewish History: Jacob Rader Marcus's Essays on American Jewry

David Zurawik
The Jews of Prime Time

Ranen Omer-Sherman
Diaspora and Zionism in American Jewish Literature: Lazarus, Syrkin, Reznikoff, and Roth

Ilana Abramovitch and Seán Galvin, editors
Jews of Brooklyn

Pamela S. Nadell and Jonathan D. Sarna, editors
Women and American Judaism: Historical Perspectives

Annelise Orleck, with photographs by Elizabeth Cooke
The Soviet Jewish Americans

Steven T. Rosenthal
Irreconcilable Differences: The Waning of the American Jewish Love Affair with Israel

Let Us Prove Strong

The American Jewish Committee, 1945–2006

MARIANNE R. SANUA

Brandeis University Press
Waltham, Massachusetts

PUBLISHED BY UNIVERSITY PRESS OF NEW ENGLAND
HANOVER AND LONDON

BRANDEIS UNIVERSITY PRESS
Published by University Press of New England,
One Court Street, Lebanon, NH 03766
www.upne.com
© 2007 by Brandeis University Press
Printed in the United States of America
5 4 3 2 1

Library of Congress Cataloging-in-Publication Data

Sanua, Marianne Rachel.
Let us prove strong : the American Jewish Committee, 1945–2006 / Marianne R. Sanua.
    p.   cm. — (Brandeis series in American Jewish history, culture, and life)
Includes bibliographical references and index.
ISBN–13: 978–1–58465–631–9 (cloth : alk. paper)
ISBN–10: 1–58465–631–X (cloth : alk. paper)
    1. American Jewish Committee. 2. Jews—United States—History—20th century. 3. Jews—United States—Politics and government. I. Title.
E184.355.S25 2007
973'.04924—dc22   2006101274

The Seal of the American Jewish Committee

חֲזַק וְנִתְחַזְּקָה בְּעַד-עַמֵּנוּ

Be of good courage,
and let us prove strong for our people
(I Chronicles 19:13)

Contents

Foreword

The first seven days of May 2006, saw close to two thousand men and women assemble in Washington, D.C., to celebrate the 100th Annual Meeting of the American Jewish Committee. An opening symposium at the Library of Congress asked: "What Will Become of the Jewish People?". In response, four of the world's greatest Jewish intellectuals debated the centrality of Zion, the distinctiveness of America, and the role of antisemitism and Jewish power in the world today. Subsequent sessions, each addressed by notable experts, focused upon Jewish spirituality, models of Jewish community, the crisis in the Middle East, the changing face of American Jewry, and the dangers facing Jews at home and abroad. At a climactic reception and dinner to honor the centennial, President George W. Bush, U.N. Security-General Kofi Annan, and German Chancellor Angela Merkel each underscored the critical role played by the American Jewish Committee in safeguarding Jewish security and human rights around the world. "For a hundred years," President Bush declared, "American Presidents have benefited from the good advice of the American Jewish Committee. . . . You have had a profound impact on American political life because you have worked tirelessly for noble goals."

The Washington gathering spotlighted the agenda and significance of the American Jewish Committee, as well as its emergence as the foremost Jewish and human rights organization of its kind. What had begun, in 1906, as a paternalistic committee of sixty American Jews, horrified by the persecution of Jews in Russia and determined "to prevent infringement of the civil and religious rights of Jews, and to alleviate the consequences of persecution," had developed a hundred years later into an organization with 175,000 members and supporters around the world, thirty-three chapters in the United States, offices abroad in Jerusalem, Berlin, Geneva, and Brussels, and association agreements with nineteen different Diaspora Jewish communities.

The growth and development of the American Jewish Committee—the issues it confronted, the changes it experienced, its successes, its failures—form the subject of this book. An earlier history of the American Jewish Committee, written by historian Naomi W. Cohen, concluded that the Committee's first six decades testified "to the clashes and adjustments, influences and pressures, mutual enrichment and absorption inherent in the confrontation between minority and majority." It showed how "the organization never ceased to remind the nation of its responsibilities to the cause of freedom," and at the same time "labored unceasingly to extend freedom's boundaries." This volume, a sequel, focuses on the Committee's more recent history; that is, its engagement with the central issues of postwar Jewish life. As the volume clearly demonstrates, the Committee played a role, frequently a decisive one, in almost every significant Jewish issue and development since World War II.

During the immediate postwar decades, Dr. Sanua shows here, the American Jewish Committee devoted a great deal of attention to the battle against domestic prejudice. "A fundamental tenet for the Committee," its honorary president, Jacob Blaustein, wrote in 1958, "has been the conviction that equality and security cannot be assured for Jews unless assured for all." To that end, the Committee sponsored social science research, advocated for new laws and policies, and authored an amicus curiae brief in 1954 that was quoted by the U.S. Supreme Court in its famous decision in *Brown vs. Board of Education* mandating racial integration of the public schools. Over time, Israel became an ever more important focus of AJC activities. As part of its program of support, it opened a full-time office in Israel in 1962 and an institute on American Jewish–Israeli relations in 1982. It likewise worked to enhance Israel's diplomatic position within the international community, taking particular pride in its campaign leading up to the 1991 repeal of the United Nations' infamous "Zionism is racism" resolution. AJC also reached out to Europe, Asia, and Africa in its continuing quest to safeguard Jewish interests and strengthen democracy. It helped to secure the historic Vatican II declaration on Catholic-Jewish relations in 1965, opened its Pacific Rim Institute in 1989, and inaugurated an Africa Institute in 2006. Notwithstanding the growing concentration of Jews in a small number of the world's most highly developed industrial centers (by 2005, more than 83 percent of Jews lived in North America and Israel) AJC has continued to focus globally.

Nevertheless, along with the American Jewish community as a whole, AJC also came to appreciate the need to strengthen Jewish life domestically. The organization's whole future, it recognized, depended on the perpetuation of a critical mass of Jews interested in leading a creative Jewish life. As a result, since the 1960s, AJC has devoted considerable resources to research, advocacy, and think-tank activities designed to invigorate the American Jewish community and to enhance Jewish continuity. Adult Jewish education, strengthening of the Jewish family, and promoting Jewish identity have all become part of its domestic Jewish agenda.

To further its agenda, AJC, as an organization committed to the power of ideas to change society, has stood in the vanguard of those taking advantage of the renaissance of Jewish intellectual life and scholarship in the United States. It has commissioned scholarly research and, through the *American Jewish Year Book*, *Commentary*, and hundreds of other publications, has provided a forum for intellectual engagement with the central issues confronting

Americans generally and Jews in particular. It has played an especially important role in producing and disseminating new knowledge concerning the American Jewish community, Jewish communities around the world, and contemporary antisemitism. Much of what we know about Jewish life in the postwar era would not be known but for the AJC and its publications.

Like every organization of its type, AJC experienced ups and downs during its postwar history; to her credit, Dr. Sanua explores the valleys as well as the peaks. She recounts, for example, the organization's "time of troubles" in the 1980s when it witnessed high-profile staff turnovers, financial woes, and considerable ambivalence concerning its agenda and priorities. She reveals how the organization, seeking new blood, opened its doors to women and to religiously traditional Jews. She also shows how, by the 1990s, the AJC righted itself, establishing a new balance between its various priorities—communal, national and international—as well as between its complementary particularistic and universalistic goals.

Historians will long be grateful to Dr. Sanua for reconstructing and recounting the AJC's decades of activity, so vital to any understanding of postwar Jewish life. AJC members will likewise be grateful to her for placing contemporary AJC policies in historical perspective. Dr. Sanua assures us that she enjoyed virtually unlimited access to AJC files and archives as well as untrammeled freedom to write and evaluate as she saw fit. As a complement to this book, AJC has also created an extensive online archive of historical materials, available on the Internet at www.ajcarchives.org.

This volume, taken together with the earlier study by Naomi W. Cohen, completes a historical record of AJC's first century, a tumultuous century that the agency helped to shape, even as it was profoundly shaped by it. As to what will become of the Jewish people in the century ahead—as it turned out, not even the participants in the "centennial symposium" were willing to guess. Assuming, however, that the past is prologue, the AJC will likely continue to offer "good advice" and seek to have a "profound impact," as it works "tirelessly for noble goals."

Dr. Jonathan D. Sarna
Joseph H. and Belle R. Braun Professor of American Jewish History and
Director, Hornstein Jewish Professional Leadership Program at
Brandeis University

Preface

This is a work of post–World War II American Jewish history, commissioned on the occasion of the American Jewish Committee's one hundredth anniversary. The general goal has been to review and analyze some of the momentous events and issues that have engaged the organized American Jewish community from 1945 through 2006 through the prism of the American Jewish Committee specifically, and also to portray some of the methods by which the AJC did its work. In doing so I have tried to answer the question of how a religious and ethnic group which represents a tiny fraction of the total American population is nevertheless able to be so effective. The relatively uncharted years since 1967 have been emphasized.

The title is taken from the Hebrew words inscribed on the first seal of the American Jewish Committee, *chazak venitchazka be'ad ammenu*—(I Chronicles 19:13)—which can be translated as "Be of good courage and let us be strong for the sake of our people." It can also be translated as "let us behave valiantly." The words are spoken by Joab, King David's general, just before the Israelites embark on an especially difficult two-front battle. The same story with similar words is told in 2 Samuel 10:12.

The American Jewish Committee was founded in 1906 in the wake of anti-Jewish riots in Tsarist Russia with the ambition of "preventing the infraction of the civil, political, and religious rights of Jews" in any part of the world.[1] Today its goals extend to the protection of human rights, enhancing the quality of American Jewish life, and deepening the ties between American and Israeli Jews. The organization began as a small group of wealthy, prominent, non-Zionist men, mostly of German-Jewish descent, who exerted their influence through personal contacts and educational programs. It evolved in the course of the twentieth and early twenty-first century into a leading multi-issue non-governmental organization (NGO). Today it has 175,000 men and women as members and supporters, offices in Israel and around the globe, and annual meetings attended by thousands of people including dozens of world leaders. With its many subcommittees, commissions, and departments, it functions not unlike a Jewish Department of State.

The fateful year of 1945 marked the point when the United States of America became a world superpower. It also marked the point where most of European Jewry had been destroyed in the Holocaust and the mantle of world political, financial, and religious leadership shifted to the Jews of the United States. The period of this study coincides with the entire cold war (1945–1991), the postcommunism years of the 1990s, and the early years of the worldwide war against Islamist terror which began in 2001. It also coincides with the growth of the Jewish population of the State of Israel from approximately 600,000 to well over 5 million, equal to or exceeding the core Jewish population of the United States.[2]

Virtually everything that happened in the American Jewish world (and indeed American history as a whole) engaged the AJC in one form or another. The issues the AJC has grappled with include aid for distressed Jewish communities around the world, the relationship of American Jews to Israel, the movement to free Soviet Jewry, the fight for civil rights and civil liberties and against bigotry and discrimination in the United States, the separation of church and state, the Vietnam War, Christian-Jewish relations, black-Jewish relations, and relations between the United States and a postcommunist Europe.

As the leading "think-tank" of American Jewry, dedicated to research and publications on Jewish life in the United States, Israel, and around the world, the AJC has since the late 1950s also confronted the issues of Jewish identity, demography, and mixed marriage with thoroughness. AJC began as a non-Zionist organization distinctly uncomfortable with its own Jewish identity and with the idea of Jewish peoplehood. An important part of its biography is its evolution through the years into a profoundly pro-Israel organization: fostering American Jewish continuity, identity, and world Jewish unity is at the top of its agenda.

My main sources have been the vast AJC archives, most of them located at the organization's New York headquarters; materials in the AJC's Jacob and Hilda Katz Blaustein Library; AJC publications; and interviews, some done on my own and others through the AJC's own oral history project.

A number of individuals and institutions contributed to the making of this book. I am profoundly grateful for the generosity of the Roy J. Zuckerberg Family Foundation for its steadfast support of this endeavor from its earliest stages up to the finished product.

Charlotte Bonelli, director of the American Jewish Committee archives, steered me to crucial material; she also served as a sounding board during long and otherwise solitary hours in the AJC collections. Her good humor and complete faith in the project were infectious. AJC archivists Kelly Chatain, Cuc Huong Do, and Claudia Olivares were of great help. My research assistant, Elie Bennett, was indispensable in opening literally hundreds of heavy AJC document boxes and doing everything asked of him with thoroughness and good cheer. The keen mind and sharp insight he revealed in researching several collections on his own were much valued. Cyma Horowitz and Michelle Anish of AJC's incomparable Blaustein Library answered scores of queries, and I am grateful for the access they granted me to some of AJC's most important documents. Gunnar Berg, archivist at YIVO and Michael Terry, Dorot Chief Librarian of the New York Public Library, were also of great help.

Also at AJC I thank Sondra Beaulieu, Roselyn Bell, Lisa Hoff, Noam Marans, Ken Schept, and Gary Spruch for their answers to my many queries. For generously agreeing to be interviewed, I thank AJC President E. Robert Goodkind, Shula Bahat, Yehudit Barsky, Morris Fine, Felice B. Gaer, Larry Grossman, and Charlotte Holstein. Larry was of particular help in reading my chapters as I went along. For extensive interviewing over several years I thank former AJC executive director Bertram H. Gold and former associate director Selma Hirsh, who provided a wealth of information about the AJC in the past. My study was much enriched by their willingness to answer questions at any time. Dr. Leonard Dinnerstein of the University of Arizona read the first two chapters and they benefited from his comments. Dr. Ruth Langer of Boston College read and commented on the chapter pertaining to the Second Vatican Council. Dr. Henry L. Feingold of Baruch College allowed me to interview him on the subject of the Soviet Jewry movement and my work is enriched by his input.

I am much indebted to Dr. Steven Bayme, director of AJC's Contemporary Jewish Life Department and Institute of American Jewish–Israeli Relations, who guided the project with tact and skill from beginning to end. Under my agreement with AJC, I was allowed complete access to all their files. They reserved the right of review and could suggest changes and cuts, but I was not bound to accept them. The chapters were much enriched by the wealth of Steve's knowledge and his long experience in Jewish communal life. He reinforced my trust in AJC by never once asking me to cut anything out.

I thank the Dorothy F. Schmidt College of Arts and Letters of Florida Atlantic University in Boca Raton, which granted me leaves from teaching and a year's sabbatical to complete the book. My colleagues there, Dr. Alan L. Berger and Dr. Lynn Appleton, always had faith in the work and appreciated its importance. Jonathan D. Sarna, Joseph H. and Belle R. Braun Professor of American Jewish History at Brandeis University, also read every chapter and was instrumental in having the book published by the University Press of New England. His reading saved me from many mistakes; any errors that remain are my own.

Finally I thank my parents, Dr. Victor D. and Stella Sardell Sanua, who lived through American Jewish history and left their own marks on it. Their reading of every chapter and their moral support during the writing of this book were invaluable. Happily my mother, who sat by my side many evenings while I wrote, lived to see the manuscript completed. She passed away, however, while it was going to press. I am greatly comforted to be able to dedicate this book in her memory.

Abbreviations

ACJ	American Council for Judaism
ACLU	American Civil Liberties Union
ADL	Anti-Defamation League of B'nai B'rith
AFL-CIO	American Federation of Labor and Congress of Industrial Organizations
AIDS	Acquired Immune Deficiency Syndrome
AIPAC	The American Israel Public Affairs Committee
AJC	American Jewish Committee
AJYB	American Jewish Year Book
AMIA	Argentine Israelite Mutual Association
AWACS	Airborne Warning and Control System
BHG	Bertram H. Gold Papers
CCAR	Central Conference of American Rabbis
CJFWF	Council of Jewish Federations and Welfare Funds
CLAL	The National Jewish Center for Learning and Leadership
CORE	Congress for Racial Equality
CUNY	City University of New York
DAH	David A. Harris Papers
DPs	Displaced Persons (usually refers to Jewish refugees from World War II)
EEOC	Equal Employment Opportunity Commission
ERA	Equal Rights Amendment
FAD	Foreign Affairs Department
FEP	Fair Employment Practices Laws
GA	General Assembly (United Nations)
HUAC	House Un-American Activities Committee
HUD	Department of Health and Urban Development
IAD	Interreligous Affairs Department
IAJIR	Institute for American Jewish–Israeli Relations
IRD	International Relations Department
ISX	Ira Silverman Papers
JCAC	Jewish Communal Affairs Commission
JCAD	Jewish Communal Affairs Department
JCPA	Jewish Council for Public Affairs

JDA	Joint Defense Appeal (AJC and ADL)
JDL	Jewish Defense League
JTA	Jewish Telegraphic Agency News Bulletin
JTS	Jewish Theological Seminary
KGB	Soviet Secret Police
LCBC	Large Cities Budgeting Council
NAACP	National Association for the Advancement of Colored People
NASA	National Aeronautics and Space Administration
NATO	North Atlantic Treaty Organization
NCC	National Council of Churches
NCRAC	National Community Relations Advisory Council
NCSJ	National Conference on Soviet Jewry
NEC	National Executive Council
NJCRAC	National Jewish Community Relations Advisory Council
NJPS	National Jewish Population Survey
NOI	Nation of Islam
OPEC	Organization of Petroleum Exporting Countries
PA	Palestinian Authority
PEJE	Partnership for Excellence in Jewish Education
PLO	Palestine Liberation Organization
SCLC	Southern Christian Leadership Conference
SEATO	Southeast Asia Treaty Organization
SNCC	Student Non-Violent Coordinating Committee
UAHC	Union of American Hebrew Congregations
UFT	United Federation of Teachers
UIA	United Israel Appeal
UJA	United Jewish Appeal
UJC	United Jewish Communities
UN	United Nations
UNESCO	United Nations Educational, Scientific and Cultural Organization
UNSCOP	United Nations Committee on Palestine
USSR	Union of Soviet Socialist Republics (Soviet Union)
VISTA	Volunteers in Service to America
WCC	World Council of Churches
WIZO	World International Zionist Organization
ZOA	Zionist Organization of America

❧ I ❧

1906–1959

❧ I ❧

Origins

From the Kishinev Pogrom to the State of Israel

[1903–1948]

On the morning of April 19, 1903, the Jews of Kishinev—a city in the southwesternmost province of the Russian Empire, bordering Ukraine and the Black Sea—were celebrating the last day of Passover while their Christian neighbors were celebrating Easter Sunday. Half of the Jews in the world at that time lived in that empire, and the Jews of Kishinev numbered fifty thousand, about a third of the city's population. The church bells pealed as the clock struck noon. Violence started when mobs in a state of holiday drunkenness began to hound Jews out of the main square. The mobs were incensed from Easter sermons about the crimes of the Jews against Jesus and rumors that the Jews kidnapped and killed Christian children to use their blood to make Passover matzohs. A pogrom—a Russian word used by Jews to describe an anti-Jewish riot—was about to start.

By late afternoon a band of close to a thousand young men descended on the Jewish quarter of the city, carrying guns, whips, iron bars, knives, and axes. They plundered and demolished property, avoiding homes that had large chalked crosses on them. They burned homes and smashed and looted Jewish shops and burned down entire libraries. They invaded the synagogues and ripped and trampled the holy Torah scrolls. They dragged Jews from their hiding places to kill, torture, and mutilate them with their bare hands. They raped girls and women within sight of their fathers and husbands, cut off breasts, chopped off hands, gouged out eyes, drove nails through people's heads, hacked bodies in half, split open bellies and filled them with feathers. The massacre went on for three days until the police, bowing to external pressure, finally intervened to stop it. At the end, forty-five were dead, six hundred were wounded and disfigured, fifteen hundred shops and houses had been gutted and destroyed, and thousands of survivors were left in the ruins, homeless, destitute, without food or clothing.[1]

Kishinev was the first of a wave of pogroms that swept Russia from 1903 to 1905, bringing in their wake similar devastation to hundreds of towns, and killing and wounding tens of thousands of people. In previous times, no one in the rest of the world would have known what was happening. But in the twentieth century the leaders of the community were able to get descriptions of the events over the telegraph lines, and the accounts hit the newspapers in London, New York, Paris, and the entire Western world. The story could still produce horror and revulsion in both Jews and non-Jews; humanity's senses had not yet been dulled by two world wars. The riots were met with a storm of protest. There were meetings, parades, demonstrations, and fund-raisings for the relief of those who were suffering. Newspapers sent eyewitnesses to provide graphic details of the disaster. In the United States, Secretary of State John Hay spoke sharply about the event to the Russian ambassador. Ex-President Grover Cleveland and other notables spoke at a mass meeting at Carnegie Hall in New York. A petition with thousands of signatures was sent to President Teddy Roosevelt.[2] In Vienna, Theodor Herzl, the father of modern political Zionism, was so distraught over the pogroms (the effects of which he witnessed firsthand on a visit to Russia) that he wanted to accept a 1903 British offer of part of East Africa to be a temporary homeland for the Jews. His proposal of the so-called Uganda plan was debated bitterly and finally rejected.[3]

Pogroms were not new in the Russian Empire, or in the neighboring areas of Eastern Europe, where many other Jews lived. They had occurred before, most notably in 1881 upon the assassination of Tsar Alexander II by Russian revolutionaries. His successor, Tsar Alexander III, wishing to crush resistance among a part of the population that he considered responsible, had instituted among other measures the infamous May Laws of 1882, which greatly intensified discrimination against Jews beyond previous levels. In the wake of 1881 hundreds of thousands of Jews fled to freedom in the United States, to the point that the Jewish population there rose from about 250,000 (mostly from German-speaking parts of Europe) in 1876 to more than a million and a half mostly Yiddish speakers by 1903. Hundreds of thousands more fled in the wake of Kishinev, a failed revolution in 1905, and the desperate poverty pervasive even in places where there were no riots. Thus was laid the basis for much of the American Jewish community in the twentieth century. More than eighty thousand Jews fled to America in 1904, some eleven and a half thousand of them in the month of July alone.[4] Until 1921 the doors of the United States were open to these refugees; no quotas or immigration restrictions barred their way. One of the first and most important functions of the American Jewish Committee was to campaign against restrictive immigration laws that would keep more Jews from finding a haven in America.

In the long tradition of mutual aid that had marked Jewish communities for hundreds of years, the wealthy and established Jews of the United States came to the aid of their brethren overseas. One in particular, Jacob H. Schiff, served as the treasurer of the ad hoc National Committee for the Relief of Sufferers of Russian Massacres, which raised and distributed more than one and a quarter million dollars. Schiff had been born in Frankfurt, Germany, where he received a traditional Jewish education, and had immigrated to the United States in 1865 at the age of eighteen. He achieved his fortune in connection with the private investment banking firm of Kuhn, Loeb, and Company. In America he also became attracted to Reform Judaism, becoming an active leader in the movement—though this did not prevent him from being a patron of the Conservative movement's Jewish Theological Seminary of America, and one of the most generous supporters of the overall American Jewish community.

It was the end of 1905; the pogroms had temporarily died down, and most of the emergency funds had been disbursed. At a gathering of men in a friend's home, Schiff made known to his associates, mostly well-to-do Jews of German descent like himself, that he did not wish to do such things alone any more. He had been strongly criticized in the Yiddish press for doing so much on his own. In addition, he was nearing the age of seventy, and he felt that some responsibility should be transferred to younger men. In any event, there was near certainty that such crises would occur soon again, and the scale and seriousness of anti-Jewish violence was growing too great in modern times for one man—or two or three—to handle alone.[5] Moreover, Jewish communities in other countries had set up organizations to help their fellow Jews in foreign lands and at home. Germany had its Hilfsverein der deutschen Juden, France had its Alliance Israélite Universelle, and Great Britain had the Anglo-Jewish Association and the Board of Deputies of British Jews. There had been national Jewish organizations formed in the United States up until that time but none had succeeded in uniting or mobilizing the American Jewish community.[6] Clearly it was time for the rapidly growing Jewish community to have such an organization, preferably one of wide geographic distribution to reach as many Jews as possible.

Schiff's friends agreed and a committee of five of them sent out a letter on January 8, 1906, to fifty-seven prominent Jews across the country, inviting them to come to New York on February 3 to discuss the "advisability of the formation of a General Committee to deal with serious problems thus presented," by the recent Russian massacres.[7] The head of the committee was Louis Marshall, a noted attorney born in Syracuse, New York, to German Jewish immigrants.

On the appointed day, rabbis, businessmen, scientists, judges, ambassadors, scholars, writers, and philanthropists gathered in New York from Baltimore, Boston, Cincinnati, Chicago, Milwaukee, New Orleans, Philadelphia, Washington, D.C., Richmond, and as far away as San Francisco.[8] It was a symptom of the times that at first they doubted if they should form an organization at all. A key tenet of the modern antisemitic syndrome as it had developed in the nineteenth century was the belief that a worldwide secret Jewish conspiracy sought world political, economic, and artistic domination, and the destruction of nations. Jewish success and achievement, whether in the financial and banking world, the arts, science, medicine, literature, music, or politics, was only proof of this conspiracy to gain submission from the Gentile world. Another national Jewish organization beyond what already existed, some believed, would just attract the attention of the antisemites, and part of the original group withdrew from the enterprise.

Through two days in February and a second meeting on May 19, 1906, the men who remained debated and argued how to organize themselves, who the membership should be, whether there would be elections for delegates or not, what to call their group, and how much attention should be paid to Jews in the United States as well as the Jews overseas. Louis Marshall weighed in on the name and extent of their group. He wanted to include "to promote the cause of Judaism" as one of the organization's goals. "If we are not Jews we are nothing," he said. "The simple and easiest thing to do is to come right out with our colors and say we are Jews. We are Jews because we adhere to Judaism. We think that there is something in regard to Judaism on which we have united for centuries. And it is because of that Judaism we would be willing to promote it in the same sense that our fellow-citizens and other denominations are able to come together to promote their specific religion."9 Marshall's phrase "to promote the cause of Judaism" was stricken but "Jewish" remained in the name.

The group was finally instituted as the "American Jewish Committee" and held its first official meeting on November 11, 1906, at New York's Hotel Savoy. The final charter described its mission as "to prevent the infraction of the civil and religious rights of Jews in any part of the world," including the United States. Membership was fixed at sixty appointees across the country, with day-to-day matters to be in the hands of a president and an executive committee. One of the first orders of business was to discuss aid to the suffering Jewish communities of San Francisco, who had been devastated by the 1906 earthquake and resulting fires. When the time came for the group to create an official seal, Dr. Cyrus Adler chose a Hebrew motto from the battles of King David (1 Chronicles 19:13): "chazzak ve'nitchazka be'ad ammenu"— "Be of good courage and let us prove strong for the sake of our people."

Harry Schneiderman, the assistant secretary of the group from 1909 to 1949 and an early editor of the *American Jewish Year Book* (whose publication the AJC assumed in conjunction with the Jewish Publication Society), recalled that first group of founders some fifty years later. As a poor immigrant growing up in the Hebrew Orphans Asylum he had seen some of them, members of the board of trustees, coming to visit on Sundays, in particular Jacob

H. Schiff. Schneiderman looked at them in awe, dressed in their silk coats and top hats. However, he noted, there was a bridge between them and the orphans they visited. "These men belonged to a generation whose members were not far removed from the knowledge or the practice of traditional Judaism," Schneiderman wrote. "Even those among the thirteen who were born in the U.S. including several leaders of Reform Judaism were punctual and regular in their attendance at synagogue services not only on holy days but also on the Sabbath. They knew the Bible, had a fair to good knowledge of Hebrew, and were familiar with Jewish history. Those who were not Orthodox were familiar with traditional Judaism and respected its sincere adherents. Several understood spoken Yiddish and a few could read it."[10] Schneiderman was already aware, even as the body was in formation, that there was much criticism of the group for their self-appointed character and their preferred method of working behind the scenes. On this he commented:

As I sat at the meeting of the Executive Committee I came gradually to understand that the leaders of the new organization aimed to make it something unusual in its class. It was to be small, only sixty members originally but it was to consist of the most influential Jews who, in an emergency, could spring into action and enlist the cooperation of their friends and associates and in turn when necessary the support of the public. The new body was not to engage in publicity except as an instrument for achieving objectives. Inasmuch as it was not to seek mass support, publicity in general would be unnecessary and only the membership would be kept informed of the activities of the Executive Committee which was to have complete discretion even in respect to informing the membership of its work. All meetings, including the one held annually of the entire Committee were to be private and open to neither press nor public. The aim of the organization was to get things done as effectively as possible; it was not to promote the renown or the aggrandizement of any of its members or even of the organization itself. This non-publicity policy antagonized a large part of the Jewish press, especially the Yiddish newspapers in New York City. These newspapers ridiculed the Committee as a "hush-hush" body and made much capital of its self appointed and self-continuing character. But the leaders of the Committee did not permit these gibes and criticism to swerve them from their course. They were confident that when at the proper time the Jewish community would learn of the results of the Committee's activities, the Jews of the U.S. would for the most part approve even though these results were achieved by an organization which was self-created and self-perpetuating.

Judge Mayer Sulzberger of Philadelphia served as the AJC's president for the first six years of its existence. The son of a cantor, he himself had been born in Heidelsheim, Germany, and immigrated to the United States with his family as a child in 1849. Schneiderman recalled that Sulzberger was a noted collector on books of Jewish subjects, "a Hebrew scholar of some distinction," and the author of several original contributions to modern Jewish scholarship. The professional scholar of the group was Dr. Cyrus Adler, who had been born in Arkansas but whose parents had also been German Jewish immigrants. Adler graduated from the University of Pennsylvania and was one of the first in the United States to receive a doctorate in Semitics at Johns

Hopkins University. He was a founder of the American Jewish Historical Society, edited the first English-language Jewish encyclopedia, and managed to work full-time and be the president of several Jewish organizations simultaneously. Other active members of the AJC Executive Committee included Cyrus Sulzberger, a successful businessman; Dr. Judah L. Magnes, who married Louis Marshall's sister-in-law and was assistant rabbi at Temple Emanu-El; and Secretary Harry Friedenwald, who was AJC's early liaison with the Federation of American Zionists.[11]

The American Jewish Committee did not have at the beginning a large office or a staff. Its scope was narrow, and it rarely intervened in events that did not affect Jews directly. Its power came from the quality and connections of its members, not sheer numbers. Dealing with the Nazi threat and the enormity of post–World War II problems would cause it to grow exponentially. Early meetings, however, had as few as a half dozen participants. Plans to broaden the base of the organization repeatedly failed to come to fruition. By 1931, the twenty-fifth anniversary of its founding, nationwide membership had grown to only 350.[12] Louis Marshall, speaking near the end of his life, said they did not mind Jewish critics who charged that the AJC was "an autocratic institution without any democratic feeling or quality . . . worthy of notice." That "just suited us," he said. "We felt that it would be very much better if our work was done quietly." Nor did they seek recognition among non-Jews. "What possible advantage," asked Cyrus Adler, "could come from making Christian clergymen and the Christian religious press acquainted with the organization of our committee?"[13]

Financial necessity might have forced a broadening of this structure, but that was also not a motivation in the AJC's early years. Mass fund-raising was not needed; sufficient funds came from assessments and voluntary contributions, and after 1941 a separate agency took care of most of the solicitations for funds. In an emergency, the eminent communal leader Jacob Schiff was always ready to dig into his personal fortune. Individuals and organizations could always be counted on to sponsor specific projects. Not until World War I did the AJC directly raise more than ten thousand dollars in any given year. Expensive offices and salaries for employees were not an issue; the original New York City quarters were modest, and the organization's general affairs were attended to successfully by one paid executive and three or four clerks. Members wrote their own letters and arranged their own meetings. The first president, sixty-three-year-old Judge Sulzberger, communicated from his home in Philadelphia and rarely came to New York. Dr. Cyrus Adler was somehow able to divide his time between AJC work in the New York office and gainful employment in Washington, D.C., and later, Philadelphia. As for procedure, decisions were usually made by consensus, rather than by formal vote taking.[14] The Executive Committee met in secret and did not always communicate fully with the general membership.

The magisterial Louis Marshall, an attorney originally from Syracuse, New York, took over the presidency in 1912 and remained at the helm until his death in 1929. Under his leadership the Committee as an organization fought to keep the gates of the United States open to immigration, recognized the Balfour Declaration, was instrumental in organizing relief for European Jewish victims, stepped in to help save the Jews of the Yishuv (as the pre-State Jewish community in Palestine was known) from starvation during World War I, and negotiated for minority rights treaties protecting Jews to be included in peace agreements made after the war. In its earliest years the AJC included relief work among its efforts, but the scale of World War I convinced them that a separate organization was needed for that purpose. In 1914 the AJC took steps that led to the creation of the American Jewish Joint Distribution Committee, which was a "sister" organization in many respects; many men sat on the boards of both organizations. Ironically, the collapse of the tsarist regime in 1917 made everyone believe for a brief period that deliverance had come in Russia and there would no longer be any need for so many Russian Jewish immigrants to come to the United States.

Also during World War I, the American Jewish Congress was founded in 1918 by Zionist Jews of East European background who objected to the self-appointed and self-perpetuating character of the "aristocratic" American Jewish Committee. It is the only one among what are known as the community-relations agencies of the American Jewish community to have been actively pro-Zionist throughout its entire history.[15] Its initial goal was to have a democratically elected organization to represent American Jewish interests at the peace conferences after World War I. At the end of the peace conferences the Congress disbanded, as the American Jewish Committee had requested. The organization reconstituted itself in 1922, however, under the charismatic leadership of Rabbi Stephen S. Wise and evolved in the 1930s into a membership organization.[16] After World War II it specialized in the use of law and social action to combat prejudice and discrimination, not uncommonly resorting to the techniques of protest and mass demonstration. The American Jewish Congress, the AJC, and the Anti-Defamation League of B'nai Brith (founded in 1913) together became known as the "big three" of the myriad of American Jewish organizations.[17] The ADL specialized in investigation, exposure, and education about antisemitism, while the AJC, which also carried on an extensive education program, at first specialized in work behind the scenes with contacts and coalitions more than litigation. The relations between the groups through the years ranged from neutrality to competitiveness to cooperation (AJC and the ADL for decades had a joint fund-raising operation) and the three frequently joined in filing friend-of-the-court briefs in major cases.

In the 1920s, when there was a steep rise in American antisemitism, Louis Marshall of the American Jewish Committee took on the Ku Klux Klan, the presidents of Ivy League universities, and automobile magnate Henry Ford.

One of the most popular industrialists in America, Ford claimed in his mass-circulated newspaper the *Dearborn Independent* that Jews were taking over America and that Bolshevism was part of a worldwide Jewish conspiracy. Ford would eventually be decorated by Nazi Germany in 1938. Before then, however, in the 1920s, Louis Marshall personally demanded a letter from Ford of retraction and apology.

The second AJC president left his law practice to travel the world for weeks and months at a time in order to secure these achievements, and he set a precedent of walking with presidents and kings. Historians have judged Marshall as one of the greatest Jewish leaders of the twentieth century. Indeed, he was such a commanding figure that when the British Jewish author Israel Zangwill came to visit the United States in 1923, he was moved to say that America was run by "Marshall's Law."[18] Some also spoke of American Jewry as being ruled by "Louis XIX."[19] By then, to the general public, Louis Marshall *was* the American Jewish Committee. His sudden death in Zurich in 1929, on the very eve of the Great Depression and the rise of Nazism, was a grave blow. Historians have speculated how American Jewish affairs might have developed differently had Louis Marshall been spared just a few more years. For the AJC itself, Marshall's legacy would serve forever after as a symbol of AJC's best moments; at the time, however, his departure very nearly crippled the organization.

On the Eve of World War II

The leaders of the AJC were products for the most part of the nineteenth century. They believed in the principles of enlightenment, emancipation, reason, American democracy, and the liberal tradition. It was hard for them to come to terms with the rise of a new and lethal fascism overseas and a corresponding rise in antisemitism in the United States. At first the civilized world was reluctant to do anything to stop the rise of Adolf Hitler, much less take action on behalf of the Jews of Germany or of Eastern Europe. Such was the background against which the Committee and other Jewish communal leaders were forced to conduct their activities. The Great Depression at home, the general feeling that World War I had been a colossal waste, and the failure of the peace treaties drove America's retreat into isolationism. A Gallup poll taken in 1937 showed that a majority of Americans thought entrance into World War I had been a colossal mistake.[20] Thousands of Americans and millions of Europeans had been killed or grievously wounded for a purpose no one was sure of any more. Opinion was widespread that the entire affair of the Great War of 1914–18 had been orchestrated by profit-hungry munitions manufacturers and financiers. Congressional investigations were held to expose these alleged dealings.[21]

These were not propitious circumstances under which to enter another military conflict. Jews found themselves open to the charge that they themselves were fomenting this new dispute. "The three most important groups who have been pressing this country to war are the British, the Jewish and the Roosevelt administration," stated the influential aviator hero Charles Lindbergh in September 1941, speaking on behalf of the America First committee.[22] FDR's New Deal was routinely referred to as "The Jew Deal." American leaders were extremely sensitive to accusations, especially before the bombing of Pearl Harbor in December 1941, that all of World War II was being fought for the benefit of the Jews.

The minority-rights treaties so painstakingly negotiated by Louis Marshall had been ignored or repudiated throughout Europe, and the League of Nations, in the face of assorted threats to world peace, had become little more than an international debating society. Tens of thousands of German Jews, once the envy of world Jewry, were desperate to leave their country, particularly after the passage of the racial Nuremberg Laws in 1935. The problem was not Germany's unwillingness to let them leave. Until October 1941 Jews were physically free, even encouraged, to leave the German Reich if they left all their property behind. The problem was that no nation, including the United States, was willing to take them in appreciable numbers. At a conference held in Evian, France, in 1938 for the express purpose of alleviating the refugee crisis, only the Dominican Republic agreed to admit a significant number of Jews.

From the late nineteenth century the Land of Israel had increasingly beckoned, and the modern Zionist movement had been founded as a way of reconstituting the ancient homeland. When Palestine became a mandate under Great Britain, under terms that called for the facilitation of Jewish immigration and settlement of the land in that country, hopes were high that the former Ottoman province could become both a haven and a cultural and spiritual center for Jews throughout the world. The Yishuv had made impressive strides. Yet through the years the British authorities had gradually retreated from their earlier promises. In the 1930s, Arab anti-Jewish riots convulsed the country and British officials would only dole out immigration certificates for Europe's Jews at the rate of a few hundred per month. Britain could not see itself as maintaining order in Palestine while needing to fight Hitler as well, and Jews were hardly in a position to question that need. In 1939 the British issued the notorious MacDonald White Paper, which shut the gates of Palestine at the very moment the Jews of Europe needed it most. Millions needed haven, but under the terms of the White Paper no more than seventy-five thousand Jews would be admitted over the following five years and then no more after March 1944 unless the Arab population acquiesced.

Even these restricted numbers on Great Britain's part demonstrated more generosity than the U.S. government was willing to extend. The era of mass Jewish immigration to America had ended abruptly in 1924, when Congress placed strict limits on the numbers that could come from any country. Only 150,000 new immigrants from everywhere in the world could be admitted each year (a number that was often not filled) under a quota system that deliberately discriminated against newcomers from eastern and southern Europe.[23] The battle to change this immigration law consumed much time and energy of the Committee until 1965, when under President Lyndon B. Johnson the quota system was finally eliminated.

In the 1930s, when millions of Americans were unemployed, public and congressional sentiment in the United States was overwhelmingly in favor of drastically cutting those immigration quotas that did exist, if not slamming the door altogether. Franklin D. Roosevelt, who came to power the same year that Hitler did, was forced to put his energy into getting his New Deal programs accepted over the opposition of the judges on the Supreme Court. While the situation in Europe escalated, Congress passed the Neutrality Acts, tying the hands of FDR and of any other government officials who wished to intervene overseas. As for the State Department, officials there might consider Nazi activities regrettable, but they also considered them an internal German affair beyond the jurisdiction of the United States.

Worst of all, the level of anti-Jewish feeling in the United States was rising at precisely the time when organized American Jewry had lost much of the resources it needed to combat it. Louis Marshall was gone and voluntary contributions to Jewish organizations fell off drastically as the Depression worsened. Nazis had established an international headquarters to aid anti-Semitic groups throughout the world and its effects were being widely felt; in the United States, anti-Jewish and pro-Nazi propaganda was fed by funds that came straight from Berlin. There had always been a strong correlation between bad economic times and anti-Jewish feeling. If Jews fought back with conspicuous anti-Nazi activity, they ran the risk of confirming anti-Semitic charges and strengthening pro-Hitler sentiment in their own country.

These concerns were partly behind AJC's desire in general to remain as unobtrusive as possible in conducting its work, preferring to use the names and addresses of supposedly nonsectarian organizations instead of its own. In general, standard operating procedure dictated not using the organization's name at all, or using it only in conjunction with other Jewish groups, or using it in conjunction with non-Jewish groups, and, when necessary, creating the name of an essentially fictitious organization to hide the fact that American Jews were behind the effort at all. Such policies often meant that the AJC or individuals associated with it did not get public credit for what they did—causing problems at fund-raising times when communal recognition was important.

Behind the scenes AJC members and staff worked to expose Nazi agents working in the United States, frequently in cooperation with the police and the FBI, going undercover and infiltrating anti-Semitic organizations when necessary. Milton Ellerin, who was working for the FBI as an infiltrator of Nazi organizations and who later joined the AJC as its expert in antisemitism, noted that at first in the late 1930s and early 1940s the U.S. government had very little information on these foreign groups. Most of their attention went to the great gangsters of the era, such as John Dillinger, Baby Face Nelson, and Pretty Boy Floyd. "The FBI at that time was politically unsophisticated," he recalled. "It paid little or no attention to political movements, with the result that when they began to look into the backgrounds of groups and individuals who now were becoming suspect [that is, Nazi agents] they had no information. And let me here say that if it were not for the Jewish agencies who had accumulated this information, they would have been lost."[24] Ellerin also noted that when he started working at the AJC in 1948 there were "hundreds of antisemitic groups in the United States." By the 1980s, with the exception of a half dozen Nazi groups and a half dozen Ku Klux Klan groups that phenomenon "totally disappeared."[25]

On a more overt level, AJC's Survey Committee, so named because of its first assignment of doing a survey of antisemitism in the United States, undertook a program of public education and a campaign through the press, radio, advertisements, and even comic books to counteract Nazi and antisemitic propaganda. At its height the Survey Committee, itself composed largely of volunteers, employed more than one hundred men and women. Women were active in the Survey Committee and during World War II sat on AJC's Executive Committee for the first time. An allied Community Service department spread materials and counseled concerned Jews across the country on how to deal with the crisis. Leading the Survey Committee was Richard Rothschild, a product of the advertising world who had also authored two books on philosophy. When he started the job he articulated what came to be known as the "Six-Point Plan," a set of principles that remained the basis of AJC public activity for many years.

In the view of Rothschild and those who succeeded him, the AJC should not and could not fight antisemitism most effectively unless they believed and portrayed it as an *American,* and not specifically a Jewish, problem (one more reason to keep the name of the American Jewish Committee out of the headlines). Obviously no one in the wider world could be expected to care about anything that was happening only to Jews. Americans, however, could be educated to see anti-Jewish hatred and discrimination as a defect in American democracy and a violation of all the values of liberty that the country held dear. Apologetics and direct refutations of antisemitic canards—that the Jews were warmongers, international bankers, "Jew Deal" conspirators, and/or communists in search of global domination—also would not be effective, although such responses might make them as the victims feel better. Such charges should not even be dignified with an answer and a direct response to them would never accomplish the desired objective for the confirmed antisemites anyway. Instead, Rothschild counseled, the AJC should expend most of its energy on the majority whose opinions were still open to outside influence. They should do what they could to portray Jews in a positive light for the sake of the general public, seeking the cooperation of non-Jewish and nonsectarian agencies when possible (for example, highlighting the achievements of Jewish war heroes or comic book and short-story good characters with recognizably Jewish names), while at the same time discrediting and exposing the brutality of antisemitism's main sponsors. Exposure to influential members of the media and political leaders would bring public opinion to bear on their side. Assiduous investigation of the most violent groups was bound to find them in violation of the law and lead to their defeat. In the case of antisemitic groups, incitement to riot, disturbing the peace, sedition, treason, as well as immigration violations and tax and other financial irregularities, were always likely charges.

AJC's legal and investigative division was charged with that particular responsibility. In the 1930s and 1940s its attorneys and agents brought charges, went undercover, infiltrated meetings, and compiled a list of fifty thousand offenders whose names were shared with the FBI and other government authorities. Scores were sent to jail because of the efforts of the AJC, and the activities of this unit continued after the war. Again, secrecy and behind-the-scenes work was the key. Most of the written records of these activities remain closed to the public to the present day.

In general, Rothschild held that "constructive" methods were the ideal in fighting antisemitism. And, true to sound principles of market research, he also believed that the AJC must never proceed blindly but must find ways to test and poll periodically the exact attitudes they needed to change. Only thus would they find out if their strategies were effective, and they would be able to devise new ones when necessary. Rothschild's emphasis on social and scientific research was especially embraced by John Slawson, a psychologist who was named the executive vice president of the American Jewish Committee in 1943. He replaced Morris D. Waldman, who served as the first executive head of the AJC from 1928 until 1943 and whose autobiography *Nor By Power* (1953) contains many details about Jewish communal life and firsthand knowledge of the inner workings of the early AJC.

Serving as executive vice president until 1967, Slawson became in effect the architect of the post–World War II AJC. Almost no one at the Committee was aware of his humble beginnings or the fact that he had not been born in the United States. "Slawson" was an Anglicization of the family name, and his original first name, changed to "John" in his travels through the Midwest, had been Jacob. Slawson was born in a small village in Ukraine in 1896 and fled to America with his family by steerage when he was seven years old to escape pogroms in the region. His notably short stature was probably due to malnutrition in childhood. What he lacked in height he made up for in presence; staff members recall that when John Slawson was around "the floors shook," and he was capable of reducing workers to tears, although he would always apologize. Slawson was forced to seek employment at an early age to help his family, and only through great effort was he able to obtain his education. He worked his way through secondary school and attended college for several years at Valparaiso University in Indiana and the University of Kansas before working his way back to New York. There he was accepted at Columbia University where he received his B.A. and his doctorate in psychology in 1927. After years of experience in social work and Jewish communal affairs he came to the Committee in 1943 determined to apply his social scientific training to the problems of antisemitism and prejudice.[26] Slawson brought with him from his previous position Dessie Kushell, who became AJC's respected and influential director of personnel.[27]

The Committee was one of the best organizations in the Jewish communal world for conducting scientific research. Time and again the crucial memorandum or research report that convinced those in power to undertake concrete change, whether used exclusively by AJC or not, was written by AJC staff and generated from the materials in the Committee library. In the view of the founders, "enlightenment" went along with education; the organization was after all born during America's Progressive Era, when science and social planning were seen as key to improving people's lives. In order to conduct their work properly, AJC leaders needed to know the exact situation of Jews abroad or at home; they needed to have non-English periodicals translated for them and their contents summarized. Research was needed to reform, persuade, or arouse public opinion. Whether to refute or to advance issues concerning Jews, they needed precise statistics and information on such subjects as racial classifications, Jewish military service during wartime, the number of Jewish criminals, and legal precedents for the abrogation of treaties or for U.S. intervention in foreign affairs. Detailed investigation was required to expose the *Protocols of the Learned Elders of Zion* as a Russian forgery that claimed that a group of Jewish elders was meeting in secret to plan world domination. In time, the AJC set up a Bureau of Social Research and Statistics (the forerunner of the Library for Jewish Information), which assumed responsibility for the publication of the *American Jewish Year Book*. This Jewish almanac was of use not only to all Jewish communal organizations but to the general public as well. Thus the AJC early established itself as a research bureau whose information was utilized by Jews and non-Jews alike.

The Outbreak of War

The outbreak of World War II in September 1939 and the entrance of the United States into it in December 1941 did much to curtail open Nazi activity in America, but it also reduced the possibilities of helping European Jews directly. Appealing to the Allied governments and pleading with them to include the rescue of Jews in their military plans became the main focus of activity.[28]

The Survey Committee continued its work on the domestic front. The number of committees and staff members grew in response to new challenges. In 1941 the organization joined with the Anti-Defamation League of B'nai B'rith in forming the Joint Defense Appeal (JDA), a vehicle for cooperation and common fund-raising. This meant that until the early 1960s when the partnership finally dissolved for good, the American Jewish Committee was blessedly limited in the amount of direct soliciting it was supposed to do.

When word came through the British press and the Jewish Telegraphic Agency that the Nazis were planning and conducting mass extermination of the Jews, rabbis called for a national day of mourning and fasting on December 2, 1942. AJC president Maurice Wertheim, the son-in-law of Henry Morgenthau Sr., joined the representatives of four other organizations, including the World Jewish Congress and Rabbi Stephen Wise of the American Jewish Congress, in the Oval Office on December 8, 1942. At least two million Jews were already dead by that time. President Roosevelt chatted politely with the group, made vague promises, and then sent them away. Any attempts to suggest avenues of rescue or increase Jewish immigration to Palestine were met by Allied leaders and the State Department with claims that these would be inimical to the war effort.[29] The best way to save anyone from Hitler, they said, was to concentrate on military objectives and win the war as quickly as possible.

The AJC helped form a Joint Emergency Committee with the leaders of the Zionist and other major Jewish organizations, worked desperately behind the scenes with the Joint Distribution Committee and other Jewish relief agencies to help those Jews who managed to escape to neutral territory, and composed a detailed twelve-point plan of action and rescue that was to be brought before a special conference on refugees held on the isolated island of Bermuda in April 1943. As had been the case in Evian, no country, including the United States, was willing to take in Jews from Europe. Several mass demonstrations took place at Madison Square Garden in New York for the purpose of calling for the rescue of Europe's Jews; the AJC broke with its tradition by participating fully in them and joining the roster of speakers. U.S. Undersecretary of State Breckinridge Long, a State Department official in charge of visas (and who was responsible for keeping what quotas for refugees did exist 90 percent unfilled), was removed from his post after false testimony before a congressional committee, in part because of AJC efforts. The staff, working in concert with other Jewish organizations, had researched an exhaustive statistical memorandum, exposing Long's blatant falsehoods about the number of refugees the United States was actually admitting. They sent it to Long himself, respectfully requesting an explanation, and then strategically sent copies of the memo to as many influential leaders as possible. Long's demise followed not long afterward.

Still, by the spring of 1943, after the Warsaw Ghetto Uprising (despite heroic resistance the ghetto was razed to the ground), millions more had perished. To save the remnant by removing them from Europe appeared hopeless. Jews had not been wanted as immigrants before, when shipping routes were still open. Even if, in wartime, millions or even hundreds of thousands of destitute Jews could be snatched from Hitler's grasp, what nation would be willing to take them in?

In January 1944, near the end of the war, when victory was certain for the Allies, FDR was finally convinced to establish an organization known as the War Refugee Board. The name "Jewish" was deliberately omitted from the name, although it was understood that its main purpose would be the rescue of Jewish refugees; indeed, 90 percent of the organization's budget came from Jewish contributions. Raoul Wallenberg worked to rescue the Jews of Hungary under the aegis of the War Refugee Board; in all the WRB is credited with saving hundreds of thousands of lives. For the vast majority of Hitler's victims, however, the WRB did too little and came too late.

Zionist, Non-Zionist, and Anti-Zionist Conflicts

Within the American Jewish community despair and devastation bred disunity. Differing philosophies regarding Zionism became the heart of the communal conflict and the subject of complex negotiations. Rabbis and organizations, even Zionist ones in the United States and around the world, differed on whether they should call for the immediate establishment of a Jewish state or whether a separate Jewish army fighting under a Jewish flag should be part of the Allied military forces. The lines were drawn among three groups: the Zionists, who were themselves divided into "maximalists" and "minimalists"; the non-Zionists, a position that had been practically invented by the AJC; and the anti-Zionists. By the early 1940s the Zionists were in the majority.[30]

"Maximalist" Zionists at the time believed that the Jewish people constituted a nation wherever they were, that they were essentially in exile, and that their problems could and would only be solved worldwide if they called for a sovereign state of their own immediately. The worldwide attempt to exterminate the Jews proved this view conclusively. "Minimalist" Zionists shared basic Zionist ideology and the ultimate goal of a Jewish national home, but believed that it was inexpedient to agitate for one in the middle of World War II when Great Britain, Palestine's mandate authority, had its back against the wall fighting against Hitler, and the policy did not yet have the approval of the U.S. government. It was best for the time being that the British mandate be allowed to continue in power and to continue pushing for the admission of as many Jewish refugees as possible under the prevailing political authority.

Non-Zionists endorsed and looked with sympathy upon Jewish settlement in Palestine and indeed were generous in philanthropic contributions to its upbuilding. They endorsed the Balfour Declaration in principle, opposed the

British White Papers that sought to limit immigration, and supported continued Jewish settlement and land purchases. Zionists and wealthy non-Zionists,
including the American Jewish Committee, had served together for a time in a
combined and enlarged Jewish Agency for Palestine. For a variety of reasons,
however, non-Zionists questioned the core of Zionist ideology or the immediate demand for a Jewish state. They could not agree that life outside a Jewish
homeland, especially in the United States, was a curse or a form of exile that
would lead inevitably to assimilation or physical destruction. Like the minimalist Zionists, some believed that a self-governing state was desirable and
obtainable in the far-distant future, but that it was inexpedient to call for a
state in the middle of a war, when all communal energy should be diverted toward winning the conflict and rescuing the remaining Jews. Britain might still
be convinced to permit more Jews to immigrate to Palestine. For the time
being, they believed, the issues of rescuing Jewish lives and the ultimate political goal of having a state ought to be kept separate. After all, what good would
a Jewish state be if there was no one alive left to live in it?

Another major point of disagreement, articulated in the "Basel Platform"
of the first World Zionist Congress in 1897, was the concept that Jews constituted a single national entity wherever they lived and that one single country
or entity could or should speak for them. The concept of Jewish nationalism
was especially distasteful in view of what was happening in Germany (*Nazi*,
after all, was an abbreviation for "National Socialism" in German) and nationalism gone wild was causing nations to eat one another alive. Why should
Jews join the crowd by adhering to such a destructive philosophy?[31]

More important, the concept of Jewish nationalism also appeared to repudiate and endanger efforts to gain Jews full rights in the countries where they
already lived and to raise the specter of dual loyalty. It did not take into account the unique position of Jews in America. There was an additional danger, some non-Zionists feared, that a Jewish state would claim Jews the world
over as its own citizens, and that antisemites would see such a state as the fulfillment of all their accusations, demanding that all Jews depart and go live in
it. American non-Zionists also questioned the establishment of a sovereign
Jewish state in Palestine when two-thirds of the population consisted of Muslim and Christian Arabs.

Anti-Zionists shared all these objections and took things a step further.
They were ideologically opposed to the existence of a Jewish state anywhere,
at any time, and under any circumstances. Such a prospect was to be fought
with every tool available. They consistently denied or disavowed that Jews
anywhere else had any special connection at all to the Land of Israel and they
opposed the very concept of Jewish peoplehood. For them, history had made
its decision two thousand years earlier when Jewish sovereignty in that area
came to an end; now Judaism stood on a higher and more spiritual plane.
Moreover a Jewish state might reverse the process of emancipation and be a

mortal danger to the millions of Jews living elsewhere in the world. In the modern era any suggestion that Jews were more than a religion dedicated to universalist, ethical, and prophetic ideals, was abhorrent. ("Americans of the Mosaic faith" or "persuasion" were common terms of self-reference among this group). The American Council for Judaism, which represented this view and was in some ways an offshoot of the AJC, lobbied ceaselessly against the creation of a Jewish state. After Israel was founded, they went out of their way to condemn it and loudly disavow any connection American Jews might have with it.

Wartime was perhaps not the best time to conduct these ideological battles. Joseph Proskauer, who was chosen as AJC's president in 1943, stressed the primacy of the rescue issue on humanitarian grounds. He later declared the entire debate over a Jewish state while the conflict was still raging as "academic," and the fulfillment of the antisemite's desire to "divide and conquer" the Jews.[32] But on the debate went.

A series of showdowns on these issues took place from 1941 to 1943 that were to have longtime repercussions for the AJC. Behind the scenes Zionists, headed by David Ben-Gurion, were undertaking protracted negotiations with the traditionally non-Zionist American Jewish Committee in order to arrive at some form of agreement. The negotiations were for mutual benefit; the AJC wished to exert its influence and maintain the cooperation and deference of the rest of the organized Jewish community. At the same time, the Zionist movement wanted and needed the power and wealth of AJC members, many of whom had acted and contributed generously toward the well-being of the Yishuv. No matter how much enmity might exist between the two factions, no plan was likely to work unless the AJC cooperated with it.

At the Biltmore Hotel in New York, May 9–11, 1942, an extraordinary World Zionist Congress consisting of every delegate who could find his or her way to the United States (some had been fortuitously stranded there when the war began) passed a maximalist resolution openly calling for free Jewish immigration to Palestine and the establishment of a "Jewish Commonwealth." At that time, even Zionists hesitated to use the word "State." Largely a reaction to the 1939 White Paper, this resolution represented a radical break with previous mainstream Zionist policy, which was based on the presumption that the British mandate would continue. The battle then came to rally the rest of the American Jewish communal world behind the Biltmore Program.[33]

At the 1942 convention of the Reform Central Conference of American Rabbis, a resolution stating that the Jewish population had the right to create an army under its own flag passed with sixty-four affirmative votes and thirty-eight opposed.[34] Reaffirming the position of classical Reform Judaism, which was on the decline in the CCAR at the time, the dissenting rabbis withdrew to form the American Council for Judaism (ACJ). The ACJ was the only national organization ever founded specifically to battle the idea of a Jewish state, and its membership and leadership happened to include a good number of men and women who were or had been associated with the American Jewish Committee. Indeed, by 1943 the directorship of the ACJ had passed to Lessing Rosenwald, a member of the AJC Executive Committee. Soon, facing continued isolation and a deliberate effort of the AJC to purge its ranks of a group they considered as bad as that of any antisemitic organization, Rosenwald and others would be compelled to withdraw from the AJC.

The Cos Cob Formula and Withdrawal from the American Jewish Conference of 1943

Maurice Wertheim, AJC president from 1940 to 1943, had been leading negotiations with the Zionists for several years; in 1941, he declared that in terms of the ongoing debate, it was by now entirely inconsistent to back the Jews in Palestine while withholding support for their political aspirations:

In my opinion there are only Zionists and anti-Zionists. I say this because up to twenty years ago with very small numbers of Jews in Palestine, we could all sympathetically regard the settlement there as a possible cultural and religious center, but now with almost six hundred thousand Jews residing there and a strong political party working day in and day out for the establishment of a self-governing community there, I think the possibility of a spiritual center is nothing more than a comfortable delusion. It just will never be that, and the Jews in Palestine will perforce take things into their own hands, whether we extend support to them or not. . . . It is entirely illogical for anyone to be pro-Palestine and anti an eventual self-governing community there.[35]

A modus vivendi along the Zionist, non-Zionist, and anti-Zionist spectrum appeared to have been reached on June 7, 1942, when Zionist and American Jewish Committee leaders met informally at Wertheim's summer home in Cos Cob, Connecticut. David Ben-Gurion, future prime minister of Israel, who had found himself in the United States at the beginning of the war, played an important role in these secret negotiations. Under the terms of the "Cos Cob Formula," as it came to be known, the AJC would accept the Zionist program for a Jewish state, while the Zionists in turn would renounce the idea of Diaspora nationalism. In the Jewish commonwealth all inhabitants, without regard to race or religion, would enjoy complete equality of rights. According to the formula, the establishment of the commonwealth also should in no way affect the status or the allegiance of any Jews who were already citizens of countries outside it. Only those who resided in Palestine were eligible to become citizens there. In effect, the Zionists would take responsibility for all matters affecting Palestine, while the AJC's main sphere of influence would remain in foreign affairs outside of Palestine.[36] Such was, in fact, the general path that the American Jewish

Committee sought in the late 1940s and early 1950s, after the State of Israel had been established.

In June 1942, however, three prominent AJC representatives at that meeting, including Joseph M. Proskauer, dissented strongly from the Cos Cob formula. They threatened to resign from the AJC and to fight the measure wholeheartedly if it passed as a matter of general AJC policy. The struggle set in motion a bitter controversy among Committee members and led to prolonged debates on the questions of Jewish statehood, Arab-Jewish relations, and Diaspora nationalism.[37]

Morris Waldman, the longtime secretary and executive vice president of the American Jewish Committee, supported Wertheim and urged him to stand firm.[38] In the end, however, Maurice Wertheim refused to stand for reelection and backed away to devote himself to wartime concerns. The AJC presidency went to Proskauer, a prominent judge born in Mobile, Alabama (his grandfather had fought for the Confederacy), who had worked closely with Alfred E. Smith during his years as governor of New York and during his 1928 presidential campaign. Proskauer's administration ran from 1943 to 1949, critical years that encompassed World War II and the creation of Israel, and he remained an "elder statesman" of the organization well into the 1960s. He had become active in the AJC soon after the Nazis came to power in Germany in 1933 and began his public life in the anti-Zionist camp, believing that a Jewish state would be a "catastrophe" for the Jewish people.[39] As a condition of his election Proskauer called for a compromise formula, the 1943 "Statement of Views with Respect to the Present Situation in Jewish Life," which he and three other Committee officers had drafted.

The Statement of Views called for the abrogation of the White Paper and free Jewish immigration into Palestine; it stopped short, however, of endorsing a Jewish commonwealth, instead calling for a U.N. trusteeship over Palestine. Wertheim gave his assent to the plan, noting that it was the product of negotiations between Zionists and non-Zionists. Indeed, from the Zionist point of view, the 1943 Statement of Views could have been far worse (as Proskauer himself acknowledged). "I am sure that you will agree with me that [the Statement] shows an ever-narrowing gulf which it is my fervent hope may some day be bridged forever," Wertheim declared at the AJC's 1943 annual meeting. "A way must be found for us and I am confident that it will be found."[40] At the time, however, to call for any kind of external trusteeship over Palestine was contrary to the view of the majority of the organized American Jewish community, where maximalist Zionists were gaining increasing influence.

As the full awareness of what was happening in Europe spread, the need for American Jews to unite became more urgent. In August 1943 the most representative Jewish body ever in the United States convened under the name of the American Jewish Conference.[41] Eight months in the making, the

Conference included 501 delegates from across the country. Proskauer, unlike some of the AJC membership, supported the participation of the Committee in the Conference and took part in the negotiations preceding it. To preserve a united front, Nahum Goldmann and Rabbi Stephen Wise of the American Jewish Congress agreed to AJC conditions: the conference would deal with questions of rescue; discussions on Jewish statehood would be postponed. In exchange the AJC would put its full weight behind the call for abrogation of the White Paper and for unlimited Jewish immigration to Palestine.

The agreement fell apart when Rabbi Abba Hillel Silver, a Zionist leader and one of the most outstanding orators of his time, seized the floor and gave a speech that ranked as one of the high points of his career.[42] Rejecting all compromise, he described "national homelessness" as the very root of the Jewish tragedy, claimed that a national home was the only true solution, and called for an immediate declaration in favor of a Jewish commonwealth in Palestine. "If we surrender our national and historic claims to Palestine," he declared, "We will lose our case as well as do violence to the historic hopes of our people."[43] He thereupon, in clarion tones, read his "Declaration on Palestine," which incorporated the Biltmore Program. The audience was moved to tears as they rose and sang "Hatikvah," the Zionist anthem, over and over. On the following day, September 1, 1943, the American Jewish Conference voted almost unanimously to adopt Silver's statement on Palestine. The only two major Jewish organizations that voted against it were the Jewish Labor Committee and the American Jewish Committee, whose delegates, including Joseph Proskauer and Jacob Blaustein, registered their dissent and then walked out of the room. The AJC officially withdrew from the American Jewish Conference a month later. The official reason they gave, then and later, was that the Conference—which took place in the middle of World War II—was supposed to discuss the rescue of Jews in Europe; moreover, it was impossible to have a democratic, sovereign Jewish state in a country where the majority of the population was not Jewish.[44]

This was not to be the last time that the AJC, carefully guarding its own autonomy, departed from a representative American Jewish organization. It was, however, by far the most notorious. It can be said that the AJC never truly recovered from the publicity that ensued. In two days it received more attention than it had in thirty years, but the attention was overwhelmingly negative.[45] In the American Jewish Anglo and Yiddish press, Proskauer's name was cursed and the American Jewish Committee leaders were damned as self-appointed oligarchs who were anti-Zionists, traitors, and destroyers of Jewish unity at a critical time. At AJC meetings passionate pleas to reenter the American Jewish Conference for the sake of unity were heard, and 10 percent of the membership resigned in protest against the withdrawal. Proskauer and Blaustein refused to relent. "The American Jewish Committee stands for certain ideals," Proskauer stated, "and they will survive over and above all the attacks that have been made on us. . . . Indeed, it is my belief that out of this turmoil will come the rebirth of the American Jewish Committee as an agency for good."[46]

Within five years no one would have recognized Proskauer's behavior. Against the wishes of a strong faction within the AJC that opposed the idea of Jewish nationalism or the creation of a Jewish state—some hoped for peace between Jews and Arabs in a binational state—Proskauer became convinced that partition of Palestine and the creation of a Jewish state was the only solution. Hundreds of thousands of Jewish Displaced Persons were unable to find a home anywhere, and there would never be free immigration to the one place that wanted them unless that immigration was in Jewish hands. Moreover, Proskauer was able to convince his followers that if the refugees themselves and the majority of the American Jewish community wanted a Jewish homeland, it was not for the American Jewish Committee to stand in the way.[47]

The change came gradually, although during Proskauer's presidential administration and that of Jacob Blaustein afterward the AJC never made peace with the central Israeli concept of *Galut*—the idea that all Jews living outside Israel were in "exile." Nor could they ever accept the idea that Diaspora Jews might owe some sort of political allegiance to the Jewish state. In many ways the complex attitude of the AJC toward the Yishuv and later the State of Israel remained a touchstone of the organization's developing Jewish identity.

Proskauer and the leaders of the AJC took every opportunity, including their connections with President Truman and the highest levels of government, to advocate for abrogation of the White Paper and for the immediate and unconditional admission of at least one hundred thousand Jews into Palestine. In many ways, their independence from the organized Zionist movement permitted them more freedom to work and to be heard among government officials. For a time, the AJC held firm to the Statement of Views policy of a U.N. trusteeship, preferring to postpone political arrangements until later. Two-thirds of the country's residents were still Arabs and too few who advocated statehood took seriously the question of what the Arabs' fate would be in a Jewish state or what sort of state could result under such circumstances. The situation of the DPs in Europe was dire, Palestine was becoming more unstable by the day, the Jewish underground groups Irgun and the Stern Gang were wreaking havoc, and Jews all over the world were protesting British policy. Further, Great Britain was nearing the end of its rope as the mandatory authority in the country and was getting ready to throw the entire affair over to the United Nations. Order had to be restored and lives had to be saved; the U.N. appeared to be the only authority that could do that, at least temporarily. "When the house is burning down, you don't stop to argue what kind of house you want to put in its place," Proskauer testified before the Anglo-American Committee of Inquiry in January 1946.[48]

By the following year, however, a new item was officially on the agenda, one that went back a decade to a previous investigative commission: the idea that Palestine could be partitioned into two states, one Jewish, and the other Arab. Under such an arrangement, which was supported and advocated by the Jewish Agency, Jews would constitute a majority in their part of the country and they would have free control over immigration. It was this solution that the majority of UNSCOP (United Nations Committee on Palestine) recommended in September 1947. No one saw the proposal as ideal, but Proskauer became convinced that it offered the only way out of an unbearable situation. That President Truman and the State Department appeared to be amenable to the suggestion increased its attraction. The Committee's leaders immediately sent a telegram to the secretary of state urging "speedy and vigorous" adoption of that measure; to the shock and dismay of his anti-Zionist associates, AJC President Joseph M. Proskauer and his second-in-command, Executive Committee chairman Jacob Blaustein, threw their full weight behind partition and the creation of a Jewish state.[49] Proskauer in particular used all his contacts at the State Department and Blaustein his contacts in the White House and the Democratic Party to assure that end.

On November 29, 1947, the resolution on partition, number 181, came up for a vote in the United Nations General Assembly. The measure passed, with thirty-three in favor, thirteen opposed, and ten abstentions. There was little evidence to support later interpretations that sympathy and guilt for the Holocaust had very much to do with the decision at the time. The very word "Holocaust" as a common reference for what had happened to Jews did not as yet exist. Fighting was occurring in Palestine, and partition seemed the best way to end it. According to one Israeli historian who studied the extensive debates surrounding the U.N. resolution, "factors such as the historical connection of the Jewish people to Palestine, or feelings of remorse because of the recent Jewish tragedy, were hardly heard, if at all."[50] Still, the resolution passed. Jewish communities around the world went wild with joy. "Those of our contemporaries who fear Jewish nationalism," wrote Milton Himmelfarb, an AJC staff member who was at the time secretary of its foreign affairs committee and of its Staff Committee on Palestine, "cannot avoid being stirred by the establishment of a Third Commonwealth two thousand years after the destruction of the Second and three thousand after the founding of the First."[51]

The overwhelming joy was premature. The million and a half Arabs in Palestine and those in the surrounding Arab nations were not willing then nor afterward to recognize any kind of Jewish state, which they regarded as a Western Jewish knife thrust into the heart of the Arab world. They vowed to fight against implementation of the U.N. decision. No clear peace agreement or undisputed borderlines resulted when what became Israel's War of Independence finally ended.[52] No arms were forthcoming from nations that would later be falsely credited with having made the Yishuv's ultimate military victory possible. Until the spring of 1950, when the United States, Britain, and

France joined in a Tripartite Declaration to guarantee Israel's borders and maintain balance of arms between Israel and the Arab nations, there was in fact an arms embargo against the Yishuv and later the State itself. Jews in Palestine scrounged their arms from Czechoslovakia and from World War II leftovers; any American Jews caught smuggling military equipment to Palestine were arrested. Furthermore, as the fighting went on, it became clear that while the U.N. was willing to vote for a partition leading to a Jewish state, neither they, nor the British, nor any other nation was willing to do anything to enforce that decision. The British had announced their intention to leave on May 14, 1948, and there was every reason to believe that chaos at best and a Jewish massacre at worst would result when the mandatory authorities finally withdrew.

"It was not contemplated that the UN resolution on partition was conditioned on the consent of the two groups in Palestine," declared the AJC in a March 28 statement in which it called upon the Security Council to step in and fulfill the UN charter: "to take effective collective measures for the prevention and removal of threats to peace, and for the suppression of acts of aggression or other breaches of the peace . . . If those two groups were brought into agreement there would be no necessity for action by the assembly. Action by the Assembly was necessitated by the very fact of disagreement." The statement continued:

The exact situation is that the Arabs threatened violence, and subsequently have employed violence, to defeat the implementation of the Assembly resolution. Some authority must use force to suppress such violence. We quite understand and applaud the desire for peaceful solution, but we urge that the UN cannot with dignity or safety be put in the position of arriving at a decision and then submitting to internal and external violence in Palestine to thwart it. Peace will not result from condoning violence. It can only be achieved by suppressing violence. . . . The necessity of such action was clearly envisaged prior to the passage of the Assembly resolution. . . . The danger calls for immediate, firm and statesmanlike action. In parts of Palestine today, the British have already withdrawn and the ordinary functions of government are being exercised by Jewish bodies. . . . There is now the danger that the Jews of Palestine have been deserted by the democratic nations.[53]

As the date for termination of the British mandate drew near and word came that the Jews in Palestine intended to take matters into their own hands and declare an independent Jewish state, Proskauer and Blaustein had a meeting with Zionist leaders in February 1948. They wished to be consulted about the name of the state, the constitution, and its system of government. The name the "New Judea" was used by many in the Anglo-Jewish press between December 1947 and May 1948. Blaustein discussed several ideas, remarking that "it appears to me now that "the Jewish State" or "Judea" for obvious reasons, would be undesirable." (The joke spread among American Jews of East European descent that the American Jewish Committee did not care if the new state was named "Irving," so long as it was not called "Judea.")[54] The name "New Judea," he thought, might be somewhat better. The name "Eretz Israel" had been one option. Blaustein himself preferred "Zion."[55] Proskauer and Blaustein also hoped that the new state's government would have a constitution and a bill of rights modeled after that of the United States, with separation of church and state and complete equality for all the inhabitants.

On May 14, 1948, the Jews of Palestine took matters into their own hands when Prime Minister David Ben-Gurion, speaking at four o'clock in the afternoon from the Tel Aviv Museum, read the Declaration of Independence of the State of Israel. An empty space was left in the original document for the actual name of the state to be filled in; until the last moment there were still discussions and debate over what that name should be. The surrounding Arab nations refused to accept the partition resolution or the existence of a Jewish state in their midst and their armies attacked Israel. Fighting continued until January 1949, when the last cease-fire was declared and Israel was left in control of eight thousand square miles including all of the Negev, eighteen hundred miles more than had been set in the U.N. General Assembly Partition resolution.

In October 1948 the Executive Committee of the AJC met in Chicago to discuss what its relationship to the new country would be and to hammer out a statement. Proskauer declared, first of all, that all the conflicts on whether there should be a Jewish state or not were over; by its very existence, the State of Israel had settled the controversy. Moreover, he said, the State "presented the Committee . . . with one of its greatest opportunities in its entire history for rendering service to Jewry." While he declared that the State "creates new problems for us," he also admitted that it had brought great benefit to the position of Jews in America. "The heroic and successful resistance of the Israelis to Arab aggression has been a great blessing to Jews everywhere," he said, "and should go far toward killing the stereotype that Jews lack courage."[56]

The group adopted several resolutions, among them that Truman should continue backing partition, that the area allotted to the new state should be sufficient to absorb a large influx of immigrants, and that Israel be granted de jure recognition and financial aid from the United States—which it achieved the following year.[57] The resolution led to a new AJC Statement of Views in 1949 that differed considerably from the statement of 1943. The statement spoke of AJC's commitment to combating bigotry, prejudice, and discrimination, as well as the organization's dedication to achieving full human and civil rights. It also spelled out an official position toward Israel. "We hold the establishment of the State of Israel to be an event of historic significance," the Committee declared. "We applaud its recognition by our own and other governments. We look forward to Israel's assumption of its full place among the family of nations as a government guaranteeing complete equality towards all its inhabitants without regard to race, creed or national origin. . . .

Within the framework of American interests we shall aid in the upbuilding of Israel as a vital spiritual and cultural center and in the development of its capacity to provide a free and dignified life for those desiring to make it their home."[58] The State of Israel had been born. Now AJC assumed responsibility for helping build it and for working out the relations between the new state and the Jews who lived elsewhere in the world.

"With Ever-Increasing Vigor"

The Science of Hatred, the Displaced Persons, and the Blaustein–Ben-Gurion Statement

The withdrawal of the AJC from the American Jewish Conference in 1943 was in many ways the first step on the road to a "new" American Jewish Committee, one resembling the large national organization of the twenty-first century. AJC leaders spoke of their determination not to permit such a rupture and isolation to occur again; cooperation with other sectors of the Jewish community would be sought whenever necessary and possible. They were also driven by an awareness of their inability to stop the slaughter of Jews abroad and a determination never to permit such a thing to recur. The AJC was completely reorganized and expanded near the end of the war and the principles developed between then and 1950 guided it for the next twenty years.

Reorganization

After spending a year examining every detail of the agency's operations, an AJC Committee on Reorganization, chaired by Jacob Blaustein, delivered its recommendations. The new executive vice president, John Slawson, was behind many of them. The first recommendation was that AJC members were forbidden to despair. They had to strengthen their hearts to go on in the face of catastrophe overseas and the rise of antisemitism in the United States. Bad though the situation was, it would have been "considerably worse," the report noted, had the AJC not already been engaged in the fight against it. They could not permit despair precisely because "the forces against us are so stupendous." These words were written when World War II was still being fought and the death camps were still in operation: "The difficulties with this problem, which at times seem so insurmountable and heart-breaking, must not discourage us into an attitude of defeatism. We cannot afford such an attitude. It would be suicide. To the contrary, because of the very magnitude of the problem and the destructive consequences thereof, the AJC, in the opinion of the Committee on Reorganization, must not only continue its activities in the domestic field but must do so with ever increasing vigor, application and courage."[1]

Then came concrete policy suggestions. Until then, the report read, the fight against antisemitism had been conducted on a short-term emergency basis, with efforts largely directed toward adults whose "conditioned minds furnish strong resistance to our counter-propaganda." While short-term action was essential, in the future more attention had to be paid to the prevention of the transmission of prejudice to the younger generation: hence, a new emphasis on the power of education. Also, the AJC had been concentrating on reaching the mass American population. Better results would be had by concentrating on *groups*; that is, tailoring each campaign to appeal to influential sectors of society such as war veterans, foreign-language groups, labor unions, industrial leaders, and women's organizations. The AJC should also mobilize the resources of the social sciences to study in a scientific way, for the first time, the problem of "intergroup and interracial disharmony" from the psychological, social, and cultural points of view.

It was also essential, according to the reorganization committee, that the AJC increase its presence overseas, by establishing a network of permanent offices in foreign cities as well as one in Washington, D.C. The writers also noted that AJC should not hesitate to become more activist in its work, marshaling public opinion and working through diplomatic channels "as energetically as possible," rather than always pursuing, as its enemies would have called it, the "hush-hush" approach. The organization itself would have to have some kind of publicity department that would act in a "dignified manner" to handle the AJC's public relations. "It is not intended," the report cautioned, "that there shall be any fundamental departure from the long and honorable tradition of modesty regarding efforts and achievements of the AJC which has consistently refrained from doing anything merely for the publicity it would derive."[2] Some publicity was necessary, however, in order for the organization to do its job most effectively and to raise the funds that it needed to do its work.

After the war the library, research, and publications programs of AJC were all enlarged and strengthened. *Commentary,* a new magazine under the editorship of Elliot E. Cohen debuted in November 1945.[3] Soon, multiple languages were covered. *Commentario* in Spanish and *Yedies* in Yiddish (meant for distribution in Latin America) and the French-language *Evidences* (Europe) also began publication shortly after.

By far the most fundamental change John Slawson called for was the establishment of American Jewish Committee local chapters across the country,

similar to those of the American Jewish Congress and many other Jewish organizations. Officers openly discussed the isolation the organization had suffered during the American Jewish Conference episode, the loss of ten percent
of its membership, and the need to broaden its membership base in order to
refute accusations that their group was nothing but a small group of oligarchs
unrepresentative of the Jewish community at large. Members undertook a
massive recruitment drive, gaining new "like-minded" adherents through letters, personal solicitations, receptions, and meetings in people's homes. Many
American Jews were receptive to AJC's message. Within three years, the AJC
had thirty-two chapters and thousands of new members across the land.

While there were many reasons to join an AJC chapter, among them the
search for fellowship, deep anxiety over what had happened during World
War II and a desire not to see it repeated in the United States were apparently
powerful motivations, as can be seen from some of the recruitment literature
of the era and the testimony of the members themselves. Norman Rabb, who
helped to form the Boston chapter in 1945 and went on to become a national
officer, recalled a quarter century later: "I became interested in the AJC in the
final analysis because I felt that it was beneficial to me and to my family. I
began to be concerned as to how as an individual I could go about protecting
my rights as a Jews, and I came to the conclusion that I really wouldn't know
where to begin; but through the American Jewish Committee at least I had a
chance. What had happened in Germany was very fresh in my mind. If it
could happen there to an influential and well-integrated Jewry, it could happen anywhere. I began to wonder, are our rights less important than our
homes, our furs, our jewelry and furniture, which we are so very careful to insure? Without our rights what do we really have? Without their rights, what
did the Jews of Germany have? Quite frankly, I looked upon the American
Jewish Committee as an insurance investment on my rights to live in freedom
as a Jew and as an American."[4]

Jacob Blaustein

Another step toward a new AJC was reached in 1949 when Joseph Proskauer
retired from his post as AJC president and was replaced by Jacob Blaustein,
who had been chair of the Executive Committee. He served in that post until
1954 and was a dominant figure in the organization until his death in 1970.
Blaustein's presidency represented several "firsts" for the organization. He
was the first president of Eastern European descent, he was not a New Yorker
and, in contrast to several of his predecessors, he was not a lawyer or judge.
He did not come from German Jewish wealth and rose from humble origins.
His father, Louis Blaustein, had immigrated to the United States from Lithuania virtually penniless and began as a peddler in the farming area of eastern

Pennsylvania. He moved to Baltimore in 1888, where Jacob was born in 1892. Jacob as a child helped his father sell kerosene in the streets of Baltimore from a horse and buggy.[5]

It was from that position that Jacob Blaustein rose to immense wealth, power, and influence. In 1910, before most Americans had cars, Jacob and his father founded the American Oil Company which began as two men and a horse-drawn tank wagon and went on to become one of the giants of the petroleum industry. By the 1950s it was one of the largest oil companies in the United States with twenty-six thousand employees. The company established the first drive-in gasoline station in the United States and it was their gasoline, Amoco, that powered Charles A. Lindbergh's historic solo flight to Paris in 1927.[6] Later the company diversified into trading, shipping, and real estate. During his business career Blaustein owned a fleet of tankers, oil wells in Texas and Louisiana, and several manufacturing companies; he also had vast real estate holdings in Baltimore, San Diego, Dallas, and Los Angeles. He was a generous contributor to the Democratic Party and became known nationally and internationally as an adviser to and diplomatic representative for several American presidents. He was an advocate of both Jewish and general humanitarian causes with world leaders, and was appointed in 1955 by President Dwight D. Eisenhower as a regular member of the U.S. delegation to the United Nations. In his Jewish activities he was best known worldwide for his role as a leading figure of the Conference on Jewish Material Claims Against Germany, which negotiated with West Germany for reparations for Israel and Holocaust survivors.[7]

Helping Jews versus Helping Humanity: The Move to "Intergroup Relations"

After the end of World War II, there were continual debates at annual and committee meetings on how involved the AJC should become in fighting for liberal causes and the civil and political rights of people who were not Jewish. Against opposition by some who claimed that the AJC could best stick to its charter by engaging only in those issues that affected Jews directly (what might be called the traditional "defense" posture) other Jewish leaders and social scientists spoke for a movement that was sweeping religious, civic, and Jewish organizations after World War II. This movement was known as "intergroup relations" and its goal was to eliminate prejudice and bigotry against all racial, religious, and ethnic minorities.[8]

At the heart of intergroup relations was what historian John Higham has called a "theory of the unitary character of prejudice," which saw antisemitism, racism, and all other forms of bigotry as a single type of hatred with a single cause.[9] There was in fact, according to this view, no true division between helping two kinds of people, just as there was no longer so sharp a difference between events affecting Jews overseas and events that affected them at home. The best and only way to protect all Jews was to fight for the civil and political rights of all people. In this sense, the new ethos of AJC and other Jewish organizations was not that far from some of the ideology of the Jewish socialist movements, which held that only the achievement of universal justice would eliminate antisemitism and be the sole and complete salvation of the Jewish people. It became a matter of faith at AJC, borne out by contemporary social science, that nowhere would Jews be safe, not in the United States or elsewhere, so long as human rights were infringed upon anywhere. The specific Jewish focus of this view, which became for many a fundamental part of their ethnic identity, was that Jews, because of what they had suffered and the experience they had gained thereby, had a special responsibility and privilege to help all of humankind fight for those rights.[10]

It was under the influence of these views that Joseph Proskauer and the AJC delegation to the United Nations founding conference in San Francisco in 1945 fought to have an International Declaration of Human Rights written into the U.N. charter, against the desires of the Soviet Union and other nations who saw such a declaration as interfering with their internal autonomy. For years, as long as the American Jewish community looked to the U.N. for leadership, this success was considered as one of the crowning glories of Proskauer and the AJC's career.[11]

The internal debate between those who wanted AJC to work only on behalf of other Jews and those who wanted to broaden the scope to include human and civil rights in general came into the open at an Executive Committee meeting in January 1947, not coincidentally at a time when violent organized antisemitism was on the decline. By that point major AJC meetings were held at hotels and clubs and more than one hundred people attended routinely. The annual meeting of the entire Committee, required under the bylaws, had grown from one Sunday afternoon in Louis Marshall's library to a gala event at a major hotel attended by hundreds of people. By the 1990s the number attending would be in the thousands and it would become the major social and policymaking event of AJC's entire year.

The year 1947 was a turning point in the nascent American civil rights movement. Only a few years earlier, during World War II, the government had brought its power to bear against racial, ethnic, or religious discrimination, because the cause of unity and production needs had caused recognition of a need for "fair employment" practices. State and local governments soon followed federal practices. Then President Truman, who had seen the rise of the Ku Klux Klan in his own home state of Missouri, became acutely conscious of the role that racism had played in the recent struggle with the Japanese and the Nazis. In 1947 he created a special committee of prominent blacks and whites, including representatives of Jewish organizations, to assess the state of civil rights laws in the country and suggest ways to improve them. The document this committee produced, "To Secure These Rights"—subsequently incorporated into the Democratic Party platform for 1948—had called for far-reaching reforms. These included a permanent commission on civil rights, fair employment practices, federal anti-lynching legislation, elimination of the poll tax, and an end to segregation in education, the armed forces, housing, health care, and public services. Much of the wording came directly from material and testimony submitted by the American Jewish Congress and the American Jewish Committee. "To Secure These Rights" set the agenda in the government and the courts for the civil rights movement and the main Jewish defense agencies for the next two decades.[12]

At its own Executive Committee meeting in January 1947, the AJC was considering how far it should go to support this national effort. On the table was a specific request by the NAACP and prominent civic, religious, and labor groups that AJC join in efforts to get an anti-lynching bill passed by Congress.[13] There was an extended discussion, led by Ely M. Aaron of Chicago and Alan M. Stroock of New York, on what they called the "scope" of AJC's activities. Those who favored an extension of the AJC's activities argued that any social pattern that limited the rights of any minority threatened the security of all minorities. Therefore, the AJC should take clear stands on the poll tax, on federal anti-lynching laws, on fair employment practices laws, on racially restrictive covenants, and on any number of similar legislative and litigation goals.

Those who supported the opposite position disagreed, saying that AJC members were of varying opinions on general matters, and it was their mandate to deal with Jewish matters only. Furthermore, the job of fighting hatred against Jews already consumed a considerable part of their time, money, and energy. By extending its activities, didn't the AJC risk spreading itself too thin and doing a poor job in everything?[14] The debate concluded at a two-day Executive Committee meeting in Chicago ten months later where the advocates of fighting for all minorities won the day. Referred to thereafter as the "Chicago Mandate," those assembled passed the following resolution: "That the executive committee recognizes that there is the closest relationship between the protection of the civil rights of all citizens and the protection of the civil rights of the members of particular groups; that it is a proper exercise of the powers of our charter that the AJC join with other groups in the protection of the civil rights of the members of all groups irrespective of race, religion, color or national origin; and that it is our general policy so to do; and further resolved that the officers and appropriate committees are authorized within their sound discretion and with proper means, to implement this policy."[15]

From then on the AJC turned its efforts and its energies to a wide variety of social causes. In doing so, they were also following the lead of NCRAC (National Community Relations Advisory Council, pronounced "nack-rack") an umbrella group of American Jewish defense and intergroup relations agencies formed in 1944 for the purposes of coordinating policy. NCRAC played a decisive role in working for civil rights legislation. Relations between NCRAC and the AJC were to remain tense, however, in part because of what AJC considered encroachments on its autonomy and community insistence that all the constituent NCRAC agencies allot duties among themselves for the purpose of avoiding duplication and waste of money. Just as in the case of the American Jewish Conference, the AJC felt itself forced to withdraw in protest from NCRAC in 1952. The reason was the ill-fated MacIver Report, a document whose recommendations were never fulfilled but that set up a model of what might happen if organizations like the American Jewish Committee and the American Jewish Congress merged.

NCRAC and the MacIver Report

During and after the crisis of World War II American Jewish communal leaders in local areas began to question the multiplicity of agencies that existed for Jewish defense and the maintenance of good intergroup relations. Why should American Jews and the local federations and welfare funds be asked to foot the bill for the American Jewish Committee, the American Jewish Congress, the Anti-Defamation League, the Jewish Labor Committee, the Union of American Hebrew Congregations, and a score of other groups? How could such a plethora of agencies carry on such important work with economy, efficiency, effectiveness, and accountability? Surely the situation would be improved if the work of defense agencies was better coordinated. In the Yiddish newspapers, there were open calls in so many words for American Jews to establish a proper *kehillah,* the type of all-encompassing Jewish community that had existed in Europe. Thus in a movement spearheaded by the American Jewish Congress, NCRAC commissioned in January 1950 an evaluative study of Jewish communal organizations by Robert M. MacIver, emeritus professor of sociology at Columbia University. AJC, a constituent of NCRAC at the time, supported the idea of the study but opposed the choice of MacIver to do it, whom they considered an outsider to Jewish communal life. The resulting MacIver Report, which attracted attention in non-Jewish circles as well, came as a bombshell to the AJC and to other organizations that had come under its scrutiny.[16]

MacIver criticized what he saw as the waste, competition, and inefficiency of the organizations as they were. In a long, complex, and controversial report he called for a system of overall financing for the organizations under the aegis of NCRAC and recommended specifically how different responsibilities should be apportioned among the different groups. Everything to do with labor, for example, would be handled exclusively by the Jewish Labor

Committee; everything that had to do with interreligious affairs would be handled by the rabbis of the Union of American Hebrew Congregations. NCRAC would be made far more centralized and decisions that bound its constituents would be made by majority vote.

The American Jewish Committee had a tradition of treasuring its autonomy and would not agree to this type of arrangement. "I think that Dr. MacIver has grossly underestimated the importance of Jewish ideological and factional differences," commented one AJC member in a letter to Jacob Blaustein discussing the impact of the report.[17] And NCRAC, after all, was supposed to be an *advisory* committee, not a supra-agency with complete control over the activities and finances of all its members. In its reorganization AJC had taken steps to abandon some of its customary aloofness and to reach out to the wider Jewish community more; it was for this reason that they had joined NCRAC in the first place. However, the leaders of the AJC did not want to be bound by the will of other agencies whose methods and philosophy of Jewish life were at complete variance with their own.[18]

The study provided an occasion for self-reflection among AJC leaders in considering just how different they were in approach and organizational "personality" from the other constituent groups of NCRAC. Judge Proskauer referred to the report as a "wave of totalitarianism repugnant to everything the AJC stands for" and said that the recommendations would turn NCRAC into a "Sanhedrin." "The AJC will never surrender," he said in a stirring speech to the leadership. "Do you choose your doctor by majority vote? Do you choose your lawyer that way? Do you determine the principles which your conscience dictates to you by going out and calling for a majority vote?" After a particularly bitter meeting held in Atlantic City, AJC formally withdrew from NCRAC over the MacIver Report in 1952. Fourteen years passed before it would rejoin.[19]

Antisemitism Abroad: The "German Problem"

No matter how and with whom the American Jewish Committee chose to fight anti-Jewish activity and antisemitism, the organization had its hands full overseas throughout the 1940s and 1950s. The citizens of Europe and especially Germany did not immediately drop all hatred of Jews on VE-day. On the contrary, Nazi propaganda had made vast inroads into the Continent, entrenching itself deeply in the minds of Europeans. There was much concern that Germany would continue to be the source of such propaganda.

According to AJC analysts, the United States had five goals in its postwar German policy. The most immediate goal was to disarm Germany. Second, Nazi leaders had to be sought out and punished. Third, the United States had to encourage a responsible democratic government to replace Nazism. The fourth goal was to revive the German economy. Because the Marshall Plan to reconstruct Europe was a keystone of American foreign policy, it was easy for the fourth goal to take precedence over all the rest. Elected officials were particularly strong advocates of this point because reconstruction would relieve the American public of a grievous tax burden. A fifth goal, crystallized some time after the end of the war and not unrelated to the fourth, was to prevent all of Germany from falling into the hands of the Soviet Union or precipitating a third world war—fought this time with nuclear weapons.

As early as the March 1945 AJC annual meeting, John Slawson warned that Nazi-inspired antisemitism was continuing to spread across Europe, and that the AJC might be required to expand its activities. As the European war drew to a close, according to two assistant secretaries of state, Archibald MacLeish and Julius C. Holmes, who stated their views on April 7 in an NBC radio broadcast, Nazism had not disappeared. It had simply slipped underground. Holmes maintained that the Germans had known since 1943 that they were going to be defeated, and had made plans accordingly. By 1944 German industrialists and technicians were being sent to places of safety "so that they could be used another day." Holmes also spoke of a plan the Germans had to set up technical schools and scientific laboratories in foreign countries. These schools would be staffed by German teachers and technicians, thereby providing a haven for the scientific talent that was a major component of German industrial superiority.[20]

As for the Jews in postwar Eastern Europe, all over the stories were similar. Any Jews who tried to return to their former homes found others living in them who would not give them up. Polish Jews who had escaped the gas chambers still feared for their lives; AJC field representatives noted that anti-Jewish feeling had grown to "alarming proportions" among the Polish masses. In August 1945 the *New York Times* reported that 150 Jews had been murdered since the liberation of Poland.[21] Worst was the city of Kielce, where forty-five Jews were killed by a Polish mob on July 4, 1946. Noted, too, was persistence of virulent antisemitism in Austria, making restitution difficult or impossible. Despite Austrian government promises, no action had been taken to return Austrian Jewish property. In eastern Slovakia, Jews were being terrorized by bands of antigovernment, antisemitic, and anticommunist Poles. In Hungary there were pogroms and charges of ritual murder. The Hungarian foreign minister, when confronted by AJC representatives, explained that the country was in dire economic straits and that the alleviation of his country's distress would minimize the hatred.[22]

In panic, hundreds of thousands of Europe's surviving Jews fled to what they believed was the closest haven: the displaced persons camps of the U.S.-occupied zone in Germany. However, the presence of a U.S. military government provided only partial protection from a hostile native population. The

U.S. government goal of rebuilding Germany and encouraging its independence seemed to be taking precedence over all else. Two years after Germany was defeated, AJC representatives observed, antisemitism was still virulent there. National Socialism was too deeply rooted. "If we build up Germany materially at the present time without doing a complete spiritual and educational reorganization job," stated John Slawson in September 1947, "we are building up a Frankenstein monster who will infect and menace the world." Slawson had just returned from a tour of Europe, where he had opened the AJC's first Paris office. He commended the "courage and vitality" of the Jewish DPs who had created their own machinery for self-government, religious, vocational, and cultural activities, and who were even publishing their own newspapers. However, as he informed the AJC Executive Committee, "There is unanimous agreement among not only the DPs themselves but also among German Jews and workers for the Joint Distribution Committee and other American agencies that antisemitism is so rife that all Jews must leave Germany."[23]

The Berlin airlift in the winter of 1948–49, and the perceived bravery with which the Germans withstood the Soviet blockade, made many Americans regard their former enemies as heroes. Among the Germans themselves it did nothing to lessen the legacy of Nazism; in fact, it increased the feelings of intense German nationalism that were growing all the stronger as the Federal Republic of Germany moved closer to independence. In its meetings the leaders of the AJC took the position that in the East-West conflict only a new, democratic, and liberal German government could be a reliable ally, and that to support such tendencies there would provide the best protection against totalitarianism.

In the fall of 1949 Zachariah Shuster, AJC's European representative stationed in the Paris office, reported that there had been no change of heart in Germany. As the war receded into memory, Germans were beginning to feel that overall the Allies had committed so many sins that it canceled out any errors the Germans had made. Even "decent" Germans felt that they had paid enough for Hitlerism and were "fully entitled to enter the family of nations as an equal." The "denazification" process that the Allies had put in place after Nuremberg was becoming the butt of jokes. There was no enthusiasm for the process in any case, he reported, and given the East-West conflict, many a German was heard to say that it made no sense to become denazified if it only meant being "de-Americanized" by the Soviets later. The simple truth, Shuster wrote, was that "Germany is being rebuilt, but not changed one bit." A high American denazification officer summarized the situation: "We are building democracy with Nazi bricks. . . . The facts are that more than fifty percent of the top bracket of German civil service officials in Hesse are former Nazis; eighty percent of the Nazis ousted by the Americans from government positions have been reinstated; sixty percent of the Bavarian judges and seventy-six percent of the prosecutors faced de-nazification courts themselves;

and more than fifty percent of private industry is estimated to be in the hands of former Nazis."[24]

Meanwhile, back in New York, AJC leaders and their consultants were forbidden to despair, or to take the attitude (as almost all other Jewish organizations did) that they should not have anything to do with Germany. Whether they liked it or not, Germany was going to be the center of a rebuilt Europe. That meant that they had to do something, even if they had to be careful not to reveal their activities to other segments of the American Jewish community. A special Committee on Germany was formed, chaired by Arthur L. Mayer and including General Telford Taylor among its members. Early on they helped to organize and promote (both practically and financially) the liberal German element through a group known as the Lessing Association for the Promotion of Tolerance. By 1948 the group had branches in Frankfurt, Munich, Würzburg, and other localities. Endowing scholarships for German students to study in American universities was one idea broached at an executive committee meeting, although doubts were expressed that they would do much good. Dr. Ray Daily, a chapter representative from Dallas, wondered whether attendance at American colleges "where discriminatory admissions policies and social segregation are so rife, would discourage antisemitism on the part of German exchange students." Others remarked that the atmosphere of American colleges was nonetheless so much freer than that of Germany that the results could only be positive.[25]

Questions arose when Nazi-associated musical artists came to perform in the United States, or when an international industries fair in New York included ex-Nazis. Should the AJC officially condemn such proceedings? If so, then how? Rabbi S. Andhil Fineberg of Community Services, one of the AJC's foremost staff members in confronting domestic antisemitism, invoked what had become a familiar dictum that this should be seen as an American and not a Jewish problem. To receive former Nazis with high honors posed a clear danger to American society, he said. This was not a Jewish versus German controversy. "To emphasize WHO wants to exclude former Nazis can result only in deafening the public to the argument of WHY they should be excluded," he declared.[26]

Activities in connection with "the German problem" were ceaseless, if behind-the-scenes. There were constant visits to Germany, reports and surveys made, conferences with government officials and heads of other organizations to push them toward the values of democratization. AJC production personnel even translated and subtitled into German their literature and films and blanketed the country with new textbooks, reading matter, radio recordings, and films, including *Make Way for Youth* (1948), one of the most successful educational films the AJC ever produced. Observers kept remarking that no progress was being made and that things were in fact getting worse, not better. Still, the efforts continued.

The Jews of North Africa and the Middle East

In the field of foreign affairs, the Middle East and North Africa were turning into areas of crisis. Just as the displaced persons problem appeared to be moving toward a solution, the approximately eight hundred thousand Jews in these countries (often known as the "Forgotten Million") were facing acute danger to their lives and property. Through good fortune and the military might of the Allies, the Jewish communities of these countries had managed to escape from the Nazis and from the Vichy administrations relatively unscathed. During the war the "Crémieux Decree," which had granted French citizenship to the 130,000 Jews of Algeria, had been revoked by the Vichy government, and it took a year of effort after Vichy's defeat on the part of AJC and its partners to restore it. But the closer the world's Jews came to the realization of a state of their own in Palestine, and the closer these Muslim countries grew to independence from their former colonial masters, the more precarious the position of Jews in Muslim countries became.

The months and years after the November 27, 1947, U.N. partition vote were especially perilous. Judge Philip Forman, chair of AJC's Foreign Affairs Division (FAD) in delivering his report in February 1948, noted that efforts in Washington were in high gear; urgent requests had been made to the State Department and all diplomatic offices in those countries to intervene as soon as possible "and not to wait for the blood to flow." Periodic reports to and from the FAD described Jewish quarter bombings, pogroms, evictions, arrests, special taxes, Jews placed in concentration camps, and systematic impoverishment. The seventy-five thousand Jews of Egypt were in special danger. In Damascus, the Jewish quarter was cleared of Jews in order to house Palestinian Arabs refugees, and the Jews were removed from their homes and placed in camps. Close to half the Jews of Turkey, including two-thirds of the population of Izmir, fled to Israel at one time; no one knew what to do with the eighteen synagogues, yeshivot, and 240 Torah scrolls that they left behind. The Palestinian refugees were now being taken as cause for anti-Jewish measures. Even before the Palestinians fled, however, in secret discussions held in Bludan in 1947, the Arab League had laid plans for "systematically looting of the property of all Jews in the Arab countries." "The plan is now in action," reported AJC agents from overseas. "It provides for many large and small, but hazardous, ways of dispossessing Jewish property in ways which are not reported in the world press."27

Marcel Franco of the Alliance Israélite Universelle, chair of AJC's new committee on Near Eastern Affairs, declared a year after Israel's independence that American Jews must now duplicate, if along different lines, the efforts they had made to rescue European Jews. Discrimination and pogroms in the Muslim countries had to be fought with the same energy displayed when similar outrages took place in other countries, he declared. Financial and technical efforts must go for "exactly the same purposes that were pursued in Europe—relief, rehabilitation, and emigration."[28]

AJC efforts in the Middle East were not limited to public relations campaigns or meetings in Washington and with overseas consulates and relief agencies. When Iraq declared martial law against the Jewish threat at the end of 1949 and the Iranian government called for the expulsion of Jews of Iraqi nationality, Jacob Blaustein personally met with the Shah of Iran on December 23 and got his assurance that the edict would be repealed and that Iran would permit its territory to be used by Jews who needed to flee Iraq.[29]

Antisemitism at Home

Even as they fought for the restoration of rights to Jews in liberated Europe, the AJC and its associate organizations found themselves confronting on their very own soil hate groups, antisemitic street meetings, hate literature, anti-Jewish candidates for public office, and antisemitic political parties—much of it, before and during World War II, funded by virtually unlimited Nazi money. Just how much was made clear when Dr. Herbert von Strempel, former first secretary of the German Embassy in the United States, was interrogated on the subject in February 1946, in connection with the Nuremberg trials. Back at AJC headquarters, members pored over the transcript of his testimony. Using his immunity as a cover, Strempel had transmitted these funds, known as "Kriegskostensonderfonds" (special war-rations funds) from Berlin to U.S. propagandists—including American Nazi leader George Sylvester Viereck, who received five and ten thousand dollars at a time to publish antisemitic and pro-German literature through his publishing company Flanders Hall.[30] Before the war the funds also helped to shore up the "radio priest," Father Charles Coughlin, who fulminated against "international bankers," praised Hitler and Mussolini as anticommunist forces, and gave weekly radio sermons from Detroit that reached as many as forty million listeners (he reportedly received more than eighty thousand letters a week). Approximately one million Americans belonged to Coughlin's organization, the National Union for Social Justice. Not until 1940 did Coughlin's superiors order him to go back to parish work and cease his national broadcasts and publication of his newspaper.[31]

The Nazi money had been put to extensive use, and the AJC had striven mightily to subvert its influence. After the bombing of Pearl Harbor in December 1941 and the entrance of the United States into World War II, many Nazi agents in America found themselves jailed or under indictment for seditious activities; nonetheless, organized antisemitic activity continued underground. There were fears that as the war went in the Allies' favor and wartime restrictions were lifted, these activities would be out in the open again. There was also fear that the American economy might plunge with the peacetime de-mobilization sure to come, and that the population might be tempted to take out its frustration on the Jews. Antisemitic leaflets, doggerel, and cartoons were still being distributed near war plants and army and navy camps, issued anonymously and cheaply printed or mimeographed, sometimes reprinted in newspapers. Such literature had grown especially plentiful during the presidential campaign of 1940, when Franklin Roosevelt and his "Jew Deal" stood for reelection, and the Committee had braced itself for even more antisemitic campaign literature in the presidential election of 1944. In addition, 1944 was a congressional election year, and some of the candidates had been outspoken in their attacks on Jews.

Much of this campaign literature was distributed by the America First Party, an organization with several branches headed by the notorious Gerald L. K. Smith, who addressed large audiences each week and published the blatantly antisemitic *Cross and the Flag* newspaper. In 1944 he ran for president and polled 1,530 votes in Michigan. AJC observers were pleased at the decline; when Smith had run for the U.S. Senate from Michigan in 1942, he had garnered 130,000 votes.[32] Undercover AJC agents attended the America First Party's first national convention, held at the Leland Hotel in Detroit, August 29 and 30, 1944, where Smith and a list of candidates for Michigan state offices were nominated. The criteria for attendance were simple; "anyone who did not look Jewish" was permitted to enter the hall and vote.[33] The crowd, the agents reported, consisted of middle-aged and elderly people, eighty percent of them women. As part of the proceedings Homer Maertz of Chicago, formerly a member of the German American Bund introduced a resolution that all Jews should be deported and those who remained in the country after five years should be sterilized.[34]

The AJC did what it could to encourage a congressional inquiry into Smith's campaign finances; the inquiry took place on October 3, 1944. In five hours of testimony to the House Committee to Investigate Campaign Expenditures, Smith repeatedly referred to "the Jewish problem" and charged that 95 percent of communists were Jews. He condemned all Jewish groups, including the ADL, with accusations that with millions of dollars at their disposal, they were "hounding innocent Christian nationalists with their Gestapo techniques."[35] On January 30, 1946, he repeated similar charges, this time before the House Committee on Un-American Activities (and the AJC pulled all their strings in Washington to put him there). Words like "communist" and "Jew" fell regularly from his lips, AJC observers reported. Smith insisted that he was a "poor, white Christian" being hounded by the "Gestapo" of Jewish organizations. He insisted that he was not an antisemite, though in his next breath he accused the Jews of "controlling the press, radio, and motion pictures."[36]

When the results of the 1944 election were in, the AJC found reason to be relieved at the results. Senator Rufus C. Holman of Oregon, an open antisemite and member of the Ku Klux Klan, had been defeated in the Republican primaries. Congressman Lewis Thill of Wisconsin, who was remembered for inserting Nazi propaganda into the *Congressional Record,* was defeated in the November elections. Congress now included eight Jewish members, five reelected and two new ones. On the other hand, Mississippi was a disappointment: John Rankin, notorious for his antisemitic speeches on the floor, had been reelected. And Mississippi Senator Theodore G. Bilbo was still in power, a man accustomed to using the expressions "My dear Dago," "My dear Kike," "darkies," and "nigger" openly on the floor of the Senate.

Sporadic efforts to form reactionary third parties that were antisemitic in effect, if not always in name, continued in the United States. Not long after Smith's America First Party disintegrated, ex-Senator Robert Rice Reynolds of North Carolina, who had declined to run for reelection, formed the basis of the Nationalist Party (publishers of the *Nationalist Record*), the tone of which was decidedly isolationist and antilabor. Among the twelve planks in its platform was a call against an "international police force" (in other words, the United Nations), a demand that all immigration to the United States be stopped immediately (thus shutting the doors against any refugees from Europe), and an appeal to the United States to conserve its resources and not play "Santa Claus" to the whole world.[37] This party intended to support candidates who followed its views in the 1946 congressional elections and had hopes of running a national ticket in 1948. Reynolds was a particular threat, according to AJC's Department of Civil and Legal Affairs (headed by George Kellman), because he was a prominent, nationally known figure with ample funds who appealed to dissatisfied voters in both parties.

In combating such entities as the Nationalist Party, the AJC followed a well-worn course: portray the problem as an American, not a Jewish, one; bring the details of a person's life or party forward and let them express themselves while the AJC remained in the background; mobilize the writers and leaders of public opinion. Carefully crafted letters and memos filled with evidence went out to newspapers, magazines, press, business, and veterans' organizations across the country warning against the intentions of these groups and suggesting that surely any fair-minded institution would not wish to support them. An exposé of the Nationalist Party ran in the *Cleveland Press,* with the reporter using material and undercover information that the AJC provided. The articles were then translated by AJC personnel and reprinted in foreign language newspapers across the country. Soon Better Business Bureaus and Chambers of Commerce in a dozen cities were warning members against making any contributions to the Nationalist Party; veterans' organizations passed resolutions condemning it. Hotels where Reynolds and Gerald L. K. Smith were scheduled to speak canceled their contracts, and mayors of cities refused to allow them entrance. As a political party, the Nationalists were soon out of business.

Action was also called for in the case of the Columbians, Inc., a "storm trooper organization," as AJC sources referred to it, organized by former Princeton University student Homer L. Loomis Jr. and incorporated in August 1946. Loomis's stated aim was to make the Columbians politically dominant in all forty-eight states, working for "an American nationalist state" and a "one-race nation." The group was clearly modeled along the Nazi pattern, with uniforms similar to that of the Hitler Youth. Indeed, their tactics were not dissimilar to those of Hitler's Brownshirts. One seventeen-year-old Columbian was convicted of attacking a Negro man with a blackjack, and the organization made a habit of boycotting and picketing homes and businesses owned by blacks.

During that same period the Ku Klux Klan, which had expanded its aim in the post–World War I years against Catholics and Jews as well as blacks, was making a comeback. At a convention of Klan leaders in Atlanta, five hundred new members were initiated, assisted by seven hundred Klansmen and witnessed by more than one thousand of their friends and relatives. Their meeting in May 1946 was the first held in Georgia since the bombing of Pearl Harbor. "White Supremacy" was the theme of much of the keynote address there, given by the KKK's Grand Dragon. AJC agents also noted with alarm increased Klan activity in Alabama, Michigan, Tennessee, and Key West and Miami in Florida. In fact, the Imperial Wizard of the Klan was a Miami veterinarian. Two KKK chapters in Tennessee were distributing postcard advertisements for the *Protocols of the Elders of Zion* at two dollars a copy. The *Protocols* were a notorious antisemitic forgery, created in tsarist Russia, that purported to be the minutes of a meeting of Jewish elders plotting world domination. In one telling case, Mrs. Kate Robbins, a Jewish woman, was forced to sell her dry goods store in a suburb of Chattanooga after a cross was burned in front of the store and, several days later, hickory switches were tied to the door knob with the note "We mean business. No Jews here. KKK."

Home-front antisemitism did not manifest itself only in the Midwest or the South, where the number of Jews was relatively small. In New York City (or "Jew York" as its detractors called it), such actions were brought right up to the doorstep of the AJC. The Yorkville neighborhood with its demonstrations by the German American Bund and other street-corner meetings was a relatively short distance away. The Christian Front, which had gone underground during the war, tried to make a comeback in New York in the late fall of 1945, starting with a Saturday-night rally in Queens Village announced by circulating leaflets. The three main speakers included Homer Maertz of Chicago, who had earlier introduced the resolution at the Nationalist Party convention that American Jews be sterilized. Two AJC agents were there, saying nothing but taking in every word. At one point, the report noted delicately, "members of the AJC present concluded that violation of the law had been committed and that the speaker should be arrested." They thereupon remonstrated with the policeman present, who at first refused to act but who was somehow convinced by the end of the speech. At the conclusion of the meeting all three speakers were led away in handcuffs.[38] Also in New York, the AJC through its sources got word that an order to print five thousand copies of the *Protocols of the Elders of Zion* had gone out to a Staten Island printing shop, at the request of a former Nazi leader in the United States. The mayor's office was alerted and a municipal representative persuaded the printer to cancel the order. These efforts also resulted in a resolution adopted by the New York Employing Printers Association that its six hundred members not accept contracts for printing un-American or "hate" literature; an editorial to that effect was printed in the union's newsletter. The AJC calculated that 85 percent of all the printing in New York was done by this group.[39]

This approach against antisemites and ex-Nazis was known as the "quarantine treatment," a term popularized by S. Andhil Fineberg of the community relations division of AJC, who elaborated upon it in a September 1946 *Commentary* article. The approach was eventually endorsed by NCRAC and spread across the United States by workshops and clinics on antisemitism that Fineberg and the AJC staff gave throughout the country.[40] Detractors referred to the quarantine approach as the "hush-hush" or "Sha, shtil!" (Yiddish for "be quiet!") method, and the American Jewish Committee as a "Sha, shtil!" organization. Nevertheless, the AJC workshops were always well attended—not infrequently people had to be turned away for lack of space—and they helped to gather many new members. In Baltimore in 1946 fifteen hundred people attended one clinic in a hotel ballroom, hundreds had to be turned away, and one hundred new members were signed up.[41] The main point of the quarantine approach was to deny the offender any publicity. According to Fineberg, defensive and apologetic literature and counterdemonstrations against antisemitic speakers were not beneficial but harmful, and only served to give the subject the attention he craved. With the excitement of an open picket line, twice as many people might show up to the meeting as might have come otherwise. Skillfully placed information was a much more effective weapon.

Violent, public, politically organized antisemitism began to decline in the years after World War II, and groups such as the AJC played no small part in that fact. Still, as members reported in March 1949, such groups were still active abroad; indeed, international groups were organizing for a comeback. AJC members had their hands full just keeping track of all the antisemitic periodicals published in the United States (copies of which are today kept locked in the AJC archives, away from public view). In 1949 there were still fifty such periodicals, with a circulation of approximately two hundred thousand.[42]

Discrimination in Employment, Housing, and Higher Education

Even as antisemitism of the political and rabble-rousing kind was abating, it was continuing in a less violent, albeit still disturbing, form in the areas of employment, housing, and higher education. These were areas vital to the American servicemen returning from the war, who faced the prospect of establishing themselves and their families. Finding a job once out of the army was a burning need. A severe housing shortage made finding shelter especially difficult. Returning servicemen also wanted to be able to take full advantage of the G.I. Bill of Rights, which was supposed to guarantee them the means to pursue a university education if they so wished.

For this reason the AJC, along with NCRAC and its constituent organizations, threw themselves into the effort to pass FEP (Fair Employment Practices) laws, on both the state and federal level, that would outlaw discrimination in employment based on race or religion and guarantee a job to qualified applicants as a civil right. In those days applicants were subjected to questions and inquiries that today would be considered no one's business, if not actually illegal. The problem was acute even before the end of the war, when one might have expected more forbearance with so many able-bodied personnel still at the front. Yet men and women, including demobilized servicemen, in the summer of 1944 found themselves facing application blanks that asked for personal information on race and religion. Even the employment blanks of federal and civil service agencies included such questions. There were also unjustified rejections due to mandatory physical examinations, disqualification on the grounds that someone had relatives in Axis countries and was therefore a security risk, and special IQ or "mechanical aptitude" tests that were deliberately designed to weed out Jews. The Federation Employment Service, the central Jewish employment and guidance center in New York, reported that there were thousands of firms in the New York area that would not take advantage of qualified Jewish personnel no matter how bad the wartime labor shortage was.

After VE- and VJ-days (the accepted way of referring to victory in Europe and Japan) the discrimination actually grew worse. A special committee of NCRAC did a survey of fifteen major centers in the United States that accounted for 80 percent of the Jews in America. Using data gathered by the Jewish War Veterans and local agencies, the committee found a marked increase of antisemitism in employment agencies and also in newspaper advertising. Newspapers had agreed not to run discriminatory ads during wartime, but now the ads began to reappear. Want ads would say "Gentiles only" "Christians Preferred," or other euphemisms that left no doubt who the firm was and was not looking for.

Discrimination after someone answered an ad was less easy to measure, but was clear nonetheless. Employment agencies simply refused to consider Jews for certain occupations or for jobs over a certain level. In one of the largest employment agencies in Chicago, according to the results of one survey, it was found that 60 percent of the executive jobs, 50 percent of the sales executive jobs, 41 percent of the male clerical and 24 percent of the female clerical openings were closed to Jews and fully 38 percent of all orders for jobs were overtly discriminatory. Anxious to please their clients, the subtlest methods might be used. One director reported, "Nothing is ever said outright. They simply reject all Jewish applicants. If you send over a Christian, the personnel director phones back and says, 'Would you please send over some additional people of the same type.'" A direct survey of 1,251 Jewish job seekers in New York, half of them veterans, revealed that more than one-third of them had to state their religion either on an application form or a personal interview at one or more firms.[43]

Even after finding a job, a Jewish veteran could be stymied by the inability to find a place to live. It was not uncommon in those days for advertising for rented homes to include the words "Christians" or "Gentiles only," just as ads for summer camps and hotels and resorts would carry the words "Selected clientele"—code words that meant, no Jews. It was significant that in May 1945, the month the European war ended, the AJC had to publicly praise the *University of Minnesota Daily*, one of the largest college newspapers in the country, for announcing that it would no longer accept "rooms for rent" advertisements that said "Christians Only."[44] Elsewhere, however, the biggest issue house seekers had to face was that of restrictive covenants: that is, agreements in real estate transactions that an owner would neither sell or rent that home to any but white Christians nor allow people of nonwhite blood on the premises (unless, for example, they were servants or tradesmen and left after dark). Covenants of that era routinely referred to "Jewish" and "Semitic" blood as a condition for exclusion.

In 1948 the issue went to the U.S. Supreme Court, with the AJC filing a friend-of-the-court brief. Restrictive covenants were struck down as unconstitutional and unenforceable. At the time, however, the decision was open to question: it did not state that the covenants could not be made—only that they could not be enforced by the courts. President Harry Truman, determined to push through his own program of civil rights, caused an uproar in December 1949 when he announced that the U.S. government would refuse to insure mortgages on housing where written restrictive covenants were in force.[45] Nonetheless, persons involved in real estate transactions were endlessly creative in finding ways to enforce these types of covenants by other means.

The AJC and others concerned with civil rights also had to be vigilant in the area of higher education. It was telling that in discussing the possibility of educating German students through American student exchange programs, AJC members had expressed doubts that former Nazis would be reformed by spending time in U.S. colleges and universities, where antisemitism was so wide-spread. Quotas, formal and informal, were common at the nation's most exclusive schools. Prospective students from New York, the majority of them Jewish, were in a double bind: out-of-state institutions did not want to have them because they were New Yorkers; New York institutions spurned them because they wished to be "national" institutions and to attract students from a wider "geographical distribution." Supposedly nonsectarian institutions routinely excluded or discouraged Jews and other students considered "undesirable" by applications requesting information on race, religion, place of birth of the applicant and his parents, photographs, and personal interviews. Once on campus Jews, along with others who did not qualify as white Christians, were segregated through fraternity systems and separate living and social arrangements.

The battle was long and hard to strike down all these things as illegal. It was in part to find a haven for such students that the AJC supported in 1950 the establishment of a State University of New York system that would bring thirty-two separate institutions under one umbrella for the purpose of providing education that did not discriminate on the basis of race, religion, or ethnic group. The move, they observed, was long overdue; at that point New York was the only state in the union that did not have a public college or university bearing that state's name.[46]

University professional schools too, where so many young Jews were seeking their way up the socioeconomic ladder, were also subject to these types of restrictions. The war had not yet ended in Europe when representatives of the American Dental Association issued an open report recommending that there be a reduction in the number of students of Jewish and Italian ancestry admitted to dental colleges.[47] In January 1945 an unsigned editorial appeared in the *Journal of Clinical Psychology* proposing restrictions on the admission of a certain "racial group" to professional psychological training programs. The editorial disavowed that this constituted racial intolerance, but stated that it was "unwise" to let any one group dominate and "the profession should not be exploited in the interest of any one group in such a manner that the public acceptance of the whole program is jeopardized."[48]

The AJC took immediate action and won a retraction from the editor and publisher, Dr. Frederick C. Thorne, who was a professor of psychiatry at the University of Vermont Medical College. John Slawson himself, who had his doctorate in the field and had been a distinguished clinical psychologist himself before coming to head the AJC, wrote a scathing letter of criticism to Dr. Thorne and all six members of the editorial board, accusing him of swallowing "Nazi racial nonsense." Dr. Thorne wrote back that the wording had been "unfortunate," that it had escaped editorial scrutiny, and that it did not reflect editorial policy. All six members of the board claimed that they had not seen the editorial before publication. Shortly afterward, the Eastern Psychological Association passed a resolution condemning race quotas in the field of psychology. Three of the editorial board resigned, including Dr. Carl R. Rogers, formerly a professor of psychology at Ohio State University.

Policies and Techniques: The Power of Science

The strength and effectiveness of AJC did not lie only in what the organization did directly, although that was a great deal. In what might be called the "multiplier" effect, its strength lay in making its specific techniques and masses of material available at cost or free of charge to anyone who might be willing to cooperate. For example, a Jewish organization of a few thousand members might be expected to accomplish little. But every organization had its own publication and newsletter. One article there could reach hundreds of thousands, even millions. One article or column in a mass circulation magazine or newspaper could reach millions in one blow. Labor unions alone represented fourteen million Americans, and they were a receptive channel for AJC's material. The National Education Association represented hundreds of thousands of teachers, who had millions of children in their care. The entire organized Methodist Church likewise represented millions of Americans. A few thousand sympathetic clergymen in a frantic search for themes for their upcoming Sunday sermons, if properly prepared, could reach millions of people. Thousands of local chapters of national groups searching for an activity for next week's meeting welcomed AJC discussion guides. Local chapters in every state could organize or be organized to campaign for beneficial state legislation. Through careful co-optation and alliance with preexisting political, religious, fraternal, and service organizations in a country filled with organizations, the AJC was able to package its philosophy and penetrate the farthest corners of the United States.

The first weapons in the battle were social science and librarianship. During and after World War II the Library of Jewish Information (founded in 1930) located on the sixteenth floor of a New York office building, serviced a growing stream of patrons: writers, speakers, columnists, college students, ministers and laymen, government agencies, news services, organizations, and schools. People wanted and needed material and the AJC was there to supply it. In one year the library dealt with more than eight hundred inquiries from writers, commentators, rabbis, ministers, and Jewish and non-Jewish organizations. The staff served as a "listening post," gathering every piece of information that was published about Jews anywhere. One of the obvious fruits of this was the annual "review of the year" published in the American Jewish Year Book. The library had one of the most comprehensive collections of antisemitica anywhere, including Nazi propaganda, and works on antisemitism going back many centuries.

During the war, science had unleashed terror and destruction upon the world. The Nazis had employed pseudoscience to support and buttress their programs of annihilation. Now the AJC embraced science along with the infant fields of psychiatry and psychoanalysis in order to bring the greater good to all humankind. This mission was of particular importance to John Slawson, Ph.D., who initiated the project. He constantly spoke of antisemitism as an "emotional disease" in search of the right antitoxin. With patience and analysis the patient might someday be cured and all of prejudice and bigotry might be erased, even if the AJC had to put the entire world on the couch.

Here he had the help of some of the finest social scientific minds in Europe that had been forced to find refuge in America: psychologists, psychiatrists, anthropologists, experts in social work, public relations, and allied fields. Many of the scientists came from the Institute of Social Research, which had been founded in Frankfurt, Germany, in 1923 but was closed with Hitler's advent to power in 1933. Members moved first to Geneva, Switzerland, then to New York and California where Columbia and other universities granted facilities to continue their work. Their numbers included Max Horkheimer (former rector of the University of Frankfurt) and Theodor W. Adorno, joined by such American luminaries as Otto Klineberg and Margaret Mead.[49] One sociologist whose work the AJC sponsored, Kenneth Clark, had the results of one of his studies cited in the U.S. Supreme Court case *Brown v. Board of Education* in 1954.[50]

The AJC took all these social scientists under its umbrella. As medical doctors labored to find a cure for polio, so did these scientists labor to discover the exact origins and possible cure of hatred for Jews. All of this activity was in contradiction to the classical Zionist doctrine of Theodor Herzl, which held that antisemitism in the Diaspora was inevitable and incurable and could only be avoided by residence in the Jewish homeland. The first Conference on Research in the Field of Antisemitism was held in New York in May 1944, while the war was still going on, and evolved into a semipermanent organization producing a series of studies, including the landmark Studies in Prejudice, which consisted of five massive volumes. The last of these volumes, *The Authoritarian Personality,* published in late 1949, became perhaps the most well known.[51] The depth and seriousness with which these scientists did their work is indicated by the following passage, which was taken from a paper published by Drs. Nathan W. Ackerman (practicing psychiatrist and chief psychiatrist at the Jewish Board of Guardians) and Marie Jahoda (a member of the AJC staff) entitled "Toward a Dynamic Interpretation of Antisemitic Attitudes." The data was derived from case studies of thirty psychoanalysts in New York and was later published in a book-length work:

Antisemites, the study found, are fundamentally weak, immature, dependent and unhappy persons whose prejudice against Jews results from dissatisfaction with themselves coupled with envy for others. They lack direction and confidence, fear failure and avoid competition. Insecure and pursued by a feeling of "not belonging," they are often unhappy in their marital relationships and seem unable to maintain intimate friendships. *The violence of the individual's antisemitism, the study found, is directly related to the depth of sickness of the personality.* [Emphasis in the original.] Antisemitism plays a role of a defense against self-hate. The incomplete person finds a spurious relief in expressing hatred against Jews, and a spurious satisfaction in the false feeling that he is a member of the dominant group in society. Thus antisemitism becomes, for the sick personality, a compensation for his unrealized desire for status, power, money, social advantage and privileges of all sorts.[52]

Such research findings, gleaned from a sample pool of patients who were already ill enough to have sought treatment, buttressed the idea of John Slawson and other social scientists that antisemitism, and indeed bigotry against anyone, was not a "respectable" prejudice but a sign of mental illness. This idea was put to immediate use by AJC public relations, media and advertising experts, and production staff who churned out books, pamphlets, discussion guides, posters, illustrations, newspaper columns, speeches, sermons, award-winning radio shows, award-winning television shows and spots, award-winning films, museum exhibits, and even comic books and cartoons in the great battle to stamp out bigotry and prejudice, to totally discredit and stigmatize bias against anyone, to combat antisemitism and to immunize Americans against it. *Superman* and the *Howdy Doody Show* had AJC pro-democracy, anti-prejudice material written into the scripts and shown during commercial breaks—a sure way to reach the nation's young people.

The main technique, as perfected by Richard Rothschild and John Slawson, was known as "salting in." Values of pro-democracy, anti-discrimination, and positive portrayals of Jews were worked into every avenue of the mass media from the highest brow to the lowest until the producers of culture believed they had thought of it or read it themselves and any trail back to the AJC was long gone. AJC production staff scripted shows on Jewish holidays, ceremonies, and Jewish heroes. They gathered writers together of all kinds—radio and motion picture writers, authors, pulp-fiction icons, editors, advertising agency executives, copywriters—and urged them to stop using stereotypes that portrayed the Anglo-Saxon as heroes and heroines and non–Anglo-Saxons as menial servants, racketeers, thieves, gamblers, shady nightclub proprietors, and crooked prizefight managers. Gradually positive portrayals of characters with Jewish names began to crop up in short stories, novels, comic books, and radio shows. "The first time that the pretty secretary who finally marries the boss is called 'Miss Horowitz' will be the dawn of a new era," said one AJC chairman of these efforts.[53] Later they did the same for the infant TV industry, doing their best to make sure that the new medium started out fresh with as few of the old stereotypes as possible.

The AJC sponsored articles written in journals and magazines, feeding the material to be written up by cooperative reporters and editors—though the AJC name was never on it. They worked to have questions about Jewish holidays and about Israel included in radio and TV quiz shows. They prevailed upon the publishers of dictionaries to remove "name-calling" terms. From the 1945 edition on, words like "coon," "Sheeny," and "Dago" were removed from the pages of the Merriam Webster dictionary. "We want so to saturate the very air which people breathe, with a message of wholesome group relations," stated John Slawson, "that they will be reluctant to give expression to antisemitic feelings. . . . we will have reached the level of adequate coverage only when the cumulative effect of our materials will have so terrific an impact on our everyday living experiences that by the sheer force of these external stimuli the average American will begin to incorporate into his own mental apparatus a healthy conception of intergroup relations."[54]

The Displaced Persons

The antisemitism that permeated American society in those days had a direct effect on the rescue or loss of Jewish lives: it was a motive either to keep foreign Jews out altogether or to draft immigration legislation in such a way that as few Jews as possible would be admitted. AJC's developing attitudes toward Israel and their attitude toward other countries that might become havens, were dominated by this issue above all: what should be done for the approximately 250,000 Jewish survivors who languished in DP camps in Germany and Austria and who had no homes to go back to? Their situation was desperate, as we have seen (chapter 1). At war's end most of the refugees were homeless, sick, and emaciated, and many were still living in the concentration camps where they had been prisoners. As winter approached, tens of thousands who had survived the war were in danger of death by disease, starvation, or exposure; indeed, many thousands who had survived Hitler did die in the years immediately after the war. Proskauer and Blaustein, in reporting on their visit to the DP camps to the Executive Committee in 1946, warned of "catastrophic consequences" if the DPs were forced to remain where they were any longer.[55]

Until Israel's independence, the gates of Palestine, the one country that wanted the refugees, had been shut by the British White Paper of 1939. In 1947, Palestine-bound Jewish refugees on the ship *Exodus 1947* had been removed from the ship and forcibly sent back to Germany. Thousands more who tried to run the British blockade were interned in camps on Cyprus. These conditions had led to a massive illegal immigration effort, known in Hebrew as the *bricha* ("escape" or "flee.") As for the United States, its doors had been shut against mass immigration since 1924, and it appeared that nothing could convince the nation's leaders to open them again.

The nation's educational system both represented these attitudes and played a role in perpetuating them. In an address entitled "The Immigrant in Our Textbooks," Edward N. Saveth, a member of the AJC Library staff, informed a national group of social studies teachers that the portrayals of immigrants he had found in investigating school texts were "downright prejudiced." Attitudes of writers, he noted, changed markedly between the "old immigration" of northern and western Europe in the early nineteenth century and the "new immigration" from southern and eastern Europe that came after 1880. Usually the "old" immigrants were said to have come for idealistic reasons, while the "new" immigrants had come mainly for economic reasons; that is, to make money. These conclusions were in direct contradiction to those of immigration scholars, who had written that the majority of immigrants to America were attracted by the economic opportunities it offered them.

Textbook writers also tended to confuse race with nationality, as in the following passage found in a public school history textbook in 1950: "In Europe the population of each country is largely of one race. In Spain, Italy, France, Germany, and others, all the work of every sort, the lowest as well as the highest . . . is done by people of allied blood." Race had been a common term applied to people of many backgrounds before the war, and had been a central concept of Nazism, but by 1950 no competent anthropologist would accept this usage. Other texts, Saveth found, identified immigrants as "willing to work long hours for low wages" and creating "new slum areas." He also quoted one particularly objectionable passage by a well-known textbook writer, who was concluding his section on the "new" immigration: "The ranks of anarchy and riot number no Americans. . . . the leaders boldly proclaim that they came here not to enjoy the blessings of our liberty and to sustain our institutions but to destroy our government, cut our throats and divide our property."[56]

At war's end such attitudes toward immigrants and other obstacles to liberalizing American immigration law were formidable. Other countries were making it clear that they themselves would not accept refugees on more than a temporary basis as long as the United States did not step in and lead the way. Since 1929, however, the yearly total U.S. quota had been set at 154,000 immigrants a year from all countries and backgrounds. That quota had never been filled, AJC immigration committee members reported to the executive committee, quoting data collected by the library staff. Only 7 percent of the allowed immigrants—some ten thousand per year—had been able to come to the country during the war years. The law was filled with restrictions, limiting the numbers of immigrants from specific areas and making inflexible the time within which quotas must be used. The largest quota allotments were given to England, Germany, and Ireland. According to AJC research on the subject, all of southern and eastern Europe, precisely those areas with the greatest need for immigration opportunities, was allowed 23,235 visas per year.[57]

In actuality, not even that number was admitted from the nether regions of Europe. Many were disqualified because of careful screening and interviewing by officials, who were required to ascertain if the potential immigrant lived up to certain standards of health, morals, "democratic political beliefs," and the ability to become self-supporting. "Democratic beliefs" meant not being a communist, and many antisemites considered "Jew" and "communist" to be synonymous. William Zukerman, an Anglo-Jewish journalist relayed this report from Munich in 1950:

Since the outbreak of the Korean War American immigration authorities in Germany have practically discontinued issuing visas to Jewish DPs who are fully entitled to them on the wholesale suspicion that all Jewish DPs are communist. Every Jewish DP who applies for a visa now is subjected to an inquisition by the Counter Intelligence Service (CIS) which would be comical if it were not so terribly pitiful. Applicants are asked: "Why don't you emigrate to Israel instead of the United States? What would you do in case of war between the United States and Israel? Who do you think will win the war in Korea? Who is the greater statesman, Stalin or President Truman?" Even if an applicant succeeds in convincing CIS that he is not and has never been a communist, he is refused a visa on the grounds that for that very reason he was chosen by the Comintern to go to the United States. Another unfortunate aspect of the new situation is that the CIS now has a number of Jewish spies in the DP camps who inform on the prospective applicants. This has demoralized the atmosphere in the camps, apart from the fact that it has practically suspended Jewish immigration to the United States.[58]

It can be speculated that such a careful screening process at the time left its mark on the character of those who successfully made it to the United States. Such questioning and security clearance procedures might weed out refugees with strong left-wing political beliefs. Those postwar Jewish refugees who were able to settle in America might tend as a group to be more politically conservative than those Jews who came during the great migration of 1880–1924.

President Truman fervently desired a liberalization of the laws from Congress and issued an order in December 1945 calling for preferential visas to DPs, but that move accomplished little. Only some five thousand additional Jews were able to enter the United States that year because of it. Of the 3,900 visas allowed altogether each month for natives of Central and Eastern Europe, more than two-thirds were set aside for natives of Germany and Austria. The quota for Poland was less than 550 per month, even though perhaps the majority of Jewish DPs had been born in Poland. The aggregate quotas of six other countries with a sizable prewar Jewish population were barely five hundred per month. The law forbade shifting of quotas from country to country, pooling of monthly or yearly quotas, and use of leftover visas or borrowing on future permits. On the principle that the country not be unduly swamped by immigrants at any one time, not more than 10 percent of a country's annual quota could be used in any one month—and there could be no carryover from one month to the next. This restriction meant that thousands of immigration permits were allowed to lapse due to accidents and delays. With these laws in place, therefore, the only way to get any large number of Jews into the country would be for Congress to pass emergency legislation authorizing entry of a fixed number of persons at a specific time.

Yet the exact same attitudes that had been prevalent before the Holocaust were still solidly in place. Restrictionist, isolationist, and antisemitic congressmen did everything possible to prevent, stall, or provide their own alternatives to such legislation. At the new congressional session of 1945, several bills were presented affecting Jewish refugees. Representatives Leonard A. Allen (Democrat, Louisiana) and Stephen Pace (Democrat, Georgia) wanted to prohibit any immigration at all to the United States as long as there were one million citizens unemployed (in a nation as it was then of 145 million people, the unemployment figure rarely fell below that). One bill sought to reduce immigration to one-half the current quota. Another sought to reduce it by 75 percent for the following ten years, in effect forcing all the displaced persons of postwar Europe to look elsewhere for new homes. Another bill was introduced calling for all Japanese to be deported, and representatives from West Virginia and Michigan introduced bills that would make it a crime for aliens to become active members of labor unions. A congressman from California wanted to make it a criminal offense to operate or participate in the activities of a foreign language school. This ruling would affect Hebrew and Yiddish schools and afternoon Talmud Torahs.[59] Only one in twenty such bills would ever make it to the president to sign; nonetheless, the overwhelming sentiment in Congress was clearly against liberalizing immigration laws. Indeed, more than half the battle of such organizations as the AJC was not for improvements, but for preventing U.S. immigration restrictions from being made any worse than they already were.

In July a Displaced Persons Act of 1948 was finally passed by both houses of Congress, the aim of which, in effect, was the exclusion of Jews. The majority of Jewish DPs were disqualified under its provisions. The bill maintained obvious favoritism to Balts or eastern Poles, preferential treatment for agricultural workers, and the requirement that DPs have both security clearance as well as homes and jobs assured them in the United States as a condition for granting visas. It also set as a condition of eligibility that in order to come to the United States, refugees had to have been physically in the displaced persons camps by December 22, 1945. Of course, many of the Jewish DPs, as the drafters of the bill well knew, had been residing in the Soviet Union and/or had attempted to return to their lost homes in Eastern Europe first. For example, the Polish refugees terrified by the pogrom at Kielce in 1946 did not turn around and make it to the DP camps until 1946–47. A fair bill would have to extend the deadline to April 21, 1947, when the displaced persons camps were officially closed to newcomers. The bill further set aside 50 percent of the German and Austria quotas specifically for the Sudetens and other Europeans of German ethnic origin—in effect, for German Christians only.[60] Under this law a Jew had a harder time immigrating to America than an ex-Nazi.

The obvious racism of the bill applied to several other groups. There was no quota for Asians; Asians were not admitted as immigrants at all, and there were thirty thousand Japanese-born residents of the United States who could not get citizenship. Moreover, the quota for the entire West Indies was one hundred immigrants per year. In the six months after the bill was passed not more than twenty-five hundred DPs of all backgrounds made it to the United States.

In 1950 a bipartisan bloc of senators managed to pass an immigration bill that removed some of the worst features of the previous one. The cutoff date for arriving in the camps was extended, and the preference given to agricultural and Baltic DPs was removed. But by this time, as the legislators were well aware, the new State of Israel had already admitted the majority of the Jewish DPs. Out of all the millions of Jews who had once lived in Europe, not more than approximately 140,000 survivors reached the United States in the decade after the war.[61]

Israel and the Displaced Persons

Indeed, the establishment of the State of Israel solved the Jewish DP problem with astonishing swiftness. A field representative in October 1948 predicted that within two years there would be virtually no Jews left in Germany (at the time, 150,000 were still there).[62] Dr. William Haber, advisor to the U.S. military governor on Jewish affairs and a member of the AJC Executive Committee, stated in a report to the foreign affairs committee that the entire Jewish DP problem might be liquidated by November of the following year. Israel, he reported, was determined to bring in from ten to fifteen thousand refugees per month; the only ones who would remain in the camps were those who were absolutely determined to immigrate to other countries.[63]

The Israeli economy all but buckled under the strain of fighting a war and seeing its population double in three and a half years. Food and all consumer goods were severely rationed for both longtime residents and newcomers. An egg equaled six olives, and Israelis could go weeks without seeing an egg or a piece of chicken. It was an indication of conditions in Israel's first years that the *AJC Committee Reporter* in September 1949 carried an announcement that beginning September 12, CARE, under an agreement with the Israeli government, would be providing kosher food package service to that country. Two packages would be available: baby food and adult food. Each cost ten dollars, which covered all costs including guaranteed delivery. The packages would be admitted to Israel tax-free and ration-free, but under the *tzena*, or the prevailing austerity program, individuals in Israel would be limited to the receipt of one kosher care package monthly.

Still, the mass immigration continued, in what the Israelis called "the in-gathering of the exiles." Jacob Blaustein, who had been invited to visit the new state by David Ben-Gurion and saw conditions there firsthand, reported with some wonder at Israel's open policy. "The basis of this immigration policy is

purely humanitarian," he noted. "No attempt is being made to select immigrants for the contribution which they can make toward the upbuilding of
the country. And a haven is being offered to the aged and the sick as freely
as to the able-bodied and productive." Outsiders might wonder, he said, if
this policy was not unwise—if some regulation ought not to be introduced
into the process. But "the official Israeli point of view is that no obstacle
should be put in the way of Jews from any part of the world who want to
come to Israel."[64]

The Executive Committee was gratified, in hearing this, that its earlier decision to support partition and the creation of a Jewish state in Palestine against
detractors within its own ranks, had been entirely justified. There was celebration at the hour of victory, joy that the DPs finally had a place to call home, a
determination to aid the fledgling state politically and financially, and an expectation that an AJC office would be established in Israel soon.

In Washington, D.C., new issues were on the agenda: loan guarantees and
agricultural equipment for Israel, and the quest for de jure recognition of the
country. There were also efforts to have Israel admitted to the U.N., and diplomatic efforts to ensure that Israel kept full sovereignty over at least the new
section of Jerusalem along with the Negev desert. Concerned parties around
the world were still calling for the establishment of an international trusteeship over *all* of Jerusalem, both the Old and the New City, and Israeli possession of the Negev was being hotly contested by Egypt. Without the Negev,
the Egyptians insisted, the Arab world was cut in two; they demanded it as a
"land bridge" between itself and Jordan. David Ben-Gurion, who had always
had a special personal connection to the desert anyway, responded by putting
up as many new towns and settlements in the Negev as he could, to
strengthen Israel's hold over the land. There were also renewed efforts to end
the embargo on sending U.S. arms to Israel. Far from being a military patron
to the new state, during Israel's War of Independence the U.S. government
had sent nothing; for Americans, smuggling arms to Israel had been a criminal offense.

The AJC and the American Council for Judaism

In 1949 Jacob Blaustein, Irving Engel, and John Slawson visited the new country for the first time at the personal invitation of Ben-Gurion, and came back
enthralled with what they saw. Still, in those years of Israel's infancy there was
some uncertainty among the Jewish community of the United States as to just
how they should relate to a sovereign Jewish country, and how that Jewish
country in turn should relate to them. The question cut to the core of their
identity as Americans and as Jews. The AJC found itself in the middle of a painful cleavage between the majority, who did not view patriotism for America

and support for Israel as contradictory; and those, represented most clearly by the American Council for Judaism, who considered any relation to Israel at all as a manifestation of dual loyalty akin to treason.

Throughout the late 1940s and 1950s the ACJ carried out a strenuous political and diplomatic campaign of confrontation and disassociation from the new state, implying in its publicity that American Jews were endangering their status severely unless they all did the same.[65] The matter was complicated by a confluence and juxtaposition of events calculated to arouse fear in the heart of every thinking American Jew. These were some of the grimmest years of the cold war, and the phenomenon known as McCarthyism was in full swing. Alleged communists and communist ideology were being rooted out vigorously everywhere in the United States. President Truman was demanding loyalty oaths of federal employees; teachers, writers, and Americans of all backgrounds were losing their jobs in what observers termed an anticommunist "witch-hunt." On August 29, 1949, the Soviets exploded their first atom bomb, years before the United States had believed they would be capable of doing so; it soon became apparent that only espionage had given them the knowledge. In October 1949 mainland China was "lost" to the communists when Chairman Mao Tse-tung declared the People's Republic of China. In February 1950 former State Department official Alger Hiss was convicted of perjury for denying that he had passed secret information to a communist agent. Three weeks later Senator Joseph McCarthy of Wisconsin made headlines by claiming that the State Department employed more than two hundred communists, and thus began his anticommunist campaign. On June 25, 1950, North Korea invaded South Korea, a conflict that many feared would involve both China and the Soviet Union and lead to a third world war. And on July 17, 1950, Julius and Ethel Rosenberg were arrested on charges of leading a Soviet spy ring. Julius was the son of a Polish Jewish garment worker living on the Lower East Side, and had been a dedicated member of the Young Communist League since his days as an engineering student at the City College of New York. He appeared to embody the worst charges of the antisemites of those days, many of whom considered the phrase "Jewish communists" as a redundancy.

This was no time for American citizens, and especially American Jews, to permit any doubts about where their loyalties lay. According to the American Council for Judaism and its supporters, Zionism could no longer be excused as a purely humanitarian cause. It was participation in a foreign nationalism and as such forbidden by U.S. law. Faithful American Jews had to regard themselves as nationals of the United States and as Jewish in religion only. Such acts as the UJA (United Jewish Appeal) declaring its slogan of 1949 to be "A Year of Homecoming" were enough to send such people into convulsions of terror and rage. Moreover, the ACJ, which included within its ranks several former members of the AJC (including its director, who still insisted

on coming to AJC Executive Committee meetings and speaking his peace)
loudly and consistently accused the American Jewish Committee of having
"sold out" to the Zionists.

Striking back at the ACJ in a speech made at an Israel Independence Day
UJA gathering in Philadelphia, Joseph Proskauer (who had once counted
himself among the anti-Zionists) counseled "restraint and wisdom" and
urged an end to the impugning of American Jewish loyalty, the full-page ACJ
advertisements, and the intracommunal acrimony that had sullied the nation's
press on these issues. No one but the antisemites, he said, could rejoice in
these things. He and Jacob Blaustein had not approved of the slogan "A Year
of Homecoming" either, he pointed out to the crowd. They had considered
the words unwise and too easily "misconstrued by the ill-disposed." Their response, however, had not been to take out full-page ads in the mass media and
all but march in the streets. Instead, they had written a friendly letter to the authorities suggesting that they reconsider having such slogans in the future. To
all the arguments over what contemporary Zionism was or was not, he had
this to say: "I do not know what Zionism means anymore. I do know this: the
time has come when controversy on the basis of Zionism or anti-Zionism is
an anachronism that belongs to a dead age."[66]

Yet the American Council for Judaism would not let the issue rest. Only a
few days after the Soviets exploded their first atom bomb, the ACJ views
achieved nationwide coverage, in the September 1949 issue of *Readers' Digest*.
The magazine's circulation numbered in the hundreds of thousands. The title
of the article was "Israel's Flag is Not Mine" and it was written by ACJ counsel
Alfred M. Lilienthal, in the form of a letter to his mother. In Lilienthal's view,
the Zionists wanted him to consider himself "a backsliding member of an
Oriental tribe." When Israel's flag was raised in the streets, he wrote, he had no
impulse to dance in the street with hysterical joy, as did so many in New York
and London. "Whenever I read of Americans singing 'Hatikvah,'" he confided
to millions of Americans, "I am outraged." So sharp was his anger that in the
article Lilienthal compared that day's Zionists with the racist and nationalistic
German American Bund that had flourished in the 1930s.[67]

The Blaustein–Ben-Gurion Joint Statement of 1950 and the Reaffirmation of 1961

America had been very good to Jacob Blaustein. He was especially sensitive to
charges of having "sold out" to the Zionists, and resentful that anyone should
even suspect that American Jews were not completely faithful in their alle-
giances. Blaustein took almost as a personal affront every pronouncement by
the Israeli prime minister David Ben-Gurion and his government that Israel
was superior as a home for the Jews and that Jews were ultimately doomed

both physically and spiritually if they remained in the Diaspora. For a time John Slawson, AJC's executive vice president, shared Blaustein's views. In time, others in the AJC who held these views regarding Israel mellowed, but Blaustein remained vigilant almost to the end of his days in the organization. The very word "home" used in connection with Israel was a red flag to him. Aside from the dual loyalty issue, Blaustein and others in the AJC feared and resented the idea, common among Israelis, that the Holocaust had proved once and for all that Jews were not safe in the Diaspora; that the only place Jewish life could flourish physically and spiritually was in the new state, and that mass Jewish immigration from everywhere, including the United States, should occur immediately. Such opinions and values, in the AJC's view, were not only untrue but acted to retard the proper integration of American Jews into the mainstream of their country.

Under Blaustein's direction, a new 1949 Statement of Views contained praise for Israel. Nevertheless, the drafters of the text also went to great lengths to state that Israelis were Israelis and Americans were Americans, that there could be no political identification of American Jews with Israel, and that the AJC leadership should be continually on its guard against any such statements from Israel to the contrary. A resolution was also passed at that annual meeting that the AJC would start its own "Jewish education" program, an "American-centered" project that would serve as a counterweight to Israel's influence and work to ensure the "wholesome integration and adjustment" of Jews in America. AJC had already started this discussion only a few months after the end of World War II, by convening the Conference on Jewish Adjustment in America, a gathering that discussed in part how American Jews could develop a feeling of security in the wake of the Holocaust.[68] Herbert B. Ehrmann of Boston, who would go on to become AJC's president (1959–61) served as chairman of the Jewish Education committee charged with the responsibility of improving the "attitudes," as they put it, of American Jews.[69]

Blaustein personally sought and obtained periodic reassurances from Israeli diplomatic officials that there would be no movement to encourage mass *aliyah* or immigration from the United States, or that Israel would presume to speak in the name of any Jews other than its own citizens.[70] It was shocking, therefore, and the prelude to a crisis when a headline appeared in the Jewish Telegraphic Agency daily news bulletin (JTA) on September 1, 1949: "BEN GURION URGES U.S. PARENTS TO SEND THEIR CHILDREN TO ISRAEL FOR PERMANENT SETTLEMENT."[71] The implication of the statement was that Israel might snatch American Jewish children against the wishes of their horrified parents. "Although we realized our dream of establishing a Jewish state, we are still at the beginning," the Israel premier was quoted as saying to a visiting American Histadrut delegation. "Today there are only nine hundred thousand Jews in Israel while the greater part of the Jewish people is still abroad. Our next task will not be easier than the creation of the

Jewish state. It consists of bringing all Jews to Israel. . . . we are determined to bring in millions more. . . . We appeal chiefly to the youth in the United States and in other countries to help us achieve this big mission. We appeal to the parents to help us bring their children here. Even if they decline to help, we will bring the youth to Israel, but I hope that this will not be necessary." David Remez, Israel's minister of communications, made a similar appeal to the Jews of the United States to send American Jewish youth to Israel. The impact of these statements was magnified when the American Council for Judaism in San Francisco, seeing new ammunition in support of its cause, used parts of this statement in a large advertisement in a local Anglo-Jewish newspaper.

A flurry of meetings, denials, and retractions followed. As Blaustein reported later in detail to the Executive Committee, on September 11, he had met with Aubrey (later Abba) Eban, Israel's representative to the U.N., and stressed that Israel had a responsibility "not to embarrass or offend the sensibilities of Jewish communities from other countries."[72] On September 19, he had sent a "friendly but firm" letter to Ben-Gurion, with copies generously distributed to key personnel, reporting on the consternation that these statements had caused among AJC members and other sincere friends of Israel; he "intimated that if Israel's official policy was reflected in the purported statement, we might find it necessary to reconsider our position with respect to Israel." On October 16, Israel's ambassador to the United States Elath assured Blaustein that the prime minister had been misquoted and that an appropriate statement would appear in a couple of days. This assurance was followed by cablegrams from Ben-Gurion's office stating that the JTA report was unauthorized and incorrect. The government of Israel certainly had no desire to intervene in the internal affairs of the American Jewish community. However, as Blaustein concluded his report, "in general there are tendencies in the Zionist movement to which we must be alert." After his report, Joseph Proskauer rose and counseled, "I agree we need to stay on alert, but let us cross our bridges only as we come to them." An appropriate resolution was passed reinforcing the recent Statement of Views.

Hardly had the dust from this incident settled, however, when the JTA and the Anglo-Jewish press ran the item: "'YOM KIBBUTZ GALUYOT'—DAY OF THE INGATHERING OF THE EXILES was celebrated throughout Israel on December 19, 1949 on the occasion of the Jewish population of Israel passing the one million mark."[73] The Israelis were also setting up offices in European countries and attempting to set up offices in the United States to encourage and facilitate mass immigration to their country. This appeared to be a clear violation of the understanding Blaustein had previously reached with Israeli diplomats and with Ben-Gurion. This time the matter could not rest with intercessors or transatlantic cablegrams. This time Ben-Gurion would have to give his retraction on the record and in person. The showdown came in the

form of a historic meeting in Jerusalem. On August 11, 1950, just two weeks
after the Korean War began, Blaustein flew to Israel at the ostensible invitation
of Ben-Gurion so that, as the AJC's newsletter phrased it, he "could clarify certain aspects of the relations between Israel and American Jews for the benefit of
both groups." A luncheon in Blaustein's honor was arranged at the King David
Hotel in Jerusalem on August 23, 1950, to which various Israeli government,
diplomatic, and UN officials were invited, along with members of the press.[74]
The statements which were given there became among the most famous documents in all the history of American Jewish–Israeli relations.[75]

David Ben-Gurion spoke first, using at certain points the precise language
that had been drafted in Blaustein's correspondence to him. He opened by
praising highly the role that American Jews in general and Jacob Blaustein in
particular had made to Israel. He said that he welcomed this opportunity to
clarify some of the misunderstandings that had arisen in the relationship
between the people of Israel and the Jewish communities abroad, as these
misunderstandings were likely to "alienate sympathies and create disharmony
where friendship and close understanding are of vital necessity":

To my mind, the position is perfectly clear. The Jews of the US as a community and as
individuals have only one political attachment and that is to the United States of America. They owe no political allegiance to Israel. . . . The State of Israel represents and
speaks only on behalf of its own citizens and in no way presumes to represent or speak
in the name of the Jews who are citizens of any other country. . . . Our success or failure depends in a large measure on our cooperation with, and on the strength of, the
great Jewish community of the US, and we, therefore, are anxious that nothing should
be said or done which could in the slightest degree undermine the sense of security and
stability of American Jewry.[76]

A key part of Ben-Gurion's statement was his assertion that Israel sought no
mass migration of Jews from the United States, but only a "selective" repre-
sentation, whether on a permanent or temporary basis, of those whose
"know-how" would benefit the new country: "In this connection let me say a
word about immigration. We should like to see American Jews come and take
part in our effort. We need their technical knowledge, skills, vision. . . . The
tasks which face us in this country are eminently such as would appeal to the
American genius for technical development and social progress. But the decision as to whether they wish to come—permanently or temporarily—rests
with the free discretion of each American Jew himself. It is entirely a matter of
his own volition."

At the conclusion of Ben-Gurion's address Blaustein arose to make his
reply. He began by praising the progress that had been made in Israel since his
first visit, but quickly shifted to implications that the Israelis would be jeopardizing American Jewish aid, endangering American Jewish security, and
undermining their own position if they did not conform to his wishes. He
spoke pointedly of how gratifying it was to be on the scene and to observe

firsthand to what good use the Israelis were already putting the support they had received from Americans, including American tractors and other machinery and equipment acquired through the loan granted by the Export-Import Bank (a loan that Blaustein had personally helped to effect). The AJC and other organizations, he pledged, would continue, "within the framework of American citizenship," to render every possible support. Now that Israel's birth pangs were over, however, that nation also had a responsibility not to "affect adversely the sensibilities of Jews who are citizens of other states by what it says or does." He then delivered, for the benefit of his Israeli audience, a passionate defense of the viability of Jewish life in the United States:

I would be less than frank if I did not point out to you that American Jews vigorously repudiate any suggestion or implication that they are in exile. American Jews—young and old alike, Zionists and non-Zionists alike—are profoundly attached to America. America welcomed their immigrant parents in their need. Under America's free institutions, they and their children have achieved that freedom and sense of security unknown for long centuries of travail. American Jews have truly become Americans, just as have all other oppressed groups that have ever come to America's shores. To American Jews, America is home. . . . They believe in the future of a democratic society in the US under which all citizens, irrespective of creed or race, can live on terms of equality. They further believe that, if democracy should fail in America, there would be no future for democracy anywhere in the world, and the very existence of an independent state of Israel would be problematic. The future development of Israel, spiritual, social as well as economic, will largely depend upon a strong and healthy Jewish community in the US and other free democracies.

This was followed by a direct, unveiled warning:

We have been greatly distressed that at the very hour when so much has been achieved, harmful and futile discussions and misunderstandings have arisen as to the relations between the people and the State of Israel and the Jews in other countries, particularly in the United States. Harm has been done to the morale and to some extent to the sense of security of the American Jewish community through unwise and unwarranted statements and appeals which ignore the feelings and aspirations of American Jewry. Even greater harm has been done to the State of Israel itself by weakening the readiness of American Jews to do their full share in the rebuilding of Israel, which faces such enormous political, social, and economic problems. . . . Your statement today, Mr. Prime Minister, will, I trust, be followed by unmistakable evidence that the responsible leaders of Israel and the organizations connected with it, fully understand that future relations between the American Jewish community and the State of Israel must be based on mutual respect for one another's feelings and needs, and on the preservation of the integrity of the two communities and their institutions.

There is evidence that David Ben-Gurion did not take the exchange with complete seriousness. Selma Hirsh, who was hired by John Slawson as his executive assistant in 1945 and during almost forty years with the AJC went on to become associate director, recalled the scene in Jerusalem just after the public speeches had been made. Blaustein had been accompanied on the trip by his son-in-law, David Hirschhorn, and Ben-Gurion had been introduced to him. Blaustein was shaking Ben-Gurion's hand, saying words about how good the agreement was, how much cooperation it showed, and so forth. Ben-Gurion turned to the son-in-law and said, "So nu, David, when are you coming to live in Israel?"[77] Blaustein did not laugh. He returned to the United States, convinced that this time his wishes would be carried out. (David Hirschhorn went on to become an important leader and benefactor to the AJC in his own right. He passed away in 2006 at the age of eighty-eight.) Periodically, however, well into the 1960s, Blaustein would follow up by correspondence and additional meetings every time he suspected that the Israelis were not living up to their part of the bargain. Blaustein and those who worked for him would scrutinize every statement by Israeli leaders published in the major newspapers, including the *New York Times,* and the responses took up "enormous amounts of time and energy," in the words of Israeli historian Zvi Ganin.[78] AJC, through Blaustein, would charge that Ben-Gurion had violated the "firm understanding" of the joint statement and Ben-Gurion would be asked to reaffirm it.[79] That bargain included the provision that American Jews would only continue to support Israel on the condition that Israel made no overt moves to call for or facilitate the mass *aliyah* of Jews from America.

Jacob Blaustein called for a reaffirmation of the statement in 1957 and in late 1960, in an incident that was followed soon after by the announcement that AJC would be opening an office in Israel. There had recently been an epidemic of swastika daubings and antisemitic vandalism around the world, and the capture of Adolf Eichmann was causing the events of the Holocaust to receive closer attention (see chapter 4). Israel herself was enduring world condemnation for having allegedly violated Argentinian sovereignty by snatching Eichmann. Ben-Gurion and Israeli officials had apparently been making statements implying that the Jews of the United States were in danger and that they should immigrate to Israel. Indeed, Ben-Gurion made a speech blatantly calling for *aliyah* from the United States at the World Zionist Congress. He announced to the five hundred delegates assembled, in a speech that was cited in the *New York Times*: "Since the day when the Jewish state was established and the gates of Israel were flung open to every Jew who wanted to come, every religious Jew has daily violated the precepts of Judaism and the Torah of Israel by remaining in the Diaspora." Citing the authority of the Talmud, he declared: "Whoever dwells outside the land of Israel is considered to have no God." In his view Jews in Diaspora were facing "extinction" one way or another. "In several totalitarian and Muslim countries Judaism is in danger of death by strangulation," he said. "In the free and prosperous countries it faces the kiss of death, a slow and imperceptible decline into the abyss of assimilation."[80]

The anti-Zionist American Council for Judaism loudly denounced both the statements and AJC's inability or unwillingness to stop them.[81] Blaustein, in his capacity as honorary president of the AJC, then wrote to Ben-Gurion in December 1960, seven months after Eichmann had been captured, "During these past few months, to our deep chagrin, there have been a number of violations of your August 1950 statement. These departures are causing serious embarrassments and consequences. . . . I assure you that if you wish your country to retain its friendship—at a time when you sorely need it—it is essential that you promptly correct the wrong impressions to which I have referred—and I earnestly urge you to do so (1) by letting me have a reaffirmation of the Statement you gave me in August 1950 and (2) by impressing upon the people in your government the necessity of avoiding conflicting statements and actions in the future."[82] In the confrontations that followed, AJC issued several public statements and press releases. One read:

The American Jewish Committee and Jews throughout the United States and the world are both grieved and shocked by the reported statement of David Ben-Gurion, Prime Minister of Israel, that Jews wherever they are have an obligation to emigrate to Israel. The American Jewish Committee has always maintained that emigration to Israel must be an act of free choice, within personal discretion of each individual, and certainly cannot be considered a necessary and vital aspect of his religious faith. Whatever authority Mr. Ben-Gurion may have to speak for Jewish citizens of Israel, he has none whatsoever to speak for Jews in other parts of the world. We confidently assert that, contrary to Mr. Ben-Gurion's reported statement that Judaism will suffer "a kiss of death" outside of Israel, Judaism is in fact a flourishing religion which, in democratic countries such as the United States, enjoys equal rights and opportunities with all other religions.[83]

Herbert B. Ehrmann wrote his own letter to Ben-Gurion, stating AJC's position:

The American Jewish Committee is deeply concerned about the promulgation by Israel officials of a philosophy to the effect that Jews cannot live in a full Jewish life and that Judaism cannot flourish elsewhere than in Israel. In our view, this denotes a lack of understanding of Jewish life in a free society such as the United States. The fact is that Judaism can and does flourish in the United States. We know from our own experience and observation, as well as from our religious teachers, that a full, vital, Jewish spiritual life may be ours in our own country. However, we hold that emigration from one country to another must be an act of free choice within the personal discretion of each individual. It is not a moral obligation because of religious or ethnic ties.

Ben-Gurion finally agreed to make another joint statement, and this was duly announced in another press release by AJC:

The relationship between Israel and Jews in other free democracies, which provoked strong controversy earlier this year, has been clarified by a firm understanding in the form of a joint statement by Israel Prime Minister David Ben-Gurion and Jacob Blaustein,

US industrialist and Honorary President of the American Jewish Committee. On December 30, 1960, the American Jewish Committee, a non-Zionist human relations agency, charged Mr. Ben-Gurion with violating the agreement made in 1950 with Mr. Blaustein as to the relationship of American Jews and Jews residing elsewhere throughout the world and the State of Israel. At the time, the Committee said it was shocked by Mr. Ben-Gurion's statement, as reported, that Jews throughout the world were obligated to emigrate to Israel and Jews could not lead a full life in the context of their Judaism outside of Israel.[84]

That very month, April 1961 (which also happened to be the month the Eichmann trial began), AJC announced that it would be opening an office in Israel. John Slawson had discussed doing so as early as 1949, but the plan had not come to fruition, partly for budgetary reasons. The office actually opened in Tel Aviv in 1962. One justification given for it was "to strengthen the links between the United States and Israel, to interpret the realities of American life in Israel, and to make available to Israel some of the lessons learned by AJC during its more than half a century of activity in intergroup relations throughout the world."[85] Another memo spoke of the three-fold necessity of the Israel office "to arrest the narrow parochialism of the younger generation of Israelis; to guard against the possible "de-Judaization" of Israel; and to build up the cultural reserves within the state to withstand the forces of Levantinization."[86]

At AJC functions, until the 1990s, the "Hatikvah," the national anthem of the State of Israel, was never sung (as it customarily was at the functions of other Jewish organizations), nor was the Israeli flag ever displayed next to the American flag. The record shows that through wars and recessions and every possible crisis when the nation was in danger, the AJC was at the side of Israel, rendering its political, diplomatic, financial, and moral support. But it would take many years before the organization as a whole felt truly comfortable with the existence of Israel. The Blaustein–Ben-Gurion statement, its reaffirmations, the legacy of AJC's non-Zionist philosophy of the 1930s and early 1940s, the failure of the Cos Cob formula, sharp memories of its refusal to support the Biltmore Program at the American Jewish Conference in 1943, AJC's cooperation with the authorities in helping to root out communists from American Jewish life, and AJC's particular "Jewish education" program—all caused much resentment from other organizations and lent support to the stereotype that was still current in the twenty-first century that the American Jewish Committee was actually an anti-Israel, anti–Jewish peoplehood organization led by stuck-up German Jews.

Much later, in the early 1980s, a staff member at the AJC New York office was making *aliyah* to Israel and the office gave a going-away party for her. "That sound you hear," remarked Bertram H. Gold, who was John Slawson's successor as AJC executive vice president from 1967 to 1982, "is the sound of AJC founders turning in their graves."[87] By that time AJC had weekly lessons among the staff, one on Talmud and one on the Hebrew Bible, celebrated all the Jewish holidays and even had a *sukkah* on the roof.[88] It took many years, the waning of John Blaustein's and John Slawson's influence and the strengthening of Bertram Gold's before the AJC eventually entered the mainstream of American Judaism and became as passionately pro-Israel as any Zionist organization.

↭ 3 ↮

"This Is Our Home"

[1951–1957]

B y 1951 the majority of displaced persons that had flooded the American zone of postwar Germany had found homes, in Israel and other countries. The resettlement had happened so quickly that the participants hardly had time to take cognizance of it before moving on with their lives. Nonetheless, Zachariah Shuster, AJC's indefatigable European office director (headquartered in Paris, he and his assistant Abraham Karlikow throughout the 1950s were the only two AJC professionals directly responsible for three continents) spared a moment in 1952 to reflect on the mighty deed that world Jewry had done. Directly after the war, he said, he had felt like Noah stepping out of the ark and contemplating all that was left. Now, however, "the Catastrophe is over," he remarked at the Committee's annual gathering that year. "And here is another thing which I do not think has been realized in this country. A gigantic task was accomplished by American Jewish organizations . . . in this great population movement. It was a saga. I witnessed the great historic movement of people from Europe to Israel or to other places. That was an odyssey which needs another Homer to describe it."[1]

Germany: New Realities

An immediate task, after the American zone was evacuated, had been to establish and refine AJC's policies toward postwar Germany. That the nation was filled with unregenerate Nazis was clear enough to them: among all the expectation was that Germany would have to remain occupied for a long time before change could occur (see chapter 2). In the 1950s the phenomenon of Holocaust denial had already made its appearance. A leading neo-Nazi publication in the summer of 1953 claimed that the number of Jews exterminated had been exaggerated; "only" one and a half million, not six million, was the correct number of Jewish victims.[2] The average German refused to acknowledge that anything had happened. "The Christians who lived across the street from any of Germany's synagogues on November 9, 1938, when every synagogue in Germany was set afire, were evidently not at home that evening," remarked community affairs consultant Rabbi S. Andhil Fineberg sarcastically after a six-week visit to Germany in 1954. "Most Germans were presumably out of town when their Jewish neighbors vanished. Nor did they glimpse the frightened groups huddled at dawn at the railroad stations, awaiting deportation."[3]

With the outbreak of the Korean War, however, Germany's endangerment and strategic value made it impossible to keep at arm's length any longer. A militarily strong Germany was deemed vital to the defense of all Western Europe against Soviet incursion. In his report on what they termed the "German problem" Dr. Herman A. Gray, chair of the Foreign Affairs Committee, reminded them that "geopolitical considerations" of the time might require that the AJC "rethink and clarify" its position on the subject of Germany and German affairs. The first question officers and members had faced was whether the organization should simply ignore Germany and refuse to have anything to do with it, as many in the American Jewish communal world and in Israel felt. A good number believed that Germany was "eternally damned" and that nothing could or should be done. Besides, the problems relating to it were exceedingly complex, and what good could a private organization like the AJC hope to do anyway?

The majority, however, took the view that Western Germany, whether it deserved to take a position in the civilized world or not, was being readmitted, and that it would be both "futile and self-defeating" to ignore it. To do so might bring about the very results they feared. Furthermore, direct negotiations with Germany would be necessary to secure the one admission price the AJC and others insisted upon for Germany's reentry into the family of nations: acknowledgment of responsibility for what it had done and the payment of proper restitution and reparations to its victims. AJC president Jacob Blaustein, an experienced arm-twister who never hesitated to walk with kings, shahs and presidents, played a major role in these negotiations.

Numerous behind-the-scenes talks, in which representatives of the U.S. government applied their own pressures, bore fruit on September 27, 1951, when German Chancellor Konrad Adenauer, who had been imprisoned by the Nazis during World War II, declared before the Bonn Parliament that Germany intended to do all in its power "to make material and moral amends" for the "unspeakable crimes" perpetuated against the Jews. He pledged both "unrelenting" prosecution of antisemites and a rapid and just completion of restitution. He added that making the "spirit of humane and religious tolerance . . . reality among the entire German people" was incumbent upon the nation's educational system. This declaration was followed by the establishment of the Conference on Jewish Material Claims Against Germany, sponsored by twenty-three Jewish organizations from nine countries. Zionist leader Nahum Goldmann was president of the Conference and Blaustein was senior vice president; in that role Blaustein negotiated directly with Adenauer and the German authorities. Ultimately the Germans agreed to pay, over a period of twelve to fourteen years, close to one billion dollars of restitution and reparations payments to Israel and to victims of Nazism around the world.[4]

Jews of Latin America and the Middle East

The matter of German reparations was thus settled, but in those uncertain and unstable years of the "hot" war in Korea and the cold war that followed, there was no end of Jews around the world who deserved and required AJC help and intervention. In Latin America, during the Korean War, there was a possibility that the majority of Jews (who were of East European origin) might be interned en masse and their property confiscated if war with the Soviets broke out. The AJC alerted the State Department and ensured that Latin American countries issue internal security clauses that would prevent such an outcome.

Of the 627,000 Jews in Latin America in 1952, more than half resided in Argentina, and these lived under the precarious domination of the dictator General Juan Perón. With Perón and Catholic groups clashing, according to Maximo Yagupsky, AJC's representative in Buenos Aires, cries of "Down with Peron and his Jewish friends" were heard. The continent saw abundant anti-semitism sponsored by Latin America's Arab communities, Italian Fascists (tens of thousands of Middle Easterners and millions of Italians had migrated to Latin America), and Nazi expatriates. The position of the Jews was still uncertain when Perón was finally ousted in 1956. The following year AJC officers undertook a mission to the Vatican for a private reception with Pope Pius XII, the first to be given to an official Jewish delegation in the eighteen years of his pontificate. They asked for, and received, his intercession on behalf of the Jews of Poland, Hungary, and Latin America.

The Jews of the Middle East had been terrorized even before the U.N. vote partitioning Palestine into a Jewish and an Arab state in 1947. In March 1951 the situation of the Jews of Iraq suddenly worsened. The Iraqi parliament passed new laws freezing the assets of Jews registered for emigration to Israel and penalized others outside the country unless they returned within sixty days. The day of May 31, 1951, was set as the termination date of legal immigration to Israel. Jacob Blaustein negotiated with U.S. government officials, who asked the Iraqis to reconsider, and the date was indefinitely extended. The AJC also acted on Iraq's arrests in 1951 of scores of Jews on charge of treason, terrorist acts, and subversive political activities. Two Jews were sentenced to death and executed; the only hope was that the twenty or more Jews convicted for other crimes would receive relatively light prison sentences. Subsequently, AJC's staff was relieved to hear through "reliable information" that many other prisoners had escaped and had since found their way to safety outside Iraq.[5]

The situation of Jews in North Africa grew increasingly perilous in the postwar years as the age of colonialism drew to an end and the control of European governments—with whom most Jews had identified themselves—gave way to the rise of independent Arab countries. The desires of Arab nationalists, the French empire, and American defense aspirations clashed, and the Jews found themselves in the middle of it all. In Libya, the first North African country scheduled to become independent, AJC's European staff in the early 1950s worked with the U.N. and the Community Council of Libyan Jews to draft additions to the nation's new constitution that would guarantee human, civil, and religious rights to the Jewish community. By 1953, however, it was clear these efforts had gone for naught. Only three thousand Jews from a once-flourishing community were left in Libya by then; the rest of the prewar population of thirty thousand had fled to Israel.[6]

The 140,000 Jews of Algeria enjoyed some protection, as they were almost all French citizens and were welcomed by the mother country when the time came to evacuate (Pierre Mendès France, the premier at the time, was himself Jewish, which had incited antisemitic radio broadcasts by Moroccan exiles to their home country). Still thousands, facing Muslim attacks in remote areas, fled to the large cities, where they faced increasing pressure from the Algerian Liberation Front to take an open stand on their side against French rule. The ultimate fate of the 240,000 Jews of Morocco and the 80,000 of Tunisia was even less certain. Muslim mobs scapegoated them after the failure of an attack on the French authorities: Jews were attacked and killed, and Jewish property destroyed. The deposing of the Sultan of Morocco in 1954, after twenty-five years of rule, did not add to the stability of the area. Irving M. Engel, former head of the Executive Committee and Blaustein's successor as president of the AJC, reported in 1955: "This past year North Africa like a massive atomic pile reached a critical stage. Around them swirls a contest between a France reluctant to yield her power and increasingly restive and impatient Arab nations-to-be. Between both forces are the Jewish communities, eager to stay if assured full rights, fearful of what the future may bring in the wake of a French withdrawal or waning influence."[7]

In 1955, at the behest of AJC's Executive Committee, Jacob Blaustein, John Slawson, Irving Engel, and staff members Zachariah Shuster and Abe Karlikow went on an extensively covered two-week fact-finding mission to

North Africa—inquiring, negotiating, intervening, and seeking the assistance of the U.S. State Department wherever they could. All that time, the AJC position was firm: the Jews of North Africa should be guaranteed full and equal rights if they chose to stay and free emigration with their property if they chose to leave. But no one should accept the situation without a struggle. There should be no panicked calls for mass emigration, even though French rule was evaporating faster than anyone had anticipated. "To view the forced flight of Jews from another corner of the world as the *only* solution," stated Engel, "would represent a victory for Hitlerian concepts."[8] Still, as the situation deteriorated and Tunisia showed signs of wanting to join the Arab League, the AJC urged all American Jews to support the United Jewish Appeal's emergency $10 million campaign for the transportation and resettlement of Jews from North Africa.

Of all those caught in the Middle East, the fifty thousand Jews still left in Egypt after Israel's War of Independence had perhaps the worst fate in store. Under Gamal Abdel Nasser, severe anti-Jewish measures followed in the wake of the Suez-Sinai campaign of October 1956, in which the Israelis, along with Great Britain and France, invaded the Sinai Peninsula. The invasion was, in large part, a response to *fedayeen* raids from Egyptian territory (*fedayeen* were members of Palestinian militias, refugees from the 1948 war, who infiltrated Israel). Despite a curtain of secrecy, reports leaked through of mass arrests, internment in concentration camps, torture, confiscation of Jewish businesses and assets, bank accounts blocked, destruction of property, and expulsion. Under the new Egyptian Nationality Law, anyone who was suspected of "Zionist" loyalties was singled out for harassment, and Egyptian firms were forced to fire employees who were not citizens of the country—a category where most of Egypt's Jews found themselves, having preferred the protection of French, British, and Italian consulates rather than being subject to local Arab law. Overnight thousands were thrown out of work with no other means of support in sight. Egyptian police would periodically visit Jewish homes either to arrest people or to grant a few days to sell one's belongings and leave the country. Those about to be expelled were asked to sign documents that they were leaving voluntarily, had no claims against Egypt, and would never return.[9] Departure of all Jews as quickly as possible was the only eventuality the Egyptians would accept. The AJC made repeated representations to the State Department, asking the United States to place pressure on Egypt to stop the persecution. Their intervention managed to secure one thousand visas for Egyptian Jewish refugees to Brazil and at least one thousand to the United States, but there was not much more they could do. Within a year the members of a once-prosperous community were scattered to the four corners of the earth, about half finding refuge in Israel.

Behind the Iron Curtain

Of a world Jewish population of only eleven and a half million according to the *American Jewish Year Book* of 1953—with mass immigration, Israel now held 12 percent of that number—it was estimated that two and a half million of them were trapped behind the Iron Curtain. This had been Winston Churchill's term for the Soviet Union and the eight "satellite" countries it swallowed up after World War II: East Germany, Poland, Hungary, Rumania, Czechoslovakia, Bulgaria, and Albania. Civilization in Europe, in the words of one AJC staff member, ended at the Brandenburg Gate in Berlin. There was no official contact at all between western cities and cities of the Soviet sphere—and the Soviets, unlike the Nazis, were armed with atomic weapons. John J. McCloy, former U.S. High Commissioner for Germany, in a 1953 address to the AJC stated that only eight years earlier "we had hoped we were finished with purges, concentration camps, racial hysteria, and secret police. We had defeated Nazi Germany and we were trying to build a new world. But it was soon apparent that the old patterns were being applied by the Soviet Union so that today we may be on the verge of a full repetition of the Nazi disgrace in the form of anti-Semitic persecution. The Kremlin preaches brotherhood and peace, and practices brutality. Millions of people are suffering. . . . The Jews of Eastern Europe are undergoing the added torment of racial persecution. Those who escaped Hitler's concentration camps are now heading for Stalin's."[10] John Slawson stated the matter more succinctly: "Two and a half million Jews are in danger of extinction."[11]

The persecution of Jews living under communist rule caused fear in the hearts of AJC leaders as nothing had since the days of Hitler. An AJC fact sheet in 1953 documented that under thirty years of communism, entire populations had been obliterated; six or more ethnic groups had already been wiped out.[12] The common pattern under Stalin was denunciation, dismissal from jobs, arrest, family members held as hostages, staged trials, confessions and signed declarations of guilt extracted under torture, and execution or mass deportation to slave labor camps in Siberia. As many as twenty million people died under his regime, and those two and a half million Jews were one of his main targets—although officially there was supposed to be no such thing as antisemitism in the Soviet Union.[13]

The "declassing" of Jews was part of the phenomenon. To help complete the communization of the country, Hungarian authorities rooted twenty-four thousand to thirty-five thousand mostly middle-class persons out of their urban homes on a few hours' notice in 1952, then dumped them in a remote area on the Soviet-Hungary border where they faced the threat of exposure and starvation. By the following year there were reports that the Hungarians had deported as many as eighty thousand people, including Jews, and sent the better part to slave labor camps in the Soviet Union. NCRAC and AJC placed the matter before President Truman and the State Department; Jacob Blaustein also sent a wire to Secretary of State Dean Acheson. President Truman issued a statement denouncing the deportations.[14] In Rumania, tens of thousands of Jews had already been deported in September 1949. In February 1952 at least a hundred thousand more men, women, and children, mostly from Jewish middle-class families, were expelled from the cities either to isolated regions of the country or to slave camps. The measures coincided with the mass arrest and imprisonment of Jewish communal leaders.[15] In East Germany a "blacklist" of the secret police was drawn up of persons of Jewish or partly Jewish origin; hundreds, including children, were arrested and put in concentration camps. The Nazi racial laws were applied to decide who was "Aryan" and who was not.[16]

Purges of Jews from public life were one of the first things to come to the world's attention. In 1951 Rudolf Slansky, the secretary-general of the Communist Party of Czechoslovakia, was accused of plotting against the Stalinist government, along with fourteen co-conspirators in the party—eleven of them Jewish. Some had survived Nazi concentration camps. The shock of the Prague public show trial reverberated around the world. Slansky was executed in December 1952. On January 13, 1953, the TASS News Agency reported the "arrest of a terrorist group of physicians, uncovered by the State Security Organs of the U.S.S.R." "Vicious Spies and Killers Under the Mask of Academic Physicians" read that day's headline in *Pravda*. Six of the physicians were Jewish, among the most prestigious practitioners in Moscow. The doctors had supposedly poisoned Soviet leaders and planned, either by poison, misuse of drugs, or improper medical treatment, to murder more, including Stalin himself. The indictment left no doubt that the doctors' Jewish identity was at issue, and specifically targeted the American Jewish Joint Distribution Committee (the "Joint"). The "Joint" was in those days a favorite subject of the ubiquitous Soviet anti-Jewish and anti-American propaganda that filled radio airwaves around the world and appeared in communist-sponsored newspapers and news agency publications:

Whom did these monsters serve? Who directed the criminal, terrorist, and harmful activity of these vicious traitors to the Motherland? . . . It has been determined that all participants of the terrorist group of doctors were in the service of foreign intelligence, having sold their bodies and souls. . . . They were recruited by a branch-office of American intelligence—the international Jewish bourgeois-nationalist organization called "Joint." The filthy face of this Zionist spy organization, covering up their vicious actions under the mask of kindness, is now completely revealed. Relying upon a group of corrupt Jewish bourgeois nationalists, the professional spies and terrorists of "Joint," through assignments from and under the direction of American intelligence, extended their subversive activity even into the territory of the Soviet Union. . . . Unmasking the gang of poisoners-doctors struck a blow against the international Jewish Zionist organization. . . . Exposing the gang . . . struck a shattering blow to the Anglo-American war mongers. Their agents were captured and neutralized. Again the true face of the slave-holding cannibals of the U.S.A. and England appears before the whole world.[17]

The announcement was followed by mass imprisonment of Jews. Rumors flew around Moscow that the Jews were to be deported to Siberia; it was widely believed that a new camp in Siberia with room for hundreds of thousands of inmates was being made ready for them.[18] Just days before the doctors' trial was set to begin, however, Stalin collapsed on March 1 after a dinner with his closest advisers, Lavrenty Beria, Georgi Malenkov, Nikolay Bulganin, and Nikita Khrushchev. His body reportedly lay unattended for twelve hours because doctors feared to treat him. On March 5 he died, officially of a stroke. No hard evidence ever surfaced that he might have been deliberately done to death. A month later, *Pravda* announced that the doctors were innocent and had been released (although, as it happened, two had already died in prison). Whether or not Stalin was indeed murdered, compassion for Soviet Jews was not a motive. The Soviet leaders, who were going through their own power struggles, might well have feared that deportation on that scale would provoke war with the United States, which they truly believed was controlled by Jewish Zionist financiers. In any event, a catastrophe was averted.

Observers spoke of a "New Look" in Soviet policies after the death of Stalin, but AJC reports indicated that very little had changed, as its representatives testified before congressional committees. ("New Look" was a popular term at the time, introduced by *Life* magazine in 1947 to refer to the innovative couture of Christian Dior.) The denunciation of Stalin and the slight opening up of the Soviet Union that followed under Khrushchev, who had become the U.S.S.R.'s premier, was only enough to confirm their fears about the situation.[19] By then it was not just physical extinction but communal, cultural, and spiritual extinction that Soviet Jews were facing. The greatest Yiddish writers and poets had been killed; Jewish schools, publishing houses, newspapers, and libraries were closed down; and Jewish organizations of every kind had been either disbanded or absorbed by non-Jewish ones. Religious observance after Stalin was limited to a few synagogues—all the easier for the Soviet secret police to keep an eye on the participants—and studying Hebrew or giving religious instruction to young people in groups larger than three was a crime. Emigration for anyone was forbidden. The old rabbis were dying and Soviet Jews were not permitted to form a seminary to train new ones. There was a sudden upsurge in Jews arrested for "economic" crimes—speculation, bribery, theft, or black-market activity—and their names were repeated over and over in the newspaper and on radio broadcasts.

Anti-Jewish propaganda soaked the communist media: the "Joint" was an American intelligence agency; Zionism was the same as fascism; Jews were "rootless cosmopolitans"; the prime minister of Israel was an agent of U.S. imperialism; the reparations agreements were an exploitation of the German people; the entire American justice system was criminal because it had sentenced Julius and Ethel Rosenberg to death.[20] The AJC was occasionally included in such attacks. "The oil magnates and Wall Street bankers who rule the American Jewish Committee needed a black book of Soviet activities against the Jews," said one party-line newspaper, criticizing the AJC's books and many publications on the subject. A Radio Warsaw broadcast of June 6, 1955, in a violent attack on AJC, referred to the organization as "Yahudish asses in the stables of the American State Department."[21]

Rabbi Morris N. Kertzer was an AJC staff member who visited the U.S.S.R. in the summer of 1956 as part of a delegation of the New York Board of Rabbis. In a small synagogue room he noted piles of Torah scrolls against the wall, all taken from synagogues that had been closed permanently. "There must be three hundred of them," he guessed. "Shhh!" cautioned a bystander. "There are spies in this room." The local rabbi had spent three years in jail after two congregation members testified that he had given an antigovernment speech. In another service, as he described it, a group of people gathered admiringly around a nine-year-old boy, who managed to stumble through a one-line "Shema" (a basic Hebrew prayer) and then haltingly pronounced the blessing over the bread. "He's one in a thousand!" someone whispered, and the older people there beamed with joy. "But they must have remembered in their own youth," observed Rabbi Kertzer, "that a nine-year-old would have already been introduced to the intricacies of the Talmud."

Walking down a Leningrad street after the service, a middle-aged man told the rabbi of his experiences trying to teach his son the rudiments of a Jewish education. "My son is almost bar mitzvah age," the man said. "It hurts me to think that a boy in my family shouldn't know an aleph from a bet. I got hold of a Hebrew primer a few weeks ago and sat down with him. After ten minutes of frustration, the boy cried out, 'Leave me alone, Papa, this doesn't mean a thing to me.'"[22]

Although by the 1950s only a small minority of Jews as a whole were active in communist causes, among those who were active, Jews were disproportionately prominent. Jewish informants and members of the secret police behind the Iron Curtain used their knowledge of the community and its language to uncover illegal Jewish activity. The Yiddish newspaper *Freiheit* followed the party line faithfully; many of its articles were identical to those in the *Daily Worker.* Many idealistic Jews around the world could not bring themselves to believe that the nation that had posited itself as the protector of workers, minorities, and liberalism—that had actually outlawed antisemitism in the 1920s—could be capable of such evil. The Soviet Union had been an ally of the United States during World War II. The victories of the Red Army had saved Soviet Jews from total extermination. Israeli kibbutzim, where photos of Marx and Lenin were displayed on dining room walls, were torn apart in the conflict between Stalinists and anti-Stalinists. Louis Harap, editor of the magazine *Jewish Life,* declared before the House Un-American Activities Committee that he had been summoned before it not because of his procommunist propaganda activities but because he was a Jew. He also stated the Jews were "better off" in the U.S.S.R. than they were in the United States.[23] These events made it all the harder for the AJC to disprove the common antisemitic charge that "Jewish communists" was an oxymoron. In the late 1940s and early 1950s, AJC took upon itself the goal of dispelling, once and for all, the public's equating of Jews with communists. And they strove to convince Jews who might still be "receptive" to communist ideology that their loyalties should lie elsewhere.

AJC representatives, in particular Rabbi Dr. S. Andhil Fineberg of the Community Affairs Department—and head of the AJC's Staff Committee on Communism—met with other Jewish organizations to convince them to purge known communists and communist sympathizers from their ranks and from their unions. His book *The Rosenberg Case: Fact or Fiction?* disputed, as Soviet propaganda and American Jewish protesters claimed, that the Rosenbergs were the victims of an antisemitic frame-up.[24] AJC cooperated fully and shared information with the House Un-American Activities Committee. For these efforts, communists labeled the AJC as representatives of "big business" interests, collaborators, Red-baiters, and informers on Jews to Gentile authorities (in Hebrew, *mosrim*).[25] When Julius and Ethel Rosenberg were condemned to death in the electric chair, AJC's leading officers would not even consider asking for clemency; the overwhelming opinion was that the two had been duly convicted and deserved their fate.

Declassified material in the 1990s proved that Julius Rosenberg was in fact guilty, although his wife Ethel Greenglass Rosenberg was not, having been convicted on perjured testimony. The investigators' policy at the time was to use her as a lever against her husband, who unlike others in the spy ring had refused to confess or to cooperate with the authorities in any way. The two had been arrested only a few weeks after the beginning of the Korean War, and Judge Irving Kaufman specifically referred to that event when he sentenced them. "Your crime is worse than murder," he declared at the time, accusing them of having allowed the Russians to perfect the A-bomb years before America's best scientists had predicted that it would. "The bomb has already caused the Communist aggression in Korea, with the resultant casualties exceeding fifty thousand and who knows but what that millions more innocent people may pay the price of your treason."[26] After two years of appeals, the couple was executed on June 19, 1953, a short time before the war ended.

In fighting Soviet communism the weapons in the AJC arsenal included information for the American press, radio, and TV, the marshaling of world opinion, utilization of every diplomatic channel at their disposal, and publications and radio broadcasts of their own to counteract Soviet propaganda. Passover was considered a particularly appropriate time for such broadcasts. In April 1953, for example, Rabbi Kertzer delivered a message of hope and a warning to the Soviet Union through a Voice of America broadcast that was translated and repeated at least fifty times during the holiday. In May 1956 AJC president Irving Engel delivered a similar Passover greeting transmitted by Voice of America and Radio Free Europe.

Two books, *The Jews in the Soviet Union* and *The Jews in the Soviet Satellites,* fully documented what was truly going on,[27] as did articles in *Commentary* and other AJC publications that were regularly distributed by State Department officials abroad. When the first book came out in 1951, referring to the millions in slave labor camps, John Slawson noted that the AJC had been accused by several newspapers of "fomenting hysteria."[28] *Harvest of Hate: The Nazi Program for the Destruction of the Jews of Europe* by Leon Poliakov — at the time a definitive history of the Nazi anti-Jewish program from its inception to the final liquidation of the Jews — was sponsored by AJC and published by Syracuse University Press in 1954. Its timing was calculated to warn the world what had happened barely a decade earlier and that antisemitism had been the glue that held a global conflict together.[29]

Recasting the problem in its true world context was an important goal. "By adopting racism and antisemitism the Red leaders are trying to lure extreme neo-Nazi and neo-Fascist groups into an anti-American bloc," noted Zachariah Schuster. "They are also trying to win the support of fanatic Arab nationalists in the Middle East. By this tactic they hope to frustrate America's policy of wielding a democratic coalition strong enough to thwart their aggression. In short, and this should be clearly recognized, the real target of Soviet antisemitism is the United States."[30]

International Human Rights

The anticommunist attitudes that prevailed during the era of McCarthyism made it more difficult for AJC leaders to take action that would have protected Jews. Circumstances brought to the fore American isolationists and xenophobes who feared the United Nations as a world government plotting to undermine U.S. sovereignty. The U.N., UNESCO, public schools and teachers that taught about the U.N., "subversive" textbooks, programs on intercultural education, even the Girl Scout handbook (which was accused of advocating "internationalism") — all came under aggressive attack by elements that attracted the nation's antisemites. With the "New Look" of antisemitism, AJC officers believed, the more crude and overt "rock-throwing" kind of Jew-hatred had gone underground to assail institutions upon which the security of Jews and other minorities rested. The AJC responded with articles, sheets, pamphlets, articles, radio and TV programs, an alliance with the National Education Association, and conferences with labor educators, youth leaders, veterans, and other civic groups.

Leaders of the AJC themselves were becoming disillusioned with the U.N., as the Soviet Union and the bloc of Arab and the new "non-aligned" nations increasingly blocked U.S. measures and passed anti-Israel resolutions. At one time AJC had been one of the most passionate supporters of the United Nations, and promoting it had been a basic part of their program. For U.N. Week in 1952 the AJC prepared radio and TV spots, newspaper features, cartoons and leaflets, all stressing the relationship between human rights and the maintenance of peace. AJC radio recordings were heard over a thousand radio stations and "The U.N.: What's in it For You?" a feature written in AJC offices, appeared in 325 newspapers. An eighty-two-page guide to social action entitled "You Hold the Key to Human Rights" was authored and sponsored by AJC (as usual, however, the name of the organization was not on it). This time the imprint was the Women's Division of the Methodist Church, and fifteen thousand were printed and distributed—again paid for by AJC—to women's church groups across the country.

Blaustein, reminiscing in 1956 about the role he and Judge Proskauer had played in forming the U.N. charter in San Francisco, addressed the issue of their disappointment with the U.N. He was more convinced than ever of the necessity of the U.N., despite "frustrations from time to time." "In addition to the many accomplishments in the economic, social, health and cultural fields," he said, "let me put it very simply this way: I would rather there be the battle of words and ideas in the world forum than fighting on the battlefields in fact." He claimed it was unlikely that the atom and hydrogen bomb would be used in war because "largely through the U.N. and its related agencies, each side has learned enough to know the strength of the other and the complete ruin that would ensue to both."[31]

Once the U.N. had adopted the Universal Declaration of Human Rights, the hope and expectation among AJC leaders was that binding covenants for human rights and against genocide would be adopted by the United States and all the nations of the world. But in 1953 Secretary of State John Foster Dulles announced a reversal of U.S. policy, stating that the administration would not sign any U.N. human rights covenant or recommend ratification of the U.N. Genocide Convention. Instead the United States would rely on "educational" means to bring about the desired ends. The reversal was in part a reaction to an amendment to the Constitution proposed by Senator John Bricker (Republican from Ohio) that would have cut off the president's treaty-making rights. At issue was President Truman's actions in considering U.N. membership as a treaty obligation and sending U.S. soldiers into Korea without requesting Congress for a declaration of war. The Bricker amendment, which would severely limit the president's autonomy in foreign affairs, had garnered the support of scores of senators in 1953 and there was serious danger that it might pass. A successor to the amendment some time later was vetoed by the president. With a two-thirds majority needed to override the veto, the measure failed to pass in Congress by a single vote.

Immigration

U.S. immigration and naturalization law, which the AJC had fought so extensively throughout the late 1940s and early 1950s, only became worse with the passage of the McCarran-Walter Immigration and Nationality Act of 1952, authored by Senator Patrick McCarran (Democrat, from Nevada) and Representative Francis Walter (Democrat, from Pennsylvania). McCarran was chairman of the Senate Internal Security Committee, which had investigated the administrations of Franklin Roosevelt and Harry Truman for alleged communist influence. The act, which set up what some termed the "Golden Curtain," and added the phenomenon of "McCarranism" to "McCarthyism," retained the nationality origins quotas of the 1924 act, whose effect had been to reduce immigration from southern and eastern Europe. It put even more obstacles in the way of potential immigrants to the United States and included procedures that permitted deportation of aliens without judicial review and a distinction between native-born and naturalized American citizens. Would-be immigrants had to fill out visa applications specifying their race and ethnic classification, and authorities evaluated them in light of a "Dictionary of Races or Peoples." Americans living abroad could far more easily lose their citizenship. Under the years the act was in effect, American citizens who had immigrated to Israel had to return to the United States every eighteen months or risk losing their American passports. The act indirectly facilitated the immigration to the United States of those who had supported Nazism while excluding those who supported communism. Each year 26,000 Germans were permitted to enter but only 5,600 Italians, 3,200 Poles, 300 Greeks, and 100 from the West Indies.[32]

AJC representatives testified in congressional committees to oppose the act and began an extensive public relations campaign including radio, TV ads, fact sheets to members of the press, and even cartoons to convince American public opinion that the act was wrong. The act provided grist for the Soviet anti-American propaganda mill and, in the evaluation of AJC honorary vice president Senator Herbert H. Lehman, had cost the United States much of its prestige abroad. "Never has a great fund of good-will such as we had abroad after World War II . . . been dissipated so quickly," he declared.[33] He later termed the act "a scandal at home and abroad. We should all be ashamed for our country."[34]

Antisemitism

Crude and overt bigotry may have been less fashionable in the United States in the 1950s. It may have been played down by Jewish leaders for fear of being disloyal to the United States: acknowledging the bigotry would supply material for Soviet propaganda and harm U.S. efforts abroad to convince the world that the United States was not truly a racist, imperialist, warmongering, or hypocritical country. In those years, whenever possible, AJC and other Jewish leaders preferred to subsume attacks on Jews and Jewish institutions under the classification of general antiminority violence. Progress *was* being made, after all. In 1953, Irving Engel noted with pleasure that for the first time in seventy years not a single lynching was reported anywhere in the United States.[35] Granted, there were incidents, such as the time in Cicero, Illinois, in 1951 when three thousand white citizens rioted to protest a black family moving into their town and then-Governor Adlai Stevenson had had to call out the National Guard; a not dissimilar scene occurred during the attempts to integrate Little Rock High School in 1957. Still, segregation was on its way to being outlawed. Blacks, especially in the diplomatic neighborhoods of Washington, D.C., and New York, were supposed to be able to enter a public restaurant or hotel or movie house without having to sit in separate sections or entering through the back door. Parks, pools, and other recreational facilities controlled by the Department of the Interior were supposed to be open to blacks as well. In 1953 when a convention of fifteen thousand black Baptist ministers could not find a hotel in Florida that would house their convention, the Miami AJC chapter stepped in to remonstrate with local hotel owners, many of them Jewish. The convention found a hotel. Restrictive covenants in housing were no longer enforceable. More Jewish students were able to attend medical school.

But antisemitism of the old-fashioned kind, including the scapegoating of Jews, was still there. During this decade Jewish boys in Boston were assaulted in the streets and a young rabbi was murdered. In Philadelphia, high school students organized a Hitler Youth gang and staged a demonstration. Other Philadelphia gangs beat up Jewish students and vandalized synagogues.[36] Anti-Jewish violence was especially sharp in the South, where an added rationale was Jewish support for the desegregation movement. If antisemitism was lessening everywhere else, in the South it was getting worse. Miami Beach was still a predominantly Christian community, and signs and advertisements that read "No Jews Wanted," "Christians Only," and "Restricted Clientele" were widespread. From April to December 1951, sixteen bombings occurred in the Miami area; eight were against Jewish centers and synagogues. In November 1957 a bomb was discovered outside Temple Beth El in Charlotte, North Carolina. In February 1958 another bomb was found at the entrance to Temple Emanu-El in a suburb of Charlotte. In March, a bomb caused extensive damage to Miami's Temple Beth-El and an anonymous caller threatened more bombings against anyone who advocated integration. On the same day, the Jewish Community Center in Nashville was also damaged by a bomb. In April, bombs damaged the Jewish Community Center in Jacksonville and Birmingham's Temple Beth El. Rabbi Rothschild of Atlanta's oldest synagogue, the Temple, repeatedly sermonized in favor of integration; in 1958 neo-Nazi extremists also bombed his building.[37]

Terrified and angry, the AJC Atlanta and other chapter members in the South pleaded with the national AJC to show some restraint in its advocacy of civil rights and desegregation. Panicked American parents withdrew their children from universities all over the South. AJC had, after all, written a friend-of-the-court brief in the *Brown v. Board of Education* decision in 1954, and the justices had made their decision based in part on research done by psychologist Kenneth B. Clark—research that the AJC had sponsored.[38] Official AJC policy, supported by Alabama-born Joseph Proskauer and Irving Engel and Georgia-born Morris B. Abram—the director of AJC's newly established Atlanta regional office—was that no Jew could stand by and *not* become involved in the desegregation issue. There was no other "honorable or decent reaction in the sight of God who has made all men brothers."[39] This policy was taken with the "Chicago Mandate" of 1947. Where one minority was threatened, *all* minorities were threatened. If any minority anywhere was not safe, then the Jews were not safe.

In that era antisemitic and white supremacist publications—if not mass meetings, as had been the case in earlier years—still flourished. Jews were accused of taking part in a Red conspiracy to "mongrelize" the nation and incite racial strife. The Ku Klux Klan included anti-Jewish bias as much as antiblack in its speeches. The Salk polio vaccine and fluoridization of the water were allegedly part of the international Jewish conspiracy and a "super-secret world government" to harm Gentiles.[40] President Eisenhower was a "tool" of the Jews. John Owen Beaty, a professor of English at Southern Methodist University, produced a volume entitled *Iron Curtain Over America* (25,000 copies), which was distributed by scores of Protestant clergymen and businessmen. The book was both a diatribe against the New Deal and a rewrite of the *Protocols of the Elders of Zion*. Conspiracy theorists, in backing up their charges of world Jewish domination (especially in financial affairs) drew attention to the fact that among all of FDR's Jewish appointees the Treasurer of the United States had been Henry Morgenthau, and his signature was on every piece of paper currency that had been printed during the FDR administration.[41]

Also in connection with FDR, in 1951 *Figaro*, a prominent conservative paper in Paris, reproduced a letter allegedly from President Roosevelt to the president of Young Israel, asking the organization to act as a mediator between himself and Stalin in a plan to divide up the world between the United States and Russia. Within a few days the AJC European office had secured a repudiation of the letter, but the story was picked up by the Hearst newspapers in the United States and reprinted on the front page of every newspaper in its chain from Boston to Los Angeles. AJC along with the other agencies then in NCRAC convened to convince the Hearst organization that the document was forged. On the following Sunday each front page carried a retraction with the comment that Young Israel was "an honorable, patriotic organization."[42]

The Arab Boycott

The chorus of denunciation was joined by pro-Arab propagandists, who emphasized alleged desecration by Jews of the Holy Places and the plight of the then 850,000 Palestinian refugees. The refugees in camps were being cared for at the largesse of the U.N. and other nations including the United States, which had given 150 million dollars toward their care by 1955. It was political suicide for any Arab leader even to speak about resettling the refugees; to do so would be to admit defeat and dash the dream of winning back the whole of Palestine.[43] Being viewed as too conciliatory to the Israelis had cost King Abdullah I of Jordan his life. He was assassinated by a Palestinian on July 20, 1951, while visiting the al-Aqsa mosque in Jerusalem.

The information office of the Arab League in New York and the Egyptian embassy spent vast sums on disseminating anti-Israel material.[44] Traveling Arab diplomats and spokesmen accused American Jews of "dual loyalty" and "dual allegiance," and alleged that support of Israel was not in America's best interests, proving only the "sinister influences" in Washington and power of the "Jewish vote." Farid Zeineddine, the Syrian ambassador to the United States, expounded in his speeches the theory that American Jews were not really "Semites" at all, but descendants of Russian Slavs who had embraced Judaism. "Why not let New York be a homeland for the Jews?" he asked.[45] The word "Zionist" took in all the Jews of America. In October 1955, for example, Egyptian premier Gamal Abdel Nasser told the *New York Post*, "All the Arabs are feeling that America is under the guidance and domination of strong Zionist organizations to help Israel against us. . . . Everyone is trying to have the Jews on their side, and the Arab world is suffering from this competition for the Jewish vote."[46]

The Arab world did not limit its attacks on American Jews to words. From 1950 onward the Arab League nations instituted a strict boycott on Israel and anyone who did business with Israel; this ban automatically included anyone who was Jewish. American Jewish citizens were denied visas to visit Arab countries; potential visitors had to prove that they were Christian. Boycott officials kept a blacklist of what they believed were Jewish-owned or -operated business firms; chambers of commerce and trade associations, when asked, supplied the information about the firms' identity. Cairo would not permit Jewish firms to bid on contracts to transport American wheat to Egypt. Jewish personnel were barred from Saudi Arabian air bases and military installations. American Jewish civilians could not be assigned to work in Saudi Arabia anywhere, either under contract with the federal government or under the auspices of private American business. Known American Jewish citizens, including congressmen, were not even permitted to land in an Arab country. If their plane did land they were not allowed to get off. U.S. government officials at first acquiesced, stating that being non-Jewish was a "bona fide job qualification" for working in the area, and the restriction against Jews was explicitly noted in the U.S. Air Force handbook.[47] As a result of AJC's protests to the White House, the State Department, and other government officials, the words were eliminated from the handbook in 1957 and the U.S. Senate condemned the discrimination. But the practices continued.[48]

Anti-Jewish Bias in Christian Textbooks

Anti-Jewish bias in Christian textbooks and teaching materials commanded the attention of AJC staff, as studies at Drew Theological Seminary and Yale University Divinity School on those materials bore fruit. AJC initiated these studies, and bore much of the cost for them, and its staff supplied much of the data (although again the imprint of AJC was seldom if ever on the resulting publications). The studies analyzed texts that went out to hundreds of thousands of Sunday school students and their teachers. "The Jews turn their backs on God, they refused His Son, they worshipped pagan gods, and they have been sorely punished for centuries as a result. . . . they are not really wanted anywhere," read one book. "With full knowledge of the consequences, Israel repeatedly turned her back on the God who led her out of slavery into freedom. Thus the Israelites became 'wandering Jews,' living in any foreign country willing to take them. Even in the United States, which has been called the world's melting pot . . . Jews still tend to locate in communities and districts of their own, not fully mixing with the people around them," read another. "They have slain Messiah and have therefore been sorely punished for centuries," read another. Jews were commonly referred to in Christian texts as "immoral," "materialistic," "self-seeking," "proud," "deceitful," and "wicked." Though one textbook writer rejected prejudice and urged students to "present a faithful Christian witness" to their Jewish acquaintances by their word and action, the author nevertheless taught that persecution suffered by Jews was "part of their suffering caused by disobedience."[49] John Slawson and AJC representatives met with Christian educators and publishers to convince them to revise the objectionable wording or to remove it completely.

In one instance, Slawson blamed limited AJC funds for the organization's inability to head off at the source a Crucifixion film released by the National Council of Churches of Christ (considered one of the more liberal church organizations). The film was made for use on TV and showed Jews in such an unfavorable light that two of the leading national networks on their own volition decided against showing it, to the dissatisfaction of the film's sponsors.[50] The AJC persuaded them to withdraw the film.

Anti-Jewish portrayals might have been expected in Christian material, but AJC staff were surprised when it emerged in a monumental work of world history by one of the most famous historians and intellectuals in the world at the time, Arnold Toynbee (1889–1975). Toynbee was an Oxford-educated professor at the University of London; in a survey of twenty-six civilizations, he considered Western Latin Christendom to be the only one that was still truly living. A devout Christian, Toynbee saw Judaism as a "fossilized relic of a civilization that was extinct in every other shape." Jews had made a fatal error of looking upon a "momentary spiritual eminence" as a privilege conferred upon them by God in an everlasting covenant. They themselves had created the bigotry against which they suffered. He blamed Israel's creation primarily upon England but also on America, specifically American Jews, who "were fearful lest their own security might be jeopardized by the admission of many DPs to America." In their establishment of the State of Israel, it was the Jews' "supreme tragedy to imitate some of the evil deeds that the Nazis had committed against the Jews." "We hope these views will not become popularized and distorted," read an AJC 1955 analysis and refutation of the work. "This may ultimately be reaped as a terrible new harvest of hate."[51]

AJC staff and lay leaders keeping watch on all such material took comfort that it did not reach the level of Nazism; nonetheless, they were always prepared for another Holocaust. "In spite of the fact that—partly as a result of our own efforts—overt antisemitism is being contained, and is becoming understood by a growing number of Americans as evidence either of maladjustment or insecurity, hate peddlers still find a market for their attacks on Jews," noted AJC administrative board chairman Ralph E. Samuel in 1956. "But we are thoroughly prepared should antisemitism flare up on the domestic scene as it did to such a worrisome extent in the 1930s."[52]

Employment, Housing, and Education

In the perhaps more mundane area of discrimination in employment, housing, recreational facilities, and education, AJC in the 1950s began to confront directly the heads of major corporations and utilities. The action was deemed especially important because at that time the country's economic elite appeared to be switching from entrepreneurial to managerial. Research had revealed that in banking, insurance, engineering, and advertising, "non-Jewish" firms were unlikely to employ Jews; if they did employ Jews, they put them in "inside" jobs where they would not come into contact with clients.[53] In 1955 John Slawson committed the AJC to fighting what members considered to be the last barrier: social discrimination, or the gentleman's antisemitism of the country club.

In housing and resorts, real estate authorities were getting around the issue of restrictive covenants by portraying themselves as "clubs," granting "membership" to those who completed an application that inquired about religion and race. Under such "club" plans, recreational facilities and certain services, including a private commuter bus, were available only to club members. Gentlemen's agreements and the phrases "selective" and "nearby churches" had replaced "Gentile clientele." AJC representatives tried to convince advertisers to replace these with the words "nearby churches and synagogues" or "nearby all houses of worship" and to convince advertisers of counterpart Jewish suburbs to remove the words "within walking distance of synagogues"; they had relatively little success. According to an AJC survey more than a score of U.S. cities with populations between 250,000 and 500,000 had residential neighborhoods restricted against Jews. A square mile of the Upper East Side in Manhattan north of 57th Street was found to be "almost solid" with such restricted buildings. In Southern Florida, the creators of a $100 million subdivision in Fort Lauderdale restricted access to nearby beaches to members of their club. Any Jews who might buy homes there would find themselves boxed in. In Seattle's Sands Point suburb, a Jewish family who bought a home there was advised that it was "making a mistake." The Homeowners' Association was prepared to withhold access to garage space, garbage disposal, and other necessary services. Some victory was achieved when, on the basis of an AJC test complaint against a specific resort, the New York State Commission Against Discrimination struck down the pretext of "club" membership as a discriminatory device; it also ruled that the phrase "a strictly selected clientele in a Christian community" could not be used in advertisements in the State of New York.[54]

In education AJC's campaign against discrimination in college fraternities, promoted by its National Committee on Fraternities in Education, was meeting with some success. One-fourth of the nation's undergraduates at the time belonged to fraternities. The number of fraternities that had restrictive clauses in their constitutions or rituals decreased steadily. In 1955 the organization sponsored an NBC television broadcast about college life entitled "The Battle of Fraternity Row" in which fifty students, most of them veterans, fought to eliminate racial and religious discrimination in their school's fraternities.[55]

Discrimination in medical school admissions was one target the AJC went after, in part because of the burning desire of so many young Jews to become doctors. In 1953 there were 7,600 places in medical school first-year classes in the entire country, and at some schools as many as half the applications each year came from Jews. An AJC survey revealed that one out of five Jewish high school seniors expressed the ambition of studying medicine, compared to less than one out of ten of his non-Jewish classmates.[56] The legend among Jewish students was that only a few of the very top students had any chance at all to enter an accredited medical school, and the best they could hope for was a quota of 10 percent. Here careful research by AJC staff uncovered the facts of the case and methods for counteracting it.

Limited access of Jews to medical education had begun in 1933, when economic conditions caused the American Medical Association to issue a report advising medical schools that the training of physicians should be "drastically curtailed." From 912 in the freshman class of all medical schools in 1933, Jewish students dropped to 617, a reduction of almost one-third. Yet total national enrollment in medical schools dropped by only 5 percent. Evidently "drastic curtailment" was interpreted to mean drastic curtailment of Jews. Throughout the 1950s "geographic distribution" formulas that avoided eastern urban areas and "personality" criteria were applied to candidates, including "diction, voice, physical appearance, and grooming." Jewish students were presumed to be disproportionately deficient in these areas. Students of Italian ancestry were also hard-hit. In 1950 an Italian Catholic had less than half the chance of other Catholics to gain admittance. Here AJC staff met with medical school deans, members of the board of trustees, and university presidents, bringing the evidence to their attention and requesting that the standards be changed. Some victory was measured in 1955, when the freshman class at Cornell Medical School was 35 percent Jewish. Previously Cornell had had a Jewish quota of 10 to 15 percent.[57]

Separation of Church and State and Civil Liberties

In addition to its stance during the desegregation crisis, in the 1950s there was another area where AJC held firm while risking anger from non-Jews. That was maintaining the separation of church and state in public schools, where 90 percent of America's growing population of children received its education. With facilities strained to the breaking point, the AJC in 1955 endorsed federal aid for construction of the nation's public schools and "fringe benefits" for private and parochial schools, allowing that tax money could be used to provide medical services and lunches and possibly bus transportation and free textbooks. But AJC and its local chapters firmly opposed, and took concrete steps to prevent, the use of the public classroom for Bible reading, the distribution of Gideon Bibles in the schools (which occurred mainly in San Francisco and Philadelphia in 1957) organized prayer, religious holiday observances, and the teaching of religion in any form. To combine Christmas celebrations with Chanukah was only to compound the error.

AJC also opposed, and lent their support to Supreme Court cases concerning, the phenomenon of "release time" in which some students were dismissed early for the purpose of receiving religious instruction, sometimes on the actual grounds of the public school itself. This they considered unconstitutional, though it brought them charges of secularism, godlessness, and consorting with communists. "The public school, traditionally free of sectarian divisions, is one of the chief instruments for developing an informed citizenry and achieving the goals of American democracy," declared John Slawson in 1957.[58]

The one warning the national officers gave was against trying to do anything to change or eliminate Christmas celebrations anywhere in the temporal vicinity of December 25. "Rightly or wrongly, the observance of Christmas has a long and deeply embedded tradition in our schools," they declared in December 1955. "For many people, the holiday has assumed the character of a national as well as a sectarian event; in the responses it evokes, it resembles the fourth of July. To assume that so widely accepted and esteemed an occasion can be totally erased from the school program is unrealistic." Sometimes the only choice was for a Jewish student to invoke the right to abstain from such activities. Whatever they did, members were cautioned not to wait until holiday time to make an issue of it. Anyone who did ran the risk of "incensing his neighbors against the interloper who seems to be threatening their deepest social and religious values." The best time to begin a program about Christmas was in July, as part of a year-round campaign to acquaint Christian clergy, school personnel, and others with the views held by Jewish organizations. Non-Jewish communal members were bound to be more receptive to requests for change in July than they would be in December.[59]

Civil Liberties

On taking a stand in the continuing conflict between national security and civil liberties, AJC ran the risk of not appearing to be sufficiently zealous against communism on the one hand, and on the other hand enduring criticism from other Jewish groups that it was collaborating with the enemy. It was not easy to adhere to the warning of Jacob Blaustein. "In eagerness to root out the cancer of Communism," he said, "we must be careful not to tear healthy tissue." The AJC staff was deeply divided on the issue of civil liberties overall, and stressed the values of caution and judiciousness when dealing with individual cases. Officially they opposed self-appointed censors and compilers of blacklists in public employment, particularly in the entertainment and academic worlds. Individual chapters were given careful guidance on how to react to persons being charged with communist activity in their local areas. Rather than attacking the House Un-American Activities Committee head-on, as other Jewish organizations did, AJC convinced the congressmen to do an investigation of far-right, neo-Fascist, and hate groups, as well as groups on the left.[60] Edward R. Murrow, in supporting this action in a speech before AJC, said of it: "Democracy is in much the same position as a man crossing the street. We must look to both right and left if we don't want to get killed."[61]

American Security and Freedom, a popular AJC-sponsored book by Maurice J. Goldbloom, took a stand against loyalty oaths in areas not directly connected to national security. True communists would have no compunctions about lying, he pointed out. Furthermore, Goldbloom came out against cases where subjects under investigation were neither informed in detail of the charges against them nor allowed to cross-examine witnesses. Senator McCarthy came under criticism for doing "far more damage to the innocent, and the reputation of the U.S. abroad, than to any guilty individuals or to the Communist movement." (The book was reviewed in the Sunday *New York Times* book section on January 9, 1955.) Whatever each individual's views had been, the entire AJC rejoiced when McCarthy was censured by the Senate in 1954. "As anti-communists, we have rejected, and we have resented, that political delinquent, the junior, the very, very junior Senator from Wisconsin," stated David Sher, member of the Administrative Committee, "not only because he made a career of hitting below the belt, not only because he had a genius for making innocent people look guilty and guilty people look innocent, but because he 'loused up' the fight against communism. I believe he has been the greatest gift to the communist cause since the German General Staff sent Lenin in a sealed train to St. Petersburg."[62]

What to do when someone pleaded the Fifth Amendment was a particularly thorny problem and the subject of intense debate among the officers. The divisions among members were settled for the most part when Judge Simon H. Rifkind, then chair of the Administrative Committee, made a passionate speech on the subject at the annual meeting of 1955. The Fifth Amendment, he said, was one the most cherished provisions of the Constitution and represented "the high point of our judicial civilization." "Are we not going too far," he demanded, "when we declare that the invocation of the most sacred instrument in our American constitutional system, the Constitution itself, is itself an act of subversion? . . . To say, as some do, that the assertion of this high privilege is in itself an admission of guilt, is a startling innovation. Either the courts are all hypocrites or the public does not understand the significance of the Fifth Amendment. One thing is sure, we cannot play it both ways. . . . So either we should make up our minds that the Fifth Amendment means what it says, that it is a shield and that it may be freely used without legal consequences, or it is not, in which case it has lost all significance. I shall not debate the issue. I assume that the Fifth Amendment is the kind of plea from which no inference of guilt may be drawn."[63]

Relations with Israel and the American Jewish Community

In the same speech Judge Rifkind had begun by saying that he was accustomed to giving all parts of the title "American Jewish Committee" equal weight and value; hence the suitability of their being concerned with the rights of all American minorities. Since 1947 the AJC had deliberately widened its scope to include these issues. At the same time AJC was still a Jewish organization, dependent upon the American Jewish community for much of its financial support. Therefore, how and where it stood with the rest of that community mattered deeply.

Surveys, informal inquiries, and any review of the Yiddish or Anglo-Jewish press revealed that the rest of the American Jewish community might respect AJC's work, particularly in the intellectual and publications sphere, but they also felt envy, resentment, and distrust of it. Much of it was based on class conflict. AJC's assumed wealth and the perceived snobbery of its members did not win it friends in many corners. The rest of the Jewish community remembered with bitterness AJC's pattern of seeking to impose its will and then withdrawing from umbrella organizations, as it had done in the case of the American Jewish Conference and NCRAC. Others who preferred a more open, activist approach to their work despised AJC's preference for quiet, behind-the-scenes work instead of public demonstrations and litigation. The AJC was also continually denounced for its "assimilationist" approach to American Jewish life. It was not uncommon in other organizations for AJC members to be referred to as "goyim,"[64] a term John Slawson said resulted "out of ignorance more often than malice." The AJC always rejected that label and referred to themselves as "integrationists."

Another point of division was the agency's attitudes and public pronouncements on the subjects of Israel and Zionism. After 1948 most American Jewish organizations were swept by a wave of fervor toward Israel, but the AJC leadership did not approve of this. The State of Israel, in their view, did not represent the final Redemption. Its main purpose had been to serve as a haven for Jewish refugees. Israel was also the ultimate manifestation of Jewish nationalism, an ideology that AJC officers frankly loathed. They never lost an opportunity to condemn it or to take active steps to combat it. In addition to their vigilance on maintaining the Blaustein–Ben-Gurion understanding, the leadership of the Committee on Israel into the mid-1960s regularly criticized Israel for its Nationality Law, which automatically granted Israeli citizenship to any Jew arriving in the country. They spoke out against the lack of separation of church and state in Israel, defended the rights of Conservative and Reform Jews, and worked with Israeli government officials to improve the status of the Arab minority.

Jewish nationalism, it should be noted, in those days did not mean only Zionism. It was an important underpinning to the ideology of many anti-Zionist Bundists and Yiddishists, who believed that Jews were not only a people but a national minority deserving their own separate language, schools, and cultural institutions. This ideology was almost extinct by the end of the twentieth century, but in the 1950s it still held considerable force. By AJC's own estimates, the majority of the Jews in Latin America followed it. In the United States thousands of Jewish children still attended afternoon Yiddish schools, such as those run by the Workmen's Circle, and the *Forward*, the Yiddish newspaper, still published a daily edition. But to the AJC, if Jews went out of their way to behave like a "nation within a nation," or allowed others to view them that way, then they denied the AJC's trust in America that was so central to their worldview. It also complicated their efforts to fight modern antisemitism, where the view of Jews as a disloyal fifth column and international conspirators was so central.

Israel could be a sore point in that regard. When it came to the issue of political loyalties or lack thereof to Israel, Jacob Blaustein in particular jealously guarded the integrity of the "Clarification Statement" (as he himself referred to it) of August 1950 that he and Prime Minister Ben-Gurion had exchanged (see chapter 2). He insisted that it be reprinted in its entirety in the *American Jewish Year Book*, and in one of his last speeches as AJC president he referred to the agreement as "one of the highlights of my stewardship." As has been noted, during his presidency (1949–54) and even after, every speech and public pronouncement that Ben-Gurion made was combed and analyzed for possible "deviations" from the agreement. Blaustein never failed to respond with protests, letters, cables, and resolutions from the Executive Committee, reaffirming the agreement and stating that America was their only home and American Jews were most definitely not living in Exile. Blaustein's insistence in this area confirmed the AJC's perceived anti-Israel stance long after the organization had moved to join the American Jewish mainstream.

Not all the officers of AJC shared Blaustein's and others' distress. In one debate on the subject, Edward A. Norman of New York suggested that the world Zionist movement was already suffering enough internal problems of its own, and to make any statements on the subject might just "supply fuel to a dying fire." Joseph Willen of New York questioned the desirability of negotiating with Israel over its pronouncements, claiming that they would not do so with any other country. Fred Lazarus Jr. suggested that Israel's formative period was now over and that perhaps the time had arrived "when we should let the country go its way ideologically while we go ours." Henry L. Kohn of Chicago expressed his doubts that a statement by Israel, "distasteful though the underlying ideology may be to us," justified the charge that American Jewish interests were being imperiled. Blaustein adamantly opposed all these views. When Israel said or did anything that presented an image of Jews as an international group acting as a unity, he claimed, "they are confirming the most serious charges exploited by the anti-Semites." It was therefore not only the right but the duty of AJC to protest, he said, just as they would protest actions of any other foreign country that threatened the position of Jews anywhere in the world.[65]

John Slawson, in reporting on Zionist and pro-Israel activities in the United States in 1957, was also notably cautious on the subject of Israel. The view was becoming too widespread that the United States and the West would fare better against the Soviets in the Middle East if not for Israel, he stated. Furthermore, from the viewpoint of current events it was possible that recent Russian missile accomplishments "will so sensitize the public to loyalty and security matters, that false charges of Jewish dual nationalism may find undue acceptance." In his mind, these were real threats; during the height of the McCarthy years in the early 1950s, he had once brought up the internment of Japanese Americans during World War II as an example of what could conceivably happen to American Jews. Modification of attitudes toward Israel was therefore in order. "Even if statements in the press are not negative in themselves," he declared, "the very large number that reflects an almost exclusive concern with Israel, fundraising for Israel, and so forth, on the part of Jewish organizations, is enough to create a negative impression." To deal with the problem, Slawson suggested that AJC discourage the holding of pro-Israel demonstrations when under solely Jewish auspices and geared to Israel's needs without reference to American concerns.[66]

A motive for this hands-off public posture may well have been to soothe troubled consciences: the fact of the matter was that the AJC *was* showing increasing loyalty to Israel. Blaustein himself had justified his concern with publishing various versions of the Clarification Statement with the words, "so that our non-Jewish fellow citizens who are aware of the vast contributions made by American Jews to Israel, will realize that American Jews are *true Americans*."[67] For some time it had been clear that on the chapter level, particularly in the South and West, some members belonged to both the AJC and the anti-Zionist American Council for Judaism, and the ACJ periodically raised the subject of an organizational merger. ACJ activities in 1949–50 had been the goad that convinced Jacob Blaustein to go to Jerusalem to meet with Ben-Gurion. Now in the months before the Suez War of 1956 this confusion was considered enough of a threat for the AJC to prepare a paper for its members delineating the differences between the two groups and sending the word out to chapters that membership in the ACJ was *not* compatible with membership in the American Jewish Committee.[68] AJC in effect purged members of the American Council of Judaism from its ranks.

On the all-important diplomatic front, the AJC had a longer and closer relationship with the State Department than any other Jewish organization. The AJC was always arguing on Israel's behalf, in the halls of Congress, in the White House, and everywhere else in the corridors of power, including personal conferences with the president and with the secretary of state. AJC President Irving Engel, who succeeded Blaustein, met with John Foster Dulles and John F. Kennedy to plead on Israel's behalf,[69] and President Eisenhower was the guest of honor at AJC's keynote dinner celebrating the Tercentenary of Jewish settlement in the United States in 1954. The non-Zionist heritage of AJC even became an asset in the fractured world of Zionist and Israeli politics. Because it had never been a Zionist organization, it had never been affiliated with Mapai or Herut or any of the many parties and factions that competed for primacy in Israel and in world Zionist politics. Thus the AJC could always maintain a useful neutrality.

The support of the AJC became crucial during and after the Suez War of 1956—also known as the Sinai Campaign or, by the Israelis, as "Operation Kadesh"—a conflict that has been called by some historians a "dress rehearsal" for the Six-Day War of 1967. The Arab world had never recovered from the humiliation of having lost the war in 1948 and refused to acknowledge the defeat. Egypt had become increasingly bellicose after the coming to power of Gamal Abdel Nasser and fellow army officers in a coup d' état in 1952. The leaders of Egypt and other Arab League countries left no doubt that they were readying for a "second round" against Israel; at one summit meeting in 1954 the Saudi Arabian representative vowed that "ten million Arab lives" would be worth it to exterminate the country, and that remark was not untypical of Arab League pronouncements.[70] Nasser, along with Jordan, for years continually sponsored or condoned *fedayeen* raids into Israeli territory. Hundreds of Israeli civilians died in terrorist attacks between 1949 and 1956. Nasser also blocked the Suez Canal to Israeli shipping and ultimately the Straits of Tiran, which were Israel's only water outlets to Asia and the Far East.

By 1954, when the Arab-Israeli situation had deteriorated to its lowest point since the War of Independence, Nasser had also turned away from the West and begun to receive shipments of Soviet arms through Czechoslovakia. There was no doubt that he intended to use these arms against Israel as soon as his armed forces learned how to use them. Now little Israel was at the center of the world's eye. The Middle East had replaced the Balkans and Korea as the "tinderbox" of the world, and observers feared that in the context of the cold war a clash of U.S. and Soviet power could take place there that might lead to Armageddon.

In the years and months leading up to the Suez War, AJC representatives lobbied for the military parity of Israel through the sale of defensive weapons from the United States, its protection through regional pacts such as NATO and SEATO, and large U.S. loans to aid Israel in the compensation and resettlement of Palestinian refugees, a plan John Foster Dulles endorsed in 1955. Ralph E. Samuel, chair of the Administrative Board, which was supposed to see to all important AJC business in between formal meetings, spoke of being on the "dawn patrol" with other members—who during that time habitually found themselves at breakfast meetings with Prime Minister Sharett, Ambassador Abba Eban, and other spokesmen. "The Arab-Israeli crisis," he reported in January 1956, "represents far and away our greatest problem and at the same time our greatest opportunity for usefulness."[71]

When the Israelis, with the backing of Great Britain and France, did attack Egypt on October 29, 1956, the action enraged President Eisenhower. The action had been unilateral, in one of the most dangerous parts of the world. None of the parties had informed him about the plan, and it was barely a week before election day. An anti-Soviet revolution was already going on in Hungary and the last thing Eisenhower wanted was a potential widening of the conflict. In the one week that the war actually lasted, Israel conquered Gaza and the entire Sinai Peninsula. Afterward Eisenhower and Secretary of State John Foster Dulles publicly threatened Israel with sanctions if she did not withdraw.[72] The pressure was successful. By March 1957 Israeli soldiers had withdrawn, albeit reluctantly, from all the new territory they had occupied, after receiving guarantees that her waterways would remain open. A few thousand U.N. peacekeeping troops took their places on the Israel-Egypt borders of Sinai and the Gaza Strip and some guarded the Strait of Tiran at Sharm al-Sheikh at the tip of the Sinai Peninsula.

After the war, Irving Engel and Jacob Blaustein successfully helped to "mend fences" with the president. As for Israel, the resulting peace lasted only a decade. Within a few years the *fedayeen* attacks resumed, this time gathering under the aegis of the PLO (Palestine Liberation Organization, founded in 1964). In 1967 Nasser requested that the U.N. troops depart and proceeded to block the Strait of Tiran again, an event that helped precipitate the Six-Day War. After that war, Israel was not so quick to give up the land it had captured.

Competition with Israel and Jewish Integration in America

Ultimately it was not the military, political, or diplomatic aspects of Israel that concerned AJC the most. Israel also represented a psychological, emotional, and religious challenge. The existence of the State touched the AJC's identity profoundly. In the aftermath of the Holocaust both Americans and Israelis were wont to say, competitively, that no further proof was needed that Jews could not live safely anywhere but in their own country. What had happened to the Jews in Europe was bound to happen eventually to the Jews of the United States as well. John Slawson was clearly shaken when, during a trip to Israel, his group came face-to-face with this attitude, as he reported to his fellow staff members and AJC lay officers:

The other day an Israeli, a member of the Knesset, made a statement to several of us verbally that pointed out our challenges rather sharply. He said that Israel needed much more Jewish immigration—the population would have to be far in excess of two million—for purposes of defense, among other reasons. But a large Jewish population in Israel was not only their need, he said, it may be OUR need. "What is the future of American Jewry?" he queried. He pointed out historically what had happened in 2000 years.

We said to him, "Well, you know there is a difference historically between post-Emancipation and pre-Emancipation Jewish history—between the latter part of the 18th century and the preceding periods."

His answer was: "Look at Germany."

Then what we have to say to the Israelis is that America is different. And we must mean it when we say it, and we must prove it to them and to ourselves, that this is our home, and wherever a Jew lives throughout the world, is the home of that Jew. This is the great mission to which this organization is dedicated.[73]

Partly as a result of these attitudes, the greatest anxiety of John Slawson and others of the American Jewish community in the 1950s was not survival or the need to promote their greater solidarity. When they addressed the question of Jewish education in those days, it was not to debate its quality or rigor. Their main anxiety was that because of misplaced fear and a heritage of thousands of years of persecution Jews were not integrating themselves into mainstream U.S. life quickly or well enough. Not just antisemitism from Gentiles but the Jews' own attitudes and reliance on obsolete European community models were seen as the culprits preventing their full absorption. AJC members were also not concerned that Jewish youth were receiving an insufficient Jewish education. They were concerned that the Jewish education that did exist was having a deleterious effect by promoting separatist, self-segregating, and nationalist tendencies among the children.

Much of the data that supported AJC's concerns was gleaned from the Riverton Study, an in-depth examination of a "typical" American Jewish community. The study, among the first of its kind, took its cue from the famous "Middletown" studies of sociologists Robert and Helen Lynd, and included information gleaned from more than four hundred interviews and questionnaires from both parents and their teenage children. The anonymous "Middletown" had in fact been Muncie, Indiana; "Riverton" was Trenton, New Jersey.[74] At the time, there had been many intensive studies of the attitude of non-Jews toward Jews, but almost nothing about the modern Jewish community itself. The study, published in 1955, revealed among other things that both the parents and their teenage children felt far more comfortable among Jews than among Gentiles, and preferred to live in virtually all-Jewish neighborhoods.

Indeed, there was reason to fear overall that the particularist and parochial tendencies of different religions—including Judaism—were worsening, not improving, in the decade after the end of the Second World War. These were the years when "Under God" was added to the Pledge of Allegiance and "In God We Trust" to U.S. currency; when John Foster Dulles regularly condemned "atheistic communism" with equal stress on both words. Religion and religious institutions were becoming more important, not less. In 1956, according to Slawson's denominational statistics, of the four million Jews affiliated with synagogues in the United States, the Reform movement claimed one million, the Conservative movement claimed one million, and the Orthodox movement claimed two million.[75] Between 1937 and 1953, church and synagogue membership had grown from 45 to 58 percent of the total population. One hundred years earlier only one of of six Americans was affiliated with a church; now the proportion was six out of ten, or eighty-five million people. Such statistics did not bode well for an organization that placed such stress on nonsectarian communal organization. What, if anything, should the AJC do about it?

In a 1953 "roundtable" debate, a popular form of membership participation at annual meetings, members discussed the "problem" of separatism in inter-religious relationships. One part of the group expressed the opinion that the trend to separatism itself could not be halted and, as a matter of wisdom, the Jewish group should "adjust itself to this trend and devise ways of strengthening its own inner resources." Another group maintained that separatism and sectarianism was an unhealthy trend that the AJC, as an organization concerned with improving group relations, should resist.[76] At a similar round-table discussion in 1954, members expressed concern about the growing influence of religion in the life of the nation, and the increasing tendency of religious separatism. Several cautioned that a "too-rigid application of [the] principle of separation of church and state might be self-defeating." The group also suggested that the growing phenomenon of the Jewish all-day school be studied: since 1948 the number of American Jewish children attending them had grown from eighteen thousand to thirty thousand. Why did Jewish parents select them? And what were the "public relations" aspects, if any, of their operation in the local communities?[77] It was clear that the group did not consider Jewish all-day schools as a positive development. Herbert B. Ehrmann, AJC's future president—who among his other duties was chair of AJC's Committee on Education and Jewish Attitudes—said in so many words that all-day Jewish schools were a "divisive influence"; nonetheless he and his associates supported the right of parents to send their children to whatever school they chose.[78]

AJC members were concerned most of all with the effects of the move to suburbia, which initiated a flurry of building, including the establishment of religious and sectarian institutions. The transformation happened with astonishing swiftness. In 1956, as Slawson noted, 20 percent of the entire Jewish population of Buffalo now lived in the suburbs, as opposed to only fifty Jewish families ten years earlier. In the "Five Towns" area of Long Island, there were fewer than 3,000 Jews in 1937 and 21,000 in 1955. In the Hempsteads, also on Long Island, there were 3,100 Jews in 1937; now there were more than 27,000.[79] Up went scores of new synagogue-centers, Hebrew schools, Jewish community centers, Jewish country clubs, and golf clubs. In addition, separate Jewish professional associations, veterans' associations, and Jewish Boy Scout and Girl Scout troops were established. In AJC's view, all these sorts of things, especially when they supplied so many completely secular services and facilities, "unnecessarily" set off Jews from their Christian neighbors. The ideal was for all, Christians and Jews, to join together in nonsectarian institutions.

The growth of new Jewish institutions made it more imperative than ever, in the eyes of AJC's leadership, that their "American-centered" approach to Jewish life find wider acceptance. Research showed that anti-Jewish attitudes were clearly declining and acceptance of Jews was comparatively greater than it had ever been. Separatism could no longer be blamed solely on the Gentiles; Jewish attitudes played a role too. Social antisemitism and self-segregation were in fact two sides of the same coin, in their view. One reinforced the other, and the diminishing of one would lead to the diminishing of the other.

The stakes were high for eliminating all barriers between Jew and non-Jew, regardless of which side built them. To Slawson, who invoked the case of the Dreyfus trial in France, it was not enough to settle for full political, legal, and civil rights, or for equality in employment, education, and housing. Unless social discrimination against Jews was eliminated root and branch from American society, their safety could never be guaranteed. Full integration into all aspects of American life, in his view, was in fact vital to their survival:

Unless the concept of individual inferiority inherent in social discrimination is eliminated, we have no assurance that the present security of American Jews will be permanent. One hundred years of goodwill and equality enjoyed by French Jews did not forestall the decade of virulent antisemitism at the turn of the past century initiated by the Dreyfus affair. To achieve permanent security, not merely safety, social discrimination must be fought. The fact that overt bigotry receives no public approval today makes it propitious to attack this last barrier. Continued work in the field of Jewish attitudes is also essential in order to overcome tendencies toward self-segregation in "gilded ghettos" and through other associations which are essentially a retreat before the artificial barrier of social discrimination . . . elimination of social discrimination . . . would root out antisemitism at its source in the sphere of the mental attitude itself.[80]

With these ends in view AJC staff threw themselves into new media and education projects in the 1950s, especially celebrations of the 1954 Tercentenary of Jewish life in America. The purpose of these publications and productions was not just to educate non-Jews about Jews and Judaism. The goal was also to make American Jews feel more secure about themselves. A ten-pamphlet series, called "This Is Our Home," (40,000 copies each) which ran from 1952 to 1957 was designed to convey "a better understanding of the Jewish heritage and the consonance of Jewish values with American democracy," as Herbert Ehrmann, who oversaw their production, put it.[81] The pamphlets, he said, were supposed to stress in every word that American Jewish roots were firm and deep, that Jews were not in the United States on a temporary basis and that they were not in "Exile." It was a falsehood to say that Jews had to choose between being Jewish and participating fully in American life. AJC proceeded on the assumption that both goals were fully compatible and that one could even reinforce the other. Ehrmann was fond of quoting, as John Slawson was, the work of Will Herberg, whose classic *Protestant-Catholic-Jew: An Essay in American Religious Sociology* (1955, reissued 1983) posited what came to be known as the "triple melting-pot" theory: American culture was divided into these three subcultures, and that one affirmed one's Americanism and middle-class status by joining a house of worship and identifying with one of these three.[82] The "This is Our Home" pamphlets were used widely in Jewish adult education programs, university campuses, temples, synagogues, and local community centers.

AJC also sponsored research by historians John Higham and Oscar Handlin, a professor at Harvard and winner of a 1952 Pulitzer Prize. They described serious American antisemitism as an outgrowth of post-1880 class competition, and suggested that these conditions no longer existed in contemporary American life.[83] Nationally broadcast radio and TV programs celebrated such events as the first Passover in America, and Jewish services were broadcast on the national "Morning Chapel" TV program. An article by Rabbi Morris Kertzer, "What is a Jew?" published in *Look* magazine in 1954, was turned into a popular book of the same name. All of these were designed to inject Jews and Judaism into the American mainstream.

The 1954 Tercentenary, coordinated by the AJC, included special programs, exhibitions, and concerts. Originally, as Tercentenary committee chair Ralph E. Samuel had noted, not everyone in AJC was certain that the presence of Jews for three hundred years on American soil was something to be celebrated. "Perhaps we should keep quiet about it," remarked one member at a Saturday night dinner at the 1953 annual meeting.[84] This type of insecurity was one of the very phenomena the celebrations had been set up to address. One of the reasons for the Tercentenary observances, Samuel continued, was to give the Gentile a "far more accurate" image of the American Jew. Equally important, it gave the American Jew a greater sense of security and confidence. "Psychologically," Samuel noted, "it did him a great deal of good to learn that he and his forebears have been in this land for three centuries and have participated in every phase of American life."[85]

The Tercentenary was followed soon after by AJC's Golden Anniversary, an event that was duly celebrated; it culminated with a four-day meeting at the Waldorf-Astoria in April 1957. That year was marked by three notable internal developments: a complete reorganization of the Committee on a scale such as had occurred in 1943; the establishment for the first time of a Department of Jewish Communal Affairs, for the purpose of "extending education on Jewish communal issues, the Jewish heritage, and Jewish integration into American life";[86] and finally, the announcement that the AJC was going to be moving into its own headquarters.

The organization's new home would be an eight-story air-conditioned building on the northwest corner of Third Avenue and East 56th Street. Moreover, the building was to have a special name. "Unless man can learn to get along with his fellows, unless we can get rid of the millstones of hate and bigotry which have weighted men down for centuries, all the great scientific and industrial progress of which our age can boast will avail us little," read the official announcement (which might be read as an implication in 1956 that the AJC could help save humanity from a nuclear war). "This then—science of human relations—is the goal to which we must dedicate the next several decades of Committee labors. After more than three years of careful consideration, your Administrative Board has decided to create the kind of setting that will enable us to become in the fullest sense what we already are: an *Institute of Human Relations,* an Institute dedicated to improving man's understanding of his fellow man and removing the roadblocks of ignorance and bigotry which lie in the way of understanding."[87]

The change inaugurated a brief period when the very name "American Jewish Committee" was in danger of disappearing. The AJC then and into the present day was always being confused with the American Jewish Congress; at the time, that was given as one reason to adopt a new name. The change, however, was more the result of the universalization of the organization's mission and the frank discomfort some of the members still felt with the title "Jewish." For a time there was concern that AJC might evolve into a totally nonsectarian organization. The faction that supported such an outcome, however, did not prevail.

❧ II ❧

The 1960s

⁂ 4 ⁂

The First Jewish Continuity Crisis and the Triumph of Vatican II

[1960–1965]

Since that meeting in Chicago in 1947, the AJC leadership had taken it as axiomatic that the best way to fight for equal rights for Jews was to fight for the rights of all human beings. In the late 1950s they saw no discrepancy between establishing a special department of Jewish Communal Affairs and at the same time erecting a multimillion dollar Institute of Human Relations. Contributing a cutting-edge social scientific institution to work for "man's understanding of his fellow man," as the institute's motto went (the name "Institute of Human Relations" and the motto now greeted visitors each time they entered AJC's lobby) was seen as an expression of the organization's Jewish heritage. A passionate belief in rights for all—especially African Americans—and not just Jews, continued to inform AJC's participation in the civil rights movement during its heyday in the 1960s. When this stance was challenged, as it sometimes was, the challenge was greeted with equally passionate claims that there was in fact no conflict between the two goals.

During the tumultuous years of the 1960s, however, in that campaign as in several others that the AJC pursued, tension began to grow between those who believed that a more "particularistic" approach to Jewish affairs would best fulfill their charter and serve the organization's agenda (that is, direct action to preserve the lives, rights, property, and culture of Jews), and those who believed that the postwar universalistic attitude was still the best approach. At the same time, the organizational attitude toward Israel and to Jewish tradition and observance went through far-reaching changes. While the AJC never then or later abandoned its goal of achieving a just and healthy society for all, circumstances and internal communal changes drove the organization—not without considerable internal dissent—into becoming a more

self-consciously "Jewish" organization and abandoning much of the aloofness
that had governed its relations with other groups within the Jewish communal world. AJC's own identity, its "image," and its commitment to the affirmative values of Jewish education and culture became matters of prime concern.
The head of a rival agency, referring to the role that AJC's executive vice president had played in the direction of the organization, called the process "the
conversion of St. John."[1]

The question of just how "Jewish" the American Jewish Committee should
be colored all of its activities during those years, including the civil rights
movement, increased interaction with Roman Catholics in the wake of the
Second Vatican Council (1963–65), and the emerging movement to save Soviet Jewry. There were several causes of concern at this time, including fears
for Jewish survival (provoked by new studies revealing plunging fertility and
rising intermarriage rates among American Jews), the stubborn persistence of
neo-Nazism, and the tensions in the Middle East that led to the Six-Day War
(June 1967). The issue mattered less in the struggle against anti-Jewish discrimination against Jews at home and aiding Jews abroad. AJC's overseas programs had always had as their aim the well-being of Jews specifically, and
fighting barriers and restrictions against Jews in employment, housing, and
education was as "particularistic" a goal as the agency could follow. The debate was more problematic in the drive to reform Catholic teachings on Jews
and the drive to fulfill all the promises of the civil rights movement to African
Americans. In the end, the Six-Day War led to a general resurgence of Jewish
pride and identification—but tempered by disillusionment that the AJC's allies in the Christian world and in the civil rights movement did and said so little to defend Israel in the hour of her greatest need.

Opening and Dedication of the Institute of Human Relations

The building of AJC's new Institute of Human Relations, an eight-story
glass-and-marble structure on the northwest corner of Third Avenue and East
56th Street, represented the highest values of universalism as well as the faith
that social science could be harnessed for the ultimate eradication of all prejudice from the world. Reflecting the interests of psychologist John Slawson, its
name and stated function bore more than passing resemblance to the psychoanalytic institutes that served as centers of training and research. Here, however, the goal was to cure the sicknesses of society, not just the sicknesses of individuals. AJC leaders spoke of it as a "gift" to America from a group with
special sensitivities, responsibility, and knowledge in these areas. For a time in
the 1960s insiders seriously discussed the possibility of AJC leaving its Jewish
roots and evolving into a nonsectarian social service agency, with membership
open to non-Jews as well as Jews. A step in this direction was taken when they

amended the bylaws in 1966 to open membership not only to Jews but to Gentile spouses and children. The move was a compromise to appease a minority that expressed its consternation that the membership rule changes were not moving far enough; membership in the American Jewish Committee, they said, ought to be open to all non-Jews who identified with their work.[2] In the meantime, some AJC employees were pleased to be able to state at parties and on application forms that they worked at the "Institute of Human Relations" rather than at an identifiably Jewish organization.[3]

Slawson and AJC officers had the foresight to purchase the new building's property when the tearing down of the Third Avenue elevated train in 1955 transformed the spot from an area of dirt and noise into a prime piece of real estate. In the nineteenth century it had been the site of the Bloomingdale family home and the location of one of its first New York stores. Previous AJC headquarters had been in a dilapidated building on Park Avenue South. Now, office dwellers on the top floor could see the United Nations building from their windows, and the rooms provided a dignified setting for the many meetings, conferences, and symposia the Committee hoped to sponsor. The building itself cost $2,500,000, of which Jacob and Hilda Katz Blaustein contributed a quarter of a million dollars, although Blaustein held off for two years before fulfilling his pledge. He hesitated, thinking that it was unseemly for the AJC to pursue such ostentation as having its own building, and that the funds might be better spent elsewhere.[4]

More than 250 national and communal leaders attended the cornerstone ceremonies for the Institute of Human Relations in the spring of 1959. The proceedings included Judge Proskauer's depositing of a time capsule containing historic Committee documents. The week the actual building was dedicated, in January 1960, two hundred social scientists, theologians, educators, and media leaders were invited for a mass conference. The event was extensively covered by the press, including a segment on NBC's *Today* show that featured a montage of the building. Dedication week ended with a special ceremony at the White House where Slawson, A. M. Sonnabend, and Frederick F. Greenman named President Dwight D. Eisenhower the first Honorary Fellow of the Institute and presented him with a fifty-four-volume set of human relations books for his presidential library. One of them, of course, was the renowned *The Authoritarian Personality*, which had recently been reprinted in paperback for use as a textbook in university social science courses.

The 1963 "Image Study"

The point of all this celebration, however, was lost on much of the organized American Jewish community, which did not fully understand the purpose of such an institute nor exactly what the American Jewish Committee was doing, or why the organization deserved their support through contributions and allocations from local federation and Jewish welfare funds. In the two years he spent raising funds for the building, A. M. Sonnabend, who became AJC's twelfth president in 1962, became increasingly aware of the need, as he put it, for the "improvement of the image of AJC in the community." What AJC did and what it stood for was, in his view, being misinterpreted or misunderstood, "and I believe it is the way we present ourselves to the Jewish public." A specially commissioned "Image Study," in which three hundred Jewish leaders across the country who were *not* associated with AJC were interviewed in depth, was conducted and presented to the Executive Committee in 1963.[5]

The results gave AJC a chance to see itself the way others saw it. AJC in respondents' minds was a group of wealthy, socially exclusive, self-sufficient, upper-class German Jews—the so-called Jewish four hundred—drawing membership from the ranks of Reform Jews only. It was simply a "defense" agency, similar in function to the Anti-Defamation League. Very few had any knowledge of its overseas or Jewish communal activities. The leaders were viewed as anti-Israel and "confirmed assimilationists"; the organization kept itself aloof and, rather than concerning itself with Judaism and the perpetuation of Jewish tradition, spent more time and energy talking to non-Jews than Jews. In addition, the Image Study made clear that AJC was paying a price in community effectiveness by remaining disconnected from Jewish umbrella organizations such as the National Community Relations Advisory Council (NCRAC) and the Large Cities Budgeting Council (LCBC). The researchers of the study also confirmed the relative coolness of the organization toward Israel by surveying both a group of AJC members and a group of members from rival organizations, giving them a list of behaviors and asking which were essential to being Jewish. AJC members clearly ranked the item "Support Zionism" lower than the others. The survey authors recommended that AJC become "more sympathetic to and understanding of the mass appeal which Israel has had for Jews in America, and therefore give greater recognition and aid to Israel."[6]

AJC's departures from the rest of the Jewish community were becoming increasingly untenable, especially when, at the end of 1963, the former fund-raising partnership with the ADL through the Joint Defense Appeal dissolved. Since 1941 the JDA as an independent entity had raised funds for both the ADL and the AJC, thus leaving officers free to work at their day-to-day tasks without being too concerned about where the money was going to come from. Rank-and-file members were thus not accustomed to being asked to contribute funds; the JDA arrangement fed the illusion that the American Jewish Committee enjoyed such wealth that concerns for its solvency were not necessary. The JDA agreement, however, only recognized AJC's domestic defense functions without taking note of its needs in foreign and Jewish communal programs, and restricted the amount of outside funds it could raise. In 1963 AJC terminated the contract, and from then on it was on its own when it came to fund-raising.

In the wake of the Image Study AJC went through a deliberate campaign to change its image and reality, letting itself be seen and heard in ways it had not been accustomed to previously. The Public Relations Department launched a campaign to familiarize the Jewish community with AJC's work and to galvanize younger chapter members. A new membership drive sought to recruit Conservative and Orthodox as well as Reform Jews. Instead of "Application for Membership"—with a blank for "Sponsor," implying that one had to be passed upon before joining the club—the new recruitment forms were titled simply "Enrollment Form." More attention was paid to the Jewish Communal Affairs Department and AJC leaders spent more time than ever talking about and proposing programming in the area of Jewish identity and Jewish education—although these programs were directed as much to the education of AJC's own membership as they were to the rest of the community. Chapters in Milwaukee and St. Louis sponsored chairs in Jewish learning at the University of Wisconsin and Washington University, in part to give new respect to Jewish studies as an academic discipline and in part to try to reach the thousands of young Jewish college students who, by all accounts, were becoming alienated from their heritage. The agency drew physically closer to Israel than ever before, pouring resources into its office there.[7] AJC began arranging trips to Israel for members and their children. In 1961 John Slawson, executive vice president, deliberately chose Theodore Tannenwald (who had served in the State Department during World War II) as the chair of AJC's Israel Committee. Unlike the great majority of AJC's lay members, Tannenwald had close ties with top Israeli officials.[8] The AJC also hired George E. Gruen, who had recently received his Ph.D. from Columbia, as their first staff specialist in Middle Eastern affairs; Gruen also happened to be one of the first Orthodox Jews to serve on the staff.

AJC leaders also began to reconsider the value of their accustomed autonomy. They drew closer to other Jewish organizations, rejoining NCRAC in 1966—an organization that had revealed its own squeamishness about using the word "Jewish." The word "Jewish" as in National Jewish Community Relations Advisory Council, was added in 1968. In 1997 it became simply the Jewish Council for Public Affairs. In announcing the return to NCRAC, John Slawson said, "We are getting back into the fold."[9] AJC was to move even further in this direction with the retirement of John Slawson, the appointment of Bertram H. Gold as AJC's next executive vice president, as well as the hiring of Yehuda Rosenman to serve as director of a reinvigorated Jewish Communal Affairs Department in 1967 (see chapter 5).

Old and New Leadership

Several factors beside its Image Study and the dissolution of the JDA drove the AJC to rejoin communal umbrella organizations and to stress Israel, Jewish identity, and Jewish education more. As early as 1963 the first of many discussions arose that AJC might consider merging with the American Jewish Congress, its traditional archrival. The Congress had been far removed from the Committee in its class and ideological background, yet as AJC's own statisticians and sociologists noted, American Jewry had become altogether more homogenized, and the differences between organizations was narrowing. The old downtown-uptown, Russian versus German, mass versus class distinctions were ceasing to matter and, with the existence of the State of Israel, the old Zionist–anti-Zionist–non-Zionist divisions had been rendered moot. In particular the gap that separated the AJC's official attitude toward the State of Israel from that of the majority of the American Jewish community began to narrow perceptibly. Israeli Prime Minister David Ben-Gurion himself saw little difference between them. When he claimed in a speech made at the World Zionist Congress in December 1960 (reprinted in the *New York Times*) that Jews were violating the precepts of the Torah in remaining in the Diaspora and that whoever dwelled outside the Land of Israel had no God,[10] an irate Jacob Blaustein insisted that Ben-Gurion publicly reaffirm his 1950 statement, which he did. Nahum Goldmann and other Zionists, who also objected to the speech, claimed that their movement was being ignored and that Ben-Gurion should never have come to an agreement with a group that was, as Goldmann put it, "not representative of American Jews." Ben-Gurion's reply was that he doubted any organization could be representative of all American Jews. As for Jacob Blaustein, Ben-Gurion said, "He is not one of those Zionists who are called Zionists in America. In my eyes, they are not Zionists either." The American Jewish Committee was a Jewish organization, he insisted, even if its members did not speak Hebrew—but neither did the members of the Zionist Organization of America make *aliyah* or speak Hebrew.[11]

The old German Jewish family names were still to be found among the ranks of officers and members, but now almost all of AJC's staff and much of its lay leadership, including Jacob Blaustein and Irving Engel, was drawn from formerly Yiddish-speaking families of East European origin who had enjoyed the blessings of upward mobility and who had joined Reform Jewish congregations in their adulthood. Before, only a small percentage of American Jews had been wealthy, college-educated, or professionally trained as the founders and early leaders of the AJC had been. Now, that profile was becoming the norm. Most American Jews were quickly approaching AJC's own socioeconomic level and, through active recruiting practices, thousands were joining the AJC membership rolls. All this led inevitably to the end of the stewardship ideal and the drifting of AJC into the mainstream of American Jewish life.

A crisis in the organization's own leadership pool led to a sharper awareness of the values of transmitting Jewish identity to the coming generations. A series of deaths, retirements, and resignations among the lay and staff people drew attention to the aging of that pool, as well as the ability of AJC staff members to find work elsewhere in the burgeoning number of social service bureaus, civil rights agencies, and academia. There was an urgent need to search for new and younger talent.

After three long-term presidents—Joseph Proskauer (1943–49), Jacob Blaustein (1949–54), and Irving Engel (1954–58)—the AJC was headed by a number of notable leaders who retired after a short period or died in office. Herbert B. Ehrmann, a native of Kentucky, assumed the presidency in April 1959; at the time he noted that all of AJC's post–World War II presidents had been born and raised in southern cities. He had achieved renown for his work on the team defending Sacco and Vanzetti in the 1920s and more recently in the U.S. district court's (Massachusetts) Lord's Day case, which gave Jewish storekeepers in that state the right to keep their establishments open on Sunday. Fighting for what in those days were called "fair Sabbath laws" occupied a good part of his and the AJC legal division's time and energy—and necessarily so; until 1963 it was against the law in New York State to keep one's business open on Sunday.

After one year Ehrmann stepped down from the active presidency because he was unable to commute from Boston. Another Harvard Law School graduate, and a veteran of both world wars, Colonel Frederick F. Greenman took his place. (It was no longer German Jewish origin but Harvard Law School, along with southern roots and military service in those years that became a common denominator among AJC's top leadership.) Greenman died suddenly in 1961, at the age of sixty-nine; Louis Caplan, who stepped into his place, declined to serve another year. In 1962 A. M. Sonnabend, a leader in the hotel industry and the main proponent of the Image Study, was named president. In his short time in office he exerted a strong influence, but he too died suddenly in 1964. At one point all three of the organization's top positions were vacant; at a meeting of the Executive Committee in 1963 it was noted that five members had been lost since the previous meeting.

The streak was broken in 1964 when famed civil rights attorney and former Rhodes scholar Morris B. Abram, a native of Georgia who had served most recently as the director of AJC's Atlanta office, assumed the presidency and kept the position for four years.[12] Abram himself noted what a novelty he was at the time, recalling that before he came the president of the AJC was inevitably "from the East Coast, very rich, and very old."[13] At forty-five, he was the youngest man ever to hold that position and John Slawson referred to him as "our Lochinvar from the South." Younger, future presidents such as Richard Maass, Elmer Winter, Maynard Wishner, and Theodore Ellenoff also became active during this period, serving as chapter chairmen or as members or chairmen of national committees. In general, scores of younger faces were in evidence at the 1965 annual meeting (the first at which the new state of Hawaii was represented) and AJC's old-timers felt reassured that the organization was building for its future.

Other factors drove AJC in the direction of making Jewish programming and education for future generations a higher priority within the organization. The election of John F. Kennedy, a Roman Catholic, to the presidency in 1960 was greeted with elation by AJC members, who perceived this as the end of dominance by the Protestant majority and permission for other minorities to acknowledge their distinctiveness more openly. In addition, the children of the baby boom generation had to be raised and cared for. By 1961, some 80 percent of American Jewish children were attending Jewish school at one time or another. Spending on Jewish education reached an all-time high, and the Ramah summer camps of the Conservative movement had more applicants than they were able to handle. Jewish education, Eugene Borowitz noted in an *American Jewish Year Book* article, was on the verge of achieving a "new and exalted status."[14] Quite simply, more time, energy, and funds were available to see to the education of the next generation. Physical rescue, the emergency redemption of thousands of Jews in one land or another, was no longer so urgent. Israel was there to accept refugees and was making progress in carrying her own economic burdens. In meetings, conferences, conventions, and coordinating sessions, educators were able to debate how best to go about their tasks, dealing with problems, as Borowitz put it, that the American Jewish community "finally had the good fortune to achieve. . . . these are the symptoms of its potential maturation."

The Swastika Outbreak and the Eichmann Trial

A new awareness of the Holocaust (a word that did not even pass into common usage until the 1960s) along with a sensitivity to renewed Nazi activity and the revelations of the Eichmann trial also led to greater discussion about the world that had been lost and the need to foster the continuity of Jewish life. For a decade and a half the events of World War II had been relegated to the background as the Jewish world tried to pick up the pieces and the survivors struggled to rebuild their lives. Overt antisemitism in the United States had been declining since World War II, but the American Jewish community was shocked in 1959–60 when an epidemic of swastika daubings, desecrations, and antisemitic vandalism began at a synagogue in Cologne, Germany, on Christmas Eve and spread rapidly throughout the world from Germany to cities including London, Oslo, Johannesburg, Vancouver, Hong Kong, and New York. Eleven days after the Cologne incident, when it became clear that this was not an isolated event, a four-man AJC delegation led by president Herbert Ehrmann traveled to Washington, D.C., to meet with West German Ambassador Wilhelm G. Grewe. In this meeting and in a series of later conferences with West German leaders, AJC documented the resurgence of neo-Nazi activity in Germany and publicly criticized that nation for maintaining Nazis in high government posts, dealing leniently with neo-Nazi crimes and tolerating a burgeoning number of antisemitic groups, including some composed of refugees from Hungary, who felt free to spread Nazi propaganda around the world. AJC also created an annual program to train West German educators in American methods of social and civic education, coordinating their trips around the country to visit American schools and holding all-day conferences at the AJC headquarters to discuss their findings. They also did an in-depth study of people caught drawing the swastikas, who were mostly teenagers.[15]

The swastika epidemic may have lent special urgency to the Israeli effort to apprehend Adolf Eichmann, who had been Hitler's chief adviser on the "Jewish problem" and had been in direct charge of killing the Jews of Germany, Austria, Czechoslovakia, and Hungary. The announcement by Ben-Gurion on May 23, 1960, that Eichmann had been captured in Buenos Aires by his country's security agents and was being flown to Israel for trial led to world condemnation, an anti-Israel resolution in the U.N. Security Council, and the expulsion of the Israeli ambassador from Argentina. Israelis were portrayed around the world as violators of international law, seeking bloodthirsty vengeance. "The accusations that have been made against Israel," wrote David Danzig and Milton Himmelfarb in a memo on the trial, "are so lacking in substance, especially in moral substance, that we must attribute them to the regret that Eichmann was caught at all."[16]

At the AJC, some were concerned at first that Israel was being portrayed in so unfavorable a light and that the trial might bring to the public eye testimony and photographs that would better remain hidden. Why should Jews go out of their way to publicize material that might give contemporary antisemites any more ideas about how Jews should, and could, be treated? The organization's first official response was to privately convince Prime Minister Ben-Gurion to allow an international tribunal to try Eichmann, both to allay charges that Israel was behaving in an "eye for an eye" fashion and to deemphasize Israel's role of speaking for all the Jews in the world.[17] This position changed only when it became clear that Israel was holding firm and that no one else was willing and able to try him. Afterward, AJC was very clear on what direction they wanted the world media coverage to take. "Undue emphasis," as new AJC president Frederick Greenman said with delicacy in 1960, should not be placed "on the lurid details of Nazism, of the death camps, of the concentration camps, nor should undue emphasis be placed on the legal and jurisdictional aspects of the trial." In its numerous publications and press releases concerning Eichmann, the only correct approach was to stress the Western world's responsibility to treat genocide as a crime against all humanity.[18]

The resulting trial, which opened on April 11, 1961, was televised around the world. Professor Salo W. Baron, Columbia professor of history and AJC consultant and committee member, was one of the first witnesses, giving testimony on the world of European Jews that had existed before the war. A version of his testimony was published in that year's *American Jewish Year Book* and it provided a valuable historical overview for a new generation of American Jews.[19] In Israel and all over the world, exactly as Ben-Gurion had hoped, the trial served an important educational function, especially among young people who began to ask questions of their parents. Eichmann was convicted and then executed by hanging on May 31, 1962; his body was cremated and his ashes dropped overboard from a police boat in international waters three miles past Israel's coastline.

By that time, there was a sense that some small justice had been done and that the event that was soon to become universally known as "The Holocaust" could be talked about openly. There was a new attitude of respect for the old world and an awareness that American Jews could not rely much longer on the reservoir of refugees who had survived to provide religious, scholarly, and cultural guidance. New generations would have to be trained to take over the functions of the world that had been lost. Academic research into the history of the Holocaust gained new impetus with the publication of Hannah Arendt's coverage of the trial, *Eichmann in Jerusalem*, which used the phrase "banality of evil" to describe him and implied that the Jewish councils had been complicit in their own deaths by cooperating with the Nazis. Authors rushed to write books and articles refuting her and new interest was displayed in documenting instances of active resistance to prove that Jews had not gone to their deaths, as some charged, "like sheep to the slaughter."

The Eichmann trial also had far-reaching effects on other events during the decade. Roman Catholic officials all over the world were preparing for the convocation of the Second Vatican Council at the time (the four sessions of the Council ran from 1962 to 1965), an event specifically dedicating to reforming and modernizing the Church. The trial increased the urgency in their eyes of dealing with the role that ancient Christian anti-Jewish teachings had played in the perpetration of the Holocaust. In addition, the Eichmann trial, along with the fervor of the contemporaneous civil rights movement, played a role in arousing Jews of all ages but especially the younger generation to help free the Jews of the Soviet Union. They were filled with shame and guilt that American Jewry had been unable to prevent the murder and suffering of millions of Jews during World War II. In the early 1960s almost three million Jews lived behind the Iron Curtain in the Soviet and satellite countries and they were now facing, in Jacob Blaustein's words, "spiritual genocide." Few aware American Jews could tolerate the idea that the history they were now learning in such excruciating detail might someday be repeated, and the Eichmann trial increased their resolve that the Jews of their country would not be found wanting a second time.

The "Last Barrier" of Social Discrimination and the
Executive Suite Program

As the decade progressed, the voices of those concerned for Jewish identity could also be heard in the reaction to the spectacular success the AJC and other American Jewish organizations were enjoying in removing any and all barriers that prevented Jews from living, working and networking, studying, or playing in any venue they pleased in the United States. Exclusionary practices in corporations, banks, university administrative posts, utilities, insurance companies, clubs, residential areas, professional associations, and recreation and leisure facilities were exposed, attacked, and eliminated. First came scrupulous research, which was either performed by AJC's own staff, assigned to well-known individual writers or journalists, or conducted under grants that enlisted the aid of such universities as the Harvard School of Business, the University of Michigan, the University of Pennsylvania, UCLA, and Cornell. Then the information was disseminated, through conferences, press releases, public programming, personal persuasive interviews with those in power, and publications, including books, pamphlets, fact sheets, TV and radio scripts, articles fed to leading newspapers and magazines such as the *New York Times* and *Business Week*, and hundreds of editorials and letters.[20] Legal testimony on behalf of corrective legislation—which gained new impetus after the passage of the 1964 Civil Rights Act—occupied a good portion of the time of both staff and lay leaders. Then there were a variety of techniques that hurt the offending institution in the pocketbook. These could and did include convincing large associations not to hold their conventions or conferences at a certain club or hotel. Local chapters organized by writing letters of protest to local clubs, warning prospective guests and speakers of the club's prejudicial policies, and threatening public exposure. The Los Angeles chapter successfully broke the restrictions of three of the most important clubs in the city this way. In one notable instance, intervention by AJC president Morris B. Abram in 1965 caused the American Bar Association to cancel all social events scheduled at the discriminatory Miami Beach Bath Club during its annual convention in August. In the 1960s, two full-time staff members at AJC headquarters kept track of all these cases.[21]

In Grosse Pointe, for example, a Detroit suburb, the screening committee of the Brokers' Association in 1960 subjected potential homebuyers to a personal investigation to determine education, kind of friends, number of children, dress, grammar, accent, and swarthiness of skin—in the case of Jews, this inquiry included the question "How much like a Jew does he look?" Points were deducted for each negative characteristic. For white Protestants, fifty was the necessary score; for Jews, it was ninety. A prominent psychiatrist from Wayne State University was told "that I could not buy or even look at a house in Grosse Pointe because I was Jewish and could not qualify."[22] In testimony before the U.S. Commission on Civil Rights, Irving Engel pointed out that in Washington, D.C., alone there were at least fifteen residential areas where Jews were still excluded by overt or covert means. All were in the desirable northwest quadrant, within a three- to five-mile radius of the White House. They included Kenwood, Hamlet, Spring Valley, Wesley Heights, Crestwood, Sumner, Woodacres, Springfield, Colony Hill, Berkeley, Kent, Brookdale, West Moreland Hills, Beacon Hill, and Yorktown Village. Many government officials of both political parties occupying some of the highest posts in the land, Engel pointed out, lived in these exclusionary areas.[23]

In the case of social institutions, investigation revealed that there was a close connection between social discrimination and discrimination in business and industry. At the beginning of its long-running Executive Suite program in 1958 (which at the time was limited to finding jobs for Jewish men), AJC studies showed that Jews made up less than one-half of one percent of executives in major corporations, even though they made up 8 percent of the college graduates and 25 percent of Ivy League college graduates. Contacts that were crucial to success in the business world were made in social clubs and, as one interviewee pointed out, a banker or a high-level executive *had* to belong to all the right clubs in town—it was integral to doing business. The Jew's inability to join disqualified him from the top positions. Other obstacles uncovered included stereotypes that Jews were "too aggressive," "too noisy," would not "fit in" to the executive family and did not "look like us"—or that the man might be suitable but his wife might be objectionable.[24] Jews were only acceptable in research or specialist jobs, where they did not have to work with the general public, and these were generally not management positions. The belief (or rationalization) was also widespread that Jews wanted to establish their own business and didn't care for the slow climb to the top necessary in big organizations. In the case of universities, where a 1966 AJC study revealed almost no Jewish presidents of universities or colleges, the stereotype was simple: "Jews don't want to be college presidents."[25]

Sometimes the massive publicity alone was enough to lead many well-meaning executives to mend their corporation's ways. More than one conscience-stricken corporate recruiter began to go out of his way to post notices at the local campus's Hillel House. In cooperation with Jewish vocational guidance experts, a full-time counselor, funded by a foundation grant, was assigned to increase the flow of Jewish applicants at the management trainee level to major companies in the Philadelphia area. Similar efforts occurred in other cities, on the theory that the reputation of these companies was leading Jews not to apply and thus setting up a vicious cycle. Special training programs were set up for AJC leaders in the communities to give them the background necessary to confront corporate leaders and urge them to change their recruitment and promotion practices. By 1967 AJC representatives had held discussions with more than one hundred corporations—fifty of them in 1966 alone—and had held conferences with the secretary of labor.

All these efforts bore fruit, symbolized by two great victories: in 1968 Edward Hirsch Levi, grandson of Rabbi Emil G. Hirsch, who had been dean of the law school and provost for the University of Chicago, became the first among many Jews to become president of a major university;[26] and in 1973 Irving S. Shapiro became chairman and CEO of the Du Pont Corporation.[27] Numerous similar victories followed. The question was now becoming, however, if young Jews could work, live, and associate with anyone they chose, what was going to happen to their sense of community? And what would happen when it became time for them to marry and establish families of their own?

Jewish Survivalism

At the turn of the decade AJC lay leaders and Executive Vice President John Slawson had been interested above all else in "American-centeredness" and the successful integration of Jews into the American landscape. All the social science research and programming on Jewish identity that they had conducted up to that point—including the Riverton, Lakeville, and Southville studies— were concentrated on that end. In 1962 the rise of Orthodox Judaism and the rising enrollment of Jewish children in all-day schools were criticized as examples of "isolation and ghettoism."[28] AJC members around the country commonly put up Christmas trees and were wondering if it was all right, even though most of them followed the convention of not placing a star on the top to differentiate it from the trees of the Christians.[29] The opening of the AJC office in Israel in 1962 was, officially, not out of a rush of Zionist feeling but an outgrowth of the ongoing Blaustein–Ben-Gurion understanding, which Blaustein confirmed with Prime Minister Levi Eshkol, Ben-Gurion's successor. One of the office's main purposes, officially, was "to help clarify the relationship between Israel and Jews in other lands." ("So Ya'acov, you come to quarrel with me?" was Ben-Gurion's response in 1961 when Blaustein arrived for one of his innumerable conferences to protest one of the prime minister's pro-*aliyah* speeches). The original mandate of the office, which was not funded by the regular AJC budget until 1965, was to seek separation of church and state in Israel, work to improve the rights of the Arab minority, and guard against Israel speaking for Jews beyond its borders.[30] Rabbis delivered the invocation and said the blessing over the bread at AJC official dinners, but otherwise Jewish tradition and observance were absent. AJC staff members, concerned about the organization's image in the community, expressed consternation that the AJC had a reputation as a place where lay members could express their Jewish identity without going to synagogue and without participating in any other form of organized Jewish life.[31] The renowned

German-born scholar and theologian Abraham Joshua Heschel, addressing a plenary session of the annual meeting in 1960, gave a gentle criticism of the group when he reminded them of the famous George Bernard Shaw quip: "Youth is a wonderful thing. It's a shame that it's wasted on the young." He then said, "Judaism is a wonderful faith . . ." and let the sentence hang.[32]

Slowly, however, doubts began to be expressed that American society no longer demanded total absorption of its minority groups and that the AJC campaign to integrate American Jews had gone perhaps too far—especially when it came to the subject of marriage. "We encourage our children to have friends who are not Jews," said Max Stocks of Syracuse, New York, in 1963, decrying the rising tide of marriage to non-Jews among the young people of his community. "However, there is an extraordinary tendency among young people to marry people they know and not people they don't know." It was very difficult to blame them, therefore, if the parents were encouraging such friendships.[33] Dr. Irving Greenberg, then a professor at Yeshiva University, addressing an AJC audience for the first of many times in 1966, said, "I think one reason why the first generation had less intermarriage was because the kids knew the parents would drop dead, literally. Whereas in the second generation, they know that given the ideology of the parents in pluralism and brotherhood, it won't be quite as disastrous."[34]

The number of children that Jewish parents did or did not have, coupled with the growing tendency of their offspring to marry partners and raise children who were not Jewish at all, became subjects of intense examination, with the two factors equating to zero or negative Jewish population growth. The first blip on the screen showing that the very survival of American Jews might be in doubt had come with the publication in the 1961 *American Jewish Year Book* of "Jewish Fertility in the United States," by Erich Rosenthal, an associate professor of anthropology and sociology at Queens College. Rosenthal confirmed the estimate that there were close to five million Jews in the United States, but their rate of fertility was 25 percent below that of Catholics, 20 percent below Protestants, and overall well below replacement levels. The article ended on a hopeful note, however. American Jews were streaming to the suburbs, where the number of children they had might presumably rise—as it might also when they achieved a more secure position in American society.

Hopes were dashed, however, with Rosenthal's second article in 1963, "Studies of Jewish Intermarriage in the United States,"[35] which revealed sharply rising rates of marriage to non-Jews as Jews grew more distant from the immigrant generation.[36] Publication of this study inaugurated what might be called the first "Jewish continuity crisis" (the panic following publication of the 1990 National Jewish Population Survey being the second). The very phrase "Jewish continuity" entered communal discourse at this point, not twenty-five years later. AJC librarians forty years later reported that the organization received more requests for reprints of the Rosenthal intermarriage article than anything else the AJC had ever published in its history.

In New York City a conference of fifty rabbis and social workers convened in December 1964 to discuss strategies for synagogues and Jewish social agencies "to preserve the continuance of the American Jewish community against threats of assimilation through intermarriage"; they recommended establishing counseling centers and institutes devoted to the problem. Jewish social workers, they agreed, had an obligation to point out to clients contemplating intermarriage the consequences of such a step and to inform them of the "growing evidence" that a mixed marriage had less likelihood of success than an intrafaith marriage. Similarly, a conference of rabbis in Canada and Minnesota urged parents "to take a firm stand" against all interfaith dating and to encourage their children to date only within the Jewish fold. They too, claimed that the children of such marriages were usually lost to Judaism and gave dire warnings that there was a greater frequency of broken homes among intermarried couples than among those of common religious background.[37]

John Slawson, making a complete about-face from his concern that American Jews were not integrating into their surroundings well or quickly enough, was seized with virtual terror when he examined the available data. Introducing AJC's resident social scientist Marshall Sklare to a meeting that year, Slawson declared that he had been reading the latest Rosenthal study and woke up one Saturday morning with a start. "Does this mean extinction?" he asked himself. "I called up Dr. Sklare and woke him from his Sabbath slumber, and from what I could hear among the noises about a half dozen babies were there, and I found out that there is some hope. . . . We should be concerned about Jewish population policy, which has not occurred to anyone in the Jewish group up to this time." Sklare in his remarks confessed that it had only *sounded* as if he had a half dozen babies, and mentioned that large-scale conversion of non-Jews might be a good thing for the American Jewish population. "Once you show Jews that the *goyim* like it," he said, "they will undoubtedly be prepared to buy the product themselves."[38] The remark brought loud applause.

The Rosenthal research was picked up by *Look* magazine in early May 1964 with a cover story entitled "The Vanishing American Jew." From the perspective of the twenty-first century many historians could claim with glee that it was *Look* magazine that vanished, not American Jews. But at the AJC annual meeting of 1964 during an address and discussion entitled "What Future for American Jews? A View of the Evidence Pro and Con for the Survival of the American Jews," led by Jewish Communal Affairs director Manheim S. Shapiro, every member present had a copy of the article in front of him or her. That year six of thirteen roundtable sessions were devoted to the Jewish future in the United States. In its write-up of current Jewish events in 1965, the *Year Book* referred to "the problem of the 'Vanishing Jew,' the major preoccupation of American Jewry during 1964." In that same issue Charles Liebman's groundbreaking article "Orthodoxy in American Jewish Life" appeared, describing the flourishing of a movement whose demise had been predicted only a few years before. "The only remaining vestige of Jewish passion in America resides in the Orthodox community," Liebman concluded, "and it is passion and dedication, not psychoanalytic studies of divorce, which will stem the tide of intermarriage."[39]

Even the Zionists took alarm. Ben-Gurion had been warning for years that the Jews of the United States were doomed to assimilation and disappearance if they did not come to Israel, but no one in the movement had realized that the problem was so urgent. The World Zionist Organization (WZO) called for stepped-up immigration from Western countries as necessary for Jewish survival. In the past, emphasis had been on bringing Jews from lands of oppression, but now the countries of the free world needed to become a top priority. At its convention in October 1964 the Zionist Organization of America passed a resolution that the emigration of middle-class Americans should be encouraged and proposed that large housing projects and even new cities be constructed for the purpose of housing and employing American immigrants.[40]

Community Service

Trying to bring Jewish communities back from extinction was an effort AJC staff had long practice in, although for years that effort was extended overseas, not in the United States. The organization did not see this type of activity in the United States as its responsibility and there was always concern about encroaching on the turf of synagogues and the myriad of existing institutions. Overseas, however, there was hardly any turf to encroach on. In the late 1950s, AJC surveys indicated that some six hundred thousand Jews lived throughout Western Europe, mostly in small and dispersed communities. Of these, between 60 and 70 percent were virtually without attachment to any form of Jewish life: they did not attend synagogue, provide a Jewish education for their children, nor contribute to any Jewish charity. Even those who were more attached to their Judaism were in many cases marginal, in the process of drifting away from their heritage.

The situation was a legacy of World War II. Communal leaders and most of the prewar Jewish population were dead or gone to other countries and Jewish institutions lay in physical and financial ruin. In the decade after the war, European Jewish leaders had been so overwhelmed with the acute physical needs of the remaining population that no one had time or funds to deal with tasks of religious and communal survival. In 1958 AJC stepped into the gap with its Community Service Program, in cooperation with its sister organizations: the Alliance Israélite Universelle of France and the Anglo-Jewish Association of

Great Britain. Claims Conference payments supplied most of the funds. The program's general aim, according to the AJC European office, was "to reestablish and help develop a positive sense of Jewish identity through programs which reflect Judaism as a religion, a rich tradition and a source of creativity."[41] A typical client was a young man in 1961 that had just been elected treasurer of his Jewish community and wrote that there was "zero" left of communal life since the liberation. His town had a population of seventy Jewish families and he was a complete novice. Could anybody help?

First, Community Service produced and adapted radio and record programs (this was still the era of LP's and reel-to-reel) of programs ranging from fifteen minutes to one hour, first in English and French and later in Italian, Spanish and Portuguese. These included a history of Jewish music, tracing it through the centuries; selections of Jewish poetry from biblical to contemporary times; readings by leading performers of France's Comédie-Française from the Talmud, Midrash, the work of Maimonides, and other great Jewish figures; addresses and discussions on Jewish history; humorous plays on Jewish themes; and lectures by authorities on the Bible, Jewish literature, and related subjects. Within two years these tapes had been used as the basis for more than four hundred Jewish lectures and social programs in six countries and had been broadcast over French, Belgian, and Tunisian networks as well as local stations in Strasbourg and Algeria and for Jewish summer camps. Community Service also produced publications that were circulated throughout Europe and reprinted in Jewish community newspapers. These included pamphlets such as "For the Health of Your Child," which described from a psychological point of view a child's need for positive identification and a Jewish education ("Pour L'Equilibre de Votre Enfant"). More than ten thousand copies of this publication were distributed in French-speaking countries; an Italian rabbi translated it and three thousand copies went to Italy. There was also a brief summary of the moral values of Judaism written by a French rabbi, and a history of Jewish literature commissioned from well-known writers.

There were music reference works and song collections, bibliographies on books of Jewish interest in multiple languages, and a magazine called *Community,* distributed to thousands of people actively engaged in Jewish community work. The magazine emphasized "how-to" articles and in those pre-Internet days served as a clearinghouse for subscribers to write in with their questions and share information. The European office also published *Evidences,* a French-language counterpart to the American *Commentary,* to the Spanish *Comentario,* and to the Portuguese *Comentário.* Periodic conferences were held by lay leaders and rabbis from across the Continent to discuss their needs. Community Service also produced numerous traveling museum exhibits, on such themes as Hebrew calligraphy, the history of the Jews of Spain, Jewish books, and illuminated Passover Haggadahs. Requests for these exhibits were still coming to AJC's Paris office twenty years later, after the program had been discontinued and the exhibits had to be taken out of storage.

Community Service also worked with community center and youth center leaders, providing material for lectures, conferences, and exhibits, as well as directly planning programs themselves. They also entered the field of Jewish observance when they began to distribute and produce films dealing with the Jewish holidays as well as producing program kits. A typical kit produced for the holiday of Tu Bishvat included a description of the festival's history to be accompanied by music, pictures, slides, or a film, and relevant extracts from the Bible, Talmud, and Jewish writers. The goal of the kits was to provide enough information to the local groups to produce their own programs. At a "European parley" held under AJC auspices in 1961, European rabbis and lay leaders in attendance urged the production of new prayer books with greater uses of translations and transliterations and explanations of the liturgy, as well as the introduction of more Jewish afternoon and day schools.

In 1965 the AJC leadership voted to expand its Community Service program into Latin America, where 750,000 Jews were living a precarious existence. AJC offices there, located now in Buenos Aires, Rio de Janeiro, São Paulo, Mexico City, and Santiago, conducted Jewish education and training programs in Spanish and Portuguese; among other accomplishments, they sponsored a Jewish studies program at the University of Santiago and a school for training Jewish professional leaders in Buenos Aires. In the early 1960s AJC also stepped up its program in France to help the local community absorb and integrate hundreds of thousands of Algerian Jews and others who were in the process of fleeing from North Africa.

Soviet Jewry

The freedom and opportunity that American Jews were now enjoying to practice their traditions contrasted sharply with the situation of the millions of Jews caught behind the Iron Curtain. Some emigration was permitted intermittently from Poland and from Rumania, and most could go to Israel, *if* they left everything they owned behind them. AJC leaders periodically intervened in meetings with ambassadors, Polish and Rumanian officials and their own State Department to encourage as many as possible to be set free. At any moment, however, the authorities could close the doors and arrest anyone who sought to emigrate or helped others to do so for "illegal Zionist activity," including suspicion of contacting the Israeli embassy or reading forbidden Zionist literature. Israel was always vilified in official propaganda as an imperialist, warmongering state. While many Jewish organizations—especially the World Jewish Congress—tried to intervene on behalf of Jews in Eastern Europe, in these negotiations as well the AJC enjoyed a peculiar advantage because it had never been allied to any Zionist movement or political party.

The Soviet Union as a whole had been passing through a process of de-Stalinization and liberalization since 1956, with Premier Khrushchev's denouncing of the "crimes" of the Stalin regime and stating his goal as "victory through peaceful competition" rather than world domination. Jews, however, benefited little from the communist thaw. Jewish schools, institutions, and a revival of Jewish publishing were promised but never materialized. A visiting journalist in 1962 reported that Eastern Orthodox, Armenians, and Muslims all enjoyed beautifully maintained churches and mosques, paid for by state subsidy. There were convents, seminaries to train priests, libraries, printing plants, and other facilities, partially supported by donations and contacts from abroad.[42] Vestments, candles, church vessels and articles were plentiful. Clearly, as one AJC officer observed, religion, the proverbial communist "opiate of the people," was the opiate only of some of the people some of the time.

By contrast, crumbling synagogues could not be repaired and new ones could not be built. The authorities accused them of being covers for alcoholism or illegal activity, closed them down by the score, and dismissed or arrested congregational leaders. Soviet Jews could not obtain religious articles of any kind unless they were homemade in great secrecy or furtively passed to them by tourists from abroad: not prayer books, prayer shawls, phylacteries, mezuzot, kiddish cups, menorahs, memorial candles, or that one item that jammed American Jewish mailboxes every August—Jewish calendars. In 1961 reports reached the West of someone who risked arrest by handwriting and mimeographing a Jewish calendar for the year 5722 and distributing it through the Leningrad community.[43]

The same journalist reported that in one visit to a synagogue still in use, congregants worshiped in unheated buildings in their overcoats and that the men wore colorfully embroidered Central Asian skullcaps or Russian fur hats as head covering because yarmulkes were not available. The prayer book pressed into her hands was so old it contained a prayer for Tsar Alexander III from the nineteenth century. Kosher food was scarce and only at great personal risk could anyone observe the Sabbaths and holidays. In an especially hurtful restriction, in 1962, after hampering production and distribution for many years, the authorities completely forbade the baking or importation of matzohs for Passover. Circumcisions were rare and there were reports of some Jews being put on trial for attempting to arrange one. Bar mitzvahs and religious rites at weddings were unusual, and Jewish cemeteries were being closed down by the state on the pretext that they were full or the ground was needed for new construction. Cremation against the families' wishes was a frequent result. Few AJC members and active American Jews in general could hear such stories without feeling a greater sense of appreciation for the rights they might otherwise have taken for granted.

Late in 1958 the Soviet Jews appeared in peril of their very lives again when reliable information emerged via Israeli agents that the government was considering the revival of Jewish settlement in the so-called Autonomous Jewish Region of Birobidzhan in Siberia and that the plan would be placed before the Twenty-first Congress of the Soviet Communist Party, scheduled to meet on January 27, 1959. The prospect of mass forced resettlement of millions of Jews was frightening. An opportunity for intervention presented itself with the visit of Soviet First Deputy Premier Anastas Mikoyan, who was on a visit to the United States. Two weeks before the congress, AJC leaders managed to obtain a meeting with Mikoyan in New York—his first such meeting ever with a Jewish group—and presented a formal, thoroughly researched statement detailing the suppression of Jewish religion and culture, rumors of resettlement, the failure of previous attempts to settle Birobidzhan, the primitive conditions that prevailed there, and their insistence that further settlement of Jews there could only occur by coercion.[44] Mikoyan flatly denied the report and said that it was without foundation. Journalists were present and the AJC made sure that the event, and this pronouncement, received worldwide press coverage beginning with the *New York Times,* putting Mikoyan on public record about the matter. When the Communist Party Congress met later that month, there was thankfully no word of the Birobidzhan plan.[45]

In addition, the AJC's European office a month later relayed the information that for the first time since 1948 the Soviet Union was permitting the publication of books in Yiddish, a language that almost half a million Soviet Jews still claimed as their mother tongue. Usually the Soviets claimed, when pressed on the matter, that their Jews were thoroughly assimilated and therefore had no desire for publications in their own language. This time, it had been clearly communicated to them that the West was not buying this excuse. The Birobidzhan incident did little to change the general situation of Jews in the Soviet Union at the time, but it set a valuable precedent. The Kremlin was sensitive to and could be directly influenced by Western pressure, and AJC officers vowed to remain alert for future opportunities.

A turning point for AJC and the nascent grassroots Soviet Jewry movement as a whole came in 1962. That year, after spending two weeks in Moscow and Odessa, Senator Jacob K. Javits (Republican, from New York) addressed the Committee. Then in his first term, Javits described an escalating anti-Jewish campaign in the Soviet Union, where scores of Jews were being arrested and sentenced to long prison terms or execution for trumped-up charges. Any aspect of practicing Judaism was officially forbidden. Yet in Moscow and Leningrad and other Soviet cities, tens of thousands were turning up at the remaining synagogues for the observance of the High Holy Days and in every Simchat Torah they were dancing in the streets— even though most of them could not understand the services and had no knowledge of Hebrew or the liturgy at all. He mentioned his wonder that some Russian Jews were still managing somehow to observe Jewish ritual and tradition and pass it on to their children. Clearly these Jews were not disappearing into Soviet society: the more the authorities oppressed them, the more they were fighting back. Furthermore, Javits had found in his travels that the Soviets were surprisingly sensitive to charges of antisemitism and that when they were pressed on the subject it made a great impression. That time had come, he said, to speak out forthrightly—to press the question of the Jews at the U.N. and before all the nations of the free world. He concluded:

With the memories of the horrors of Nazi Germany and the Stalin terror still fresh in our minds, the facts which have come out are too dangerous and too damaging to halt this inquiry. There is enough to justify the government of the U.S. taking note of it. If there is one change in the world which has occurred as far as Jews are concerned and as AJC is concerned, it is to speak up. We no longer sweep problems under the rug because this is the cozy and quiet and nice way in which to either hope that they will go away or work them out with some high-level personality—which has happened before and not always unsuccessfully, I hasten to add. But the way of the world is now somewhat different. I hope . . . that the AJC after this discussion will address itself to the subject and that it will take a far more active role . . . than has so far been the case. The world has learned unfortunately . . . that these very tiny dark clouds on the horizon . . . if seized in time perhaps can avoid great catastrophes, and the worst that they can call you, is that you jumped the gun, that you were too premature, that you are hollering before you are hurt. So what? I would rather holler before I am hurt and not be hurt than to be hurt mortally as we saw so devastatingly in our own lifetimes within the last thirty years.

The result was a new Statement on Soviet Jews that was more forthright and activist in its tone than anything the Committee had ever issued on the subject. Nonetheless, Herbert Ehrmann heard complaints during the drafting that an even stronger statement would improve the image of the AJC among American Jews. He answered angrily that it was only in the past few years that other Jewish organizations had been making regular public statements about Jews in the Soviet Union. "The AJC many years ago, during the Stalinist regime and ever since, has been exposing those conditions and denounced the treatment of Jews," he pointed out with some bitterness. "And I think perhaps to those who are going to perfect this statement, something should be put into it to indicate that we are not just trying to get in line with a lot of Johnny-come-latelies who have only discovered the treatment of Jews in Russia in the last few years. We were denounced as Fascists when the AJC first exposed those conditions, by other Jewish organizations. . . . This is nothing new to the AJC; it dates back many years."[46]

That year AJC leaders began pressing and briefing anyone they could on the situation. They met with the newly appointed ambassador to the Soviet Union to present him with the case of Soviet Jewry. They criticized repression against

Jewish citizens in a cablegram to Premier Khrushchev signed by forty-six clergymen, religious leaders, and educators. The text appeared as an advertisement
on December 7, 1962, in the *New York Times*, the *Washington Post*, and two
other newspapers. In 1964 AJC joined with twenty-four other Jewish organizations—including the American Jewish Congress, the B'nai B'rith, and
NCRAC—in the American Conference on Soviet Jewry, with AJC staff member Jerry Goodman as its first coordinator. Richard Maass, AJC's foreign affairs committee chairman and later AJC president, headed the organization
when it became the reconstituted National Conference on Soviet Jewry in
1971. When he first came to AJC, Goodman recalled, he was criticized by his
friends for joining "that '*Sha, Shtil*' [Yiddish, be quiet] organization" and said
he was able to tell them how unfair that charge was. "I don't know if the older
generation of lay leadership would have done that, and if they had if it would
have been accepted by the rest of the Jewish world," he said, noting AJC's role
in the struggle for Soviet Jewry. "To become the leadership—not just another
person—but the leadership of the Conference on Soviet Jewry, speaking for
the whole Jewish community. . . . That's very, very significant. . . . it was a significant reflections of the changes [in the organization]." Like Gruen, Goodman was also an observant Jew, and successfully made leaving early on Fridays
and taking off the second day of Jewish holidays as a precondition for his
coming to work there.[47]

AJC delegates met with President Johnson and Secretary of State Dean
Rusk to plead the case of Soviet Jewry and to obtain public statements in support of their freedom. Mass demonstrations involving thousands of people
were held in New York and in cities across the country, in venues as large as
Madison Square Garden. A memo on the situation of the Jews was entered
into the *Congressional Record*. Morris B. Abram criticized anti-Jewish practices in the halls of the U.N. Resolutions were introduced in the House and
Senate protesting the ban on supplying matzohs and calling for full religious
and cultural freedom for Soviet Jews. In 1965 a national AJC delegation
headed by John Slawson participated with twenty-three other organizations
in holding a National Eternal Light Vigil for Soviet Jews in Washington; AJC
members were urged to support similar vigils around the country. The old
AJC attitude that public demonstrations were invariably unwise and dangerous was fast fading.

As a great storm of protest rose up from Jewish and prominent Catholic
and Protestant leaders around the world, the evidence was that the Soviets
were listening and that the "Jews of Silence," as Elie Wiesel called Soviet Jews
in 1966, were taking strength and hope from knowing that they were not forgotten. In 1967 some six hundred Jewish families were actually permitted to
leave the Soviet Union, the first of an exodus that would continue intermittently until almost one million had gone and an empire had fallen. Then and
for some twenty-five years to come, fighting for the freedom of Soviet Jews to

reclaim their heritage and to emigrate became central to the communal identity of hundreds of thousands of American Jews.

The Road to Vatican II

Probably no other American Jewish organization had such close ties to the Roman Catholic hierarchy as the AJC. Interfaith and interreligious work was its specialty and an integral part of its image—work that had garnered criticism from the rest of the community, which believed that the AJC spent more time talking to Gentiles than with Jews and hurled at them the charge of being "assimilationists" or "Catholic lovers."[48] For decades AJC-sponsored studies of Protestant and Catholic school textbooks had examined and rooted out teachings that were prejudicial to Jews; AJC staff members were already consultants to several such textbook publishers to ensure that such teachings did not infect future generations of Christian children.[49] AJC staff and lay leaders overall, both on the national and chapter level, had through the years made it a point to cultivate relations with Roman Catholic prelates in the United States and, in their diplomatic interventions, all over the world. In the United States, this cultivation often meant making generous contributions to Catholic causes and charities. Far from being simply exercises in good brotherhood, these relations were a life-and-death issue to the nearly one million Jews who lived in such places as Latin America, Poland, and Hungary. From the Roman Catholic hierarchy—and from the pope himself at various times—AJC leaders asked for, and received, statements calling for the protection of Jews, denunciations of antisemitism, and calls that Jews be allowed to emigrate freely to various countries.

An especially close AJC relationship with Catholic leaders went back to the time that Judge Joseph Proskauer, AJC's president from 1943 to 1949, had worked together with Al Smith in the Catholic politician's 1928 presidential campaign. Proskauer had studied Catholic teachings extensively in order to defend Smith properly against the charge that it was impossible for a Catholic to be president of the United States. His fluency in basic Catholic doctrine and terminology influenced AJC's correspondence with Catholic leaders for decades. Aside from his own ample experiences with anti-Jewish discrimination, the virulent anti-Catholic bigotry that Proskauer encountered during the Smith campaign, as he wrote in his memoirs, was a formative experience in his decision to dedicate his life to the elimination of bigotry and intolerance.[50]

Proskauer's and AJC's good relations with leading American Catholics also extended to Richard Cardinal Cushing, archbishop of Boston, and Francis Cardinal Spellman, archbishop of New York. In the 1960s Spellman, who presided over one of the richest archdioceses in the world and who counted many Jews among his supporters, was referred to in Italy as the "American Pope."

In addition, Jacob Blaustein, a leading philanthropist for causes of all kinds in his native Baltimore, Maryland, had through the years contributed generously to Catholic charitable causes in that city and enjoyed a close and cordial relationship with Lawrence Cardinal Shehan, Baltimore's archbishop. Finally, AJC enjoyed a foothold in Rome through its members' generous contributions in funds and personnel to the Pro Deo (For God) University, an institution with thousands of students from all over the world that was endorsed by the Vatican.

These relationships and others forged over the years were to prove crucial down to the last minute when in 1965 the Second Vatican Council, a worldwide gathering in Rome, at its fourth and final session voted to issue its famous Declaration on the Jews as the fourth section of the document *Nostra Aetate* (In our time), which dealt with the relation of the Church to non-Christian religions. The declaration acknowledged the Jewish roots of the Church, repudiated the age-old idea that all Jews were eternally cursed for the crime of having killed Jesus, stated that hatred of Jews should have no place in Church teachings, and called for fraternal Christian-Jewish dialogue. The declaration, though it left a bitter aftertaste in the minds of Jewish participants at the time, was a major turning point in the history of Christian-Jewish relations. "Vatican II changed my life," recalled one AJC member, remembering a childhood of having to cross the street to avoid gangs of boys who regularly attacked with the taunt, "You killed Christ!"

The declaration and the implementation of it afterward also served, ironically, as a path back to the Jewish community and Jewish education for the AJC. Determined that their input should reflect the cooperation and viewpoints of all branches of American Jewry, for the first but not the last time AJC found itself stepping into the role of interdenominational referee within a group of modern Orthodox, Conservative, and Reform rabbis, thus increasing its value to the rest of the organized American Jewish community. When the declaration finally was passed, AJC also had to look to increase the level of Jewish education of its own people in order that they might properly participate in necessary dialogues with Catholics to implement the decision. The Jewish Communal Affairs Department had to respond on both the national and chapter level with appropriate publications and workshops and outreach to the rabbinate and other resources within each community. AJC members could hardly sit down with Catholics to discuss matters of theology and doctrine and belief if, as was so often the case, they themselves had no idea what Judaism had to say about such things.[51] Therefore, the decision of the Second Vatican Council indirectly contributed to the greater "Judaization" of the organization. In addition, it created a demand among Christian seminaries and organizations for knowledgeable Jewish scholars. Requests from Catholic groups for lecturers and professors of Jewish studies streamed into AJC offices, and many Christian schools began requiring a course on Judaism for graduation. Contemporary observers spoke of the resulting "rabbi gap" and encouraged the development of Judaic Studies as an academic discipline on American campuses to help fulfill this new-found need.

Since the end of World War II, AJC had had as its target one of the oldest and most important ingredients in the antisemitism that had led to the Holocaust: the charge that the Jews had killed Jesus Christ. "When Hitlerism—an essentially pagan movement generated chiefly by social and economic forces unrelated to religion—unleashed the most terrible of persecutions," AJC researchers wrote in the first of three important memoranda on the subject submitted to the Vatican, "some devout and valiant Christians courageously saved Jewish lives; but the majority of Christendom stood indifferently by. The Jews will not forget their rescuers, but neither can they forget the six million whom no one rescued."[52] If antisemitism was to be destroyed at its source, there would have to be major changes in the way Christians in general and Catholics in particular were taught to view the Jews in their midst. To work for such a goal, in the words of one of John Slawson's favorite analogies, was the human relations equivalent of draining the swamps to prevent the spread of malaria, rather than continually dosing victims of the disease with quinine. As part of its educational efforts, AJC leaders were determined to root out these attitudes and teachings, first from Protestants and then from Catholics.

Major turning points in this effort included a 1947 conference on antisemitism at Seeligsberg, Switzerland. There Christian leaders, influenced by the writings of French Jewish scholar and author Jules Isaac—who had called attention to "the teachings of contempt" toward Jews in Christian sources—called upon churches in all lands to remember that Jesus was born of a Jewish mother, and to avoid presenting the story of Christ's Passion in such a way "as to bring the odium of the killing of Jesus upon Jews alone." Churches, the conference declared, should no longer promote "the superstitious notion that the Jewish people is reprobate, accursed, reserved for a destiny of suffering," and all Christian publications, especially those directed toward the education of the young, ought to be revised in that spirit. An AJC representative was present at Seeligsberg and provided much of the language that was used in the wording of the final declaration.[53] In 1961, at a conference in New Delhi, AJC—and in particular its new director of interreligious affairs, Rabbi Marc H. Tanenbaum[54]—was similarly involved in a declaration issued by the World Council of Churches, a body representing some three hundred million Protestant and Eastern Orthodox adherents around the world. The declaration held that antisemitism was "a sin against God and Man" and that all of humanity bore responsibility for the death of Christ, not just one people. That particular declaration did not escape notice by Catholics, who were in the process of preparing for the Second Vatican Council at the time.

The time was ripe in the early 1960s for dramatic changes within the Catholic Church. Social and technological changes had to be acknowledged; hovering above all was the specter of nuclear destruction of the world within minutes. World upheavals of the century were having their effect. There was the defeat of World War II fascist regimes in Germany and Italy, both countries where the Catholic Church played an important role. There was the loss to the Soviet Union of the overwhelmingly Catholic countries of Poland, Hungary, and Lithuania. Asian and African non-Christian countries were growing in number and power. Militant atheistic communism had to be confronted. The State of Israel had emerged, challenging previous Christian conceptions about the role of Jews in the world as homeless wanderers. Christian consciences were more keenly attuned to the fate of the European Jews. There was the example of the United States, where under a democratic government with separation of church and state, Catholicism was flourishing.[55]

Although it was probably a minor factor, the strong feelings aroused by John F. Kennedy's campaign for president in 1959–60 probably played a role in stimulating the Church to change. First, there was the wonder that not only had a Catholic been elected, as Rabbi Arthur Hertzberg noted in an AJC symposium on the election, but that he had been elected by a plurality of barely 100,000 votes out of 69 million cast, and no one—most important, not even his opponent Vice President Richard Nixon—had asked for a recount. Clearly, the Church could note, Catholics and Catholicism could function well in a free and open democratic society that separated church and state. On the other hand, virulent anti-Catholic sentiment in reaction to the campaign indicated that the Catholic Church might pay more attention to its public relations and relations with other Christians. In the course of the Kennedy campaign tens of millions of pieces of anti-Catholic literature, much of it obscene, was distributed at the cost of hundreds of thousands of dollars. Reformation Sunday, October 30, 1960—the date commemorating Martin Luther's posting of the famous Ninety-five Theses on his church door—was declared a Protestant "stand-up-and-be-counted" day by conservative Christian groups as hundreds of anti-Catholic clergymen railed from the pulpit against the election of a Catholic president.[56]

Much of the spirit of the new Catholic Church was embodied in Pope John XXIII, who was elected pope in 1958, succeeding Pius XII, who had been pope during World War II. Pope John XXIII served only four and a half years before his death in 1963, two years before the declaration *Nostra Aetate* No. 4 was passed. As Angelo Cardinal Roncalli, he had spent the years of World War II as a Vatican diplomatic envoy in Bulgaria, Turkey, and France, and had also served as the patriarch of Venice. During that time he made available church documents that enabled the rescue of thousands of Jewish men, women, and children from Nazi death camps. Shortly after becoming pope, he ordered removed from the liturgy several references that Jews regarded as offensive, such as the call for the conversion of "the perfidious

Jews" during Good Friday services. Although the Vatican still did not formally recognize the State of Israel (anger that the State did not internationalize Jerusalem was named as a factor), Israelis were aware of his actions during the war, and unofficial relations with the Jewish state became perceptibly warmer and more open.

The new attitude toward Jews was only part of Pope John XXIII's desire to bring the Catholic Church into the modern world. By summoning an Ecumenical Council in 1960 he sought an *aggiornamento;* literally, an updating of the church. When asked by a visitor for the exact meaning of the term, he was said to have gone to the nearest window to open it wide and let in the fresh air.[57]

The man Pope John XXIII chose to carry out his decision was one of his most trusted advisers, the German Jesuit Augustin Cardinal Bea (pronounced BAY-ah) the retired rector of the Biblical Institute of Rome, a renowned scholar. Cardinal Bea, who counted Hebrew and Aramaic among his many languages, was appointed president of the Secretariat, a key position for drafting and implementing the Council's pronouncements.[58] Both the pope and Cardinal Bea warmly received Jules Isaac for an audience on June 13, 1960, where the French Jewish historian spoke of the anti-Judaism inherent in Catholic liturgy and teachings and suggested that the pope appoint a committee within the planned Vatican Council to study the issue of Christian antisemitism.[59] Afterward, seeking support for his efforts, Isaac consulted with the European office of the AJC, where he was well known, having published in *Evidences* for several years.[60] Hearing a report of the meeting in New York, AJC's top leadership decided that the upcoming Ecumenical Council and the promises of Pope John XXIII and Cardinal Bea represented an unparalleled opportunity.

In the following years AJC representatives supplied Cardinal Bea with their research, suggested wording for the proposed declaration, had numerous conferences with him in Rome, and were his hosts at a gala dinner at the Plaza Hotel in 1963 during his visit to the United States at the invitation of Cardinal Cushing (the dinner was ostensibly under the aegis of the American friends organization of Pro Deo University, but AJC arranged and paid for it). Further, they invited him to an unprecedented, unpublicized meeting at AJC headquarters on Sunday, March 31, 1963.

The chairman of that meeting was Rabbi Abraham Joshua Heschel, who authored one of the three AJC memos to the Vatican and also met privately with Cardinal Bea and Vatican officials several times during the course of the Council. Those in attendance also included Rabbi Louis Finkelstein, chancellor of the Jewish Theological Seminary; Rabbi Emmanuel Rackman, former president of the Orthodox Rabbinical Council of America; Rabbi Joseph Lookstein, president of Bar-Ilan University; and Rabbi Albert Minda, president of the Reform Central Conference of American Rabbis. Rabbi Joseph B. Soloveitchik of Yeshiva University, who had read and commented on AJC's research memos to the Vatican, planned to attend but could not at the last minute because of his wife's illness. "There he was with his yarmulke, and it was red," recalled Morris Abram of Cardinal Bea at the meeting, "and there he was with a group of Orthodox rabbis, including Abraham Heschel with his yarmulke and it was black, and they were gesticulating wildly to each other, I think speaking Hebrew, and it was hard to tell who the cardinal was and who the rabbi was."61 In answer to their inquiries, Cardinal Bea pledged his support that day; to the very end he remained one of the strongest proponents of a declaration denouncing antisemitism and repudiating the charge that Jews were guilty of deicide.

Whatever Cardinal Bea's intentions were, however, the road that led to *Nostra Aetate* No. 4 was far from easy. Even getting it on the agenda, much less passing it, cost its supporters four years of hard work, with many reversals and nerve-wracking delays through the four sessions of the Council before the declaration was finally passed near the end of the final session. All work had to be done exercising the ultimate in tact, discretion, and secrecy lest it appear that the declaration could be accused of being a product of the Jews rather than an authentic decision by the Church. The process was severely complicated by the death of the saintly Pope John XXIII in 1963 and the succession of Pope Paul VI, who was far less committed to the change and more likely to accede to international pressure to squash the document. As late as the weekend before the vote, newspapers were speculating that the section on the Jews would be reduced to a single sentence, or that the entire declaration would be shelved.62 The declaration that was finally passed was itself a compromised, watered-down version of an earlier draft that fell far short of AJC's hopes. In fact, it left the door open at several points for Christian antisemitism and proselytizing of Jews to continue.

The Second Vatican Council was not a monolith but a legislature of more than two thousand bishops and hundreds of church leaders from all over the world meeting to discuss and vote on overall far-reaching reforms. The Jewish issue dramatically illustrated a split between liberal and conservative wings of the Church. The latter did not want to see any change in Church doctrine or in the literal interpretation of the New Testament; indeed, a significant minority disapproved of the entire purpose of the Council. Bishops gathered in Rome were also subjected several times to antisemitic propaganda. At the end of the first session, for example, every bishop found in his mailbox a privately printed 900-page volume entitled *The Plot Against the Church*, which rehashed *The Protocols of the Elders of Zion*, charged that there was a Jewish fifth column among the Catholic clergy, and drew attention to the Jewish birth of two of the bishops on Cardinal Bea's staff. At later points, Cardinal Bea himself was accused of being Jewish, and Pope John XXIII was accused of being a communist. An Italian neofascist organization was eventually found responsible for the book, although it turned out that the printing had been financed by Egypt. Only a few days before the vote, a pamphlet was anonymously distributed to the bishops calling on them not to vote for the declaration "because it would betray Christianity to the Jews."[63] Within the Church itself, the strenuous exertions of the American bishops proved decisive in convincing many of their more conservative brethren from Europe, Latin America, and the Middle East—and last but not least Pope Paul VI himself—to support the change.

The issue also divided American Jewish rabbis and leaders, who had varied opinions on how far Jewish leaders should try to influence the outcome—or whether Jews should have anything to do with the Second Vatican Council at all. The debate was at times acrimonious and the AJC came in for strong criticism for its efforts. On a number of occasions President Morris Abram had to make public statements justifying the organization's involvement. Rabbi Tanenbaum, fielding questions from AJC's own membership on the suitability of their acting as de facto theologians for the entire Jewish community—and probably infringing on the turf of rabbis—defended the effort as a legitimate exercise of AJC's mandate to eliminate the sources of antisemitism. There was obviously no future for Judaism in the lands of Islam, he noted, nor in the once "secular Utopia of the Proletariat," the Soviet Union. The overwhelming majority of Jews in the world, including those in Israel, now found their destiny profoundly linked with the Christian West; thus the relationship of Jews to the Christian world was not merely a theological question but a key to the existence of the entire Jewish people.[64]

Charges were also common from others, including the Orthodox rabbi Eliezer Berkovits, that antisemitism was inherent to Christianity and the New Testament and that the whole effort at dialogue was impossible and hopeless. Critics from all sides claimed that despite any theological justifications, it was undignified and debasing for Jews to "plead" their case in Rome in such a way. One rabbi at a NCRAC meeting remarked, "I don't feel that I have to be exonerated. I didn't crucify anyone." The author Harry Golden suggested that a Jewish Ecumenical Council be held to "exonerate" Christians for everything they had done against the Jews through the millennia, including the Crusades and the Spanish Inquisition. The Yiddish press published a cartoon that showed Pope Paul VI holding Rabbi Marc Tanenbaum on a leash.[65]

Some rabbis believed that the Council was an internal Christian matter and that Jews should not be involved. Others feared that the document was preparation for wide-scale proselytization of Jews. The renowned halachic authority Rabbi Moshe Feinstein, partly in an attempt to convince his equally renowned Orthodox colleague Rabbi Joseph B. Soloveitchik not to cooperate with the AJC (which he was indeed doing), went so far as to write an edict declaring that it was a sin for Jews to be conferring with Catholic priests on anything, whether it be matters of faith or matters of common social and political concern. For Feinstein and others, the process revived unpleasant memories of the notorious medieval disputations between rabbis and priests. The only purpose of such conversations, he declared, was to attempt to convert the Jews. Feinstein wrote:

Concerning the matter of ecumenicism that has been spread through the conspiracy concocted by the leaders of the Christian faith, whose only intent is to cause Jews to apostatize, God forbid. This act of Satan has succeeded in enticing a number of rabbis to join with priests in joint fellowship on permanent committees established in every locale, as well as in conventions held here in this country and in Europe. Behold, we declare that there is an absolute and clear prohibition against joint meetings of rabbis and priests. One should not participate in the convention to be held in Boston, nor anywhere, either in this country or any countries. Just as it is forbidden to dialogue on matters of faith and religion, so there should be no joint discussion on matters of social-political concern and there should be no excuses or rationalizations offered for it. Indeed, it is prohibited to aid the project of ecumenicism in any manner. . . . On account of this, we have come to sign this document so as to proclaim the *issur* [prohibition] against this to all rabbis who preserve the religion of our holy Torah, and we stand up against the breach on this day of the Fast of Esther, 5727.[66]

The text of *Nostra Aetate* No. 4 also became a focus of international diplomacy as heads of Arab states exerted every pressure they could to see that the declaration was shelved. The Arab states made it officially known to the Vatican that any statement in favor of the Jews would be considered by them unfavorably, and hints were made threatening the persecution of the Catholic Church and its institutions in Arab countries. The threats were taken seriously; at least nine million Catholics resided in the Middle East in overwhelmingly Muslim countries, and the Church had a system of schools and institutions that had been built up for centuries.

"Arab diplomats, emissaries were sent from Cairo, from Beirut, from Amman, Damascus, to Rome during the Council," recalled Rabbi Marc Tanenbaum in 1972. "They brought enormous pressure to bear, especially on Arab Christian bishops, some of whom were told that if you don't defeat this declaration you might as well not try to come home."[67] The Voice of the Arabs, the station of Egypt's Gamal Abdel Nasser, broadcast on November 7, 1963, that there was a "world Zionist plot to capitalize on the Vatican Council to further the oppression of the Palestinian refugees."[68] The Syrian prime minister, speaking before Arab Christian leaders, criticized the proposed declaration and asked all the heads of Syria's Catholic communities to urge Pope Paul VI not to exonerate the Jews of deicide. President Charles Helou of Lebanon, who was Christian and a former ambassador to the Vatican, was formally charged by the Arab League with the duty of expressing their opposition to the pope.[69] The *New York Times* of April 25, 1965, reported that under Nasser's direction Arab opposition had advanced to a full-scale political and economic offensive, with countries threatening to cut off trade or to defect to the Soviet Union. Prime Minister Bourguiba of Tunisia took a more conciliatory tone, suggesting at one point that Arabs and Israelis come to Rome for a summit meeting under the aegis of the Vatican; he was promptly condemned by the Nasserites. The Muslim mayor of East Jerusalem, which was under Jordanian control, announced that the bells of the Church of the Holy Sepulcher—regarded by most Christians as the site of Jesus' tomb—would toll in protest against Vatican endorsement of the declaration.[70]

It was here where AJC's Catholic contacts and experience in the corridors of world diplomacy proved crucial in providing counterpressures to Arab opposition. In May of 1964 an AJC delegation managed to obtain an audience with the new Pope Paul VI through the good offices of the head of Pro Deo University. The delegation consisted of AJC president Morris Abram, John Slawson, Zachariah Shuster, Phil Hoffman, Ralph Friedman, and Mrs. Leonard Sperry, widow of the former head of the Los Angeles chapter who was endowing a chair at the Pro Deo university in her husband's memory. The purpose of the visit, which achieved its goal, was "to pin the Pope down," as Morris Abram recalled. After the Pope gave them a grudging endorsement of the idea that Jews should not be held guilty of deicide, a visit to Secretary of State Dean Rusk—who had just been given AJC's highest award, the American Liberties Medallion, at that year's annual meeting—got the State Department on AJC's side, with promises that President Kennedy himself would make their views known to the U.S. ambassador to Italy. This visit was quickly followed by a grand tour of Latin America, papal endorsement in hand, to line up support for the declaration from Catholic leaders who would shortly be traveling to Rome for the next session of the Council. "We visited the Primate of Argentina," Abram recalled. "He was conservative as hell, but how was he going to disagree with the Pope? . . . We visited the Primate of Chile, the Primate of Peru, the Primate of Brazil, and we saw the presidents of every single one of these countries."[71]

Matters grew increasingly tense as the fourth and final session of the Council neared its opening in September 1965. In August the AJC received word through its European office of an authoritative report that a prelate who was "an intimate friend of Pope Paul VI" had met with him recently; at the meeting, the pope related the great pressures that had been brought to bear on him by Middle East leaders. The Pope, he reported, had stated to him clearly that the Vatican Council could not pass the Jewish decree in its present form because it would adversely affect the diplomatic and economic relations of the Church in the Middle East.[72] It happened that in the interests of world peace Pope Paul VI planned to make a visit to the United States and address the United Nations the first week in October. The visit provided an opportunity to warn the Pope of damage to his international standing if he gave in to these pressures. Jacob Blaustein was asked to intervene with his friend and fellow Baltimorean Lawrence Cardinal Shehan, who wielded strong influence as one of the presidents of the Vatican Council. "It is of the greatest importance," Rabbi Tanenbaum instructed Blaustein, "that the Cardinal organize a group that will call upon the Pope very shortly, and stress that it will be a catastrophe if he yields to naked political pressures. His moral standing as arbiter of the peace among nations will be profoundly compromised if he allows principle to be sacrificed to political expediency. If he compromises on the Declaration, his visit to the UN will be greeted with widespread resentment, and will become a diplomatic disaster in the powerful West."[73]

Blaustein asked for and immediately received an audience with Cardinal Shehan, shortly before the latter departed for Rome, and gave him that message to convey to the Pope. Blaustein spoke of the experience that he and AJC had in dealing with Arab threats, and offered to provide proof that these threats against Middle East Christians were unlikely to materialize:

I told the Cardinal [that] it is hoped the Pope will not take the Arabs too seriously and will realize that the Arabs have a record of bluffing and blustering on a number of issues and then backing away on every issue when strength was shown. I mentioned that this had been the case with my own experience—when the Arabs at the outset in 1952 expressed dire consequences to West Germany if it went through with the restitution and compensation for the victims of the Nazi persecution; and again recently when Germany exchanged diplomatic relations with Israel; also in the appointment of Arthur Goldberg as the U.S. Representative of the UN etc. His Eminence said that this was important information to bring to the notice of the Pope and he would make some notes of these instances. I then told him that I was having a documented report prepared on these instances of Arab smoke without fire—and he asked me to be sure to get it to him and gave me specific instructions as to how to send it so that it would be sure to come into his hands personally. It is imperative therefore that this report be prepared promptly and that I get several copies of it.[74]

Writing from Rome, Shehan later reported that he had held the requested audience with the Pope and, along with several of his fellow American prelates, had made it clear that they had no intention of returning to the United States without a version of *Nostra Aetate* "that they could live with as American Christians who attach great importance to their relationship with the Jewish community."[75] With this and other pressures, the Pope relented and the declaration was back on the agenda. (After the Council was over, the AJC presented plaques to each of the five American cardinals in acknowledgment of their role in making the passage of the Jewish declaration possible.) After a strong plea for its acceptance by Cardinal Bea, the Council finally voted on October 15 to approve the document by a vote of 2,221 to 88; the Pope formally promulgated it, along with four other Council documents, on October 28, 1965.[76]

The final declaration was not so clear or so strong as its supporters wished; it did not specifically mention the word "deicide," as earlier drafts had. Nevertheless, it marked a radical break with nineteen hundred years of Church history and offered much hope for the future. At AJC's anniversary celebrations in May 1966 Joseph Proskauer (by then approaching ninety), perhaps caught in the glow of the moment, stated of *Nostra Aetate* No. 4 that if the AJC had done nothing else in the sixty years of its history, "dayenu" (it would have been enough).[77] Much work still remained in improving and maintaining good Catholic-Jewish relations and actually implementing the declaration. The internal Jewish debate would continue. But the highest authorities of the Roman Catholic Church had taken a major step along a road from which it would be difficult ever to turn back.

Text of Final Declaration of *Nostra Aetate No. 4*

Voted Oct. 14–15, 1965 and promulgated on Oct. 28, 1965

As the sacred synod searches into the mystery of the Church, it remembers the bond that spiritually ties the people of the New Covenant to Abraham's stock.

Thus the Church of Christ acknowledges that, according to God's saving design, the beginnings of her faith and her election are found already among the Patriarchs, Moses and the prophets. She professes that all who believe in Christ—Abraham's sons according to faith are included in the same Patriarch's call, and likewise that the salvation of the Church is mysteriously foreshadowed by the chosen people's exodus from the land of bondage. The Church, therefore, cannot forget that she received the revelation of the Old Testament through the people with whom God in his inexpressible mercy concluded the Ancient Covenant. Nor can she forget that she draws sustenance from the root of that well-cultivated olive tree onto which have been grafted the wild shoots, the Gentiles. Indeed, the Church believes that by His cross Christ, Our Peace, reconciled Jews and Gentiles, making both one in Himself.

The Church keeps ever in mind the words of the Apostle about his kinsmen: "theirs is the sonship and the glory and the covenants and the law and the worship and the promises; theirs are the fathers and from them is the Christ according to the flesh" (Rom. 9:4–5), the Son of the Virgin Mary. She also recalls that the Apostles, the Church's mainstay and pillars, as well as most of the early disciples who proclaimed Christ's Gospel to the world, sprang from the Jewish people.

As Holy Scripture testifies, Jerusalem did not recognize the time of her visitation, nor did the Jews in large number, accept the Gospel; indeed not a few opposed its spreading. Nevertheless, God holds the Jews most dear for the sake of their Fathers; He does not repent of the gifts He makes or of the calls He issues—such is the witness of the Apostle. In company with the Prophets and the same Apostle, the Church awaits that day, known to God alone, on which all peoples will address the Lord in a single voice and "serve him shoulder to shoulder."

Since the spiritual patrimony common to Christians and Jews is thus so great, this sacred synod wants to foster and recommend that mutual understanding and respect which is the fruit, above all, of biblical and theological studies as well as of fraternal dialogues.

True, the Jewish authorities and those who followed their lead pressed for the death of Christ; still, what happened in His passion cannot be charged against all the Jews, without distinction, then alive, nor against the Jews of today. Although the Church is the new people of God, the Jews should not be presented as rejected or accursed by God, as if this followed from the Holy Scriptures. All should see to it, then, that in catechetical work or in the preaching of the word of God they do not teach anything that does not conform to the truth of the Gospel and the spirit of Christ.

Furthermore, in her rejection of every persecution against any man, the Church, mindful of the patrimony she shares with the Jews and moved not by political reasons but by the Gospel's spiritual love, decries hatred, persecutions, displays of anti-Semitism, directed against Jews at any time and by anyone.

Besides, as the Church has always held and holds now, Christ underwent His passion and death freely, because of the sins of men and out of infinite love, in order that all may reach salvation. It is, therefore, the burden of the Church's preaching to proclaim the cross of Christ as the sign of God's all-embracing love and as the fountain from which every grace flows.

We cannot truly call on God, the Father of all, if we refuse to treat in a brotherly way any man, created as he is in the image of God. Man's relation to God the Father and his relation to men his brothers are so linked together that Scripture says: "He who does not love does not know God" (1 John 4:8).

No foundation therefore remains for any theory or practice that leads to discrimination between man and man or people and people, so far as their human dignity and the rights flowing from it are concerned.

The Church reproves, as foreign to the mind of Christ, any discrimination against men or harassment of them because of their race, color, condition of life, or religion. On the contrary, following in the footsteps of the holy Apostles Peter and Paul, this sacred synod ardently implores the Christian faithful to "maintain good fellowship among the nations" (1 Peter 2:12), and, if possible, to live for their part in peace with all men, so that they may truly be sons of the Father who is in heaven.

(Source: Vatican Archives)

5

Disaster and Deliverance

Jewish Identification and the Six-Day War

[1967–1968]

The months and years immediately following the promulgation of *Nostra Aetate* were a whirlwind of activity, with leaders throughout the Roman Catholic Church, especially those of the United States, acting to implement it when the ink on the declaration was barely dry. Even before the final vote the American hierarchy created a Subcommission on Catholic-Jewish Relations and AJC in March 1966 set to work creating new guidelines for relations with Jews.[1] Previous efforts at improving Catholic-Jewish relations had been piecemeal, varying from parish to parish and from publisher to publisher. Within a year of *Nostra Aetate*, however, as Rabbi Tanenbaum reported, the first guidelines went out to all forty-six million Catholics in the United States, specifying that proselytization of Jews must be carefully avoided and that all school texts, prayer books, and other materials must be examined to remove anything that depicted Judaism in a negative light.

The influence of the declaration was felt around the world, even in countries where Catholic leadership tended to be far more conservative than that in the United States. In the years immediately after the Council, Catholic textbooks in Belgium, Spain, Italy, and Latin America were either rewritten or removed from the curriculum. The Vatican II declaration also set in motion serious reformation of such phenomena as the annual Passion play at Oberammergau, Germany.[2] Villagers performed this pageant of the last days of Jesus every ten years as part of the fulfillment of a medieval vow made when Oberammergau was delivered from a plague. By 1950 the event was drawing hundreds of thousands of visitors and millions of dollars in revenue. But the Jewish characters' dress and makeup appeared to be taken straight from antisemitic propaganda: Jews were portrayed as despicable, bloodthirsty people, jealous and cruel, who willfully condemned and killed Jesus and accepted upon themselves God's curse for all time for having done so.[3] The AJC and Anti-Defamation League led mounting world protests condemning the pageant and requesting that the text be revised for future performances, and in 1968 the AJC was first invited to submit suggestions for possible changes. The process of negotiation and change went on for many years and it was not until the performance in 2000 that sufficient changes had been made to justify the claim that most of the innate antisemitism of the pageant had been removed. Without the papal authority of the Vatican II declaration, however, it is doubtful the changes in this and similar Passion plays around the world would have taken place at all.

It was in the United States, as we have seen, where what some observers termed "ecumania" reached its height. Jewish laymen scrambled to become more knowledgeable about Judaism so that they could participate in the dialogue process, and scholars who could lecture or teach courses on Judaism were in high demand. Scores of institutes and workshops for Catholic educators and teacher trainers, where they learned to teach about Jews and Judaism in new ways, took place; and scores of Jewish-Christian dialogue programs for laymen were established in every place in the country. In his report on AJC's Interreligious Affairs Department in January 1967, Rabbi Marc Tanenbaum enumerated eighty-one projects in various stages of planning across the country under AJC's aegis alone. These included twenty-three interreligious institutes for laymen in twenty-one cities, eight teacher- and clergy-training projects in seven cities, thirteen Catholic-Jewish institutes at seminaries in twelve cities, and five textbook reform projects.[4]

Four months later, however, something occurred that brought these efforts on the part of Jews to a grinding halt. In the six weeks preceding and then the week during the six-day Arab-Israeli war of June 1967, Jews expected that their newfound Christian allies would come to their aid with enthusiastic declarations and offers of support while Arab forces armed with Soviet weapons were massing on the borders of Israel and threatening, in speeches repeated on TV and radio, to annihilate the Jewish population of the State of Israel. Instead, Christian organizations for the most part responded with lukewarm support, pleas for neutrality, pro-Arab resolutions, or outright silence.[5] According to the AJC, apparently a vital ingredient had been missing in Jewish efforts to educate Christians about Judaism: the centrality of Israel in the lives of American Jews. One reason they may not have communicated better on that point, staff and laymen concluded, was that until the Israeli nation was on the verge of extermination in May and June 1967, many American Jews themselves—and certainly the balance of AJC's membership—did not realize just how important Israel was to them.

Prelude to War

For almost two decades, from 1952 until 1970, the history of the Arab world was dominated by the charismatic Gamal Abdel Nasser, an Egyptian army officer who had fought against the British, sought collaboration with the Nazis, and experienced defeat as a soldier in the 1948 war against Israel.[6] With a group of fellow officers he overthrew the Egyptian government in the summer of 1952 and eventually became president and dictator of all Egypt. Nasser dreamed of uniting all the Arab countries under one authority with himself as the head; indeed, there were unsuccessful experiments during his rule to combine Egypt and Syria and then Iraq and Jordan into single countries.[7] Reasons for this pan-Arabism movement included (1) a desire to recapture the glories of the precolonial Arab world of ages past, and (2) the rationale that disunity had contributed to the utter humiliation of the Arab world's inability to defeat Israel.

Dreams of Arab unity proved elusive, however. The leaders of Iraq (which experienced a revolution and several coups and countercoups in these years), King Hussein of Jordan, and Tunisia were especially resistant to letting Nasserism dominate the region. In 1958 President Eisenhower set a precedent for U.S. intervention in the Middle East when he sent U.S. Marines to Lebanon in a successful attempt to stabilize the region temporarily and prevent an Iraq-like coup from happening there. In 1962 a tribal and civil war broke out in Yemen that found Egypt and Saudi Arabia backing opposing sides. In all inter-Arab rivalry, competing dynasties, fervent nationalism, vast disparities in wealth, and civil war ensured that in the decade between the end of the 1956 Suez War and the year before the outbreak of the 1967 war, the Arab world was embroiled in internecine conflicts that at times left Israel on the periphery though there was never a moment when she was not subject to terrorist attacks and ambushes along her borders.

The years from 1957 to 1966, despite one major recession, were in fact a period of relative economic, political, and diplomatic growth for Israel. New allies were gained when hundreds of students from Africa and Asia came to learn from the Jewish state and hundreds of Israeli advisers and technical experts were sent abroad to assist other new, developing countries. Israeli ships and ships carrying cargo from Israel were forbidden to sail through the Suez Canal—contrary to pledges Nasser had made to the United States and the United Nations after the 1956 war—but Israeli ships sailed the Gulf of Aqaba and the Red Sea freely. In the United States, the lack of a full-scale war against Israel left more energy to concentrate on the "continuity crisis" and the state of Jewish education in the early 1960s. Still, common hatred of Israel and a desire to eliminate it was the one thing that united the Arab nations; the sharper the rivalry between opposing Arab countries, the more keenly they competed in their expressions of inflammatory statements against Israel.

The consequences of this hatred went far beyond the borders of the countries directly involved. In the summer of 1955 the Middle East conflict moved beyond its geographical boundaries and became part of the global cold war struggle, thus leading to fears that World War III could erupt at any time in that area—fears nearly realized during the 1956 conflict. Wishing to strengthen his hand in the region, and rebuffed at the U.S. refusal to help him build the great Aswan Dam on the Nile River, Nasser in 1955 had turned to the Soviet Union as an ally. The Soviets saw the strategic value of the Middle East in its role as supplier of the majority of the world's oil, and Nasser's ambitions were their point of entry. Economic and military aid flowed in: Soviet advisers offered to train Egyptian troops both in Egypt itself and in the Soviet Union's own military academies. Syria and Iraq also became clients of Soviet largesse. The United States countered with attempts of its own to woo Egypt from Russia's embrace with food and economic aid (which in actuality allowed Nasser to use even more of his national budget to buy weapons) and to form alliances of its own with friendly Middle Eastern countries such as Pakistan, Iran, and Turkey—though not, at first, with Israel. Egypt replied with periodic barrages of anti-American, anti-Israel, and anti-Jewish propaganda, accusing the U.S. presidency of being in the pay of the Jews and the Zionists of being the true rulers of America.

Seeing the quantitative and qualitative superiority of Soviet arms that these Arab nations were enjoying, AJC leaders in this period voiced concerns either that Nasser would soon be in a position to launch another anti-Israel war or that the Israelis themselves would have to launch a preemptive strike before it was too late. "Why should Israel be waiting longer until the Arab countries will get stronger? Egypt is proclaiming every day that it wants to destroy Israel and throw out the Jews," reported Maximo Yagupsky from AJC's office in Israel in 1963.[8] It did no good to rely on promises, as Ben-Gurion received from American presidents, that U.S. help would be forthcoming as long as Israel herself did not provoke the attack. It took five minutes to fly by jet from Cairo to Tel Aviv and outside help might not come in time. AJC leaders and Jacob Blaustein in a private capacity spent much time and energy during this period on consultation and communication with the State Department, the president, and other officials advocating against further "appeasement" of Nasser and warning that the United States should sell weapons to Israel so that the balance of power could be maintained.[9] Irving Engel stressed the matter in a private meeting with Kennedy in 1962. Finally, later that year President Kennedy approved the sale to Israel of Hawk ground-to-air defensive missiles. Offensive arms were forthcoming during the administration of Lyndon Johnson, and by the Nixon administration the United States had become the major arms supplier of Israel.

The arming of Egypt through the 1960s continued, aided not only by the Soviets but by hundreds of German scientists working to perfect Egyptian rockets. In 1964 the Arab League authorized the founding of the Palestine Liberation Organization (PLO), at first under the leadership of Ahmed Shukairy, and began arming Palestinian refugees for the goal of attacks against Israel; the hope persisted that through armed conflict they might reverse the effects of the 1948 war. Another organization that conducted attacks against Israel was Fatah (Arab Liberation Movement), sponsored by Syria and and formed from Palestinian refugee recruits. Syria carried out a constant barrage against kibbutzim and villages in northern Israel down from the Golan Heights—to the point that trips to the bomb shelter were common and tractors were fitted with armored plating. Syria, Lebanon, and Jordan also cooperated in efforts to divert the sources of the Jordan River and let the flow go to waste, thereby cutting off Israel's main supply of water. In May 1967, for example, King Hussein of Jordan laid the foundation stone for a planned $32 million dam on the Yarmuk River, the Jordan's principal tributary; in his speech, he urged the Arab states to bury their differences and cooperate "to eliminate the Zionist threat."[10] Israel retaliated by shelling and bombing the engineering installations, tractors, bulldozers, and other construction equipment to prevent these plans from being carried out.

The Six-Day War, June 5–10, 1967

The immediate impetus for war came in May 1967 when, after months of rising tensions, Nasser demanded the removal of the United Nations Emergency Force, a 3,400-man entity that had helped keep the peace along the Egypt-Syrian border since 1957. As the U.N. peacekeepers evacuated without a backward glance Egyptian troops began massing along the border. On May 23 Nasser announced a blockade of the Strait of Tiran, the waterway leading out to the Gulf of Aqaba and the Red Sea that was Israel's lifeline to Africa and Asia. The strait was guarded at Sharm es-Sheikh, an old Egyptian fortress. "The Strait of Tiran is part of our territorial waters," Nasser announced. "No Israeli ship will ever navigate it again."[11]

As the AJC convened for its annual meeting on May 18–21, 1967, the U.N. Security Council was debating Arab terrorist raids and armed clashes along the Syrian and Jordanian frontier, to no conclusion. The council voted to adjourn on June 3. Abba Eban, at the behest of Israeli Prime Minister Levi Eshkol, was making the diplomatic rounds of the world's capitals, seeking aid. All he received were promises of help as long as Israel did not shoot first. Vague promises from Great Britain and the United States that an international maritime flotilla would run the blockade on Israel's behalf evaporated (when conflict did erupt, the State Department declared its neutrality). Israel's apparent helplessness only fed their enemies' appetite for the one final conflict that would erase the humiliation of 1948. "The problem presently before the Arab countries," Nasser declared on May 25 before the Egyptian parliament, "is not whether the port of Eilat should be blockaded or how to blockade it—but how totally to exterminate the State of Israel for all time."[12]

As the crisis deepened, AJC's leadership sent a strongly worded statement and telegrams to President Lyndon Johnson and Secretary of State Dean Rusk, calling on the United States to issue "an immediate and unequivocal re-affirmation of the fundamental United States commitment to Israel." Jacob Blaustein on his own sent a telegram to the president urging him to state "publicly and privately" to the Arab states and the Soviet Union that if no ac-tion were forthcoming from the U.N., the United States would "act on its own to prevent aggression"; he followed this with two days of meetings with officials in Washington.[13] Meanwhile the vise tightened around Israel, with the Arab media openly making bloodthirsty speeches and threatening to kill all the Jewish population of Israel (which only recently had passed the two million mark). On the day the war broke out, on June 5, 1967, the full forces of Egypt, Syria, Jordan, Iraq, the Palestine Liberation Organization, and Fatah allied against Israel; troops and support were promised by Lebanon, Saudi Arabia, Algeria, Kuwait, Yemen, Morocco, and the Sudan. On her borders, Is-raeli forces were outnumbered by Arab forces three to one.[14]

At that point, Israel had been mobilized for war for three weeks and normal life was at a standstill. Families cemented the windows of their children's rooms to protect them against enemy fire. Public parks were designated as emergency cemeteries. Mimeographed pamphlets on corpse identification and burial instructions were distributed by the civil defense offices. Nylon sheeting was stockpiled for the wrapping of bodies and blank death certifi-cates were prepared.[15] Three years earlier new chief of staff Yitzhak Rabin had testified before the Knesset security and foreign affairs committee that Israel's limited resources made her unable to sustain a war for more than a few days. Also, given the close proximity and overwhelming numerical and military superiority of the enemy, the country could not afford to stay purely on the defensive. In the case of a major confrontation, only a preemptive strike could possibly save the country. Israel would have to wait until the very last mo-ment, however, to avoid alienating world opinion.[16] This meant that forever after, the Israelis would be accused of having fired the first shot in the 1967 war. After a cabinet meeting that ran for seven hours through the night of June 3–4, Israel's leaders voted to go to war before Egypt and Syria attacked first. The next day, Israeli jets, flying close to the ground to evade radar, in the space of two hours bombed almost the entire Egyptian air force while it was still on the ground.

Victory after victory followed. After five more days of fighting, ended by a cease-fire resolution issued by a suddenly active U.N., Israeli forces had demolished the enemy on all three fronts and had more than tripled its size through the capture of the entire Sinai, the Golan Heights, the Gaza Strip, the entire West Bank of the Jordan River and, most important of all, the Old City of Jerusalem, from which Jews had been expelled in 1948. A quarter of Israel's casualties on the Jordanian front had died in the battle for the Old City; General Moshe Dayan had ordered no artillery or air support to avoid damaging the holy places, which reduced soldiers in many instances to hand-to-hand combat. War with Jordan and capture of her territories had not even been part of Israel's war plan at the beginning. On the first day of the war, Israeli Prime Minister Levi Eshkol had sent an urgent message to King Hussein of Jordan that Israel would not attack him if he did not enter the hostilities. The Jordanians opened fire anyway, beginning by shelling West Jerusalem. Every town and city in Israel along the armistice line was in the sights of the Jordanian army. The Israelis had to counterattack. "We have unified Jerusalem, the divided capital of Israel," announced Defense Minister General Moshe Dayan at a visit to the Old City on June 7. "We have returned to the holiest of our Holy Places, never to depart from it again."[17]

The threat had been so grave and the victory so complete that the religiously minded could easily see the Six-Day War as a case of divine providence and a possible harbinger of the messianic era. Indeed, to Israelis and Jews around the world, the victory, following the traumatic weeks of worry, appeared as a miraculous deliverance. And no less so to the leaders of the AJC: John Slawson recalled the first day of the war, when all the top officers gathered for a meeting to figure out what they could do to prevent Israel's destruction. "It was almost a foregone conclusion that the combined forces of Egypt, Jordan and Syria would penetrate and be able to destroy Israel" he remembered. "What could we do?"[18] Many Jews, including members of AJC formerly sympathetic to the American Council for Judaism position, were frightened at the specter of Israel's plight. AJC president Morris Abram recalled that "there appeared in the halls of the American Jewish Committee Americans of Jewish ancestry so totally assimilated as to have changed the actual pronunciation of their names." One of these was Ambassador Lewis Strauss (he pronounced his own name as "Straws") who joined the high-level meeting. They discussed whether they should ask the American government to send ships through the Mediterranean, and thus show its strength. Former AJC president Irving Engel recalled that all during the tense hours of that meeting, there was no news from Israel over the television and radio, only announcements from Egypt of the tremendous victories the Arab forces were achieving. He described the scene that day:

It was finally decided that we would try to have a private conference with President Johnson to discuss the situation and urge that something be done to see that Israel was protected. The best contact for that purpose seemed to be Eugene Rostow, who was then Assistant Secretary of State but previously had been Dean of the Yale Law School and in that capacity I had gotten to know him quite well. [Engel was an alumnus of Yale Law School] So I called him and explained the situation. I said we didn't want any publicity; we would come in by the back door, or whatever way he wanted, but if we could just have a little of the president's time we would appreciate it. Rostow said he would see what he could do and call me back. Well, I didn't hear from him. That evening I had a dinner party here, I think sixteen people and they were all greatly concerned . . . here in this room where we could see the television and still the news was all coming out of an Arab victory and nothing from Israel. . . . While we were at dinner the telephone rang and there were two calls in quick succession. One was from David Ginsberg, who was the Counselor to the Israeli Embassy in Washington, and he told us that we had no reason for further concern; there was no reason to trouble the president, because Israel had achieved a great victory. And a little while later, Joseph Califano, who was one of the special assistants to President Johnson, called up and I think his exact words were "Israel has won the greatest victory in the shortest campaign in all history." And again, it wasn't necessary for us to come down.[19]

The sense of relief was so intense that Engel and all the guests at dinner never forgot the moment those phone calls came. Both they and the American Jewish public in general would never have believed that danger to Israel could so dominate their thoughts and emotions. As AJC research director Lucy Dawidowicz described it in her report on the matter, American Jews surprised even themselves with their intense response to the war. "American Jews were sleepless," she wrote. "The volume of transistor radios on New York streets rattling off news reports drowned out the city's habitual noises. Strangers asked each other if there was news. Day and night people sat before their TV sets watching the emergency sessions of the UN Security Council, whose protocol became familiar and comic, but whose impotence was exasperating, even agonizing. American Jews with relatives and friends in Israel clogged the telephone lines with long distance calls." Jews congregated, going to meetings and going to synagogue in numbers that exceeded attendance on Yom Kippur—first to pray for Israel's survival and afterward to give thanks. Some went to Israel themselves. College men and women jammed Hillel houses to fill out applications for volunteer work in Israel; in all, more than seven thousand college students volunteered. Mount Sinai Hospital in New York sent medical equipment and pledged to pay the salaries of doctors for up to three months if they went to serve in Israel. At Yale, thirteen senior faculty from the medical school flew there.[20]

There were massive contributions of money, often in cash, with a desperation and religious fervor unmatched in American Jewish history, even during Israel's War of Independence in 1948. In less than a month, from the day Nasser ordered the U.N. troops to depart to the day the war ended, the United Jewish Appeal had raised more than one hundred million dollars; within weeks, it would raise up to four hundred million more. Campaign offices reported that their tabulations could not keep up with all the contributions pouring in, some of it from people who had never donated to the UJA in their lives. Banks hired scores of temporary employees to help the UJA catch up, and a major Cleveland Bank set aside a million dollars in loans for people who could not otherwise pay their pledges. In a Baltimore bank a UJA volunteer saw donors line up to liquidate their accounts; in some cases, they emptied the contents of their safe-deposit boxes directly into the hands of collection agents. Some contributors reportedly cashed in securities and life insurance policies. Children donated the contents of their coin boxes, and teenagers their bar and bat mitzvah money. Boy Scout troops and Jewish youth groups donated their treasuries. A small Jewish congregation in Oklahoma sold its synagogue and wired the proceeds to Tel Aviv. Throughout New York City, teenage volunteers with shopping bags collected money at subway and bus stops. Jewish schools canceled graduation parties and skipped the traditional cap and gown, donating the money saved to the Israel Emergency Fund.[21]

Marshall Sklare, in a follow-up study of "Lakeville" in the wake of the Six-Day War, wrote that respondents who contributed money saw themselves as having helped to ensure Israel's miraculous victory. He added, however, "The miracle is that our respondents can, even today, connect their own actions with an Israeli victory. If the winning of any war ever depends upon superior financial means, the Six Day War was not such a war. By the time the first public fundraising meetings could be convened, victory was a foregone conclusion. But sober businessmen long experienced in problems of manufacturing and transportation acted as if the money they contributed today would somehow miraculously be turned into the sinews of war tomorrow."[22] Lucy Dawidowicz suggested a more sober explanation for this activity: "Perhaps for many their contributions were an expiation for their indifference 25 years earlier."[23]

Perhaps of more immediate use was the wave of political activity and public assertiveness from American Jews on behalf of Israel, as pro-Israel rallies drawing tens of thousands of people proliferated and thousands of letters and telegrams flooded the White House, offices of elected officials, and the editorial desks of newspapers and magazines. In this the AJC joined to an extent never seen before. Reflecting the attitude of the "old" AJC, the earlier May 1967 annual meeting had been concluded by a statement from the Foreign Affairs and Israel Committees that they were "strongly opposed" to the organization of mass meetings or public demonstrations, and any telegrams to government officials should be "moderately worded." AJC President Morris Abram, however, who had been a declared anti-Zionist in his youth, could not remain immune to the sweep of enthusiasm. The tradition of caution and the fears of showing dual loyalty in public were thrown to the winds. When NCRAC and the Conference of Presidents announced a massive rally in solidarity with Israel for June 7 in Washington, D.C., Abram, without seeking approval from the board of governors, endorsed it immediately and urged AJC chapters to encourage their members to attend and provide the greatest possible turnout for the event. More than one hundred AJC members from twenty-four communities were there in Washington that day, and Morris Abram was a featured speaker.[24]

In the immediate aftermath of the war, AJC staff began to monitor the media and prepare quick responses to anti-Israel and antisemitic statements. National AJC called a meeting of high-level public relations professionals, including officers from Ruder and Finn, on July 6 to plan a campaign that would portray Israel's viewpoint to the world. Some laypeople would have preferred that the AJC keep its head much lower. For example, at the first full board meeting after the war on June 20, Alan Stroock, who had once thought of joining the American Council for Judaism, stood up and declared that perhaps the AJC was identifying itself too strongly with Israel and that a mood of caution and "reassessment" was in order. The world was calling Israel a "conqueror," he said, and "the fate of five million Jews in the United States is being relegated to the fate of two million Jews in Israel."[25] John Slawson replied, "We have a great stake in Israel; we were very important in its creation and we must now be concerned about its preservation." AJC's present task, he said, was to support Israel and help her achieve a lasting peace. There was no further debate, and AJC's board of governors, some albeit reluctantly, in effect endorsed everything that the staff leadership had done.[26]

On the issue of the newly conquered territories, AJC abandoned its former paternalistic attitude (which implied that it knew best what was good for Israel) and also showed a willingness to take a position contrary to that of the State Department. In 1956, an angered President Eisenhower threatened to block UJA funds as a way to punish Israel and American Jewry for a war conducted without his knowledge and approval, and he demanded that the Israelis withdraw from the territory they had conquered. AJC urged Secretary of State Dulles to remove the underlying causes of the conflict by insisting that the Arab states negotiate peace with Israel. Nonetheless, AJC told the Israelis to comply with Eisenhower's demand and then did their best to "patch up" relations with Washington. However, when on August 10, 1967, Eugene Rostow called in a delegation of AJC leaders to get them to exert pressure on Israel to compromise with Jordan on the status of Jerusalem, they refused. Only Israel could formulate policy on this issue, they replied. Moreover, a newly united Jerusalem under Jewish control was of such profound religious and historical significance that it would be a wasted effort to try to get Israel and the American Jewish community to accept a return to Jordanian control of the city.[27]

AJC further underlined its support of a united Jerusalem when it moved its Israel office there from Tel Aviv in October 1967, and approved the placement of a full-time professional to work in the office of Jerusalem Mayor Teddy Kollek. When the Israel office had been announced in the spring of 1961 one motive was to be on the scene to enforce the Blaustein–Ben-Gurion understanding. As mentioned earlier, its mission, according to the founding memo, was to "strengthen the link between the U.S. and Israel, interpret the realities of American Jewish life in Israel, and make available to Israel some of the lessons learned by the AJC during its more than half a century of activity in intergroup relations throughout the world." The office was also supposed to funnel to the AJC information on which its activities in Washington, D.C. and elsewhere would be based.

Under M. Bernard Resnikoff, who became director of the office in 1967 and stayed in that role until 1984, while the office remained true to its mission its activities expanded. It became more of a place where Americans and Israelis could get to know one another in an atmosphere of mutual respect, rather than a base for the AJC to teach Israelis.[28]

Previously Israel had ranked close to the bottom of the list on AJC's annual activity reports. The annual addresses of Slawson and AJC presidents did not include substantial discussions of Israel. AJC's program director had rejected an article on Israel for the front page of the September 1966 AJC newsletter, explaining, "I'm not clear as to what qualifies it as a lead article after a summer of Argentina, race riots, burgeoning conscious of Jewish identity, a Congress in session, and a growing right-wing extremism."[29] With the Six-Day War, however, Israel became a top priority. AJC expanded all its activities there and set the goal not only of bringing American and Israeli Jews closer but of introducing Israel to non-Jews by paying for trips to bring black leaders, educators, Christian clergy, and civil rights activists to Israel (Vernon Jordan was one of the early beneficiaries of a free trip to Israel, courtesy of the AJC). Previously only a handful of the top laypeople had visited Israel regularly; in 1968 AJC began an annual monthlong summer seminar in Israel for its staff members, in recognition of how important it had become to all their work; in 1979, it began a similar program for its lay members. The Jewish Communal Affairs Department called for members to study modern Hebrew, read Israeli literature, and invest in Israel.

Previously activities related to Israel had constituted a minimal segment of AJC's annual budget; by the mid-1970s, the proportion of Israel-related expenses rose to between 25 and 50 percent.[30] After the 1973 Yom Kippur War, Norman Podhoretz, writing for the *New York Times Magazine*, noted that while the AJC still tried to pursue an independent line rather than automatically back Israeli government policy, "the American Jewish Committee today is at least as fervent in its devotion to Israel as the Zionist organizations themselves."[31]

The Christian Response

The fervor with which American Jews spoke and acted in regard to safeguarding Israel, however, was nowhere near matched by the official church organizations with which AJC and others had been working for years. Dr. James W. Parkes, a Church of England clergyman and historian, told a meeting of Christian and Jewish scholars at the AJC that September: "the most monstrous recent example of how even latent antisemitism can affect judgment of Christian churches has been their silence during 1967 when the Arabs were threatening . . . to kill every Jew they could in Israel."[32] Until 1967, recalled AJC President Philip E. Hoffman in 1970, the dialogue between Christians and Jews had been "one of the most promising developments in the ecumenical trend." With the trauma of the Six-Day War in 1967, he observed, "as many American Jews recognized—some for the first time—the depth of their ties with the fledgling state, the indifference of many Christian leaders to the question of Israel's survival was a source of deep, and in some instances, bitter disappointment."[33] Indeed, the overall mood in the Jewish communal world regarding organized Christianity during and after the Six-Day War was one of abandonment and betrayal.[34]

Among American Christians in general, there was no lack of support. Rabbi Tanenbaum noted that public opinion polls showed that more than 80 percent of the American people supported Israel's position, and prominent leaders had spoken out in Israel's favor. [35] Surveys showed that Israel enjoyed a favorable press during the war, with much of the media taking an anti-Soviet, anti-Arab, pro-Israel position. Marshall Sklare noted in his "Lakeville" study that American Jews felt that they had achieved new respect in the eyes of Gentiles because of the Israeli victory. "You Hebes really taught those guys a lesson," said one non-Jewish business associate to a Temple officer.[36] Jokes abounded about sending General Moshe Dayan to help the United States with its war in Vietnam. The Unitarians in Lakeville, whose ranks included many ex-Jews and many intermarried couples, were unusually helpful; the mood in that church, according to a local rabbi, was that "we Jewish Unitarians do our part."[37]

When AJC and other Jewish organizations sought statements or petitions on behalf of Israel, however, key Christian bodies—the National Conference of Catholic Bishops (whose members had voted in favor of *Nostrae Aetate*), the National Council of Churches, whose constituents included the main Protestant denominations (including the Episcopalians, the Presbyterians, the Methodists, and the Quakers), and the World Council of Churches—were ambivalent, silent, or blatantly anti-Israel during and after the struggle. Their reasons included missionary interests in Arab countries, little appreciation for Jewish nationalism, and deep unease at the idea of Jews controlling all of the Holy City of Jerusalem, the site of Jesus' Passion and crucifixion. Here, deep theological divisions that had been papered over but never solved played a role in some Christian reactions. As Rabbi Irving Greenberg pointed out in an evaluation a year after the war, the State of Israel itself had been a fundamental challenge to the Christian understanding of Jews. Once upon a time, starting some forty years after the crucifixion of Jesus of Nazareth the Judeans had lost their temple and their sovereignty in two bloody wars against the Roman Empire that took the lives of up to a million people and sent hundreds of thousands of survivors into slavery. "It is a fact that the Christian covenant was based upon the assumption of the disappearance of the Jewish people," Greenberg stated at an AJC gathering. "Exile of the Jews was interpreted as the punishment for the rejection of Jesus. . . . It is this issue and not just the presence of Arab Christians which has influenced the Vatican's refusal to formally recognize the State of Israel. The great challenge of June 1967 is that it will force Christianity to confront its own conscience, to discover whether or not it can define its own validity not at the expense of Judaism."[38]

At the time of the war, the National Council of Churches adopted a resolution supporting U.N. peacekeeping troops and calling on President Johnson to maintain "even-handed neutrality." The National Conference of Catholic Bishops issued a statement on June 8 opposing the war in general, and designating June 11 as a day of prayer for peace. In July the NCC Executive Council met to consider the Middle East crisis and adopted a resolution that was blatantly anti-Israel.[39] A past president of the Union Theological Seminary, reacting to Jewish criticism of the Christian reaction, wrote in a letter to the *New York Times* on July 7, "All persons who seek to view the Middle East problem with honesty and objectivity stand aghast at Israel's onslaught, the most violent, ruthless and successful aggression since Hitler's blitzkrieg across Western Europe in the summer of 1940, aiming not at victory, but at annihilation—the very objective proclaimed by Nasser and its allies which had drawn support to Israel."[40] Both Jews and Christians were shocked at the comparison of the Israeli army to Nazis. In late June the Pope called for the internationalization of Jerusalem to ensure the safety of the holy sites and their access to all faiths; the NCC and the WCC also called for the internationalization of Jerusalem.

Jews took note that Christians had said nothing about Jordan's expulsion of the Jews from East Jerusalem after 1948, the destruction of more than fifty synagogues, the denial of Jewish access to their holy places for nineteen years, or the desecrations they found of the Jewish cemetery on the Mount of Olives when they were finally able to visit it again. A common excuse for not speaking up during threats to annihilate Israel was that this was a political issue and as ministers of the gospel they could not take a position. Yet these same people, pointed out Jacob Neusner of Brown University, had regularly solicited Jewish help on other issues such as Vietnam and race relations, "which are no less political."[41] Said one rabbi of the UAHC (Union of American Hebrew Congregations): "Christian leaders worried about Arab refugees . . . but not about clear pledges to exterminate and massacre the people of Israel. . . . [W]as the Christian conscience so ambivalent on the question of Jews that once again, a pall of silence would hang over the specter of Jewish suffering, until later, condolences and breast-beating and epitaphs and the croaks of guilty consciences would fill the air?"[42] The outcry became so intense that UAHC president Maurice Eisendrath had to counsel, "Let us not behave toward the church as if it had reinstituted the Inquisition. . . . Not every Christian whose conscience compels reservations regarding Israel's policies is an anti-Semite."[43]

In the wake of the empty response of Christian organizations, some rabbis called for a suspension of the Christian-Jewish dialogue. "American Jews are taking a new—and long—look at the practice of holding dialogues . . . with Christian churchmen," declared one UAHC spokesman. "Many Jews, already cool to what they considered unwarranted 'ecumania,' are now turning to us with 'I told you so' tone asking: where was the Christian community during the last few weeks when Israel in the cause of world peace so desperately needed visible support?"[44]

The overwhelming response of the AJC, however, was to take the opposite position: on the contrary, the lack of Christian support only indicated the need to continue the dialogue with greater intensity, this time stressing the things that they had come to know truly mattered: the State of Israel, the city of Jerusalem, the concept of Jewish peoplehood, and the nature of Jewish identity. The targets were the national church organizations, the general public, and—last but not least—their own membership. For the second time in six years, a major impetus to changes in AJC's internal policy was confrontation with the Christian world. "We need to enhance, not abandon, the dialogue process in which we pioneered," stated Philip E. Hoffman, at the time chairman of AJC's Executive Board. Rabbi Tanenbaum called on AJC and other concerned Jewish organizations to "step up" both the interreligious dialogue and internal Jewish education "to create understanding with respect to the concept of Jewish peoplehood and the role of Israel and religion in Judaism."[45] Almost overnight, the phrase "Jewish peoplehood," words that would have been shunned by AJC in earlier years, found their way into the organization's every public and private pronouncement. The job of interpreting Israel to the mainline churches, which were becoming the target of virulent anti-Israel and antisemitic propaganda, would become an ongoing concern. In the meantime, the AJC as a whole saw a need to educate and Judaize itself for the sake of their own people and to be better able to educate others.

New Leadership

Along with Rabbi Tanenbaum the major spokesman for change within the agency itself was Bertram H. Gold, the new executive director who took over from a retiring John Slawson immediately after the Six-Day War with a specific mandate to bring the AJC into the American Jewish mainstream. "In 1966 the agency was far on the periphery of Jewish life," recalled one staff member who saw the change. Under Bert Gold, he said, "The AJC began to remember that its middle name was 'Jewish' and began to act that way." Bert Gold reportedly stopped the drift toward calling the agency the "Institute for Human Relations" and insisted on keeping the name "American Jewish Committee."[46] Revamping the Interreligious Affairs programming to include more emphasis on Israel and Jewish peoplehood was a top priority. "We need to do a much better job of interpreting to our Christian friends the concept of Jewish peoplehood and what this means to us," he said. "We need to give them a much better understanding of the central role Israel plays within Judaism and the very special role that Jerusalem has always played and will continue to play for us. . . . Formerly we made a conscious choice allowing Christians to view us as if we were another denomination in Christian terms. We chose to do this because it gave us parity with the Protestants and the Catholics. In this way we derived much greater strength than our numbers would warrant. Suddenly we realized that this parity has not had significance attached to it because it has been achieved at the expense of the Christian clergy neither understanding our attachment to Israel, nor comprehending the nature of the historical and cultural bonds which bind Jews together."[47]

Gold, who took office on August 1, 1967, was director of the Jewish Centers Association of Los Angeles when he was tapped for the position of John Slawson's successor. He had grown up in Toronto attending the Workmen's Circle school where Bundist ideology—a strong belief in Jewish nationalism and in the importance of Yiddish language and culture—had held sway. Having attended a non-Zionist socialist school, he observed ironically, "I must say I never thought then that when I was arguing against the need for a Jewish state that I would spend a good part of my professional life working on behalf of such a Jewish state."[48] Gold had been so well known in the Jewish communal world that as far back as 1953 John Slawson had sought him out in California as a possible staff addition to the New York office. At that time, however, he recalled, "I knew I would not feel comfortable" working for the American Jewish Committee, and he turned Slawson down. Fourteen years later things had changed enough for him to say yes.[49]

The hiring of Yehuda Rosenman as the new director of Jewish communal affairs was also indicative of an organizational change in attitude. Born in Poland after World War I, Rosenman had grown up in a traditionally Jewish, Zionist, and Hebrew-speaking home. He left Poland for a visit with relatives in the United States one week before World War II broke out; with the exception of one sister, who had immigrated to Israel two years earlier, he lost his entire family in the Holocaust. He obtained a degree in social work and worked in Baltimore for many years as the executive director of the Jewish community centers there, where he became known to the Blaustein family. He was just finishing a two-year stint working for the American Jewish Joint Distribution Committee in Geneva and Paris when Zachariah Shuster recommended him for the Jewish communal affairs position. As in the case of Bert Gold, he recalled that if he had been asked to join the Committee years earlier, he never would have accepted, "but then in 1967 I had no problem." He said in later years that the fact that he never changed his first name was the greatest contribution he ever made to the Committee. People would always ask him where the name came from and the resulting discussions were invariably educational for the inquiring party.

At one point Rosenman's name had been a serious issue to him. In an early interview with John Slawson, he offered to anglicize his first name, feeling self-conscious about his European birth and accented English and fearing that a "Yehuda" might not be appropriate in the halls of the American Jewish Committee. There was no need, Slawson answered him; the AJC had changed a great deal and needed to change more. "John Slawson became very Jewish in the last years of his stewardship of the AJC," Rosenman recalled, citing his many speeches and publications on Jewish identity, Jewish culture, and Jewishness generally. "After I came here I used to kibbitz with John and say, why the hell didn't you do it twenty years ago? You remind me of the man who before he dies, suddenly comes back to his religion."[50]

Like Bert Gold, Rosenman's specific purpose was to bring "more Jewish consciousness and more Jewish life" into the organization. This goal encountered some resistance, especially from some of the staff in other departments. Many were accustomed to working on antisemitism, intergroup relations, and the rights of all minorities; they lacked convictions or skills in the area of affirmative Jewish life per se. Moreover, they did not all believe that such activities were the business of the AJC. In previous years Jewish matters were thought to be the province of the synagogues, Jewish educational institutions, and Jewish community centers. The directors and staff of the Jewish Communal Affairs Department had frequently complained that their division was the "stepchild" of the organization, at best a "separate but equal" compartment that did not permeate the entire organization.

There were also misgivings on this new direction from the extended lay leadership. In that area, both Rosenman and Gold had a strong lay ally in the person of Maynard I. Wishner, a graduate of the University of Chicago Law School, who became the new head of the Jewish Communal Affairs Department and eventually president of the entire organization (1980–83). Wishner carefully shepherded a new resolution on "commitment to creative Jewish continuity" through the labyrinthine layers of AJC lay boards to make sure that all segments of the Committee were in agreement. Wishner himself symbolized the decline of the German Jews and the rise of the Eastern Europeans. Like Bert Gold, Wishner had gone to Yiddish schools as a boy and had even acted in the Yiddish theater, a legacy that equipped him with a measure of public charm and great skill at joke- and storytelling. In a visit to address an AJC gathering in 1968, Elie Wiesel was seated at the same table as Gold and Wishner and exclaimed with delight that here, at the Committee, he could speak "such beautiful Yiddish!" with the two of them.

The "Scope Committee"

Almost as soon as the Six-Day War was over, both John Slawson—who remained on for a time as director emeritus—and Bert Gold organized what came to be known internally as the "Scope Committee," a body with thirty-four staff representatives from all departments of the agency who were charged first with the task of orienting Gold, and then with determining what the scope and priorities of AJC activities should be in the years ahead. The Scope Committee was aided by a professional advisory board that Rosenman convened for the JCAD, made up of twelve prominent thinkers and academicians including Daniel J. Elazar, Rabbi Ben Zion Gold (director of the Harvard Hillel), Irving Greenberg, Jacob Neusner, Gerson D. Cohen, Leonard Fein, Paul Ritterband, Marshall Sklare, and AJC's own iconoclastic director of information services, Milton Himmelfarb. In a series of meetings through fall 1967 and early 1968, including two weekend retreats, the Scope Committee task forces produced a flurry of background papers and memoranda evaluating every aspect of AJC's workings and in almost all cases describing and carrying out specific ways to increase the "Jewish identity" of the organization. They called for AJC to sponsor more educational programs for members and their friends, to encourage AJC chapters to become more involved in local Jewish institutions, to initiate and support chairs and lectureships in Jewish studies at secular universities, to reach out to Jewish youth, to become more involved with Israel in myriad ways, and to become a "think tank" that would sponsor research of specific interest to the Jewish community. The JCAD professional advisory committee in its first meeting called for the outright "Judaization" of the AJC, saying it should become a "deliberately Jew-producing" organization.[51]

AJC's very survival, according to community services director and Scope Committee member Nathan Weisman, depended on a more active embrace of Judaism and Jewish values and joining the mainstream of American Jewish organizations. Jewishness was the only aspect that would motivate potential members to join AJC rather than some other organization. By that period, Weisman pointed out, American Jews and the best AJC staff, actual and potential, had ample opportunities to express their political idealism in numerous nonsectarian institutions and a multitude of new government organizations. Members were demanding and needed more Jewish educational content to remain motivated to stay, and recruiters had to seek out new members who were drawn to expressing themselves through a specifically Jewish organization. Strong support for Israel appeared to require a more united American Jewry. Also, in order to be more effective, AJC needed to have leaders from all segments of the American Jewish community within its ranks, including New York. For example, nearly half of American Jewry lived in New

York but only 15 percent of AJC's membership in 1967 came from there. "To influence Jewish public opinion, we require a constituency which has roots in every significant part of the community," Weisman wrote. "When it comes to getting things done with the government, the day of the 'court Jew' is long past. As never before, government asks whom you speak for, how large is your group, where do they live?"[52]

Since 1963 the AJC had already been stressing Jewish continuity and identity more, and it had already begun drawing closer to Israel: as already mentioned, it established an office there in 1962 and had it fully funded by AJC's regular budget in 1965. In these post–Six-Day War days, however, concerted effort to increase Jewish activity among the members met with even greater success. Yehuda Rosenman was pleased to report at the Scope Committee's second staff retreat in January 1968 the number of chapters that had "stepped up Jewish education and commitment." A chapter in California had spent a weekend at the Brandeis-Bardin Institute and enjoyed it so much that they planned to make it an annual event; the San Francisco chapter was sponsoring lectureships on Jewish studies at Berkeley; Boston was holding a regular discussion group on major Jewish philosophers, including Philo, Maimonides, and Martin Buber. One chapter had met with local Jewish schools to see if AJC input and materials could enrich the curriculum. Southwestern chapters, rather than concentrating solely on Christians, had begun holding interdenominational Jewish dialogues, with rabbis and member representatives from the Reform, Conservative, Orthodox, and Reconstructionist branches. Chapters were also sponsoring histories of their local communities and setting up oral history libraries. The crown of these efforts was the William E. Wiener Oral History Library in New York, with a mission to concentrate on American Jewish biography and areas of interest to the Committee, such as civil rights and fighting antisemitism.[53] By 1970 the JCAD had two Jewish educators on its staff along with three part-time consultants in three cities whose specific purpose was to educate members and to strengthen AJC's presence in the Jewish community.

Signs of deeper Jewish observance became apparent as well in the day-to-day activities of the organization. Leaving early for the Sabbath, taking two days off for the Jewish holidays, and asking for kosher food at official AJC functions became not only allowed but encouraged.[54] Previously the only concession to the "December dilemma" at AJC headquarters was holding a New Year's party every year instead of a Christmas party. Yet in 1967, when December 29 coincided with Chanukah, staff members asked for and received a candle-lighting ceremony and for someone with a guitar to sing Chanukah songs.[55] Rosenman felt comfortable suggesting the introduction of a one-hour study period before AJC board and chapter meetings. When race riots in Newark necessitated the moving of AJC's chapter office to a new location in New Jersey, the opening was marked by a ceremony in which a local rabbi in the presence of 150 members and guests conducted the traditional "dedication of the house" and affixed a mezuzah to the doorpost.[56] In the annual meeting program for May 23–26, 1968, the following notice appeared: "American Jewish Committee members and friends are cordially invited to attend Sabbath services at the synagogues listed below." The names of nine synagogues—Reform, Conservative, and Orthodox—followed, with the exact times of services for both Friday evening and Saturday morning. The "Oneg Shabbat Roundtable Discussions" on Saturday morning were preceded by a Sabbath study-discussion led by Dr. Abraham Aaroni, a professor of Hebrew at the Hebrew Union College. He presented an overview of the week's Torah portion (Leviticus 25:1–24) and spoke about the traditional Jewish outlook on the ownership of land and property, the preservation of natural resources, and the dignity of the land.

Young Jewish college students, including the children of AJC members, also became a priority in the late 1960s. Irving Greenberg described college as a "disaster area" for Jewish identity. "It has been said that the British Empire was lost and won on the playing fields of Eton," he wrote, in an article that was extensively discussed by the JCAD professional advisory committee. "The crown of Judaism and Jewishness will be won or lost on the campuses of America."[57] America's campuses, convulsed by protest, were filled with Jewish students and faculty who were militants and activists in the "New Left" (as opposed to the "Old Left," who had been communists and socialists in the 1930s) and saw their Judaism as spiritually and intellectually irrelevant. At the very least, Jewish youth everywhere were rebelling against middle-class values—and that included the synagogue. In an address entitled "Our Alienated Jewish Youth: Challenge for AJC," Dr. Alfred Jospe of the B'nai B'rith Hillel foundations contrasted the shallow and sometimes "grotesque" bar or bat mitzvah education that most American Jewish youth received with the intellectual richness of the university. Jewish youth in general and college youth in particular had been sadly neglected by the Jewish community, he insisted, and education and work with Jewish college students should be the top priority in Jewish communal programming and financing.[58]

AJC responded to this challenge with a national convention of Jewish college students at Tarrytown, New York, in November 1968; it was attended by thirty students from ten universities across the country.[59] Advisers called for every AJC chapter to underwrite the cost of sending at least one college student on a trip to Israel. Numerous JCAD youth-oriented activities included sponsoring a Hebrew House at Oberlin College, fostering the study of Hebrew on college campuses, and convening a colloquium of Orthodox Jewish scientists to emphasize how traditional Jewish observance and values could coexist with a contemporary "relevant" scientific and intellectual life.

Advisers in the post–Six-Day War period also recommended that AJC reassess its research focus. Research on such topics as war and peace or urban life or the roots of poverty would now be supported by the federal government and large foundations; AJC's contribution in those areas would be "a drop in the bucket," according to consultant Paul Ritterband of Columbia University. "Our mandate and concern is the welfare of the Jewish people and its physical and cultural continuity," he wrote. "AJC must apply the criterion of the possible utility of the research product to the Jewish people. This perhaps sounds reminiscent of the Elephant and the Jewish Problem syndrome, or 'is it good for the Jews?' In a sense this is precisely what is meant." In order to have research one must have researchers, and Ritterband cited a recent article by Seymour Martin Lipset that commented on the dearth of sociologists at that time willing to write about the Jewish community. Non-Jewish sociologists, Lipset observed, saw so many Jewish colleagues and did not feel themselves qualified to write on Jewish subject matter. Jewish sociologists, in turn, did not want to seem parochial, and so they conducted research on blacks. The end of the matter was that no one conducted research on Jews. Ritterband therefore recommended that AJC work to get more Jewish scholars "hooked" on Jewish research.[60]

From 1963 on, as a subject for research, intermarriage became and remained an important preoccupation. The first step was acknowledging that intermarriage was happening at all and realizing that some of AJC's own policies might have helped to bring it about. It had never occurred to them that so many Christians would be so eager to wed Jews. Addressing the Scope Committee on how developments in the community should affect "AJC program emphases," the director of the Community Services Department, Samuel Katz, noted that a fundamental change had taken place in the Christian world in terms of its own attitude toward Judaism and that this change was reflected in polls the AJC had taken on Christian attitudes toward intermarriage. There was a notable shift away from rejection and condemnation of marriage with a Jew toward a willingness to tolerate it. In other words, intermarriage was rising not only because more Jews were willing to tolerate the idea, but because more Christians who previously would have been appalled at the idea of marrying a Jew, were now willing to accept them as mates and in-laws.[61]

Rosenman elsewhere pointed out that previously AJC's policy for protecting Jews at home and abroad had followed two approaches, neither of them directly helpful for Jewish continuity: (1) the idea that security for Jews could be obtained by working for universal equality and justice, and (2) that Jewish equality could best be achieved by working to help Jews become fully integrated in American life. In the past, commitment to Jewish life had been taken for granted and AJC leaders assumed that in a free society American Jews would feel comfortable accepting and acting upon their religion. However, "present day trends in Jewish life do not bear out this assumption," he wrote. "The danger today is not lack of Jewish equality and opportunity, nor lack of integration, but rather the ability to continue to preserve and insure Jewish continuity. Unless the Jewish group survives there may no longer be a need for organizations to protect Jewish rights."[62] Milton Himmelfarb challenged outright AJC's long-standing work in Executive Suite and social discrimination programs. "Achievement in this area might be at odds with a desire to perpetuate Judaism," he advised. "We should possibly reevaluate this program to give it a lower priority than we did at first or not engage in it at all."[63]

Sociologist and AJC consultant Marshall Sklare was one who had long researched Jewish themes; his post–Six-Day War follow-up study on "Lakeville," a northern suburb of Chicago, provides a valuable portrait of American Jewish intermarriage circa 1968. Tellingly, the results were published in a condensed version in 1969 titled "Not Quite At Home"—in contrast to the "This is Our Home" series AJC's JCAD had published in the 1950s.[64] Sklare reported that every one of his respondents had more personal acquaintanceship with the phenomenon of intermarriage than a decade ago, when he had first started his studies of the community. "So commonplace is the phenomenon," he wrote, "that a respondent characterized the opening of a wedding invitation or announcement received from Jewish friends as 'the moment of truth.' Since he has found that in only fifty percent of the announcements he receives are both bride and groom Jewish, he and his wife have made a kind of game of predicting whether or not each new envelope contains the news of yet another intermarriage." Respondents felt that intermarriage was "in the air" and might strike at any time; their main concern was maintaining the child-parent bond. Even those who said they opposed intermarriage and had told their children they would not accept one said they would avoid estrangement should their child intermarry. One respondent whose own sister had been driven to psychiatric treatment over the intermarriage of her daughter vowed that she herself would react more "intelligently" if it happened to her, and she now had a Gentile son-in-law.

Lakeville's Jews did attempt to forestall out-marriage by first giving their children a "good" Jewish education to bar or bat Mitzvah (confirmation). Thus they afforded the child every opportunity to become "immune" to intermarriage. "If the serum was not effective," Sklare observed, "it is because the doctor failed. If Dr./Rabbi/Institution had been more competent or 'inspiring,' the result might have been different. In any case, the parent did his duty." Stage 2 consisted of what Sklare called the "unhappiness" argument: parental advice and discussion about intermarriage, warning that the marital relationship was already fraught with enough traps without introducing yet another source of disharmony. This argument, Sklare wrote, was familiar from a decade ago, but was now being repeated with "a growing sense of unreality . . . when probed, some respondents revealed that while they do not stress the fact with their children, they do know of happy intermarriages. While those who feel strongly about combating intermarriage may tell their children that most such marriages end up in the divorce courts, it is quite possible that in their own thinking they no longer are capable of believing that such marriages are doomed to failure." Another issue he discovered was the unanimous desires of Lakeville's Reform congregants to have a rabbi officiate at mixed-marriage ceremonies and their denunciation of the majority who still refused. Perhaps, Sklare reflected, by having a rabbi there parents could fantasize that a "normal" marriage was in fact taking place, that the marriage was similar to the parents' own and that the child was not really leaving the fold. One rabbi in an adjoining suburb was agreeable to officiating at intermarriages and was reportedly doing a "land-office business"; one respondent who had used his services remarked that this rabbi was accomplishing more for Jewish survival than any of his Lakeville colleagues. "We do not know, however, to what extent this man is considered a kind of rabbinical 'abortionist' either by his colleagues or those who utilize his services," Sklare observed. "In any case this particular rabbi's name seems so widely known that referrals appear unnecessary; the abundant life in Lakeville now includes the phenomenon of intermarriage with rabbinical sanction."[65]

In the decades to come AJC research studies would be among the chief sources for information about intermarriage among American Jews. The organization would be hobbled in taking any policy against it, however, because AJC's own board members were intermarrying, too. Milton Himmelfarb delivered a sharp rebuke about this when he advised at a "Scope" meeting that a primary principle applied to doctors should also apply to AJC: "Whatever else they do, they shouldn't spread the disease." "We give positions of honor and respect to men whose children are Christians," he accused, "or rather men who have deliberately consented to having their children brought up as Christians. These men may be admirable human beings from all other points of view, but from the point of view of an organization that professes to be concerned with the future of Judaism, they are not the right people to appoint to high office. An organization that wants to take itself seriously in these matters can't have it both ways. Either it is serious or it can appoint such people."[66]

Forces within the AJC calling for more positive Jewish programming were also tempered by concern from non-JCAD staff that the organization might abandon or lessen its long commitment to the goals of urban affairs, rights for the poor, civil rights—in particular the fight for equality of African Americans—and general social action. Bertram Gold noted that it was in these areas where the greatest ideological differences by far existed between staff members.[67] The Six-Day War and AJC's internal reorientation were in fact taking place against a backdrop of a divisive war in Vietnam, urban violence, a growing "Black Power" movement, white ethnic backlash, and white exclusion from the civil rights movement. All these strained AJC's commitment to a political liberalism that had become, parallel to support of Israel, part of the religious faith of non-Orthodox American Jewry.

Significantly, AJC as a whole reacted to these challenges with an attitude similar in many respects to that it had shown in the face of perceived Christian abandonment of Israel during the Six-Day War. The tendency was to accept guilt and blame upon the AJC itself and upon the entire American Jewish community for being insufficiently committed to the cause of true equality and to pledge to work even harder at this cause. Never before had it been more important to "implement the moral imperatives of Judaism on the American scene," in the words of one AJC Scope Committee member. Far from abandoning the struggle to improve life for African Americans, official AJC policy in the late 1960s and early 1970s was to expand these efforts and work even harder. Whatever more AJC did in the area of Jewish programming was an addition, not a replacement. They saw no discrepancy at all in both working for civil rights and being Jewish. In fact, whatever the frustrations, rather than giving up, AJC members as a whole were ready to double and redouble their efforts in pursuing liberal political programs. They considered those efforts the deepest expression of a Jewish identity.

6

The Civil Rights Movement and the Great Society

[1960–1970]

As we have seen, when the AJC pledged in 1947 to work for the rights of all minorities at its Executive Committee meeting in Chicago, and in the 1950s when it took a public stand on the burgeoning Civil Rights movement, the southern contingent did not accept it happily. According to Selma Hirsh, at the time assistant to John Slawson, executive vice president, the issue was debated "hot and heavily," with many of the southerners arguing against it. "They couldn't imagine that we would put our fate on the line with the fate of blacks," she recalled, "and at the time of the 1954 Supreme Court decision on desegregation in the schools, our southern chapters virtually seceded."[1] John Slawson recalled that AJC leaders in the North were accused of "sticking their long noses" where they had no business.[2] On the other hand, four of AJC's post–World War II presidents were from the South or border states, and they all led AJC in support of the movement. These were Joseph M. Proskauer (1943–49) from Mobile, Alabama; Jacob Blaustein (1949–54) from Baltimore, Maryland; Irving M. Engel (1954–59) from Montgomery, Alabama; and Herbert B. Ehrmann (1959–61) who had been born in Louisville, Kentucky. Later presidents would include Morris B. Abram (1964–68), who was born and raised in Georgia.

As long as he was active whenever anyone in the organization expressed doubts about AJC's possibly moving beyond the boundaries of its charter by fighting for the rights of all minorities, Irving Engel would always invoke "the mandate of 1947." He invoked it again as the South was torn over the desegregation of its public schools and Jews were blamed with siding with the northerners (see chapter 3). Two weeks after a year of violent antidesegregation attacks culminated in the bombing of Atlanta's oldest temple on October 12, 1958, he addressed a special meeting in New Orleans of AJC national officers and the southern chapters. There was no question in Engel's mind where a Jew should stand on desegregation. "The anti-Semite will attack the Jew whether he speaks or whether he is silent, whether he fights or whether he shrinks from battle," he declared, claiming that any Jew who "dared" remain indifferent to the issue of desegregation was denying the values and ideals that had made possible Jewish freedom in America.[3] Joseph Proskauer counseled courage and "serenity" in New Orleans. Southern delegates were shaking and had tears in their eyes, claiming that if AJC came out publicly in favor of school desegregation the White Citizens' Councils would put an end to them. "We took that position anyway," Selma Hirsh recalled, "and as it turned out, they survived."[4]

When the civil rights movement in the South had entered a new, activist phase, AJC president A. M. Sonnabend (1962–64) addressed internal critics early in 1964 about the organization's activities in the field of civil rights. "The question people ask me is—why is the AJC so deeply involved in this race crisis?" he asked. "Why should we be concerned with the Negro problem? What business is it of ours? The answer is simple and emphatic. The AJC is committed to the advancement of human rights for all people in this country and throughout the world. . . . we will use all of our energies and all of our resources to safeguard the sanctity of the human being and to fight against any force which violates it. . . . Our responsibility to the Negro is really no more or less than our responsibility to ourselves."[5] Later that year Philip Hoffman, then chair of the domestic affairs committee, tried to allay the fears of members who complained that civil rights and the War on Poverty were possibly becoming the "only thrust" of AJC. He noted that their ecumenical, Executive Suite, and entire overseas programs were solely Jewish in their impact and purpose and had "nothing to do with the Negro problem." However, he continued, "Not that we ever can, have, will or intend to ignore civil rights or the Negro question. It is without any shadow of a doubt the burning question of the day. It is basic to everything we do, for if we can't achieve full equality for all Americans, it goes without saying that we can't achieve welfare and safety for the Jews."[6]

With great fanfare, AJC awarded its highest honor, the American Liberties Medallion, to those in the forefront of the civil rights struggle: to Thurgood Marshall, the attorney and later Supreme Court justice who argued *Brown v. Board of Education*, in 1962, and to Martin Luther King Jr. in 1965, one year after he had been awarded the Nobel Peace Prize. In introducing him, Joseph Proskauer invoked the Hebrew Bible: "He is a modern Moses and the modern Pharaohs must give way." In 1966, the award was given and accepted by President Johnson himself at the annual meeting in Washington, D.C., and the program also included a special tribute to Chief Justice Earl Warren. A few weeks after King's assassination in 1968, AJC invited the Reverend Martin Luther King Sr. to address a dinner in honor of Morris B. Abram, who was shortly departing as AJC's president to serve as president of Brandeis University. "I don't know many who could sit where you are sitting," the father said to Abram and the assembled crowd. "We felt your support. You honored my son here and I want to thank you. If everyone had done as Morris Abram and this organization did Martin Luther King, Jr. would be living tonight."[7]

Morris Abram of Georgia had direct knowledge of the evils of segregation and spoke most fervently for the AJC as a whole, including its southern contingent, to wage an all-out battle against it. He recalled that before the celebrated "Freedom Summer" in the small town where he grew up, where half the population was not white, blacks were barred from all places of public accommodation including parks, playing fields, and the public library. There were separate schools. There were separate taxicabs for whites and blacks. When blacks felt like attending a movie at the local theater they had to enter through the back door and sit up in the balcony. In the county courthouse there were separate seats and washrooms, and no black person had ever sat on a jury. Almost 90 percent of the blacks were not registered to vote.[8] Attorney General Robert F. Kennedy, in addressing an AJC gathering, described how poll taxes and literacy tests kept even those registered from voting. Puerto Ricans in New York who knew only Spanish were disqualified. In the 1960s the Department of Justice had hundreds of cases in its files of literacy tests being enforced so as to disqualify national grant winners, college professors, schoolteachers, and ministers, while whites with a second- or third-grade education were permitted in.[9] Most loathsome were the lynch mobs that regularly did black men to death in the most brutal possible ways for real or imagined violations of "Jim Crow etiquette." The U.S. Civil Rights Commission counted 2,595 lynchings of blacks in southern states between 1882 and 1959. Not one resulted in a white man's conviction.[10]

There were international concerns as well. At the time, civil rights was also a major front in the cold war against the Soviet Union. AJC leaders constantly justified their actions in light of the need to defeat communism and defend U.S. leadership. This was a world in which dozens of newly independent, "non-aligned" developing countries in Africa and Asia were overcoming their former colonial status and joining the U.N. General Assembly. Jewish leaders constantly reminded one another that two-thirds of the world was not white. In the twenty years after the end of World War II, the number of independent nations in the U.N. went from 51 to 114. In 1960 alone nineteen new nations were admitted to the U.N., and eighteen of them were in Africa. In a new era of mass communications, when American blacks and civil rights demonstrators were spat upon and attacked with billy clubs, tear gas, police dogs, fire hoses, and electric cattle prods, the pictures and stories were beamed not just into the living rooms of shocked Americans but around the world. They provided ample fodder for Soviet anti-American propaganda. Of particular resonance had been the September 1957 attempt to integrate Central High School in Little Rock, Arkansas. With hundreds of media outlets watching, a small group of black teenagers attempting to enter the school were met with a mob of hundreds of whites that pelted them and the reporters with rocks and bottles. The next day Arkansas Governor Orville Faubus called out the National Guard to prevent their entrance. Federal troops had to be sent by President Eisenhower to finally escort the teenagers into the school; angry whites had to be prevented from attacking them at the point of rifles and bayonets.

"On the world stage we have been the most prominent champions of democratic and humanitarian values," declared Irving Engel at the same New Orleans meeting after the 1958 synagogue bombing. "But in our own land we have continued to deny the most elementary of human rights to large segments of our own population. . . . Every foreign demagogue, every foreign dictator, and every would-be dictator in the world today is making the most of this defect. . . . If this link were recognized then acts of deliberate defiance of the Supreme Court's decision would be properly appraised as acts of subversion and sabotage as dangerous as any our country has ever sustained."[11] In addressing the AJC in 1966, then U.S. representative to the U.N. and former Supreme Court justice Arthur J. Goldberg declared, "The better we do in civil liberties at home, the more persuasively our voice speaks in the councils of the world." The name of Earl Warren, he said, "is a household name in Asia and Africa" and the message of *Brown v. Board of Education* "has hurdled the barriers that separate us from Moscow and Peking."[12]

The AJC worked nationally and locally to advance civil rights through the traditional means of education, research, negotiation, legislation, and finally litigation. The Anti-Defamation League and the American Jewish Congress also worked ceaselessly at these efforts, although the style of the Congress, as always, was to stress public demonstrations and litigation more. AJC leaders testified before both House and Senate committees on behalf of proposals that eventually resulted in the passage of the Civil Rights Act of 1957. This was the first such legislation passed in the United States since the end of Reconstruction. The act established a bipartisan commission on civil rights appointed by the president with power to investigate violations of voting rights and a committee to ensure that nondiscriminatory policies would be followed in the allocation of federal contracts. Locally, chapters lobbied for antidiscrimination bills in state and municipal bodies. The New York chapter was especially active in promoting passage of a state law prohibiting racial or ethnic discrimination in the sale of rental or private housing. When Governor Nelson Rockefeller signed the bill in 1961, it was heralded as the first law of its kind in the United States; indeed, the *American Jewish Year Book* noted that year that more state civil rights laws were enacted in the United States from 1960 to 1961 than in any similar period in American history.[13] What the country still lacked, however, was a comprehensive civil rights act that would make racial discrimination a crime on the federal level.

School Desegregation in the North

AJC in particular took desegregation of public schools as a goal. In 1954 the Supreme Court ordered such desegregation to proceed "with all deliberate speed," and not only south of the Mason-Dixon Line.[14] In 1957 AJC's research department released one of the first statistical surveys of the subject, showing how residential patterns, and not Jim Crow, were causing racially segregated schools in the North as well as the South. The AJC affirmed that segregation had to be opposed regardless of the cause. In 1958, after months of discussions with the chapters on how to proceed, the national organization released the statement "A Proposed Guide for Community Activity on Integration in Northern School Systems." The statement was thereafter expanded into a community how-to guide and published in 1962. One of the main purposes of the public schools, it said, was to educate for civic competence; "that means the ability to understand and work with diverse peoples. . . . The public schools, therefore, must impart this ability by having a heterogeneous student body."[15]

Throughout the late 1950s and 1960s several AJC northern chapters, including Westchester and New York City, conducted "human relations" training for teachers and others on how to deal with their new students, and worked to desegregate their local schools. The means they endorsed included district rezoning, strategic location of new schools, open enrollment, pairing schools in adjacent districts racially to balance the school population, and (when necessary) transport of white and black children outside their neighborhoods. Results were slow in coming. Local parents, including many Jews, frequently objected to these measures, and both northern and southern school districts proved themselves adept at avoiding compliance. In 1964, the tenth anniversary of the *Brown* decision, AJC's Edwin J. Lukas, director of the national affairs department, observed, "fewer than ten percent of the children eligible for appropriate school transfer have been so accommodated." Furthermore, the spirit of resistance to it "[created] a half-dozen new suits per month" that embroiled human relations agencies in litigation and taxed their manpower and budget resources.[16]

A New Activism: "I Have a Dream"

By 1960 the slow rate of change had caused the emphasis of the American civil rights movement to shift from legislation and litigation to protests in the street. "Sit-ins" were the first tactic. Groups of black college students would sit at the whites-only lunch counters of southern drugstores and department stores, requesting to be served. The sit-ins began in Greensboro, North Carolina, and spread swiftly to seven states. Physical clashes, beatings, and riots erupted when the protesters refused to leave. In May 1961 the "Freedom Rides" began. Black and white demonstrators from across the country converged in Washington, D.C., and began traveling on special buses through the South, demanding service at segregated lunchrooms, shoeshine stands, barbershops, and restrooms. Opponents rioted, firing shotguns at the buses and slashing the tires. One bus was firebombed.

To exert pressure on Congress to pass a more comprehensive civil rights bill, more than two hundred thousand Americans—including two hundred rabbis of all denominations—participated in the August 28, 1963, March on Washington for Jobs and Freedom, seen by many as one of the most memorable events of the twentieth century. The year happened to correspond with the one-hundredth anniversary of President Abraham Lincoln's Emancipation Proclamation. Dr. Martin Luther King Jr.'s "I Have a Dream" speech on that day, which emphasized the ideal of full integration, marked the apotheosis of the black-white and black-Jewish alliances. Rabbi Joachim Prinz, a former refugee of the Nazis, who was one of the organizers of the march and who served from 1958 to 1966 as the president of the American Jewish Congress while holding a Newark pulpit, immediately preceded King. His speech evoked the connections that many American Jews were drawing between the struggle for civil rights and the Holocaust. "When I lived under the Hitler regime, I learned many things," he told the crowd. "The most urgent, the most disgraceful problem is silence. A great people had become a nation of silent onlookers. They remained silent in the face of hatred, brutality, and murder. America must not become a nation of onlookers. It must not be silent. Not merely black America, but all of America. It must speak up and act, from the president on down to the humblest of us, and not for the sake of the Negro, but for the sake of America."[17]

A few months after the march, the "Mississippi Freedom Summer" was announced by four organizations, all except the last with a sizable proportion of Jewish members and supporters: SNCC (the Student Non-Violent Coordinating Committee; pronounced "snick"), CORE (Congress for Racial Equality), the NAACP, and the Southern Christian Leadership Conference (SCLC), which was headed by King. The goals during that summer of 1964 were desegregation and massive voter registration. AJC's director of research and information Milton Himmelfarb, making the point of how much a thirst for social justice was part of the Jewish heritage, estimated that young Jews made up two-thirds of the white freedom riders and up to one-half of the Mississippi summer volunteers (he also noted that young Jews made up to 60 percent of Peace Corps volunteers).[18] Attacks and beatings of volunteers were frequent; two Jewish young men, Michael Schwerner and Andrew Goodman, along with black civil rights worker Tom Chaney, lost their lives that summer. Schwerner, who had just spent six months in Mississippi along with his wife Rita at the time he went missing, was particularly targeted by the local Ku

Klux Klan, who were convinced that their state was being invaded by "Yankee beatniks, Jews, and other scum."[19] A statewide investigation by the FBI led to the discovery of their three bodies six weeks later.

AJC as an organization, despite its traditional preference for quiet intervention, supported the shift to mass demonstrations in the early 1960s. This support stood them in good stead when they rose to the challenge of freeing Soviet Jewry and later when the Six-Day War loomed. Both the lay Executive Committee and the staff endorsed the 1963 March on Washington and the fifty-four-mile march for voting rights—from Selma to the state capitol in Montgomery—in March 1965, requesting that AJC personnel be represented there. Nonviolent demonstrations, they declared, were a "proper and indeed characteristically American" method to petition the government for redress of grievances; indeed, they had become "an essential technique for the achievement of social change." They cautioned, however, that public demonstrations should not become standard AJC policy in every situation; every case should be viewed individually.[20] AJC also played a leading role in establishing the Lawyers Constitutional Defense Committee, one of several groups sending scores of attorneys south—90 percent of them Jewish—to aid and represent civil rights workers who were going south.

A third phase of the civil rights movement came after the long-sought passage of the Civil Rights Act of 1964 followed by the Voting Rights Act of 1965. Five days after President Kennedy's assassination, President Lyndon B. Johnson had gone before a joint session of Congress and stated that "no memorial oration or eulogy could more eloquently honor President Kennedy's memory than the earliest possible passage of the Civil Rights bill for which he fought so long." He then pulled out every stop he could to ensure the bill's passage in February 1964. The law prohibited discrimination on the basis of race, color, religion, or national origin in places of public accommodation. Employers, labor unions, and employment agencies were additionally forbidden to discriminate on the basis of sex (the word "sex" was added to parts of the bill at the last minute), ensuring that white women in the workplace would become among the primary beneficiaries of the law. The act also put teeth in the 1954 *Brown* decision and established federal guidelines for the desegregation of public schools.

The Urban Crisis

It was soon realized, however, that all these rights made no immediate change in the daily life of millions of poor African Americans. Automation and new technology had been rapidly eliminating the very unskilled and semiskilled jobs that poor people (including Jewish immigrants) had always depended upon to get a foot up on the economic ladder. Nor did the end of Jim Crow in the

South solve the problem of discrimination nationally. There had been a mass movement of blacks out of the south and into northern inner cities, creating ghettoes of the poor and unemployed that demanded national attention.

Before World War II, almost three-quarters of American blacks had lived in rural areas below the Mason-Dixon Line. By the early 1960s, in a mass movement not unlike that which had brought immigrants to American shores, almost half lived in the Northeast and West and more than 75 percent lived in urban areas—taking up residence in the inner cities while millions of white Americans streamed to the suburbs. Similarly, nearly a million Puerto Ricans from the island were moving to the mainland, and in the West millions of Spanish-speaking people from Mexico were on the move as well. AJC research analysts reported estimates in 1959 that within thirty years the nonwhite population of ten of the fourteen largest cities in the United States would be between 25 and 50 percent.[21] At the same time, some one million migrants— poor whites fleeing the Appalachian mountain areas of Kentucky, Tennessee, and West Virginia—also streamed to the cities in search of work and a better life. These migrants were Protestant Americans, many with roots going back to the origins of the nation. The derogatory term for them was "hillbillies." They settled in the cities of the North and Midwest, particularly Cincinnati, and the Cincinnati chapter developed special programming to preserve the culture and deal with the problems of these "country cousins."[22]

As early as 1959 Philip Hoffman, then chair of AJC's domestic affairs committee and future president, warned of developing slums and ghettoes. He alerted his audience that vast sections of the major cities were becoming "wastelands." "A half century of criminal neglect and planning," he said, "is leading to serious intergroup tensions and dangerous race relations problems in the nation's large cities" that were of concern to all Americans. He urged an immediate conference of mayors to deal with the program and called for massive federal aid to cities.[23] His speech anticipated Lyndon Johnson's Great Society programs—and its central focus, the War on Poverty—which were to leave as deep a mark on the United States as Franklin Roosevelt's New Deal. Johnson first outlined his plans for what he called the "Great Society" in a speech to students at the University of Michigan on May 22, 1964. He talked about using American wealth "to enrich and elevate our national life, and to advance the quality of our American civilization . . . for in your time we have the opportunity to move not only toward the rich society and the powerful society, but upward to the Great Society." Johnson foresaw massive government programs that would solve the problems of the nation's cities, eliminate poverty, make America beautiful, and increase the level and quality of education.[24] Along with other Jewish organizational constituents of NCRAC, the AJC fervently embraced the Great Society program. From 1964 onward, the AJC put achievement of the program's goals—including economic equality for all and not just civil rights—at the top of the organization's agenda.

The War on Poverty: "Full" Employment, Housing, and Education

"We can see that the initial phase of the civil rights struggle is well on its way toward completion," declared Minnesotan Vice President Hubert Humphrey in addressing the Committee in May 1965. Humphrey himself, as mayor of Minneapolis, had been largely responsible for getting civil rights in the 1948 presidential Democratic platform; he was also an architect of the 1964 Civil Rights Act. He would pursue an unsuccessful run for the presidency in 1968, narrowly losing to Richard Nixon. His remarks that evening reflected the high idealism of those days, the confidence that the federal government could and should eliminate poverty in the United States—and the cold war prism through which so much of American policy was viewed:

> But I ask you this: Where is the justice in a situation which permits a Negro to eat in a restaurant of his choice, but denies him the opportunity to earn enough money to pay for his dinner? More than the law is needed. What is needed is the implementation of the law, the flesh upon the bone structure. . . . It is to weaken the shield of our defense, it is to weaken the moral fiber of our character, to permit even a scintilla of discrimination that denies human equality. Now we have come face to face with the greatest challenge. Does this nation have the capacity and courage to bring disadvantaged Negroes and others fully into the mainstream of economic, political, economic and social life? I am confident the AJC will be on the frontline of this struggle. . . . One fact is beyond dispute: Our commitment to achieve full equality of opportunity is unmistakable. We have burned the bridges behind us. We cannot turn back. We can only move forward in this noble work.[25]

Humphrey also described in this speech a new entity established under Title VII of the Civil Rights Act that was to become of special interest to American Jews: the Equal Employment Opportunity Commission (EEOC). This commission, he said, would have the task of working with state and local authorities, employers, trade unions, and employment agencies to see to it that "people are employed on the basis of merit." Just how the EEOC should go about fulfilling its mandate and whether preferential treatment based on race and/or specific quotas were a permissible way to remedy past discrimination, would become one of the sharpest topics of debate and division among blacks and Jews and the general body politic in the coming years. Humphrey ended by calling on his audience to help find jobs for the more than two million teenagers—a "substantial portion" of them black—who would otherwise be unemployed in the coming summer.

Finding jobs for minority workers had already become a priority for the AJC in the days of Kennedy's presidency. In 1963 national AJC held a conference for Jewish business leaders from all over the country, encouraging them to provide employment and on-the-job training for African Americans. The various chapters held follow-up conferences and periodic job fairs. Later on, chapters worked with the Small Business Administration to enlist Jewish lenders in the Title IV program of the Economic Opportunity Act, which provided loans to poor members of minority groups and others wishing to start businesses of their own. At the May 1965 meeting where Humphrey spoke, the organization as a whole moved even beyond civil rights for all minorities to the statement of policy that "equal opportunity for all" could not be achieved unless there was "*full* as well as *fair* employment, housing, and education." Members and staff were charged with exploring "every possible legislative, administrative and private approach for the achievement of that goal." When the White House held a planning conference in 1965 to discuss implementation of the acts, AJC president Morris Abram was one of the co-chairmen. He, along with honorary chairman A. Philip Randolph, called for a $100 billion "Freedom Budget" for eliminating slums and segregation and creating jobs for the poor.[26]

Within the framework of President Johnson's War on Poverty programs, AJC chapter members set up tutorial centers for ghetto children, pushed for nursery and pre-kindergarten programs, and sat on the advisory boards of VISTA (Volunteers in Service to America). They lobbied for subsidized housing, rent supplement programs, a federal minimum wage, federally subsidized medical care, and the raising of levels of public assistance and social security grants. They cooperated with government agencies to help channel the hundreds of millions of dollars available in federal grants through local social service and philanthropic agencies. They pressured traditionally Jewish social service agencies to take non-Jews as clients and Jewish housing developers to expand the supply of low- and middle-income housing. Under the direction of John Slawson and Max Birnbaum (AJC's director of education and training), the Institute for Human Relations, in cooperation with private foundations, fulfilled its mandate by training hundreds of teachers, lawyers, social workers, Peace Corps veterans, union organizers, voter registration workers, and economists to fill the positions opening up in business, labor, government, and community organizations.

The AJC–government agency line ran both ways. AJC recruited Jews who already held important positions in urban affairs, government, private planning, and universities into AJC programs. In 1967 Hyman Bookbinder, assistant director of the Office of Economic Opportunity, left to become AJC's new representative in Washington, D.C. Conversely, the AJC was making its contribution to the War on Poverty, Slawson complained, by losing some of its best staff members to positions in government programs.

Dedication to these goals was total. AJC's leading officers and urban affairs staff, along with countless other idealistic Americans, set themselves to uproot the ghettoes and cure all the illnesses of American cities with imaginative programs and massive funds, with some staff calling for nothing less than "a domestic Marshall Plan."[27] The national organization strove to enlist influential Jewish businessmen and community leaders across the country, along with the federal government, in the complete transformation of America's cities. When in 1965 President Johnson created a new cabinet post, the Department of Housing and Urban Development, AJC responded in 1966 by setting up its own Department of Education and Urban Programming, headed by director Irving M. Levine. "The AJC, actively engaged as it is in the battle against prejudice, discrimination and racism, recognizes its goals can hardly be achieved in these complex times through a fragmented attack on symptoms," read the department's founding statement. "It must organize its future program by viewing the metropolis as an interlocking system, which can bear the fruit of equal opportunity for all only if we intelligently utilize the creative minds of the finest social engineers with the highest technical competency."[28] One of the plans the department devised was the building of an educational complex combined with an industrial complex in order to provide both schools and jobs in the slum area of Brownsville, Brooklyn. In 1967 Levine's department produced the "Statement on Slums and Housing Development," which endorsed and included guidelines for advancing home ownership among the poor and increasing the supply of moderate and low-income housing.

Both Irving Levine's department and the AJC New York chapter endorsed Mayor John Lindsay's "Scatter Site housing" program announced later that year, the aim of which was to further integration by locating low-income housing projects in white middle-class neighborhoods. Opponents to these programs included numerous Jews; nonetheless, in the face of bitter controversy, the chapter defended and negotiated one such low-income housing project to be built in a Jewish neighborhood of Forest Hills, Queens. Largely because of the Forest Hills project, the AJC headquarters in New York found itself besieged with mail from middle- and lower-middle-class Jews in Queens. These residents charged that an organization supposedly founded to protect Jewish interests was actually betraying them, and putting the interests of blacks ahead of the interests of its fellow Jews (see chapter 8).[29]

The Radical Right

"White backlash," as observers called it, against school and housing desegregation, the apparent rising crime rate, and the creation of lavish federal programs — at the taxpayers' expense — that appeared to benefit blacks only, had become a serious concern at AJC. Not only was it a local obstacle to the fulfillment of the Great Society's goals; it also appeared to be feeding the potentially antisemitic far-right movements and candidates that the agency had always eyed with anxiety. Working-class northern whites were making common cause with southern segregationists and creating a new political force. In the recollection of one AJC area director, "The smell of Fascism hung in the air."[30]

White backlash was evident in the growing strength of the John Birch Society and the surprising success of Alabama Governor George Wallace in several northern states in the Democratic 1964 presidential primaries. AJC analysts noted that several traditionally antisemitic figures and organizations were backing his candidacy. In 1968 Wallace, running for president this time under his own American Independent Party, won nearly ten million votes (13 percent of the total), five states, and forty-six electoral votes. As it was, the election went to Richard Nixon, a conservative Republican who pledged to be the voice of the "silent majority" of Americans who were not protesting; Nixon promised to restore "law and order." It was Governor George Wallace who had ordered Alabama state troopers to attack peaceful civil rights marchers in Birmingham and Selma; Wallace who in his gubernatorial acceptance speech had vowed, "segregation now, segregation tomorrow, and segregation forever!"; and Wallace who in June 1963 had personally blocked a doorway at the University of Alabama to prevent two black students from registering.

Also in 1964, archconservative Barry Goldwater, son of an Episcopalian mother and a Jewish father, headed what appeared to be a radical-right minority takeover of the Republican Party. ("I always knew the first Jewish president would be an Episcopalian," quipped the southern writer and humorist Harry Golden.) When he won the Republican nomination for president, Naomi W. Cohen wrote, "Many Committee leaders were convinced that their recurring nightmare about racists and bigots capturing a major American political party had become a reality."[31] Goldwater lost the presidential election, but was to become known as one of the fathers of modern political conservatism, paving the way for the victory of Ronald Reagan in 1980. "Sometimes I think this country would be better off if we could just saw off the Eastern seaboard and let it float out to sea," Goldwater once declared in a news conference.[32] As senator from Arizona he had voted against the Civil Rights Act, and was branded as being far too casual in his talk of resorting to nuclear war against America's communist enemies. "In your heart, you know he's right," went his campaign slogan. Democrats, including countless Jews, countered this with "In your heart, you know he might" and "In your guts, you know he's nuts." In 1967 members of AJC's Executive Board were asked to rank what they believed were the greatest threats to American Jews. "Political extremism" and the radical Right ranked first in line; black nationalism, second; and Arab anti-Israel and anti-Jewish propaganda, third.[33]

Black Power as Anti-White and Anti-Jewish

The term "Black Power" came into use in 1965–66 through the writings and speeches of SNCC's new director, Kwame Ture, then known as Stokley

Carmichael. "If we are to proceed toward true liberation, we must cut ourselves off from white people," Carmichael declared in his first SNCC position paper on the subject.[34] He objected to what he saw as the relative passivity and docility of blacks in organizations run and funded by "paternalistic" whites. SNCC adopted this radical philosophy and effectively ejected all whites from its ranks by 1967 (the organization went out of business altogether some four years later). As in the case of the student volunteers who went south, the white membership and financial supporters of SNCC were predominantly Jewish.

"Black Power," which became an umbrella term in the late 1960s, also included an explicit rejection of the Martin Luther King Jr. approach of integration and nonviolent protest. As an example of his declining influence, when King attempted to address a political conference in 1967, which had Black Power advocates in the audience, he was shouted down by black militants yelling, "Kill Whitey!"[35] The "Someday" at the end of the "We Shall Overcome" song was replaced by the cry, "Freedom now!" "Black Power" called for unity, economic and political strength, black separatism to the point of nationalism, and, in its most extreme form, physical violence and revolution. Bertram Gold in 1968 expressed his fear that some black leaders were attempting to make the term "synonymous with anti-white sentiment and with revolutionary plans for guerilla warfare to tear America asunder." Gold predicted, as polarization between black and white communities increased, that more blacks would be drawn to violence and more whites would respond with repression.[36]

Revolution, whether on an American or an international scale, was indeed rapidly becoming part of the rhetoric of the Black Power/black nationalists and their sympathizers in the late 1960s. Hatred of white oppressors frequently either crossed the line or became synonymous with hatred of Jews and/or hatred of the United States as a whole. As in the case of the cold war, the protests and conflicts that tore America apart during these years of upheaval were being viewed in a global context. The growing influence of Islam and Muslims in the United States, symbolized by the popularity of Elijah Muhammad, added to the explosive mix. Blacks of strong Christian heritage, it had been noted in light of AJC's ecumenism drive, were already predisposed to see Jews negatively, and antisemitism served as a link between them and the white non-Jewish majority. Black clergy in general had no more to say about the peril of Israel's Jews in 1967 than white clergy. Then, as the religious alternative of the Black Muslims grew stronger among them, adherents were prone to adopting traditional Muslim ideological and religious views regarding Jews and the State of Israel, views that accorded well with preexisting Arab anti-Israel propaganda. When Palestinian immigrant Sirhan Sirhan assassinated presidential candidate Robert F. Kennedy in 1968, for example, the AJC was concerned not that popular opinion would turn against Arabs but that anti-Jewish and anti-Israel attitudes might intensify as a result. "The upcoming trial of the assassin may well spark a sharp increase in Arab propaganda," AJC declared, "and AJC has collaborated with other Jewish agencies in plans to counteract any injection of antisemitism into the trial and the nationwide publicity that will surround it."[37]

Among radicalized black nationalists and the followers of the New Left, the alleged crimes of American Jews—which in the 1980s were extended to include the founding of the slave trade—became part of an entire complex of antisemitic, anti-Israel, and anti-Zionist attitudes that were to become an almost permanent part of the American and world landscape. Adherents linked themselves with the struggle of all "Third World" peoples throughout the globe against what they considered colonial oppression, most notably the victims of apartheid in South Africa and the Palestinian Arabs living under Israeli occupation in the West Bank and Gaza. This allegiance dovetailed well with Soviet and communist-bloc antisemitic propaganda, which had raged for years. Americans activists' attitudes crystallized during a series of visits by SNCC, CORE, and Black Panther leaders to Africa, Cuba, and North Vietnam in the mid- to late 1960s. The radicalism extended to the halls of the United Nations and would eventually lead to the "Zionism equals racism" resolution in the General Assembly in 1975. AJC was destined to spend almost two decades to have it rescinded.

Black nationalists did not see in Zionism similarity to the nationalist movements that had created dozens of new countries in Africa. For them, Israel became an outpost of Western imperialism, supported by a warmongering United States. They thus interpreted the rush of American Jewish identity and pride in the wake of the Six-Day War as the actions of racist colonializers. SNCC's June–July 1967 newsletter, for example, accused Jews of committing atrocities against Arabs and included several antisemitic cartoons that likened Israeli soldiers to Nazis. At their Labor Day meeting, the same one where Martin Luther King was shouted down, caucuses in the audience passed resolutions condemning the "imperialist Zionist war." Many, but not all, Jewish delegates still in attendance walked out in protest. Indeed, the AJC and the American Jewish communal world as a whole noted with sorrow that, despite all this antisemitism, a number of young Jews never left and were still to be found in these circles. In 1970 AJC president Philip Hoffman commented on these young people who were "very pro-Palestinian, anti-Israel, anti-imperialist, anti–United States, who have sympathy for the Arabs, the Vietcong, the Black Panthers, the Chicago Seven, and who are stonily indifferent to the fate of the Jews." He attributed this in part to their immaturity and suggested that it was incumbent upon the AJC "to find more constructive things for our youth to do."[38]

CORE, IFCO, and Ocean Hill–Brownsville

Black antisemitism became widely discussed among the organized Jewish community when organizations where they had made common cause with blacks drew to the Left and rejected them. One of the most important instances was during a debate on the use of busing to achieve school desegregation in Mount Vernon, New York, in February 1966. This project was strongly supported by the national AJC and the Westchester chapter. When the Jewish president of the Parent-Teachers' Association spoke out against busing at a public meeting, the educational chairman of the local CORE chapter shouted in response, "Hitler made one mistake when he didn't kill enough of you!" Shocked at the comment, the AJC and Jewish organizations expected that CORE's national leadership would apologize and repudiate the remarks immediately.

CORE was slow to respond, however, and only issued a lukewarm statement four days later. With the exception of a public statement criticizing the CORE representative from former major league baseball player Jackie Robinson, not a single black leader in any of the civil rights organizations spoke up in rebuke. In protest, Will Maslow, the executive director of the American Jewish Congress and the architect of much civil rights legislation and litigation, resigned his membership on CORE's executive board. It was observed at the time that about 80 percent of CORE's support came from the white community, and these whites were primarily Jews. With this incident, CORE lost their support.[39]

In another instance, Rabbi Marc Tanenbaum of AJC's interreligious affairs division had been a proud founding member and was president of the Interreligious Foundation for Community Organization (the IFCO), which originally was supposed to work peaceably to bring the resources of churches and synagogues to local black community organizers. In 1969, however, the IFCO convened a conference in which militants issued a "Black Manifesto" that called for armed confrontation and state socialism through revolutionary seizure of power. They also demanded a nationwide seizure of America's churches and synagogues as part of a $500 million reparations package for black oppression. After consulting with the AJC Executive Board, Tanenbaum regretfully resigned as IFCO president. Also, the Synagogue Council and NCRAC (of which AJC was a member) issued a joint statement disassociating the Jewish community from the tactics and programs of the Black Manifesto.[40]

The New York City teachers' strike of 1968, which centered on the largely black school district of Ocean Hill–Brownsville in Brooklyn, erupted after years of boycotts, sit-ins, and clashes between angry local parents and community activists, the board of education, and later the system's teachers. When New York Jews had been barred from entrance into other businesses and professions, thousands had streamed into the public education system. As a result, two-thirds of New York's teachers and most of the principals and vice principals were Jewish. A walkout by their union, the United Federation of Teachers, led by Albert Shanker, kept more than one million students out of school over a period of two months and led to a surge of antisemitism expressed in the streets and amply covered in the media. At issue was no longer desegregation, but the otherwise laudable goal of "decentralization" of the city's school system into local school boards that would be fully representative of the city's minority population and answerable to the parents and superintendents of the neighborhoods.

The UFT had not originally been opposed to the idea; some members had even lobbied for Ocean Hill–Brownsville to be among the first experimental districts to be decentralized. Shanker was also an unlikely opponent against a measure that would clearly advance the power of the local black community; he had been a socialist in college, had raised money for Freedom Summer, and had marched with Martin Luther King Jr. in Selma. The immediate conflict was set off when the local Ocean Hill–Brownsville board, under the direction of superintendent Rhody McCloy (an admirer of Malcolm X, frequenter of a Harlem mosque, and Black Power advocate), seized control of the curriculum and set about replacing white teachers and principals with black and Puerto Rican ones. In the process his board called for the transfer (in effect, the firing) of nineteen teachers, all but one of them Jewish. Some 350 other teachers walked out in sympathy, but these were replaced by nonunion teachers. Shanker, almost universally condemned by public opinion, then began to prepare to shut down the entire system over the matter.[41]

During the conflict teachers found antisemitic statements in their mailbox that made direct reference to the Arab-Israeli conflict. One declared that black children should be taught by Afro-Americans rather than "Middle East murderers of colored people." Another read, "Cut out, stay out, stay off, shut up, get off our backs, or your relatives in the Middle East will find themselves giving benefits to raise money to help you get out from the terrible weight of an enraged black community." Shanker reacted by reprinting one hundred thousand copies of these handbills and announced on TV that his union was trying to prevent "a Nazi takeover of the schools."[42] The most memorable low point of the strike was reached when Leslie Campbell, a leader of the Afro-American Teachers Association, read aloud on listener-supported FM radio station WBAI a poem allegedly written by a fifteen-year-old girl:

> Hey Jew boy, with that yarmulka on your head
> You palefaced Jew boy—I wish you were dead.
> I can see you Jew boy—no, you can't hide,
> I got a scoop on you—yeh, you gonna die. . . .
> I'm sick of seeing in everything I do
> About the murder of six million Jews;
> Hitler's reign lasted only fifteen years. . . .
> My suffering lasted for over 400 years, Jew boy. . . .
> When the UN made Israel a free independent state

Little 4- and 5-year-old boys threw hand grenades.
They hated the black Arabs with all their might,
And you, Jew boy, said it was all right.
Then you came to America, land of the free,
And took over the school system to perpetuate white supremacy,
Guess you know, Jew boy, there's only one reason you made it—
You had a clean white face, colorless and faded.
I hated you, Jew boy, because your hang-up was the Torah,
And my only hang-up was my color.[43]

In the words of one observer, when the strike finally ended in November, the cause of school integration and race relations in New York City had been set back at least twenty years.[44]

The New York chapter of the AJC, which had gone on record as favoring the decentralization measure "with modifications," took the approach of trying to lessen the tension and avoid "over-reacting." They urged the union to end the strike, "conditioned upon assurances from the Board of Education for continuing negotiations by the school authorities for the protection of teachers' rights and due process"; at the same time, they called for Mayor Lindsay to condemn the "bullying tactics" of the local board. They also took out a full-page ad in the *New York Times*, signed by Jewish, Catholic, Protestant, and black leaders, calling for "reason and moderation." In the aftermath they supported Mayor Lindsay's Special Committee on Racial and Religious Prejudice to investigate the nature and extent of antisemitism in the city.[45]

The "Long, Hot Summers"

In other instances, calming tensions hardly seemed possible. Beginning in 1964, blacks' hatred of Jews became a serious concern. Black ghettoes across the nation erupted into four years of intermittent summer rioting that killed and injured hundreds of people, cost hundreds of millions of dollars in damage, and frequently required armed force to restore order. Between 1964 and the summer of 1968 (before the New York teachers' walkout) there were 329 riots in 257 different American cities, costing more than three hundred lives. The white targets and victims, as it turned out, were disproportionately Jewish.[46] The riots were most often touched off by encounters, arrests, or shootings of black residents by white police officers (in the case of Newark, inaccurate rumors spread that one arrestee had died in custody), leading to charges of police brutality and calls by civil rights activists for civilian review boards of police actions. Most of these ghettoes had once been Jewish neighborhoods. Some Jews still lived there and those Jews who did not still owned the stores, businesses, and buildings.

The first of what came to be known as "the long, hot summers"—in 1964—saw violence in New York, Rochester, and Philadelphia. In Philadelphia it was estimated by the Jewish Telegraphic Agency news organization that 80 percent of the wrecked and looted businesses were owned by Jews; it was reported that businesses displaying the sign "This is a Negro Store" were not touched while adjoining Jewish-owned stores were destroyed.[47] In August 1965 the most violent explosion was in the Watts section of Los Angeles: thirty-four people died, more than one thousand were wounded, and four thousand were arrested. Some forty million dollars in property damage was reported. The rioters targeted food markets, liquor stores, clothing stores, department stores, and pawnshops. Arthur Groman, the chairman of the Los Angeles AJC chapter denied that stores owned by Jews had been singled out. He expressed his regret that the riots might "provide a field day for the bigots and extremists in the white community," declaring that it would be "tragic if we allowed the Jewish community to ally itself in any way with such elements."

Newsweek, on the other hand, wrote that the looting revealed "a virulent strain of antisemitism—not so much blind race hatred as fury against individual Jewish storeowners. The liquor store boss who refuses to cash checks, many of which would bounce, and the pawn broker." One ghetto inhabitant told *Newsweek,* "They put the NAACP sticker in the window and pat us on the back and say, 'We know how it is because we have been persecuted too.' But every day they put the money in the sack and get in their 'Jew canoes'—those damn Cadillacs—and drive on out of here."[48] "The Jew is the landlord. He is the merchant. He is the white man the Negro sees," declared one black attorney in the aftermath of a riot in New York—in which "we gotta take Harlem out of Goldberg's pocket" became a rallying cry.[49] Malcolm X, commenting in a press conference in 1965, specifically took the more international view. "These Jewish people conduct their businesses in Harlem, but live in other parts of the city," he said. "They enjoy good housing. Their children attend good schools and go to colleges. This the Negroes know and resent. These businessmen are seen by the Negroes in Harlem as colonialists, just as the people of Africa and Asia viewed the British, the French, and other businessmen before they achieved their independence."[50]

In the aftermath of riots in Philadelphia, the local chapter of CORE distributed mimeographed leaflets demanding that the Jewish community "censor" Jewish merchants—listed by name—"who rob and cheat black people," as well as "Jewish slumlords" and those who "continually scream antisemitism as a defense for their own injustice against black people."[51] "If one is a simple, uneducated Negro with no future," explained civil rights leader Bayard Rustin in addressing the AJC, "he is bound to meet four kinds of white people who have a terrifying effect upon his life. One is a policeman; one is a schoolteacher; one is a welfare worker; and one is a small businessman. Except for the policemen, the majority of the teachers, welfare workers and businessmen are Jewish. . . . These are the people who often exploit them, and when they do not in fact exploit them, the very nature of their situation leads them to feel that they are being exploited."[52]

Whatever the reasons, massive rioting and looting broke out again in the summer of 1966. A Jewish newspaper in Minneapolis commented on all the "for sale" signs in the ghetto and noted that while in the aftermath help was forthcoming for the black residents, nothing was being done to help the victimized businessmen, nearly all of whom were Jews.[53] Rioting, looting, and arson erupted yet again the following summer, this time leaving eighty-five dead, thirty-two hundred injured, sixteen thousand arrested, and more than half a billion dollars' worth of property damage. The worst upheavals occurred in Newark, once home to the seventh-largest Jewish population of any city in the United States and more than forty synagogues. Starting on July 12, 1967, the rioting there continued for five days and destroyed several city blocks. One of those arrested and sentenced to two years in prison for incitement and weapons possession included black activist and playwright LeRoi Jones, who later changed his name to Imamu Amiri Baraka and lived to become the poet laureate of New Jersey. Newark's remaining Jews fled to the surrounding suburbs of South Orange, West Orange, and Livingston, and the former AJC chapter of Newark became the "Metro West" chapter.[54] Later that month, riots in Detroit, also home to a significant Jewish population, left forty-one dead and property damage of $500 million—the greatest destruction in any single city during those four years. As in the case of Newark and other cities, Jews fled the central city for the surrounding suburbs, with many eventually ending up far away in the gated communities of America's Sunbelt: California, Arizona, and above all South Florida.

Rioting by blacks in 1968, which was a year of political upheaval and protest on all fronts, was touched off in particular by the assassination of Martin Luther King Jr. in Memphis in April. Similar violence, on a lesser scale, continued for several years. AJC's Philadelphia director Murray Friedman estimated that in that city alone twenty-two Jewish merchants were killed and twenty-seven shot or beaten in slum areas from 1968 to 1972. There was good reason to believe that the Jewish death toll was similar in other cities.[55]

Taking note of the destruction of the nation's cities, in August 1967 President Johnson convened the National Advisory Committee on Civil Disorders to examine the origins of and possible ways to remedy the riots. It was popularly known as the Kerner Commission, after its chairman Otto Kerner, governor of Illinois. Mayor John Lindsay of New York was the vice chair of the Commission and a driving force behind the 500-page report issued eight months later in March 1968. The report became a bestseller, with more than two million copies sold in trade paperback. White racism, the report declared, was at the root of the conflict. It concluded that the United States was moving toward two societies, one black and one white, "both separate and unequal."

"What white Americans have never fully understood—but what the Negro can never forget," the report's memorable conclusion read, "is that white society is deeply implicated in the ghetto. White institutions created it, white institutions maintain it, and white society condones it."

The AJC, which otherwise embraced the Kerner report and made it a center of its policies in the late 1960s, had one important criticism. In the chapter on "merchants," the report singled out Jews: it described them as "proportionately overrepresented in ghetto business," and it confirmed the black belief that businessmen exploited their black customers. Poor people paid more for their services, the report declared, because they were, in the words of AJC's staff summary and critique, "cheated, duped and exploited by unscrupulous merchants who grow fat on the profits from the poor."[56] The explanation that the riots were largely the result of justified fury at white exploitation by landlords and merchants in the ghetto was to find its way into standard American textbooks.

Responses

Responses among AJC members and officers to the riots and rejection from the black organizations varied. Large numbers of Jews, reported Bertram Gold in October 1968, "feel that their national leaders are more concerned with bettering intergroup relations than with protecting the interests of the Jewish community and they are increasingly demanding that Jewish organizations withdraw from the civil rights struggle and serve, instead, as a counterforce against rising black militancy."[57]

Within the ranks of the AJC throughout the years of the riots, however, there was ambivalence in admitting that there was a problem at all (an early attempt to pass a resolution in 1965 condemning black antisemitism was struck down on the grounds that it might actually help bring about the phenomenon it was meant to confront). There was a tendency to excuse or justify the rioters, as the Kerner Commission had done; a penchant for writing off the tension as a form of "sibling rivalry"; and a stubborn persistence in the belief that the best way to protect Jews and be true to Judaism was to help all others. Leaders stressed that it would be a tragedy if Jews were seduced into antiblack feelings because of the actions of a few. There was a call for an "attitude-changing campaign" against white backlash among AJC members, other Jews, and the white community in general. Most prominent were exhortations to double and redouble efforts to solve the problems of the day, which were the actual root causes of the violence. Only then would the carnage in America's cities cease. Consequently, it was said that calls for establishing "law and order" and "cracking down" on rioters would only cause the conflagration to burn even higher. Accordingly, there was an almost frantic embrace of the recommendations of the Kerner report, as if these alone were the key to saving the country from utter destruction.

Antisemitism or "Legitimate Protest"?

After June 1967 and especially after the Ocean Hill–Brownsville strike, journalists tended to cover most closely expressions of radical black antisemitism on the one hand and Jewish "paranoia" on the other. *Time* actually ran a cover story on the alleged end of the black-Jewish alliance in January 1969, which suggested, "In light of Judaism's centuries-long experience of persecution, it is not surprising that some of the reactions to anti-Jewish statements made by black leaders have verged on hysteria."[58] But the reaction of AJC staffers and lay leaders, none of whom was actually a victim of the riots, was hardly hysterical. When urban affairs staff member Seymour Samet went to meet with residents of Washington, D.C., after a riot he reported frankly at the weekly staff advisory meeting: "The Jewish community felt the rioting was anti-Semitic in intent and likened the situation to Nazi Germany and the smashing of Jewish stores."

Nevertheless, Samet's recommendation to the residents and to the Washington chapter did not at all depart from classic AJC ideology. The goal here, as in other such encounters, was not to start a program to help inner-city Jews, but to convince inner-city Jews that it was as much in their interest as anybody's for integration to succeed. Samet outlined for the staff the reply he had made to the Washington, D.C. Jews:

1. This is an urban crisis, not a Jewish issue, and should be so identified.
2. The Apartheid system in America must be stopped. Jews should align themselves on the side of an integrated society.
3. The Jewish community must respond speedily both with funds and with personal and group effort (i.e. to repair the damage caused by the riots).

A sharp exchange ensued. Dr. Simon Segal of the foreign affairs committee criticized these guidelines and asked whether this meant that the AJC was encouraging these Jews to stay in the ghetto after what had happened to them. Indeed, if they wished to remain in the "slum areas," Samet replied, Jews should "begin making plans for a more viable atmosphere." Bertram Gold intervened in the dispute by saying that while they all recognized the importance of integration as a principle, they should encourage Jews to leave the slums "for safety's sake." At the same time Nathan Perlmutter suggested an "unpublicized" meeting of AJC with Jewish merchants from the New York ghetto areas to let them know that AJC was actually concerned with their situation.[59]

Part of the coolness may have stemmed from embarrassment at the role Jewish businessmen had played in the ghettoes, as implied in the Kerner Commission report. There was also shame that so many inner-city white

Jews who had the means to do so were defeating the goal of integration by fleeing from their old neighborhoods. At several points Morris B. Abram (who lived with his wife Jane and two children in a Westchester suburb) openly criticized Jews who tried to escape integration by moving away from blacks or sending their children to private school. Some placed indirect and sometimes direct blame on Jewish businessmen that they had brought the situation upon themselves and that by their actions and by their leaving, they were worsening black-Jewish relations for everyone. Although the AJC itself did not issue such statements, representatives from other Jewish organizations did, challenging "Jewish slumlords" to end unfair business practices. For example, Albert Vorspan, director of the UAHC's Commission on Social Action, called for congregations and rabbis to put moral pressure on "Jewish slumlords and ghetto profiteers" and implied that such slumlords should be excommunicated by their rabbis.[60]

Excuses for black excesses, as well as ambivalence toward speaking up about black antisemitism—for fear that it might be used to divert Jewish groups from their traditional devotion to civil rights concerns—were commonly expressed. "We have heard the bloody screams of defiance against 'Whitey,'" read an AJC editorial in 1965 after the second summer of riots. "Are not the outbursts of anger against the 'oppressors' also cries for attention and help? If attention is finally paid to the city and its festering problems, perhaps the long frustrated energies can work toward changing this desperate scene."[61] As time went on, AJC and other Jewish organizations that were part of NCRAC had to answer the charges that they were tolerating anti-Jewish expressions from blacks that they would never tolerate from whites or radical-right spokesmen. AJC carefully qualified its official position in a 1968 application for an allocation from the LCBC (Large Cities Budgeting Conference): "Increasingly we have been departing from traditional 'liberal' ranks which preferred to sweep Negro antisemitism under the rug. We have been speaking out plainly and aggressively as a signal to the leaders of the Negro minority groups that they too must be heard and as an expression to Jews of our refusal to countenance antisemitism regardless of its source. We have been weighing very carefully all that we say because we are well aware that our reactions could feed backlash and we are also not unaware that there are some who almost welcome Negro antisemitism as a rationale for pulling back from the civil rights movement. We therefore will give this a great deal of thought in the coming year."[62]

AJC's president and executive director led AJC officers in repeatedly excusing, rationalizing, or even justifying the rioters, and insisting that AJC must stay the course no matter what happened. "We can't escape responsibility for the masses of our citizens who live in agony on earth while the Glenns hurdle toward the moon," declared Morris Abram, after hearing a report of terrible rioting in Philadelphia in which hundreds of Jewish establishments were

stormed, looted, and destroyed. "You can't expect these people to reach a responsible maturity until they have developed self respect and a feeling of self
worth. And in the growing up process there are going to be these tensions,
these confrontations and these times of trouble."[63] A month after the Ocean
Hill–Brownsville strike, he talked about the necessity of blacks becoming educated, insisting: "There will be many black-white confrontations and much
friction between Negro and Jew—but we must pay the price of past
wrongs. . . . We must recognize that not every conflict and confrontation sig-
nifies antisemitism."[64] Referring to the "cry of separatism" from blacks, he
said, "One is a racist cry which I reject totally; but the cry of identity and pride
is something I accept and applaud."[65]

Abram took every occasion to denounce white backlash and criticize those
who had "backed away" from ideas of equality because they had "not been
prepared to face up to the radical reforms our society must undergo to make
of the white and the Negro America one nation." In a speech before the AJC
executive board, he declared: "We in the AJC must not, shall not, and do not
intend to withdraw from this struggle. Rather, we shall intensify all our efforts
to create fair and full housing, full employment, and integrated quality
schools. . . . The surest way for the north to inflict upon itself a grievous
wound from which it will never recover is to grasp the unworthy traditions of
prejudice and discrimination that the south did during the days of reconstruction."[66] U.N. Ambassador Arthur Goldberg—who succeeded Abram as AJC
president for one year (1968–69), resigning to run for governor of New York
State—would express similar sentiments when he denounced "the evil and
sickness of racial discrimination." The former Supreme Court justice further
declared that "if, because of excesses on the part of the Negro community and
its struggle for emancipation, the American Jewish Committee were to retreat
from its pioneering position in the field of human relations, instead of intensifying its efforts in the interest of justice for all, it would be the greatest mistake this organization ever made."[67] After Abram's presentation in October
1966, the entire board passed unanimously the "Resolution on Civil Rights,"
which spoke of their determination not to be deterred from their chosen path
no matter how "obnoxious" either side became:

The development of extremism on both sides of the civil rights question has caused
even moderates of good conscience to "sit this one out." We would like to make very
clear the position of the American Jewish Committee.

This is not the time to diminish our efforts. We must intensify all programs in this
fight for human rights and equality. The issue is not "black power" vs. "white power."
Regardless of militant positions, no matter how obnoxious on either side, we must keep
in focus the true issue: the achievement of human rights and equality for all people.

We therefore call on all our members to maintain a firm position. This is the time to
fight for what is right.[68]

In his last years as executive director, John Slawson kept repeating like a mantra that what was bad for America was worse for Jews, and that it was more important for Jews to be concerned with the sicknesses of society than with specific Jewish issues. He maintained these themes concurrently with his increase in concerns about Jewish continuity and identity and the general "Judaization" of the Committee. Slawson exhorted his followers to maintain their optimism in 1965. "Yes, the civil rights movement has been changing and we have been experiencing a rebuff," he declared. "In spite of this frustration, however, I say that our efforts in this area must not only be continued but redoubled. . . . there is a moral imperative that we do this regardless of the difficulties, even if the difficulties are being caused by those who would most benefit. . . . The most effective way to reduce this danger is to work for the elimination of the conditions that breed such anti-social and abhorrent attitudes." He indirectly implicated the escalating Vietnam War as a factor in the rioting when he commented, "We must ask ourselves to what extent we have helped to legitimize violence as a means of political action." When criticism was voiced by board members that through the War on Poverty programs the AJC was perhaps overstepping its bounds, Slawson set forth "how far we should venture outside the specific area that is designated as 'Jewish.'" He referred to all their work in the United States and around the world as being of one piece with their organization's mission:

The question is still argued although by now it should be apparent that our own best interests are served when we promote human understanding and human rights for all. . . . We of the American Jewish Committee must address ourselves not alone to the needs of the Jewish community but to those of the total American community as well. In so doing, far from jeopardizing our special and primary purposes, we advance them by enhancing Jewish security and Jewish dignity. . . . Now a criticism we hear fairly frequently is that the AJC is "all over the lot." Yes, in a sense we are. We are concerned with further ecumenism in Rome and in our own country, stemming the menacing resurgence of anti-democratic forces in Argentina, helping stabilize the international position of Israel, remedying dangerous failures in intergroup and interracial relationships in our own country, advancing human rights through international law throughout the world, just to cite a few examples. Yet though seemingly disparate and widely separated, none of these concerns is actually far removed from the others. Experience has taught us that all are related to our security and dignity. . . . If we are indeed all over the lot, it is because this is a very imperfect world. Naturally we must be careful to reserve our resources and not spread ourselves too thin. But if we dig too deeply into any one area, to the exclusion of all others, we may well be overwhelmed and dig ourselves into our own graves.[69]

All of the major American Jewish organizations, not just AJC, kept their pledge not to depart from their previous policies in spite of rejection from the civil rights organizations and the violence in the nation's cities. After the summer riots of 1967, NCRAC—at the time made of up nine national Jewish

organizations including the AJC and more than eighty local community councils—issued the "Guide to Program Planning for Jewish Community Relations, 1967–1968," which spoke of the urgent need for Jews to take the responsibility of improving black-Jewish relations. American Jews should intensify
their efforts to help blacks achieve full equality, the guide instructed, despite
the antisemitism heard from "black demagogues." While it was agreed that
Jewish organizations had a "continuing obligation" to "interpret intensively
to the Jewish community the facts of antisemitism among Negroes, its nature,
its origins, its real significance, and effective ways of combating it," the guide
also warned against "exaggerating" the problem's true dimensions and mis-
taking "legitimate protest" for antisemitism. The guide also gave a dire warning of what the consequences might be if Jews abandoned the struggle: "For
the Jewish community to be deflected from its support and advocacy of equality for Negroes on the ground that Negroes are anti-Semitic would not only
be self-defeating but to repudiate a fundamental tenet of Jewish tradition—
equal justice for all."[70] "Even before the riots of last summer," observed the
chairman of NCRAC in mid-1968, "our Joint Program Plan read to a remarkable degree like the report of the Kerner Commission."[71]

Criticism from Within and Without

In May 1968—shortly after the Kerner Commission report had been released—a notable symposium entitled, "Pieties and Realities: Some Constructive Approaches to Negro-Jewish Relations," was held. AJC officers and
members in attendance sat and received little but criticism from leading
African American and Jewish guest speakers. The balance of their addresses
focused not on black antisemitism but on its flip side: accusations that the AJC
was condoning the descent of the American Jewish community into white racism. "You ought not to be in the civil rights movement to be thanked, to be
rewarded, to be respected, to be loved," said Bayard Rustin, then executive director of the A. Philip Randolph Institute. Rustin spoke of how middle-class,
well-educated blacks felt stifled in their own entrepreneurial desires because of
the Jews they found everywhere above them: "You ought to be in it because
there is injustice to your brother, and regardless of his behavior you continue
to be dedicated to the prophet. . . . No one ought to permit verbal violence,
rioting, or even overt antisemitism in the Negro community to become an excuse for Jews opting out of this struggle. I think that if there is a backlash
among Jews as a result of all this, we are all damned."[72]

Psychologist Kenneth B. Clark, who was also a guest speaker, denounced
the ambivalence of northern whites, including Jews, "who were apparently
totally committed to the civil rights struggle as long as the emphasis was
southern." The mass media, he charged, were giving maximum coverage to

the most aggressive and hostile expressions of black extremists in part because they judged it newsworthy and in part because it concentrated discussion on the statements rather than on the real problems that needed to be addressed. "Related to this kind of game-playing is what seems to me to be a particularly perverse form of game, what I call the sado-masochistic charade," he continued, in effect referring to himself, "where the black militant is often hired by white backlashers who are ambivalent about their backlash to engage in an orgy of verbal flagellation. There is a cathartic component here; the whites have their guilt alleviated by the verbal flagellation, by having the Negro militant in effect drive out the devils. But here again verbalizing a problem is an excuse for not addressing oneself to the difficult task of doing something about it." He then addressed the topic of antiblack attitudes among Jews, expressed resentment against Jewish paternalism, attacked Albert Shanker and the UFT, and demanded that AJC take a stronger stand on the issue of school decentralization in New York City:

I come now to the point of why I am here discussing what could very well be part of this charade—a discussion of Negro-Jewish relationships. There is no point in discussing antisemitism among Negroes without at the same time discussing anti-Negro feelings among Jews. And there is no point of discussing anti-Negro feelings without talking about fundamental problems which society must solve without regard to whether people like other people or don't like them, or whether Jewish organizations are going to participate in a "Be-Nice-to-Negroes" week, or whether you can get the black militants to smile whenever they see a white person who has contributed to the Urban League. There are fundamental problems that must be dealt with regardless. First, education. Second, economic. Third, housing. . . . The decentralization problem is critical in terms of the stagnant, unresponsive, dehumanizing public educational system in New York City. . . . I am not talking just about the Brownsville–Ocean Hill problem. I am talking about the long history of hostility toward the legitimate aspirations of the parents of children in public schools that have long been used to dehumanize these children rather than to educate them. There is no evidence that Albert Shanker, the Board of Education of the City of New York and the United Parents Association, which have been very strong in fighting any serious and effective decentralization, had ever raised their voices in trying to develop a program to educate these children, to raise their reading and arithmetic level from the present disgracefully low criminal level, which until now has been accepted tolerantly. And now they expect the people of the community not to be hostile toward them. I for one cannot afford the luxury of hostility, but I certainly will use every bit of intelligence I can possibly find, borrow, steal or pay for, to render them impotent to continue to shackle on powerless children of the ghetto in a criminally inferior school.[73]

One Jewish speaker at the symposium went so far as to claim that the Jews' very survival in the United States was threatened by the encroachment of racism among them, which he seemed to equate with apostasy. This was sociologist Charles E. Silberman, author of a 1964 study on race in the United States entitled *Crisis in Black and White*. Silberman would explore issues of Jewish continuity and survival seventeen years later in a well-known book, *A Certain People: American Jews and Their Lives Today*.[74] In his view, racism—

not intermarriage—was the main threat to Judaism, particularly as it had recently been displayed by Jews in school desegregation and busing controversies. "Our survival as a people is gravely threatened," he declared to his AJC audience. "For us, in the U.S., the principal threat no longer comes from antisemitism. For us in 1968 the greatest threat to survival comes from assimilation—assimilation to the dominant attitudes, values and mores of American society—to the materialism and the hedonism, and increasingly, to the prejudice and discrimination, to the racism of white America. . . . It is a form of assimilation, I am sorry to say, that affects a large and rapidly growing proportion of American Jews."

Silberman believed that the AJC should turn its long-lauded talents in the field of scientific research to solving the problem of racism among Jews. "It's time to begin talking *tachlis* [getting down to business] to one another," he said, using a Yiddish expression. "It's time—no, long past time—to face up to the raw, rank, anti-Negro prejudice that is within our own midst. We talk—endlessly—about Negro antisemitism; we rarely talk about, let alone try to deal with, the Jewish anti-Negroism that is in our midst and that is growing very rapidly. . . . We American Jews more than anyone else should avoid the sins of indifference and silence because of the six million." He spoke of Jews' opposition to desegregation and school busing in such white northern suburbs as Mount Vernon, Great Neck, Scarsdale, and Shaker Heights. In these communities, he said, the realities of racial conflict "have stripped away the veneer of liberalism." Something had to be done to prevent this if American Judaism in its pure nature was to be preserved. "I therefore call upon the AJC to give the highest priority to the development of programs to combat this growing Jewish anti-Negroism. . . . I am suggesting that this defense organization give equal priority to the defense against *ourselves*—the defense against our own prejudice, our own bias, our own racism. I am suggesting that equivalent resources—intellectual as well as financial—be devoted to diagnosing the sources of Jewish prejudice and finding means of reducing or eliminating it. I am suggesting that we devote more effort to persuading ourselves that we are different, that our Jewishness if it means anything at all means a commitment to 'do justice.' Such a program will contribute to the survival of Judaism in America as something more than a quaint folk culture. More important, it will be the right and the just thing to do."[75]

Professor Leonard J. Fein, at the time associate director for research at the Joint Center for Urban Studies at MIT and Harvard, similarly equated Jewish distinctiveness with refusal to descend to the level of white backlashers. He also downplayed or excused expressions of anti-Jewish hatred from blacks, and accused the Jews of being paranoid. The reality, he said, was that the Jew was "the central representative of a largely oppressive society, a role which is a fact of public life in New York City." He referred to the "often incidental damage" to Jewish establishments that resulted from the riots: "We may empathize with the paranoid streak which is so much a part of Jewish communal life, paranoia come upon quite honestly, a paranoia which makes of every whispered unpleasantry an organized campaign of malice, of every minor act of rudeness an onslaught of aggression." Fein asserted that Jews might actually find themselves to be the unexpected beneficiaries of black power and black assertiveness, rather than undeserving victims; this new presence could be an indication that Jews could now assert themselves and their distinctiveness too:

Why? When Jews arrived in this country in their masses the basic tactic we employed to gain admission to American society was a denial of our difference. We threw off our kapotes with alacrity, shaved our side curls, studied English, took pride in the German Jews who had already made it as gentlemen, sought out rabbis to lead our congregations who could impress others with their accents and their elegance. In time America dropped its barriers, allowed us to join its country clubs, decided that we were NOT, at least not all of us, wild-eyed and bushy headed, and made its peace—a peace nowhere better expressed than our elevation from a paltry three percent of the country's population to full partnership status in its religious community. What more could we have sought? What more could we have expected? What more could we have achieved? The problem was embedded in the success. For we convinced not only our neighbors but also ourselves and our children. We began by thinking "If it will help us to survive, let's tell them we're not different." But we said it so well, and so persuasively, that our posture soon was changed and we thought to ourselves; "We are not different, so why are they oppressing us?"

Fein equated the new assertiveness not only with expressing a distinctive Jewish identity per se but also in continuing to fight for social justice, thus refusing to be assimilated to the majority white racist culture. The recent response to the Six-Day War was, in his view, a laudable example of how Jews could be distinctive and assertive, and he believed this assertiveness should be matched in the area of fighting racism. It was also an example of how American society was now willing to accept such responses from its minorities. "For a brief moment last June there seemed to be a change," he said. "We threw caution to the winds, we became petulant, aggressive, temperamental. When Israel was threatened, we violated every cautionary precept of that sophisticated public relations we had learned so well to practice. And the roof did not cave in on us. On the contrary, most of our neighbors understood our anguish and some even shared it. Yet it now seems most likely that we are returned to business as usual, which is to say, business which seeks to mask the difference, differences between Jews and Christian, rather than asserting them." Jews "were not white and should not become white," he insisted; they should instead take a lesson from black militancy and make it their own. "If that militancy succeeds, it will succeed because Americans will have learned to live with difference," he declared. "If therefore it succeeds, we ourselves will be among its unintended beneficiaries. I must answer that we may die of success just as surely as we may die of struggle, that to suppose that America cannot contain a Jewish community that dares to assert itself, in all its distinctiveness, is to sell this country short and to mistake the powerful new mood of these days. . . . We and Negroes have a common purpose at last, the purpose of teaching America at long last what pluralism is all about."[76]

Exceptions to the Rule

Not all AJC leaders continually blamed Jews or excused and rationalized the deeds of the rioters. Nathan Perlmutter, Marine Corps veteran and associate director of the Committee (he would later become national director of the Anti-Defamation League), took issue with criticism of Jewish "slumlords" and said the slogans of "Whitey" and "Goldberg" were getting out of hand. "The word "slumlord" has become synonymous with property owner in the ghetto and "ghetto merchant" has seemingly become synonymous with exploitation," he said in an address on civil rights to AJC in 1967. "There are rent gougers in the ghettos but ghetto landlords and merchants are no more *ipso facto* slumlords and exploiters than are ghetto Negroes prone to crime, addiction or easy virtue." He pointed out that a recent four-year experiment by a New York civic group concluded with a determination that it is "virtually impossible" for a landlord to maintain decent living conditions in a slum area and make a fair profit, he said. "As far as the ghetto merchant, he stayed. Give him a plus for that. He gives credit. His insurance rates are higher. His pilferage loss is higher. The people who talk indiscriminately about the white presence in the ghetto might consider what effect this stereotyping has on the lives and safety of ghetto merchants, lives no less precious than those that have been lost and mutilated as the result of white demagoguery in Mississippi."

Perlmutter also defended Jews against charges of "flight to the suburbs," saying that it was people's right to move where they could find more and cleaner space, cleaner air, better schools, and safer streets. He urged more sympathy for low- and lower-middle-income whites that "constitute an alienated and powerless group. . . . Liberals can no longer be content to dismiss this large group as backlashers and bigots. Instead they need to confront such issues as crime in the streets rather than allowing them to become the exclusive province of the right wing."[77] Finally, he voiced strong objection to those who romanticized the rioters—as had author and activist James Baldwin who likened Watts and related riots to the uprising of the Warsaw Ghetto. "A hoodlum, regardless of the sociological and psychological clay that shaped him, remains a hoodlum," Perlmutter insisted. "He is not simply for being black, therefore a freedom fighter. To liken the at once glorious and pitiable heroes of the Warsaw Ghetto to looters of fifths of whiskey and television sets is a gross obscenity."[78]

Bertram Gold spoke of the need to balance AJC's priorities and commitments when he declared late in 1968—a few days before the U.S. presidential election—that the organization would not be fulfilling its leadership function if it were deterred "from our efforts to secure a just society . . . but neither will we be if we ignore the legitimate fears and apprehensions of Jews who are victimized by violence and affected by the demands for greater power by the Negro community at the expense of hard-won gains made by many individual Jews." The AJC could no longer assume that what was good for blacks was automatically also good for Jews. In his view AJC would function best when it honestly examined each issue that produced tension and conflict with the black community and made deliberate choices, "sometimes in open disagreement with black groups and other times making necessary compromises." At another time, he admitted "we will increasingly face the problem of conflicting group interests . . . and there may be times when we will have to speak up for Jewish group interests even though this might bring us into disagreement with some elements of the Negro community."[79]

AJC President Philip E. Hoffman made reference to beleaguered inner-city Jews in his presidential address of 1970 when he referred to the formation of Meir Kahane's Jewish Defense League, whose main function at its beginning was to serve as a civil patrol to protect elderly Jews from crime. Many Jews, he said, "have made no secret of the fact that they look upon our dedication to the goal of equal opportunity for all—and especially for the Negro—as too often being at the expense of Jewish rights and Jewish interests. Such in fact is the reason for being of the militant organization known as the Jewish Defense League. Much as we may deplore their tactics, we cannot ignore the problem that brought them into being." The AJC, he reported, was at the present moment expanding its role in "keeping civic peace and domestic tranquility." This was out of enlightened self-interest and "an immediate concern for the safety and well-being of thousands of our urban dwelling Jews."[80]

It was for the sake of these Jews that AJC issued a groundbreaking report in January 1968: "The Invisible Jewish Poor." The report, written by staff member Ann G. Wolfe, estimated that in New York alone there were some fifty to a hundred thousand Jews, many of them elderly, whose income put them below the poverty line. Because of administrative criteria geared toward blacks these poor Jews were receiving no help from government antipoverty programs, and neither were many poor Irish-, poor Italian-, and poor Polish-Americans.[81] AJC also in the late 1960s began to take up the cause of "white ethnics" in general, who had been bypassed by much of the new government legislation. "The insensitive handling of older and poor sections of white, urban, ethnic America by community officials and planners is . . . a national scandal," wrote Murray Friedman, AJC's area director in Philadelphia, in his study of Kensington, a white, predominantly Catholic, low-income area of that city. "Kensingtonians are beset by economic problems and status anxieties," he said. "These anxieties are increased as they watch—in their opinion—the lawlessness of Negro violence in Watts and Detroit being rewarded by special federal and city efforts."[82]

Norman Podhoretz, editor of *Commentary* magazine since 1960, departed earliest from AJC's predominant universalistic and integrationist philosophy; in February 1963, to the great anger of John Slawson and many others in the organization he published the article "My Negro Problem—and Ours." The article spoke of his experiences growing up in a mixed black-white working-class neighborhood in Brownsville, Brooklyn, and the terror and hatred he had felt toward blacks who had beaten and robbed him. In the article he predicted the failure of integration as a movement, forecast the rise of the Black Muslims and Black Power, and concluded that the only way the race problem could be solved eventually was through miscegenation. "It was a piece written at the height of the integrationist enthusiasm in the liberal community," he recalled some years later, "when everybody was saying that if only Negroes and whites could go to school together and live together, they would discover that all their prejudices were based on misconceptions and they would all live happily ever after."[83]

Commentary had been controversial from the day it had been founded, with some officers seeing it as an uncontrollable extravagance that the Committee could ill afford. During Podhoretz's tenure it became even more so, and there were numerous efforts to jettison the magazine; the prestige the magazine enjoyed, however, and a powerful group of supporters within the Committee prevented that from happening. By 2006, *Commentary* was mostly self-supporting through donations and advertising (though it got its office space and services free from AJC). Podhoretz claimed that paradoxically *Commentary*, which took a strong stand against classic liberal politics and affirmative action, became much more controversial within the AJC when it began to speak up more aggressively on Jewish interests. "AJC was in those days . . . a liberal organization," Podhoretz recalled, "and they tended to have what they regarded as a universalistic idea about Judaism and about Jewish interests. . . . AJC was basically a defense organization and the view was that discrimination against anyone is discrimination against everyone, and I think in those years certainly more energy was being spent fighting discrimination against Negroes than fighting discrimination against Jews, but in all good conscience on the theory that this was part of the same fight."[84] Podhoretz, under his agreement with AJC, enjoyed complete editorial independence, and many of *Commentary*'s articles took positions that were not in keeping with AJC official policy.

Responses to the Kerner Commission

The attitudes of Perlmutter, Podhoretz, Hoffman, and at times Bertram Gold, were, however, as we have noted, exceptions to the rule. For the most part national AJC and its chapters in 1968 grasped the responsibility of saving the country from itself and did not for a moment cease their efforts to bring peace and justice to the nation's cities. They would not let evidence of black antisemitism slow them down at this point any more than they had accepted silence from Christian leaders during the Six-Day War. "In the malaise which hangs over the nation, it is only too easy to yield to a sense of futility and powerlessness," declared an AJC editorial to its members. "The alternative is to go to work." In the aftermath of Robert F. Kennedy's assassination in June, barely two months after the death of King, a similar editorial acknowledged the "pall of despondency and collective self-reproach" that had descended, but nonetheless insisted that "the best cure for the emotions of the day is concerted action. . . . It is nonsense to say—as desperate groups on slums and campuses would have it—that all the doors are locked and nothing will do but to set fire to the house." Nowhere else was this stubborn optimism clearer than in AJC's response to the recommendations of the Kerner Commission. In both large and small ways, AJC members and chapters across the country poured their energies into a massive effort to implement the recommendations in any way they could.

Even before the report, through the years of the riots, AJC through its twenty field offices and one hundred chapters sponsored endless black-Jewish dialogues and exchanges of pulpits between black churches and synagogues. They had already been doing the things the Kerner Commission called for. They had long been working with Jewish businessmen to find employment for blacks, especially youths, and participated extensively in Head Start and similar community programs. In New York City, Cleveland, Phoenix, and indeed all over the country, chapters took special interest in conducting human relations training programs for police officers, as most of the race riots had been sparked by hostile confrontations between blacks and the local police. The New York chapter in particular was asked, and agreed, to put four hundred leading members of the police department through their training. AJC's Philadelphia chapter produced the pamphlet "Case Study of a Riot: The Philadelphia Story," which analyzed the social and economic factors that led to the North Philadelphia riot of August 1964 and contained a detailed guide on ways to reduce the likelihood of riots recurring. The pamphlet was used as a training handbook for VISTA volunteers, police recruits, and federal, state, and local government personnel.

AJC had also joined the Urban Coalition, a group of business, labor, political, religious, nonprofit organization, and civil rights leaders pledged to attack the problems of the cities as revealed by the Newark and Detroit riots. In radio and TV spots, car, bus, and subway posters, and newspaper advertisements in New York City and around the country, residents were urged by their local Urban Coalitions to "Give a Damn" about people who lived in the nation's slums.[85] In January 1968, the coalition was already preparing to head off another summer of violence. Under the auspices of Vice President Hubert

Humphrey, Hyman Bookbinder was called to chair a special task force of urban leaders from fifty cities with the goal of dealing as much as possible with the immediate problems of the cities before riots erupted again.

The Kerner Commission Report, which concluded that white racism was at the root of the riots, came out in early March 1968. Warning of impending disaster and destruction if the decay of the inner cities was not halted, its recommendations included broad government initiatives to relieve the plight of poor blacks in housing, education, and jobs. Specifically, it called for national welfare reform to provide basic sustenance to all, the creation of two million jobs within three years, remedial training and special programs for the hard-core unemployed, and the creation of pre-kindergarten programs in the ghetto as part of a general improvement of the public educational system. It also called for better riot control training of local police and National Guardsmen, rapid arrests, and use of tear gas or other nonlethal weapons to subdue offenders. Bookbinder, who had been assistant director of President Johnson's Office of Economic Opportunity before becoming AJC's Washington, D.C., representative, called on the American Jewish community to support the recommendations. The programs would be costly, he admitted, but "the cost of not meeting the challenge will be even costlier—costlier not only in dollars but in honor and in conscience. It will cost the nation its very soul."[86]

Within three weeks of the report's appearance, telegrams were sent by Morris B. Abram to three hundred AJC leaders, calling them to four emergency regional meetings to discuss and implement the report immediately. "There is evidence that the country does not in fact or in feeling comprehend the urgency of the Kerner Report's recommendations," Abram wrote. "We must take dramatic and visible action. . . . The AJC has given the problem of coping with race relations the highest possible priority. For the next several months, all of AJC's resources are being mobilized in order to be of the maximum possible help." The release of the report earned a thank-you letter to Governor Kerner from Bertram Gold: "We in the AJC were deeply moved by your Commission's acutely perceptive findings and were so motivated as to deploy our total resources in an accelerated and concentrated effort to do our modest share toward confronting your Commission's recommendations."[87]

At the emergency meetings, 235 lay AJC leaders from fifty cities responded. The meetings convened the very week after Martin Luther King's assassination on April 4, 1968. This led to fresh outbreaks and fears that the coming summer would be even more violent than previous ones. Delegates prepared a checklist of programs to be undertaken by that time. They emphasized public education, or "keeping the Kerner Report alive"; improving police-community relations; intensifying and expanding urban programming; evidencing "visible commitment and concern from the Jewish community as a whole"; and supplying emergency relief where necessary.[88] National AJC took out full-page ads in the local newspapers of twenty communities supporting the report and urging its immediate implementation.[89] AJC, ADL, and twenty-five other organizations joined in sponsoring a mass printing of three hundred thousand copies of the report to be used in discussions, meetings, and planning conferences throughout the country.

That month's *AJC Newsletter* announced the formation of task forces and outlined short-term ways for members to help. In "Implementing the Kerner Report: What You Can Do," the editors urged readers to advocate aid to riot victims.[90] During the Washington, D.C., outbreaks, for example, AJC worked with Catholic and Protestant groups to shelter and feed those who had been burned out of their homes. Members were told to use their business connections to help displaced businessmen get loans either to reopen their stores or to move. They could support state legislation for pooling ghetto insurance risks, create jobs, round up other AJC members who were employers and ask how many jobs *they* could offer, and help black-owned businesses get off the ground through advice, aid, loans, and purchases. They could not only use black suppliers and contractors whenever possible but urge others to do so as well. They could help in freeing mothers to work outside the home. "Many Negro mothers could hold jobs if they had someone to take care of their children," the guide recommended. "Find out how your city is supplied with day care centers and assist in setting up centers where needed." In the media, they should promote "responsible reporting" of black affairs and urge wider employment of blacks in TV, radio, and newspapers. They could help with recreation: in several cities, AJC was already talking with Jewish federations or other Jewish organizations about giving or leasing unused land they still owned near ghettos for local black residents to use as clubs or playing fields. They could also take ghetto youngsters on trips and provide places in day or sleep-away camp for them during the coming summer.

Over the next few months, AJC was proud to report an impressive record of hands-on action in implementation of the Kerner report's recommendations. AJC reports depicted how over and over again, chapters and members answered the question of exactly what they could do, in the most concrete of terms.[91] Units located near Washington, D.C., and state capitals lobbied for government legislation that would help the poor. In New York members provided counseling and bank contacts to help Puerto Rican residents in their businesses. Based on a report prepared by AJC's race relations coordinator, Harry Fleischman, Mayor Lindsay issued an executive order for minority preference in the awarding of contracts for municipal work; chapters pressed for similar measures in other cities. Also based on the report, New York employers doing business with the City agreed to hire 175 additional black and Puerto Rican workers. Seymour Samet coordinated a program with the Economic Development Corporation to train blacks interested in buying small businesses that whites wished to give up. In the garment district, AJC apparel manufacturer Lawrence S. Phillips spearheaded a venture to form a $20 million credit pool to help black merchants stock new clothing stores in nonwhite areas of the City. He set his goal at five hundred new stores. AJC's Long Island chapter funded scholarships for blacks to attend the Brooklyn College of Pharmacy; they had discovered that there were only twenty-nine licensed black pharmacists in New York and not one black-owned pharmacy. White pharmacists who wanted to leave the ghetto had to find trained registered pharmacists to buy their businesses, and this program helped fill that need.

In New Jersey, the Essex County chapter in cooperation with the local Jewish Community Council collected money, food, clothing, housewares, and furniture for families in Newark's ghetto. Businessmen arranged for groups of black teenagers to get school credit for spending several hours each week in their business offices and factories, as a way of acquainting them with job procedures and duties. The Philadelphia chapter bought a badly decaying building and renovated it to be used as a recreation and training center for neighborhood youngsters. Elsewhere in Pennsylvania, the Harrisburg chapter joined with Protestant and Catholic groups to sponsor the building of 175 units of low-cost housing. Pittsburgh chapter employers recruited black workers and provided on-the-job training and transportation from ghetto areas to factories and plants. In Baltimore, AJC members were among the businessmen, lawyers, tax experts, insurance men, and executives who served on a panel set up by the Baltimore Associated Jewish Charities to provide guidance and aid to businessmen hit by rioting. In Chicago, AJC members arranged loans and foundation grants for blacks wishing to invest in small businesses, and set up a revolving fund for small loans up to fifty dollars for the needs of minority youth that the big programs did not cover—for example, art courses, a musical instrument, or a new suit for going out on a job interview.

The St. Louis AJC chapter recruited thirty-five black children, raised the money to pay their fees, and then enrolled them in three previously all-white suburban day camps. They also arranged educational trips for sixth-grade children from the inner city: one Saturday a month they would be taken to such places as the zoo, the planetarium, or a baseball game. Also in the area of recreation, the Cincinnati AJC chapter set up and coached sixteen baseball teams in the black ghetto, providing an average of three hundred dollars per team to cover uniforms and equipment. The Detroit chapter, as part of an Interfaith Action Council, collected relief supplies for riot victims, and individual chapter members cosigned loans from the Hebrew Free Loan Society to help needy minority students pay for counseling or job-training fees. They also worked with the local Volunteer Placement Corps to find summer jobs for almost five hundred Detroit high school students.

The Milwaukee chapter similarly sponsored a program to prepare high school students for college, and thirty-five AJC women with teaching experience offered to be tutors with the Upward Bound program at the University of Wisconsin in Milwaukee. Meanwhile, chapter president Elmer L. Winter and others raised seed money for a nonprofit corporation that would build one-family houses to rent at ninety-five dollars a month under the provisions of the Federal Housing and Urban Development program. In Los Angeles, the chapter was cosponsor of a housing corporation that planned to build 176 units of integrated, moderate-cost housing; members provided seed money and guaranteed bank loans to potential buyers. In Texas, AJC joined with Mexican American groups, the State Catholic Conference, and the Texas Council of Churches to hold leadership workshops for young Mexican Americans. In Dallas, the chapter supported a job fair sponsored by the local Urban League that found jobs for more than thirty-five hundred poor white and black young people aged sixteen to twenty-two. Some 440 employers, the largest number of them Jewish, sent interviewers, and one hundred AJC members worked as fair volunteers. Their most important contribution turned out to be the orientation on how to behave on a job interview. Given in advance to applicants, this orientation was credited with making the placement rate so successful. Other Dallas AJC employers provided on-the-job classes in communications for their employees who were functionally illiterate. And Stanley Marcus, head of Neiman Marcus in Dallas, wrote to his thousands of suppliers that his store would "look with favor" upon companies that took positive measures toward employing and training minority group members. Neiman Marcus itself had gone out of its way to hire blacks in previous years and by 1968 had four hundred and fifty on its staff, some in executive jobs.

Inward and Rightward?

Historians of American Jewry, in looking back at so formative a decade as the 1960s, have tended to describe an American Jewish community that turned "inward and rightward" after the terror and salvation of the June 1967 war. Indeed, pride and concern for Israel became and remained a unifying principle and point of identification in ways it never had before. That concern would be tested again soon enough during the 1973 Yom Kippur War, when AJC and the American Jewish community in general rallied with even greater fervor to Israel's cause. The streets of the nation's ghettoes were noticeably quieter in the summers of 1969 and 1970, though civil protest remained strong on all other fronts.[92] In the meantime, the Vietnam War drained funds and energy from the War on Poverty, which fell victim to its own ambitions. A Republican sat in the White House. AJC pledged to make Soviet Jewry its highest priority when word came in 1970 of threats of a rebirth of Stalinist policies and further arrests and show trials for Jews.

Yet even when the days passed when all the world's problems seemed solvable, AJC and the greater part of organized American Jewry remained solidly committed to the liberal agenda it had so long pursued. This commitment continued into the 1970s and long afterward. In an address delivered on December 5, 1970, Philip E. Hoffman, AJC president, declared: "More than a decade ago we pledged ourselves unequivocally to the achievement of successful integration for blacks and other groups into our society." Hoffman bemoaned the unhealthy "tribalism" that seemed to have replaced the pluralism they had had all hoped for, yet concluded, "We could not then have done otherwise—and we cannot today do otherwise."[93] A famous saying often quoted in those days was that of the liberal first-century sage Hillel, who often disagreed with his stricter rival, Shammai: "If I am not for myself, who is for me? But if I am only for myself, who am I? And if not now, when?"[94] Even in the aftermath of the Six-Day War, when American Jews became so determined to "be" for themselves, they remained at the same time firm in their religious devotion that they must be for others as well.

❧ III ❧

The 1970s

7

New Challenges

The Energy Crisis, Jimmy Carter, the Rise of the Evangelicals, and Cults

[1970–1979]

Very soon after the end of 1968, Jewish leaders and scholars acknowledged that one age had ended and another had begun. They looked back to the years from 1945 to 1967 as the "Golden Age" or the "Golden quarter century" of American Jewry. Certainly Bert Gold, AJC executive vice president, did so in his annual address to the AJC in 1972: "This approximately twenty year period, which has been characterized as the golden age of Jewish life in the United States, saw a tremendous upward mobility in Jewish life and the virtual end of overt antisemitism. . . . It was a period in which virtually all American Jews believed that American growth and prosperity and the Jewish interests were congruent, and that an expanded welfare state with broadly conceived liberal goals would free man everywhere. . . . Those were heady, optimistic days. Convinced that our country's economic growth, together with goodwill and solid motives, would produce miracles, we all fought the good fight—for the expansion of civil rights, for fair opportunities, and then for full opportunities for all. And since we were all singing the same song, it mattered little who sang the loudest."[1]

Now the American economic pie was contracting, not expanding; the need to pay for both the war in Vietnam and the programs of the Great Society, along with a rise in the price of oil and other geopolitical factors, brought inflation, recession, and unemployment. AJC itself had to lay off thirty-three of its staff in 1970, eliminate several programs including community service in Europe, and close its overseas offices in Santiago, Montevideo and São Paulo, leaving Mexico City, Buenos Aires, and Rio de Janeiro to service all of Central and South America. Throughout the United States faith in the value of traditional political liberalism was shaken. The euphoria caused by Israel's victory in the Six-Day War was short-lived as Jews came to realize that for the second time in a quarter century millions of Jews had been in danger of death and the world had done nothing to stop it. Israel, once the underdog, was now viewed by many as the imperialist Goliath, oppressors of the Palestinians on the West Bank and Gaza. When it became evident in 1973 that they could not destroy the country physically, Arab nations and Palestinian groups fought Israel with diplomatic isolation, seeking to obtain through negotiations and terrorism that which they had been unable to obtain on the battlefield. Under the administration of President Jimmy Carter, criticism of aid for Israel and calls for recognizing the PLO increased. Although organized antisemitism and discrimination in housing and employment was almost a thing of the past by the 1970s, American Jews at home faced a host of new anxieties. These included the Watergate scandal, the rise to power and politics of Evangelical Christianity, the loss of their children to unorthodox religious cults, a reprise of rioting during a 1977 blackout in New York, and a fracturing of the black-Jewish alliance over the issues of affirmative action and the resignation of U.N. Ambassador Andrew Young.

The Growth of Palestinian Terrorism

Prior to 1967, the terms of the Arab-Israeli conflict were simple: the desire of the Arab nations to destroy Israel. Afterward, there were new and more complicated issues including rule over a million Palestinian Arabs, settlement in the West Bank of the Jordan, rising Palestinian nationalism, and disputes on the sovereignty over the Old City of Jerusalem. The Six-Day War set the stage for the fantasy that if only Israel would withdraw to the borders of June 4, 1967, then peace would reign and all would be well in the Middle East. The Six-Day War did not really end. A three-year War of Attrition in 1967–70 with Egypt sapped Israel's strength and cost even more casualties. The Soviet Union continued to fund the Arab side, the Americans countered, and the threat of World War III breaking out in the Middle East was ever present.

While armed *fedayeen* had been engaging in attacks against Israeli civilians since the establishment of the State, terrorism in the name of Palestinian liberation and the release of prisoners held by Israel also entered a new phase in the late 1960s and early 1970s. The Palestine Liberation Organization (PLO), which had been founded in 1964, was reorganized in 1968 under the leadership of Yasir Arafat's al-Fatah faction. Along with several other Palestinian factions with different ideologies but similar goals, it waged a war of terror against Israeli targets at home and abroad, pursuing a specialty in airplane piracy, hostage-taking, and the sending of letter and parcel bombs to Jewish and Israeli leaders throughout the world. The new wave began in 1968, when terrorists hijacked an El Al flight and diverted it to Algiers, where they held thirty-two passengers and crew hostage for more than a month. In December gunmen opened fire on an El Al jet in Athens about to take off for New York, killing one passenger and wounding two others. In 1969 terrorists attacked an El Al passenger jet at the airport in Zurich and hijacked a TWA flight from Los Angeles to Damascus where they held two Israeli passengers hostage for forty-four days. There were grenade attacks on Israeli embassies and El Al offices in Europe. In 1970 a bus containing El Al passengers at the Munich airport was attacked, causing the death of one passenger and the wounding of eleven others; a Swissair flight bound for Israel was sabotaged and crashed, killing forty-seven; and in early September, terrorists hijacked no fewer than five passenger jets (Pan Am, TWA, Swissair, and BOAC) and blew up three of them in a Jordanian airport.

In response to the September 1970 attack on his soil, King Hussein of Jordan, with the quiet assistance of the Israelis, waged a war to expel Palestinian terrorists from Jordan. In the process, Israel's mobilization prevented a Syrian invasion of Jordan on the Palestinians' behalf. Despite the lack of a formal peace treaty between Israel and Jordan, an informal state of cooperation existed between them. The Israelis preferred King Hussein to other radical Arab leaders who were always eyeing Jordan. An Israeli journalist in 1981 claimed that without Israeli protection, Hussein would have been deposed long ago. Allegedly the Israelis saved him from at least five assassination attempts by informing him of plans to kill him that were caught by the Israeli intelligence service.[2] The Israelis also warned Hussein that if he did not get rid of the terrorists, they would. Most of the Palestinian terrorists left Jordan for haven in southern Lebanon, where they took up residence in what came to be known as "Fatah-land." One group formed a faction called Black September in memory of the expulsion; in addition to killing Jews they vowed that they would someday get King Hussein as well.

Israel was far from rid of the terrorists when they went to Lebanon. In the first five months of 1971 more than 140 attacks against Israel were carried out from Lebanese territory. The U.N. Security Council would never condemn them, although it would pass resolutions condemning Israel for reprisal bombing raids in Lebanon and Syria.[3] Of the constant attacks on Israeli citizens from Lebanon, two of the most notorious took place in 1974 in the border towns of Kiryat Shemona and Ma'alot; in the latter, terrorists took a school building with one hundred children hostage and threatened to blow it up.[4] Lod Airport (later renamed Ben-Gurion Airport) in Israel was the target in May 1972, when on May 9, four terrorists hijacked a Sabena jet there and threatened to blow it up. On May 30 three Japanese allied to the Popular Front for the Liberation of Palestine opened fire at the same airport, killing twenty-three and wounding seventy-eight. Most of the victims were from a Puerto Rican Christian pilgrims' group.[5] The Israelis fought back by installing state-of-the-art security procedures on Israel-bound flights and intercepting terrorists before they could strike. One moment of triumph in this constant struggle took place in July 1976, when before the eyes of the whole world Israeli forces successfully flew all the way to Uganda to rescue Jewish and Israeli hostages being held at the Entebbe airport. Symbolically the news of the rescue broke on July 4, the Bicentennial of the United States.[6] Israelis and Jews everywhere erupted in jubilation, and fantasies ranged freely on how many could have been rescued had there been such a thing as an Israeli Air Force during World War II.

A major sporting event also became a target of terrorism. At the 1972 Summer Olympics in Munich, as millions of TV viewers looked on, eight terrorists disguised as athletes invaded the Olympic compound, took eleven Israeli athletes and trainers hostage, shot two and then grenaded the rest during a failed rescue attempt by the German police. Few missed the symbolism of such an event happening in Germany. On AJC's part, President Philip E. Hoffman joined in the voices calling upon the governments of the world to impose international sanctions on countries that aided and abetted such terrorism. Rabbi Marc H. Tanenbaum provided a running commentary on NBC's *Today* program on the return of the Israeli dead to Israel; researchers prepared a detailed memorandum on terrorist groups that was distributed to the media; and the Interreligious Affairs Department joined with leaders of the major Christian churches in special memorial services for the victims.[7]

The Olympic Games went on, with no formal acknowledgment of what had taken place. Again, the U.N. did not condemn the act. Instead, there were more resolutions of condemnation for Israeli attacks on terrorist bases and an invitation in November 1974 for PLO Chairman Yasir Arafat, as the leader of a liberation movement, to address the U.N. General Assembly. Now the diplomatic war against Israel was in full swing. The following year the PLO was granted "observer status" at the U.N. and on November 10, 1975, the General Assembly—with the votes of the Arab nations, the developing world, and the Soviet bloc—passed Resolution 3379, which equated Israel with apartheid South Africa. The resolution concluded with the words "Zionism is a form of racism and racial discrimination."

Israeli U.N. ambassador Chaim Herzog, noting the coincidence that November 10 was the anniversary of Crystal Night in Germany in 1938, made a speech defending Zionism as the "national liberation movement of the Jewish people"; at the end, he ripped the resolution to shreds in front of the assembly. U.S. delegate Daniel Patrick Moynihan said the resolution gave the appearance of "international sanction" to the "abomination of anti-Semitism"; he announced that the United States "will not abide by, will not acquiesce in this infamous act."[8] The PLO and their supporters exulted. To them the resolution was far more than a piece of paper. A few days after the resolution passed a group of PLO members set off a bomb in West Jerusalem's Zion Square that killed six youngsters aged fifteen to seventeen and wounded dozens of others. The Israeli consulate then passed on to AJC the words of a

broadcast they had heard and transcribed from the "Palestine Corner" of
Radio Damascus:

The *fedayeen* take one copy of the resolution adopted at the UN, mix it with TNT, and
blow up Zion Square! . . . These resolutions were adopted at the UN in order to enable
each and every inhabitant of the stolen land to carry a copy that will convince him to
join the *fedayeen*, mix it with dynamite and blow up . . . one of our other occupied
squares or streets. Now the resolutions of the UN are turning into deeds under the
leadership of the Arab people—at whose head marches the Palestinian people. . . . The
important aspect of the assembly resolution is the negation of any moral, human, or
social basis for the existence of Israel. This resolution condemns the ideological foundation upon which Israel arose—namely the Zionist idea and movement. What this
resolution says in effect, is that Israel has no right to exist.[9]

After a long struggle in which AJC played an important part, the "Zionism is
racism" resolution was rescinded by the U.N. General Assembly on December
16, 1991 (see chapter 11).

The Yom Kippur War and the OPEC Oil Embargo

President Anwar Sadat of Egypt, who had succeeded Nasser in 1970, had
vowed since the 1967 defeat that he would win back the territory lost to Israel.
The Soviet Union aided him in his plan. On October 6, 1973, Israel was subject to a massive surprise attack by both Egypt and Syria in the Sinai and the
Golan Heights. It was the afternoon of Yom Kippur, one of the holiest days in
the Jewish calendar, when most Israelis were in synagogue and many soldiers
demobilized. Despite numerous intelligence warnings, it had become clear
only that morning to the Israeli leadership that the Egyptian and Syrian armies were massing for an attack. Israel's Prime Minister Golda Meir, under
warnings from U.S. Secretary of State Henry Kissinger, denied an appeal by
members of her cabinet that Israel launch a preemptive strike and awaited the
first Arab attack. (After the war she was denounced for her position and resigned under public pressure.) First the Soviet Union and then the United
States were ready to intervene. Once again the world was brought to the brink
of nuclear war.[10]

Ultimately, Israel prevailed, but there was no repeat of the 1967 thrashing
that so many expected. Israel's losses were heavy in the first days of the war,
and only a massive airlift of supplies and ammunition authorized by President
Richard M. Nixon enabled Israel to turn the tide.[11] The event marked an ex-
ponential rise in the amount of U.S. aid to Israel and a new reliance in the following years of the Jewish state on the Americans. The United States became
Israel's chief arms supplier and aid to Israel shot up to billions of dollars a
year. Nixon, whom many American Jews loathed for his social policies and his
past as an anticommunist hunter in the 1950s, saw Israel as a factor in regional

stability and an obstacle to Soviet expansionism. So too did his secretary of state and former national security adviser Henry Kissinger, who had come to the United States as a refugee from the Nazis and who rose to the highest level in U.S. government that any Jew had ever reached before.

The flow of U.S. arms strengthened Israel; at the same time, paradoxically, it brought new anxieties to American Jews. No other nation but the United States had come to Israel's side in her hour of need. The amount of dollars the U.S. government was capable of sending dwarfed the amount all of American Jewry could send through private contributions. American Jewish organizations now felt an enormous sense of responsibility to keep that U.S. government aid flowing through numerous obstacles, opponents, and changes in administration. The new situation also left the United States with greater leverage to pressure Israel to make political and territorial concessions in subsequent negotiations with her enemies.

In the Yom Kippur War, Israel faced the combined armies of Egypt and Syria, equivalent to the entire forces of NATO. Iraq, Saudi Arabia, Kuwait, Libya, Algeria, Tunisia, and Morocco gave troops and financial backing. In its course almost three thousand Israeli soldiers were killed (given the small Israeli population, this was the equivalent per capita of all the deaths the United States had suffered in Vietnam over ten years) and more than three hundred were taken prisoner. The gravest concern was for the prisoners who had been taken on the Syrian front. Shortly after the cessation of hostilities forty-two Israeli soldiers were found shot dead on the Syrian front, blindfolded with their hands tied behind their backs and with signs of torture. The Syrians for months refused to give any news about the more than one hundred other prisoners they had or even to hand over a list of their names.[12] In this case AJC was able to intervene directly by mobilizing its interreligious network. A group of French priests, nuns, and laypersons appealed directly to French President George Pompidou for France to use its good services for their return. Scores of human rights and religious organizations sent appeals to the U.S. government to persuade Syria to release the information. AJC convened a special meeting on the prisoners of war at its headquarters on February 12, inviting ninety-one people, including the families of some of the prisoners; two days later the pope intervened with Syria on the prisoners' behalf.[13] The May 1974 disengagement treaty with Syria, negotiated by Henry Kissinger, included the exchange of prisoners.

The effects of the Yom Kippur War were felt not only in the Middle East but around the world. Oil was the lifeblood of modern technological society and on October 17, 1973, seven Arab member–nations of OPEC (Organization of Petroleum Exporting Countries) called for an oil embargo against the United States and its Western European allies.[14] The Netherlands in particular was singled out for its support of Israel during the war. President Nixon and Congress responded with calls for such actions as voluntary rationing, an extension of daylight savings time, a maximum of ten gallons at a time for gasoline purchases, and a complete ban on gas sales on Sundays. Long lines snaked around blocks at gas stations across the country. Congress also approved plans for the Trans-Alaskan oil pipeline, designed to supply two million barrels of oil a day (the pipeline was completed in 1977). In the meantime, gasoline and heating oil shortages in the United States aroused fears of an antisemitic backlash among the major American Jewish organizations. What should they do, their leaders wondered, if Americans, furious at waiting in long lines for their gas or finding themselves on the unemployment line, blamed Israel and the Jews for their plight? Rumors spread of bumper stickers reading "We Need Oil, Not Jews" or worse, "Burn Jews, Not Oil," although no one ever found hard evidence of them.[15] That many Jews alive then are convinced to this day that those bumper stickers existed exemplifies their continuing anxiety about antisemitism even when it has not been reflected in the reality of American society.

The term "energy crisis" was in fact already well established in the American vocabulary. The Arab oil-exporting nations had already begun to raise the price of oil in the face of higher demand, and shortages were already developing in the winter of 1972–73, almost a year before the Yom Kippur War broke out. Schools and factories closed because they did not have enough heating oil; diesel trucks sometimes lacked fuel to deliver the oil they had on hand; jetliners had difficulty fueling their tanks for nonstop flights from the East to the West Coast. Senator Henry M. Jackson referred to the energy crisis in January 1973 as being "the most critical problem facing the nation today."[16]

Shortages were only the beginning of the problem. Arab oil-producing nations could not absorb the tens of billions of dollars of profit pouring into their countries.[17] The solution—to which businessmen and corporations eagerly responded—was to turn around and invest these "petro-dollars" in financial dealings and academic institutions in the United States and around the world. This new source of capital led to unprecedented economic and political power—and fears that Jews or Israelis, or anyone doing business with them, would be shut out of these investments through the long-standing Arab boycott. Petro-dollars led to a decline in the security of Israel because the oil-producing nations were able to spend billions in acquiring arms and military equipment. Petro-dollars also fueled the effort to disseminate pro-Arab and anti-Zionist, anti-Israel propaganda in the world media and in diplomatic circles. The ADL in 1976 estimated that OPEC nations were spending forty-five million dollars a year on pro-Arab publications, newspaper advertising campaigns, and efforts to bring the Arab viewpoint before business, financial, political, academic, and church communities.[18] Saudi Arabia also used its petro-dollars to fund Islamic schools and institutions in the United States and around the world, including in sub-Saharan Africa—in the process spreading its own brand of puritanical Islam.[19]

In reaction to the business aspects of the boycott, AJC and other Jewish organizations in NCRAC mounted a two-year effort to push Congress to adopt
a major antiboycott law. This law would make it illegal for American companies (1) to refuse to do business with Israel as a condition of doing business
with Arab states; (2) to refuse to do business with another American firm because the latter was owned by Jews or was on an Arab blacklist; and (3) to
practice any form of ethnic and religious discrimination to meet boycott re-
quirements. The resulting Williams-Proxmire Bill was signed by President
Carter in June 1977.[20]

Even months before the Yom Kippur War began, the Houston chapter of
AJC, concerned that in a few years Kuwait might become a major stockholder
in Shell Oil, insisted that the energy crisis be placed firmly on the agenda of
the AJC annual meeting in May 1973. In the long term, they insisted, something would have to be done to increase domestic oil production—or, better
still, to develop alternative energy sources. "Nobody at all," protested Billie
Stern to the national office from Houston, "is contemplating a Manhattan or
NASA type project for a massive national effort toward making ourselves self-
sufficient in energy resources by, say, the mid-1980s." Even if there were to be
an immediate large-scale crash program involving both government and private industry, he wrote, the solutions would still be ten to fifteen years away:
"The consequences may very well be much higher product prices, rationing of
fuel, head to head conflict with Japan and Europe for energy, and the incessant
devaluation of the dollar. Gas may be $1.25 per gallon in the near future, creat-
ing a major transportation crisis in the U.S. . . . People in our cities and suburbs will be unable to use their cars to get to work, let alone for recreation, at a
time when virtually nothing is being spent on the development of mass rapid
transit systems."[21]

Such fears moved closer to reality when war broke out and the actual embargo was declared in October, only a few days after Nixon had authorized
the massive arms airlift to Israel. Predictions were made that by the spring of
1974 up to ten or fifteen million people might be thrown out of work as a result of the embargo and the country might be headed for double-digit inflation. From the Dallas chapter came reports that people were "scared and
worried" and that for the first time in many years Jews were talking openly
about antisemitism. Busy executives were talking about volunteering their
services and anxious people were calling up the local Jewish welfare federation just to have someone to talk to about it. The energy crisis and concern
for Israel was uppermost in their minds. "Israel has always been a concern,"
said one member, "but it has been something that was 'over there.' All of a
sudden it is hitting home."[22] "American Jewry is in trouble," announced an
officer of the Los Angeles chapter, inviting members to his home for an
emergency meeting. "I deeply hope I am wrong. If, however, there is only a
five percent chance of trouble, we must start now with a program of: 1. trying

to avert the problem before it happens and 2. If we cannot avert the problem, we must have an advance plan of action as to how to handle the situation the moment it develops."[23]

AJC's response was a case study of its operations at the height of their power. The organization's ability to invest extraordinary time and effort and to marshal every bit of wealth, power, influence, and intellect it could in pursuit of its goals, suggests how organizations representing less than 3 percent of the American population were nevertheless able to be so effective. By the first week of December the national office had sent out a dozen background memoranda stating Israel's case to fifteen hundred newspapers and all Israeli consulates in the United States and Canada, so that Israeli officials would have usable material to handle any inquiries. The Israelis, in other words, were dependent on AJC for their own public relations material. Spanish translations were sent to the Israeli ambassador in Mexico. Programs stressing Israel's need for "defensible borders" were broadcast on forty-two black radio stations. In the perennial effort to demonstrate that this was an American and not only a Jewish problem, staff and laypeople solicited and publicized statements of support from prominent Christians and set up the Interreligious Task Force for a Fair Energy Policy (in which AJC would stay behind the scenes as much as possible).[24] As usual AJC would do everything it could to get Christians to agree to issue statements, or allow statements to be issued that AJC would write under their names.[25]

Through its National Project on Ethnic America—which had been founded in 1971 under the leadership of Irving Levine to support and form coalitions with America's ethnic groups—similar statements of solidarity were solicited from Greek, Italian, Japanese, and Polish groups. To gain the support of academics and the intellectual Left, they arranged publication in the *New York Times* of a letter signed by a group of Israeli professors associated with Israel's peace movement. AJC members across the country were urged to write or send telegrams to their elected officials; some sent delegations to visit their senators and their congressional representatives. Hyman Bookbinder in the Washington office kept track of the tone of congressional mail and met daily with his counterparts from the ADL, AIPAC, and other national agencies. Staff at the national office daily monitored opinions expressed in the nation's leading newspapers—editorials, letters to the editor, essays by national and local columnists—quickly preparing and sending replies to any charges that Israel or American Jews or "pressure groups" were responsible for the embargo or that U.S. support of Israel was against the interests of the United States. Area officers monitored local radio talk shows and called in themselves where necessary. The major goals were to combat any antisemitic or anti-Israel propaganda, to stress that an energy crisis existed independently from the Middle East conflict, and to call for America to become completely independent of foreign energy supplies.[26]

So desperate did the energy crisis appear that Richard C. Rothschild, who had headed the AJC's Survey Committee against Nazi Propaganda in the 1930s, was called out of retirement to advise on the formation of what AJC now called "Survey Committee II." (The name originated in a "survey" of antisemitism in the United States, but it had soon moved from simple surveying to taking action). The techniques he recommended using were exactly the ones that AJC had used with such success in the 1940s and 1950s: educating the public to view prejudice and antisemitism as wrongs and mental disorders. A confidential "white paper" prepared with his help—entitled "A Tactical Program Plan to Combat Anticipated Anti-Semitic Fallout from the Energy Crisis"—noted that all surveys done so far showed that the bulk of the American people were not blaming Israel or American Jews to any degree. All polls showed that hatred, if any, was being directed against the oil companies and/or the Arab countries. Potentially, however, the situation was not dissimilar to conditions that had existed during the Nazi era.[27] The Great Depression of the 1930s had schooled American Jews in the idea that in times of economic crisis, they were likely to be made the scapegoats. "We must launch an immediate, vast, and subtle program of interpretation," the memo declared, "vast because of the infinite complexity of the problems we face and subtle because most of what we say should be 'salted into' the mainstream of American thought so that our messages will be carried, for the most part, by non-Jewish organizations and individuals, coalitions and citizen's committees."

In order that the campaign not appear to be "a Jewish self-interest effort," the writer recommended, a "non-partisan Committee of concerned citizens" should be recruited to act as signatory to any letters or advertisements. The ideal was to get ideas into the public domain without anyone knowing that AJC lay at their source. If AJC had to publish anything in its own name, the imprimatur "Institute for Human Relations" should be used. Pertinent materials would have to be prepared for all of the "opinion-molding forces" on the American scene, including television, newspaper editorials and columns, magazine articles, speeches by national, state, and local officials, trade organization publications in the fields of labor and business, and churches. "Salting in" would also include comments, asides, even jokes in radio and TV entertainment.[28] The AJC, the writer suggested, should consider engaging the Advertising Council or an appropriate agency to prepare a campaign using newspaper and magazine ads, TV and radio spots, jingles, billboards, store posters, bumper stickers, and even buttons. Long, intellectual-oriented articles (such as those in *Commentary*) were unsuitable for this purpose. The message should be delivered as much as possible in simple slogans or near-slogan style. Selma Hirsh polled all the staff at national headquarters and they came up with the following suggestions:

"Israel or not, the crisis had to come."
"Israel, America's natural ally."
"The Arabs — pawns in the Soviet's Mideast Game Plan"
"U.S. Foreign Policy must be 'Made in the U.S.A.'"
"We can solve our energy problem."
"Economic terror is still terror."
"Without meaning to, the Arabs did us a favor, by alerting us NOW."
"Let's not rely on suppliers we can't trust."
"Yielding to blackmail invites more blackmail."
"Let's not look for scapegoats."

To fund all this, the memo concluded, a budget of one million dollars for the first year and a full-time staff, financed separately from AJC's regular functions, was desirable. And time was of the essence: "One blow against the enemy *now*," the author noted, "is worth a dozen blows after his propaganda takes full effect."

Indeed, private donations of ten thousand dollars or more were forthcoming from prominent individuals recruited or solicited by AJC. Judge Simon H. Rifkind chaired the executive board of Survey Committee II. Members included William Bernbach of Doyle Dane and Bernbach; David Finn of Ruder and Finn; Robert L. Bernstein of Random House; Gustave L. Levy of Goldman Sachs and Co.; Lou R. Wasserman (chairman of the board of MCA), Eli M. Black of United Brands; Lawrence A. Tisch of Loew's Theaters; Louis G. Cowan, Fred Klingenstein, and John H. Steinhart.[29] Abe Fortas, Arthur J. Goldberg, and Eugene Rostow were available for consultation. Others recruited included Sol P. Steinberg, Irving Goldman, Robert Tischman, William S. Paley, Charles H. Revson, Meshulam Riklis, Lawrence A. Wien, Arthur Krim, Irvin S. Chanin, Nathan Cummings, and Leonard H. Goldenson of ABC, as well as several others active in the fields of communications, public relations, real estate, law, or publishing.[30]

During the year and a half that Survey Committee II was in operation, AJC public relations director Morton Yarmon, the staff member who coordinated the effort, maintained a file of scores of index cards, keeping track of his contacts with cooperative writers, editors, producers, correspondents, and commentators in a multitude of media. Either Yarmon and AJC leaders would contact or have lunch with them, encouraging them to do stories or feeding them material. Or they would approach AJC, seeking ideas, material, and spokesmen for upcoming articles, editorials, broadcasts, documentaries, and books on any aspect of the energy crisis or Arab investment in the United States. An AJC pamphlet or a deftly written and well-researched memo in the mailbox was especially vital in those days; there was no e-mail or Internet to provide the latest information. Occasionally AJC staff would appear on talk or radio shows, or they would suggest non-Jewish allies who were willing to appear (Eugene Rostow, Frank Gervasi, Vernon Jordan, and Bayard Rustin appeared when asked). Contacts included the producers of *60 Minutes,* and the news at CBS TV and radio; *Eyewitness News,* the documentary unit, and the Washington correspondent at ABC TV News and radio; the *Today* show along with the news executive director and producer at WNBC TV; and the director of the New York bureau of National Public Radio. A January 28 briefing with Chaim Herzog convened by AJC at the Israeli consulate drew representatives from all three major networks.

Major newspapers, magazines, and even book publishers were in AJC's sights. The *Washington Post,* the *New York Daily News,* the *Boston Globe,* the *Philadelphia Inquirer,* the *Los Angeles Times,* and the *Wall Street Journal* received regular phone calls and offers of background memoranda for their stories; so too did Gus Tyler, a columnist for United Features. So did *Newsweek, U.S. News and World Report,* the *Christian Science Monitor,* and *Readers' Digest.* Newspapers carried advertisements prepared by AJC (though their origin was not indicated). Yarmon suggested to an editor at Macmillan that they expand a front-page *New York Times* story on the energy crisis into a book. An editorial director at Bantam Books told him they were about to publish a book by Ralph Nader on the subject and would see if AJC material could be incorporated into it.

Contacts with the *New York Times* were especially fruitful. Harry Schwartz, a member of the editorial board who had written a piece on energy exploration, after one conversation said he would be available for further discussion and possible writing. Leonard Silk, also on the editorial board, called to ask for material and used it to write a front-page story. Linda Charlton of the Washington bureau called to discuss doing a story based on an AJC pamphlet she had received. Herbert Mitgang of the Op-Ed page said that he already had too much on energy, but the pamphlet was so good that he had passed it on to other *Times* writers. Kalman Siegel, the letters editor, said he was getting on average a letter a week with antisemitic overtones and would consider a letter from AJC. So in February, AJC President Elmer Winter sent out a letter to the *Times.* Yarmon checked on its progress, only to be told that the letter was "in the works" and was being circulated to appropriate editorial writers. The letter finally appeared on March 24, 1974, warning that the energy crisis represented a "made-to-order opportunity" for the "peddlers of bigotry" and suggesting various means of dealing with it, including possible rationing and price controls and the expansion of mass transit.[31]

Economic dislocations, inflation, and recession—caused in part by the high price of oil—continued, however, and there were fears that the embargo might be reimposed. Survey Committee II kept up its activities for more than a year until it was officially disbanded on May 1, 1975.[32] The same techniques were then used in 1979, when another energy crisis developed under President

Carter. Once again lines for gasoline went around the block and schools closed for lack of heating oil.[33] That time there were not even rumors about bumper stickers that spoke of burning Jews.

Watergate and New Presidents

In the meantime President Nixon, who had been reelected by a historic margin in 1972 (though not by American Jews, who voted overwhelmingly for George McGovern), was suffering a crisis of his own. The two-year series of events that came to be known as the Watergate scandal had begun during Nixon's campaign on June 17, 1972, when five men with close ties to the Republican president were caught breaking into the offices of their competition, the Democratic National Committee. The headquarters were located in the office complex of the Watergate Hotel in Washington, D.C. Thereafter, the suffix "-gate" entered the language as a way to name any political scandal. One of the burglars was a leader of the Committee to Re-elect the President (CRP), which subsequently came to be both spelled and called "CREEP." The question arose whether Nixon had known about or actually ordered the break-in and other nefarious activities that were subsequently uncovered. The investigations that followed, culminating in a U.S. Supreme Court decision and impeachment hearings by the House Judiciary Committee broadcast on TV, revealed a pattern of presidential corruption, abuse of power, and possible criminal activity. Facing certain impeachment and possible criminal prosecution, Nixon resigned effective August 9, 1974. He was succeeded by Vice President Gerald R. Ford, who had formerly been a congressman from Michigan. The investigations ended when Ford granted Nixon a full and unconditional pardon for any crimes he had committed during his time in office.

That year AJC gave its highest award, the American Liberties Medallion, to Katharine Graham, chief executive of the *Washington Post* company, honoring her for her "defense of free speech in the face of one of the most vicious, insidious, concentrated attacks upon the First Amendment this country has ever seen."[34] Aside from the national upheaval and irreparable tarnishing of American government that resulted from Watergate, those at AJC who kept their eye on antisemitism were most directly concerned with the question of whether Jews would be blamed for Nixon's impeachment and resignation. A careful survey revealed that the answer was no. Milton Ellerin, head of what AJC called its "Trends Analysis Division," had begun his career as a special agent for the FBI, infiltrating American Nazi organizations in the 1930s and 1940s. Part of his job was to read, digest, and assess every single publication put out by every antisemitic organization or any movement or group that might be of concern to the Jewish community.[35] To be sure, he did find writings that claimed Watergate was "A Jewish conspiracy. . . . A diabolical plot by

Jews to take over the country," or "a smokescreen for the consolidation of power by the Jewish governmental clique." The *Washington Post* had reported that "a small number of Arab leaders are firmly convinced that Watergate is yet another Zionist plot aimed at heading off Middle East Peace moves," and Saudi Arabia's King Faisal had told foreign visitors that "Zionists are behind all America's current internal problems." Nixon's supporters were convinced that "the media" was the president's chief tormenter, Ellerin reported. Happily, however, the charges had been free of "any intimation that it [the media] is Jewish owned or operated." Polls revealed that most Americans placed direct responsibility for Watergate and its aftermath at the White House.[36]

As for the Jewish community, Ellerin noted that the AJC itself never issued any statement calling for the president's resignation. Neither had any other major Jewish agency or organization. Jewish congresspersons, with the exception of Representative Bella Abzug of New York, had either been silent or had taken minor roles. The first resolution calling for Nixon's impeachment was introduced in the House by Representative Robert Drinan, a Jesuit priest from Massachusetts. Organizations that had come to be known as "the impeachment lobby" included the AFL-CIO, the ACLU, Common Cause, the ADA, and Ralph Nader's group. "While many of these organizations have Jewish members and in some instances even in substantial numbers," Ellerin wrote, "in the main they have not assumed nor are they presumed to have leadership roles in the demand for the president's removal." Moreover, one of Nixon's principal defenders, who led a massive newspaper advertising campaign in favor of the president, was Baruch Korff, who identified himself as an Orthodox rabbi. Ellerin therefore concluded that the AJC had nothing to fear: American Jews would not become the scapegoats for the tribulations of Richard Nixon.

Nor, as it turned out, had they much to fear from his successor, Gerald Ford. Reporting from AJC's Washington office, Hyman Bookbinder confessed that because of the low Jewish turnout for Nixon and his own history of working for the Kennedy and Johnson administrations, he had feared that he and the AJC would be "frozen out" of a Republican White House. Fortunately, such fears had proved groundless. Bookbinder reported that he had been able to maintain "extremely good relations both with the White House itself and with all of the executive departments with which we had business," and there was no reason to expect a change with the new administration. This positive relationship, he noted, was made possible "because of the long established reputation that AJC enjoys in the nation's capitol for fairness and nonpartisanship as well as expertise in various fields and the efforts of some very key AJC lay people." These included Max Fisher, a Republican philanthropist and donor from Detroit, whose title was honorary chairman of AJC's National Executive Committee. He had personally pleaded with Nixon to send aid during the Yom Kippur War and, as it turned out, was a good friend of the new president, a fellow Michiganian. Moreover, Bookbinder reported, at least two of Ford's principal staff were Jewish, and AJC enjoyed "good entrée" to both of them. He promised to forward more names and information about Jews in Ford's administration as they became available.[37]

Ford addressed the AJC at its seventieth anniversary and U.S. Bicentennial annual meeting in May 1976 and was well received. Despite moments of tension over concessions that Israel was being called on to make, during the Ford presidency the first disengagement treaty between Israel and Egypt over the Sinai Desert was concluded (by Henry Kissinger, using his technique of "step-by-step shuttle diplomacy"). Israel's value as a strategic asset against Soviet expansionism remained part of American foreign policy.

President Jimmy Carter

Gerald Ford, however, was not elected in his own right in 1976, and the Watergate-weary American public gave the presidency to a relative Washington outsider, former governor of Georgia Jimmy Carter. Carter also happened to be a born-again Southern Baptist who spoke publicly and often about his religious beliefs. Rabbi Tanenbaum of the Interreligious Affairs Department found it necessary to issue a statement during the campaign warning Jews and others against undue stereotyping or prejudice against Evangelical Christians. Carter, according to a CBS–*New York Times* poll, received 68 percent of American Jewish votes in 1976. For a time he was popular with them for his strong stand on human rights (which boded well for the Soviet Jewry movement) and for his strong words against the prospect of an Arab oil embargo during the campaign. He earned glory as a peacemaker when he brokered the Camp David Accords in September 1978 and later the first peace treaty between Israel and Egypt, signed on the White House lawn March 26, 1979. That great moment had been preceded by an unprecedented visit by Egyptian president Anwar Sadat to Jerusalem in November 1977, where his motorcade was greeted by crowds of Israelis waving Egyptian and Israeli flags and where he walked right into the Knesset to speak directly to the nation.[38] Sadat was prompted by a desire to get the Sinai back, the economic instability in Egypt, the fact that Egypt always bled disproportionately in all the Arab-Israeli conflicts, and the impression that Egypt had actually won the Yom Kippur War, which bolstered his nation's pride and dignity. During the negotiations, Israel agreed to give the entire Sinai Peninsula back to Egypt.

When the Camp David Accords were signed, M. Bernard Resnikoff of AJC's Israel office spoke of the great excitement in the streets and of the reported reaction to the news in one Israeli multipassenger taxicab: one passenger broke down crying, two passengers embraced, and the other two started to argue.[39] "The 'impossible' has been achieved between Israel and Egypt," declared AJC President Richard Maass about the peace treaty, in his address at that year's annual meeting. "Let us hope for more miracles! We must pay tribute to President Carter, without whose dogged determination, persuasive skills, and unflagging optimism there would have been no treaty."[40]

These moments of joy, however, were overshadowed by months of apprehension, anxiety, and deep divisions among American and Israeli Jews—and much vilifying of Egypt. Opponents in Israel considered the Camp David Accords "national suicide." Conversely, the newly formed Peace Now movement, which called for territorial compromise on the West Bank and self-rule for the Palestinians there, felt that the accords and the treaty were not going far enough or fast enough and that the prime minister of Israel was destroying the Zionist dream through his stubbornness. American supporters of Peace Now, many of them prominent in the Jewish community and in Jewish organizations, did not hesitate to take out full-page newspaper ads expressing their agreement. Anwar Sadat paid heavily for his recognition and peace with Israel: Syria declared a national day of mourning, and five other Arab nations broke diplomatic relations. Egypt was expelled from the Arab League until 1989, and Sadat himself was assassinated in 1981.

As for Carter, who worked under the guidance of his mentor and national security adviser Dr. Zbigniew Brzezinski (pronounced zeh-big-ni-EV Bruh-ZHIN-ski), the negotiations turned into occasions to exert pressure on Israel to make more and more concessions at every turn. He gradually went further than any other president before him in advocating implicitly or explicitly that Israel withdraw to its pre-1967 borders, that settlements on the West Bank were illegal and should be dismantled, that a Palestinian state should be established, and that the PLO, which continued its terrorist attacks against Israel, should be recognized as the legitimate representative of the Palestinians without requiring that the organization change its charter. The charter, or "covenant," which had been written in 1968, declared the State of Israel illegal and called for its destruction.[41] The disengagement treaties negotiated by Henry Kissinger under President Ford had specifically promised that the United States would not extend recognition to the PLO unless it renounced its charter and recognized Israel's right to exist.

These changing attitudes became clear to AJC leaders in Carter's public pronouncements and from the several meetings they held with him, either alone or in conjunction with the Presidents' Conference and other Jewish organizations. The change also became clear in the public pronouncements and activities of Carter's U.S. Ambassador to the U.N., the Reverend Andrew Young, whom Carter appointed in 1977. Bert Gold in an AJC press release accused Carter outright of moving from being a "mediator" in the negotiations to being an "advocate" for Egypt.[42] At one point Carter shook hands with the PLO observer to the U.N. and likened Palestinian demands to those of the civil rights movement in the United States. Bert Gold responded with a statement that by so doing,

Carter was "doing an injustice" to the movement.[43] A statement released by the Conference of Presidents of Major American Jewish organizations declared: "we are dismayed and disappointed that the President should even think of the civil rights movement, characterized by non-violent means and seeking the liberties that our Constitution promises to all Americans, in the same breath as the obscene acts of a terrorist gang which seeks through violent means to eliminate the Jewish State."[44]

Carter and Brzezinski, unlike Nixon, Ford, and Kissinger, did not view Israel as a wonderful strategic asset; indeed, they considered that Israel might be helping to bring the Soviets into the Middle East, not keep them out. In a meeting of Brzezinski and Vice President Walter Mondale with AJC leaders Hyman Bookbinder, Bert Gold, Morris Fine, Jerome Shestack, and AIPAC Executive Director Morris Amitay, Brzezinski said outright that while support of Israel was essential to the United States in terms of its interest in keeping the Russians out, "the argument could also be turned around, with validity to both positions." He did not think that it was "fruitful" to pose the U.S. interest in Israel as a "military asset."[45] "I can remember the days when he would make an occasional major address to the AJC and when we all marveled at the astuteness of his mind and perceptions," reminisced Morton K. Blaustein, in speaking about Brzezinski (who turned down an invitation to address the annual meeting in 1977). "It would seem that this has all changed since his office has moved to the White House. In my opinion, he is one of the many disasters surrounding President Carter."[46]

Jewish anxiety about the Carter administration reached a peak when word leaked out in August 1979 that Ambassador Andrew Young, in direct violation of State Department policy, had had a secret meeting on July 26 with Zehdi Labib Terzi, the PLO's representative to the U.N., and had failed to give his superiors a full and accurate account of it. Amidst embarrassment to Secretary of State Cyrus Vance and protest by Israel, Young was forced to resign on August 15.[47] With the exception of one organization (the American Zionist Federation) Jewish leaders had only protested Young's action; they knew better than to call for his resignation. Nevertheless, most of the African American community blamed Young's demise squarely on the Jews. Carter, glad to see the blame for Young's departure placed somewhere other than on his administration, waited six weeks before making a public declaration that "any claims or allegations that American Jewish leaders or anyone else urged to ask Andy for his resignation are absolutely and totally false."[48]

"If Andy Young is shot down on this one," warned a black reverend in New York, speaking to the head of AJC's New York chapter on the day the resignation was announced, "it will come across that the Jews shot him down. Now it may well be that Young is the fall guy for the State Department, but that is not the way the black community is going to see it. We are less and less pro-Israel and more and more willing to hear the Arab side. I have already talked with CBS to let them know that there is a mobilization going on to support Young and I just wanted to emphasize to you the dangers of the situation. . . . Young is a symbol to us and we don't have many symbols."[49] A mass meeting of black leaders on August 22, held at NAACP headquarters and attended by more than two hundred people from across the country, turned from a discussion of Andrew Young's resignation to a forum for black grievances against Jews. These included the Jewish stand on affirmative action, relations between Israel and South Africa, and Jewish intellectuals, who allegedly had become "apologists for the racial status quo." There was also a declaration that only blacks themselves could decide the role they would play in foreign policy and that they would not hesitate to differ with Jewish organizations and leaders if they were not perceived as acting in blacks' best interest. "It was our declaration of independence," asserted Dr. Kenneth B. Clark, who was one of the signatories of the statement.[50]

In the ensuing weeks several notable black leaders drew closer to the PLO. The Reverend Jesse Jackson on TV accused Jews of being unwilling to share their "power" and said they could not place their own interests above that of the country. In September a delegation of ten blacks representing the SCLC visited Yasir Arafat in Lebanon, where the entire group kissed, embraced, linked arms and sang "We Shall Overcome."[51] Expressions of black anger against Jews frequently crossed the line into antisemitism and black leaders who had formerly worked closely with Jews did not denounce it.[52] Black-Jewish relations in New York were also poisoned by a series of confrontations in Crown Heights between blacks and Hasidim, and ire at Edward I. Koch, who became mayor in 1977. He set a consistently negative tone against blacks when during his campaign he denounced "poverty pimps" as part of his promise to trim the welfare rolls.[53] Judge Simon H. Rifkind and the leaders of the AJC decided it was time to revive the Survey Committee again, this time calling it "Survey Committee III." "Black-Jewish relations have entered a new and unacceptable phase," they concluded at their first meeting. "Restoration of a cordial alliance on issues of common concern would be beneficial to both groups."[54]

The following year Jimmy Carter failed to win reelection, not winning a majority among Jews or the general public. He was replaced by Republican Ronald Reagan. Carter's share of the Jewish vote, set by polls at 45 percent, marked the first time a Democratic candidate had failed to carry at least 60 percent of the Jewish vote since 1924.

Prime Minister Menachem Begin

American and American Jewish-Israel relations under Carter had already become strained while Yitzhak Rabin and Shimon Peres of the Labor Party were in power. Matters grew worse when on May 17, 1977, Menachem Begin, leader of the opposition Likud faction, upset twenty-nine years of Labor rule and became prime minister of Israel. It was said that the Carter administration's moves toward recognizing the PLO may have played a role in convincing Israelis to vote for the hard-line right-winger. Precisely such a "tough" character was needed to stand up to American pressure in the upcoming peace negotiations.[55]

The AJC—and American Jewish organizations in general—already struggling with Carter, had great difficulty accepting that Labor, with whom they shared so many affinities, was no longer in power. Begin, with his conservative economic and social views, was the very antithesis of American Jewish liberalism.[56] While Labor as a whole had expressed a belief in "territorial compromise" and did not establish settlements in areas with large Arab populations, Begin was a Revisionist Zionist who believed that the territories captured by Israel in 1967 were an indivisible part of the Jewish homeland, as they had been part of the British mandate, and they should be settled as much as possible. He also supported the efforts of "Gush Emunim" (Bloc of the Faithful), who believed that the capture of Old Jerusalem and the West Bank in 1967 had been divinely ordained and that settlement of the entire Holy Land would help to bring on the Messiah.

The American media took a distinctly negative stance toward Begin and the Israelis. It did not bode well when *Time*, in reporting on Begin's victory in its May 30, 1977, issue, headlined his face on the cover with the words "Trouble in the Promised Land" and began the story thus: "His first name means 'comforter.' Menachem Begin (rhymes with Fagin) has been anything but that to his numerous antagonists." Carter's and Brzezinski's views clashed sharply with Begin's, and American Jews found themselves uncomfortably in the middle, with both sides exerting pressure on them to take sides in the conflict.

It was not only Begin's right-wing policies and religiosity, but his appearance and manner that irritated people. Robert Goldman, a member of the board of governors and the foreign affairs commission of the AJC, referred to this in his essay defending Begin "A Jew First, an Israeli Second." Praising Begin's "Jewishness" and care and concern for the Jews of Diaspora, in comparison to the arrogance and indifference of Israeli officials under the Labor government, he claimed that while American Jews "pegged" their hatred of Begin to his politics it was really Begin himself that gave them trouble. "It's uncomfortable to see this quintessential, short, bald, Polish Jew as the leader of Israel," Goldman wrote. "He is too Jewish. Too easy to feel antisemitic about, too easy to become embarrassed about. Good Americans, particularly in the Eastern establishment, want to support Israel; it's part of their cultural furniture. But when it becomes *this* Jewish . . . and the upper levels of American Jewry with links to the establishment . . . feel the same way. It was all so easy when we had Golda Meir, the wonderful and lovable Jewish mother who had a Midwestern twang and who could easily fit into the cast of characters in

American ethnic folklore. Yitzchak Rabin with a slightly different accent, could have been Prime Minister of Norway or Holland."[57]

AJC and the American Jewish community were caught in a painful dilemma. On the one hand, Begin was the duly and democratically elected head of the State of Israel and deserved the honor and respect of that position; not to support him fully could mean giving aid and comfort to Israel's enemies—and there was little doubt among them that some of Carter's policies and pronouncements were harmful. On the other hand, many American Jews, including members of the AJC, strongly disagreed with Begin's West Bank and Gaza policies and felt uncomfortable being the ones who had to explain them to the American public. They agonized over whether they should make their displeasure known publicly. AJC took the view that the American Jewish organizations should provide a united front on Israel's behalf and that criticism of Israel should be done cautiously (and preferably in private).[58] Even they found it difficult to stay quiet, however, when Begin announced that he was encouraging Jewish resettlement in the ancient town of Hebron—right in the middle of a hostile Arab population.[59]

Menachem Begin, who was reelected in 1980, resigned in despair from public office in 1983 after the failures of Israel's invasion of southern Lebanon and the death of his wife. He went into seclusion, but the electoral revolution he represented continued. From then on, in addition to the traditional Labor alignment, the Likud was a serious and legitimate contender on the Israeli political scene.

Jews and the Rise of Evangelical Christianity

President Jimmy Carter's status as a born-again Southern Baptist also symbolized a striking phenomenon in American religious life: the renaissance and rise to power and politics of conservative Evangelical Christians, who stressed the need for a personal relationship with Jesus and the authority of the Bible in all matters.[60] At one time, AJC reports noted, such groups had been on the periphery of American life; many such Christians had not even registered to vote. Now, this group of American citizens was growing at a rate faster than that of the mainline Protestant denominations (such as the Methodists and the Episcopalians, whose membership was actually declining) and becoming a larger proportion of the general population.[61] Part of the growth was fed by the coming to maturity of millions of Americans from such states as West Virginia, Kentucky, Tennessee, and Alabama—the so-called country cousins—who had migrated to the cities in the 1950s and 1960s. Evangelicals became particularly prominent during the election of 1972, when Republicans leaders campaigning for Nixon sought to capitalize on their conservative values by calling George McGovern the "Triple A Candidate"—Acid, Amnesty and

Abortion.[62] Richard Nixon, on the other hand, cultivated the Evangelicals, and evangelist Billy Graham was a confidante and frequent visitor to the White House.

While such fervent Christians could be found around the world (including the Soviet Union), such movements were by far most popular in America, commanding the allegiance of tens of millions of followers. At their core were descendants of the immigrants of the colonial period and the early years of the republic, who had come as members of dissenting churches, suspicious of the authority of the established church. With their emphasis on personal commitment to God (rather than through intercession by clergymen) and their reliance on Holy Scripture, Evangelicals were especially well suited to the American environment, as Lucy S. Dawidowicz observed in a history of U.S. Jewry that she penned for AJC's seventy-fifth anniversary:

These churches, it turned out, were best adapted to survive under the rigors of life on the frontier or the vast prairie. Few learned ministers or theologians were available to guide these Methodists, Baptists, Presbyterians, Evangelicals, and Revivalists, even if they had wanted such guidance. These men had already learned to depend upon themselves not only in their struggle with the wilderness, but also in their encounter with God. For them the Bible sufficed as the word of God. The Bible became their ultimate authority and they required no mediating or interpreting minister. They conducted their own services and allowed their religious feelings full and free expression. These religious feelings became the hallmark of frontier Revivalism and Evangelism, the articulation of which these frontier Christians believed to be more authentic faith than the rituals of the established churches. This free will individualistic religion owed much to America's political ethos which declared that all men were created equal.[63]

From the perspective of AJC, ADL and the rest of the organized Jewish community, Evangelical Christians were a potential threat in numerous ways. First, many of their leaders tended to view "Christianity" and the United States as synonymous, and were open in their desire to "Christianize" the country. AJC had to work to preserve the pluralistic character of American society while not violating these groups' freedom of religious expression. Second, some were frank in their desire to "save" the Jews by converting them; AJC had to maintain good Jewish-Christian relations while making it clear that they rigorously rejected such campaigns. Third, although many Evangelical leaders were pro-Israel and considered Israel's success in 1967 as a fulfillment of biblical prophecy,[64] they also often took positions on social issues that were sharply at variance with the American Jewish liberal tradition. Finally, the AJC had after many decades secured from the Catholic Church and the mainline Protestant denominations written repudiation of the charge that all Jews were responsible for killing Jesus. On the tenth anniversary of Vatican II, for example, the National Conference of Catholic Bishops, taking its clue from a Vatican statement, removed any doubt remaining from *Nostra Aetate* and declared that "the Jewish people never were, nor are they now, guilty of the death of Christ."[65] Now AJC's interreligious affairs division had to work to secure that kind of cooperation and repudiation from Evangelicals.

One of the most prominent offenders was President Carter himself, who was overheard giving a Sunday School lesson in his church in 1977 about Jesus driving the moneylenders from the Temple. During it, he made the statement: "there was no possible way for Jewish leaders to avoid the challenge, so they decided to kill Jesus." The words were picked up by the national newspapers and brought forth strong reactions in the Jewish and Christian communities. Rabbi Marc Tanenbaum reportedly had several "conversations with the White House staff" about it. The result was a personal letter by Carter, written to an AJC ally and Lutheran minister, the Reverend John Steinbrook. "The Christian religion, according to my understanding, holds that Jesus of Nazareth, who was a Jew, gave his life to redeem the sins of humanity," Carter wrote. "The Gospels declared that His death was foreordained, and without that death and the resurrection which followed it, Christians would not be saved in Christ." Yet, he continued "the crucifixion required human instruments. Among these were Judas, who was a Christian Disciple, Caiphus, who was a Jewish priest appointed by the Roman authorities, and Pilate, the gentile who actually condemned Jesus to death. In accordance with the Gospels, I know that Jesus forgave the human instruments of His death, but I'm also aware that the Jewish people were for many centuries falsely charged with collective responsibility for the death of Jesus, and were persecuted for that unjust accusation which has been exploited as a basis and rationalization for anti-Semitism."[66]

Reverend Steinbrook wrote back, thanking Carter for his letter, and declaring it a "historic repudiation of the Christ killer canard that has so long and unjustly been a burden of the Jewish people, our older sisters and brothers." The whole incident was duly publicized in a *New York Times* story headlined "Carter Denies He Believes Jews are Guilty of the Death of Jesus."[67]

Even before Carter was elected, Evangelicals were frank in their desire to spread Christianity throughout the land. They planned a program called "Key '73," in which they would "blitz" the continent with an Evangelistic crusade in 1973, "to share with every person in North America more fully and more forcefully the claims and message of the Gospel of Jesus Christ, to confront people with the Gospel of Jesus Christ by proclamation and demonstration, by witness and ministry, and by word and deed."[68] Techniques were to include mass media, mass rallies, and door-to-door canvassing. The campaign turned out to be of limited success, but it caused concern to Jewish groups nonetheless. In 1976 William Bright, a key figure among a group of business, professional, and political leaders, planned a worldwide Evangelical campaign. He announced that his group would work to elect as many "born again" Christians as possible to public office.[69] Also of concern were the "Christian Yellow Pages," and the "Christian Business Directory," which accepted advertisements and listings only from those who signed an oath that they were "born again Christians." By September 1977, these directories were circulating in fifty-seven cities. Jewish and mainline Protestant leaders attacked them as offensive to Jews and other non-Christians and divisive among Christians who did not accept the concept of a "born again relationship with Christ." That year ADL units in three cities filed suit against the two directories on the grounds that they violated statutes on unfair business competition and religious discrimination.[70]

As the 1980 elections approached, the conservative Evangelicals, now known as the "New Right," became even better organized, and Ronald Reagan became their chosen candidate. In 1979, the Reverend Jerry Falwell of Lynchburg, Virginia, founded the group Moral Majority, a coalition of conservative Evangelical political action committees. They lobbied for the restoration of school prayer and Bible readings in public schools, the teaching of the biblical story of creation rather than Darwinian evolution, and censorship of entertainment material that was not "pro-family." They were against abortion, homosexual rights, pornography, treaties with the Soviet Union, gun control, and the Equal Rights Amendment.[71] Falwell's *Old-Time Gospel Hour,* was carried weekly on nearly seven hundred TV and radio stations and reportedly raised one million dollars a week, while Pat Robertson's *700 Club* was seen on 150 TV stations and three thousand cable stations in 1980–81.[72] Other well-known Evangelical political leaders included Richard Viguerie, Paul Weyrich, Terry Dolan, and Howard Phillips, all engaged in a massive effort to get Evangelists to donate and vote and to get as many faithful Christians as possible into office. "It's interesting at great political rallies how you have a Protestant to pray, a Catholic to pray and then you have a Jew to pray," noted the Reverend Bailey Smith, president of the thirteen million-member Southern Baptist Convention. In front of fifteen thousand people in September 1980 at the height of the presidential campaign, Smith declared: "With all due respect to those dear people, my friends, God Almighty does not hear the prayers of a Jew."[73]

Rabbi Alexander Schindler, former head of the Conference of Presidents and head of the UAHC, called for a "coalition of decency" to fight the effects of the Moral Majority;[74] and Rabbi Balfour Brickner condemned Jewish organizations such as the Zionist Organization of America who gave people like Falwell awards because of their staunch support for Israel. "Some Jews seem willing to ignore or forgive anyone anything so long as they gather that some kind of support for Israel exists," he wrote. The Christian fundamentalist, he insisted, was no Zionist; his interest in Israel was part of this theology according to which the *parousia,* or End of Days, would arrive only after the Jews of the world were gathered back in the land of Israel. "Then," he continued, "after the Battle of Armageddon, when the forces of good will triumph over the forces of evil, paving the way for the second coming of Christ, all humanity will become 'One in Christ.' At that moment Jews and all others will give up their particular identities. Thank you—but no thank you. We need not enhance the 'fundies' for momentary love of Zion which, in the end, advocates the demise of Judaism." He called the Christian fundamentalists "an effort to drive us intellectually back to the Middle Ages" and said that they were attempting to restore "the medieval idea of 'church-state fusion.'" If they succeeded, he warned, "Kiss goodbye our commitment to the prophets of Israel. Kiss goodbye our children's future. . . . We cannot squander our position and we certainly need not retreat in fear. What is at stake is not a renaissance of some 'liberal agenda' or even the future of Jews in America, but the future of America itself."[75]

The domestic affairs division of the AJC was and remained as wary as the ACLU of the possible threat to pluralism and separation of church and state that the Evangelicals represented; it was this division that took up the legal battles they posed. The job of the interreligious affairs division was to educate, build bridges through dialogue, seek out cooperative Christians, and secure statements speaking to the physical and spiritual safety of American Jews. As early as 1970 more than seventy Jewish and Baptist theologians met formally for the first time in a conference sponsored jointly by the AJC and the Southern Baptist Convention. In the case of Baptists, a strong connection existed because there were Baptists in the Soviet Union who, like the Jews, were being persecuted for their religion. The conference passed a resolution calling for a common defense of Baptist rights. Resolutions also called for greater involvement of religious bodies in the nation's social problems (another common cause between AJC and Christian groups) and, finally, a joint effort to end antisemitism.[76]

The Baptist alliance paid off during Key '73. AJC alerted them to Jewish apprehension, and the result was a statement by the Baptist national planning committee, printed in the June 1973 issue of *American Baptist,* that they did not view Jews as specific targets for Christian conversion. "Our devotion to religious freedom and our respect for the rights of other religious communities are rooted in the life and work of Jesus Christ, who invited and persuaded persons but did not coerce or take unfair advantage of them," the statement read. "We believe it is inappropriate for Christians to single out Jews as Jews or indeed to single out any racial or ethnic group as such, for special Evangelistic attention."[77] In 1978, urged on by the presence of Jimmy Carter as a born-again Baptist president, AJC again sponsored Jewish-Baptist conferences across the country, the most important taking place at Southern Methodist University in Dallas. The conferences concentrated on such common issues as human rights, religious liberty, and the role of women. Through the contacts and cooperation secured through these conferences AJC reaped a revision of Baptist liturgy that might reflect insensitivity to Jews, and a full-page ad in the *New York Times* and other newspapers in June 1978 signed by fourteen prominent Evangelicals declaring support for Israel and her rights to an undivided Jerusalem and the West Bank of the Jordan River.[78] When Bailey Smith made his remark about God not hearing Jewish prayers, meetings with AJC, ADL, and other Jewish officials at first failed to get a retraction; all he would say was "I am pro-Jew. . . . I believe they are God's special people, but without Jesus Christ, they are lost." The better-known Jerry Falwell, however, was persuaded to say that he "strongly criticized" Smith's suggestion, that God did indeed hear the prayers of all people, and that he rejected the idea that the United States should become a "Christian republic."[79]

Billy Graham proved to be an exceptionally strong friend and ally; there were rumors that Billy Graham had been the one to soften the heart of Richard Nixon—who was no lover of the Jewish people—on behalf of Israel. At one point Graham offered to be a speaker for the UJA. The AJC considered this "inadvisable" because it would expose him to "further attack and harassment from professional-Arab elements in the Protestant community" and conceivably could "limit his influence in Washington, where it is really needed."[80] At another time Billy Graham himself turned down an offer to speak, writing "at this point I do not think it would be wise for me to get involved in the political specifics of the Middle East—better wait and see what develops concerning Geneva."[81] At the onset of Key '73, AJC needed a statement from a prominent Evangelical that Jews would not be targeted for conversion. Marc Tanenbaum was able to write Graham the following letter: "It has been on my mind for some time to be in touch with you about the possibility of our having a conversation regarding Key '73. The problems of proselytization and respect for conscience require some basic clarification between the Evangelical and Jewish communities. From my recent travels around the country, I am persuaded that the earlier it could be done the better for everybody concerned." Shortly thereafter Billy Graham issued a press release: "Along with most Evangelical Christians, I believe God has always had a special relationship with the Jewish people, as St. Paul suggests in the Book of Romans. In light of that, I have never felt called to direct my Evangelistic efforts to Jews or any other particular group."[82]

Billy Graham was rewarded with AJC's Interreligious Award at its October 1977 National Executive Council meeting in Atlanta. In accepting the award—Marc Tanenbaum introduced him as "the greatest friend to the Jewish people since Reinhold Niebuhr and Pope John XXIII"—he made a speech that drew repeated standing ovations and was widely reported in the newspapers. In it, he pointed out that almost the entire New Testament—with the exception of the books of Luke and Acts—had been written by Jews. "As soon as I began to study the Bible in earnest I discovered the debt I owed to Israel, to Judaism and to the Jewish people," Graham declared. "I realize that the record of relations between Christians and Jews makes unpleasant and at times horrifying reading." He continued:

Millions who profess Christianity could not possibly be true Christians in the Biblical sense. For example, if a professing Christian is not dominated by love for his neighbor, then he cannot possibly be called a Christian. Thus many of the persecutions of history were caused by false Christians who dragged the name of their Master into the mire of bigotry, antisemitism and prejudice. Evangelical Christians especially have an affinity for the Jews because the Bible they love is essentially a Jewish book written under the influence of God's spirit. It is to the lasting glory of Judaism and Christianity that they have their roots in the Old and New Testament scriptures written so largely by Jews. . . . There are theological differences that we may never agree on, but there are certain things we can work together for now that may make a better America."[83]

Having this image of Billy Graham, AJC leaders were shocked to read twenty-five years later, in a story first uncovered by James Warren of the *Chicago Tribune*, that Graham had been caught on tape exchanging antisemitic remarks with President Richard Nixon during a conversation in the Oval Office in 1972. Graham spoke then about the Jews having a "stranglehold" on American life and expressed the hope that Nixon might be able to "do something" about it. Later, he referred to Jewish friends he had who "swarm around me and are friendly to me," but, as he confided to Nixon, "[t]hey don't know how I really feel about what they're doing to this country."[84] When the remarks came to light, a very embarrassed Graham apologized profusely. American Jews were angry, although some observers said that Billy Graham's private words so long ago did not reflect his current views and should not negate the good deeds he had done on behalf of Israel and the Jewish people.

Cults and Missionaries

Not all Christian leaders were so benevolent as Billy Graham and the American Baptists, who swore that they would not target Jews for conversion. No number of statements could prevent Jewish youth from being exposed all around them to the attractions of Christianity. Also vying for their attention were new religions and new cults. For example, representatives of Jews for Jesus, founded by Moishe (Martin) Rosen in San Francisco in 1973, could soon be found on every street corner and in every shopping mall in cities with large Jewish populations.[85] From the 1960s through the 1970s hundreds of new religions and cults appeared drawing millions of adherents: TM (Transcendental Meditation; introduced to the West through the Maharishi Mahesh Yogi) yoga, Hare Krishna, Children of God, Scientology, "Jesus Freaks," variants of Buddhism, Sufism, Hinduism, various forms of mysticism, astrology, and the Reverend Sun Myung Moon's Unification Church. Tourist travel to India to study with various gurus—and swamis and perhaps experience living on an ashram—became a well-organized business. A Gallup poll done in 1976 revealed that up to 12 percent of Americans were engaged in a variety of movements that had been introduced in recent years, TM and yoga being the most popular.[86]

Jewish communal workers all agreed that Jews were represented in these movements well out of proportion to their less than 3 percent of the population.[87] A local AJC leader in Hartford, Connecticut, estimated that at least 60 percent of the members at the local Divine Light Mission were Jewish; anecdotally, the proportions were similar in other groups. "The reporter mentioned name after name after name," recalled Professor Leon Jick at an AJC panel, commenting on a *New York Times* article about gurus in India that he had recently read. "I began to get uneasy shivers up and down my spine, and finally he [the reporter] left nothing to the imagination. The overwhelming majority of Americans in these places are upper middle-class American Jewish young men and women. What a shocking testimony that is to the vacuum we have created by our universalism."[88] No one was immune: one such conversion occurred in the family of AJC member George Alpert, distinguished Boston attorney, railroad president, and founder of Brandeis University. His son, Richard, was expelled from the Harvard faculty after advocating the use of LSD; Richard then went to India and came back transformed into guru Baba Ram Dass.

The "Jesus Revolution" was one of the first and most widespread of the religious movements to come to the notice of AJC's Jewish Communal Affairs Department. "During the past several months various religiously oriented youth movements which seek to relate the role of Jesus as a contemporary answer to the student community have begun to develop," reported Milton Ellerin and Steven Windmueller (a new program specialist in the JCAD) in the spring of 1971. "One movement has involved young people who are seeking an alternative to drugs, and as a response are 'turned on' to Jesus." Reflecting this new zealotry was a movement within the rock music field to retell the life of Jesus in contemporary musical style, as in the musicals *Jesus Christ Superstar* (by Andrew Lloyd Webber and Tim Rice) and *Godspell*. Jewish students might be stirred to rethink their own tradition, Ellerin and Windmueller wrote, and should be provided with answers by the community "in order that they might respond to some of the pressures that may be brought against them by these new Jesus fanatics."[89]

To AJC, *Jesus Christ Superstar* fell under the heading of "Passion plays," dramas portraying the last days of Jesus' earthly life that tended to provide antisemitic accounts of the Jews' role in it. In addition to the most famous one in the village of Oberammergau, Germany, the AJC in the 1970s was keeping track of more than fifty Passion plays in the United States and around the world, monitoring their scripts, calling for revisions if at all possible, and—when all else failed—taking steps such as convincing travel agents not to put such plays on their itineraries.[90] *Jesus Christ Superstar*, which the NJCRAC called "a catastrophe" for Jewish-Christian relations and a "setback in the struggle against the religious sources of antisemitism," became the biggest Passion play of all time when in 1973 it was made into a movie viewed by millions of people, including impressionable young Jews.[91] AJC planned a nationwide education campaign to coincide with the movie's opening. Gerald Strober, an ordained Presbyterian minister who worked as a consultant to the IAD, wrote an analysis of the film that was distributed to all the newspapers, magazines, and TV and radio stations in the country. In New York City, the day before the film opened AJC held a press conference attended by representatives of all the major news media, AJC President Elmer Winter outlined a four-point program drawing attention to the film's inaccuracies and speaking to its effect on antisemitism. Much of this material turned up in newspaper and magazine reviews that millions of Americans read before they went to the movie.[92]

The involvement of Jews in Christian cults also attracted the attention of *Newsweek*. American Jews were alarmed when it ran an article in its April 17, 1972, issue that described the activities of the American Board of Missions to the Jews, an institution headquartered in New Jersey. The article claimed that the institution had been specifically founded to target Jews for conversion, and that it had been successful in thousands of cases. As many as one hundred thousand former Jews, the article claimed, were attending Sunday services at Protestant churches. It quoted a Rabbi Shlomo Kunin, who estimated that young Jews were converting at the rate of six to seven thousand a year.[93] A well-financed, nationwide campaign of TV, radio, and newspaper ads by the American Board of Missions began "So Many Jews are Wearing that Smile Nowadays . . ."[94] At the earliest AJC conference on cults and missionaries, it was noted that Jewish converts were spending time in Israel, learning Hebrew, and returning with Israeli credentials that helped them in their efforts to convert more Jews. On the West Coast it was estimated that several thousand Hebrew Christians were living on communes. In discussing alternatives and outreach efforts, special mention was made of the Chabad Lubavitch, who were showing great success in bringing some of these young people back into the Jewish fold.[95]

In response to reports of mass conversions at colleges and universities, the B'nai B'rith Hillel Foundations decided to conduct a survey of more than eighty campuses in order to determine whether such reports were accurate. They found evidence of "significant conversion" on only fifteen campuses, and still in much lower numbers that "flatly contradicted" *Newsweek*'s claim.[96] This reassurance did not dissuade the missionaries from their pursuit—nor did it comfort American Jews who did not want to lose even one child to such groups.

The Hebrew Christian groups moved into high gear in 1976 when they targeted Long Island's six hundred thousand Jews for conversion. The groups did extensive advertising and flooded streets, shopping centers and college campuses, handing out leaflets. Christian coffeehouses were established in East Meadow and Smithtown, and it was announced that one of the major messianic groups, B'nai Yeshua was relocating its headquarters from Graham, Texas, to Stony Brook. The group had spent more than eight hundred thousand dollars to purchase and renovate a parcel of twelve acres there. The purchase included a dormitory that housed sixty students, and Stony Brook was to be the site of a national conference of Hebrew Christians that summer. Rabbis in more than half the one hundred and twenty synagogues and Temples in Nassau and Suffolk Counties began education programs designed to counter and refute conversion techniques. "A third of our people were lost in World War II and another third were lost behind the Iron Curtain where they can't practice their religion," noted Rabbi Elliot Spar of Smithtown. "That's why we view this conversion effort as a serious threat."[97]

The Unification Church was especially popular with young Jews. Rabbi A. James Rudin and his wife Marcia did a special report on it, in the process interviewing scores of members. Rudin, a former Air Force chaplain, was assistant director of the Interreligious Affairs Department and became director in 1983. Their review of the movement's writings revealed that the Jewish people were supposed to be the allies of Satan and were collectively responsible for Jesus' crucifixion. The Reverend Moon's church, charged a Jewish Queens College student who had escaped and come to testify before the AJC, was nothing less than a political movement that exploited and manipulated its members for fund-raising and proselytizing. "Reverend Moon considers himself to be the Messiah," she warned, "and his goal is to take over the whole world."[98]

The Hebrew Christians, also known as Messianic Jews, were considered the greatest threat because they used Jewish tradition and rituals and lulled adherents into the belief that they were not really being converted; they were just becoming more "fulfilled" as Jews. Arguments over the meaning of the fifty-second and fifty-third chapters of Isaiah fueled the general missionary effort. AJC responded to the threat with conferences, statements, discussion guides, policy guides, task forces to combat cults in communities across the nation,[99] and surveys, reaching out to make coalitions with Protestant and Catholic groups, who also opposed the cults. In the wake of the Rudins' study on the Unification Church, for example, AJC convened a meeting of the National Council of Churches and the Roman Catholic Archdiocese of New York. The Jewish, Protestant, and Catholic leaders all denounced the movement as antisemitic, anti-Christian, and in direct conflict with the basic teachings of Christianity; representatives of the media were on hand to record their views.[100] Dr. David Singer, who had recently joined the Jewish Communal Affairs Department as a program specialist (he subsequently became AJC's director of research) addressed Isaiah 53 and other questions in the article "The Jewish Messiah: A Contemporary Commentary." The article was printed in

Midstream (and AJC mailed five thousand reprints to Hillels, Jewish youth organizations, professors, bureaus of education, rabbis, and Jewish community centers around the country).[101]

As for pastoral work, Rabbi Rudin recommended as an antidote to the cults and missionaries special counseling, "meaningful camping experiences," a guide to the cults for every Jewish high school and college student, telephone hotlines, urban hostels to care for Jewish runaways, intensive Jewish education, and an increase in the number of fellowship groups for young Jews.[102]

The research and survey materials produced by AJC became even more important to the entire American population after a shocking event catapulted the cults to national and international attention. On November 18, 1978, in the jungles of Guyana, South America, it was discovered that 913 men, women, and children, led by the Reverend Jim Jones in a cult known as the People's Temple, had committed mass suicide at the command of their leader. Because cult members lived in a sealed-off compound called "Jonestown," the event became known as the Jonestown Massacre. (Members had killed themselves by drinking poisoned grape Flavor-Aid, which was similar to Kool-Aid). There was a congressional investigation into the incident: before the massacre the People's Temple had assassinated a congressman and several associates who had come to Guyana to investigate the cult. Cults had become literally a life-or-death matter; taking legal action against them now became acceptable. The FBI had more than a dozen cases under investigation involving alleged assaults or kidnappings by cults, and at least six state legislatures were contemplating resolution to limit and investigate cult activities.[103]

In the wake of the Jonestown massacre, the Rudins wrote a new and more detailed study and discussion packet on the cults.[104] (Their study was later expanded into the book, *Prison or Paradise? The New Religious Cults* [Philadelphia: Fortress Press, 1980].) They had to warn their readers that no matter how deeply parents or family members might feel, it was unacceptable to remove captive children forcibly from these organizations. "AJC is deeply committed to the first amendment and the concept of religious liberty," they wrote. "In fact, that is a vital part of our reason for being. The Constitution does not and cannot 'pick and choose' as between competing religious groups. . . . Kidnapping and forcible detention violate the law and cannot be condoned, notwithstanding the parents' deep feelings, any more than they could be condoned if a wayward son or daughter were to join the Communist Party or on the verge of entering into a marriage which the parents view as a disaster. But there are other methods, all quite legal, that can be used." The legal methods were not dissimilar to the techniques AJC had advocated against antisemitic organizations, such as catching their members in violation of the law and having them arrested. Any amount of detailed investigation could bring these cults down. Did they make full financial disclosure? Were their methods of financial solicitation legal? Did they have minors who worked for no pay? Were their educational institutions accredited? Were members free to leave? Could some more accurately be called "business enterprises" than religions? Did they extort money from their members? Did they obey U.S. immigration laws? Did they spend time on political propaganda, or intervening in political campaigns? If the answer to any of these questions was yes, then legal action could be taken against them. This was no guarantee, however, that the children would return to their families and synagogues.

Some time during all this activity had to be devoted to the question, why were so many Jews attracted to the cults in the first place? "I assure you that those Jewish parents who deprive their children of any Jewish knowledge did not dream that it was going to end up that way," suggested Leon Jick gloomily, in his remarks about the Jewish names in the *New York Times*. "Obviously we have created a spiritual, intellectual vacuum, and now that vacuum is filled by the most spurious kinds of things."[105] Rabbi Rudin wondered, not for the first or last time in American Jewish history, whether all the attention on external threats, such as antisemitism and Israel, might have come at the expense of American Jews' inner lives. "We have neglected the religious and spiritual side of Jewish life, and this is what Jewish children seem to be looking for," he said. "The phenomenon of the cults is a stunning indictment of our inability to relate to our children on a spiritual level."[106] Whatever the reasons, it was clear in the 1970s that for some time to come the American Jewish agenda would be crowded with many issues. Only a limited amount of the community's time, energy, and will was available to devote to something as intangible as the souls of its children.

8

Internal Divisions

Vietnam, Affirmative Action, Housing, Aid to Private Schools, and the Rights of Neo-Nazis

[1970–1979]

From the days of John Slawson the American Jewish Committee had ceased to be a committee and had become a highly complex organization, with numerous lay subcommittees, many separate departments, and dozens of chapters and regional offices spread across the land. For certain matters—such as immediate danger to Jews anywhere—the AJC could act swiftly, with the president, the highest lay officers, and the executive vice president empowered to move on their own. Other decisions, however, could take a great deal of time. Before national AJC could take a stand on any new issue the matter had to be thoroughly researched by the staff, thrashed out to the top of one of four commissions set up in 1970–Domestic, Foreign, Interreligious, or Jewish Communal Affairs—and then passed on by the supreme governing bodies, the board of governors and a body that met once a year, the National Executive Council. On some matters AJC was unified and resolutions passed swiftly through the ranks with few if any modifications. In other cases the organization was torn by internal disagreements, with much individual soul-searching required. In the 1960s and 1970s such internally divisive issues included the Vietnam War, affirmative action, public housing, the question of government aid to private schools, "scatter-site" housing, whether and how much support AJC should give to Jewish all-day schools, and whether the right of neo-Nazis to march in Skokie, Illinois, was protected by the First Amendment.

The Vietnam War

A centennial review of the *American Jewish Year Book*, the annual write-up of the year's events of Jewish interest (prepared in large part by AJC staff), revealed a curious omission. From the Gulf of Tonkin Resolution on August 7, 1964, which gave President Lyndon B. Johnson authorization to send American military forces to Vietnam (there was never an official declaration of war by Congress) and the fall of Saigon in April 1975 that ended the war, the word "Vietnam" appeared in the index exactly three times.[1] Vietnam was the longest war in U.S. history, a war whose toll on U.S. servicemen was more than fifty-eight thousand killed and more than three hundred thousand wounded. The war virtually tore American society apart for eight years. Yet in such an important annal of AJC and the American Jewish community, it was barely mentioned.

The silence in fact hid an intense struggle going on behind the scenes. AJC staff, lay leaders, and the rank and file in the chapters agonized for years on the question of whether they should make a public statement about the Vietnam War and what exactly the wording of such a statement should be. This distress was based on the idea that a statement by AJC one way or the other carried great weight in the country's political life and would affect its relations with allies, government officials, and the rest of the Jewish community.

Some members—especially staff—felt that the organization would be damned if it did not stand up and oppose what they felt was a crime being perpetrated in the name of their country. An additional concern was that their children and Jewish youth in general, who were so prevalent among the antiwar protesters, would be completely alienated from the "Jewish Establishment" if AJC and other Jewish organizations failed to react in a strong manner. Indeed, the 1970 annual meeting was interrupted by two young protesters of the Radical Jewish Union of Columbia University, who had been arrested at Temple Emanu-El the previous night for attempting to speak out against the war during services. Their demands included that synagogues and temples across the country be open as sanctuaries for those wishing to resist the draft, that the AJC constitute itself as a center for antiwar activity, that AJC divest of all stocks and bonds in war-related industries, and that they and all Jewish organizations immediately take out full-page ads in the *Times*, the *Washington Post*, and other newspapers calling for "immediate and unilateral withdrawal from Southeast Asia."[2]

Another group in AJC, which included members equally opposed to the war, argued that a public antiwar statement was unnecessary and irresponsible and would open them to charges of hypocrisy. As individuals, AJC members could, and did, engage in antiwar activity through any number of other channels. There are numerous mentions in AJC records of staff and members of the board of governors on their own marching, protesting, and participating in moratoriums against the war. But for the American Jewish Committee as an organization to publicly oppose their country's president on this issue was to risk alienating him on military aid to another country they cared very much about: Israel. The Israelis themselves were concerned about this, and officials and embassy personnel were known to remonstrate with American Jewish leaders and Jewish youth in a (usually) vain attempt to get them to keep quiet about their opposition to the war.[3] "This organization ought to preserve its access to the President of the United States and to the Secretary of State on issues which are of vital importance to 2,600,000 Jews who are the remnants of six million that were destroyed," declared one AJC member in 1970, literally begging the AJC not to pass a statement against the invasion of Cambodia.[4] There was also concern that if American Jews came out too far against their government, it would affect the well-being of the Jews in the Soviet Union.

Under President Johnson, who took criticism of his war personally, these risks were quite real.[5] During 1966 other Jewish organizations—the American Jewish Congress, Union of American Hebrew Congregations, the Central Conference of American Rabbis, the Synagogue Council of America, and the National Council of Jewish Women—all passed well-publicized antiwar resolutions. Johnson took notice.[6] Addressing the AJC annual meeting in May 1966, on the occasion of being awarded the American Liberties Medallion (AJC's highest award), Johnson partially expressed his feelings when he told the crowd that "your people" who had suffered so much over the centuries while others stood by, should be the first to understand "that the threat to your neighbor's freedom is only a prologue to an attack on your own freedom." This was a clear hint that he expected some quid pro quo from his audience on Vietnam in return for his strong support of Israel.[7]

Johnson's feelings came further out into the open on September 6, 1966, when the newly elected commander of the Jewish War Veterans and several of his officers paid a courtesy call to the nation's commander in chief at the White House. Their organization had just passed a resolution strongly in support of the war and they took the occasion to present it to him.[8] Johnson in turn took the opportunity to vent his disturbance over the lack of support for the Vietnam War he was noting in the rest of the American Jewish community at a time when he was increasing military and economic aid to Israel. The meeting was "highlighted," the Jewish attendees reported, by "the strong conviction on the part of the President that Jews who seek U.S. support for co-religionists in Russia and for Israel should vigorously identify with Administration actions in Vietnam." Johnson, they claimed, had called on the JWV officers to "launch a campaign in the Jewish community to rally support for the Vietnam War."[9] The report appeared first in the Jewish press and a substantiating account appeared in the September 11 *New York Times*. There, Johnson was reported to have said that the preponderance of antiwar Jews puzzled him since he knew Jews to be "highly compassionate, among the best-informed on foreign affairs, deeply concerned about Communist rule in other nations, and eager for the U.S. to support other small countries, such as Israel."[10]

Jews were in turn anxious and outraged—anxious that aid for Israel might be in jeopardy and outraged that among all American citizens who were protesting the war, the President had singled out Jews for their behavior. More meetings and denials and counterdenials followed.[11] The heads of B'nai B'rith demanded a meeting with the president for "clarification" and then issued their own statement that President Johnson had been either "misunderstood or poorly interpreted" by his other Jewish visitors, and that any inference of a relationship between future America-Israel affairs and support among Jewish organizations for the administration's policies in Vietnam was "as inaccurate as it was unfortunate."[12] Other Jewish leaders, however, were not convinced that the president had been misunderstood. "When the President talks about Jews," said one rabbi, "he generalizes much too freely. When he seems to suggest that American policy toward Israel depends on Jewish good behavior, on support for his policies, he is going too far." Abraham Joshua Heschel, a well-known opponent of the war, was less cautious in conceding a specific Jewish viewpoint on Johnson's policies. "If Abraham had no hesitation about challenging the judgment of God over Sodom and Gomorrah, lest it would sweep away the innocent with the guilty, " he declared, "should not an American have the right to challenge the judgment of our President when horrified by the war in Vietnam?"[13] Other leaders spoke about "political blackmail" and charged that Johnson was trying to stifle opposition by threatening to punish Israel.[14]

In an effort to de-escalate what had by now become a front-page story, Arthur J. Goldberg, then head of the U.S. delegation to the U.N. (he later served as AJC president, 1968–69) and one of the highest-ranking Jews in Johnson's administration, held an off-the-record meeting at his hotel attended by forty representatives from the Conference of Presidents of Major American Jewish Organizations. Goldberg insisted later that Johnson himself had played no role in the meeting.[15] After a two-hour discussion, the participants left reassured, convinced that the president knew that not all Jews opposed U.S. involvement in Vietnam, that he respected the right to dissent, and that he had no intention of linking support for Vietnam with assistance to Israel.[16] "I've been backing the President and I'm a Jewish Senator," said Jacob Javits (of New York) in a press conference following the meeting.[17] Some antiwar activists started wearing buttons with the slogan "You Don't Have to be Jewish to be Against the War in Vietnam."[18]

Some weeks later Johnson announced that the United States would lend Israel six million dollars to expand its electric power facilities. The press release stated specifically that Johnson was taking this action to prove that his displeasure over Jewish attitudes toward the war in Vietnam would not affect his commitments to Israel.[19] This disclaimer was no doubt welcomed by Jewish leaders, but could hardly serve to remove all doubt on the issue. In the meantime an AJC member from Atlanta presented a resolution at the board of governors meeting in October 1966 that the organization issue a statement in *favor* of the Vietnam War. The consensus then was that the issue was "extraneous to the competence of the American Jewish Committee" and that they should make no statement regarding the war at all.[20] This silence remained AJC policy for the rest of the Johnson administration.

Vietnam came up again on the national AJC agenda in October 1969, when Johnson was no longer in power and Richard Nixon had won the presidency on a platform promising to get the United States out of the war. Bert Gold and leading members of the board agreed that "the situation had changed substantially" since 1966 and members should have a chance to make their views known.[21] "The war has become the overriding moral issue of our time," read a discussion guide on the subject. "For AJC to remain silent in the face of this reality would be an unconscionable evasion of moral responsibility. . . . If AJC fails to make a contribution to the public dialogue in terms of our affirmation of a desire to peace, we will regret it years from now and when we face our children today." On the other hand, the guide also stated in a long list of pros and cons, "a public stand on Vietnam would also impair AJC's leverage in high places of government, diminishing our ability to influence and inform administration officials and political leaders on issues that concern us including Israel."[22] After months of polling members in every chapter and hour upon hour of debate at national meetings, again the final decision was to say nothing. The predominant view, according to AJC's Ad Hoc Committee on Vietnam, was that "the American Jewish Committee's reputation for probity, reasoned judgment, and prudent statesmanship might well be called into question were the Committee to issue a statement, either pro or con."[23] Instead, national AJC issued a compromise statement on the right of Americans to dissent and debate without being considered disloyal to their country.

There was, however, during this time an agreement that regardless of political differences on the war, AJC leaders could make a contribution to humanitarian aid for Vietnamese refugees. A group of representatives from AJC and the American Jewish Joint Distribution Committee chaired by Morris Abram formed, calling themselves the American Jewish Service Committee on Civilian Relief in Vietnam. Members of the executive committee included Jacob Blaustein, Simon Segal, and Eugene Hevesi of AJC's Foreign Affairs Department.[24] Abram and two others actually traveled to Vietnam in January 1968 to visit refugee camps and to determine the feasibility of a Jewish welfare and rehabilitation program there. Upon their return they reported almost two million refugees—the great majority women and children—living in dire poverty and filth and racked with disease. Dozens of social welfare and religious organizations were already active in refugee work, they said, but the need was so great that there was ample room for Jews to make a contribution. Plans were made to incorporate the group, start fund-raising among the Jewish community, and set up a small office and staff with a representative in Vietnam. Twenty young emissaries for work in the camps were to be recruited from "returnees from Peace Corps service which include a large number of Jews," along with men and women who had kibbutz experience in Israel.

As for official public statements on the Vietnam War, AJC's silence finally came to an end in the spring of 1970. Many who up until that point had been firmly opposed to saying anything about it changed their positions. On April 30 President Nixon announced the invasion of a neighboring country, Cambodia. Nixon had been elected on a promise that he would end U.S. involvement in the war; instead, he was expanding it. The invasion triggered massive protests on campuses across the country. At Kent State University in Ohio, students burned down the campus's ROTC building, and the National Guard was sent in to keep order. On May 4, 1970, only a few days before the opening of AJC's annual meeting, National Guardsmen fired into a protesting crowd, killing four students and wounding nine others. A nationwide student strike resulted, causing hundreds of campuses to shut down. "I have been distressed as have all of us by the events of the last ten days and by the seeming reluctance of the agency to react in a constructive way to the events in Cambodia, the rest of Southeast Asia, and Kent State," wrote Ann G. Wolfe of the intergroup relations and social action division to Bert Gold the day before the May annual meeting was to start. The staff in that section had been pressing for years for the organization to come out against the war in Vietnam. "I must express my own sense of disappointment and dismay at the possibility that AJC may choose to sit this one out, as we have so many others in the past, silent and uncomfortable, because the most conservative of our elements want it so. . . . Our silence on these matters may well be louder than any words we may choose to speak. I would urge you to help us not condone murder by our silence."[25]

At the annual meeting itself, after two days of debate and no less than seventeen drafts, the delegates produced the compromise "Statement on Cambodia," which called for the removal of all U.S. personnel from that country—but ended with the proviso "we must not let the nightmare of Vietnam be replaced by the delusion of isolationism." The statement reminded the United States not to forgo its responsibilities in other parts of the world. Similar cautiously worded and long-debated statements followed in May 1972 and early January 1973. Some members resigned in protest and complained that the organization was not going far enough. "AJC must decide sooner or later, and now is the best time, whether it is to remain the American Jewish Committee or be named the Israeli Jewish Committee," wrote one member in 1972, denouncing the incumbent White House leadership that used the situation in the Middle East "as a sword of Damocles over the heads of the American Jewish population." "AJC must be for the good of Israel," he wrote, "But it must also be for the good of humanity."[26] Staff and lay leaders were still debating the issue of what to say and what not to say back and forth when a cease-fire in Vietnam was declared and the war was officially over on January 27, 1973.[27]

Even when the United States was no longer in Vietnam the issue remained of what to do with the hundreds of thousands of draft evaders, many of whom became exiles in Canada.[28] An unknown but not inconsiderable proportion of them were Jewish. An AJC staff meeting in New York in the spring of 1973 yielded the following statement: "It was decided that in view of the Jewish component, i.e. the number of Jewish students involved, that Jewish agencies should be concerned with the issue and should go on record in favor of granting amnesty."[29] Murray Polner, staff member and editor of AJC's magazine *Present Tense*, wrote an entire book, *When Can I Come Home? A Debate on Amnesty for Exiles, Antiwar Prisoners, and Others*.[30] But what kind of amnesty? Should those who declined to serve in Vietnam receive an unconditional pardon? Or should they be forced to do public service or pay some kind of penalty for their actions?

Some Jewish groups, including the American Jewish Congress, called for complete and unconditional amnesty.[31] The AJC did not, taking into consideration among other factors the "majority public opinion which seems to support conditional rather than unconditional amnesty" and "the possible effects of an unrestricted amnesty on the armed forces in the event of need for future draft and mobilization, e.g. Israel."[32] In the end they voted only to send a letter to President Ford urging that "the issue of amnesty be approached in a compassionate manner" and took no further action.

The one exception was the member of the amnesty subcommittee whose son was an exile in Canada and who lobbied unsuccessfully for his organization to call for an amnesty that was unconditional. "I don't think I have to recite for you the disastrous effects that the war in Vietnam has had on America, both at home and in the world community," the father wrote to Bert Gold, pointing out that Israel had never requested any American soldiers. "Nor should I have to argue that our undeclared war was at best an error and at worst a bare-faced imperial gesture without justification of any sort. Under these circumstances, for the AJC to take the position that we are not interested in the fate of those who resisted, either as 'draft dodgers,' deserters or draft non-registrants or in any other way, seems to be callous and out of character with our other activities. . . . I am aware of the argument that unconditional amnesty will encourage future draft resistance. If we have another war like Vietnam, I hope it does. . . . Bert, I ask you with all the sincerity of a father who now has a son living in Canada as a draft resister, to use your influence to see that this matter is reconsidered."[33] In 1977, the day after his inauguration, President Jimmy Carter followed through on a controversial campaign promise and granted a full pardon to those who had avoided the draft during the Vietnam War by not registering or by going abroad. Those exiles who wished to were able to return home.

As in the case of aid to the refugee camps in Indochina, the only issue related to the aftermath of Vietnam that was hardly debated at all was the need to render humanitarian assistance, this time for the hundreds of thousands of refugees and "boat people" that the war had produced. Chapters organized to help refugees, and some members took refugees into their homes. AJC's President Elmer Winter (1973–77) issued a strong statement calling for President Ford to allow immigration to the United States of 120,000 refugees in 1975. "We cannot forget the hundreds of thousands if not millions of Jews who arrived in this country penniless who found here a haven for themselves and their children," he announced. "Whatever our differences and disagreements may have been about this country's involvement in Vietnam—and our membership, like the nation as a whole, has been sharply divided on this issue—there is no division among us as to the urgency of humanitarian aid to these refugees. We call upon all Americans to open their hearts to them as the people of this country have always opened their hearts to human beings in need."[34]

Affirmative Action and Black-Jewish Relations: The Bakke Case

Another issue that caused passions to rise and long-standing positions to be questioned was the entire complex of government rules and regulations relating to affirmative action and its extension into preferential treatment or quotas for members of certain groups. Some called this "reverse discrimination." The term *affirmative action* had first been used by President Lyndon B. Johnson in 1965 in Executive Order 11246, which required federal contractors to "take affirmative action to ensure that applicants are employed, and that employees are treated during employment, without regard to their race, creed, color, or national origin."[35] AJC had long been devoted to the principle of equality for African Americans and had fought with these groups for all the gains of the civil rights movement. In the late 1960s and early 1970s, however, the idea arose that simple equality for individuals under the existing civil rights laws was not sufficient; black Americans were, in effect, being thrown into the race bound and shackled from hundreds of years of discrimination and were expected to perform as well as advantaged whites.

One way to rectify this negative legacy was to establish group recognition and to set aside a certain number or proportion of places for minorities in job hiring or school admissions. Some activists and officials, with the support of social scientists, also proposed doing away with written and oral tests as the sole basis for positions in the civil service or in school admissions on the grounds that such tests were culture-bound and thus favored middle-class applicants. Affirmative action guidelines could also interfere with the rights of seniority, as the economy was contracting and many people were being fired in the 1970s. Normally on the principle of last hired, first fired, more minorities who had recently gotten their jobs would lose them. But the affirmative action principle required that whites who had more seniority be fired so that a sufficient percentage of minority members could keep their jobs.[36]

The preferential treatment technique, first used in the awarding of government building contracts, made its way to America's institutions of higher education in the academic year 1970–71. American Jews were especially sensitive to its presence in academia as higher education had played such an important role in their upper mobility. The admission of their children to universities and law and medical schools—ideally the most prestigious Ivy League ones—also served as the arbiter of a family's success and an informal barometer of the fall of antisemitism. Now the City University of New York system, which had once been more than 80 percent Jewish, announced a policy of "open enrollment." All black and Puerto Rican high school graduates who applied were admitted until their proportion went from 15 percent of the CUNY student body to 40 percent, their approximate ratio in the public school population. Stony Brook University, part of the State University of New York system, announced in 1972 that it would fill one hundred faculty positions in the next three years with blacks—of whom half would be women—and that it would downgrade high school averages and SAT scores in favor of motivation, past employment, and community service until the percentage of minorities in its student body reached 30 percent. The law school at the University of California, Berkeley, also announced that it would set aside 30 percent of its admissions for minority applicants.[37]

An extensive debate on how to react to this turn of events took place within the domestic affairs and legal divisions of the AJC. The view was generally favorable toward affirmative action through such means as remedial training or specialized recruiting. The majority, however, held that rigid quotas by race or ethnic group were illegal and unconstitutional on principle, would increase intergroup tensions, would unfairly stigmatize minorities who benefited from them, and finally would be of potential harm to Jews. AJC did not stress the last factor in its various briefs and reports. Nonetheless, Jews had everything to lose if hiring and admissions were to be done less on merit and more on the proportion of one's group in the population. Jews, less than 3 percent of the American population, were represented in education, professions, and other desirable positions far beyond proportion to their numbers. For example, they were 60 percent of the teachers and principals in the New York City public school system and, among those professors who received their training after World War II, up to 25 percent of the faculty at the nation's colleges and universities.[38] If the quota principle in hiring, promotion, and admissions took hold they feared they and their children might be pushed out of their rightful places. Furthermore, the very idea of quotas unearthed traumatic memories of the measures that had been used for generations to keep Jews out of educational and social institutions, which the AJC, the ADL, the American Jewish Congress, and similar groups had been fighting against for the better part of their collective existence.

For African American civil rights groups, however, which had fought shoulder to shoulder with Jewish groups for so many years, Jewish opposition to quotas was hypocritical, self-serving, and a betrayal of everything Jews were supposed to stand for. (The very word "quotas" was offensive to them and they themselves did not use it). The debate became heated. For example, in early August 1972, AJC president Philip E. Hoffman wrote letters to both presidential candidates urging them to "reject categorically the use of quotas" in "implementing vitally essential affirmative action programs."[39] (A rumor had spread during the campaign that McGovern had pledged 10 percent of federal patronage jobs to blacks if he were elected; he denied it). Both of the candidates responded with positive letters, and the exchange received extensive attention in the media. Some black leaders, however, feared that a presidential ban on quotas would slow down the vital process of affirmative action when the economy was contracting—and under Nixon the government already appeared to be pulling back from a dedication to civil rights. Representative Louis Stokes, chairman of the newly formed Congressional Black Caucus, attacked the AJC letter as "high-handed at best and racist at worst," criticizing the organization for believing that "by crossing our fingers, closing our eyes and hoping for the best, minority, poor and disadvantaged Americans will receive a fair share of opportunity."[40] When affirmative action–related cases began to be heard by the courts, with black leaders supporting one position and some Jewish leaders the other, veteran civil rights leader the Reverend Jesse Jackson at the national convention of the National Urban League demanded a "summit meeting" with AJC and ADL to "reassess" their relationship. "People who marched with us and demonstrated with us ten years ago are now meeting us in the Supreme Court" as adversaries, he declared.[41]

The first court case Jackson was referring to was *DeFunis v. Odegaard*, which was argued and decided in the U.S. Supreme Court in the spring of 1974. In 1970 Marco DeFunis, a Phi Beta Kappa and magna cum laude graduate of the University of Washington, applied to the university's law school and was rejected, although black, Filipino, Chicano, or American Indian students with lower grades and test scores were accepted. DeFunis declared that the law school's practice of preferential admission on the basis of race violated his rights under the Fourteenth Amendment to the Constitution, which provided that no state shall deny to any person equal protection of the law. A lower court decided in his favor and ordered the school to admit him, but the University of Washington appealed the decision to the U.S. Supreme Court.

Jewish organizations were divided on the case. At that point, the AJC, the ADL, and the American Jewish Congress filed an amicus curiae (friend-of-the-court) brief supporting DeFunis while the National Council of Jewish Women, the Union of American Hebrew Congregations (UAHC), former AJC President and Supreme Court Justice Arthur Goldberg, and other individual Jews supported the position of black leaders, which was to uphold the university's preferential admissions program.[42] Ill-feeling by black Americans against the stand of the AJC, American Jewish Congress, and ADL was compounded when it became clear that DeFunis was Jewish (he came from a Sephardic family in Seattle). As it developed, the Court in *DeFunis* endorsed neither position. As in the meantime, owing to the decision of the lower court, DeFunis had been enrolled anyway and was about to graduate, the U.S. Supreme Court declared the whole matter moot on April 23, 1974.

The decision allowed for a rapprochement. Black-Jewish relations and alliances appeared to be improving in 1974–75, as Milton Ellerin noted in his write-up on intergroup relations in the *American Jewish Year Book* for that year. There were expressions of sympathy in black periodicals about terrorist acts committed against children in Israel. Black leaders such as Bayard Rustin, Roy Wilkins, and Vernon Jordan (executive director of the National Urban League), frequently and publicly issued statements calling for Israel's right to exist as a sovereign nation. Jordan in particular expressed understanding of Jewish feelings regarding quotas, appreciated the Jewish organizations that had supported the law school's position in *DeFunis*, and stressed the need to avoid conflict.

In May 1974 the ADL, the AJC, and the American Jewish Congress joined the National Urban League, the Puerto Rican Legal Defense Fund, and the NAACP in lobbying the director of HEW (Health, Education and Welfare) to issue concrete guidelines on methods educational institutions could use to recruit students and faculty from previously excluded groups.[43] The Reverend Jesse Jackson and a leading rabbi convened a two-day conference in June of fifty Jewish and black leaders, including the AJC, that ended with a public affirmation that there were "more things to unite us than divide us." A joint statement called for full employment, national health programs, and an "effective" affirmative action program. In June 1974, AJC and Fisk University, a historically black institution, cosponsored a conference on black-Jewish relations.[44] In 1975 Bayard Rustin, at AJC's behest, got the signatures of thirty-eight black leaders (Jesse Jackson declined to sign) to form BASIC: the Black Americans in Support of Israel Committee. Their founding statement condemned the Arab blacklist, declared support of Israel's right to exist, pointed out that OPEC oil policies had a "disastrous" economic effects on blacks both in America and in Africa, and supported the "Palestinian right to self-determination" while opposing the PLO.[45] Signers included future mayor of New York David Dinkins, and Congressman Andrew Young.

Then came the case that reopened old wounds. Many considered it the most important civil rights case since *Brown v. Board of Education* and also one of the most difficult ever heard by the U.S. Supreme Court.[46] Allan Bakke, a white, thirty-two-year-old male, had an excellent academic record at the University of Minnesota and Stanford University, and was a veteran of the Vietnam War. At a relatively advanced age, he decided he wanted to pursue a career in medicine. In 1973 and again in 1974, he applied to the University of California, Davis, Medical School and was rejected both times; in both years special minority applicants were admitted who had significantly lower grades and scores. The university was setting aside sixteen out of one hundred places in its entering medical school class for members of minority groups: blacks, Chicanos, Asians, and American Indians. Bakke brought suit, claiming that he had been rejected solely because of his race. In doing so, Davis had denied him his rights under the Equal Protection Clause of the Fourteenth Amendment and had also violated Title Vietnam of the Civil Rights Act of 1964, which barred any discrimination "on the ground of race, color, or national origin in any program receiving federal financial assistance."

The case began to attract national attention when it reached the Supreme Court of the State of California. In September 1976 that court ruled that the program favoring students from minority groups for admission to state medical schools was indeed unconstitutional and that Bakke should be admitted. The regents of the university, however, decided to appeal to the U.S. Supreme Court. They took on Archibald Cox, former Harvard Law School professor and most recently special prosecutor at the Watergate hearings, to argue their case. Bakke's attorney was Reynold H. Colvin, who happened to be the chairman of the San Francisco Bay Area chapter of the AJC. In February 1977 the Supreme Court agreed to hear the case in its upcoming October term.

At first it was not clear whether national AJC would file an amicus brief in the landmark case of *University of California Regents v. Bakke* at all—and if it did, which side it would support. There were views expressed from all sides, along with concern for the reactions of minority allies. Legal director Samuel Rabinove began polling the chapters to get their views on the question. Seymour Samet, director of the domestic affairs division, pointed out that the case was different from *DeFunis*. In *Bakke* the university flatly admitted that its special admissions program was based on racial and ethnic considerations. The lower court had ruled against DeFunis, but it had ruled in favor of Bakke. "A reason for concern by many minority group leaders," Samet wrote, "is that the composition of the present Supreme Court is likely not only to rule in favor of Bakke, but also to declare affirmative action programs to be illegal where they give preference on the basis of race, creed or color." In the view of these minority leaders, such a declaration would be a "serious step backward": there were many such affirmative action programs through the country that had made it possible for a "substantial number" of minority group people to enter professional schools, at a time when admissions to such schools was becoming increasingly competitive. So afraid were they of a negative ruling that the National Urban League originally urged the U.S. Supreme Court not to review the case at all. They would prefer that California universities be subject to a "painful legal rule" rather than risk having it made the rule for the entire country.[47]

The question of whether to enter the case—and on whose side—was still unresolved at the beginning of a stormy meeting of the Domestic Affairs

Commission in May. "The Bakke case is a matter in which intelligent people of good will strongly disagree," noted Seymour Samet.[48] Several high laymen and staff of the AJC, including Hyman Bookbinder, wanted to file a brief *against* Bakke.[49] Many felt that race was a valid preferential criteria and that "we should face our past history of slavery squarely. . . . It is necessary to be color conscious now in order to be color blind in the future," and that it was legitimate to have such a preference "for a limited period of time."[50]

Even after the brief was written members continued to disagree with it, including one female AJC member who saw quotas in affirmative action as being beneficial to women, who had suffered so much job discrimination in the past. "I am sure you realize that this was fully discussed at the Domestic Affairs Commission meeting in Atlanta and had previously been discussed in great depth at earlier meetings, Board of Governors, Executive Committee, etc.," wrote Charlotte Holstein, in an effort to assuage the objections of Harriet Alpern. "Reaching an agreement or consensus with the AJC membership is a difficult assignment on any issue, and the Bakke case has clearly been one of the most difficult. However, a clear majority of the members . . . as well as the general membership approve and applaud the AJC position. It will also interest you to know that a high proportion of the members of the Domestic Affairs Commission are women and they are part of the decision-making process for the Commission."[51]

AJC's final decision was to submit, along with the American Jewish Congress, a brief supporting Bakke that upheld their previous position: quotas were objectionable, but other forms of affirmative action were not. Fearing the onus that might be placed on them as Jews for taking what might be considered an antiblack position, the legal department sought to get as many other parties as possible to support them. Eventual cosigners of the brief included the Hellenic Bar Association of Illinois, the Italian American Foundation, the Polish American Affairs Council, and the Ukrainian Congress Committee of America. Alan M. Dershowitz of Harvard Law School was listed "of counsel."[52] Not all Jewish groups supported Bakke. The Union of American Hebrew Congregations and the National Council of Jewish Women filed in favor of the position of the University of California.[53]

A summary of AJC's brief in conjunction with eight other groups was released to the public in August 1977 under the headline "Speed Entry of Minorities into Universities on Basis of Disadvantage, Not Race."[54] The brief was written by lay leaders and staff lawyers of both the AJC and the American Jewish Congress. "We submit this brief," it began, "because we believe that our system of constitutional liberties would be gravely undermined if the law were to give sanction to use of race in the decision-making process of governmental agencies and because we believe that disadvantaged students can be aided by other procedures that are both constitutional and practical." Racial quotas were "factually, educationally, and psychologically unsound, legally and constitutionally erroneous, and profoundly damaging to the fabric of American society." AJC could endorse special education preparation and tutoring prior to admission and during school attendance, but such a system would have to be based on the individual's degree of disadvantage, not race. Furthermore, it was permissible to take into account factors other than grades and test scores only. Schools could evaluate candidates in terms of their background; whether they came from a "culturally impoverished home:" the nature and quality of schools attended, whether the student had to work while in school, whether he/she had done voluntary work in the community, whether the student showed exceptional "leadership, industry, perseverance, self-discipline, and intense motivation," and whether the student had to surmount handicaps as might be caused by discrimination, poverty, or chronic illness. If the lack of minority professionals to work in underserved areas was at issue, then preference could be given to candidates who entered into a binding commitment to serve in an urban ghetto, a barrio, or an Indian reservation after graduation. "All of these factors may constitutionally and legitimately be considered by the school," the brief concluded. "But what the school may not do, we submit, is to classify applicants for admission on the basis of race or ethnicity and so structure its selection process as to admit an essentially predetermined proportion of members of certain groups."

The AJC also took extensive political action in addition to submitting the amicus brief. During the spring and summer of 1977 Hyman Bookbinder and other AJC leaders held a series of meetings with Joseph A. Califano, President Carter's secretary of health, education and welfare to impress their position upon him. They took credit for "helping to mold" a strong anti-quota speech Califano subsequently delivered that was given wide attention by the media. They also decided that in "a series of discussions with White House advisers" they would seek a letter from President Carter similar to the one on affirmative action that they had obtained from the two candidates during the 1972 presidential campaign. Carter obliged in October 1977, as the case was being argued, in a letter to AJC President Richard Maass commenting on AJC's brief: "I appreciate your informing me of the American Jewish Committee's strong support for affirmative action programs. As you may know, I share the Committee's view that such programs are necessary. . . . The brief recognized that programs using rigid racial quotas are exclusionary and are therefore unconstitutional. I support the position which the brief took, recognizing the distinction between flexible affirmative action programs using goals and inflexible racial quotas. It is my understanding that you take the same position." Press releases about the exchange were duly sent to all the nation's media outlets and all national and state legislators. The original letter from Carter was handed over for safekeeping to Cyma Horowitz, director of AJC's Blaustein Library, who kept it in a locked room in a box marked "Contracts" and a folder titled "Special Letters."[55]

On the other side of the case, black leaders were fearful that if the Court ruled against quotas and in favor of Bakke, affirmative action programs of any kind would disappear. A coalition of fifteen prominent black leaders sent a telegram to President Carter warning that the wrong decision would "sabotage Black advances and frustrate minorities who look to your administration for help."[56] In a column appearing in the *Amsterdam News*, a leading New York lawyer attacked the Jewish community for supporting Bakke. "Organized Jewry," he wrote, "has taken the position that affirmative action to remove the vestiges of four hundred years of white racism is acceptable, but that preferential treatment to achieve a specific goal is somehow un-American."[57]

In the months before the case was to be argued, expressions of pro-Bakke and anti-Bakke forces grew louder and more numerous. By the end, at least fifty-seven friend-of-the court briefs were filed in the Bakke case, more than in any other case in the previous two decades. The briefs came from 162 organizations and individuals; forty-one supported the University of California's quota system while sixteen argued that Bakke's constitutional rights had been violated.[58]

The decision the Supreme Court finally handed down on June 28, 1978, was so divided and complex that at first it was not clear to observers what they should make of it. In a 5–4 vote the Court ruled that Bakke's constitutional rights had been violated and that the university should admit him. At the same time, it held that it *was* constitutional for schools to use race as a factor in weighing the qualifications of applicants, thus overturning the decision of the California Supreme Court.[59] "Both sides won," declared Bert Gold, pleased that the Court had essentially taken AJC's position: anti-quota but pro–affirmative action. He called for "all parties involved" to "renew the inspiring civil rights coalition of the early 1960s" and spoke of "healing wounds."[60]

Most black Americans, however, did not take it that way. "Bakke: We Lost" read the headline in New York's *Amsterdam News* the following day. The paper editorialized that the Bakke decision placed every affirmative action program in jeopardy, whether in academic institutions or in private business and industry. One of the paper's columnists blamed key AJC ally Bayard Rustin "and his friends from B'nai B'rith and the American Jewish Congress" for undoing enforceable affirmative action programs.[61] Jesse Jackson likened the impact of the decision to a Nazi march in Skokie, a Chicago suburb with numerous Holocaust survivors, or a march of the Ku Klux Klan in Mississippi. There were angry protest rallies in San Francisco, Los Angeles, and New York. The main point for them was not that race was still a legitimate factor to take into account in hiring and university admissions, but that Jews and Jewish agencies had backed Allan Bakke and won.[62] So great was the uproar over Bakke that when the following year another affirmative action/quotas case reached the U.S. Supreme Court—*United Steelworkers of America v. Weber*—both the AJC and the American

Jewish Congress voted to stay out of it to avoid causing further alienation of the black community.[63]

The sting from the Bakke affair, combined with the Andrew Young affair, the Zionism-is-racism movement, and the renewed energy crisis were apparently fueling such an upsurge in black anti-Jewish expression that AJC's legal director seriously suggested that they review their stand on quotas as a way to stem it. According to Samuel Rabinove, in a document entitled "Affirmative Action for the 1980s: Options for AJC," prepared in December 1979, AJC leaders had several alternatives to consider in the coming decade. First, of course, they could stay where they were. Or they could harden their policy further, holding that quotas were bad for America and worse for Jews. Or, they could "soften" their policy: "Accept that quotas and preferences are a matter of simple justice. Quotas might be both necessary and appropriate in some cases and therefore AJC ought to support them." They might go even further and support the notion that achieving "at least a rough proportionality" for minority groups was overall a legitimate national objective. "Since our society has condoned preferences for white males in the better jobs since time immemorial," he pointed out, "it is no more than right to grant similar rights to those groups which have been shut out for so long." Furthermore, while quotas and preferences might be injurious to individual Jews, there was no evidence that Jews as a group had been disproportionately hurt; in fact, quotas and affirmative action programs had already benefited many Jewish women. If AJC eliminated all its opposition to quotas and preferences, he concluded, it would produce "one very substantial boon–a renewal of broken ties with our erstwhile friends and allies in the black community as well as enhancing the prospects for forging stronger relationships with the burgeoning Hispanic community."[64]

AJC over the years did not change the position it had taken in *Bakke;* it remained against quotas while affirming and supporting other forms of affirmative action. Racial quotas remained illegal and unconstitutional. Twenty-five years after *Bakke* the U.S. Supreme Court again considered the constitutionality of affirmative action programs through two suits brought against the University of Michigan.[65] This time AJC filed in *favor* of the university's program, as there was no rigid quota and an applicant's minority status was only one factor among many considered. "Disallowing the consideration of race as one factor among many in university admissions would have the effect of eliminating meaningful diversity on American campuses," announced Jeffrey Sinensky, the general counsel for the AJC, in February 2003.[66] In a split decision the Court ruled in favor of the university: race could still be used as a factor in admissions. "Twenty-five years from now," the justices wrote in their opinion, "the use of racial preferences will no longer be necessary to further the interest approved today." The AJC and many other Americans of all backgrounds shared in that hope.

Forest Hills and Busing

The old vision of an integrated American society was still driving Haskell Lazere and members of AJC's New York chapter to support the building of a low-income housing project in Forest Hills, Queens, but there was controversy within the ranks and criticism from outsiders about how far to support the project or whether to support it at all. The white, middle-class neighborhood was popular with Conservative and Orthodox Jews who had established a network of institutions to which they could walk. Much would be lost if the neighborhood "changed" and they had to move. Jewish residents who were not motivated by the vision of integration castigated Mayor John Lindsay, a proponent of the project, for not pressing for low-income housing in such places as Manhattan's Upper East Side or in the Riverdale section of the Bronx.[67] The controversy was an occasion for Jews to express abundant racism against blacks. During demonstrations some threw rocks and hurled racial epithets. Some also had strong words for the AJC. One couple wrote to resign their membership because of AJC's stand on Forest Hills. "The Jewish families in Forest Hills are entitled to pleasant and safe living just as much as the high income Jewish families in Scarsdale or Great Neck," they wrote. "Perhaps it is noble for rich Jewish people to show the world that Jewish people are so fair—but we believe that it is more important to have conditions favorable to the middle class Jews. In a choice between the happiness and comfort of slum welfare families vs. the Jewish middle class families, we expected you to be in favor of the Jews."[68]

In the face of such reactions, the AJC staff decided to form a committee to consider the "implications" of its stand and a possible revision of policy.[69] The New York chapter tried to negotiate a modification of the original housing plan. They recommended that the whole project be scaled down to many fewer units than had originally been called for and that 40 percent of the units be set aside for the elderly (who, it was assumed, would be largely Jewish). The prospect was met with a blistering condemnation by Joseph Willen, a layman who had served on AJC's highest executive committees since 1943 and had been executive vice president of the Federation of Jewish Philanthropies in New York. He was of the opinion that AJC should support the Forest Hills housing project as it was originally planned. As he expressed it, the fate of the organization depended upon their decision. "The Forest Hills community attitude toward the low income housing project that the city has approved and that a large majority of the community deeply resents remains, in my judgment, one of the acid tests of the validity of much of what the AJC believes in," he wrote. "Its failure to act courageously and forthrightly in this situation raises questions as to our future usefulness." He cited the conclusions of the Kerner Commission in insisting that the very fate of the country was at stake and that they must support the housing project wholeheartedly no matter what the cost:

AJC should endorse the project without any reservations whatsoever. It should support Mayor Lindsay's position even if every fear materializes. It may very well be that the only way our country will ever solve the problem of segregation is through the painful and at times disastrous experience of the kind that could very well develop in this area. I would not for one moment compromise the proposition that the greater threat to America is what the Kerner report really fears, a black and white community occupying the same national boundaries but not of the same country. I am not unmindful of the fact that very few of the people that would vote for my views in the American Jewish Committee live in this area. I wonder how the bill of rights would be defended if in every instance local communities had to be consulted. . . . I repeat, I would not compromise one inch with the inalienable right of breaking up ghetto areas and economically isolated ghettos. The threat to America is rich neighborhoods, poor neighborhoods, black neighborhoods, white neighborhoods, Jewish neighborhoods, Catholic neighborhoods, WASP neighborhoods etc. We must undertake the long difficult struggle and difficult it will be, for some deeper understanding of how these ethnic and colored ghettos should be broken up and what must be if America is to emerge as a healthy nation. As we struggle and go through the agonies of finding an answer to this problem, we dare not in my judgment equivocate or be vague about our total and complete endorsement of the project in the Forest Hills area no matter what the risks might be.[70]

The AJC as an organization also suffered internal division and the criticism of outsiders on the busing of schoolchildren to achieve racial desegregation — a central issue in the 1972 presidential campaign. At that point, public schools that had been desegregated through busing were beginning to become segregated again as white parents pulled their children out of the public schools and sent them to private academies, or moved to the suburbs. The Republican platform flatly declared that it was "irrevocably opposed to busing for racial balance." The Democratic candidate, George McGovern, on the other hand, stressed throughout the campaign that busing was a "legitimate" tool to achieve racial desegregation.[71] AJC compromised by issuing guidelines to suggest when busing should and should not be used. However, on the constitutional amendment to ban busing that was on the agenda in 1972, there was no argument: they strongly opposed it.

"We do not believe children should be bused into inferior schools," declared Bert Gold, in a standard letter to those advocating a different position. "But what the AJC is also saying is that busing, as one possible instrument for accomplishing integration, should not be ruled out, particularly since approximately forty percent of public school pupils are normally bussed to and from school, and usually for reasons having nothing to do with racial integration." For many years, he pointed out, busing had been used in a number of states "solely to perpetuate the existence of segregated schools. . . . There is no question that it is vitally important for middle-class white people not to be placed in intolerable situations which impel them to withdraw their children from public schools. But it is also vitally important, we feel, that white children and black children who, after all, are the adult American citizens of tomorrow, come to know each other as human beings in a racially integrated setting where quality education is available to all."[72]

Church-State Separation, Aid to Private Schools, and Jewish Education

As in the affirmative action case of *Bakke*, where the Equal Protection Clause was central, issues pertaining to constitutional law could be especially divisive. Perhaps the most cherished constitutional right for American Jews was the establishment and free exercise clauses both contained in the First Amendment—or, as Thomas Jefferson described it in a letter in 1802, "that act of the whole American people which declared that their legislature should make no law respecting the establishment of religion, or prohibiting the free exercise thereof, thus building a wall of separation between church and state." The words are etched in stone on the walls of the Jefferson Memorial in Washington, D.C. Jews had been able to flourish in America as nowhere else in good part because there was no established national church and no religious test was required to hold public office. Many saw a high wall between church and state as a major guarantor of American Jewish safety and freedom. Preserving and defending this separation had always occupied a good deal of the time and energy of the Jewish defense agencies, in particular the American Jewish Congress, which took the lead in bringing litigation in church-state cases.

A myriad of issues fell under the category of church-state legal activity, including prayer and Bible reading in the public schools, religious displays in public places, compulsory chapel services, Sunday closing laws, birth control, abortion, and censorship. After World War II a substantial part of church-state litigation centered on the issues of keeping expressions of Christianity out of the public square and preventing any government aid to private sectarian schools (which were often in financial trouble, servicing many parents who had difficulty affording the tuition). In comparison to other Jewish groups, AJC did not take the extreme separationist view on school aid. It was a matter of pride to the organization that the first amicus curiae brief it had ever filed was in the U.S. Supreme Court case *Pierce v. Society of Sisters of the Holy Names of Jesus and Mary* (1925), which defended the right of parents in Oregon to send their children to Catholic schools. As a matter of policy AJC had been willing to accept aid to sectarian schools for bus transportation, school lunches, some medical services, and secular textbooks, which the U.S. Supreme Court had allowed on the basis that these benefited the child, not the school. AJC was also willing to advocate "dual enrollment" or "shared time" arrangements, in which children would receive secular education in the public schools and religious instruction elsewhere off public school premises.

Further than that, however, AJC majority policy was not willing to go. There were staff and lay members who wanted it to go further, and others who did not even want it to go that far. In general, aspects of church-state relations caused a long-standing debate within the AJC and within the entire organized Jewish community between what were called the *separationists*, who took the establishment clause as most important, and the *accommodationists*, who were willing to make some compromises on the side of the free exercise clause. The urgency of this issue only became stronger with the years, and it was still being debated at the turn of the twenty-first century. Howard I. Friedman and Robert Rifkind, two former presidents of the AJC, took opposing sides on the issue in a session of the May 3, 2000, annual meeting. The session was so memorable to the delegates that upon request AJC issued the verbatim transcript as a separate publication entitled "The Great Debate."[73]

In 1970, American Catholic schools were experiencing a financial crisis, in part because of a developing shortage of teaching nuns and priests and the need to hire teachers at laypeople's salaries. The accommodationists within AJC, and in particular members and staff of the interreligious affairs division, wanted to soften the organization's stance on church-state separation to avoid losing support from Catholic allies who so badly needed help with their school system. After all, they pointed out, AJC was constantly asking Catholic representatives for statements on Jewish issues such as Israel, Soviet Jewry, and revision of liturgy and textbooks in the wake of *Nostra Aetate.* How long could this go on without giving Catholics something in return? How could they answer charges that Jews were simply anti-Catholic and anti-Christian? The Jewish communal affairs division, for its part, wanted AJC to soften its stance on aid to private schools in order to avoid alienating Orthodox Jews, who were also seeking aid for their own growing day school system. They also had an ongoing desire to show the rest of the community that the AJC was, contrary to the image it still had, truly interested in Jewish matters. In response to all this, AJC national officers in 1971 formed a special Committee on the Community Relations Implications of AJC Policy on Aid to Private Education, which recommended greater sensitivity to Christian feelings but otherwise did not call for any change in basic AJC policy.[74]

Against the background of this conflict, Yehuda Rosenman and the Jewish Communal Affairs Department in 1970 began a campaign to get AJC to issue a policy statement supporting Jewish education in general and endorsing a primary role for Jewish all-day schools in particular. Jewish day schools were viewed with suspicion by many in the American Jewish community: they were perceived as being for the Orthodox community and most American Jews were not Orthodox. Through the years AJC's lay leadership slowly moved away from its original antagonism to these schools toward the position that such schools were of primary importance and should be supported by local Jewish communal and philanthropic agencies. Ironically, for many of the "separationists" within the AJC and the organized Jewish community as a whole, the rationale of demanding communal support for Jewish day schools was not because day schools were inherently desirable, but because they wished to "restore the Jewish consensus" on church-state issues and stop Jewish day schools from the "temptation" of going to the government for funds.[75]

At first, it was not even taken for granted that defense and community relations organizations such as AJC or NJCRAC (since 1968 the National *Jewish* Community Relations Advisory Council) should involve themselves in Jewish education at all. Their main purpose was supposed to be relations with non-Jews. When the subject of funding for Jewish day schools came up on the agenda of a NJCRAC commission meeting in 1971 attended by Yehuda Rosenman and Samuel Rabinove, some in attendance—not from AJC—protested the idea of even issuing a statement on the subject. Why, they asked, did the community relations field seek to concern itself with Jewish education; in any event, why the day school rather than Jewish education in general? One delegate thought that "NJCRAC is entering a field that is foreign to its responsibilities" and urged that rather than approving a policy statement, it should "give further thought to the appropriateness of its role in this area. . . . It is not the responsibility of NJCRAC to pass on every question that may come before the Jewish community, any more than it should make judgments on how synagogues should be organized, or what the content of the synagogue service should be, or what rabbis preach."[76] The chair of the meeting responded to this protest by claiming that they had to consider the subject because of concern with the Orthodox community's efforts to get state aid for their day schools. In order to stop this, it was necessary for NJCRAC to help day schools get more funding from within the Jewish community.

At another interorganizational meeting on church-state relations and aid to religious schools, Rabinove noted that the most interesting recommendation came from Leo Pfeffer, who had headed the American Jewish Congress's Committee on Law and Social Action and who was virtually the architect of church-state separation law in the United States. Pfeffer's suggestion was that rabbis collectively impose a requirement that at each bar mitzvah and wedding at which they officiated, 5 percent of the anticipated cost of the celebration or the wedding reception must be earmarked for Jewish day schools. Such an arrangement, Pfeffer pointed out, would render it unnecessary "to seek money for Jewish day schools from any other sources, whether public or private."[77] A variation on this theme was that wealthy Jews should set aside 5 percent of their estates to support Jewish day schools. This idea became known as the "Five Percent Plan" and was still being debated in 2006, with the focus on how exactly all of America's wealthy Jews would be persuaded to participate in this plan. By that time an AJC study had been done that showed the current cost of tuition for the two hundred thousand children in the existing Jewish day school system to be some two billion dollars a year, and at least an additional billion a year would be necessary to expand that system to accommodate another one hundred thousand children. In comparison, all the federations in the United States together allocated approximately seven hundred million dollars a year. The question of where in the world of Jewish philanthropy anyone could obtain the additional needed billions was never answered.[78]

First, however, the leadership of the predominantly secular Jewish organizations had to be convinced that Jewish education and in particular Jewish day schools were causes worth fighting for at all. At AJC's National Executive Council meeting in Houston in 1970, the first attempt was made by the Jewish Communal Affairs Commission (chaired at the time by Maynard I. Wishner) to get through a policy statement endorsing Jewish education and especially Jewish day schools. After much controversy over its wording and emphasis, the statement was eventually killed, with a referral for "future study." The problem was that it placed too much emphasis on day schools. Objections included: (1) an increase in Jewish day schools would weaken the public school system; (2) day schools would isolate Jewish children from the community and hurt desegregation efforts; (3) such commitment by AJC would weaken its position on separation of church and state; and (4) that it was not certain if day schools actually accomplished all that their supporters claimed they did.[79]

When the statement at first did not pass, Bert Gold felt the need to explain why, both to the membership and to the general Jewish public, where such apparent lack of support for Jewish education on AJC's part did not play well. There was no question, he noted, that Jewish day schools were booming and springing up all across the country; in the New York area alone, of the 150,000 Jewish boys and girls who were getting any kind of Jewish education, one-third were attending such schools in 1970. It was not surprising that these institutions were beginning to bid urgently for community support through federations and other philanthropic sources. "What made the fur fly at Houston," Gold explained, "was a paragraph in a proposed statement that said that Jewish day schools deserved AJC's moral and financial backing, being 'an important vehicle for future Jewish scholars, communal workers, and lay leaders.' No one questioned that the Jewish day schools could be all this and more. But many vehemently objected to thus singling out one phase of Jewish education for special endorsement—especially one which might seem to ally AJC with tendencies toward cultural separatism." AJC's task, these critics insisted, was rather to help improve *all* options for Jewish education; hence the statement was turned down for further work. "But the reason was not that AJC loves Jewish day schools less," concluded Gold, "[i]t is rather that AJC loves the totality of Jewish education more."[80]

Following the NEC's recommendation for "further study," in 1972 Jewish communal affairs set up a colloquium on Jewish education and Jewish identity that collected a wealth of hard data on what was otherwise an abstract subject. Its specific recommendations were released in 1977 and encapsulated in a statement on Jewish education and Jewish identity that AJC's NEC, meeting in Atlanta, passed that same year. The statement indeed addressed the "totality" of Jewish education. Home and family, it was found, were in fact the primary framework in which Jewish values were acquired; quantitatively, home background was found to be two and a half times more important than Jewish schooling in developing a Jewish identity. Therefore, it concluded, formal and informal educational experiences that involved the entire family, such as weekend retreats, camping, and group trips to Israel, should be encouraged. The studies also found that "a minimum of three thousand hours of Jewish schooling is essential if it is to have an impact on forming a positive Jewish identity" (less than that, some concluded, could actually do more harm than good). Jewish schooling should therefore be continued into the adolescent years, rather than terminating at bar or bat mitzvah age. That numerical conclusion gracefully led into the final recommendation: "Since Jewish day school education provides students with the requisite minimum hours of Jewish study and a total learning environment in which Jewish education is effectively integrated with secular education it should be given the special consideration of Jewish parents and the support of the Jewish community as a logical and effective educational alternative."[81]

The statement, copies of which were distributed to several hundred people across the country including the trustees of bureaus of Jewish education and the religious education committees of all the synagogues, was greeted in some quarters with jubilation. "MESSIAH IS HERE! COMMITTEE: MORE MONEY SHOULD GO TO JEWISH EDUCATION" read the headline in the Atlanta *Jewish Post*. The author wrote: "What many would have predicted even as short a time ago as two years would be if not the coming of the Messiah, at least the prelude of his coming, took place here when the American Jewish Committee went on record calling on the Jewish community to give 'top priority' to Jewish education and in the allocation of communal resources for domestic needs. . . . That the resolution included support—'special consideration'—for Jewish day schools education is another indication of the revolution in the body considered the mouthpiece of the Jewish wealthy."[82]

One member in San Francisco, however, expressed his skepticism of the statement, accusing it of "lacking a sense of reality" when it came to Jewish day schools. "What is the AJC prepared to do about it," he asked, "except to provide abstract, high-level, 'Policy' advice? How, I wonder, does this differ from kibitzing, expensive kibitzing, but kibitzing nonetheless? . . . I don't know how many children attend Jewish day schools around the country, but I assume that the numbers are rather modest despite some recent dramatic growth. . . . It would seem that the statement is urging parents to give their children the same amount of education—three thousand hours—that students get at Jewish day schools. This is another example of the sort of 'good idea' in the form of a 'policy' which seems to me to be not much more than a rhetorical flourish. The day schools don't exist, the commitment on the part of the parents doesn't exist, most of the federations have provided subventions to day schools only after great pressure and conflict, etc. In short, this is a good idea which doesn't inspire confidence that AJC is really serious about what it means to recommend a course of action. . . . An organization with AJC's power, muscle, and intellectual resources can do better."[83]

The AJC as a whole reaffirmed its commitment to the totality of Jewish education and to the important role of day schools in 1982. By 1999 it was calling for a communal endowment fund for the purpose of providing children and youths with scholarships for any form of "quality" Jewish education. It also called for establishing a communal fund to help parents working in the Jewish communal field (most of whom earned modest salaries) to pay for the tuition of their children. The average supplementary afternoon Hebrew school provided an average of four contact hours a week—and this at a time when children were already tired from their secular school day. "Quality Jewish education" to this group meant only one thing: day schools, at tuitions running from eight thousand to twenty-five thousand dollars per year. In the same statement, AJC also reiterated its opposition to any form of government aid to religious schools. By 2006, the communal fund that could financially guarantee a Jewish day school education for every Jewish child in the United States had never materialized and was nowhere on the horizon. Jewish organizations were working harder than ever to fortify the wall between church and state, so government support for day schools appeared to be out of the question. Debates back and forth continued. Philanthropic organizations and family foundations were indeed putting more money into day schools. New institutions were established specifically to aid day schools, such as the Avi Chai Foundation and the Partnership for Excellence in Jewish Education. Their contributions, however, were but a drop in the proverbial bucket compared to the real cost of tuition for hundreds of thousands of Jewish children. The church-state separation–funding Jewish day schools dilemma appeared not much closer to solution in 2006 than it had in 1970.

Nazis Marching in Skokie—Protected by the First Amendment?

Constitutional law, this time the free speech clause of the First Amendment, also came into play during the threatened march of Nazis in front of the Village Hall of Skokie, Illinois, a heavily Jewish suburb with approximately seven thousand Holocaust survivors living in it. Frank Collins, the leader of the neo-Nazi group, first applied to march in Skokie on May 1, 1977, but faced legal obstacles at every turn. In a perverse twist to the story, it was discovered that Collins was the son of a German-born Jewish father whose name had originally been Kohn and who had spent time in the Dachau concentration camp.[84] The survivors of Skokie and their many supporters were determined that every legal means to stop the Nazis should be used and a large counter-demonstration should meet them if they did come.

After a year of appeals by Collins's representative, the American Civil Liberties Union (whose executive director, Aryeh Neier, had also been born in Germany to refugee parents), the march was finally set for Sunday afternoon, June 25, 1978—coincidentally three days before the Supreme Court handed down its decision in *Bakke*. Eugene DuBow of AJC's Midwest regional office, who was granted leave by AJC to be the coordinator of the event, was by then prepared for a crowd of fifty thousand people (DuBow joined the national staff of AJC in 1980 and in 1998 became the first director of the organization's new office in Berlin.) Twenty speakers were scheduled for the program including the governor of Illinois and the vice president of the United States. Special shuttles would operate to bring in demonstrators from O'Hare Airport. Meir Kahane and the Jewish Defense League were promising to show up. Two hundred off-duty Jewish policemen were enlisted to serve as marshals. DuBow arranged to have a field hospital ready to deal with five thousand casualties, staffed with volunteer doctors and nurses. The governor called on the National Guard to be prepared to intervene if necessary.[85]

In the preceding months AJC, all the organizations and federations of NJCRAC, and American Jews in general found themselves highly divided over the Skokie issue. Many believed that the Jewish community should do what it had usually done in such cases: ignore the antisemites and deny them the media attention they craved. "A lot of American Jews were saying, 'Listen, why don't we do what we've always done, leave these twenty creeps alone, let them have their march and be done with it,'" reported Gene DuBow, asserting that it was Sol Goldstein of Skokie and his fellow survivors who had pushed the Jewish community into departing from its previous practice.[86]

Indeed, AJC's first tactic was to use the tried-and-true "silent" or "quarantine" treatment that had been developed by Rabbi S. Andhil Fineberg in the 1940s and 1950s. "I want to assure you that the AJC does not ignore this phenomenon, yet it does try to keep it in proper perspective," Bert Gold wrote to S. R. Hirsch of Milwaukee, who had noted increasing instances of neo-Nazism around him and wanted to know what the AJC was going to do about it. Gold reassured him that they had done several studies of the American Nazi Party and had found that they did not number more than two hundred people in the entire country and that they were torn by dissension. "At the present time we are actively attempting to arrange a conference with key newspaper publishers and other media representatives on the way in which the Nazis have in our judgment exploited the media to their advantage. I would also point out that the totality of our program is targeted toward establishing a climate in America where the loathsome ideology of the Nazis cannot and will not flourish, and to that end I am convinced that we, and other Jewish agencies, have been successful," he wrote.[87]

There were many questions about the propriety of the ACLU deliberately choosing to defend the Nazis, and thousands of American Jews resigned from the organization in protest. From a constitutional perspective, the field was divided between those who thought the Nazis marching was protected by the First Amendment and those who felt it was not. A few changed their minds, such as AJC's Maynard I. Wishner of Chicago, who at first advocated that the Nazis be allowed to march but felt differently after talking to the survivors' group. "We listened to the survivors," he wrote, "and instead of engaging in a fruitless battle over tactics, we came to understand what they were feeling. . . . Why should we think in terms of stopping the victims who were expressing what every normal human being should feel? What is wrong with thinking about stopping the Nazis? . . . In First Amendment terms, the Nazi plan to deliberately affront and taunt Jews in Skokie is not a protected right."[88]

This matter elicited strong dispute within the ranks of AJC. The tension reached its peak at the May 1978 annual meeting, which took place five weeks before the expected march and before the courts had handed down all of their decisions regarding the constitutionality of the case. Milton Ellerin, AJC's expert on antisemitism, announced that he had just come from a conference on neo-Nazism in Vienna and the consensus was that the Nazis were of no immediate threat and had "no political significance at this particular time." That did not stop the assembly from treating the matter at hand with deadly seriousness. In introducing the resolution to be debated that day by the NEC, Sholom Comay—who was then head of the Domestic Affairs Commission—noted that the board of governors had already held "a long, passionate, ambiguous debate on this matter" and that views had been expressed on both sides. Some believed that the resolution before them, which stated that the Nazis marching was *not* constitutionally protected free speech and that AJC could take or cooperate in legal steps to prevent it, was "violative of the First Amendment and of grievous harm to the traditional and proper position of the AJC." On the other side, he reported, there had been many who felt that the resolution did not go far enough, that it was an "inadequate response to those who threaten the very freedom of our society itself." As a result the resolution had been reworded, but its basic point remained the same. "You're being asked to consider a position that some may, indeed some do, believe is a break with the past," announced Maynard Wishner, as the debate began.[89]

Some of the arguments against the resolution focused on the fallacy of equating Frank Collins and his twenty-five fellow demonstrators with a potential Nazi invasion of the United States. Rabbi S. Andhil Fineberg himself, who had served as a community relations consultant to AJC from 1939 to the time he retired in 1964, was present that day and opened the debate by warning that AJC should not yield to "hysteria" and that it should act on the basis of the American experience and "not on the basis of what had happened in Germany or elsewhere." In Germany, Fineberg pointed out, fourteen years after Hitler joined the Nazi Party it garnered 230 seats in the Reichstag and millions of votes. By contrast, in the twenty years since George Lincoln Rockwell had founded the American Nazi movement, it had not even been able to nominate anyone for Congress. People were forgetting that the situation in Germany was "totally different" from what was happening in Skokie, he said. "The fear that has been instilled in the whole Jewish community by the Nazis going into Skokie is almost incredible," Fineberg asserted. "I sympathize profoundly with those refugees. I certainly do, but to think that by that little trick the Nazis were able to get the American Jewish community to fall into what Richard Rothschild in 1939 called falling into the Nazis trap . . . seems almost incredible. . . . We had it thirty-five years ago with Joe McCarthy and Father Coughlin. We had it with all the other antisemites, none of whom became another Hitler. The idea that anybody who waves a stick at the Jews is going to be another Hitler is absurd." Abe Karlikow, who was head of AJC's Paris office at the time, reassured the audience that in Europe, where neo-Nazism was a real threat, Europeans had allowed the democratic process and free speech to "bring them into the sunlight"; as a result their institutions had gotten nowhere.

The balance of the other arguments centered on the idea, not dissimilar to that of the church-state separationists, that in the long run devotion to the principle of free speech was the only thing that would keep Jews safe in America, whatever the short-term pain might be. Fears were expressed that any restrictions would eventually boomerang against the Jews. "I believe at the outset that this resolution should be defeated, defeated resoundingly and not just amended," declared Miles Jaffe of Detroit, who asserted that free speech should be "the central organizing principle of our world." "No one ever said that free speech was without risk," he said. "No one ever said that free speech would never hurt anyone. All that has ever been said about free speech is that it is essential for the existence of groups like us. If there is one difference that will abide between this country and Germany, it is that there are those among us who in any circumstances, at any costs of pain or suffering to ourselves or to our friends, will insist that this principle at least is inviolable. . . . I strongly urge, more strongly than anything I've ever said in this body, that in this area, at least, we maintain the wall, not the constitutional wall, but the wall of the only principle that will keep us and others like us safe." A speaker from Indianapolis repeated the words she had heard from a Holocaust survivor who lived in that city, worked for Jewish organizations, and had lived in two countries with communist regimes before coming to America. "I experienced what Nazism does," he had said. "I lost my family . . . but then I also had the experience of living under the forms of government in which no free speech was allowed, and if I lived in Skokie. . . . I cannot tell you how I would feel to see a brown shirt walking down the street. I don't know whether I would have the self-discipline to know what to do; what I know I must do . . . turn my back. I would not permit those vermin to . . . undermine those things that keep me free."

Several speakers referred to the current Jewish agenda of speaking out in favor of Israel despite the "annoyance" it might be causing the president and the non-Jewish population. Any restriction of free speech on groups like the Nazis, they warned, might eventually be used against Jews when they wanted to speak out about Israel. "Throughout the entire history of Jewish community relations," declared a professor, "we have operated on the assumption that Jewish security is inevitably dependent upon the constitutional liberties that keep us free, that we have no stronger armor than the constitutional liberties of the Bill of Rights. It therefore seems to me that at a time when the strength of those constitutional liberties may well be required to protect the Jewish community in the fulfillment of its own agenda, we must be especially vigilant against any erosion of those rights. . . . We can't say that when we are at odds with a situation that we consider particularly painful then the Constitution has to be set aside. In all of our plans, in all of our tactics for responding to those who would inflict pain on us or even destroy us, despite all provocation, we must remain steadfast in our support of the Bill of Rights."

A man from Chicago who was a lawyer declared that any modification of free speech would "backfire" against AJC in the future. "We have brilliant lawyers who have written this wonderful document," he said, "but I want you to know that the people who don't like the Jews have brilliant lawyers too, who know how to write and twist words beautifully. Anything that attempts to attack or cut back on the fundamental law of the U.S. we should not be in favor of." Similarly Charles Tobias of Cincinnati said, "It's perfectly clear to us that the Constitution does not protect Nazism, but it's going to be perfectly clear to someone else out there that something we hold very dear is not protected by the Constitution either. I don't want to see AJC carving out exceptions because it happens to be our particular sensibilities which are hurt." Lester Hyman of Washington, D.C. mentioned a friend who had told him, "I don't understand you bleeding heart liberals. I know what's wrong, and the march of Nazis in Skokie is wrong and therefore we must prevent it." "But the problem is what he knows is wrong," concluded Hyman, "might not be what someone else knows is wrong."

A number of speakers warned that the resolution was a case of "prior restraint"; that is, cutting off speech because it *might* escalate to the doing of physical harm. That argument had been used by Southern white leaders against the speech of civil rights demonstrators and might again be used against Jewish interests, they pointed out. If any abridgment of freedom of speech were allowed, what would happen in the future when people wanted to demonstrate on unpopular causes? Suppose demonstrations against future wars were forbidden on the grounds that they constituted a threat to the lives of American soldiers? What if people who thought abortion was murder were

in power and they restrained the free speech of people who wanted to demonstrate in support of abortion?

Denying the Nazis the publicity they were seeking, in an affirmation of
Fineberg's warning, was the motivation for several others who warned against
passing the resolution. "What will the result be if the AJC adopts this or something like it?" wondered Howard Smith of Los Angeles. "It's certainly not
going to stop the American Nazi Party from doing anything. If anything, I
think it will simply give the American Nazi Party a bigger forum, more access to
the courts, more access to the press, and a way to get publicity for themselves."
A speaker from Washington, D.C., claimed, "If I were a member of this neo-
Nazi movement . . . I think what I would want more than anything else is for
this AJC to support this resolution and go to court and try to prevent that
march because that guarantees them the publicity that they want and need."

On the other hand, some of those who supported the resolution—that is,
wanted to take legal action to prevent the Nazis from marching—argued that
since some forms of speech, such as obscenity, were not protected, speech as
heinous as that of the Nazis could not possibly be supported either. These
speakers were disproportionately from the Chicago AJC chapter, the ones
physically closest to the survivors of Skokie, and they tended to draw connections between the Nazis there and the Nazis of World War II. "I might be accused of being overly simplistic," said Solomon Fisher of Philadelphia, "but it
seems to me that when Nazis walk in brown shirts carrying the symbol of the
swastika, what they are saying to me at least, and I think to most people, is let's
kill all of the Jews. Now, if one believes that, I find it very hard to find in any
case of the Supreme Court to say that it is constitutionally protected free
speech. . . . I think it is fundamental to our democratic country that people
should not be allowed to go around and say let's kill other people because of
their ethnic identity." Elaine Wishner of Chicago pointed out that the AJC
had been trying and hoping for years to get the United States to ratify a U.N.
convention against genocide, "and yet we're sitting here debating whether a
group that has been espousing genocide for the last 40 years has a legal right
in this country. . . . I find no struggle with the First Amendment, in being able
to stand up in court and say that there is something special, something different [about] the worst crime ever committed in the history of human beings. . . . That's not protected by the First Amendment, and I want to be able
to argue that in the name of the American Jewish Committee."

Speaker Robert Jacobs, also from Chicago, actually said he wished he could
go back to the McCarthy era and the days of the 1950s "when we could enjoy the
luxury of clarity"; nonetheless, he still supported the resolution. "These people
are not exercising First Amendment rights of free speech," he declared. "They
are suggesting action which in the past has led to the deaths of six million or
more Jews and countless millions of others. They are the philosophical heirs to
those people and I think we are entitled in our own self-interest, self-defense,

and in the interest of maintaining a strong and secure America to raise this issue in the courts. We need not stand by once again and listen to the Nazis start down the road that they went down thirty-forty years ago."

One young speaker alluded to the comments by opponents to the resolution that any compromise on free speech now might hurt American Jewish interests later, particularly when it came to their outspoken support of Israel. "There is another fear operating here, which Maynard Wishner spoke of," he noted, "and it's one that perhaps I don't feel because of my age, but many others do. It's the fear that we as Americans are going to be perceived as a nuisance, and it's the fear that we have to, therefore, be more American than the Americans. And I would just like to say that, if we were as much purists about our Jewishness as we are about being American, then there would be no question in our minds as to how to handle the Nazis."

Near the end of the debate, Jules Whitman stated he did not feel the resolution went far enough. He also denied that Nazis marching was protected free speech, equating it instead with the already forbidden obscenity. "The Constitution is a moral document," he said. "It says we can all have life, liberty and the pursuit of happiness. . . . It does not believe that everything is equal in terms of speech. It does not believe that any course of conduct is tolerable." He continued, his words increasing in intensity:

Is there no speech or symbol so gross, so vicious, so uncommunicative of any idea or worthy of propagation that it does not deserve the First Amendment protection? Is there no limit to the infliction of harm and trauma by barbaric speech and symbols? Would the Nazis march down Seventh Avenue and would the Jews be protected by the First Amendment? Can the Klan burn the fiery cross at 125th Street? What is there left? What is there that we are protecting in the marketplace of ideas? Is it the right to have freedom destroyed? Is it the right to preach and achieve genocide and mass murder, concentration camps, and the brutalities of the Nazis? . . . The First Amendment has never been absolute. Obscenity is prevented and indeed in one opinion, just as Chief Justice Burger stated, he had no doubt . . . that fornication in Times Square at high noon could be stopped by court action, even though those fornicating were speaking about a political message, and I would go further in suggesting that they could stop, even though they believed that the act of fornication in public was the way to happiness and success, and I suggest to you that the Nazis marching in Skokie is more obscene than fornication in Times Square.[90]

Whitman also began equating the Nazis in Skokie with the Nazis of Hitler's time, in the process perhaps displaying the trauma that the Holocaust had inflicted on American Jews and their determination to act so that it should never happen again: "Remember, we are all victims. If the Nazis had succeeded, we would be in the gas chambers with the Jews of Europe. . . . Let us fight back with the law. . . . Let the Supreme Court tell us if we are wrong. . . . Let us have faith that the Supreme Court treasures the First Amendment as much as we do, and will protect it in a manner consistent with democracy and freedom. Be proud. Win or lose, but let us not surrender to the Nazis."

The debate was finally over and the vote was called. Near the end of the process, someone from Chicago was heard to joke, "I'm from Cook County—we always vote twice." The vote was close: 118 in favor of the resolution to try to stop the Nazis and 108 opposed.

Thereafter, the delegates adjourned for lunch, but the matter was not yet settled. By custom AJC did not decide matters by such close votes, and several members, according to Maynard Wishner's recollection of that day, were so devoted to the ideal of free speech that they threatened to resign from AJC if the resolution went through. What could they do to avoid a crisis? Over lunch, Wishner, Bert Gold, and several others came up with an idea: declare that it was up to each individual chapter to study and implement the resolution if they wished. How to react to the situation in Skokie would be up to them. That way, the Chicago chapter could go ahead and do what it wanted to help the cause of the survivors in Skokie, and the rest of AJC would not be "tainted."[91] A resolution to that effect was proposed after lunch and it was unanimously carried by voice vote. In the aftermath of the annual meeting, chapters took this obligation to heart. The Washington, D.C., chapter, for example, went so far as to obtain a cassette of the plenary session at which the issue was debated, playing portions of the pro and con speakers as a background for their own debate.[92]

In the meantime, all legal efforts of the village of Skokie to deny the Nazis a permit for their march, including an appeal to the U.S. Supreme Court, came to naught. There was no constitutional way to stop them. Frank Collins and his followers, however, had heard about the preparations for a counter-demonstration of up to fifty thousand people and were beginning to have second thoughts. Collins was ready to make a deal. At a press conference on the evening of Thursday, June 22, 1978, he announced that he was calling off his plans to demonstrate in Skokie that following Sunday and was accepting the offer of the city of Chicago—which Collins himself had solicited—to let him demonstrate in the non-Jewish area of Marquette Park instead. He claimed that all the efforts of the past months had been "pure agitation on our part to restore our free speech" and that, having won the yearlong battle in state and federal courts, he had proved successful. The threat of a march in Skokie, he warned, had not disappeared. "The minute I suspect that our free speech is being blocked again," he said, "I will reschedule the Skokie demonstration. I am only canceling this one march."[93] The Jewish community of Skokie announced immediately afterward that it was calling off its counterdemonstration. "I consider this decision a victory for the American way of life and a victory for the freedoms guaranteed by our forefathers," stated Skokie's mayor, Albert J. Smith. "We look forward to a return to peace and tranquility."[94]

In the weeks preceding the proposed march another factor had intervened to focus the country's attention even more closely on Skokie. On the nights of April 16 through 19, the NBC network broadcast a four-part, nine-and-a-half-hour docudrama, *Holocaust*, based on a book by Gerald Green. While it was a smaller ratings success than *Roots*, which NBC had broadcast the year before, its ratings were high: NBC estimated after the 1979 rebroadcast that as many as 220 million viewers in the United States and Europe had seen the series.[95] AJC and much of the organized Jewish community threw itself into the promotion and the production of educational materials in connection with the program, showing an almost "desperate need"—in Eugene DuBow's evaluation—to sensitize the general public on the subject.[96] The broadcast was a milestone in the development of what has been called "Holocaust consciousness" in the United States. Constitutional, political, and denominational issues might still divide Jews in the United States, but remembering and commemorating the Holocaust—especially after the trauma of Skokie—became for many years something almost all could agree on as a fundamental part of their Jewish identity.

⋇ 9 ⋇

Jewish Identity, the Women's Movement, Intermarriage, and Soviet Jewry

[1970–1980]

As striking as any activity AJC ever sponsored was the continuing evolution of the agency's own Jewish identity and the development of its
programming in areas of direct concern to Jewish culture, education,
and family life. In this respect it reflected and boosted similar changes in the
American Jewish community as a whole. Although the Six-Day War in 1967
has usually been pinpointed as the turning point in this process, in AJC the
evolution began several years earlier. In 1963, Erich Rosenthal's research showing rising intermarriage with each generation, coupled with other research
showing that Jewish women's fertility was well below replacement level, led to
publicity about "the vanishing American Jew." It was then that AJC executive
director John Slawson, to whom integration and adjustment of Jews to their
American surroundings had been primary goals, looked at the numbers and
feared that his campaigns had been so successful that American Jews might be
headed for extinction.[1] In the same year, AJC's "Image Study" was completed,
and Slawson became determined to refute the apparent stereotype that his organization was a haven for "assimilationists." Intensifying Jewish programming and stressing AJC's identity as a Jewish organization were important
ways to disprove the stereotype.

The full blossoming of AJC's Israel office began some time before 1967, as
did the hiring of more Jewishly observant personnel. The 1967 war, however,
greatly accelerated the process and the change was evident both in AJC's external programming and internally in the day-to-day operations of its headquarters. In the 1970s there was more active recruiting of traditional Jews and the
adoption for the first time of full Sabbath and holiday observance and the
serving of kosher food at AJC-sponsored events. AJC's overwhelmingly male
leadership also began to recognize fully the female half of the Jewish people,

and Jewish women participated equally in these new religious observances. AJC women organized themselves to bring more of their number to leadership positions and the AJC began to wield its power in the cause of women's issues, beginning with the ERA (Equal Rights Amendment). Direct concern for Jewish community and continuity was discernible in AJC's attention to inner-city Jews (a group that included many Orthodox) and its studies on the Jewish family and intermarriage. The organization's commitment to Jewish survival was evident above all when it assumed leadership in the burgeoning movement to save Soviet Jewry.

Kosher Food

AJC had actually served kosher food at its functions during the days of Cyrus Adler and Jacob Schiff, but very early on in the history of the organization this ceased to be the case. Classical Reform Judaism, in which most of the early members had been schooled, did not require adherence to Jewish dietary laws. A suggestion in the 1950s during an AJC board meeting that the organization make its events entirely kosher was immediately and vociferously voted down. In addition, there had been little or no Sabbath observance as part of the programming; at weekend meetings, working sessions were held as readily on Saturday morning as on Friday or Sunday. When observant Jews began to join the staff in 1964, or an occasional Orthodox guest was present at an AJC meeting or function, requests for kosher food brought forth plates of fruit and cheese or similar limited fare. Student activists protesting at a 1970 AJC meeting, among their demands, voiced criticism that it was necessary to "go out of the way" to get kosher food there.[2]

This policy continued to arouse surprise and dismay in some quarters through the 1970s until Rabbi Marc H. Wilson, an active AJC member who was also chairman of the Atlanta Rabbinical Association, took AJC to task in 1979. All the members of that association had recently endorsed a letter calling on all Jewish functions in the area to be kosher and not in violation of the Sabbath or the Jewish holidays. "At a time when Jewish solidarity is so crucial," the letter noted, "it is vitally important that we make every effort to make our communal activities accessible to all members of our community from the most observant to the least." Soon thereafter Rabbi Wilson, in preparing to attend the annual meeting (which was to be held in Atlanta that year), made an inquiry about the food and found out that it would not be kosher. "The lack of kashrut at the forthcoming AJC dinner is particularly unconscionable," he wrote, "particularly after the letter on kashrut policy I recently sent to all local Jewish organizations. . . . It is exceedingly difficult to support an organization like the AJC that claims such lofty aspirations for world Jewry while being so myopic and negligent in its own Jewish policies.

You have effectively disenfranchised many of the very people who could have served you best."[3]

At the same time William Katz, who had been director of membership and community services at AJC since 1965, was following a mandate to increase AJC's dues-paying membership to fifty thousand persons by 1981; he wanted specifically to target Conservative and Orthodox Jews. Some progress had already been made. A survey of AJC national and chapter leadership found that 80 percent were Reform and 25 percent were attorneys. The same survey showed that newer members—those who had joined only since 1977—were 38 percent Conservative, 9 percent Orthodox, and only 7 percent attorneys. Moreover, Jewish concerns, as opposed to energy policy or human rights, ranked much higher on their list of priorities.[4] (By 2005 the proportion of Reform Jews was back to 80 percent.) A letter went out to chapter leadership in 1979 directing the recruitment of more Orthodox Jews. "Were we to campaign for their membership specifically we would have to change some chapter practices, specifically chapter dinners," responded chapter head Bernice Newman. "I think we would also have some difficulties with our intermarriage recommendations . . . and our support for Medicaid and abortion would also cause problems. Lastly, nobody on our chapter board is a member of any of the Orthodox synagogues in the area."[5]

The letter was turned over for comment to Yehuda Rosenman, director of the Jewish Communal Affairs Department (JCAD), himself an adherent of Jewish traditions, who had been scrupulously careful not to impose his ways on the organization as a whole. He stated his opinion that the presence of modern Orthodox Jews would not be a problem for AJC's political agenda and would in fact "make our discussions about controversial issues more exciting by introducing different points of view." The food, however, was an obstacle. "It is very simple," he wrote to Will Katz. "We cannot eat the cake and have it. If you want to recruit Orthodox members, we have to, as a minimum, serve kosher food at meal functions. By the way, independent of the question of recruiting Orthodox Jews as AJC members, I believe the time has come for us to make a policy decision on the questions which were raised again in Atlanta, namely the serving of kosher food at AJC public functions, and AJC activities on the Sabbath and Jewish holidays. I recommend that a group of us get together to consider these issues. I would appreciate your taking the initiative in convening such a meeting."[6]

Another voice in a growing chorus came in the form of a letter from long-time member Solomon Fisher of Philadelphia, who also observed the dietary laws, to AJC President Richard Maass. The letter pointed out that three of AJC's sister organizations—the ADL, the American Jewish Congress, and the NJCRAC—served only kosher meals. "Over recent years I have noticed an important trend in the AJC which includes more and more emphasis on issues of Jewish identity," Fisher noted. "I believe this emphasis to be proper and correct, as I believe that the survival of our people depends on this issue of greater Jewish identification." He also noted with approval the recent attempt by the membership program to reach out to more Conservative and Orthodox Jews. Consistent with that, he continued, "I would recommend that very serious consideration be given to converting our kitchen in New York to a kosher kitchen and observing the rules of kashrut in all official AJC functions. As you know, there are a number of us for whom eating kosher is a religious conviction. There are none of us for whom it is a mitzvah to eat treif. I believe that as a Jewish organization desiring to stress Jewish identity and to reach out to all Jews, we should express our Jewishness via our sensitivity to fundamental Jewish sancta. We have done this in a number of ways and I think it is important that we add kashrut as an additional factor."[7]

Within a week of receiving this letter the Jewish Communal Affairs Commission was working on a proposal regarding AJC observance of Jewish holidays and kashrut. One member wondered if the additional cost of kosher dinners might hurt AJC's fund-raising efforts and another wondered if holiday observance could be made optional for the chapters. Eventually they came to an agreement. The proposal was passed in September 1979; the commission was informed that the AJC kitchen at national headquarters was already being converted to conform to the dietary laws and would be serving dairy meals.[8]

Inner-City Jews

AJC in these years also began to take more interest in the welfare of Jews living in the inner city, many of them lower income and/or Orthodox, particularly those living in the outer New York boroughs of the Bronx, Brooklyn, and Queens. AJC members in the New York area were drawn overwhelmingly from the city's suburbs or from the Upper East or Upper West Sides of Manhattan (of the New York chapter in 2006, 75 percent of the members lived in Manhattan and only 15 percent lived in the Bronx, Brooklyn, and Queens combined; the other 5 percent lived in the suburbs). The inroads of the militant Jewish Defense League among the poor and lower-middle-class Jewish population in these areas and the resistance of such Jews to housing integration programs were two motives convincing AJC that they should pay attention to these groups.[9] Also, with the Domestic Affairs Commission's concern for government social welfare programs, AJC could hardly ignore the needs of Jews at its own doorstep.

In 1971 AJC broke ground with the study "The Invisible Jewish Poor," authored by Ann G. Wolfe of the intergroup relations and social action division, followed by a national conference on poverty in the Jewish community that brought together academics, communal workers, and others who could shed light on the subject.[10] The study estimated that up to 800,000 Jews lived near

the poverty line.[11] While critics charged, correctly, that this figure was in-
flated and that the actual number of Jewish poor was under 200,000, the
study and the conference left no doubt that the problem existed. It was clear
also that the majority—approximately two-thirds—of the poor were in their
sixties or older, mostly members of the immigrant generation who were left
behind when their neighbors made it into the middle class. Women in this
group far outnumbered men. "Many of the aged poor live in wretchedly neglected houses in neighborhoods no longer Jewish," reported Bert Gold.
"Many are so afraid of crime in the street—and for good reason—that they
rarely venture out even to shop or to see the doctor and do not visit with
friends at all. Most Jewish institutions—synagogues, community centers,
Y's—moved away when the majority of Jewish residents did, and their services have not been replaced." Of the other third, some were poor literally
because they were Jewish. The Hasidim and other strictly Orthodox Jews
held religious beliefs that obligated them to raise large families, consume
only kosher food, and send their children to private rather than public
school. The Hasidim were additionally held down in their earning capacity,
Gold noted, "by the deep rooted tradition of limiting secular education, of
excluding certain aspects of the modern world from their society and their
children's schooling."[12]

AJC's recommendations were that government poverty program guidelines should be rewritten or reinterpreted to cover Jews in their neighborhoods, that more private aid should be forthcoming, and that Jewish social
agencies should rethink their agendas to take such Jews into account, particularly the elderly. As for the Hasidim, AJC (against the strong objections of at
least one board of governors member) lent its support to the efforts of the
Metropolitan Coordinating Council on Jewish Poverty, an organization for
poor Jews founded in the 1970s, to have Yiddish-speaking Jews classified as a
minority under state and federal guidelines. Some of the Hasidic groups,
such as the Satmar and the Belz, were entirely Yiddish-speaking. Such a classification would make them eligible for government assistance in such areas
as housing, medical care, job training, and small business support. The impetus for this inclusion came from the broadening in 1973 of the definition of a
minority from being only "American Indian, Negro, or Oriental" to including "or Spanish language and members of any additional limited English
speaking groups designated as a minority within the state by the state
agency." Because the new definitions specifically mentioned the Spanish language, the Metropolitan Council declared, "It should follow logically that all
similar future legislation should similarly cite the Yiddish language within the
framework of the definition." The letter called on all Jewish communal
groups to petition government authorities for this inclusion. Bert Gold, who
was himself a fluent Yiddish speaker, said that he saw no reason why the AJC
should not support this inclusion.[13]

The July 1977 Blackout

The New York chapter of the AJC also took a stand in direct support of inner-city Jews when it reacted to the city- and suburbwide blackout on the night of July 13–14, 1977. Unlike the Great Blackout of 1965, which had happened on a cool November evening (in that case the lights went out across eight states and two Canadian provinces), the July 1977 blackout, which took place during a heat wave, was marked by looting, plundering, and arson on a level not seen since the urban riots during the summers of the 1960s.[14] It was a time when the national economy was marked by high unemployment and high inflation (the Dow Jones Industrial Average sank to 800 that year) and New York had barely recovered from a fiscal crisis that left the city on the brink of bankruptcy. That summer more than sixteen hundred businesses across the city were completely destroyed and whole neighborhoods were left without essential services. "Many of the owners may not want to reopen," warned Haskell Lazere, this time taking the lives of middle-class Jewish merchants very much into consideration, "and certainly, if there is a delay in getting restarted, many others will drop out of the neighborhoods. This will accelerate neighborhood deterioration and create new slum areas if tangible assistance as well as public display of volunteer and governmental concern for small businesses are not delivered quickly." He proposed that to minimize business flight and maximize reopening of businesses, there be created as soon as possible neighborhood emergency assistance centers to process insurance claims and loan applications, provide tide-over funds until these came through, and expedite repairs.[15]

The plan was presented to Mayor Abraham Beame and immediately approved. Lazere volunteered to lead the operation and was given a room and a phone at the Office of Economic Development. Within one week eleven storefront assistance offices were set up in the hardest-hit neighborhoods, including one in Crown Heights. Telephones were installed, materials developed for client intake, volunteers recruited, and the operation begun. In all, there were 170 volunteers from some dozens of corporations, law, and accounting firms. Some volunteers responded to a letter sent out by the New York Federation of Jewish Philanthropies. Flyers were written in English and Spanish and passed out to advertise that technical services were available. Most clients needed money urgently to resume business or to tide them over until insurance money came in. Some required help filling out insurance claims. Others were helped by securing for them moratoriums on bank loans and mortgages. Some got help restoring financial records that had been destroyed and without which they could not apply for a Small Businesses Administration loan. Some needed help from the city tearing down or boarding up partially destroyed and dangerous buildings. One volunteer personally visited seventy merchants to see if any aid was required. In the two weeks these assistance centers were in operation, they provided counseling to some four hundred clients, visited another four hundred, and responded to about six hundred telephone inquiries.[16]

The success of the program caused AJC to be showered with accolades in the weeks after the July blackout. One letter came from Mayor Beame. "I want to express my heartfelt gratitude and the gratitude of all New Yorkers for the invaluable assistance which the AJC has given and is giving in the effort to help our city recover from the recent blackout," he wrote. "Although AJC can be credited with a long list of accomplishments, your organization's speedy, constructive and selfless response to this crisis is certainly deserving of a special thanks from all of the citizens of New York City."[17]

The "New Ethnicity" and Jewish Programming

As Solomon Fisher had observed, AJC had indeed been paying more and more attention to the goal of enhancing Jewish identity. The times were ripe for it. American society was becoming altogether more accepting of ethnic distinctiveness, as the old "melting pot" theory gave way to what observers and scholars termed the "New Ethnicity" or the "New Pluralism."[18] Publication of such books as Michael Novak's *The Rise of the Unmeltable Ethnics: Politics and Culture in the Seventies* (New York: Macmillan, 1972) set the tone. There were protests and programs to eliminate ethnic prejudices from school textbooks and the media, and ethnic studies programs became popular on American campuses. In 1972 the Ethnic Heritage Studies Programs Act, sponsored by Senator Richard S. Schweiker (Republican, from Pennsylvania) and Representative Roman Pucinski (Democrat, from Illinois) made federal money available to make information about ethnic minorities part of school curricula and teacher training. Organized ethnic groups were given a choice of what part of their history and culture they wished to put forth in the curriculum and the Jewish community for the most part "chose the Holocaust as that aspect of the Jewish heritage which they wanted highlighted."[19] Ethnic parades became popular and distinctive dress or hair in public no longer drew condemnation. Jews as a group became less self-conscious about asserting themselves in public. In two notable examples, the annual Salute to Israel Parade in New York, which had begun in 1964 (another pre-1967 innovation) on an unobtrusive street, moved in the 1970s to Fifth Avenue and came to attract tens of thousands of people. Also, young modern Orthodox Jewish men and college students who in previous years would have worn hats or gone bareheaded now did not hesitate to wear crocheted *kippot* on their heads in public.[20]

AJC reached out with programs for Jewish college students, some of whom were becoming communal activists and were embracing the causes of

Zionism and Jewish education with the same fervor with which they had formerly protested the Vietnam War. AJC delivered literature to Hillel Foundation houses and arranged for speakers to give lectures on college campuses.
The Boston chapter started the *Jewish Student Press Digest*, a collection of articles taken from some sixty Jewish student newspapers that were springing
up.[21] AJC contributed to the Jewish Student Press Service and sent them material to be used as articles. AJC sponsored, helped to promote, and arranged
speaking tours for the authors of *The New Jews*, a book of essays by college
students on contemporary Judaism edited by James A. Sleeper and Alan L.
Mintz.[22] Steven Windmueller, an associate of the Jewish Communal Affairs
Department, prepared taped radio programs on subjects of Jewish interest
and sent them to sixty-five college stations.[23]

When local federations and Jewish communal institutions took up the goal
of reaching out to students, AJC turned its attention to Jewish faculty. As men
and women of science, many viewed themselves as elevated far beyond Jewish
parochial concerns. David Singer noted this attitude when he went on a field
trip in 1974 to the Midwest with the goal of getting local academics to work
more closely with the Jewish community. "What I found out is that the more
things change, the more they remain the same," he reported. "Specifically,
many Jewish academics would like to move closer to the organized Jewish
community, but will first have to overcome their snobbishness about rubbing
shoulders with 'pants manufacturers.' Academic elitism is, unfortunately, alive
and well and will not be easily overcome."[24]

Begun in 1969, the Academicians Seminar Program in Israel recruited Jewish professors via local chapters and sent them on a two-week, intensive, all-
expenses-paid trip to Israel. Funding came partly from national AJC and
partly from foundations and local communities. By 1979 the program had
touched the lives of more than two hundred faculty. Questionnaires and
follow-ups revealed what an impact the trip had upon them. One "young, universalist, liberal professor of modern history" as Rosenman described him,
"changed from one who regarded Israel as "too narrow and tribal" to its de-
fender at public meetings. . . . He has also obtained permission to teach a
course on Israel."[25] Others spoke of it as the most important experience of
their lives. Graduates of the program joined AJC chapters, made themselves
available as resource persons, and planned courses on the Middle East and Israel through their disciplines.

Capitalizing on the popularity of *Roots*, the 1977 miniseries based upon
Alex Haley's novel that traced his African ancestors through seven generations, the Jewish Communal Affairs Department prepared a booklet called
"Jewish Roots: Guidelines to Tracing Your American Jewish Past." "What do
you know about the world of your fathers and mothers?" the book began.
Readers were instructed in all the details of doing genealogy, from what materials they needed and what documents to collect, to how to do an oral history.

Readers were supposed to ask older family members: How did your family come to this country? Where did they settle? What did they do for a living? The booklet provided the template for a family tree, a selected bibliography, and a sample questionnaire to use for interviews.[26]

Aside from serving kosher food, other matters of Jewish religious observance became legitimate topics of concern for AJC. Observers of the Jewish community noted that a polarization was taking place. On the one hand, intermarriage, assimilation, and sheer indifference appeared to be increasing; on the other hand, there was an unmistakable renaissance in Jewish religion and culture among the core community. Yehuda Rosenman spoke of it as "new pockets of Jewish energy" where young people were actually returning to Judaism, albeit in their own style. If the ingredients that made for these "pockets" could be found and distilled, other sections of the community might benefit.[27] One such "pocket" was the *havurah* movement, which had begun among college students and recent graduates in Boston. *Havurot* were small, informal groups where members gathered for prayer and study; they were becoming increasingly popular in the 1970s. Intensive interviews and observations were made of these groups in Boston, New York, and Philadelphia.[28] There was also a noticeable trend at the time toward young Jews becoming what was called *baalei teshuva;* that is, "newly penitent" souls who formerly had been nonobservant but now were becoming Orthodox Jews. JCAD proposed seeking out ten such individuals to write autobiographical essays about what influenced them to become religious and what problems they faced in doing so.[29]

Also of note in these studies were special synagogues that reached out to young people, the best known being Lincoln Square Synagogue in New York, led by Rabbi Shlomo Riskin. The congregation had begun with fifteen people; by 1979, it had hundreds of members. In an address to AJC entitled "How to Reach the Uncommitted," Rabbi Riskin declared that the major threat to Jewish survival was no longer external but internal; that is, the threat of assimilation. "The threat is very serious," he said, "and this generation may represent the last chance to win the battle. . . . We are currently fighting a nuclear war with pea shooters." The distinctions among Orthodox, Conservative, and Reform branches of Judaism had very little meaning in these circumstances, he declared, when the real issue was Jewish survival. He distinguished only between religious Jews and "not yet" religious Jews—religion being defined by Rabbi Riskin as a "sense of being bound to the Jewish people and the land of Israel." Once exposed to the "riches" of Jewish life, there was reason to be optimistic about young people. "Young Jews have a thirst for learning and the word of God," he asserted. "They want to find meaning and purpose in their lives above and beyond the search for pleasure or power. American society cannot satisfy the search for meaning. Judaism can."[30]

Fostering Sabbath observance among AJC members and the extended Jewish community was the goal of JCAD's Sabbath Haggadah project. Modeled after the Passover Haggadah, it was designed to provide Jewish families with reading and discussion materials with which to celebrate the Sabbath together. Michael Strassfeld, coeditor of the highly successful *Jewish Catalog*, was commissioned to do the text. The project also included several cassette tapes: candle lighting on one, blessings over wine and bread on another, grace after meals on a third, and songs on a fourth. "I've discovered that a very pleasurable side use of the tapes is as background music while I work," wrote Rosenman to Rabbi Albert S. Axelrad of Brandeis University, whose students were assisting in the creation of the tapes. "My long-term goal (very long term) is to make your tapes the Muzak of the AJC. No telling what their subliminal effects on this place might be."[31]

The 1968 annual meeting had been the first where local synagogues were listed in the program and where a traditional Torah study session was held before commencing with Saturday's business meetings. In May 1974 for the first time a full Sabbath service was made part of the program. It took place in the Sutton Ballroom of the New York Hilton Hotel with staff taken from Central Synagogue, Temple Emanu-El, and the Park Avenue Synagogue. Rabbi A. James Rudin, then assistant director of AJC's Interreligious Affairs Department (he later succeeded Marc Tanenbaum) directed the service, which was composed in gender-neutral language by Dr. Gladys Rosen of the JCAD. A female cantor, Mimi Frishman, led the singing in Hebrew and English and members Mildred Grossman and Hannah Baum read the Torah and Haftorah portions. The service concluded with the traditional Mourner's Kaddish, with reference to "our sisters and brothers who fell in the Yom Kippur War and our younger sisters and brothers who were taken from us at Kiryat Shemonah and Ma'alot."[32]

The Impact of the Women's Movement

The innovation of having a full Shabbat service at an American Jewish Committee meeting in 1974 came simultaneously with other religious innovations. The presence of a female cantor, liturgy rewritten in gender-neutral language, the reference to "sisters and brothers" and the full participation of female congregants in the service were all signs of a phenomenon that was transforming American Jewish life: the impact of the second wave of feminism (the first had won women the right to vote).[33] The first female rabbi in American history had been formally ordained by the Reform movement only two years earlier.

AJC in its first quarter century was entirely a male affair, yet from the mid-1930s women had never been absent from its ranks. It was a matter of pride in the organization that it never had a separate women's division or auxiliary. It was an important influence that the membership was overwhelmingly from the Reform denomination, a movement that had made religious equality of women one of its central tenets. Women had been part of the old Survey Committee that in the 1930s and early 1940s had worked round-the-clock to fight the inroads of Nazism in the United States. One in particular, Madeline (Mrs. Sidney C.) Borg (1879–1956) was central to the entire effort. "During that period, we drew from her store of wisdom in our councils, and we fired our spirits from the flame of her dynamic energy, in effectuating and making vibrant the policies which her wisdom had aided us in forming," recalled Joseph Proskauer in a special tribute to her at the annual meeting the year she died. "We shall not look upon her like again. And of her, as of few people I have ever known in my long life, it could be said that none knew her but to love her, none named her but to praise." There was a moment of silence in her memory.[34]

On the staff, Selma Hirsh, a graduate of Oberlin College, was a professional writer who had been working as the executive director for the Writers' Board of the Office of War Information in Washington, D.C., when John Slawson recruited her to work for him as his righthand woman at the AJC in 1945. He valued her so highly at the time that he matched the starting salary that had been offered to her by a prestigious advertising company—seven thousand dollars a year, which was more than most of the men in the agency were making. Selma Hirsh's career in the AJC spanned five decades and she, along with Slawson, set the tone and level for much of the agency's activity. One of her first jobs, because she knew so many writers and editors, was to contact them and encourage them to "salt in" Jewish names and positive images of Jews in their work. She was also for many years the "ghost speechwriter" of the organization.[35] She was offered (and turned down) the post of executive director when John Slawson stepped down and eventually rose in her own right to the title of assistant and then associate director of the entire organization.

From the 1940s one of John Slawson's slogans, repeated by officers after him, was "Husband and wife are equal at the AJC." When a married man joined AJC his wife became a full member as well; this practice was criticized as sexist in the 1970s but was nonetheless progressive for its time. It was true that through the 1960s never more than a handful of women sat as full voting delegates on the executive boards; in committee assignments they were most conspicuous as hostesses at the annual meeting or on the hospitality committee. Whenever AJC's governing boards met, however, wives were always invited to attend as guests. They participated during debates and made their opinions known to their husbands. Lists of guest attendees showed that a majority of the men's wives were there. As Emily Post etiquette dictated at the time they were inevitably listed under the title "Mrs." and their husband's first name. The only time a woman was listed as "Mrs." with her own first name was if she was divorced.

Without doubt the most powerful woman in AJC's early years who sat in her own right and not as a wife was Judge Caroline Klein Simon (her husband's first name happened to be Leopold), who became active in AJC immediately after World War II. She graduated from New York University Law School in 1926 and was admitted to the New York State bar. She overcame all obstacles to become a female judge, politician, state official, and a drafter and advocate of laws against discrimination in housing and jobs. She was the first woman to run for citywide office in New York when she sought the presidency of the City Council in 1957. A series of state posts culminated in Governor Nelson Rockefeller naming her as secretary of state of New York in 1959. She remained active in legal work into her nineties. Within the AJC she was an active member of the national board and chair of the New York City chapter. "There are four things a woman needs to know," Simon said, reflecting on her career in a widely quoted 1959 speech. "She needs to know how to look like a girl, act like a lady, think like a man, and work like a dog."[36]

When Caroline Simon retired from AJC, however, the number of women even approaching leadership positions in the AJC could be counted on the fingers of half a hand. Then the first impact of the women's movement was felt. The issue of modern feminism officially hit the AJC on September 22, 1970, when a vote on endorsing the Equal Rights Amendment (ERA) came up on the board of governors' agenda. The ERA was a proposed constitutional amendment that would guarantee equal rights under the law to Americans regardless of sex. It required passage by both houses of Congress and ratification by thirty-eight states to take effect. Getting it passed was the ultimate goal of the movement. Presumably, endorsement by AJC would have some impact. However, the vote that day by the almost all-male AJC board was to take no action. "We were very disappointed that the Board of Governors decided not to take any action on it and that upset a whole group of women who were always spouses but never board members," recalled Charlotte Holstein, one of the earliest leaders in the fight to enhance the role of women within AJC.[37]

The wives made their opinions known, the women leaders of the Detroit and Philadelphia chapters began to organize, and Mildred Grossman of Detroit made an ardent presentation at one of the next national board meetings of the impact of the women's movement in the country and how much it should mean to their work. By then the ERA had been passed by both houses of Congress and ratified by thirteen states. These all had their effect. At the annual meeting in May 1972 the issue came up again and this time a statement endorsing the ERA passed unanimously. From then on it would be a matter of human rights. "AJC's position and supporting programs over the past many decades have consistently supported the underlying concept of equality of rights under the law regardless of race, creed, or national origin," the statement read. "We wish to underscore this principle by our support of this right without regard to sex. . . . We believe that the issue of equality of rights for women will be a major social issue in America during the 70s. AJC cannot stand aside when an issue affecting fifty-three percent of the population is in question. . . . We believe that the consequences of the passage of such an amendment are overwhelmingly positive. It will release the untapped talents and energies of a portion of American society to the betterment of all."[38]

The following year AJC's National Committee on the Role of Women was established, under the chairmanship first of Emily Sunstein, who later rose to be a national vice president, and Charlotte Holstein, who had been chosen to be a full voting member of the national board. The goals of the committee were to improve the role and status of women, both lay and staff, in AJC so that they could participate "at every level and in all activities equally with men"; to help ensure equality for women in the Jewish community; to work for the passage of the ERA; to pursue domestic policies that would further the goal of equality for women; and to support women who were entering the workforce.[39] The very first decision that this group of women made, recalled Holstein, was to start using their own first names.

From the beginning, the National Committee on the Role of Women was designed not to serve as a separate "women's desk" but to foster change in every commission and committee in the AJC across the country. A questionnaire went out to all the women in all the chapters of AJC, asking them to detail their education and accomplishments. Answers were used to recruit women to get into the "pipeline" of national AJC leadership based not on who their husbands were but on their own potential contributions. A federal pamphlet entitled "Hints for Male Supervisors of Working Women" went out to every desk in the national headquarters ("Treat women as adult persons. Nothing is more demeaning, or as easily detected, as being treated like a child or as a person who is mentally retarded. . . . Treat women as you would male employees. Treat secretaries as full partners in the office operation and structure.") Selma Hirsh announced that AJC was "actively engaged" in a talent search for executive-level women to fill vacancies due to retirements within the next three to five years.

Within interreligious affairs, AJC women formed a special dialogue group with Protestant and Catholic women, and eighteen of them together in 1976 took a tour of the Middle East that covered Israel, Egypt, Jordan, and Syria. One of these was Mimi Alperin who went on to serve, among many AJC leadership roles, as chairman of the Interreligious Affairs Commission; eventually, she became the first woman to chair the National Executive Council. Rabbi A. James Rudin called for the abolition of Temple Sisterhoods because he thought they channeled women into exclusively "feminine" or supportive roles and deprived them of real power; he also called for the active recruitment of Jewish women to be rabbis, cantors, and executive directors in Jewish communal organizations.[40] Dr. Gladys Rosen, a program specialist with the JCAD, began with an important paper of the impact of the women's movement on the Jewish family and conducted other studies and programming that helped lead to the establishment by AJC in 1979 of the William Petschek National Jewish Family Center, which sponsored research and programs to support working parents and their children. She also authored "The Portrayal of Women and Girls in Jewish Textbooks and Curricula," a result of a 1978 AJC conference bringing together Reform, Conservative, and Orthodox leaders to discuss the question of sex stereotyping in such materials.[41] The *American Jewish Year Book* in 1977 published a landmark article by Anne Lapidus Lerner, "Who Hast Not Made Me a Man: The Movement for Equal Rights for Women in American Jewry," which described Jewish feminism as a combination of radicalism and traditionalism.[42] And within the realm of domestic policy, AJC filed amicus briefs in cases regarding women's rights and took positions on issues of women's equality in education, employment, public policy, social security, and the right for an American woman to have credit in her own name.

It was a great disappointment for the women's movement when the deadline for the ratification of the ERA passed on June 30, 1982, with the amendment just three states short of passing. "Even in the unfortunate event that the amendment is defeated," AJC president Maynard I. Wishner had announced two weeks earlier, "the struggle for equal rights will go on. It took women 72 years—from 1848 to 1920—to get the vote. We are confident that it will not take that long for American women and men, working together as they are now, to secure equality for women. Whatever the short-term set-backs, this goal will be fully realized."[43]

Study on Intermarriage

Study on Jewish women and the Jewish family led to study on one of the most personal, delicate, and controversial issues in Jewish life from 1970 on: the study of intermarriage, or marriage between a Jew and a non-Jewish partner. Such studies had to include the related issues of whether or not the partner converted and how children of such marriages were to be raised. It was unlikely, given the circumstances of AJC's formation and early history, that it would ever become one of the Jewish community's major centers for the study of intermarriage; this was a group, after all, that for decades had been labeled with the epithets "goyish" and "assimilationist." In the 1970s, however, AJC evolved as just such a center, through its interpretation and publication of data, its numerous own surveys, and the convening of rabbis, scholars, and Jewish communal leaders to discuss an issue that cut to the heart of personal identity and Jewish survival in the United States.

Until 1960 marriage between Jews and non-Jews was so rare as to be almost unthinkable. Available surveys showed that up to 1940 the proportion of Jews who intermarried was between 2 and 3 percent, a number that rose to only 7 percent from World War II to 1960.[44] According to the strictest interpretation of Jewish law, a marriage ceremony between a Jew and a non-Jew was illegal and invalid. All three major denominations in the United States—the Orthodox, the Conservative, and the Reform—forbade their rabbis from officiating at such marriages. To do so was compared to a doctor performing an abortion, an operation that except under very specific criteria, was against the law in all fifty states of the Union.[45] Those who cared less for Jewish law were nevertheless deterred by the strongest social taboos against marriage between Jews and Gentiles. Traditional parents were known to disown children who married out of the faith, and Gentiles were not particularly eager to marry Jews anyway. Erich Rosenthal's research had dealt with Indiana and Iowa, which were not considered typical Jewish communities.

Then the intermarriage rate began to rise precipitously, with evidence that in only a fraction of the cases did the non-Jewish partner convert to Judaism and/or agree to raise the children as Jewish. This was coupled with a perilously low fertility rate; in other words, American Jewish parents were not having enough children to replace themselves when they died, much less having enough children that the community would grow. Among those marrying between 1961 and 1965, some 17 percent were intermarriages; for those marrying between 1966 and 1972, the rate rose to more than 30 percent.[46] One Israeli demographer pointed out that even with these figures endogamy, or inmarriage among Jews, was still high: Jews were such a tiny minority everywhere in the Diaspora that if they married at random there would hardly be any endogamous unions at all.[47] Still, given the previous state of affairs, the numbers were alarming for those who believed that families were being lost and the Jewish population was decreasing through intermarriage.

Moreover, conditions seemed to favor a continual rise in its incidence. The vast majority (estimates were 85 percent) of Jewish youth were attending colleges and universities, where deep and intimate relationships between people of different religious and ethnic backgrounds were most likely to occur. Social barriers had fallen. Jews and non-Jews worked as colleagues instead of as merchants and customers.[48] Americanization and upward mobility had made Jewish men desirable mates in Gentile eyes. At the same time, observers speculated, Jewish men felt discouraged from marrying Jewish women because they would be entering their adulthood in a group with far higher income and vocational expectations than the American average. They would face much less pressure if they married into a non-Jewish family.[49]

Individual rabbis were not prepared to deal with intermarriage and the accompanying question of conversion on such a large scale. Hillel Foundation rabbis could not comply with the requests of frantic parents who called up begging the rabbi to break up a relationship or an impending marriage. Other parents threatened that the upcoming wedding would take place in a church if the rabbi didn't agree to officiate. One Reform rabbi, David Max Eichhorn, in

1970 circulated a list of eighty-nine of his fellow rabbis who agreed to state publicly that they were willing to officiate at intermarriage without requiring that the non-Jewish partner convert. (At the time this was approximately one-tenth of the Reform rabbinate). Reform rabbis theoretically had more freedom to act because, unlike the Orthodox and the Conservative, they were not bound by *halacha* and under civil law it was not illegal for people of different faiths to get married. "It is clear that the unrestricted availability of this list will help to combat the defection of many of our people who are being lost to Judaism because of the spiritual insensibility of so many of our colleagues," Rabbi Eichhorn wrote in the letter that accompanied the list.[50] He was lauded by some peers for his honesty and inclusiveness and criticized by others for countenancing and encouraging intermarriage.

In the 1972–73 television season the CBS network aired a popular situation comedy called *Bridget Loves Bernie,* about a marriage between Jewish Bernie Steinberg, an aspiring writer working as a cabdriver, and Bridget Fitzgerald, a teacher from a wealthy Catholic family. The pair lived in an apartment above the delicatessen owned by Bernie's parents. The diverging social, cultural, and ethnic backgrounds between the two families and their attempts to reconcile for the sake of the young couple provided most of the plotlines. American Catholic organizations protested; among the Jewish community there was uproar because on national TV intermarriage was being presented in a positive, lighthearted way. The protest occurred, AJC's legal director Samuel Rabinove noted, even though American Jews had traditionally espoused freedom of speech and expression and opposed censorship of any kind. The Synagogue Council of America, an organization comprising rabbis from all three major denominations, led a successful campaign to have the show canceled. In the same year the New York Board of Rabbis, which also had members from all three major denominations, adopted a resolution strongly condemning any of their number who performed mixed marriages or who referred couples to rabbis who did.[51]

It was against this background that Yehuda Rosenman in Jewish communal affairs convened in February 1975 the first of several "consultations" of rabbis to discuss intermarriage and conversion. Once again, AJC headquarters provided neutral ground where rabbis of differing denominations could talk to one another. Participants included Rabbis Norman Lamm, Emmanuel Rackman, Max Routtenberg, Ludwig Nadelman, Judah Nadich, Sol Roth, Harold Saperstein, and Steven (a.k.a. Shlomo) Riskin.[52] Because intermarriage on a large scale was happening whether they liked it or not, the group wanted to figure out what the reaction of the Jewish community should be and to work out a uniform conversion procedure that would be acceptable to all parties. It was hoped that such a procedure would maximize the number of conversions and ensure that more children of such marriages would be raised in Jewish homes. These rabbinic meetings were not dissimilar to those that would later take place in Israel in an attempt to reconcile Jewish law and Israel's Law of Return, which granted citizenship automatically not only to Jewish persons but to their extended family members. According to the most stringent Jewish law going back at least eighteen hundred years, conversion had to be supervised by a *bet din*, or Jewish religious court; it required ritual immersion in water or "tevilah" for both sexes and for males, ritual circumcision ("milah"). Persons born to a Jewish mother were deemed to be completely Jewish regardless of the background of the father, whereas a person born to a Jewish father but a non-Jewish mother was held to be a non-Jew.

The rabbis struggled to find some common ground. At one meeting, they debated the creation of a sort of "super Bet Din"; that is, a rabbinical court that would be recognized by all groups. Rabbi Rackman, who was himself Orthodox, disagreed, saying that it would be "almost futile in the present climate, especially in the Orthodox group" to create such a body. Perhaps, he suggested, they could all cooperate on how to deal with mixed marriages where the mother was Jewish. "Their children are not fifty percent but one hundred percent Jewish," he pointed out. "There may be fifty thousand or a hundred thousand children of such marriages who are Jewish, and we ought to do everything in our power to claim them. We don't know how these children are being raised. . . . Second, I think all the social workers in New York City ought to be sensitized to these problems. When a mixed couple comes to Jewish Family Service the social worker should know enough to steer them to a sympathetic, understanding rabbi who may reclaim the family for the Jewish community." Rabbi Harold Saperstein, representing the Reform point of view, countered that in his movement children of Jewish fathers were accepted as being fully Jewish if they underwent a bar mitzvah or confirmation, which counted as a public profession of commitment. Reform rabbis might be convinced to require ritual immersion and circumcision, he said, but in any event their feeling was that "we are saving these children for Judaism rather than closing the door to them."

Rabbi Riskin, also Orthodox, suggested that they bypass the rabbinates altogether and establish a Bet Din of three committed and observant laymen, one from each of the major denominations. These laymen could be taught all the necessary rules and rituals and the basics of keeping the Sabbath and the dietary laws, which they would require the convert to accept. Again Rabbi Rackman disagreed. "Let us not get into an area now which is as difficult as splitting the Red Sea," he countered. "Let us strike out in the one area in which we can function—reclaiming those Jews whom we have the power to bring back into the fold." Rabbi Riskin replied that Rabbi Rackman's plan was not comprehensive because the majority of Orthodox synagogues would not accept into membership anyone who was in a mixed marriage, period, even if the wife was Jewish. "I repeat, therefore, that nothing is going to happen within the three establishment organizations," Riskin declared. "We shall have to proceed on an individual basis. Let me make it clear that personally I am very stringent with conversions and I do not relax any of the halachic standards. At the same time, I believe we need desperately in America a kind of Bet Din that will require only minimum halachic standards, and I am willing to go on line saying that."[53]

This mood of desperation was so great that AJC became cosponsor of an event that united virtually every synagogue and rabbinical association and major Jewish secular organization in the United States: what was billed as the first National Conference on Mixed Marriage, convened in New Jersey in December 1976. Attendees participated in workshops and open discussions on how to combat intermarriage and how to "enhance Jewish survival." Yehuda Rosenman contributed by giving a talk on the demography, statistics, and sociology of the issue. Rabbi Robert Gordis in the aftermath of the conference suggested that they all create a national institute to deal with intermarriage.[54]

Still, both at the AJC consultations and the national conference in the 1970s there was no agreement on a course of action suitable to everyone, and the debate was still going on with undiminished force into the twenty-first century. There were sharp differences of opinion on what the Jewish community and its social agencies should be doing to meet the needs of converts and the non-Jewish partners in intermarriages. Some argued that intermarriage was actually a good thing for the Jewish population, that it resulted in a net gain of adherents, and that it was a proper use of communal resources to do as much outreach as possible to such couples. Others believed that this attitude would be lowering the religious, cultural, and social barriers to intermarriage that still existed, leading to more intermarriage and ultimately the loss of far more Jews than could ever be gained back through such outreach efforts. It would also be expending valuable and limited communal resources on the periphery of the community that might be more wisely and effectively spent on shoring up Jewish families closer to the communal center.

Yehuda Rosenman believed at the time that the arguments might be decided by getting hard quantitative data on just how many Jews were being won or lost. "We cannot determine what, if anything, should be done," he declared, "until we have the objective data which tells us what the problems are and what the plus-minus effects for Jewish continuity is, stemming from increased interfaith marriages." Pointing out that "objective research and fact-finding" had always been the hallmark of AJC, he announced that AJC was embarking on the first nationwide study of marriages between Jews and non-Jews and that they would begin in the six communities of New York, Westchester, Nassau-Suffolk, Philadelphia, Cleveland, and San Francisco. Egon Mayer, at the time a young assistant professor of sociology at Brooklyn College, was designated to direct the research.[55] He had been one of several social scientists invited to AJC for a "brainstorming" session, and both Rosenman and Milton Himmelfarb had been impressed by his work. Information was to be gathered via questionnaires and interviews conducted by volunteers who would be trained in the techniques of the study. The results of the study would be used to issue the first AJC policy statement on the subject of intermarriage.

Getting the sample and convincing people to fill out the questionnaire turned out to be the most challenging part of AJC's first foray into intermarriage research. The very process revealed almost as much about the phenomenon of intermarriage in the 1970s as the data gleaned from it. (Reviewers later criticized the "ad hoc" nature of the sample gathering and the lack of an endogamous married control group for purposes of comparison).[56] Volunteers and local project directors in each of the six communities were first asked to get names from among personal friends, relatives, and acquaintances. Then Egon Mayer suggested they make contact with both Jewish and non-Jewish clergymen, "especially rabbis who officiate at mixed marriages, Unitarian ministers, etc." and ask them to provide the project with a list of names, addresses, and telephone numbers from their records or from among their circle of acquaintances. A letter to one minister, he assured them, had yielded several hundred names. Another technique was to ask local Jewish organizations to sponsor lectures with titles such as "Intermarriage and Intergroup Relations" or "A Look at Mixed Married Life" that would be advertised in newspapers and that would presumably attract intermarried couples. A project representative giving the lecture would use the opportunity to describe the study and encourage members of the audience to participate. Cooperative subjects were in turn asked to submit more names, addresses, and telephone numbers.[57]

A master list of thousands of names was thus compiled and each one got a telephone call or a letter from Egon Mayer, reading "Dear Friend, . . . We are embarking on a nation-wide study on the effects of Jewish intermarriage so as to shed some light, rather than heat, on this issue. For the purpose of this study I need to develop a large and representative sample of families with mixed religious backgrounds. . . . You can help me accomplish this difficult but important goal by filling out the enclosed questionnaire. You may be assured that our survey will be conducted with complete scientific objectivity and the right of privacy of all concerned will be faithfully honored by us." The first survey was hampered by a low rate of response to such letters. People who had the least bit of ambivalence or discomfort about their marriages would never choose to answer it. The final sample consisted of only 446 couples from all six communities. Some recipients of the letter were enraged, as in the case of one man from Philadelphia. He made an incoherent phone call to his local AJC office and then delivered the following missive:

According to the letter from Dr. Egon Mayer on AJC stationery, my wife and I were selected from a "comprehensive" list of one thousand people in and around Philadelphia. I want to know first, how this was acquired and second, who has access to this list. As I told you before you banged down the receiver, rabbis have told me it is a sin to bring up conversion to a converted Jew. I don't care if AJC members believe in sin. But if the rabbis are correct, it is horrendous on this one point alone that the AJC should do this. But more to the point as far as I'm concerned as an individual is that this has been a tremendous invasion of the privacy of my wife, my children and myself with potential repercussions beyond what you know and which I only hope I can prevent.[58]

Other problems arose when Egon Mayer submitted a draft of his final report, which he entitled "Mixed Blessings under the Canopy," to Yehuda Rosenman and the rabbinical advisory board of the Jewish Communal Affairs Commission in March 1978. Numerically, in only one-third of the intermarriages surveyed did the couple state their intention to raise the children as Jews. In the interpretation of his data, however, Mayer took an almost enthusiastic stance toward intermarriage, holding that the old attitude toward it was obsolete. He wrote that it was a result of a climate of general tolerance for Jews and that more intermarriage only increased that tolerance. (Presumably, there would be less antisemitism among Gentiles who had Jewish relatives). He claimed, as the title implied, that intermarriage still represented a significant opportunity for American Jews to increase their numbers, that there was no evidence at all that it hurt family relations in any way, and that rabbinic officiation resulted in the couple's increased identification with Judaism. His final recommendations were that intermarried couples and their children should be brought into the Jewish community and that "there appears to be an urgent need for programs and materials which would help Jewish families integrate non-Jewish members in such a way as to make the Jewish way of life an attractive alternative to the new couple."[59]

When the consulting rabbis met to discuss the draft the response of some was to express preference that the study not be released at all or that certain parts of it be struck from the record. They spoke of their concern about the "delicacy of the topic" and fears that the study might be misused, misinterpreted, or taken out of context. They pointed out that for most American Jews intermarriage was a sociological issue, but for them it was an issue of *halacha,* or Jewish law. "Any sociological report which seems to say that we can increase our numbers through intermarriage will be used as a tool," said one rabbi. The claim that rabbinic officiation led to positive Jewish outcomes was also controversial. Another rabbi spoke of the study's potential to weaken the resolve of those rabbis who were "holding the fort" by refusing to solemnize mixed marriages. If rabbis agreed to officiate without conversion, he pointed out, then this took away the motivation of the non-Jew to convert. In the end the rabbis agreed that intermarriage was a threat to Jewish identity and that "no statement issued by AJC should be construed as indicating resignation to, or approval of, intermarriage." Neither did they view it as an opportunity to increase Jewish numbers.[60]

Yehuda Rosenman refused to remove the claim about rabbinic officiation, but on everything else he and the Jewish Communal Affairs Commission, chaired by E. Robert Goodkind, agreed with the rabbis. Egon Mayer's interpretations, in the words of another JCAD staff member, "was not one which we felt that the American Jewish Committee should associate itself with."[61] The final compromise was to issue two versions of the report. One, written by JCAD program specialist Dr. Carl Sheingold using Egon Mayer's data, was published in a pamphlet with AJC's imprimatur, and AJC took responsibility for it. The title was "Intermarriage and the Jewish Future" (1979). Egon Mayer's original, more detailed report was available in mimeograph form for anyone who requested it. Mayer was also free to publish his report elsewhere, which he did.[62]

Controversy of a different sort occurred when the Jewish Communal Affairs Commission tried to have a policy statement on intermarriage passed by AJC's board of governors. Several of these laypeople were intermarried and there was fear of insulting or alienating some key leaders. The original statement, based on the AJC report, opened with these words: "Mixed marriage is a threat to Jewish continuity. Most children in mixed marriages are exposed to little of the Jewish cultural or religious tradition, receive no formal Jewish education, and have parents who lack the knowledge to impart such an education on their own. If this pattern continues, mixed marriage at its current rate or higher will almost certainly lead to an erosion of the size, strength, and vitality of the Jewish community."[63] E. Robert Goodkind presented the statement for debate. One board member objected to the characterization of intermarriage as a "threat," claiming that it was not mixed marriage that was a threat, but rather "what could flow from a mixed marriage." Several board members requested insertion of a statement supportive of rabbinic officiation at mixed marriages. This issue was politically explosive, Goodkind explained, and had been intentionally left out of the statement. One prominent board member, who had been active in AJC for decades and headed several important committees, had an unconverted Christian wife who regularly attended and participated in AJC events. This board member also objected to calling intermarriage a "threat," and joined others in requesting language that would call for a change in communal attitudes toward mixed marriage couples. Eventually the sentence was changed to "Mixed marriage currently poses serious problems for Jewish continuity." With this and several other amendments, the statement was finally passed. The board revisited the issue in 1991 and 1997. It affirmed its opposition to intermarriage as a "serious risk" while also calling for outreach to bring about conversion of the non-Jewish spouse and exclusively Jewish raising of the children.

The Movement to Free Soviet Jewry

The anxiety about high intermarriage and low fertility rates leading to the disappearance of the American Jewish community was always compounded in communal circles by awareness of the catastrophic population loss the Jews had suffered during World War II. There was also the knowledge that some 20 percent of the world Jewish population was trapped behind the Iron Curtain where it was condemned to cultural and spiritual death.[64]

It was anti-Jewish riots and butchery that had led to the formation of the American Jewish Committee in 1906, and exposing and mitigating the effects of antisemitism on the Jews of the Soviet Union had long been a top priority in AJC's foreign affairs division. Previously, Israeli and American Jewish actions had always been tempered by fear that any missteps might lead to a worsening of conditions and further repression by the mighty Soviet Union. But in the years following the Six-Day War, a powerful minority of Soviet Jews themselves yelled out that they were still there, that they still wanted to be Jews, and began demanding the right to immigrate to Israel. They themselves began the movement that led to their ultimate freedom, and Jews in free communities around the world rushed to their aid.

In March 1970 the Soviet Union launched yet another campaign of anti-Zionist and anti-Israel attacks, pressuring Jews to denounce the "Nazi-like" policies of the Israeli government, while at the same time issuing statements that Soviet Jews were a perfectly content ethnic group and had no desire to leave the U.S.S.R.[65] Instead of being cowed, a powerful minority of Soviet Jews began to release scores of protests and petitions, signed with their names and addresses, demanding the right to settle in Israel, the "historic homeland of the Jewish people." These appeals were directed to the Soviet government, the U.N., and to Jewish groups around the world, to the president of the United States, senators, and later leading figures in the 1972 U.S. campaign. One petition called for "Israel or death." A group of Jews in Leningrad tried to commandeer a plane to take them to Israel.[66]

During the High Holy Days and on Simchat Torah tens of thousands of Jews from Moscow, Kiev, Riga, and all over the country danced and sang Hebrew songs. Jews organized protests and situation-ins, demanding exit permits. At one point sixty Jews organized a sit-in at Communist Party headquarters and eleven Jews from Lithuania who had requested exit permits went on a hunger strike in Moscow.[67] On Rosh Hashanah and Yom Kippur thousands of Jews gathered at the ravine of Babi Yar near Kiev and other sites of mass murders of Jews during World War II to mourn their deaths and to protest Soviet attempts to suppress the fact that they had been killed because they were Jews. Letters and telephone calls went out to the free world. Andrei Sakharov, a Soviet physicist who was the leading non-Jewish advocate of human rights in that country, openly appealed to the authorities to let go both Jews and non-Jews who wanted to leave.

The Soviet authorities let several thousand leave but reacted to the rest with crackdowns. At minimum, applying for an exit permit meant dismissal from one's job and expulsion from school for one's children. There was also harassment by the KGB (the Soviet secret police), interrogations, arrests, incarceration in psychiatric institutions on the grounds of fictional "mental illness," punitive drafting into the armed forces for young men, kidnapping of children from Jewish families, cutting of telephone lines, and the levying of exorbitant head taxes for those wishing to leave. This included in August 1972 the levying of a "diploma tax," or a demand that highly educated Soviet Jews reimburse the government for all the money that had been spent to educate them, a sum that could reach tens of thousands of dollars and was virtually impossible to raise.[68] Soviet authorities also tried to break the back of the dissident movement by putting its most prominent members on trial and sentencing them to long prison terms. This tactic backfired on them because the movement to free Soviet Jewry became so well organized and the channels of communication so effective that if the Soviets so much as touched a dissident, the news was all over the world press the next day.

Indeed, American Jews responded to the situation with an outpouring of emotion and support similar to what had been seen during the Six-Day War. Protests and demonstrations and letter-writing on behalf of Soviet Jewry became the order of the day. The entire American Jewish organizational apparatus moved into high gear for the sake of Soviet Jewry, and hundreds of thousands of Jews found in the movement a new outlet for their own identification. In late spring 1971 previous Soviet Jewry groups were reorganized into the National Conference on Soviet Jewry, with AJC's Jerry Goodman as executive director and Richard Maass, then head of AJC's Foreign Affairs Commission and future president, elected as chair. Thus the AJC, an organization that had once eschewed mass demonstrations, became a leader in some of the biggest mass demonstrations in all of American history. At the same time the Greater New York Conference on Soviet Jewry was reorganized to channel the energies of the nation's largest Jewish community, and Malcolm Hoenlein became its first full-time executive director.

Other Soviet Jewry groups, some with differing views on the methods to reach their goal, organized in a dozen cities. The JDL coined the slogan "Never Again!" in reference to the Holocaust and declared war on Soviet diplomats and visiting Soviet performers. The mainstream Jewish organizations both disavowed them and were driven to become more militant through their actions.[69] The national agencies—including the American Jewish Congress, the Anti-Defamation League, and B'nai B'rith—all vastly increased their budgets and programming for Soviet Jews. Sunday, April 30, 1972, was named the first "National Day of Solidarity" and parades, marches, and rallies for Soviet Jews were held in more than one hundred American cities. The occasion in New York was marked by a parade down Fifth Avenue attended by almost one hundred thousand people. Visiting troupes of Russian performers or visiting Soviet diplomats were greeted by crowds of demonstrators and full-page ads demanding freedom for Soviet Jews. When President

Nixon traveled to Moscow for a summit meeting with Soviet Premier Leonid Brezhnev he was asked to bring up the subject of emigration of Soviet Jews in a petition with more than a million and a half signatures. The petition was supported by proclamations from congressmen, governors, mayors, and state legislatures across the country.

The cause also permeated Jewish religious life. In December 1971, more than twenty-five thousand people filled Madison Square Garden in a "Freedom Lights for Soviet Jewry" Chanukah celebration. Children celebrating their bar or bat mitzvah ceremonies were paired with "twins" of the same age in the Soviet Union, in acknowledgment that there was another Jew somewhere who could not expect to celebrate that joyous occasion. During Passover, passages on Soviet Jewry were incorporated into the liturgy, and the "Matzoh of Hope" dedicated to them appeared at the Seder table in thousands of homes.[70] Passover, with its theme of liberation from slavery into freedom, and its call that each Jewish person should regard himself as if he or she personally had escaped from Egypt, was especially rich in symbolism for the Soviet Jewry movement, and special *haggadot* written for "freedom Seders" became popular. One such Seder, written by Rabbi A. James Rudin for a special Seder for Soviet Jewry held by the AJC New York chapter, recast the traditional four questions in modern terms:

Why is it that we and other Jews who live in free societies can obtain matzoh while our Jewish brothers and sisters in the Soviet Union cannot?

Why are the lives of Soviet Jews made bitter by discrimination and harassment while we enjoy freedom? Why aren't they free to leave?

Why can't Jews be free to live as Jews in the Soviet Union, studying our religion, history, and culture? Why are Soviet Jews afraid to conduct a Seder while we celebrate the Seder without fear?

In the illustrations the wicked son was pictured as a stout, Soviet army officer lighting his cigar from a lit menorah. Pharaoh's army was represented as Nazis and there was further analogy to the Holocaust in the dedication of the third cup of wine: "On this night we remember with great pride the resistance of the Jews in Hitler's Europe. Starving, weakened by disease, weighted down by oppression etc. the revolt in the Warsaw ghetto began on the first night of Pesach April 19, 1943. We drink this third of four cups of wine to honor the glorious memory of the Jewish fighters in the ghettos, concentration camps and forests of Nazi Europe. They fought and died with honor and avenged the murder of our people. Their courage and hope in the face of unutterable brutality and despair inspires us."[71]

Such outpouring of emotion and demonstration activity was not limited to the United States. The movement to free Soviet Jewry was worldwide. In Brussels the first World Conference of Jewish Communities on Soviet Jewry met, drawing some eight hundred delegates from thirty-eight countries. The meeting ended with a declaration that communities all over the world would commit themselves "by unceasing effort, to ensure that the plight of Soviet Jewry is kept before the conscience of the world until the justice of their cause prevails. . . . We will not rest until the Jews of the Soviet Union are free to choose their own identity. LET MY PEOPLE GO!"[72] Soviet Jews heard about these activities through broadcasts on the Voice of America, Voice of Israel, Radio Liberty, visitors from the West, letters and phone calls, and underground samizdat publications, and were heartened in their efforts.

"There is no doubt that what is happening to Jews in Russia is something of a miracle," said Dr. Ariel Levran, a defector from the Soviet Union, who came to address the AJC and other Jewish organizations despite the danger that the Soviet authorities might retaliate against family members still left behind. Levran's own father was one of those who had signed a petition demanding to leave. "Jews who were considered by many to be silent," he said, "suddenly became able to speak and to speak loudly." He gave his opinion why he hoped in 1970 that someday, despite all the opposition they faced, there would be a mass emigration of Soviet Jews to Israel. He explained that since 1968 the doors had been opened slightly and a few thousand had been allowed to leave. Correspondence to and from Israel was censored but it was not being blocked entirely, and Soviet Jews were now able to receive Jewish and Hebrew books from Israel without always having them confiscated. Finally, the Soviets might eventually conclude that they could "solve" their Jewish problem by letting the troublemakers go; it might come to the point that it was not worth the effort to keep them locked in. "It is the sacred duty of Jewish communities throughout the world and of non-Jewish friends in the free world to exert maximum pressure on the Soviet government on this subject," he concluded, "and I hope that in the long run we will win."[73]

Levran's companion, a recent émigré from the Soviet Union, speaking through a translator also referred to the miracle and the knowledge of the Jews there that the United States had a tradition going back at least seventy years of helping the Jews of Russia. He, too, expressed optimism. "In spite of all the evident hopelessness of the situation," he declared, "the young generation of Jews found enough strength to begin to fight for its national future. . . . At the demonstrations . . . you can hear Jews saying loudly, like as if by a choir, 'we are Jews; we remain Jews.' Thousands of young Jews are now studying Hebrew in the Soviet Union. . . . More and more, the Jews of Russia consider themselves as part of the world Jewish community. But they need the help of free Jewish communities of the world. They do not want the Jewish people in the free world to forget about their existence. They hope that free Jews in the free world will help them and will save them from national death. . . . Soviet Jews hope that you will raise your voice in their defense. They will go on struggling, and if your help will be added to that struggle, we will see the day when the part of the Jewish people, the part which is willing to remain Jewish, will have the right to do so, and the Jews of the Soviet Union will join free Jews in the free world."[74]

Richard Maass rallied the AJC delegates at this meeting, telling them "We have to let the Jews of Soviet Russia know that they are not forgotten. If they are willing to put their lives on the line, the least that could be expected of us in the free world is to give them support." They then passed the following resolution (the wording, incidentally, indicating that in 1970 the women's movement had yet to penetrate the AJC):

The AJC, which has manifested its concern for the oppression of Jews under the Tsars as well as under the Soviet regime, declares its kinship with the Soviet Jews who assert their desire to establish Jewish identity in the Soviet Union. We appeal to all men regardless of the political systems in which they live, to our own government and to the international communities to use all public and private means to restore to Soviet Jews the right to live as free men. . . . To this end, the AJC pledges to strengthen its activities on behalf of Soviet Jews in this country and abroad. We will seek to expand the creation of coalitions with individuals and groups, Jewish and non-Jewish, to continue focusing world opinion on the plight of Soviet Jews. Once again, history has determined that the struggle of Soviet Jews is also our struggle.[75]

AJC members marched in demonstrations, sent postcards and letters, and made trips to the Soviet Union to distribute Jewish articles; individual chapters "adopted" Soviet Jewish scientists. The Paris and Washington offices helped to secure visas and travel support for those who were able to leave and, through extensive interviews and debriefings, gathered information on what was still going on in the U.S.S.R. All of AJC's contacts in Washington, in the State Department, and in nations around the world, were put into the service of Soviet Jews.

In all this there was a particular contribution that AJC could make, using its historic skills in coalition building, diplomacy, and above all interreligious relations. That was to turn the issue from a Jewish problem into a human rights issue and to gather support from the non-Jewish world. Soviet propaganda had it that the effort to free Soviet Jews was simply part of the world "Zionist, imperialist, pro-Israel conspiracy" and that these Jews were spies and espionage agents of a foreign government. The desire of Jews to go to Israel was seen by them as a desire to augment the military forces of Israel, to expand out into the occupied territories, to fill the desert with people, to serve as grounds for further Israeli expansionism, and to aid and assist in the general Jewish/Israeli offense against the Arabs. Soviet leaders believed truly that every newspaper in the United States was Zionist-owned and -operated and that most of the banks were owned by Jews. To them, Soviet Jewry activism was not a religious or a human rights matter, but, according to one AJC leader who was a U.S. representative at the U.N., "essentially a political matter in which the U.S. is adding and abetting Israelis in committing aggressions and expansionism against their Arab neighbors. . . . This makes it imperative, in my opinion, for the Jewish and other human rights organizations to get to these other Western governments and try to get them interested in the questions as a purely human rights question, irrespective of whatever posture they may have on the Middle East, and whether or not they are backing Israel in any particular point of view."[76] Professor Thomas E. Bird of Queens College, a specialist on Soviet Jewry (who was himself not Jewish), reaffirmed at the same meeting that it was essential to get the non-Jewish community involved and to stress the human rights dimension of the problem. "As long as the problem of Soviet Jewry remains one more complaint of the American Jewish community," he declared, "it continues to be easily pushed under the rug. It remains vulnerable to all the tragic clichés that the Jews are complaining against; the Jews are hysterical again; the Jews are exaggerating again. You know and I know that this is not the case . . . but the message has not been gotten out."[77]

In the struggle to obtain human rights for Soviet Jews and others after them, the AJC had a new arm in the Jacob Blaustein Institute for the Advancement of Human Rights, a division that had been established in memory of AJC's former president with a one million–dollar endowment from his family in 1971. Blaustein's widow, their children, and their spouses, all of whom remained active in the organization, agreed that a contribution to the development and acceptance of human rights was the best way to commemorate him.[78] It was only in those years that the subject of human rights began to be raised at all as a subject worth talking about in international diplomacy. Largely due to the diplomatic and negotiating efforts of AJC's Joseph M. Proskauer and Jacob Blaustein, the Universal Declaration of Human Rights had been made part of the United Nations Charter in 1945.[79] However, it had received little attention during most of the cold war. People who spoke of "human rights" in a world of realpolitik were dismissed as dreamers, dogooders, or cranks. In the 1970s, by contrast, hundreds of organizations were being founded to advocate human rights and stories on the subject were making the front pages of the newspapers.[80]

Soviet Jewry was one of the earliest causes to benefit from this new recognition as the Blaustein Institute set out to enshrine their rights into international law. Its first act was to cosponsor and fund an international conference at the University of Uppsala, Sweden, in 1972, which resulted in a declaration proclaiming "the Right to Leave and the Right to Return." The right to move from one place to the other had been mentioned in the Universal Declaration but it did not receive much legal attention. Much had been written until that point on the right to freedom of speech, freedom of the press, freedom of religion, freedom to vote, and so on, but little attention had been paid to the most basic right of all: the freedom to move from one place to another, which often was prerequisite for enjoying all the other rights.[81] "Everyone has the right to leave any country, including his own," stated the declaration. "No one shall subject a person or his family to reprisals, sanctions, penalties, or harassment. . . . No special fees or taxes shall be imposed for exercising the right to leave. No person shall be denied travel documents or permits as may be required. . . . Anyone being denied these rights has the right to seek for recourse in international tribunals."[82]

The right to emigrate was subsequently included in what came to be known as the Helsinki Accords, a set of agreements signed by the Soviet Union and thirty-four other nations in Helsinki, Finland, in August 1975. The Soviets had long sought international recognition of her post–World War II borders, especially control over the Baltic states of Estonia, Latvia, and Lithuania. The other nations of the world granted the Soviets this recognition at Helsinki in return for the Soviets signing an agreement that they were bound by a basic package of human rights.[83] In the aftermath of the accords, "Helsinki Watch" groups were established around the world to monitor human rights and to hold the Soviet Union to account for what her leaders had signed. The founders of the first Helsinki Watch group formed in Moscow in 1976 included Andrei Sakharov, his wife Yelena Bonner, Aleksandr Ginzburg, and a young Jewish computer scientist named Anatoly Shcharansky (later changed to Natan Sharansky). Sharansky had been refused an exit visa to Israel in 1973 and went on to become one of the most famous political prisoners of all time. His arrest and conviction on charges of treason and espionage in 1978 galvanized the movement when it was at low ebb, and his wife Avital became a familiar figure as she traveled the world seeking help to set her husband free.[84]

In addition to establishing the Blaustein Institute, AJC's ecumenical skills and ability to keep a low profile were put to good use in Chicago where it was behind the founding of the National Interreligious Task Force on Soviet Jewry, an active group that in the United States proved more convincingly than anything else that this was not just a "Jewish problem." According to Marc Tanenbaum, the group grew out of a "long relationship" between the National Catholic Conference for Interracial Justice and the interreligious affairs staff at the AJC Chicago office, headed by Eugene DuBow. Sister Margaret Ellen Traxler, who herself achieved some fame within the movement, was the executive director of the National Catholic Conference and convened a meeting of Christians and Jews with the goal of "sensitizing and informing" the Christian communities about the problem of Soviet Jewry.[85] Encouraged by the meeting, a group of AJC staff from the Chicago office and from foreign affairs and interreligious affairs in New York labored for months to bring about the first National Interreligious Consultation on Soviet Jewry in Chicago, March 19–20, 1972. R. Sargent Shriver agreed to serve as honorary national chairman and requests for sponsorship over his name resulted in a roster of more than forty prominent Americans. That meeting, Marc Tanenbaum reported to AJC's executive director, "was widely reported in the press, but the story of its organization, not widely known, is I think a good example of the AJC in action."[86]

More than six hundred participants, mostly Christian clergy—including Roman Catholics, Protestants, and Greek Orthodox—attended that first meeting in Chicago. It ended with all of them rising to their feet to affirm a "statement of conscience" that was released to the press and was featured in the observance of "Solidarity Day" that April 30. The meeting was so successful that the group decided to form a permanent organization, and Sister Margaret Ellen recommended another nun who was to achieve fame in the movement, Sister Ann Gillen, to serve as the executive director. Ann Gillen, a member of the Sisters of the Holy Child of Jesus, had served as a Catholic college dean and principal of a parochial high school in California.[87] Rabbi A. James Rudin years later recalled the hours he spent with her in congressional offices and the State Department seeking public support. Public officials invariably underestimated this nun when they saw her, but their attitude changed quickly once she began citing statistics, her firsthand experiences in the U.S.S.R. visiting Jewish "refuseniks," biblical citations, and the human rights provisions of international treaties.[88]

The AJC paid Sister Ann Gillen's modest salary out of a foundation grant while Sister Margaret Ellen's organization donated office space and secretarial services. Thus the National Interreligious Task Force on Soviet Jewry was born and it rallied millions of non-Jewish Americans on behalf of Soviet Jewry. "This persuades me that the cause of Soviet Jewry is not just a Jewish problem, as the Soviets keep telling us, but that it is a matter of Christian conscience and American conscience," said Senator Henry M. "Scoop" Jackson (Democrat, from Washington) after meeting with the group on Capitol Hill.[89]

The task force worked well in tandem with AJC's Christian Visitors to Israel program, run by the Interreligious Affairs Department and AJC's Israel office. AJC chapters would select key Christian leaders in each community and send them on a trip to Israel with a tailor-made itinerary. When they came back, they gave speeches to church and civic groups, spreading word of what they had seen. The trips to Israel were a powerful motivator in getting these leaders to work for the cause of Soviet Jewry, and also had strong impact on their attitudes toward antisemitism and Jews in general.[90]

The Interreligious Affairs Department and the National Interreligious Task Force on Soviet Jewry also planned and coordinated a strong Christian presence at "Brussels II," the second world conference of Jewish communities on Soviet Jewry held again in Brussels in February 1976. Led by Sister Ann Gillen, more than fifty Christian leaders from nine nations attended the conference, including Roman Catholics, Protestants, and Evangelicals, and they issued a "Call to Christian Conscience" that was published and distributed throughout the world. "We Christians, Catholics, Protestants, and Evangelicals, from many parts of the world—meet in Brussels 30 years after the end of the Nazi Holocaust in Europe," the "call" read. "We are painfully aware that a majority of our fellow Christians of that generation ignored the ominous signs of the escalating Nazi attacks upon the Jewish people—attacks that culminated in the nightmare of this century: the murder of six million Jews. But today this generation of Christians will not be silent as we raise our voices in support of the struggle to prevent the cultural and spiritual annihilation of the Jews of the Soviet Union."[91]

Former Israeli Prime Minister Golda Meir was the honorary president of the Brussels event, and AJC's David Geller, working there as part of the staff of the foreign affairs division, arranged a private reception between the Christian leaders and Golda Meir, who was given special medallions to award to them. When Sister Ann Gillen presented Mrs. Meir with a copy of the "Call to Christian Conscience," the former prime minister expressed her gratitude. "I am anxious for the sake of our Jewish children to see that our very often cruel and dangerous dialogue with the non-Jewish world shall not be the only dialogue," she said. "There has never been a period of history when non-Jews came to stand by our side. . . . I would ordinarily say thank you, but I cannot say thank you about a cause of this kind. I know you are preoccupied with this problem because you have made it yours. I praise God in these hours that we are not left alone. Just as we are found together today, so also somewhere someplace may we meet again when we have won."[92]

Eugene DuBow, who along with European office head Abe Karlikow was also representing AJC at the conference, wrote this description of the event:

I don't think there is any doubt that one of the outstanding features of the meeting was the introduction of the Christian delegation for which AJC can be justly proud. Sister Ann Gillen in my opinion has established herself and the organization as the Christian voice on the subject of Soviet Jewry. She has, in her own special way, become sort of an international Jewish "superstar." The kind of reception she got from both American and European Jewish participants at the meeting left little question as to the kind of esteem in which she is held. . . . The performance of David Geller at the conference left me in awe. To see him operate with the Israelis and Europeans is to see a spellbinding performance. The meeting of the interreligious delegation with Golda Meir was accomplished only through David's monumental hard work and convincing manner. I do not think that the people around Mrs. Meir understood the importance of the Christian group until it was laid out to them by David. The arranging of the meeting and the master stroke of having Mrs. Meir award medallions to the Christian participants was nothing less than brilliant. I have seen a few emotional scenes in my day; however none have been more moving than Golda's speech and her kissing of Ann Gillen when she awarded Ann the first medallion. There was not a dry eye in the entire room including my own. The Christians to a person considered the meeting a thrilling and moving experience and I think we have solidified and strengthened the dedication to the cause of Soviet Jewry.

In addition to public relations and social action on behalf of Soviet Jewry, the AJC and much of the American Jewish community were able to wield another weapon in the battle—this time a legislative one—in the form of the Jackson-Vanik amendment to a U.S. trade bill dealing with economic relations with the Soviet Union. Sponsored by Senator Henry "Scoop" Jackson (who was backed by Senators Abraham Ribicoff and Jacob K. Javits) and Representative Charles A. Vanik (Democrat, from Ohio), the amendment made free trade with the United States conditional upon the Soviets relaxing emigration restrictions and abolishing such obstacles as the diploma tax.

In the superpower playing field this was an era of détente, or a relaxation of the cold war between the United States, the Soviet Union, and the People's Republic of China.[93] All acknowledged that concentration on producing nuclear weapons of mass destruction was endangering the world and depleting their economies. From the U.S. point of view, détente was based on the idea that that there was no hope of defeating the Soviet Union. The superpower was there to stay and the best thing to do was to come to terms with it through peaceful coexistence. As part of détente President Nixon (and later Ford) and Secretary of State Henry Kissinger were eager to open normal trade relations with the U.S.S.R. The Soviets, with their relatively weak economy aggravated by crop failures, were in turn eager to have access to American trade and industrial know-how. Most Jews favored détente and an encouragement of trade between the two countries in the hope that such would allow for more influence on the U.S.S.R.'s internal policies. The Jackson-Vanik amendment, however, put hard pressure on the Soviets to pay for the privilege of normal trade in the coin of human rights.

Senator Jackson first introduced the idea of the amendment at an emergency meeting of the National Conference on Soviet Jewry in September 1972 in Washington, D.C. The 120 participants had gathered and were outraged, as were many in the international community, by the institution of the diploma tax and the harassment of Soviet Jews who had applied for exit visas.[94] Jackson had asked to speak at the meeting; after hearing his plan, the NCSJ decided to endorse it. There was a massive campaign on the amendment's behalf and it was passed in the House of Representatives in December 1973 with a three-quarters majority. The bill then went on to the Senate, where Jerry Goodman and representatives of the National Interreligious Task Force on Soviet Jewry were among those who testified on its behalf.

It was a hard campaign. Nixon and Kissinger were appalled at the Jackson-Vanik amendment to their trade bill and did everything they could to persuade members of Congress and Jewish leaders to turn away from it. Nixon threatened to veto it if it came to his desk and even called fifteen prominent Jewish leaders including the president of the AJC into the Oval Office in April to try to persuade them to reconsider their support of the amendment. Kissinger met with Richard Maass, who as head of the NCSJ and head of AJC's foreign affairs division led the campaign, three times for the same reason. In the view of the administration, placing this type of pressure on the Soviet Union would upset the delicate balance of détente, enrage the Soviets, harm American business interests, and be counterproductive: in anger, the Soviets would probably shut off the flow of immigrants anyway. "Quiet diplomacy," the administration said, had already gotten tens of thousands out and was much more likely to lead to a positive outcome than punitive legislation. Kissinger stressed repeatedly that nuclear confrontation was the greatest threat to mankind and that détente and elimination of that threat had to be the top priority, no matter how sympathetic or concerned the United States might be with a human rights issue.[95]

Nonetheless, the AJC steadfastly maintained its support of the amendment. It did so even during the Yom Kippur War, when Israel was dependent on aid from Nixon, and when Kissinger threatened that above all he needed the goodwill of the Soviets at this time in the interest of peace in the Middle East. What good would the right to emigrate do Soviet Jews, he asked, if there were no Israel for them to go to?[96] As the months passed and pressure from the administration and from American business interests built, some in the Jewish community began to waver. Even within the lay leadership of AJC there were strong doubts. In one instance, Senator Gaylord Nelson of Wisconsin, who opposed the amendment, tried to persuade AJC President Elmer Winter of Milwaukee to convince Richard Maass and the AJC to withdraw their support of the amendment. Senator Nelson agreed with the Soviet view that her emigration policies were an internal affair and that no other country had the right to interfere with them. He also tried to persuade Winter that it would hurt American business interests, and that it ran the risk of closing the doors to emigration altogether.

Richard Maass was not convinced, and his references to the Holocaust (matched in several speeches and statements related to the Jackson-Vanik conflict) indicated just how uppermost it was in the minds of those fighting the battle for Soviet Jewry. American Jews above all did not want to face again the impotence they had felt when the State of Israel was threatened with extinction in 1967 and did not want to risk losing millions of their relatives for a second time. "The right of emigration can no longer be viewed as an internal policy," Maass insisted in a memo countering Nelson's arguments, "any more than the practice of genocide can be viewed as such. Human rights have become the concern of all. By maintaining that we have no right to interfere with the internal policies of Russia, Nelson is, by extension, advocating a hands-off position which can only encourage the replication of such horrors. . . . Further, with respect to businessmen, I can only point out that from 1933 to 1938 American business leaders fought off all suggestions that they not do business with Hitler, with the argument that if we isolated Nazi Germany, we would certainly have no influence on her racial policies. They continued to do business and either made no attempt to change policies or were unsuccessful in doing so."[97]

Maass also believed that the idea that the Soviets might react by closing the doors altogether was only a rationalization on Senator Nelson's part for his opposition to the amendment. "Unless he has direct information from the Russians which has not been made available to us, there is a risk of course, just as there is a risk in every position," he wrote. "But this is no more certain than a continuation of emigration if the Jackson Amendment is dropped." Maass then made reference to the AJC's recent contact with the most important party in the conflict: the Soviet Jews themselves, who had themselves begun the movement to gain their freedom and had not been silent on this question. A year earlier, at great risk, 105 leading Jewish activists in Moscow had signed an open letter to the U.S. Congress supporting the idea of the amendment and asking that they pass it.[98] They were still making their views known clearly. "Furthermore," Maass declared, urging his fellow AJC leaders to stay the course, "our decision to continue to push the Jackson Amendment has been made with the knowledge that those most directly concerned—those Soviet Jews who are fighting for the right to emigrate—urge us repeatedly to stand firm. This message was repeated to us within the past forty-eight hours. In the absence of a firm commitment to the elimination of harassment, and the continued flow of emigration, the Jackson amendment remains our only weapon. . . . I would strongly recommend no change in our position of support for the Jackson amendment."[99]

In the end the AJC and the majority (though not all) of the other national Jewish organizations stood firm. The complex trade bill including the Jackson-Vanik amendment was passed by an overwhelming majority of the U.S. Senate on October 19, 1974, and was signed into law by President Ford in January. At the last moment, however, in a move unnoticed and unchecked by the major players, Congress passed a bill that included an amendment— known as the "Stevenson Amendment" after the senator from Illinois—drastically lowering the amount of credit available to the U.S.S.R. It was this, and not the Jackson-Vanik legislation itself, that may have convinced the Soviets not to comply. The Soviets angrily declared publicly that they would not be bound by the principle of human rights in connection with U.S. trade relations and there was a steep drop in Jewish emigration.[100] Nonetheless, the Jackson-Vanik amendment represented a political success for the movement and also reflected the will of the dissidents themselves. In the long run the principles it embodied, along with the Helsinki Accords, would yet prove their effectiveness.

After a few bright moments in 1979—including the signing of the Israel-Egypt peace treaty and an agreement on limiting nuclear weapons signed by both the United States and the Soviet Union—a series of international events brought an end to the era of détente. The Soviet Union intervened militarily on the side of a Marxist government in Afghanistan, getting itself into a war that would last for several years. President Jimmy Carter in response announced a

U.S. boycott of the 1980 summer Olympics to be held in Moscow. The Shah of Iran was overthrown; then ensued the Islamic Revolution and the taking of American hostages (an attempt to rescue them ended in disgraceful failure). The Soviet Union, on its part, began to wield more military strength and the possibility of nuclear war once more threatened the world. In 1980, Ronald Reagan, who considered the Soviet Union an "evil empire," became president. Reagan stressed military preparedness more than negotiation; his desire was to bring an end to the evils of communism. Between 1979 and 1985 hardly any Soviet Jews were allowed to leave.

Despite Reagan's campaign rhetoric, defeat of the Soviet Union appeared as remote as ever. At the 1980 AJC annual meeting Bert Gold spoke openly about a major decline in American power and a shift in favor of the U.S.S.R. The Soviets, he said, were now operating on a scale that would have been "impossible" ten years earlier. Soviet warships patrolled the Mediterranean, the Indian Ocean, the West Africa waters and the Caribbean, where the nation of Cuba again threatened. There had been successful and well-organized Soviet operations not only in Afghanistan but in Ethiopia and Angola as well—in stark contrast to the "inept" attempt of the United States to rescue its own hostages now being taken in Iran and elsewhere. "The loss of American power has led inevitably to a diminution of American will—what some observers call a failure of nerve. . . . These new geopolitical realities have a sobering impact on us," he concluded.[101]

At that moment the future appeared bleak. However, even as Bert Gold spoke, the days of the Soviet empire were numbered. "The evil empire" was not to last forever. And the time was not far off when history would yet witness the final redemption of Soviet Jewry.

❧ IV ❧

1980–2006

A Difficult Decade

Bitburg, Lebanon, Pollard, the Intifada, "Who Is a Jew?" Soviet Drop-outs, and the Fall and Rise of AJC

[1980–1990]

The clear needs of Israel after the wars of 1967 and 1973 and the movement to save Soviet Jewry had provided points of consensus for the American Jewish community and relative unity with regard to Israeli policies. This consensus began to break down in the 1980s. After the signing of the Egyptian-Israel peace agreement, American Jews found reason for deep divisions and ambivalence in their relations toward Israel. The Likud leader Menachem Begin, who came to power in 1977, frustrated many politically liberal American Jews and was viewed as a destructive force by a significant minority on the Israeli left. He drew criticism for his policy on Israeli settlements in the territories and his reluctance to grant autonomy to the Palestinians or to negotiate with the PLO, which at no point abated its terrorist operations in Israel and around the world. Begin drew praise in some quarters when he authorized the bombing of an Iraqi nuclear reactor in 1981, but drew widespread condemnation on Israel and deeply disturbed American Jewry with his 1982 incursion into Lebanon, code-named "Operation Peace for Galilee." Begin drew even more condemnation when a massacre in a Palestinian refugee camp by Christian Lebanese soldiers took place on Israel's watch. Israelis themselves were so divided that after Menachem Begin neither of Israel's two main political divisions could put together a majority coalition in the Knesset. Instead, in a series of "national unity" governments, the two sides had to take turns leading the country.

News of religious extremism and vigilantism among Jews in Israel caused concern in the United States, as did the domination there of Orthodoxy as the established religion when the majority of American Jews belonged to the Conservative or the Reform movements of Judaism. American Jews also had reason to be concerned when a massive uprising by Palestinians in the West

Bank and Gaza broke out in 1987. Israeli soldiers defending themselves were viewed on international television fighting against civilians, including children. The rebellion became known as the "Intifada" (an Arabic term literally meaning "shaking off") and continued for several years. The arrest of the American Jonathan Pollard for spying for Israel, the implication of Israel in what was known as the Iran-Contra affair, and a 1988 attempt to amend the Law of Return to exclude from automatic Israeli citizenship anyone converted to Judaism by a non-Orthodox rabbi — all were points that caused some American Jews to react with rage toward Israel. Also on the international stage, unity on the subject of freeing Soviet Jews ironically gave way to bitter division when the doors finally began to open in the late 1980s. Cries of "Let My People Go!" gave way to arguments in Israel and America over how to fund the exodus and whether the Soviet Jews should all go to Israel or have the right to settle in the United States and other countries if they wished.

At home, matters appeared no less negative. Republican presidents were in the White House for the entire decade, at a time when American Jewish Democrats outnumbered Republicans by more than four to one.[1] While Israel had never enjoyed such a close strategic relationship with the United States as it did under Ronald Reagan, Reagan's domestic policies and affinity for the Christian Right alienated many American Jews. Reagan's insistence in 1985 on visiting a cemetery in Bitburg, Germany, where Nazi SS officers were buried, led to fears that the Holocaust was being forgotten. American Jews suffered agonies of embarrassment and fears of an antisemitic backlash when Ivan Boesky and other prominent Jewish Wall Street financiers were arrested in corruption and insider trading scandals. Among Jews themselves, there were major tensions between the three main denominations that were closely related to the idea of patrilineal descent, sectarian violence in Israel, and attempts by the Israeli Knesset to legislate Jewish identity. In addition to inter-religious dialogues with Christians and Muslims, the AJC had to spend even more time fostering dialogue among different groups of Jews.

Finally, a stock market crash in October 1987 jeopardized the philanthropic sources of American Jewish organizations as a whole and aggravated the financial and administrative troubles that they and the AJC were already having. The AJC itself went through five executive directors in eight years and was suffering from deep deficits. In order to survive, AJC was forced to undergo a major restructuring in 1990 that involved cutting six million dollars from its budget and laying off almost a quarter of the entire staff.

The Presidency of Ronald Reagan

When Ronald Reagan was elected president in 1980 the AJC board of governors was not certain at first what to do or what the election meant. From the discussion it could be ascertained that the majority of them had voted either for the Democratic incumbent Jimmy Carter or for the independent candidate, John Anderson. They definitely mourned the loss in the Senate of such longtime allies as Senators Jacob K. Javits, Frank Church, and Richard Stone. According to a CBS–*New York Times* poll, American Jews as a whole had voted 14 percent for Anderson, 40 percent for Reagan, and only 45 percent for Carter, the first time since 1924 that Jews did not vote overwhelmingly for the Democratic candidate.[2] How Jews voted was always carefully polled because even though they cast less than 4 percent of the national vote, they were concentrated in nine large states–California, New York, Pennsylvania, Illinois, Ohio, Michigan, New Jersey, Florida, and Massachusetts—that had a total of 223 electoral votes, with 270 needed to win.

Orthodox Jews, by contrast, had voted overwhelmingly for Reagan. AJC leaders wondered if Reagan's victory came from "anti-Carter" feeling or represented a true shift in the country's mood. They also wondered what his election would mean for domestic and fiscal policy. Representatives of the Committee on Women's Concerns were alarmed that the new administration and Congress would translate anti-ERA sentiment into such measures as a constitutional amendment to ban abortion. Emily Sunstein, a member of the board of governors from Philadelphia, suggested that they not drop all their old liberal contacts to "get into bed with the Moral Majority," and several others agreed that they must be wary of that group that had played so important a role in bringing Reagan to power.[3] When Reagan ran for reelection in 1984, Jews reportedly voted for his Democratic opponent, Walter Mondale, by a ratio of 2 to 1, and when Reagan's vice president George H. W. Bush ran for president in 1988, 70 percent of Jews voted for Democrat Michael Dukakis.[4]

The AJC and all the American Jewish organizations in the Conference of Presidents strongly opposed Reagan's efforts, early in his term, to sell advanced weaponry known as AWACS (Airborne Warning and Control System) to Saudi Arabia. There was great fear that these weapons would disrupt the balance of power in the region and might eventually be used against Israel. In a bruising political battle that raised the specter of dual loyalty and antisemitism, the Jewish organizations lost and the Saudis got their weapons.[5] For the rest of his term after that, however, U.S.-Israel relations under Ronald Reagan and his secretaries of state—Alexander Haig and later George P. Shultz—reached their highest point. Reagan clearly saw Israel as a strategic asset against Soviet expansionism and Islamic extremism in the Middle East and did not hesitate to show it. Israel was also a model of counterterrorist activity at a time of resurgence of international terrorism. Reagan and Shultz took a strong stand against terrorism and saw Israel as an ally in fighting it. It helped that during those years the price of oil was relatively low and there was a glut in that product in the Middle East. In an analysis written in 1985, George E. Gruen, AJC's specialist in Middle East affairs, noted all the "invaluable tangible benefits" that the United States enjoyed from its alliance with Israel. Israel provided access to captured Soviet equipment on its battlefield and technological talent as well as "vital intelligence and other forms of strategic cooperation." Moreover, Gruen wrote, aid to Israel was always paid back as the Israelis bought virtually all their arms in the United States and tens of thousands of American jobs were created for every billion dollars of U.S. assistance to Israel.[6] Shultz, who was given AJC's highest award at the 1986 annual meeting, became personally involved in Israel's 1985 economic crisis and provided the aid that helped the economy recover. U.S. aid to Israel in general was increasingly coming in the form of grants rather than loans. Strategic, economic, and trade relations between the two countries were so close and so formally recognized that Israel almost rated as a NATO ally. Israel was even given defense contracts to work on the United States' SDI (Strategic Defense Initiative, also known as "Star Wars") — Reagan's chief weapon to defeat the Soviets.

For many at the AJC, however, the good that Reagan did by his stance on Israel was canceled out, first, by his economic policies. There were deep cuts in all social programs and especially in health and welfare, which resulted in reduction in food stamps, elimination of college loan opportunities, decreases in funding for public transportation, a rise in the price of home heating oil, and an elimination of jobs and vocational training programs for minorities. At a board of governors meeting not long after Reagan was sworn in, one member pointed out that the New York Federation raised only thirty-two million out of the nine hundred million it spent on medical and social welfare services for the poor, the elderly, and the young. The difference was provided by grants from the government. Thus the impact of such cuts for the Jewish community was not theoretical but practical and immediate.[7] Others spoke of "Reaganomics" as causing social trauma and unraveling the safety net that protected the country's poorest inhabitants.

The American economy had already been in poor shape under Carter — in 1979 there was double-digit inflation — and early in Reagan's term (1981–82), the nation entered a severe recession. While the economy eventually recovered, some changes were longer-term: an increase in the gap between the rich and the poor became a feature of Reagan's presidency. Hunger and homelessness began to blight the nation's cities in ways that had not been seen before. During the winter of 1981 New York City faced a crisis in providing emergency shelter for homeless residents, and Mayor Edward I. Koch appealed to the city's religious leaders to offer temporary housing in synagogues and churches. AJC's New York chapter helped to organize the Ad Hoc Interfaith Committee on the Homeless, which represented fifty institutions that opened or expanded shelters in the following years. This committee also pushed for more permanent solutions. According to Joanne Hoffman, the coordinator of the program, there were an estimated forty thousand homeless people in New

York in 1985. Some of the causes were withdrawal of federal assistance to development of low-cost housing and land use policies that gave priority to luxury developments. The victims were single parents with young children or people who suddenly lost jobs and hadn't been able to find work again, or members of the working poor who had been "gentrified" out of the local housing market.[8] The homeless and hungry also included the deinstitutionalized mentally ill. In 1983 the New York chapter also cosponsored a meeting of private agencies and other concerned individuals to discuss what was known about hunger, how to operate a food pantry or soup kitchen, and how to run a food drive.[9]

Whether directly traceable to Reagan or not, crises in urban areas were matched by crises in rural areas of the country. Thousands of midwestern farmers were enduring farm foreclosures, bankruptcies, auctions, and repossessions by banks. These farmers were easy prey for antisemites, who claimed that "Jewish bankers" or "an international Jewish conspiracy" that controlled the nation's Federal Reserve system was to blame for their troubles. The farm crisis and the antisemitism that accompanied it drew much attention during the 1980s from such organizations as the AJC and the ADL. Rabbi A. James Rudin, now head of interreligious affairs, in August 1985 made a trip to Iowa and drove more than a thousand miles visiting farm families so that he could report on the situation back at the AJC.[10] AJC leaders lobbied for federal relief for the farmers and began a media campaign in the Midwest to educate the farmers that the Jews were not to blame for their troubles.

American Jews who for some time had occupied the highest rungs of the socioeconomic ladder were not immune to the economic conditions and government policies of the early Reagan era; in fact, they suffered all the more intensely when unemployment struck because of the high economic and educational standards of their communities. In 1983 AJC formed a new program called "Jews on the Edge," staffed by urban affairs specialist Evan Bayer, to address rising unemployment and underemployment among Jewish professionals. There were lawyers, accountants, engineers, corporate managers, business owners, social workers, and educators who had used up their savings and were facing the prospect of losing their homes. Bayer reported that some of the newly poor were becoming disconnected or alienated from the Jewish community, and synagogues and other communal institutions reported that their memberships were down. New graduates were also finding difficulty in obtaining good full-time jobs. The Jewish Vocational Service of Detroit referred to this group as "a new generation of downwardly mobile Jewish youth who now doubt that their level of occupational achievement will equal that of their parents." Bayer suggested that much of this difficulty was happening because Jews were traditionally attracted to human services, health, education, and government service; thus, budget cutbacks in social programs hit Jewish professionals especially hard.

The financial recession also hurt Jewish small business owners. And the movement of manufacturing and heavy industry overseas affected professionals in management and engineering.[11]

Reagan's alliances with the Moral Majority and the forces of the Christian Right—along with the dangers this might pose to civil rights, civil liberties, and the separation of church and state—were even more objectionable than his economic policies to many leaders at the AJC. Religion, as had begun to be the case under President Nixon, was playing an increasing role in American politics and Jews were uneasy at what they saw as an attempt to Christianize America. Antisemitism analyst Milton Ellerin distinguished between the Old Right, which was obsessed with an alleged communist conspiracy, to the New Right, which saw the "elitists, eastern liberal establishment" as the enemy and sought to restore military preparedness and a more "family-church-neighborhood oriented culture."[12] Reagan personally introduced an amendment to the Constitution that would restore prayer in the public schools, and AJC legal director Sam Rabinove, who was also a member of the ACLU National Church-State Committee, led an all-out campaign by AJC to defeat it.

At the 1984 Republican convention Christian Right leaders such as Jerry Falwell delivered benedictions and directed the party platform in favor of school prayer and against abortion, equal rights for women, pornography, and homosexuality. On these issues, the AJC—as were American Jews on the whole—was overwhelmingly more liberal than the general American public. Sociologist Steven M. Cohen's annual survey of American Jewish public opinion in 1984 found that 90 percent favored gun control, 87 percent backed civil rights for homosexuals, 81 percent approved federal funding for abortion, and 75 percent supported welfare state programs. Censorship of anything, including pornography, was overwhelmingly opposed.[13]

As early as 1974 the AJC New York City chapter had testified in support of a City Council bill that extended basic civil rights to homosexuals. When the subject was on the agenda again in 1986, chapter director Haskell Lazere called it a "sad commentary on our city" that in the last twelve years so little had been done to eliminate this form of discrimination.[14] That year the board passed a strong statement recommended by the National Affairs Commission against discrimination based on sexual orientation in employment, housing, education, and public accommodations; chapters around the country were urged to work on legislation that would eliminate it. In the debate some said that precisely because of the growing power of the Right in the United States it was important to take such action now. Alfred Moses compared the measure's importance to the civil rights acts of the 1960s that benefited Jews. David Gordis, who was AJC director at the time, stated that as a human rights organization AJC had the duty to speak up for the civil rights of every group that was denied them.[15] AJC also invited leading Protestant, Catholic, and Jewish clergy to a national interreligious conference on AIDS held at AJC headquarters in 1987.

Recommendations included (1) setting up speakers' bureaus and producing educational material so that clergy could teach more about the disease, and (2) establishing programs to help AIDS victims and their families. These programs were done against a background of criticism against the Reagan administration for saying and doing too little about the AIDs epidemic, which had been identified in 1981. They also were set in opposition to those Far Right–wing Christian leaders who maintained the disease was a form of divine punishment.

Ambivalence about Reagan's presidency and the tension that so often existed in those years between support for Israel and support for liberal domestic policies erupted into open controversy within AJC when a group of leading officers (many of them from California) voted to give the former president AJC's highest award—the American Liberties Medallion—in 1989 "for his exemplary leadership in support of the State of Israel and lifetime commitment to the freedom of Soviet Jewry." The move drew wide criticism within the organization. At least a dozen members wrote letters strongly objecting, threatening to withhold financial support, or actually resigning from AJC over the matter. AJC Executive Vice President Ira Silverman pointed out, in his response to such letters, that AJC had often been outspoken against many of Reagan's policies, particularly on domestic issues such as civil rights. On the other hand, the Committee had been equally outspoken in support of Israel and Soviet Jewry, and no administration had ever been so supportive of these two "priority issues for the Jewish community" as that of Reagan. Another important reason was "to send an important message to the present administration [that is, George H. W. Bush's] which has yet to show the same level of commitment to these issues."[16] Indeed, as Kenneth Jacobson in his 1989 analysis for the *American Jewish Year Book* wrote, "The closeness and warmth in relations that had characterized the Ronald Reagan–George Shultz years showed signs of evaporating under the tenure of President George Bush and Secretary of State James A. Baker."[17] Also under President Bush's administration, many Soviet Jews who wanted to leave the U.S.S.R. were denied the status of refugees and were not so readily accepted as immigrants to the United States.

Joan G. Schine, a member of the National Affairs Commission, was one of those who wrote in to resign her membership: "I cannot in conscience remain a member of a body that recognizes Ronald Reagan for 'exemplary leadership,'" she wrote. She was willing to recognize that Reagan had done much for Israel and Soviet Jewry. "However," she wrote, "one of the strengths of AJC for me has been the commitment to a comprehensive, rather than a parochial, view of American Jewish interests." She pointed out that AJC had in recent years recommended positions on the issues of bilingual education, equity and reproductive rights for women, separation of church and state, and had "reaffirmed a strong stand" in support of equal opportunity for minorities and the poor. "On every one of these issues Ronald Reagan has been at the opposite end of the spectrum," she declared, "and he has not hesitated to use the power and prestige of the presidency to erode civil and individual liberties and to shape the federal courts to become the voice of reaction. For AJC to pay tribute to this 'hero' of the Far Right makes a mockery of the thoughtful research and decision-making process of our commission and indeed of the stated purposes of AJC itself."[18] Mrs. Victor Shaincock of Houston charged that Reagan "falls short of the values that I hold dear and the values that the American Jewish Committee stands for," and that she wanted to resign but it would serve no purpose."[19]

Former AJC president Richard Maass wrote to say that in his opinion the decision to give the award was a sign of the decline of AJC and that he had no intention of coming to the meeting to see Reagan receive the award "which I believe under the circumstances of his presidency is an obscene gesture." "My objections are not to Reagan personally, nor to the fact that he is a Republican and I am a Democrat, for I long ago discarded partisanship for common sense," he wrote. "But I cannot ignore, the decimation of the U.S. Civil Rights Commission, the attempt to eliminate the Department of Education, the elimination of almost all housing subsidies for the poor and homeless, while at the same time sanctioning the plunder of HUD for political purposes. In sum the Reagan administration has set back human rights and civil rights 10 years or more through its deliberate actions and inaction. But, you may say, we are giving him the award because of his support for Israel and for Soviet Jewry. If this is the basis for making that award, ignoring all the other negatives, then I suggest that next year we give the American Liberties Medallion to Jerry Falwell, Jimmy Bakker and Jimmy Swaggart—all of whom support Israel and the cause of Soviet Jewry."[20]

Even the goodwill Reagan earned from Jews for his policies on Israel and Soviet Jewry were in jeopardy when it was announced in April 1985 that as an act of commemoration of the fortieth anniversary of the surrender of Nazi Germany to the Allies, Reagan would lay a wreath at a German military cemetery in Bitburg. The invitation to do so came from West German Chancellor Helmut Kohl, who believed that the gesture would serve as a formal sign of reconciliation between Germany and the United States and would stress in the eyes of the Soviet Union and all the countries of the world the strength of the alliance between the United States and West Germany. However, what should have been a routine visit, in the words of historian Deborah E. Lipstadt, "became a major international event. . . . The imbroglio over the visit threatened to seriously affect American-German relations, be a spur to antisemitism, politically alienate American Jews from the Reagan administration, and indeed color the way in which Reagan's entire presidency would be viewed in history."[21] The event was also a case study of how Jewish organizations in general—and AJC in particular—could have a strong impact on the policy of world leaders, using their contacts with sympathetic and helpful non-Jews.

There had been anger among Jews when Reagan had announced earlier that he would not visit a concentration camp as part of his visit to Germany. Anger turned to outrage when it became known not long after the announcement of the itinerary that among the approximately two thousand German World War II soldiers buried at Bitburg, at least forty-seven had been members of the notorious SS (*Schutzstaffel*, or "protective detachment"), an elite volunteer Nazi guard headed by Heinrich Himmler. Their duties included operating the concentration camps, and the group had been named during the Nuremberg trials for war crimes and atrocities against innocent civilians in Nazi-occupied countries.

Jewish organizations, including the AJC, were the first to issue strong declarations condemning the visit and calling for it to be canceled. On April 12, two days after the announcement, the National Council of Churches, the National Conference of Catholic Bishops, and the pastor of one of America's leading black congregations also issued condemnations. In the next few days Reagan received letters urging him to cancel the trip from organizations representing Polish, Ukrainian, Hispanic, Italian, Greek, Chinese, and Japanese Americans as well as the head of the NAACP and veterans' groups. More than half the members of the U.S. Senate, including forty-two Democrats and eleven Republicans, sent Reagan a petition urging him not to go to the Bitburg cemetery; later, both houses of Congress passed resolutions almost unanimously calling on the president to change his plans. The fifty-five members of the U.S. Holocaust Memorial Council, all presidential appointees, threatened mass resignation. After a meeting with a delegation from the Conference of Presidents of Major American Jewish Organizations on April 16, Reagan announced that he would visit a concentration camp on his trip after all. But he refused to cancel the trip to Bitburg and Chancellor Kohl refused to withdraw the invitation. Holocaust survivors and their supporters demonstrated against the visit in the streets and the matter was front-page news for more than a month. In Germany there were reports of an escalation of anti-semitism and talk of how Jewish power and control of the media was once again influencing Washington, D.C., and its president.[22]

Perhaps the most dramatic encounter of the Bitburg affair took place on April 19 at the White House, when death camp survivor and author Elie Wiesel was to be awarded the Congressional Gold Medal of Honor, one of the highest awards the U.S. government could give to a civilian, for his contributions to human rights and to literature. Wiesel told friends that he was thinking of boycotting the ceremony. When White House officials told him to limit his speech to three minutes and omit any direct criticism of the president's decision to visit Bitburg, Wiesel reportedly protested to Donald T. Regan, the White House chief of staff, who assured him that he could say what he wanted.[23] "The issue here is not politics, but good and evil," Wiesel finally said to Reagan when he was presented with the award, "and we must never confuse them. For I have seen the SS at work, and I have seen their victims. They were my friends. They were my parents. . . . You have told us earlier when we spoke that you were not aware of the presence of SS graves in the Bitburg cemetery. . . . Of course, you didn't know. But now we are all aware. May I, Mr. President, if it's possible at all, implore you to do something else, to find a way, to find another way, another site. That place, Mr. President, is not your place. Your place is with the victims of the SS."[24]

As soon as the story about the Bitburg cemetery broke, AJC officers and staff around the country were called upon by the media to respond. As AJC President Howard Friedman later reported to the membership, the New York headquarters prepared an extensive "backgrounder" to be sent to everybody "so that they could discuss the issues knowledgeably and effectively."[25] "As the only American Jewish organization that has been engaged in fruitful dialogue and educational programs with West Germany for years," he wrote, "we were in a unique position to explain—in dozens of newspaper stories and countless radio and television programs in the days that followed—why the Bitburg visit was not an acceptable signal of reconciliation."[26] As for mobilizing Christian and ethnic leaders to respond with letters, editorials, and newspaper advertisements opposing the visit, interreligious affairs director Rabbi A. James Rudin noted that this was not an instance where Jews had to "solicit Christian names." "They called us," Rudin observed. "My phone was ringing off the hook."[27] Several times AJC got calls from other Jewish organizations asking them to join in public counterdemonstrations against the president. "The AJC does not endorse this kind of response to the Bitburg visit," declared Executive Vice President David Gordis, "and this has been made clear to other organizations who have called to seek our support for such efforts."[28]

Howard Friedman himself, accompanied at times by AJC Associate Director William Trosten, spent more than a week shuttling between Bonn, New York, and the White House, trying to negotiate behind the scenes with the Germans and Reagan's staff a cancellation of the Bitburg visit or the choice of an alternative site for a ceremony of reconciliation. On April 23 Friedman and Trosten met with Alois Mertes, a German foreign affairs minister who was well known to them for his efforts to promote good relations with Jews and Israel, and who had already been invited to address AJC's upcoming annual meeting in New York. Mertes also happened to represent the parliamentary electoral district that included the town of Bitburg. Friedman at that point suggested that instead of visiting Bitburg, Reagan and Kohl mark German-U.S. reconciliation by laying a wreath at the gravesite of the first chancellor of postwar West Germany, Konrad Adenauer, under whose administration the first reparation agreements with the Claims Conference had been signed. Adenauer had been imprisoned by the Nazis during World War

II and was considered the architect of Germany's reintegration into the civilized world and of good relations with Jews and the State of Israel. Mertes agreed with this idea and immediately dictated a letter to Chancellor Helmut Kohl in Bonn, repeating and endorsing AJC's plan to replace the visit to Bitburg with a visit to Adenauer's grave.

An answer came back from Kohl the next morning. He was willing to accept their suggestion as an addition to Reagan's itinerary, but not as a substitute for the Bitburg visit.[29] Still, this agreement gave AJC something concrete to work with. In the meantime, back in New York on the day of Elie Wiesel's speech, Rabbi Marc H. Tanenbaum, who was now AJC's director of international affairs, received a call from the Reverend Billy Graham. As Tanenbaum reported it, Graham had called to discuss "the terrible situation" of President Reagan and his forthcoming trip to Germany and to offer his help. Graham, a confidant and adviser to both Ronald and Nancy Reagan, said that he had spoken to the president twice in the past ten days and also had had a long talk with Nancy Reagan "who is more upset than at almost any time I have known her over the past thirty years." Tanenbaum continued:

Graham said that the President was bewildered over the difficulty and does not know how to get out of it. . . . In any case Graham told me he was "very strong with Reagan—I have never been so strong with him before—and told him that this was far more a moral issue than a political one, and unless he finds a way to straighten this out it will undermine his moral authority in this country and overseas." I confirmed Graham in his assessment of the seriousness of the moral issues at stake. Nancy Reagan says she wishes Kohl would find a way to withdraw the invitation to the Bitburg Cemetery. Nancy, he said, is very angry at the staff that got him into this hole. Arthur Burns [U.S. ambassador to West Germany] said that Kohl is stubborn about going to the military cemetery which has now become a political issue in Germany and he probably will not back down.

Billy Graham's intervention resulted in another call the next day to Tanenbaum from presidential adviser Michael Deaver, who was arranging the details of Reagan's trip. Deaver invited a delegation from AJC to visit the White House on April 29 to discuss the matter. Howard Friedman, David Gordis, William Trosten, Marc Tanenbaum, A. James Rudin, and Hyman Bookbinder at that meeting again urged cancelation of the trip to Bitburg. Short of that, they requested, the visit should be downplayed, with emphasis on "other, more appropriate symbols." They informed Deaver about Kohl's agreement to add a trip to Konrad Adenauer's grave. Deaver answered that that information would make it easier for him to adjust the President's itinerary, but there was no realistic way to cancel the trip to Bitburg. He did promise, however, that the visit could be "enormously downplayed, with no speech by the President."[30] Reagan himself came in at the end of the meeting to offer his greetings and thank the AJC for their cooperation. The AJC delegation also had an opportunity to meet with Reagan's speechwriter, to whom they suggested themes and ideas for Reagan's speech at the concentration camp. The speechwriter took copious notes, and many of the ideas and themes found their way into Reagan's subsequent speech.[31]

The next day Marc Tanenbaum got word that while Reagan still would not cancel the trip to Bitburg, he and Kohl had agreed that the trip would include a wreath laid at Konrad Adenauer's grave. Tanenbaum then quickly wrote in its entirety a speech for Reagan to give at the gravesite and handed it off to the White House on May 1 just as the president was preparing to leave.[32] On Sunday morning, May 5, Reagan visited the site of the Bergen-Belsen concentration camp, where Anne Frank had died. He made one of the most emotional speeches of his career and stayed for more than an hour. Here he invoked a slogan that had originally been coined by the JDL but had become a slogan for all of American Jewry: "Rising above this cruelty, out of this tragic and nightmarish time, beyond the anguish, the pain and the suffering, and for all time, we can and must pledge: Never again."[33] This visit was followed by a trip to the Bitburg cemetery where he stayed for ten minutes and said nothing. Thousands of policemen in riot gear held back angry Jewish demonstrators by the road to and from the cemetery.

Reagan and Kohl also visited the gravesite of Konrad Adenauer, where the American president gave the speech Tanenbaum had prepared for him. Describing how Adenauer had personally expressed his sense of shame for crimes committed against the Jews by the Nazis, the speech noted, "With great tact and sensitivity of conscience, Chancellor Adenauer forged a special relationship with the State of Israel which thankfully continues to this day."[34] "Paradoxically there has been some positive fallout from this event," concluded AJC President Howard I. Friedman, in his report to the membership on AJC's activities during the Bitburg affair. (He was later awarded the Commander's Cross of the Order of Merit of the Federal Republic of Germany for his work in promoting greater understanding between American Jews and West Germany.) "The entire world has been reminded of the unremitting Jewish anguish over the Holocaust; and we have seen a heightened recognition that the lessons of that horror are universal."[35]

Menachem Begin and the War in Lebanon

As well as the leader of the United States, the leader of Israel from 1977 to 1983 also caused serious and ongoing divisions among Jews in America and in Israel and was the subject of protracted debates and close votes at AJC meetings. While U.S.-Israel relations remained close through the term of Menachem Begin, there were tensions and serious divisions among Jews over Begin's supposed unwillingness to follow through on the peace treaty with Egypt (beyond giving up the entire Sinai Peninsula), the Israeli government's policies of settlement in the West Bank and Gaza, and the 1982 incursion into Lebanon called "Operation Peace for Galilee" which was the longest and most controversial war in Israeli history (see chapter 7). When Israeli forces on June 7, 1981, bombed the Iraqi nuclear reactor near Baghdad, claiming that it was about to reach the stage where it could produce nuclear weapons, Israel was condemned in the U.N. Security Council and the United States joined in the condemnation. When Israel objected to the sale of AWACS to Saudi Arabia the *New York Daily News* ran a banner headline: "Reagan to Begin: Butt Out!"[36] *Newsweek* ran a cover story about Begin titled "Road Block to Peace" and *Time* ran a three-page essay titled "What to do About Israel" that stated flatly that Israel was a strategic liability for the United States and that relations with it should be "reassessed" because it was interfering in American domestic politics. Rita Hauser of AJC's Foreign Affairs Commission personally met to voice her objections with *Time*'s managing editor, the author of the essay, the senior editor, and the correspondence editor, who printed her letter of response in one of the next issues.[37]

At first there was widespread consensus in Israel that the armed forces needed to go into southern Lebanon in June 1982 in order to destroy the PLO infrastructure and their state-within-a-state that had been building up for years. When King Hussein expelled the PLO from Jordan in 1970 they had gone to Lebanon, upsetting the balance of power in that country and helping to set off a civil war between Muslims and Christians that began in 1975 and resulted in Syrian intervention. Soon thousands of PLO fighters with advanced weapons, aided by Syria and the Soviet Union, were using Lebanon as a base to attack Israel to the south. The Israelis had already confronted PLO forces in southern Lebanon in 1978 in Operation Litani, after which they partially withdrew and allowed the establishment of UNIFIL troops (United Nations Interim Force in Lebanon). UNIFIL, however, itself became a target and was of little use in stopping PLO attacks against Israel. Terrorists regularly infiltrated the Israeli border to attack civilians, and in northern Israel normal life became impossible because of the constant threat of rocket attacks and the resultant need when these happened to spend nights in bomb shelters. Strong disputes in Israel arose, however, in 1982 over how far the Israel Defense Forces should go in Lebanon, how long they should stay, and the mounting IDF and civilian casualties that the war and the occupation of Lebanon was causing. As AJC Associate Executive Director Shula Bahat recalled, there was concern that Israel's stay in Lebanon might turn into an indefinite situation similar to the one in the West Bank and Gaza.[38]

Israel's Defense Minister Ariel Sharon originally announced that Israel only sought to establish a forty-kilometer security zone in southern Lebanon so that northern Israeli towns would be out of missile range.[39] In his view, however, the mission would be complete only if the Israelis were able to destroy PLO headquarters in West Beirut, remove all foreign forces from Lebanon, and help establish a strong central government there that would be able to sign a peace treaty with Israel.[40] The Israel Defense Forces advanced to West Beirut where they bombarded and besieged the city, demanding an evacuation of the PLO forces. There were calls for Sharon's resignation and massive public demonstrations for and against staying in Lebanon by the Peace Now and Labor factions on the one hand and pro-government forces on the other. In the United States, images of the war were being broadcast daily on American television. There were pictures of building damage that had actually been caused during the Lebanese civil war but that was blamed on Israeli weapons, and wildly exaggerated accounts of the numbers of refugees and dead and wounded civilians.[41]

Ariel Sharon got his wish: under the supervision of a multinational peace-keeping force (which included a contingent of U.S. Marines in Beirut), Yasir Arafat and hundreds of PLO fighters evacuated Beirut, many eventually ending up in Tunisia where they set up new headquarters. Israel claimed, however, there were still thousands more PLO fighters hiding in Palestinian refugee camps on the outskirts of Beirut. On September 16, having taken control of the area, Israeli leaders allowed Christian Phalangist forces, with whom they had an alliance, to enter the Sabra and Shatila refugee camps, ostensibly to root out PLO terrorists. After years of civil war the Phalangists and the Palestinians were bitter enemies; moreover, Phalangists were thirsting for revenge at the assassination of their leader by Syrian and pro-PLO forces only two days before. Instead of just rooting out armed fighters, the Phalangists perpetrated a massacre on the civilian population. Israel forces surrounding the camp heard evidence on their radios that atrocities might be going on, but reaction was slow and it was not until Saturday that the Israelis forcefully ordered the Phalangists out of the camp.[42]

When the news broke on foreign television and news broadcasts—Begin himself learned of the massacre by hearing about it on TV—much of the world, including the Israelis, was horrified. The war in Lebanon had become increasingly unpopular in Israel and the massacre appeared to be the last straw. In the biggest public demonstration in Israeli history, some four hundred thousand Israelis, almost one-tenth of the entire population, gathered in a Tel Aviv square to demand the resignation of Begin and Sharon and to call for a commission of investigation, which was indeed subsequently appointed. A comparable proportionate American protest would have required twenty million demonstrators.[43] It did not matter that during the civil war, tens of thousands had been killed in interethnic and interreligious massacres in Lebanon, and no one had ever called for an investigation. Nor did it matter that the Israelis were not in the camps and had not personally done the deed, as the report by the Kahan Commission (after Yitzhak Kahan, president of Israel's Supreme Court) noted.[44] It did not take long for those who wished Israel and the Jews ill to repeat the story as if the Israelis themselves had shed the blood.

An early reaction of Begin's was to say "When *goyim* kill *goyim*, they come to hang the Jews."[45] The Kahan Commission held that the Israelis were "indirectly responsible" and that Ariel Sharon bore "personal responsibility" for what had happened under his command and should resign. In the commission's view, it had been a fatal error of Sharon to allow the Phalangists anywhere near the camps, knowing what they might do. Sharon had claimed to the Knesset that "we did not imagine in our wildest dreams that the Phalangists would act this way."[46]

A sad turning point in Jewish disunity was reached when, during a Peace Now demonstration in the wake of the Sabra and Shatila massacre, a grenade was thrown into the crowd from a group of Likud counterdemonstraters. Ten marchers were wounded and one was killed. The loss of thirty-three-year-old Emil Grunszweig, a graduate student and paratrooper officer who had fought in Lebanon, marked the first time in Israeli history that anyone had been killed in a peace demonstration. His funeral the next day drew ten thousand people and more calls for Begin and Sharon to resign.

As the news of the massacre broke in September 1982, Maynard I. Wishner, AJC's president, issued this statement: "The AJC is shocked at the atrocities committed in Palestinian camps in Beirut over the weekend and we grieve for the victims. No extenuating circumstances can justify such crimes. The fact that internecine warfare and fanaticism resulted in similar atrocities over the past decade does not lessen the intensity of our outrage and condemnation. . . . Every step must be taken by every party involved, directly or indirectly, including Israel, to determine how this tragedy occurred and by whom these crimes were perpetrated. . . . We call upon our government to do everything possible to speed the departure of foreign armies, and to work toward the restoration of civil order until such time as a strong Lebanese central government can establish itself."[47] A few days later six prominent American rabbis came to AJC headquarters for a standing-room-only news conference to "express the anguish of the American Jewish community over the loss of life in the Beirut massacres." Marc H. Tanenbaum was joined by Gerson D. Cohen, chancellor of the Jewish Theological Seminary, Joseph B. Glaser, executive vice president of the CCAR, Norman Lamm, president of Yeshiva University, Paul M. Steinberg, dean of Hebrew Union College, and Walter S. Wurzburger, president of the Synagogue Council of America. All called for a high-level and independent investigation to establish the facts and determine responsibility.[48] In the following months the American Jewish Joint Distribution Committee helped to distribute tons of emergency food supplies, cement, kerosene heaters, and clothing to Palestinian refugees in Lebanon. Donations came from the United States, Israel, and from Jewish communities, agencies, synagogues, and individuals from around the world.[49]

AJC staff compiled a list of "talking points" to use if anyone from the media called to ask AJC's reaction to the event. This was what they were told to answer: "1. We feel a moral revulsion against the massacre that occurred this weekend and we note that the revulsion is shared by the Israelis and particularly the government of Israel. 2. what happened flies in the face of what we know from our first-hand experiences about the nature and behavior and ethos of Israel and the Israel Defense Forces, and so it is inconceivable that they would have any involvement even passively; 3. we welcome the quick initiative of the Israeli ministry of defense in appointing a committee of officers to conduct the inquiry into what took place; 4. what makes this tragedy even more tragic is that it is not an aberration but one more horror in a series of bloody outrages that have taken place between Muslims and Christians for nearly 10 years; 5. what we all look forward to is the reconstitution of Lebanese sovereignty and a viable Lebanese government and army and the withdrawal of all foreign forces from Lebanon."

Under the pressure of the Kahan Commission's recommendations, which were released in February 1983, Sharon resigned as defense minister and was replaced by Moshe Arens. Begin, however, remained in office and Sharon remained in the cabinet as minister without portfolio. Eventually the Israelis signed an agreement with the Lebanese and withdrew to a point some twenty miles from their northern border, but the achievement fell far short of the peace that Ariel Sharon had envisioned. Syria, amply supplied by the Soviet Union, was determined to maintain its control over Lebanon. Hezbollah, a terrorist organization funded and trained by Iran, established its presence there; PLO guerillas reestablished themselves at the perimeter of Israel's security zone; and Lebanon continued to represent a danger to Israeli soldiers and civilians. In the summer of 2006, six years after Israeli forces had withdrawn from southern Lebanon, Hezbollah forces without provocation crossed the Israeli border to kill and kidnap Israeli soldiers. When Israeli forces responded, Hezbollah began firing rockets into northern Israel, hitting as far south as Haifa and Tiberias. There were fears that the rockets might have a range as far south as Tel Aviv; for the third time since Israel's War of Independence and the Gulf War, the entire civilian population of the country was in danger. Israelis in the north once again moved to bomb shelters, and Israel went to war in what some called a second "Operation Peace for Galilee" to try and put an end to Hezbollah.

The "Intifada"

The behavior of Israel's military again became a subject of strong international condemnation, pressure from the United States, and a factor dividing Jews from one another in December 1987, when an Israeli motorist in the Gaza Strip lost control of his truck and ran into two Arab vans, killing four people and injuring seventeen others. It was an accident, but rumors spread that this was a premeditated retaliation from the Israelis for the earlier stabbing of an Israeli man in Gaza.[50] The incident ignited long-simmering tensions and set off a wave of rioting that soon spread throughout the West Bank and East Jerusalem and turned into the first organized Palestinian uprising, which the Arabs called the "intifada."

While the initial outbursts appeared to be spontaneous, on December 10, PLO radio from Baghdad broadcast a message from Yasir Arafat calling on the Arab population in the territories and also the Arab citizens of Israel to "rise up. . . . The fires of revolution against the Zionist invaders will not fade out . . . until our land—all of our land—has been liberated from these usurping invaders." Arafat called for a concerted struggle until "the banners of Palestine are hoisted on the Strip and on the courageous bank and also on the minarets and churches of Jerusalem."[51] Young Palestinians, some of them children, burned tires, set up barricades, and attacked Israeli soldiers with rocks, firebombs, knives, and other weapons, endangering their lives. Israeli soldiers reacted with tear gas, rubber bullets, and then plastic bullets. The soldiers, arresting and deporting demonstrators, were under instructions to use live ammunition only as a last resort.

In January, Yitzhak Rabin, minister of defense under the national unity government, announced a new policy to deal with the uprising: "The first priority is to use force, might, beatings," he said.[52] Reports spread of hundreds of Palestinians being treated for broken bones and the U.S. government and American Jews did not take well to the news that Israel, a supposedly enlightened country, was beating up demonstrators. Military spokesmen said beatings were supposed to be a less lethal substitute for shooting at them, but Israel was still criticized for using excessive force, and TV pictures of the violence in every detail were broadcast on television screens around the world. Israel was being depicted as a Middle East Goliath fighting stone-slinging Palestinian Davids.[53] The effect on Israel's public image was as bad or worse as it had been during the war in Lebanon.

As soon as the disturbances began, AJC leaders met with U.S. officials central to Middle East policy, from Secretary of State Shultz to members of the State Department and the National Security Council. AJC denounced U.S. criticism of Israel's actions, and urged the United States to act in ways that would renew peace activities. AJC's policy, the result of many long meetings and discussions, was to advocate for "direct negotiations for a peaceful solution between Israel, the concerned Arab states, and appropriate Palestinian representatives" through an international conference if necessary. "Appropriate Palestinian representatives" did not include the PLO, which was inciting the riots and never stopped conducting regular terrorist raids on Israel. As for the Israelis, AJC President Theodore Ellenoff wrote an open letter to the people of Israel that appeared in Israeli newspapers, saying "We stand with you, profoundly sympathetic to the dilemma which you and your government face in confronting the upsurge of violence in the territories."[54] More privately, AJC officers and staff conferred with Israeli officials to offer their help, to let them know how the riots were being perceived in America, and to suggest less lethal ways of dealing with the violence. For example, they sent cables to Prime Minister Shamir, Foreign Minister Shimon Peres, and Defense Minister Rabin, expressing their concern over reports of beatings and physical violence against Palestinian protesters.[55] They also, in the words of Bertram Gold, "urged Israel to be more forthcoming, because we do not believe that time is on Israel's side." Already at meetings there had been discussion of the "demographic time bomb" that the 1.4 million Palestinians in the West Bank and Gaza represented, which in 1988 was 600,000 in Gaza and 800,000 in the West Bank. Because of their high birthrate their numbers were increasing rapidly, confronting Israel with a dilemma: either hold the population indefinitely without giving them full political rights, or absorb them and grant them Israeli citizenship, which would eventually put into question the very nature of Israel as a predominantly Jewish state.[56] Hyman Bookbinder remarked at one point that in the end there had to be some separation of Gaza and the West Bank if Israel was to remain a Jewish state.[57]

As the violence raged AJC attempted to present a united front to the outside world by joining in missions and drafting common statements with the Conference of Presidents, which was headed at that time by AJC Honorary President Morris Abram. (All AJC past presidents were given the title of honorary President). Technically AJC was only an observer and not a full member of the conference, but in this instance they acted as full members anyway. As usual, the International Relations Department wrote detailed background memoranda that were widely distributed. While AJC staff did not go out of their way to contact the media, "in an effort not to inflame an already volatile situation," they responded when the media called.[58] AJC President Theodore Ellenoff and others at AJC appeared on radio and TV programs and were quoted in newspaper and magazine articles. They held meetings with officials of all the religious, ethnic, and communal organizations in their coalition, trying to explain the complexities of Israel's situation and what was behind the images on the TV screens. They took out full-page ads in newspapers cosigned by Christian leaders with the headline "We Stand with Israel." Both on a national and chapter level, they held meetings with key executives at networks and other media, "urging them to place the situation in Israel in fairer perspective."[59] In one instance Marc Tanenbaum arranged a meeting for all the major Jewish organizations with the ABC network, in the aftermath of its Monday, January 18 *ABC World News Tonight* with Peter Jennings, which drew comparisons between Israel and South Africa. In response Allan L. Kagedan, a policy analyst in the International Relations Department, wrote a special report, "Israel and South Africa: The Mythical Alliance," which was widely distributed and published as a chapter in a book.[60] Memos to field staff and chapter leaders included lists of addresses of news department heads of networks so that members could write them, and lists of their local network affiliates as well. "While we cannot tell constituents what to write," suggested one such memo, "the consensus among mainstream Jewish organizations is not to engage in media 'bashing,' but neither to refrain from calling to the media's attention in a business-like way those reports which we consider to be skewed, biased, unbalanced, or unfair. Where you detect such a pattern in local reporting, on editorials, meetings should be set up, either independently or in conjunction with Jewish groups. Kindly keep us informed of your plans in this area and send us copies of all related materials."[61]

In the course of the intifada, King Hussein of Jordan decided to cut all legal and administrative ties to the West Bank, where most Palestinians had maintained Jordanian citizenship from the time the territory was part of Jordan. This severing eliminated for all time the chance of an arrangement—for which Shimon Peres and others had worked and hoped—for any part of the West Bank to be handed back to Jordanian jurisdiction. King Hussein recognized the Palestine Liberation Organization as the "sole legitimate representative of the Palestinian people." The United States also recognized the PLO. In December 1988, after years of pressure from all over the world including the Arab nations Arafat read a statement to reporters, supposedly backed up by a decision of the Palestine National Council, that the PLO was willing to renounce terrorism and recognize the State of Israel along with a Palestinian state. "Let me be absolutely clear that neither Arafat, nor anyone for that matter, can stop the intifada, the uprising," he added. "The intifada will come to an end only when practical and tangible steps have been taken towards the achievement of our national aims and establishment of our independent Palestinian state."[62] President Reagan and George P. Shultz believed that this declaration met the conditions they had set for talking to the PLO.[63]

Indeed, the violence in the West Bank and Gaza did not stop, continuing in force until 1991 and becoming a regular part of the background of Israeli life. It did not cease in its entirety until the signing of the Oslo Accords in 1993. Long before then, American Jews found themselves facing other crises: the Pollard affair, the Iran-Contra affair, revelations of Jewish white-collar crime on Wall Street, religious disunity, and the controversy over the so-called Who is a Jew amendment to Israel's Law of Return, which in their eyes would render Reform and Conservative Judaism invalid.

Religious Extremism and "Who is a Jew"

The AJC strongly condemned the activities in Israel of Meir Kahane, founder of the Jewish Defense League, who had enough support in Israeli society that he was able to win one seat in the Israeli Knesset in 1984 on a strongly nationalist,

nonsecular, and anti-Arab platform. He and his followers at one point marched
through the Arab section of the Old City of Jerusalem, vandalizing Arab shops,
shouting "death to the Arabs," and claiming that the way to deal with the Palestinians was to force them to leave the country. A related Jewish terrorist underground materialized at the same time. Calling themselves "TNT" for "terror
against terror" in Hebrew, they plotted to blow up Arab buses and to destroy
Arab sites on the Temple Mount. Almost all were settlers of the West Bank and
the Golan Heights.[64] The Israel security services, accustomed to dealing with
Arab threats, had to develop a special division to deal with Jewish violence. In
1988 the Knesset and the Israeli Supreme Court found a way to bar Kahane from
running for office again.

The *haredim,* or ultra-Orthodox, were also growing in power, numbers,
and assertiveness at this time and there were clashes in the streets, complete
with riots and tear gas, between them and secular Jews over such things as
"immodest" advertisements on bus shelters, movies on the Sabbath, and public swimming pools that offered mixed bathing and tried to open on Saturday.
Since the founding of the state the Orthodox had enjoyed a monopoly over
religious matters in Israel, particularly marriage and burial. In politics, the
ultra-Orthodox were also gaining power through Israel's complex political
system. There were 120 seats in the Israeli Knesset allocated toward a multiplicity of parties, so many that no one party could ever hope to have a majority. The only way a prime minister could form a government and get the minimum sixty-one seats in the Knesset was by forming coalitions, and the few
seats that a number of ultra-Orthodox parties controlled could make a difference in a government's rise or fall.

In 1988 Yitzhak Shamir tried to avoid another national unity government
by forming a coalition with the ultra-Orthodox parties. They demanded as a
condition an amendment to Israel's Law of Return that would disqualify for
automatic citizenship any Jew who had not been converted according to *halacha,* or Jewish law, which in effect meant Orthodox rabbis. In the protracted
and bitter so-called Who is a Jew controversy, American Jews understood such
an amendment as delegitimizing non-Orthodox denominations such as Reform and Conservative. The General Assembly of the Council of Jewish Federations, which happened to be meeting at the time, sent an emergency mission to Israel to protest the amendment. "Over two thousand Jewish leaders
met with Prime Minister Shamir, with Rabin, with members of the Knesset,
and with representatives of the religious establishment. . . . The office of
Israel's president was inundated with letters of protest, phone calls, and telegrams from enraged American Jews."[65] The AJC joined twenty-six other Jewish organizations in a statement on the subject read: "We are one people with
a single destiny. We reject any effort to divide our people by legislative action
of the Knesset. All Jews, including those of us who are not citizens of Israel,
are affected by the possibility of a change in the definition of 'Who is a Jew?'

under Israeli law. . . . Changing the definition of 'Who is a Jew?' . . . would inflict enormous damage, actual and symbolic, on the Jews of the Diaspora. The unique partnership between the Jewish people and the State of Israel must be preserved."[66] In the aftermath of the conflict AJC sought to open a dialogue with the ultra-Orthodox in Israel; in 1989 an AJC delegation including Theodore Ellenoff, Alfred H. Moses, Robert S. Rifkind, and Steven Bayme met with heads of the ultra-Orthodox parties and such figures as the Hasidic Belzer and Gur Rebbes.[67]

Events in Israel also affected for ill the relations between the different Jewish denominations in the United States and within the denominations themselves. Orthodoxy was split into a left, a centrist, and an increasingly assertive right wing, the latter wanting to withdraw from having any relations at all with non-Orthodox rabbis or organizations.[68] Divisions were widened in 1983 when the Reform movement, in a radical break with Jewish tradition, affirmed that they would accept the child of a Jewish father and a non-Jewish mother as a Jew, as long as the child publicly identified with Judaism. Previously in all three major denominations only the child of a Jewish mother had been accepted as Jewish. Reform establishment of patrilineal descent, as the principle was called, raised fears of a religious schism among Jews. The modern Orthodox Rabbi Irving Greenberg of CLAL—the National Jewish Center for Learning and Leadership, a group that sought cooperation between the different denominations—held a conference in 1986 and then published the famous article "Will There Be One Jewish People in the Year 2000?" Greenberg predicted, "Within decades, the Jewish people will split apart into two mutually divided, hostile groups who are unable or unwilling to marry each other."[69]

Rabbi Harold Schulweis in *Moment* magazine answered that the split might not take that long in his article "Jewish Apartheid: Terrifying Examples of Intra-Jewish Separatism." "Given the mounting polarization in the Jewish community, do we not already stand on the brink of cataclysm?" he wrote. "We have passed beyond the stage of stereotypic caricaturing, beyond the depiction of Orthodox Judaism as crazy, Reform as lazy and Conservative as hazy. The old stereotypes have been replaced by fragmentation that tears at our identity, at the continuity and character of Judaism. Today the deepest threat to Jewish living does not come from without . . . evidence of schism comes from small and large incidents." In one example Schulweis recalled the case of Bailey Smith, president of the Southern Baptist Conference, who had declared in 1980 that "God Almighty does not hear the prayers of a Jew." Jews, he wrote, had called Bailey a bigot and and antisemite and had forced him to apologize. A few months later the chief rabbis of Jerusalem announced that those who prayed in Conservative synagogues would not be fulfilling the mitzvah of hearing the shofar. "Bailey Smith knows that God does not hear the prayers of Jews," Schulweis wrote. "Jewish Orthodox authorities know that God does not hear the sounds of the shofar when it is blown in the wrong place."[70]

In 1985 AJC established the National Jewish Religious Dialogue, a committee consisting of the most prominent leaders of the major movements (with Alfred H. Moses as chair) that met periodically to keep the lines of communication open and to find areas of common concern. The National Jewish Religious Dialogue program was duplicated on the chapter level as AJC chapters located Reform, Conservative, and Orthodox leaders in their communities and formed similar committees.[71] A central goal of these committees was to keep the ties between different Jewish groups in the United States and between Jews in the United States and Israel from rupturing. In 1999 AJC reconvened a national committee of leaders from the major denominations; once again, the issue of "Who is a Jew?" had come up in the Israeli Knesset and the monopoly of the Orthodox Chief Rabbinate in Israel on religious affairs was more resented by the non-Orthodox movements than ever.

The Pollard Affair

American Jews had another reason to be angry with the Jewish homeland when news broke on November 22, 1985, that Jonathan Jay Pollard, an American Jewish man who worked as an intelligence analyst for the U.S. Navy, had been arrested selling classified information to Israel. Knowing that government agents were on his trail, he had been at the gates of the Israeli embassy in Washington when he was caught, hoping to find asylum. Pollard's claim was that he had come across information on Syrian and Iraqi missiles and nonconventional weapons that the United States should have shared with Israel but did not. An American Jewish spy for Israel was a fulfillment of the worst possible nightmare for anyone who feared that non-Jews would interpret American Jews' deep involvement with Israel as a case of dual loyalty. Putting that charge to rest had been the whole point of the joint statement Jacob Blaustein had negotiated with Israeli Prime Minister David Ben-Gurion in 1950. AJC's executive vice president at the time, David Gordis, recalled in commenting on the case that Harry Golden had once been asked what he would do if Israel went to war with the United States. After hemming and hawing, he finally declared that he would commit suicide. Harry Golden was a famed Jewish humorist, but there was nothing funny, Gordis wrote, about the discomfort American Jews felt in the Pollard case in which an American Jew was caught spying for Israel.[72] They wondered how the Israelis could have done this to them. One poll taken after Pollard's sentencing indicated that 54 percent of American Jews surveyed feared a rise in antisemitism as a result of the affair — although the same poll showed that the overwhelming majority of Americans did not even know who Pollard was.[73]

The first reaction of AJC as well as of NJCRAC and the CJF, who all met in emergency session on December 5, was to stay quiet. They would not volunteer statements or comment on the matter. If pressed, everyone in AJC had been supplied with "talking points" with which to answer. These were, as had happened, that Israel (a full ten days after the arrest) had publicly apologized, saying that this was a "rogue" operation, that it would never happen again, and that there would be a thorough investigation and anyone found guilty would be brought to justice. George Shultz had accepted the apology and Israel's pledge of an investigation. "Because of the compartmentalization of Israeli intelligence apparatus," read the talking points, "it is conceivable that Pollard's Israeli contacts acted independently and without the knowledge of their superiors."[74]

The Israelis did their best to minimize the incident, saying that Pollard had only supplied intelligence material on Arab military matters and that in contrast to other American spies he had not handed over any information that could be considered harmful to the United States. Israel-U.S. relations seemed to be as strong as ever; only a couple of weeks earlier President Reagan had officially designated Israel a major non-NATO ally of the United States. This declaration came despite the impending sentencing of Pollard, despite a State Department report on Israeli arms sales to South Africa, and despite revelations concerning Israel's role in the Iran-Contra affair, also known as Irangate.[75] The latter was a major scandal of Reagan's second term. Members of his administration, in an attempt to obtain Iran's favor so that it would intervene to free American hostages, were selling arms to Iran illegally and using the money to fund the Contras, a guerilla organization in Nicaragua that was seeking the overthrow of the Marxist leader. Israel had complied with requests to help send the arms to Iran, although Israeli officials denied transferring any funds to the Nicaraguan Contras.

Matters in the Pollard affair became more complicated when Pollard pleaded guilty to having sold classified information to Israel and, as part of a plea bargaining arrangement, began providing his interrogators with his knowledge and involvement in Israeli espionage activities in every detail. Pollard implicated four Israelis in the case and the Department of Justice named them as co-conspirators. Two of them who were in the United States at the time quickly left the country and there was greater anger among the AJC when the Israeli government, instead of dismissing these men from their posts, gave them promotions. Pollard also described a far more extensive Israeli intelligence operation in the United States, reaching up much higher in the Israeli government than had previously been suspected. There were also accusations that the Israelis had been less than forthcoming with the U.S. officials investigating the case.

On March 4, 1987, Pollard was sentenced to life in prison, a far more severe sentence than his supporters had expected and an apparent violation of his plea bargain. His wife, Anne Henderson Pollard, was sentenced to five years as an accomplice. Pollard, after all, had given information to an American ally, not to an enemy like the Soviet Union. Spies for the Soviet Union had in fact received lighter sentences. The unusually harsh sentence was based in part on intervention by Secretary of Defense Caspar Weinberger, who had written a classified affidavit to the judge claiming that Pollard had done irreparable harm to American intelligence interests and deserved to spend the rest of his life in jail. The director of AJC's Israel office was of the opinion that Weinberger had "seriously over-exaggerated" the significance of Pollard's espionage and noted that a "senior figure" in the Israeli prime minister's office believed that Weinberger was a "genetic antisemite" due to his part-Jewish background[76] (Weinberger's paternal grandfather was Jewish, although he himself had been raised Episcopalian.)

At first, American Jewish organizations were "virtually unanimous in condemning the Pollards and praising their conviction." This consensus at the time was expressed by Morris Abram, AJC honorary president and chairman of the Conference of Presidents, who declared: "Pollard pleaded guilty in an American court to a serious crime. He received due process and a just punishment."[77] In reaction to the sentencing and the resulting press coverage, AJC executive vice president David Gordis and many other heads of Jewish organizations rushed to condemn Israeli policies in print and to explain—and excuse—to their fellow Americans the precise nature of their relationship to the Jewish state. In one article, although Gordis stressed the "deep religious and emotional ties Jews feel for the land of their ancestors," he spoke more about the roots of American Jewish insecurity in the Holocaust and in Jewish history and why American Jews were dedicated to preserving Israel as a refuge for themselves. "During World War II, the doors of the nations of the world were locked to Jews seeking to escape from Hitler's murderous onslaught," he recalled. "Mixed in with this too is a deep feeling of guilt that by an accident of fate they [American Jews] did not perish as well and did not do more to help those who did. . . . The fortunes of Jews have gone up and down throughout history. Whether they prospered for several centuries before being expelled from Spain in 1492, felt integrated in the Germany of Heine and Beethoven before the 1930s, only to find the death camps waiting, or found safety, security and success in this country, there is always the gnawing fear that the situation can change virtually overnight."[78]

In another article, Gordis wrote, "Illogical though it may seem, Jews who escaped the Holocaust, and particularly American Jews, still harbor guilt over their failure to prevent that disaster. They perceive Israel as the principal guarantor that the Jewish people will survive. Even in America, Jews, conditioned by a two thousand year history of victimization, feel vulnerable. This may be unjustified by objective measures: all indicators show a steeply declining curve of antisemitic incidents and attitudes. Yet in poll after poll, despite their extraordinary success and achievement, Jews continue to express anxiety over current and anticipated acts or expressions of hatred against them. Even Jews who have no intention of living in Israel, who in fact have never set foot in Israel, perceive Israel as an insurance policy." But despite all their ardor for Israel, he continued, their most "enduring love affair" was with the United States, and their loyalty "to our own beloved country" was not compromised. "Almost always we see our two loves, America and Israel, in harmony with one another; it is inconceivable to us that the United States and Israel could be incompatible in any substantive way," he declared. Because of their loyalty to America, Jews were not prepared "to countenance any behavior that is incompatible with America's safety and security." Israelis might be disappointed that American Jews did not elect to join them in building the Jewish state, but that did not give them the right to indulge in behavior that "undermines the loyalty of American Jews to their own country, challenges American Jewish patriotism, and outrages and embarrasses American Jews." The Pollard affair, he concluded, was possible only because "Israel either failed to understand or chose to ignore the bonds between American Jews and America. It is essential that Israel now learn that lesson."[79]

In addition to writing such articles, AJC staff also flew to Israel, as did a reported sixty-five officers of American Jewish organizations, to impress upon the Israelis in private conferences, newspapers, and radio and television broadcasts how serious the spying was, how much it had jeopardized Israel-U.S. relations, and how it could affect the status of U.S. Jews in their country. They insisted the Israelis set up their own investigation into the matter.[80] George Gruen even wrote an article for the *Jerusalem Post* called "Back to Basic Principles" in which he quoted the Blaustein–Ben-Gurion joint statement of 1950 at length and described how he had received Prime Minister Yitzhak Shamir's assurances that it still held. Such conversations inevitably included expressions of Israeli resentment about why American Jews did not come to live in Israel, something Blaustein had stressed was a matter of "free choice."[81] Columnist Charles Krauthammer of the *Washington Post*, in observing these actions, wrote that while American Jewish leaders were acting properly in warning Israelis of the danger the Pollard affair represented to them, their rush to Israel "bears the sign of more than just an informational visit. There is about it an air of defensiveness bordering on panic." He cited in his column the comment by Senator Daniel Inouye (Democrat, from Hawaii) who had said, "To suggest that the act of one Jew should be borne by all Jews is an insult."[82]

Shlomo Avineri, a professor of political science at Hebrew University, was in agreement with Krauthammer, and uncharacteristically lashed out at American Jewry in a piece called "Open Letter to an American Jewish Friend," which was published in the English-language *Jerusalem Post*. In it, he accused American Jews of panicking and running over the Pollard case and thus revealing that despite their protestations they really were living in *galut,* or

Exile, in the United States. He quoted one Jewish leader who said that not since the Rosenberg case had American Jews been "so badly compromised." Avineri noted "a degree of nervousness, insecurity and even cringing on the part of the American Jewish community which runs counter to the conventional wisdom of American Jewry feeling free, secure and unmolested in an open and pluralistic society." He continued in anger:

How many times have American leaders told me that America is not another Exile, that you do not live in Galut, that you can aspire to the highest office in the land, that you are not a minority but constitute an integral ingredient of the multi-ethnic and multi-religious tapestry that makes the American matrix such a unique historical experience for Jews? And what do we see now? A person who happens to be Jewish is caught spying for Israel. You would expect that in a free and open society no guilt by association should be presumed and that nobody except Pollard himself should be held responsible for his deed. Instead we see some senior American Jewish leaders falling over each other and condemning Pollard and distancing themselves and the Jewish community from him. . . . You somehow feel deep in your heart that despite all of your material success and intellectual achievements you may not be seen by non-Jews as being truly Americans. . . . When the going is good—when being Jewish and supporting Israel go together with waving the American flag—who would be as stupid as not to wish to have the best of both worlds? But when the going gets tough, then the test arrives of being accepted, of really being equal, of really being proud and not having to look over your shoulder. . . . You are condemned by your own protestations of loyalty and flag waving. . . . One Jewish spy—and look how deep you find yourself in Galut. . . . The truth of the matter is simple: you and America are no different from French, German, Polish, Soviet and Egyptian Jews. Your Exile is different—comfortable, padded with success and renown. It is Exile nonetheless. The test of really belonging and real equality is when the going is tough. And when the going got tough your leaders reacted like trembling Israelites in the Shtetl, not like the proud and mighty citizens of a free democratic society. You too have to be emancipated from Galut and alienation and for all its achievements and promise America, it now evidently appears, may not be your Promised Land.

The Avineri piece, which questioned the fundamental relationship of American Jews to the United States, set off a long-lasting debate in the midst of all the other discussions on the Pollard affair. Hyman Bookbinder of AJC called the charges "unworthy," "absurd" and "a bum rap," adding, "I deeply resent them." Abraham H. Foxman of the ADL accused Avineri of a "cheap shot" unworthy of his talents and claimed that for someone who had spent so much time in the United States to misread American Jewry so badly was "astonishing."[83] The most extreme reply came from Brown University scholar Jacob Neusner, who answered in the *Washington Post* that not only was America not Exile, it was actually a better place to live than Israel. "It is time to say that America is a better place to be a Jew than Jerusalem," Neusner wrote. In politics, economic achievement, culture, and learning, in his view, American Jews had outdone their Israeli counterparts. "If there ever was a Promised Land," he concluded, "we Jewish Americans are living in it."[84]

Theodore Ellenoff, president of AJC at the time, noted in evaluating the overall impact of the Pollard affair that this was the first time that the entire

American Jewish community openly criticized Israeli actions; he said that this was indicative of "a shift in the Israel-U.S. relationship."[85] Mimi Alperin also commented on the increased willingness of American Jews to criticize Israel publicly. In agreeing that the relationship between the two Jewish communities had changed, she referred not only to the Pollard affair but to internal Israeli politics, the frustration that American Jews felt about working with a government of national unity that some called a "government of national paralysis"—and also to the impression in 1987 that Israel was a strong nation no longer fighting for its survival. "From the war in Lebanon to more recent issues—ranging from Israel's relations with South Africa, to its policy toward Soviet emigration, to its recent attempts to define who is a Jew, to the structure and priorities of the Jewish agency—American Jewry is becoming more assertive in expressing its point of view," she wrote. "While this new assertiveness may make some Israelis nervous, they ought to understand that the days of unquestioning adulation are over. Certainly, external threats to Israel's survival are no longer serious enough to command the kind of emotional outpouring from American Jewry that Israel grew to expect during her long and difficult struggle for existence. Many American Jews who care deeply about Israel's future are very concerned about the way in which Israel handles its internal conflicts—between Israelis, Arabs, and Jews, between secular religious Jews, between Sephardim and Ashkenazim, between doves and hawks—and especially they are concerned that Israel have a government that can govern. American Jewry has long been the forefront of efforts to perfect American democracy. We've now begun to remove the rose-colored glasses, to roll up our sleeves and, for better or worse, to pitch in to help Israel strengthen her democratic ideals."[86]

For several years after Pollard's sentencing AJC policy was to say nothing more about the affair. As the years passed, however, campaigns on Pollard's behalf by his family and by Jewish groups grew amid allegations of discrimination, civil rights abuses, and antisemitism with regard to his sentence to life in prison, where he was living in solitary confinement.[87] The end of the cold war and the collapse of the Soviet Union also had an impact. "David, isn't it about time that the AJC take the lead and join with Robertson and Wiesel and stop worrying about being 'a shonda far di goyim?'" wrote one AJC member to AJC's Executive Vice President David Harris, using the Yiddish expression for "a shame in front of the Gentiles." "Why do Christians feel this way and we can't get our great Jewish organizations to get their collective heads out of the sand and help a fellow Jew who has given his last six years as no other American Jew has done recently—I feel this is an important issue for the Committee since now it is safe to come out of the closet."[88]

Eventually after presentations by Pollard's attorneys and supporters, the AJC board of governors voted to ask the president of the United States to review the record in the Jonathan Pollard espionage case to see if the imposed sentence of life imprisonment was appropriate and if not, to reduce it. In a letter to President Clinton dated March 23, 1993, AJC President Alfred H. Moses pointed out that the cold war was over and there was no longer any chance of Pollard passing on dangerous information to the Soviets. Furthermore, he deserved a review of whether his sentence of life imprisonment was disproportionate to the crime, which had been turning over information to Israel, a country that was friendly to the United States.[89] President Clinton took no action. Subsequent AJC letters to subsequent presidents brought no results. In 2006, Jonathan Pollard was still sitting in prison.

Scandal on Wall Street

Simultaneously with the Pollard affair in 1986 American Jews were living with the unraveling details of the Iran-Contra affair and the revelations in November that Ivan Boesky, one of the richest men on Wall Street, had been arrested for insider trading and forced to pay a $100 million fine. Boesky's picture appeared on the cover of *Time* on December 1, 1986, with the headline: "Wall Street Scam: Making Millions with Your Money: Investor 'Ivan the Terrible' Boesky." In the course of the investigation several other Jewish names surfaced, such as Michael Milken, Dennis Levine, and Martin Siegel.[90] Boesky had been a philanthropist active in Jewish communal affairs and had been the campaign chair of the New York–UJA Federation from 1984 until 1986. He had been an especially generous benefactor to the Jewish Theological Seminary. As the scandal broke, students at the seminary rushed to have their pictures taken in front of the sign that said "Ivan F. and Seema Boesky Family Library" before it was removed.[91] JTS Chancellor Ismar Schorsch called together the entire student body for a special assembly to announce the steps being taken to dissociate from Boesky. He also announced that security precautions were being strengthened and warned that antisemitic action might be taken against the building. The New York chapter of AJC announced that it was going to hold a public conference on business ethics and the Jewish tradition.

Of the Iran-Contra affair George Gruen wrote to Hyman Bookbinder, in a confidential memo: "We need to monitor to what extent this, added to the Boesky and New York City corruption cases, is likely to feed antisemitic feelings that the Israelis and Jews are in general devious, preoccupied with profit, and insensitive to morality. There is also the insinuation that somehow Israel dictates U.S. policy."[92] David Gordis, in a memo to regional and area AJC directors, described the steps that the agency was taking and recommended what action chapters should pursue. "The Iran crisis continues to dominate the news, causing great concern among Americans in general and the Jewish community in particular," he wrote. "While not all the facts are yet known about Israel's involvement in either arms sales to Iran or arms transfers to the

Contras, several allegations, largely unsubstantiated, are now circulating which have the potential for harming the interests of both Israel and the Jews in the U.S. . . . In addition this crisis raises special concerns for the Jewish community; the temptation in some cases already realized, to scapegoat Israel; possible negative effects on the long-term Israel-U.S. relationship; and negative perceptions by Americans of Jews as manipulators or arms dealers, particularly as Iran shares the headlines with the Boesky affair."[93]

Freedom of Choice: The "Noshrim" Debate

Relations between Israel and the U.S. government survived the Pollard affair and the Iran-Contra affair. Nevertheless, American Jews found themselves divided from Israel in yet another issue of the 1980s: whether Soviet Jews leaving the U.S.S.R. with Israeli visas should go straight to Israel, as the Israelis desperately wanted them to, or whether they should have the right to "drop out" on the way and decide to go to the United States instead, where they would be funded and helped on their way by American relief agencies.[94] Under U.S. law, Soviet Jews were automatically counted as "refugees" and allowed in, and American Jewish organizations did whatever they could to pressure their government to keep the doors open to them. The Israelis, on their part, did everything possible to make sure the immigrants would come to Israel. The movement to free Soviet Jewry had been Zionist-inspired and Soviet Jews were being given Israeli visas ostensibly to be reunited with their brethren in their own homeland. The Israelis referred to the drop-out phenomenon as *neshira* and to the drop-outs as *noshrim:* they expressed concern that the entire emigration movement would be jeopardized if the Soviets saw Jews deserting Israel for the fleshpots of Western capitalism.

There were no diplomatic relations or direct flights between the Soviet Union and Israel, so Jews at first had to leave via a way station in Vienna. In 1976 as it became apparent that the majority of Soviet Jews wished to "drop out" in Vienna and go to the United States instead, AJC first took the position that "every Jew who gets out of the Soviet Union should be helped to reach his final destination." To refuse to render assistance to Jews who changed their minds about their destination after leaving Vienna would violate that principle.[95] Donald Feldstein, who was executive vice president of AJC in 1983, argued that there should be no conflict at all over the issue; the main point was to get out as many Soviet Jews as possible as soon as possible. "This pool of over two million Russians Jews is not a permanent reservoir waiting for a propitious moment to fill Israel's population needs," he wrote. "The pool is made up primarily of Jews who have very tenuous connections with their Judaism, if any, and who have the option of intermarriage and having their offspring not registered as Jews and not facing the disabilities which that registration entails. These Jews are a reservoir which is evaporating. If too many years pass, there will be very few Jews left to argue about."[96]

The argument receded for a time because in the early 1980s only a trickle of Soviet Jews was allowed to leave. The situation changed, however, with the ascent of Mikhail Gorbachev to power in 1985, who brought about the reforms of *glasnost* (openness) and *perestroika* (restructuring). Gorbachev established close relations with Ronald Reagan, who had been convinced to make freedom of emigration for Soviet Jews a condition of détente. One of the factors that convinced him was a massive demonstration on December 6, 1987, called Freedom Sunday for Soviet Jewry, which took place the day before a Reagan-Gorbachev summit meeting in the United States. The demonstration called for the right of Soviet Jews to practice their Judaism freely where they were as well as the right to leave. Coordinated by AJC's David Harris, who was on loan to the community for six weeks from his position as Washington representative, the event drew up to 250,000 people, a number that was "beyond the organizers' wildest dreams." It was the biggest demonstration in all of American Jewish history and marked the apotheosis in the United States of the movement to free Soviet Jewry. Moreover, an unpublicized arrangement was made with the Voice of America to broadcast live a running translation of the entire program into Russian for listeners in the Soviet Union.[97] The evening of the rally, the AJC held a press conference and banquet at the Sheraton Grand Hotel, where a recently released Natan Sharansky received AJC's highest award, the American Liberties Medallion.[98]

As more Soviet Jews were given leave to go, there was more conflict and negotiation over where they should go to. Eighty percent of those leaving were "dropping out" to go to the United States, and this proportion was unacceptable to the Israelis. The Israelis believed that the immigrants were "our people" traveling with "our visas" and that it was "absurd" on principle for the United States to call them refugees when there was a Jewish state ready and willing to welcome them.[99] Moreover, the Israelis badly needed the Soviet Jews to increase their Jewish population and for the education and technical expertise they would bring with them. In 1987 Israeli Prime Minister Yitzhak Shamir met with President Ronald Reagan and Secretary of State George P. Shultz in an effort to convince them to withdraw the "refugee" status of Soviet Jews and thus make it more difficult for them to enter the United States. Reagan and Shultz at first refused, in part because at that time the AJC and virtually the entire American Jewish community was united against Israel's claim. They did not believe on principle that Soviet Jews should be coerced into going where they did not want to go—nor did they want to awaken painful memories of earlier periods when fleeing Jews wanted to get into the United States but could not.[100] Israelis turned their attention to rearranging the travel and flight routes from the Soviet Union so that there would be less opportunity for the Soviet Jews to drop out. AJC agreed to cooperate in seeking ways to make Israel a more attractive choice for the immigrants.

In the end, the sheer numbers of Soviet Jews wishing to leave forced the issue. There were not enough refugee slots open in the United States to take all the immigrants nor were there enough funds to resettle them. The local Jewish federations were feeling overwhelmed with caring for and absorbing the Soviet Jewish immigrants they already had. Moreover, according to U.S. officials, conditions under Gorbachev in the Soviet Union had supposedly improved to the point that Soviet Jews were no longer in danger of their lives and no longer automatically deserved to be called "refugees"—although AJC reports of growing antisemitism there belied that claim. AJC delegations met with the State Department and congressional committees, urging that more places be set aside for Soviet Jews. This position over time grew more difficult because there were refugee groups other than the Soviets who needed to come to the United States (such as Cambodians and Haitians), who did not have an alternative such as Israel to go to.

In 1989 after complex negotiations with Jewish leaders the Bush administration implemented a plan to limit the number of Soviet Jews allowed into the United States to those with first-degree relatives already there, which worked out to about forty thousand a year. Yet hundreds of thousands more needed and wanted to leave. There was fear that conditions in the Soviet Union could change at any moment and the doors would be closed, or that the remaining Jews would be subject to increasingly virulent nationalist antisemitism. It was not necessary to have relatives there to go to Israel and, indeed, there was no limit at all on the numbers that the Israelis were willing to take. These financial and political realities caused a change of heart among American Jewish organizations. With the question of the *noshrim* gone and unity finally achieved, American Jews turned their energy toward raising money to help the Soviet Jews settle in Israel. When the Israeli budget and private philanthropy proved insufficient to the task, the Israelis sought, and after a prolonged political battle obtained, ten billion dollars in loan guarantees from the United States so that it could borrow the money it needed at feasible interest rates in order to meet the immigrants' needs (see chapter 11). From 1987 through 2005 close to one million Jews from the lands of the former Soviet Union immigrated to Israel.[101]

"Perestroika" at the AJC

All of these points of disunity and division took their toll on the American Jewish Committee, which was already facing problems common to all American Jewish organizations. There were well over five hundred Jewish organizations listed in the annual directory of the *American Jewish Year Book* in the

1980s and a contracting Jewish community could not support them all. Across the board, membership and fund-raising were down. Studies showed that Jewish philanthropists were giving less of their money to Jewish causes than in the past; the local symphony orchestra or museum was as likely to be the object of their largesse.[102] Changes in the tax laws in the 1980s that reduced financial incentives for philanthropy generally had their effect. In October 1987 there was a stock market crash that cost the AJC alone four million dollars on paper.[103] The realities of two-income families meant there was less time to devote to volunteer work, upon which so much of Jewish organizational life had depended.

Observers also referred to a "leadership vacuum." With the decline of antisemitism Jewish lay leaders and professionals were able to seek status and fulfillment in government and non-Jewish organizations. After a series of executive vice presidents with long tenure—John Slawson had served from 1943 to 1967 and Bertram H. Gold served from 1967 through 1982—AJC went through five executive heads in eight years. Donald Feldstein, Associate Director William S. Trosten, and David Gordis, who served from 1984 to 1987, were all asked by lay leaders not to return or were offered early retirement. The departure of David Gordis was particularly divisive within the organization since one faction of AJC lay leaders strongly wanted him to stay and another strongly wanted him to leave; the latter faction won. Bertram H. Gold was called out of retirement in 1987 to serve again as temporary executive head. The post of executive vice president in 1988 then went to Ira Silverman, who had worked for the AJC in the 1970s and had years of experience directing top Jewish communal institutions. However, he soon became incapacitated from a rare illness he had contracted during a trip to China. He had to step down in 1990 and died not long after.

Getting committed lay leaders became more of a challenge and AJC had to begin reaching out and cultivating its leadership, rather than waiting for people to come to them. One barrier was the huge investment in time and money required of AJC lay leaders. Members of the board of governors who did not live in New York spoke of spending ten to fifteen thousand dollars a year in the 1980s attending AJC meetings around the country—and as part of the reality of a nonprofit organization, they were expected to make large donations too. They had access to popes and presidents and kings but they paid handsomely for the privilege, always covering their own hotel, flight ticket, and expenses. Meetings required hours of time, a difficult prospect for someone who had a business to run or a law practice to attend to. Philip Hoffman, who served as AJC's president from 1969 to 1973, spoke of holding the office and trying to work at the same time as "holding two full-time jobs."[104] E. Robert Goodkind, president of AJC in its centennial year, spoke of the position as being "totally all consuming in terms of time and travel," albeit crucial at a time of so many "obvious threats to the Jewish people and to the State of

Israel."[105] Other former AJC presidents noted the extraordinary time commitment required. In short, it took tremendous dedication and skill to be an AJC lay leader.

In addition to staff problems, difficulties in staff-lay relations, and a shortage in leadership, the AJC was also suffering from a lack of focus and uncontrolled growth. It had long been a multi-issue organization but by the 1980s its array of interests had turned into what some members termed "the smorgasbord approach" that led to incoherence and retarded fund-raising.[106] The four program commissions—national affairs, interreligious affairs, international affairs, and Jewish communal life—had become almost independent fiefdoms, without strong central control. Partly to blame was the constant tension between universalism and particularism, between programs that aided Jews specifically and those such as social welfare that were supposed to help humanity in general. One reason the tension was never truly solved was the multi-issue, multicommission character of AJC; under such a large umbrella, members interested in particular Jewish concerns could find their home in the Jewish Communal Affairs Department, and those with less "parochial" interests filled the ranks of national, interreligious and the international human rights divisions. Milton Himmelfarb, AJC's most faithful internal critic (he edited the *Year Book* but did almost all of his writing for *Commentary*) discussed the matter in 1981, during AJC's seventy-fifth anniversary:

We will continue to suffer the necessary tension of duality. We have a Jewish agenda and a general agenda. Departments will fight over who gets more money. There will be a continuing kind of balancing or attempt to balance and the seesaw will never quite come to rest. That's in the nature of the AJC. It's American and it's Jewish and that causes creative tension. My own bias of course is on the Jewish side of things, if only on the "bigger bank for the buck" theory. With limited resources, you have some hope of affecting what goes on among Jews but much less hope of having any. . . . You know, what are we, megalomaniacs? We're going to turn America around?[107]

In 1985 AJC was buckling under the strain of trying to do everything. The treasurer announced that expenses were rising and the budget was going up by one million dollars each year. Everybody agreed that drastic cuts needed to be made, but at first there was no agreement on the agency's priorities and no clear view of what to cut and what to keep. By 1988 membership had declined to 16,000 paid units or 22,000 people.[108] The crisis came in 1989 when AJC was forced to borrow four million dollars to stay afloat, using the New York headquarters as collateral. The suggestion was raised to sell the headquarters altogether and move the entire AJC operation to Washington, D.C., but the board quickly decided against it.

A turning point for the organization came at a board of governors meeting in February 1990 at a seaside hotel in St. Petersburg Beach, Florida. Observers in the Anglo-Jewish press called it the *perestroika* of the AJC, or "restructuring," after Mikhail Gorbachev's efforts in the Soviet Union.[109] The new president was Sholom D. Comay, a graduate of Brandeis University, descended from a scholarly Jewish family whose father, Amos Comay, had been president of the National Foundation for Jewish Culture. A businessman from Pittsburgh, Comay had served as chair of the National Affairs Commission and as AJC's national treasurer, so he was well aware of the financial restructuring that needed to be done. As the meeting opened it was announced that Ira Silverman had been hospitalized and the new acting executive head was Israeli-born Shulamith Bahat, who had joined the AJC staff in 1979. She had degrees from both the Hebrew University in Jerusalem and the Technion in Haifa and had done two years of post-graduate studies at the University of Pennsylvania. Her career also included five years as a captain in the Israeli Defense Forces.

The solution to AJC's situation, Comay announced, was not just "haphazard cuts to balance an income figure." It was a reexamination of AJC's very reason for being. "By now, no one, not even the Jewish community nor we ourselves, can explain exactly what AJC does," he declared. "It has become imperative that we prune the agency to the point where we will be able to describe what we are and what we do. Unless we do the job now, we will be facing the same situation again in five years. . . . Our immediate task this weekend is to prioritize our activities and eliminate all but the essential areas of our work where we can make a difference and assume a leadership role in the effort. . . . We must carve out a role for AJC that is not duplicated by any other organization, remaining only in the areas where we are most skilled."[110] Streamlining the organization in this way, he insisted, would not only solve the immediate financial crisis but would also make future fund-raising easier. The leaders decided that AJC would concentrate in three areas only: "ensuring the security of Jews throughout the world, safeguarding and nurturing pluralism, and enriching the quality of American Jewish life."

Entire programs and departments were cut from the budget. The International Affairs program in New York was closed and moved to Washington, D.C. Some weeks earlier AJC's two magazines, *Commentary* and *Present Tense*, were told they had to become financially self-supporting. *Commentary*, which was part of a national advertising network with eight other journals including the *New Republic*, the *National Review,* and the *New York Review of Books,* and which had a nationally known editor, Norman Podhoretz, was able to obtain enough subsidies to continue publication. *Present Tense* did not, so it was discontinued. By far the most painful part of the restructuring fell upon the sixty AJC staff members (out of a total of 275) who lost their jobs. Some of them had spent all or most of their careers at AJC.[111]

The final part of AJC's restructuring was to find a new executive director. In September 1990 the job went to David A. Harris, the first in the Committee's history to be appointed from the ranks of the staff. Harris had grown up in New York, was the child of European parents, and was multi-lingual from having lived many years abroad. He attended the University of Pennsylvania and did graduate work at the London School of Economics. For many years he had worked as a professional in the Soviet Jewry movement and had been responsible for coordinating the Freedom Sunday demonstration in 1987 that brought almost a quarter of a million people to Washington, D.C. He served first as AJC's deputy director of international relations and later as Washington representative. The board of governors approved his choice by acclamation. Sholom D. Comay described Harris as "precisely the right person to lead a strengthened AJC in the years ahead."[112]

Sadly, AJC President Sholom D. Comay did not live long enough to see the fruits of his work. After two brief years in office he died of a heart attack on May 18, 1991, at the age of fifty-three. The entire organization mourned his passing but continued on the path that he had set. Others leaders would take AJC to a resurgence in the 1990s, after one of its most difficult decades.

"The Global Jewish Committee"

AJC at the Turn of the Twenty-First Century

Efforts to keep AJC afloat were successful and the organization very quickly bounced back in the 1990s to enjoy a renaissance. The agency was well able to meet new challenges. Under the leadership of Executive Director David Harris and Associate Executive Director Shula Bahat, AJC transcended the "American" part of its name and became a global non-governmental organization, with offices and alliances and formal partnerships in every corner of the world. The "Jewish" part was strengthened as well. AJC moved ever closer to the communal mainstream when it very nearly merged with the American Jewish Congress. It also gave up some of its cherished autonomy and independence when it moved from being merely an observer to being a full member of the Conference of Presidents of Major American Jewish Organizations. The Jewish communal affairs division achieved new prominence as it expanded its role from think-tank to becoming a force for communal advocacy. Its thirty years' experience stood it in good stead after the revelations of the National Jewish Population Survey of 1990 persuaded almost everyone within organized communal life to put Jewish continuity and identity at the top of the agenda. The Jewish Communal Affairs Department, renamed the Contemporary Jewish Life Department in 2000, was now a leader in what was becoming a very crowded field. As for its financial health, AJC was very soon operating on a surplus, attracting major gifts from donors, and operating from a completely refurbished New York headquarters. By 1997 for the first time it made the list of the top twenty-five philanthropies in the country.

The decade in which these transformations took place began with high hopes. For the first time Israelis and Yasir Arafat's Palestine Liberation

Organization engaged in direct talks, beginning with secret meetings in Oslo, Norway; in 1993 the two parties signed an agreement that made it appear for a time that there would finally be peace in the Middle East. Communism had fallen and, despite concerns about old national, ethnic, and religious conflicts that were rematerializing, a new world order appeared to be emerging. In numerous newly liberated countries there was movement away from totalitarianism and toward more democratic forms of government. AJC now had access to millions of Jews that had once been out of reach. After nearly two decades of activism the Jews of the Soviet Union were free to go. The mighty superpower itself was about to dissolve into fifteen of its component republics. The decades of work by AJC, the ADL, the American Jewish Congress, and other Jewish organizations and their non-Jewish allies in fighting against anti-Jewish discrimination appeared to be vindicated when an observant Jewish man came within a hairsbreadth of becoming vice president of the United States, a stepping-stone to the highest office in the land.

Then, at precisely the turn of the Gregorian millennium (a date that Jewish scholars—to little avail—insisted had no significance whatsoever in the Jewish calendar) the Israeli-Palestinian peace talks collapsed. A second "intifada" broke out, marked by increased terrorism and suicide bombings. In fact, terrorism and suicide bombings by such PLO rivals as Hamas and the Islamic Jihad had never stopped during the seven years of what came to be known as the "Oslo peace process." On September 11, 2001, Islamic terrorism and suicide bombing jumped the ocean when fourteen extremists, followers of Osama Bin Laden, successfully hijacked three planes and drove two of them into the Twin Towers at the World Trade Center in New York and one into the Pentagon building in Washington, D.C. (A fourth plane was hijacked, but deliberately crashed by its passengers before it could reach its target.) In the aftermath, Muslims and many in the West were blaming Jews and Israel for everything from the September 11 attacks to fomenting the subsequent U.S. war in Iraq that drove Saddam Hussein from power in 2003. In 2006 Iran, a chief state sponsor of terrorism in general (and, more specifically, of Hezbollah in southern Lebanon) was on its way to developing nuclear weapons and missiles to deliver them, and its president, Mahmud Ahmadinejad, had stated publicly that Israel should be wiped off the map. By its centennial year AJC was well into the new Age of Terrorism and found itself confronting a worldwide wave of antisemitism abroad, the likes of which had not been seen since the Second World War. And while surveys showed that levels of organized antisemitism in the United States had never been lower and American Jews ought to feel secure, AJC and the American Jewish community found itself facing new and intensified forms of antisemitism at home from African Americans.

Internal Growth

AJC during the 1990s very quickly regained its financial health. Only a year after the St. Petersburg meeting, the financial officers reported that they were breaking even and had a small surplus. By June 1992 AJC had paid back every penny of its $4 million bank loan, two years ahead of schedule. When in 1994 the treasurer sought a new line of credit, several banks competed to get the account—and this time the one who got it did not require the headquarters and its contents as collateral. In 1997 the American Institute for Philanthropy, which released an annual ranking based on how much of each dollar went for charitable purposes and how much it cost the agency to raise one hundred dollars, showed the American Jewish Committee among the top twenty-five philanthropies in the country, along with Memorial Sloan-Kettering Cancer Center, the Girl Scouts of the U.S.A., the Salvation Army, the Boy Scouts of America, and the American Heart Association.

Sholom D. Comay's prediction that streamlining the organization would also make fund-raising easier proved true. Major gifts the AJC attracted in the 1990s included two million dollars from Jacob Blaustein's descendants to renovate the headquarters. It was now renamed the Jacob Blaustein Building and the name "Institute of Human Relations" faded away; one of the more notable renovations was a large mezuzah affixed to the building's front entrance. There were also one million dollars from the family of Alfred E. Moses (AJC president 1991–1995) to build a new headquarters in the heart of Jerusalem, another half million from the Moses family to fund Jewish continuity programs, three million dollars from Harriett and Robert Heilbrunn to endow a humanitarian fund and AJC's international interreligious program, one million dollars from Dorothy and Julius Koppelman to endow the Institute for American Jewish–Israeli Relations, a half-million dollar grant from filmmaker Steven Spielberg to support a Catholic-Jewish education program, a half-million dollars from the family of Robert Belfer to name AJC's center for American pluralism, and several other six-figure gifts. Reflecting the growing importance of Latinos as the fastest-growing minority group in the United States, AJC also received one million dollars from Marilyn and Richard H. Davimos to form an Institute of Jewish-Latino Relations in 2001. In this work it was aided by Jacobo Kovladoff, former head of AJC's Buenos Aires office, who had escaped with his life from Argentina in 1978 and had built up a successful Spanish-language press, publications, and radio program at the New York headquarters.

As it had under Bert Gold, AJC moved closer to the Jewish mainstream when in 1992 it began to engage in serious merger talks with the American Jewish Congress. Outsiders had been complaining that there were too many Jewish organizations to support operating along similar lines since the ill-fated MacIver Report of 1951, and there had always been pressure for the AJC, the American Jewish Congress, and the Anti-Defamation League to join forces and budgets.[1] Serious merger talks in the two years following the Yom Kippur War between the Committee and the Congress had fallen apart, when the two organizations still had very different ideologies and styles. By 1993, as Robert Rifkind noted, "past ideological differences have faded or are minor"; Shula Bahat pointed out that both organizations had gone through "tremendous changes" since the 1970s.[2] This time merger talks came much closer to going through, although enough organizational and political differences remained for them to be broken off at the last moment.[3]

For years, another symbol of AJC's organizational independence and aloofness from the rest of the Jewish world was its reluctance to join the Conference of Presidents of Major Jewish Organizations, a body set up in 1954 at the request of the U.S. administration, which needed one address for the multiplicity of Jewish organizations in matters relating to Israel. While the AJC did maintain observer status in the conference, the attitude from the John Slawson days persisted among some leaders: that outright membership might dilute its distinctiveness, hamper its independence and violate the philosophy that no one organization should speak for all of American Jewry. "It is time we assert our leadership role and change our status from observer to full member," declared Alfred Moses to the AJC board of governors in March 1991, speaking of the need for a united Jewry to stand behind Israel's security. "Our continued refusal to become a full member is inappropriate and does not reflect well on our stature in the Jewish community."[4] The board unanimously voted to join the conference.

The Gulf War, the Zionism is Racism Resolution, Loan Guarantees, and Oslo

AJC's full membership in the conference was in part motivated by a desire to portray American Jewry as a united front in the aftermath of the first Gulf War with Iraq (1990–91, officially known as Operation Desert Storm). The goal was partly to counteract strong pressure that was being brought to bear on Israel to take chances with her security during peace talks. The war itself was one of the first crises that the Sholom Comay–David Harris administration had to face after AJC's budget-slashing. The forces of Saddam Hussein, Iraq's dictator, invaded and annexed neighboring Kuwait in August 1990. Hussein refused to respond to a U.N. Security Council resolution giving him until January 15 to withdraw. He portrayed himself as the liberator of Palestine in the region and said that he would not withdraw from Kuwait until Israel withdrew to its pre-June 1967 borders. He also threatened to turn his chemical and biological weapons on Israel if the United States reacted with force against him.

The administration of George H. W. Bush pledged in September to defend Israel in case of Iraqi attack, but set the condition that Israel not react on her own. True to Hussein's word, when the armed forces of the United States and a coalition of forces attacked Iraq after the January 15 deadline had passed, the Iraqi leader sent wave after wave of Scud missiles to Israel, an estimated forty in all, damaging buildings and causing civilian casualties. None of them as it turned out had chemical or biological warheads, although the Israelis had no way of knowing that this would be the case. Throughout the entire war, which ended in February (symbolically, on the holiday of Purim), the Israelis absorbed the attacks and kept their promise to the United States, letting American Patriot anti-aircraft missiles attempt to defend them. To keep still went against every Israeli instinct and principle of defense, and they very nearly broke that promise after the first missile attacks evaded the Patriots and landed on Israeli soil. *Newsweek* revealed after the war that when the first missiles fell, Israel's minister of defense notified Washington that twelve Israeli planes had been sent to bomb targets in Iraq and demanded the special codes that would allow them to avoid being attacked as enemy aircraft. The Americans refused, and the planes were recalled to Israel.[5]

In December 1990, when the threat of war hung over Israel and tourism had virtually ceased, 125 AJC leaders spent a week in Israel to show their solidarity with the country, in a trip they called Operation Undaunted. Immediately after the war broke out and the first Scud missiles were falling, Sholom Comay, Alfred Moses, and David Harris got on a plane to Israel. When they arrived at the airport they noticed that despite the war, planeloads of new Soviet and Ethiopian immigrants were still arriving. Within an hour after the three AJC leaders registered at their hotel, the sirens went off signaling another possible missile attack. As David Harris later described it, the hotel residents all made their way up to the ninth floor and were told: ten people to a room, close the door, seal the edges with tape, place a wet towel along the bottom, put on a gas mask and filter, make sure it fits snugly, turn on the radio for further instructions — and remain calm. That night a missile hit near Tel Aviv and killed three people. The next day the sirens went off again. This time they shared a sealed room with eight Soviet Jews, four of them veterans of the first immigration wave of the early 1970s and four who had arrived in Israel just two days earlier. "God did not bring the Jews back to their homeland after two thousand years to see them destroyed," said one newcomer. "I am not afraid."[6] On the final day of their trip, the three men visited the sites of the attacks.

The recent fall of communism and the alliances the United States had formed with coalition forces during the Gulf War were conducive to a goal the AJC had sought since 1975: repeal of the U.N. resolution equating Zionism with racism and racial discrimination. In 1990 the Israelis had not even made up their minds whether it was worthwhile to actively pursue the reversal of what Daniel Patrick Moynihan, U.S. ambassador to the U.N. in 1975, called "this obscene resolution." Some argued that such an effort would be counter-productive as the votes were not there and the effort would fail. Others argued that they should "let the resolution collect dust" and not reawaken "needless additional controversies."[7] Then Vice President Dan Quayle, signaling the Bush administration's support on the issue, made a speech at Yeshiva University which included a call to repeal the resolution, and the speech brought major public attention. Sholom Comay immediately reacted with a letter to Quayle praising him and followed up with a letter about the speech to the Soviet ambassador. The Soviet Union, onetime military patron of the Arab nations and with a bloc of Eastern European countries behind it, had been one of the chief sponsors of the original resolution—but now, perhaps, things might be different.

AJC leaders decided to contribute to the campaign for repeal by pursuing the issue in a series of high-level meetings in Washington, D.C., that they had scheduled. They managed to reaffirm their praise in a meeting with the vice president himself, and asked if he and other senior members of the administration would actively pursue the issue. They did; resolutions were introduced in both houses of Congress calling upon the United States to repeal the Zionism is Racism resolution. At the next board meeting AJC officers pledged to make repeal a top priority and to use all diplomatic channels and congressional contacts open to them and to seek collaboration with all the religious, civic, and human rights organizations they knew. They took out two full-page ads in the *New York Times* calling for repeal, one signed by fifty leaders of non-Jewish ethnic and African American organizations. President Bush made a call for repeal part of his speech when he addressed the opening of the U.N. General Assembly, thus throwing full American power behind the proposal. AJC sponsored a conference at the U.S. Mission to the U.N. marking the fifteenth anniversary of the Zionism is racism resolution. Several representatives of East European countries, recently emerged from communism, spoke up to explain why their nations had mistakenly voted for the resolution and why their new governments would work for its elimination.[8]

During 1990 and 1991 altogether David Harris estimated that AJC held more than one hundred meetings with foreign statesmen to argue the case for repeal. Japanese and Korean officials, whom AJC leaders had gotten to know through their new "Pacific Rim" institute (an innovation by the Los Angeles chapter leadership) promised that they would not only vote for repeal but sign on as cosponsors of the resolution.[9] Other leaders who pledged their cooperation when asked included the presidents of Poland, Czechoslovakia, and Lithuania, the chancellors of Germany and Austria, the prime minister of Italy, and the foreign minister of Hungary.[10] The day before the vote the prime minister of Greece used an AJC breakfast reception as the forum to announce Greek cosponsorship of the proposal. Finally, on December 16, 1991, the U.N. General Assembly voted overwhelmingly to revoke the U.N.

resolution equating Zionism with racism. The vote was 111 in favor of repeal, 25 against, with thirty nations either abstaining or not present for the vote. Those not present included representatives of six Arab countries. All the former Soviet bloc nations voted for repeal, and many Asian and African countries that had supported the resolution in 1975 now reversed themselves. As the results of the vote were announced, applause could be heard and well-wishers rushed to congratulate Israel's foreign minister.[11] Not failing to follow up, a few days later AJC took out another full-page ad in the *New York Times*, this time to say thank-you to the 111 countries that had supported the Israeli cause. The AJC continued to fight on Israel's behalf within the U.N. and in 1999 incorporated U.N. Watch, an organization in Geneva that had been founded by Morris B. Abram, AJC honorary president; the mandate of U.N. Watch was to monitor the performance of the U.N. and its adherence to its charter, and to work for equal treatment of member states.[12]

Securing loan guarantees for Israel to help house and absorb the hundreds of thousands of immigrants from the Soviet Union and Ethiopia who were streaming in during the early 1990s was another challenge that AJC and the organized Jewish community had to meet. The situation was dire. At one point almost forty-five thousand people were arriving each month and there were no houses or jobs for them; the estimated costs of taking care of their needs went into the billions of dollars.[13] Israel asked the United States first for four hundred million and then ten billion dollars in loan guarantees so that it could borrow money it needed at feasible interest rates in order to meet the immigrants' needs. But President Bush and his secretary of state James Baker III saw Israeli settlements in the territories as the chief obstacles to their hopes of achieving an Arab-Israeli peace agreement. They refused to give the guarantees unless Israel promised to halt construction of settlements in the West Bank and Gaza and pledged not to send any new immigrants there. In one speech, Bush seemed to indicate that he considered even East Jerusalem out of bounds for Israeli immigrants.

Israeli policy in the territories had been a source of internal controversy from the moment Israel captured them from Jordan and Egypt in 1967. Some Israelis felt that the country had already made an enormous territorial concession when it gave back the entire Sinai Peninsula to Egypt. In 1990–92 both the organized American Jewish community and the Israeli public were torn between "doves" and "hawks" on the settlements issue. There were those who believed, as did the Peace Now and Project Nishma organizations, that territorial concessions and withdrawal were desirable and necessary as much for Israel's sake as for the sake of the Palestinians and the Arab nations. Others believed that every inch of the Land of Israel was necessary for Israel's security—and to settle so many people, as Prime Minister Yitzhak Shamir continually stated. AJC's official policy under Executive Director David Harris, repeated in public statements and correspondence with Bush and Baker, was that settlements in the West Bank and Gaza were not "helpful," but that the settlements were not against international law. Indeed, some of them had existed well before the creation of the state in 1948. In any event, it was "the basic unwillingness of most of the Arab world to live with Israel in permanent peace," not the settlements, that were the true obstacle.[14] It was also AJC policy that an undivided Jerusalem was the capital city of Israel. There were no debates now over whether and how to criticize Israel in public, as there had sometimes been in the 1980s. The goal now, as one staff leader who had observed AJC before the Harris administration put it, was to be "two steps behind and not two steps ahead" of Israel.[15]

Israeli Prime Minister Shamir refused to make any compromises on the right of Israelis to settle in the territories, and he directed his associates to find other ways of raising the money in case the United States did not give in to his views. The conflict brought the relations between the United States and Israel to a historical low point. In one instance Secretary Baker was so disgusted with the attitude of the Likud government that he gave out the White House phone number during testimony in Congress. "The phone number is 1–202–456–1414," he said, addressing his comments to Shamir. "When you're serious about peace, call us."[16] Another time, at a White House meeting when others remarked on his critical attitude toward Israel and how it might upset American Jews, Baker reportedly answered "F—— 'em. They didn't vote for us." Baker denied that he had actually said this and State Department spokeswoman Margaret Tutweiler called the report "false, outrageous, and garbage."[17] Many American Jews, however, were not convinced that there was not some truth behind the reports. Some days later columnist William Safire in the *New York Times*, also not naming his sources, said that Baker had made the remark not just once but on two separate occasions.[18]

Bush himself was capable of sharp words on the matter. Israel made its formal request for the $10 billion in loan guarantees on September 7, 1991, seven months after the end of the first Gulf War, and on September 12, more than a thousand Jewish activists from across the country, including AJC representatives, came to lobby members of Congress on the issue. Bush responded with a nationally televised news conference in which he banged the podium for emphasis, calling for Congress to delay the debate on Israel's request at least 120 days and threatening to veto any earlier legislation about it that they sent his way. He stated that consideration of loan guarantees at the present time "could well destroy our ability to bring one or more of the parties to the peace talks" and furthermore complained of being overwhelmed by "powerful political forces." "I heard there are something like a thousand lobbyists on the Hill working the other side of the question," he said, while at the White House, "we've got one lonely little guy down here doing it."[19]

The general American Jewish response was dismay that Bush was refusing to give Israel what it needed and shock that the president of the United States had evoked such an antisemitic stereotype. Among the many reactions was a letter of rebuke from the AJC signed by David A. Harris and AJC President Alfred Moses, "strongly and respectfully" disagreeing with the president's position on deferring action on the Israeli request for loan guarantees. The issue of settlements, they insisted, should not be linked to the humanitarian needs of settling hundreds of thousands of Jewish refugees. They furthermore took issue with the "tone" of the comments that the president had made:

As several members of Congress on both sides of the aisle told us yesterday, one unintended consequence of the thrust of some of these comments could be an exacerbation of inter-group tensions in the United States. We were among those who participated in yesterday's meeting on the loan guarantee request. In doing so, we were exercising our right to petition our government—a right which is fundamental to our democratic process and exercised daily, thankfully, by so many Americans. To be singled out yesterday, as the participants were, with the imagery of special pleaders with a narrow agenda, seems to us be both unfair and inconsistent with the general tone of civility and mutual respect you have spoken about so often in your presidency. . . . We have always sought to express ourselves in a manner which reflects our high esteem for you and the high office you occupy. It saddens us that we feel moved to write today in response to your remarks, which we believe were a departure from the standard of public discourse that best serves the interest of our country and all its people. Thank you in advance for your consideration and the favor of your reply. Respectfully . . .[20]

An AJC delegation also had an opportunity to make their feelings known at a special meeting at the State Department for them held some weeks after reports of the "F—— 'em" comments had surfaced and seven months before the Republican president was due to run for reelection. Baker began the meeting by describing all the good things he and the Bush administration had done in the interests of the Jewish community and in enhancing Israel's security. These included billions of dollars of aid annually, defense of Israel during the Gulf War, persistent efforts on behalf of Soviet, Ethiopian, and Syrian Jews, leadership in the successful effort to repeal the Zionism is racism resolution, and support for Israel's efforts to achieve full diplomatic recognition from the nations of the world. "We're troubled by the differences that exist, and the mood in the American Jewish community. That doesn't please us," the secretary of state said. "I've enjoyed good relations with the Jewish community—and I like it that way and want to continue it that way. I'm a man who says what he thinks. . . . The record is a good record. The perception is not a good perception. Someone said, the lyrics are good; the music is not what it should be. I buy that. That is why we are having this meeting."[21] "Mr. Secretary, I have a tin ear," replied Alfred Moses, then AJC president, "so I will have to rely on you to describe the music. . . . Both what the president said at his press conference on September 12 and also statements that have been attributed to you have sent a chill through our community." When Baker asked, "What statements?" Moses alluded to the congressional testimony in which he announced for Israel's supposed benefit the White House switchboard number.

"That was one and a half, two years ago," Baker protested. Moses replied, "The Jewish community has long memories." Moses ended the meeting by requesting that Baker reconsider his refusal to extend the loan guarantees after Israel's upcoming election in June. The AJC leaders also requested, and Baker agreed, that he make more public statements in support of Israel, and that he find opportunities to become more "visible" to the Jewish community. As it happened, George H. W. Bush turned out to be a one-term president. He lost the election to Bill Clinton in 1992.

It was the results of the Israeli elections, also in 1992, that ultimately decided the issue. The Israeli voting public, fearful that their prime minister would permanently alienate the United States and leave them without any money to help almost a million new citizens, overturned fifteen years of Likud rule and elected a Labor government that brought Yitzhak Rabin back to power. Rabin had been prime minister from 1973 to 1977 and defense minister throughout the 1980s. Israel's new leader agreed to limit the building of settlements, and his country finally got its $10 billion in loan guarantees.

Yitzhak Rabin not only showed more flexibility on the settlements issue than his predecessor; he and members of his cabinet were also able to sign a peace agreement with the PLO. The agreement was secretly negotiated in Oslo, Norway, and then signed in a ceremony on the White House lawn on September 13, 1993. The photograph of Rabin and Yasir Arafat shaking hands in front of a smiling President Bill Clinton joined the historic photograph of Menachem Begin and Egyptian President Anwar Sadat shaking hands in front of U.S. President Jimmy Carter in 1979. According to the Oslo Accords, officially called the Declaration of Principles on Interim Self-Government, Israeli forces would withdraw from parts of the West Bank and the Gaza Strip and affirm the Palestinian right to self-government within those areas through the creation of the Palestinian Authority (PA). The two parties also signed letters of mutual recognition, Israel recognizing the PLO as the representative of the Palestinian people and the PLO claiming to renounce terrorism, violence, and a desire for the destruction of Israel. The agreements deliberately excluded such sensitive issues as the status of Jerusalem, refugees, Israeli settlements in the territories, security, and borders. These were to be negotiated during and after a five-year interim period during which confidence would (it was hoped) build that the agreements could actually work. For their role in the Oslo Accords, Israeli Prime Minister Yitzhak Rabin, Israeli Foreign Minister Shimon Peres, and PLO Chairman Yasir Arafat, were awarded the Nobel Peace Prize for 1994.

AJC pledged to stand behind the peace process while supporting Israel's security needs. As the AJC board watched the ceremonies on television, Robert S. Rifkind asked everyone to recite the biblical prayer of thanks to God. Alfred Moses, David Harris, and Washington representative Jason Isaacson were present on the South Lawn of the White House that day and Moses commented that the Middle East would never be the same. This could not have occurred so long as the Soviet Union was in place, he declared, nor could it have occurred before the Gulf War. At the same time, one staff member in New York voiced doubt at the reliability of Yasir Arafat as a peace partner. In Israel, AJC office director Michael Oren gave a hint of things to come when he described the three scenes he could see from his Jerusalem window. A few blocks away he could hear the sounds from the rock music bands that Peace Now had hired and see the giant television screens they had rented for all of Jerusalem to watch. In the not-so-far distance he could see the PLO flags waving in East Jerusalem. In the street below him, demonstrators from the Israeli right wing were reciting the mourner's kaddish over a cauldron of ashes.[22]

International Diplomacy

The notion of Israel as a pariah nation had been at least temporarily banished, and the peace process was on. Against the backdrop of this process and other worldwide transformations, AJC expanded its diplomatic activities and earned its nickname, "the Jewish State Department." The annual meetings, which had previously been held mostly in New York, were moved permanently to Washington, D.C., so that the hundreds of members in attendance would have greater access to foreign embassies and U.S. government officials. The meetings themselves, particularly the annual banquet, had become as much a gala social event as an event for determining policy programming; the attendance grew larger and the guest lists more dazzling. In 1994 the meeting was addressed by Vice President Al Gore, Secretary of Defense William Perry, Director General Uri Savir of the Israeli Foreign Ministry, and the keynote speaker, Secretary of State Warren Christopher. In 1995 the guest list included President Bill Clinton himself, Israeli Prime Minister Yitzhak Rabin, and Associate Supreme Court Justice Ruth Bader Ginsburg.

As part of the ceremonies commemorating the fiftieth year since the end of World War II the delegates went to Arlington National Cemetery to honor the memory of the American and Allied soldiers who had given their lives; there was also a special tribute to the numerous war veterans who were attending the meeting. In 1998, as part of the celebration of Israel's fiftieth anniversary, the meeting paid special honor to Costa Rica and Uruguay, two nations that had played an important role in passing the 1947 U.N. Partition resolution. The presidents of both countries flew in especially to attend. In 1999 First Lady Hillary Rodham Clinton was the keynote speaker and there were videotaped remarks from Secretary of State Madeline Albright (who could not be there in person because of the Kosovo crisis). More than a thousand people regularly attended the annual banquet, among them government figures and dozens of foreign ambassadors. In 1996 for the first time the guests included foreign diplomats and ambassadors from several Arab countries. At AJC's centennial banquet in 2006, the number of people present rose to two thousand, and President George W. Bush, German Chancellor Angela Merkel, and U.N. Secretary-General Kofi Annan addressed the crowd.

Before the actual meeting convened, dozens of smaller AJC delegations would visit embassies and government offices to establish relationships and advocate for issues. In 1994, for example, they met with ambassadors and other senior diplomats from Azerbaijan, Austria, Belarus, Brazil, China, the Czech Republic, Egypt, Germany, Hungary, India, Italy, Jordan, Korea, Mexico, the PLO, the Philippines, Poland, Russia, Singapore, Slovakia, South Africa, Turkey, and Ukraine. Five of these countries had not existed a few years earlier and they were eager to start off their years of independence with a clean slate. The following year AJC delegations met with senior diplomats from three countries that had diplomatic relations with Israel—Egypt, Jordan, and Turkey—as well as six predominantly Muslim and Arab countries that did not: Bahrain, Eritrea, Kuwait, Morocco, Qatar, and Tunisia. The Qatar representatives said they were firmly committed to peace with Israel and had already entered into trade agreements with the Jewish state. As the years passed the number of embassies visited grew.

The marathon meetings with embassies in the spring were matched by marathon meetings with heads of state and foreign ministers, taking advantage of the presence in New York of numerous world leaders attending the opening meeting of the U.N. General Assembly. The tradition began in 1992, when an AJC delegation held private meetings with the foreign ministers of eight countries. By 2000, fifty-five such meetings were noted, with countries spanning the entire globe from Argentina to Australia and from Thailand to Tunisia. Aside from Tunisia, AJC representatives regularly met with the top diplomats of such Muslim nations as Bahrain, Egypt, Eritrea, Jordan, Kuwait, Mauritania, Oman, Qatar, and Yemen. In addition, it was no longer a case only of the AJC going to see the U.N. The U.N. was coming to the AJC. International leaders of all kinds were increasingly making pilgrimages to the building on East 56th Street.

The items on AJC's agenda pursued in these meetings included the safety and welfare of local Jewish communities; international human rights; diplomatic recognition of Israel; support for the peace process; an end to cooperation with the Arab boycott; an end to Israel-bashing at the U.N.; dissuading governments from selling arms to Israel's enemies (such as Syria, Iran, or Libya); cooperation in antiterrorist activity; control of extremism, neofascism, and the religious fundamentalism that was cropping up after communism; agreement where necessary from a country to take responsibility for what it had done during the Holocaust; and in general to promote democracy and the rule of law. The foreign diplomats, on their part, saw the American Jews as a powerful, influential, and internationally minded force that could serve as a point of entry and contact with the only superpower left in the world. Some sought to attract American aid and investment and looked to AJC to put in a good word on their behalf. And AJC could be helpful in other ways; for example, David Harris fulfilled the desire of many of AJC's diplomatic allies when he testified in Congress in favor of expanding NATO to include the nations of Central and Eastern Europe.

Indeed, many of the new countries, especially in the former Soviet bloc, perceived that U.S. assessment of their commitment to democracy would depend, to a certain extent, on how they dealt with issues of importance to Jews, including Israel.[23] Distancing one's country from the Holocaust was also a powerful motive for nations to seek good relations with the AJC (and through them, with the United States). The Ukrainian minister of culture, for example, said that strengthening the Jewish-Ukrainian relationship was "one of the most important ideological and moral challenges facing Ukraine today," because Jews were such an intimate part of Ukrainian history—and also "the newly established Ukrainian government does not want to be held responsible for the crimes and misdeeds which occurred in the Ukraine while it was under Russian occupation."[24] Throughout much of history the Ukrainians had been notorious among Jews for their antisemitism and anti-Jewish violence, and they were particularly remembered for the role many of them had played as collaborators with the Nazis during World War II. Such declarations were important because even after the great Soviet exodus, Ukraine was still home to the fifth-largest Jewish community in the world. Overall at least a million Jews still lived in the former Soviet Union.

AJC not only expanded its diplomatic activity in the United States but also greatly expanded its travels abroad. Many of the meetings with top officials in Washington and New York ended with invitations to visit those countries, to which the AJC responded. Formerly, the delegations abroad might consist of the AJC president, executive director, and a handful of honorary presidents or top officers. Now the entire board of governors was invited. (As always on such trips, only the expenses of the staff were covered; the laypeople always paid their own way). In 1994 the board met in Jerusalem, and this meeting was followed up by a trip covering six countries in ten days, with talks with world leaders in every country. In 1995 another board meeting in Israel was followed by a trip to Germany, Poland, and the Vatican, where the AJC delegation had an audience with Pope John Paul II. There, the issues were Christian acknowledgment of the Holocaust and the opening of the Vatican archives. Another delegation visited Tunisia and Jordan, where they had a meeting with King Hussein at his royal palace in Amman. The session was given extensive publicity in the Jordanian media.

In further activity with Arab countries, in 1995 an AJC delegation visited Bahrain, Oman, and Qatar, where they spoke to American businessmen and U.S. ambassadors as well as diplomats. During the discussions Qatari officials assured them that Qatar was closing its office administering the Arab economic boycott of Israel, and Omani officials said that their country would soon do the same.[25] The following year AJC became the first Jewish group ever to pay an official visit to Kuwait. Executive director David Harris and Jason Isaacson, director of government and international affairs, traveled at the invitation of Kuwaiti Foreign Minister Sheik Sabah al-Ahmad al-Sabah, with whom they had previously established a relationship when he visited the United States for the 1995 U.N. General Assembly session. Also in 1995, Charlotte Holstein led a delegation of nine to the International Women's Conference in Beijing, where they helped to head off the anti-Israel and pro-Palestinian activity that had characterized previous such meetings in Nairobi and Copenhagen. The AJC was also represented there by Felice Gaer, director of the Jacob Blaustein Institute for the Advancement of Human Rights, who attended as part of the official U.S. government negotiating team.

AJC traveled the world and helped others travel as well, funding the trips through AJC's own budget, foundation grants, private donations, and co-sponsorships with other groups. Leaders were understandably concerned about the waves of antiforeigner nationalism and religious hatred that was developing in the new European democracies that had recently emerged from communism. A partial solution was to identify and bring emerging leaders from Central and Eastern Europe to the United States to study the American values of "pluralism and cultural diversity." In 1996, the fourth year of this program, AJC helped bring to the United States fourteen young leaders from Bosnia, Bulgaria, the Czech Republic, Estonia, Lithuania, Poland, Russia, Serbia, Slovakia, Slovenia, and Ukraine. The subjects spent time in six American cities where they met with people from politics, ethnic organizations, the media, education, and law enforcement, so they could see how things really worked in a democracy. To learn about diversity they attended interreligious dialogues arranged by AJC's Interreligious Affairs Department and visited public schools, TV stations, Capitol Hill, and finally the U.S. Holocaust Memorial Museum.[26]

In the 1960s and 1970s the AJC had sponsored frequent missions to Israel for non-Jewish Americans, but such activities had been severely limited in more recent years by lack of funds and staff. The gap was filled in 1992 when the agency absorbed Project Interchange, which had already been running extensive seminars in Israel for American non-Jewish leaders for ten years. At that point more than two hundred Project Interchange alumni were present or former congressional aides—advisers to senators and representatives who decided on foreign aid and Middle East policy. The trips, approximately fifteen each year, were funded through foundations and private individuals; through the years, they involved thousands of men and women. Special groups who got a firsthand look at Israel through the program included federal, state, and local politicians, clergymen, heads of Christian theological seminaries, teachers, professors, African Americans, leaders of the Hispanic community, and Asian Americans. The latter were particularly delighted to meet some of the two hundred refugee "boat people" who had been given Israeli citizenship after the wars in Indochina. One year Project Interchange targeted student body presidents from universities in Idaho, Iowa, Minnesota, Montana, Nebraska, North Dakota, South Dakota, and Wyoming. Many of them had never seen a Jew before they were brought to Israel to learn about the country.[27] All these subjects were Americans; in 2005 AJC leaders decided to extend the program to groups of influential Europeans, Latin Americans, and Asians as well.

Perhaps most important, AJC set its international sights on other Diaspora communities around the globe. New communities were emerging and old ones were facing the same challenges as American Jewry, such as antisemitism, Jewish continuity, the role of Jewish communities in a general society, and how they should relate to the State of Israel. One solution was to combine resources and set up a worldwide network by forming partnerships with comparable Jewish organizations in other countries. By 2006 AJC had formal alliances with Jewish organizations including those in Argentina, Australia, Bulgaria, Chile, Costa Rica (home to 2,500 Jews), the Czech Republic, France, Mexico, Peru, Slovakia, Spain, and Venezuela. AJC cosponsored— along with the American Joint Distribution Committee and local groups— conferences where the Jews of Europe and Russia could come together to discuss matters of mutual concern. This American organization also took upon itself the task of fostering Jewish communal leadership in the rest of the world. The agency held its first International Leadership Conference at the annual meeting in 1994. More than one hundred and fifty young Jewish leaders representing twenty-five countries attended, and at least fourteen of those countries had not existed as independent nations when AJC celebrated its eightieth anniversary: Russia, Georgia, Latvia, Estonia, Slovakia, Uzbekistan, Croatia, Kazakhstan, Azerbaijan, the Czech Republic, Belarus, Ukraine, Kyrgyzstan, and Lithuania. AJC arranged for the funding to bring them to America. After the sessions of the annual meeting were over, the young leaders, together with an equal number of AJC staff and members, spent the weekend in long discussions on a wide range of topics.

AJC paid special attention to the needs of the Jews of the former Soviet Union. Hundreds of thousands of them had settled in New York and other American cities, and there were estimates that they and their children made up as much as one-fourth of the entire Jewish population of the New York area. Russian speakers became ubiquitous as clients, patrons, and employees in Jewish homes and institutions. The vast majority arrived without any formal Jewish training, and the concept of Jewish activism in a democratic state was completely foreign to them. AJC's goal was to turn this human resource into Jewish communal citizens and potential leaders. Candidates were selected for leadership ability by a committee chaired by Peyretz Goldmacher, a prominent figure in New York's Russian-speaking Jewish community who had turned to the AJC for help in this area. Participants took part in days of intensive courses on Judaism and Jewish life in America; they were then brought to Washington, D.C., for a two-day program on conducting political advocacy. The first such class graduated in 1999. In 2003 Moscow-born Sam Kliger, who had been part of the Soviet Jewish underground before he left in 1990, was named AJC's director of Russian Jewish community affairs. By 2004 there were one hundred and fifty graduates of the program—nearly all the major political and organizational leaders of the New York Russian Jewish community—and plans were being made to expand the program into Boston, Chicago, and even Berlin.[28]

Germany and Poland

In its overseas work AJC paid special attention to Germany, a nation it had been cultivating since the late 1940s. In 1949 the issue they had to face was the end of the Allied occupation and the declaration of an independent Federal Republic of Germany (also known as West Germany), while the German Democratic Republic (known as East Germany) remained under Soviet control. The former capital city of Berlin, about forty miles west of the border with Poland, was split right down the middle between the two forces. Berlin was divided by a concrete, brick, and barbed wire wall and guarded by Soviet forces. Anyone who tried to go over the wall could be shot. The West German capital was set up in the Rhine Valley city of Bonn. On the unforgettable night of November 9, 1989, the Soviet forces withdrew, and East and West Berliners overwhelmed at the freedom of being able to cross at will, began to knock the wall—known in German as *die Mauer*—down. Pieces of it were subsequently sold in the street to tourists as souvenirs.

Now, forty-five years after the end of World War II, West and East Germany were about to be unified into one giant country again. The economic and military might of a united Germany would dwarf that of its European neighbors, and many observers would have preferred that it remain partitioned. By early 1990, however, that was no longer an option; the two Germanys had decided to unite, and none of the powers that had defeated the Third Reich stood in the way. Even the State of Israel gave its blessing, through a speech by Minister of Defense Moshe Arens in Bonn—a move that was widely criticized in the Israeli press. "To be sure Israel has no greater friend in Europe than West Germany," declared the director of AJC's Israel office, in his report of Israeli opinion on the subject. "It has provided economic as well as crucial diplomatic support, at times when France and England have buckled to Arab pressure. But forty years of experience as a democracy, willingness to acknowledge the responsibility for the Holocaust, attempts to make financial restitution in the form of reparation payments, and unceasing diplomatic support have not erased Israeli fears of German nationalistic aspirations." The editors of *Ma'ariv* suggested there should have been a debate or a national referendum on the issue, before Israel gave its blessing "to the creation of conditions that could lead to a Fourth Reich and a new Hitler." The approval of the Jews, they wrote, "can only be debated in another two hundred years, after twenty generations of citizens of a unified Germany have proven that this is indeed a new Germany."[29]

The officers of AJC's International Affairs Commission also viewed the end of German partition with trepidation. Soviet-dominated East Germany, unlike the Federal Republic, had never acknowledged any responsibility for the Holocaust. It had never provided any compensation to survivors, had never established diplomatic relations with Israel, had supported the Zionism is Racism resolution and had served as a benefactor to anti-Israel terrorist groups operating in the Middle East. "We cannot help but wonder where events are headed," the officers wrote in a statement on German reunification. "Will the end of Germany's division also augur the end of historical memory about the Nazi era and the incalculable tragedy and destruction it wrought? Will November 9, the anniversary date of *Kristallnacht*, now be wholly replaced in the German consciousness by November 9, the anniversary date of the Berlin Wall's first holes? Will the united Germany ever again flex its muscles and attack its neighbors as it has done twice in this century alone? It simply isn't possible to answer these questions today with any degree of certainty. Still, there is basis for hope."

An important first step had been taken in April 1991 when the first freely elected East German parliament made an official request for forgiveness from the world's Jews for the crimes of the Nazis. They had also indicated their desire to move ahead on the question of claims and compensation and to establish diplomatic relations with Israel as soon as possible.[30] All of this portended well for the future, but AJC recommended a number of concrete steps to make sure that "memory becomes institutionalized, even as the nation charts its future course." The East German educational system, they said, should be adapted to include the same programs of Holocaust education that had long been part of the West German system. There should be lectures, exhibits, and other such methods used to acquaint East Germans with "the historical and current realities of the Jewish people." Former concentration camps on East German soil should be marked with commemorative signs to show that these places had been used to kill Jews. West German laws designed to check the activities of extremist groups inciting racial, religious, or ethnic hatred or violence, or questioning the truthfulness of the events of the Third Reich—laws the AJC and other Jewish organizations had advocated for many years— should be extended to East Germany as well. In its public life, the new nation should "make appropriate statements, observe commemorative events, establish memorials and support other efforts whose aims are to remember the past and warn against any possible recurrence." It should continue to maintain a "special relationship" with the State of Israel, "based on historical and moral commitment." "The American Jewish Committee," they concluded, "is ever mindful of the horrors that befell our people during this century, and ever vigilant to the well-being of Jews throughout the world. In this spirit we shall continue our pioneering efforts to develop links with the German government, institutions and people to enhance understanding and cooperation and seek to ensure that never again in our history will we suffer the tragedy of the Nazi era."[31]

Relations were always cordial, even warm, but the AJC never took its eyes off Germany. At least once a year, and usually more often, AJC leaders and delegations would go on official visits to Germany, being received for long discussions with Chancellor Helmut Kohl and other German officials and speaking up and holding press conferences when they noted anything untoward, such as antiforeigner violence, neo-Nazi activity, or vandalizing of Jewish sites. In 1992, there was a reception in their honor at the home of Germany's president; during the trip they also made a visit to a concentration camp and recited the kaddish prayer. In 1995, as part of the commemoration of the fiftieth year since the end of World War II, David Harris spent a week speaking to high school students and army officers in six German cities and towns. In 1999 Harris himself received twenty-seven top-ranking German military officers into his own home, for an event with the Westchester chapter. The officers were part of an exchange program event held annually at AJC's New York headquarters. Several of the Jews present were children of parents who had survived the war in Europe. For many of the German officers, this was their first time in a Jewish home. The *New York Times* reporter there wrote that "clearly, it was an evening that evoked many emotions for both groups."[32]

In 1997 AJC opened an office in Berlin, at a time when a united Germany had become a leader in the European Union and the city itself, a gateway to all of Central and Eastern Europe, was becoming the nation's capital once again. AJC's new quarters were in a palatial office, once a publishing house, in a brand-new city center block built on a site once owned by a Jewish family but confiscated by the Nazis. On opening day, when a mezuzah was affixed to the door, hundreds of people crowded in, including seventy-five members of the board of governors, leading German political figures, the American and Israeli ambassadors, academics, members of the German Jewish community, and representatives of all the major print and electronic media in Germany. Thanks to the generosity of a German businessman, AJC was getting these rooms with panoramic views of the Reichstag and the Brandenburg Gate rent-free for ten years. "Few visitors," noted a report of the event, "miss either the symbolism or the irony."[33]

As Germany was a leader of Western Europe, Poland was leader of the East. It was at the head of all the countries changing from communism to Western-style democracy. The Polish Solidarity trade union movement, headed by Lech Wałesa, had played a crucial role in bringing down communist rule in Eastern Europe. Polish Americans were an important group among AJC's ethnic coalitions. The Polish Catholic church also deeply influenced the Vatican and the Catholic world. Pope John Paul II was originally from Poland. One in six priests in Europe was from Poland, where fifty-five Catholic seminaries were located, so any positive shift in the way Judaism was presented to candidates for the priesthood could have a far-reaching effect. Relations between a newly independent Poland and Israel were relatively good because Israel was viewed as an ally of the United States. The Arab nations were not viewed well because of their allegiance to the Soviet Union; the Poles deeply resented the years they had spent under Soviet domination.[34] Post-Soviet Poland also had strong motives for pursuing good relations with American Jews and the AJC: it wished to overcome its reputation for being an antisemitic country—and also for being the location of the death camps where so many European Jews were murdered.

At a meeting with Lech Wałesa, elected president of the country in 1990, AJC leaders could thank him for allowing the use of Warsaw as a transit point for Soviet Jews going to Israel, for creating a special commission to combat antisemitism, for introducing units on Judaism and the Jewish people in Polish schools, and for Polish support in repeal of the Zionism is Racism U.N. resolution.[35] Rabbi A. James Rudin, director of interreligious affairs, further strengthened Polish-Jewish relations when, in cooperation with a Polish archbishop, he arranged for annual visits of Jewish studies scholars to teach at Polish seminaries and universities. In 1996 AJC, which had a full-time consultant in Poland, began its first exchange program there, bringing influential Poles to the United States for visits and bringing American Jews to Poland. In 1997 AJC's role in Polish-Jewish affairs was recognized when it was chosen to sit on a commission of organizations, among them the U.S. Holocaust Memorial Museum and Yad Vashem in Israel, charged with discussing a permanent plan for the Auschwitz-Birkenau death camp site with the Polish government.[36]

The Holocaust

Matters related to the Holocaust figured prominently in much of AJC's public activity both abroad and in the United States. Getting some kind of apology or acknowledgment from the Vatican, making sure the events were remembered, dealing with Holocaust deniers, getting compensation for the survivors in formerly communist countries and those who had worked at slave labor for German companies, making sure that all Holocaust-era assets such as artwork and Swiss bank accounts went to their rightful owners or heirs—all were items high on the agenda of world Jewish organizations in the 1990s. The year 1993, in which the first PLO-Israeli peace agreement was signed and the Vatican officially recognized the State of Israel, was also a turning point in bringing the Holocaust to public attention. In April the $168 million U.S. Holocaust Memorial Museum opened on government-donated land, off the Mall in Washington. President Clinton, Vice President Gore, Israel President Chaim Herzog, and Elie Wiesel addressed a crowd of thousands who attended the ceremony. In December the film *Schindler's List*, by Steven Spielberg, about a German industrialist who saved one thousand Jews by employing them in his factory, was released and went on to receive seven Academy awards, including Best Picture and Best Director.[37]

Undersecretary of Commerce Stuart E. Eizenstat, who was an AJC honorary vice president, reflected in 1999 on other reasons why fifty years after the event all of these issues were becoming more important than ever before. The end of the cold war, he said, was part of it; that freed up energies for other issues and also freed up archives that previously had been closed. For a U.S. government report on the actions of Swiss banks during and after the Holocaust that he had directed, Eizenstat noted that they had declassified almost a million pages of previously classified documents. There was a sense of urgency about getting the facts before it was too late from survivors who were nearing the end of their lives, many of whom had never told their families what happened to them during the war. There was also a "millennium complex," Eizenstat suggested; that is, an attempt by their psyches to put in order the cataclysmic events of the last century before moving on to the next.[38]

Robert S. Rifkind, president of the AJC in its ninetieth-anniversary year of 1996, spoke in almost idealistic terms about the good work the organization was doing when it helped to perpetuate the memory of the Holocaust, an event he compared to the Exodus from Egypt. Indeed, he seemed to consider the perpetuation one of the Jewish people's chief accomplishments:

We have at the same time seen to the centralization of the Holocaust in the imagination of modernity. When His Holiness the Pope calls this the century of the Shoah, when the museum dominates the mall, when no conversation about the political, historical, military life of the twentieth century can progress without reference to the central fact, we know we have stamped it indelibly on the mind of modernity. And that, let's recognize it, is an event which could have be marginalized. It is an event that could have been ignored, forgotten, and there were those who sought to do so. But we have seen to it that it has become one of the core cultural facts of the modern world, and that is a major contribution to the civilization in which we live. . . . What we have done in this regard—to capture the significance of it—one might recall that four millennia ago, a small tribe wandered out of Egypt. No one might have paid any attention to it. As far as I can tell, other than in our own records, the Egyptians paid no attention to it. . . . But the fact is we transformed it into a metaphor of the Exodus, a metaphor of the quest for freedom, a metaphor for the role of moral forces in history, and it has become the symbol for all Western man, of the revolution, of the progress towards the Promised Land for all men. And that was a major cultural contribution of our people to the betterment of our fellow citizens around the world, and I think we're in the process of doing that also with the Holocaust.[39]

In relations with the Vatican one goal was to obtain some kind of expression of regret or remorse for the role organized Christianity might have played in making the Holocaust possible. In 1998 the Vatican released the fourteen-page document "We Remember: A Reflection on the Shoah." The statement acknowledged the long history of Christian anti-Jewish hatred, but did not draw any causal connection between that and Nazism, which it attributed to "neo-Pagan anti-Semitism." Rabbi A. James Rudin was part of a small group of Jewish leaders who met with the pope and senior Vatican officials to express disappointment that the document did not go far enough.[40] The best that could be said of the document, according to Martin S. Kaplan, chair of the Interreligious Affairs Commission, was that it made clear that Christianity at the present time had no place for antisemitism and that the Holocaust was a historical fact, something that would help refute the Holocaust deniers. It praised those Catholics who had risked their lives to save Jews and mentioned that others did nothing. But it fell short of being the apology they were looking for.[41]

Pope John Paul II came one step closer to an apology when he made a historic visit to Israel in the spring of 2000. He paid a visit to the Yad Vashem Holocaust memorial in Jerusalem. Then, coming to the Western Wall to pray, in accordance with Jewish tradition he placed a note in the wall that sought God's forgiveness for Jewish suffering at the hands of Christians during the "course of history."[42] The AJC took out full-page ads in the Catholic press to commemorate the visit. As important as the visit itself, observed Rabbi David Rosen, then director of the ADL's Israel office and soon to be international interreligious director for AJC, was the precedent that had been set for future popes who might not be so committed as John Paul II was to reconciliation with the Jewish people. "He set down solid foundations," Rosen noted. "It's impossible today to have a serious position in the Catholic Church and to express an anti-Judaic opinion."[43]

Other outstanding issues with the Vatican that were still unresolved in AJC's centennial year were the complete unsealing of the Vatican archives and Jewish objections to conferring sainthood on Pope Pius XII, who, despite being credited with saving Jews in quiet and discreet ways, never risked issuing a formal public condemnation of the Nazi extermination and never threatened to excommunicate anyone involved in it. The subject of what the wartime pope did or did not do remained the subject of plays, numerous books and articles, and extensive debate among Jewish and Catholic intellectuals and leaders.

As Martin Kaplan had noted, Holocaust denial was achieving more widespread acceptance during these years, and AJC devoted publications, conferences, and programs to combating it. Kenneth Stern, AJC's program specialist in extremism and antisemitism, wrote one of the first books on the subject, which included a bibliography as well as practical suggestions on how to respond to the arguments of deniers. AJC also hosted a scholarly conference on the impact of Holocaust denial on the campus, the media, and the political process.[44] In her report on the subject to the board of governors in 1993, Mimi Alperin, then national treasurer and chair of the Jewish Communal Affairs Commission, called it "a sophisticated attempt to rewrite history and a tactic to mask blatant antisemitism." These views were becoming more legitimate owing to an "intellectual climate" created by such trends as deconstructionism, an approach to literature that stated that texts had no meaning and that experience is relative.[45]

The deniers, who took on the role of pseudoscholars and held conferences and published journals on the subject, stated that the Nazi attempt to exterminate the Jews never happened. It was supposedly a lie the Jews had manufactured to win sympathy for the State of Israel and to extract financial gains from Germany. Jews were allegedly able to convince the world that this fantasy had actually happened only because they controlled the media and Hollywood. Any attempt to halt these claims, the deniers held, was an infringement on their freedom of speech. Advertisements claiming that the Holocaust never happened were especially to be found in college campus newspapers, and the AJC contacted many editors trying to convince them not to run such ads.

A turning point in the attempt to battle the deniers took place when author David Irving—who for much of his career claimed in books, articles, and speeches that the Nazi gas chambers never existed—sued American professor Deborah E. Lipstadt for libel in the British courts. In her book, *Denying the Holocaust: The Growing Assault on Truth and Memory,* Dr. Lipstadt identified Irving as one of the leading offenders in the field. Irving claimed that Dr. Lipstadt's words were part of an attempt to ruin his reputation and he was seeking damages. Under British law the burden of proof lay with Lipstadt and not with Irving, as it would have under U.S. law. It was up to her to prove the truth of what she had said. "It is a tragic absurdity that in 1998 one must prove the facts of the Holocaust," declared E. Robert Goodkind, in introducing Deborah Lipstadt at an AJC meeting. "Should Mr. Irving win this case or any element of it, other Holocaust deniers would be able to continue denying the facts of the Holocaust and still be considered credible historians."[46] Dr. Lipstadt expressed thanks to the AJC for taking the lead among Jewish organizations and quietly raising close to two million dollars to cover her legal fees. She informed them that the case seemed to be going in her favor. "We estimate that the trial will take place around this time next year and that it will last between thirteen and fifteen weeks," she told them. "I never thought I would ever have complained about having to live in London for thirteen–fifteen weeks, but I would rather visit for other purposes."[47]

Victory came in April 2000, when the judge in the case held that Dr. Lipstadt was justified in calling Irving a Holocaust denier and associate of right-wing neo-Nazi extremists in her book.[48] As for Irving's legal fees, because of the decision he was liable for the costs of the trial, which forced him into bankruptcy. For most of 2006, after trying to visit a country where he was banned, he was sitting in an Austrian jail serving a three-year term for Holocaust denial—a criminal offense in that country. Despite the curb on Irving's activities Holocaust denial publications, conferences, and websites continued to proliferate. In 2005 it was reported that the websites had the most up-to-date technologies, including streaming audio, video, background music, and original artwork.[49]

After the fall of communism, it was discovered that there were thousands of elderly Holocaust survivors living in Eastern Europe and the former Soviet Union who had never received any compensation. The German government, which had already paid out hundreds of millions to survivors, Jewish institutions, and the State of Israel, was reluctant to take on this new responsibility. AJC took on the case and pressed it during visits with the German president, chancellor, and government officials. After making no progress, in May 1997 AJC leaders launched a more public campaign to bring attention to the issue. They took out an ad in the *New York Times* that contrasted the neglect of these Jewish survivors with the payments that Germany provided wounded war veterans of the Third Reich—including members of the Waffen SS. The same day, they held a press conference on Capitol Hill, where supportive members of Germany's parliament were present. The first reaction of the German government was that while some war criminals might be receiving pensions, Germany was not in a position to provide financial help for any more Holocaust survivors. AJC stepped up the campaign by enlisting the support of President Clinton's administration and congressional leaders in the hope of reversing Germany's stand. The result was a Senate letter urging pensions for the survivors, sponsored by Senators Dodd (Democrat, from Connecticut) and Hutchinson (Republican, from Texas). Their letter, addressed to Chancellor Kohl, was signed by eighty-two senators and was featured in another AJC ad in the *New York Times* and several other major newspapers. Only then did the German government agree to begin negotiations on Eastern European survivors with the Conference on Jewish Material Claims Against Germany, the international Jewish body set up after World War II to deal with compensation and indemnification. Rabbi Andrew Baker, AJC's director of international Jewish affairs, was on the negotiating team. Germany eventually pledged to provide more than one hundred million dollars, which was sufficient for monthly pensions to an estimated twenty thousand survivors who had spent at least six months in a concentration camp or eighteen months in a ghetto or in hiding.[50]

AJC also intervened in the negotiations between Germany and representatives of former slave and forced laborers who had worked for German companies during World War II. The goal was to pressure German companies to join an industry and government fund to compensate them. Researchers and legal staff did their work: in November 1999 at press conferences held in both Berlin and New York, AJC released a list of more than two hundred and fifty contemporary German companies that had used slave and forced labor during the Nazi era. Prior to release of the list, only twenty-four companies had publicly agreed to contribute to the fund, although AJC claimed that nearly all German companies had relied on slave and forced labor during the war. By the beginning of January, one hundred twenty-three companies had publicly agreed to support the fund and more were still coming forth. Ten days after the list was published, agreement was reached to establish a compensation fund of several billion dollars, and AJC began pressing the German parliament to pass the necessary law so that payments could begin immediately.[51]

Terrorism

In its international work, even as AJC sought justice for crimes that had been committed so many years before, it found itself confronting in the 1990s a new threat against the United States, Israelis, and by extension Jews in general: international terrorism by Islamic extremists operating through new, radical interpretations of Islamic law. Their targets were Israel, the United States, and the very forces of Western civilization; indeed, these forces saw no difference between the United States and Israel, calling one "the Great Satan" and the other "the Little Satan."[52] Some of these attacks were in the United States itself, causing the AJC headquarters and Jewish institutions of all kinds to strengthen their security precautions.

One of the sources of this new terrorism had been the Islamic Revolution in Iran in 1979, when Ayatollah Ruhollah Khomeini became leader of the country; the hostage crisis that occurred in the wake of the revolution can be said to be the United States' first encounter with modern radical Islam. Hezbollah, the "Party of God," representing the Shi'a Muslim population in Lebanon, was created and funded by Iran; their first goal was to drive out the Israelis and the Americans after Israel's incursion into Lebanon that began in June 1982. In 1983 they attacked the U.S. embassy in Beirut and, later in the year, the Marine headquarters in there. The latter cost the lives of 241 servicemen. Both were some of the earliest uses in the Middle East of the technique of suicide bombing: an attack in which the bomber had no intention to escape but blew him- or herself up along with the target. Hezbollah and Iran are also considered responsible for the suicide truck bombing of the Israeli embassy in Buenos Aires on March 17, 1992 (which killed twenty-nine and wounded 242) and for the July 18, 1994, suicide truck bombing of the AMIA (for Argentine Israelite Mutual Association) building, also in Buenos Aires. The AMIA was the headquarters for the largest Jewish community in Latin America. The seven-story building was reduced to rubble; eighty-five died, and more than three hundred others were wounded. Hezbollah started Israel's second war in Lebanon in July 2006 when it attacked a division of Israeli soldiers and began to rain rockets into northern Israel.

Hamas (an acronym in Arabic for the Islamic Resistance Movement) was founded in 1987 during the first intifada and called for the destruction of Israel through armed force and the establishment in its place of an Islamic state. It, too, used suicide bombings against Israel all through the 1990s as a way to stop the Israeli-PLO peace process and as part of the second intifada, which began in the fall of 2000. Hamas and related groups, such as Islamic Jihad and the Al-Aqsa Martyrs Brigade, chose as their targets passenger buses, restaurants, cafés, and crowded nightspots, in attempts to kill and maim as many Israeli civilians as possible. Hamas was and is known also for its extensive network of welfare programs in the West Bank and the Gaza Strip. In the first democratic Palestinian elections in January 2006, Hamas as a political party defeated the Fatah organization that had been led by Yasir Arafat and won a majority of seats in the Palestinian Legislative Council. The decades of work the PLO had invested in gaining recognition as the sole legitimate representative of the Palestinian people went for naught. So too did the years of diplomacy to get the PLO to modify its charter and accept the existence of the State of Israel (a pledge that many critics of the Oslo peace process believed that Arafat and the PLO had never intended to fulfill anyway). Israel now found itself with a Palestinian authority on its borders led by a government that was bent unambiguously on its immediate destruction. Israeli forces almost daily foiled attempted suicide bombings, and the State was building a security fence to serve as a physical barrier between Israelis and Palestinians.

Another important terrorist group, Al-Qa'ida, one of whose founders was Saudi-born Osama bin Laden, had its roots in the 1979 Soviet invasion of Afghanistan. Al-Qa'ida is its secret name, meaning simply "the base": the full name of the organization is the International Front for Jihad Against Jews and Crusaders. Non-Afghani Muslim fighters flocked to Afghanistan to join the Mujahadin, the anti-Soviet resistance movement, and al-Qa'ida, at times with the support of United States and Pakistan, helped to fund and train them. When the Soviets withdrew from Afghanistan in 1989—a victory for which al-Qa'ida and similar groups claimed credit—many committed veterans of the war wanted to continue their fighting for Islamic causes on other fronts.

The 1991 Gulf War, which al-Qa'ida viewed as a U.S. invasion of the Muslim world, provided further provocation to them. Osama bin Laden in particular called for the removal from Saudi Arabia of infidel U.S. military installations, which he saw as a desecration of the holy soil of the home of the cities Mecca and Medina and a threat to other Muslim countries. The first bombing of the World Trade Center on February 23, 1993; the simultaneous bombing of the U.S. embassies in Tanzania and Kenya in August 1998 that killed 220 and wounded more than four thousand; the suicide bombing of the USS *Cole* in the port of Aden in Yemen in October 2000; the September 11, 2001, airliner attacks against the World Trade Center and the Pentagon; the bombing of a synagogue in Tunisia in 2002; the bombing of a hotel in Casablanca where Jewish guests were staying in 2003; and the bombing of a synagogue in Istanbul, Turkey, also in 2003—all were al-Qa'ida operations.

The issue of Islamic extremism and the importance of counterterrorism initiatives appeared on the AJC agenda as early as 1991. Through the decade it was a subject of newspaper ads, congressional hearings, briefings with the FBI and law enforcement agencies, and most discussions with foreign officials. In 1993, AJC released its first studies on Muslim fundamentalist organizations and state-supported terrorism. In 1998, the year of the embassy bombings, AJC published the first of several papers on Osama bin Laden and also hired as an adviser Steven L. Pomerantz, former FBI chief of counterterrorism. In 1999—almost three years before the September 11 attacks—AJC formed a Division of Middle East and International Terrorism and chose Yehudit Barsky, a recognized expert in the field who was fluent in Hebrew and Arabic. The division monitored terrorist publications and websites, provided detailed analyses and briefings on Middle East terrorist organizations and their supporters in the United States, and met with media, law enforcement agencies, and Jewish communities to discuss terrorism and ways to defend against it. This AJC division in particular found itself very busy and much in demand by other parties in the United States and around the world after the September 11 attacks.[53]

Black Antisemitism and Black-Jewish Relations

Additional threats in the 1990s were new variations of black antisemitism in the United States, including the popularity of antisemitic academic theories on college campuses and the aftermath of the Crown Heights riot that began on the evening of August 19, 1991. The effects of the riot were still being felt in the twenty-first century; among other factors it revealed a gulf between the main national Jewish organizations, headquartered in Manhattan, and the mostly Orthodox Jews living in the outer boroughs of New York. Crown Heights was a Brooklyn neighborhood that was home to a minority of Lubavitcher Hasidim and a majority of black African and Caribbean Americans. What was considered by historian Edward S. Shapiro to be "the most serious antisemitic incident in American history"[54] (the Hasidim themselves called it a "pogrom") was set off by the death of a black child, seven-year-old Gavin Cato. He was hit by the third car in the three-car motorcade of the Lubavitcher Rebbe, who was returning from one of his frequent trips to a cemetery.

As had been the practice for a decade, a police car with two officers from the 71st Precinct led the motorcade. This protection, seen by black residents as part of a pattern of preferential public treatment of the Hasidim, was a result of Hasidic claims that their Rebbe was a world figure and thus deserved such treatment—and also of fears of death threats against him that had been made by the Satmars, a rival Hasidic sect.[55] At one point the rear car fell behind the Rebbe's; as the driver tried to catch up, he struck another car and veered out of control, running up on the sidewalk where he struck Gavin Cato and his seven-year-old cousin Angela. The other two cars had already continued on their way. Gavin was killed and Angela was severely injured. A hostile crowd of black people gathered, some of whom began to beat the driver, Yosef Lifsh, and the other occupants of his car. Lifsh's alleged running of a red light was also seen as an example of Hasidic superiority and arrogance.

Hatzoloh, a volunteer Jewish ambulance service, was the first to arrive at the scene, closely followed by the police. The police feared for the safety of the Hasidim, now covered with blood, and one told the Hatzoloh driver to get them out of the area as soon as possible. The children, the policeman said, would be cared for by a city Emergency Medical Services ambulance that had just arrived. Lifsh and his companions were taken to Methodist Hospital where he received eighteen stitches to his head and face. He was also given a breath-alcohol test; the results were negative. A grand jury later ruled that he was not guilty of negligent homicide and that the incident had been an accident, a ruling that some in the black community considered a function of superior Hasidic political power.[56]

To the crowd that night, already enraged by the accident, it appeared as if the Jewish ambulance had shown contempt for the lives of non-Jews by taking the Hasidim away first and failing to treat the Cato children, thus leaving them to die. Such inaction fit into a familiar pattern of racism and unequal treatment. Rumors circulated that the Hasidic car had deliberately run down the children, that the Hatzoloh ambulance had refused to treat them, that the driver had been drunk and, later, that the results of his breath alcohol test had been changed by the office of the Brooklyn district attorney. "We can't take this anymore," yelled one man at the scene. "The Jews get everything they want. They're killing our children. We get no justice, we get no respect." Another yelled, "Let's go to Kingston Avenue [the main shopping street of the Hasidim] and get the Jews." Aroused by the speakers, young blacks went on a rampage in the neighborhood, throwing stones, bottles, and debris, and assaulting and robbing Jews, crying "Get the Jews!" and "Jews, Jews, Jews!"[57]

The cries "Heil Hitler" and "Death to the Jews" were also heard in the ensuing days, and an Israeli flag was burned.[58]

Three hours after the accident and two blocks from the scene, twenty-nine-year-old Yankel Rosenbaum, a visiting doctoral student from Australia, was beaten and stabbed by a mob that saw him and shouted, according to several witnesses, "Kill the Jews," "There's a Jew," "Let's get the Jew."[59] Rosenbaum later died of his wounds. Verbal violence against Jews continued at Gavin Cato's funeral, where eulogists referred to Hatzoloh as "an apartheid ambulance service," equated the boy's death with that of the four little girls who had died in a church bombing in Birmingham, Alabama, in 1964, and referred to the Hasidim as "Oppenheimer in South Africa [who] sends diamonds straight to Tel Aviv and deals with the diamond merchants right here in Crown Heights." Speakers also excused and even praised the actions of the rioters, threatening "the fire next time" if the supposed preferential treatment the Lubavitchers received from police and politicians continued. They also threatened that the next victims of the violence would be the Hasidim in Williamsburg.[60] Al Sharpton and Alton Maddox actually flew to Israel in an attempt to extradite Lifsh, who had fled back to his home there, and they suggested to newspaper reporters that Israelis could atone for the sin of their military and commercial relations with South Africa if they handed him over. (Israeli officials refused.)[61]

The Hasidim of Crown Heights, on their part, complained that during the whole affair the police had stood by while black and Jews clashed and had done nothing to stop it. Indeed, a subsequent state report laid the blame for the riot at the feet of Mayor David Dinkins and his aides, including Police Commissioner Lee Brown, who did not issue orders to "crack down" on the rioters until the third day, until Dinkins himself visited the scene and saw how bad the violence was.[62]

Blame and counterblame, along with a series of trials for those who had allegedly murdered Rosenbaum and incited the mobs, continued for years. Among the multiple legal actions taken by both sides was a class-action suit filed in federal court by the Crown Heights Jewish Community Council, charging that Mayor David Dinkins and Police Commissioner Lee Brown had "permitted, facilitated and effectively condoned," attacks on Hasidic people, that they had conspired not to protect Jews from the mob, and that their civil rights had been violated.[63] Dinkins's poor handling of the Crown Heights incident was a factor in his failure to win reelection in 1993; instead, the victor was Republican Rudolph Giuliani. In 1998 Mayor Giuliani announced a $1.1 million settlement in the case; with members of the Rosenbaum family at his side, he formally apologized to the Hasidic community of Crown Heights for the "clearly inadequate" city response to the 1991 riot.[64]

Fourteen years later, rage and resentment at the death of Gavin Cato was still evident. In January 2004 the play called *Crown Heights*—sponsored by nonmainstream political figure Lenora Fulani, who was known for making antisemitic statements—opened off-Broadway. In this version of the incident, the Rebbe's own car hit the young boy. Both the car and the Jewish ambulance left immediately. "There's a black boy bleeding," actors sang, "as the rabbi just runs." They referred to the Jews as "smug and safe in their white skins," who "turned their back" on a dying child. The death of Yankel Rosenbaum was presented as an accident in a fight in which Jews threw the first punch.[65]

A notable aspect of the riot itself was the relatively slow and hesitant response of the mainstream organized Jewish community, which felt distant and ambivalent toward the Lubavitch Hasidic community and was reluctant to say anything that might jeopardize already fragile black-Jewish relations.[66] Reaction was also complicated by the absence of key staff members and lay leaders, who were on vacation at the time the riot occurred. Among the articles criticizing the supposed inaction and lack of sympathy of the national Jewish organizations was an op-ed piece by *New York Times* editor A. M. Rosenthal, entitled "On My Mind: Pogrom in Brooklyn." "Some Jewish organizations acted as if Crown Heights did not concern them," he charged. "Their usually ferocious faxes were either silent or blurted out diplomatically balanced condolences to all concerned."[67] In fact, AJC's first press release after the riot did offer condolences to both sides and drew a clear moral equivalence between the accidental death of Gavin Cato and the murder of Yankel Rosenbaum. Lucette Lagnado in the *Village Voice* wrote an article, "The Jewish Non-Defense League: How Mainstream Jews Failed the Hasidim of Crown Heights." The article critiqued the ADL, the American Jewish Committee, the Jewish Community Relations Council, and the American Jewish Congress, asserting that the organizations had "failed horribly" during the riot.[68] Sidney Zion, in the *New York Observer* and the *New York Post* went so far as to compare their supposed inaction during the Crown Heights riot to an alleged "conspiracy of silence" that had caused these agencies to be ineffective in saving Jews during World War II. "Why the hell do we need these great Jewish organizations?" he concluded.[69] David A. Harris, AJC's executive director, wrote a letter in reply calling Zion's attack "scurrilous" and claimed that rather than being indifferent, "Jewish groups . . . worked feverishly behind the scenes in order to try to end the violence."[70]

Indeed, AJC leaders joined the Jewish Community Relations Council in an attempt to hold a press conference during the riot on the steps of City Hall to reaffirm the black-Jewish alliance and call for an end to the fighting. The group included fifteen black ministers, fifteen rabbis, the executive director of the New York Urban League, officers of the local JCRC, and Mayor Dinkins himself. The conference was deliberately called for eleven o'clock in the morning so that it would obtain some attention on the six o'clock news. But that night the news gave coverage, as it did throughout the riots, only to the most extreme statements from both sides and ignored the conference.[71] Within a few days after the riots AJC arranged for a full-page advertisement in the *New York Times,* headlined "We Have a Stake in Israel. America's Black Mayors," an attempt to stress that Jewish people had the best interests of black people at heart. The ad praised Israel's rescue and absorption of Ethiopian Jewry and was signed by thirty-six black mayors of American cities, including David Dinkins of New York, Tom Bradley of Los Angeles, Wilson Goode of Philadelphia, and Maynard Jackson of Atlanta.

After its initial reaction, AJC also issued a statement strongly criticizing the inadequate police response in the first few days of the riots. It called for a state investigation of the incident, demanded an inquiry into why only one arrest had been made for the murder of Yankel Rosenbaum when he was attacked by an entire mob, and offered a five thousand dollar reward for the apprehension of his killers. The AJC held meetings and exchanged letters with the leaders of national black organizations, asking why so few had spoken up to condemn the violence. It also called for greater attention to the "root cause" of inter-group hostility in urban areas, including cultural conflict and inadequate resources—especially in jobs and housing.[72] "Hatred will flourish in Crown Heights as long as government officials, clergy and community groups see the field of inter-group relations as less important than the running of schools, the protection of police and firefighters, and the regular pickups of the Sanitation Department," concluded Kenneth S. Stern, AJC's specialist in antisemitism and extremism, in his report on the riot, entitled "Crown Heights: A Case Study in Antisemitism and Community Relations." "If the black and Jewish communities do not learn what hurts each other and what each community perceives as its needs, violence and antisemitism are inevitable. Hate grows in a community where people are willing to create a moral equivalence between the tragic death of a child in an accident and a young man murdered by a hateful gang."[73]

The Crown Heights riot happened only a few weeks after another incident that put the spotlight on varieties of black antisemitism, among them an academic theory, known as Afrocentrism, which claimed that anything African was superior to anything non-African, that Africans were the original men and founders of civilization, that there was a white conspiracy to put blacks down, and that Jews were leaders in the trade that had enslaved them. The central figure in this theory—which became popular on the campus lecture circuit with such speakers as Louis Farrakhan and Khalil Muhammad—was Leonard Jeffries, a professor at City College of CUNY since 1972 and chairman of the Black Studies department there. In July 1991, Jeffries created a widespread Jewish reaction and black counterreaction when he made a speech at the Empire State Black Arts and Cultural Festival held in Albany, New York, ostensibly with the goal of defending the inclusion of multiculturalism and black studies in the public school curriculum.[74] Gary Rubin, director of AJC's National Affairs Department, in reporting on the speech described it as "classically antisemitic and every antisemitic belief throughout history was reiterated."[75]

Much of the two-hour speech was spent in attacking Jews. According to Jeffries, films that had insulted blacks were part of a "conspiracy" planned out of Hollywood "where people called Greenberg and Weisberg and Trigliani" lived. "It's not antisemitic to mention who developed Hollywood," he said. "Their names are there—Metro-Goldwyn-Mayer, Adolph Zuckor, Fox. Russian Jewry had a particular control over the movies, and their financial partners, the Mafia, put together a system of destruction for black people." He also claimed, "Everybody knows rich Jews helped finance the slave trade"; citing books of Jewish history as sources, he mentioned such venues as the colonial Jewish community of Newport, Rhode Island. The Jews there, especially Aaron Lopez, allegedly controlled "a couple of hundred slave ships" and also controlled "most, if not all, of the thirty distilleries that processed molasses from the Caribbean into rum, to be sold to the native Americans as 'fire water,' and to be sold to Africa, for enslaved Africans." Jews originally from Spain had supposedly "laid the foundation" for enslavement in the 1400s and 1500s. The sixteenth-century Amsterdam synagogue "was the center of slave trading for the Dutch. Amsterdam became a leading port in this period of time for slaving. And it was around this synagogue that the slaving system was established." "The documentation is there," he said, "We are now preparing ten volumes dealing with the Jewish relationship with the black community in reference to slavery, so we can put it in the school system, so there'll be no question."[76]

Jeffries' term as chairman of his department was up for renewal in the fall, and AJC passed a statement condemning his reappointment. In March 1992 the CUNY board of Trustees voted to remove Jeffries as chairman and put another professor in the position, while maintaining him on the payroll as a tenured professor. Jeffries sued, claiming that his demotion was punishment for controversial views and was therefore a violation of his First Amendment right to freedom of expression.[77] In the first legal round Jeffries won his case and received monetary damages and reinstatement as chairman. In 1995, when his term was up again, the trustees named another professor to the chairmanship. Jeffries remained on as a tenured professor, however, and continued to espouse his views in writing and in lectures on college campuses and at Nation of Islam events.[78]

Another instance in which AJC found itself confronting the Afrocentrist movement directly came in 1994, when it considered the case of Anthony Martin, a tenured history professor in the Africana Studies department of Wellesley College. A fellow Wellesley professor and chairman of the classics department, Mary Lefkowitz, was leading the faculty movement to discredit Martin, and she turned to the AJC board of governors for help when Martin sued her for libel. As a primary textbook for his survey course in African American history, Martin assigned volume 1 of *The Secret Relationship Between*

Blacks and Jews (Chicago: Nation of Islam, 1991), whose only author was given as "The Historical Research Department of the Nation of Islam." It is reasonable to assume that Jeffries himself was the main author and that this was meant to be the beginning of the "ten volumes dealing with the Jewish relationship with the black community in reference to slavery" that he had mentioned in his July 1991 speech. *The Secret Relationship* led to some half-dozen book-length refutations. It was eventually banned in Canada and by the Barnes and Noble and Borders bookstores, although it was still selling briskly on Amazon.com in 2006.[79]

"Most have always assumed that the relationship between Blacks and Jews has been mutually supportive, friendly and fruitful—two suffering people bonding to overcome hatred and bigotry," read the introduction to *The Secret Relationship Between Blacks and Jews*, "but history tells an altogether different story." The book's claim, buttressed by more than a thousand footnotes, was that Jews were conclusively linked "to the greatest criminal endeavor ever undertaken against an entire race of people—a crime against humanity—the Black African Holocaust. . . . They were participants in the entrapment and forcible exportation of millions of Black African citizens into the wretched and inhuman life of bondage. . . . Deep within the recesses of the Jewish historical record is the irrefutable evidence that the most prominent of the Jewish pilgrim fathers used kidnapped Black Africans disproportionately more than any other ethnic or religious group in New World history and participated in every aspect of the international slave trade. The immense wealth of Jews, as with most of the White colonial fathers, was acquired by the brutal subjugation of Black Africans."

Mary Lefkowitz outlined for AJC leaders the origins and assumptions of the Afrocentrist theory, which Anthony Martin was teaching in his class. When asked how such a false theory had gotten into the curriculum, she replied that a number of factors explained the "new academic climate of the 1990s." These included overspecialized faculty, diffuse and uncentralized curricula, lower academic standards, grade inflation, and the idea that freedom of speech guaranteed the right of a professor to teach anything he or she wanted regardless of how well grounded it was academically. The Wellesley administration, she said, did not want to criticize Martin for "fear of being called racist"; in addition, "many tenured professors do not want to disrupt the quality of their lives" and attacking even the most controversial professor would leave the door open for debate on their own quality of teaching. Martin, in the meantime, had written a book entitled *The Jewish Onslaught: Dispatches from the Wellesley Battlefront* (Dover, Mass.: Majority Press, 1993), in which he accused Mary Lefkowitz of being part of an anti-Jewish conspiracy against him arising from his attempts to prove Jewish control of the slave trade. Mary Lefkowitz later countered with *Not Out of Africa: How Afrocentrism Became An Excuse to Teach Myths as History* (New York: Basic Books, 1997).

At the board of governors meeting in 1994, the AJC leaders agreed to give Mary Lefkowitz legal assistance in the libel suit (the lawyers who eventually represented her came from the ADL) and to work on educational materials for campuses that would provide students and faculty with accurate information in order to dispute these types of arguments. They also formed a task force to investigate "trends of bigotry in academia with focus on extreme manifestations of Afro-Centrism."[80] AJC was already on guard against extreme anti-Israel and pro-Palestinian activity on college campuses, and the Nation of Islam's Louis Farrakhan—who now frequently quoted from *The Secret Relationship Between Blacks and Jews* in his public addresses—had been a popular speaker among black student groups since the early 1980s. As part of what they called their "Campus Watch" program, AJC now kept its eyes on what professors were teaching as well, making special use where possible of the many board members who were trustees of colleges and universities. In 2002 AJC's task force on antisemitism approached fifteen hundred university presidents to sign on to a letter drafted by seven current and past presidents opposing antisemitism and supporting an intimidation-free environment on campus. The letter was signed by three hundred of them and was printed in the *New York Times*.[81]

It was established AJC policy by the late 1980s not to have dialogues or meetings with anyone affiliated with the Nation of Islam. AJC and the ADL as well several times took out newspaper ads denouncing the NOI and its representatives. The general reaction of AJC in the face of such incidents as Crown Heights, Louis Farrakhan, and the antisemitic academic theories of black professors, however, was to work even harder to cultivate good black-Jewish relations with more centrist leaders. For example, four months after the riot, AJC sponsored a twelve-day study mission to Israel for eleven prominent black Christian leaders from the New York area. "It would be terribly wrong to turn our backs on people whose situation is so desperate just because their leadership is wrong or not of our choosing," declared Mimi Alperin—at the same board of governors meeting where Mary Lefkowitz presented her case. "We should know the long-term psychological effects of historical victimization. . . . We should not lose hope in the black community simply because of who we perceive as heading it." She reminded them that Jews had come willingly to America and had succeeded, but blacks had been brought in slave ships.

Stephen Steinlight, director of national affairs in 1994, said in another of numerous discussions on the subject that it was "essential" not to abandon relations with the black community, even though many in the Jewish community were "tired" of reaching out to them. Precisely because surveys showed that antisemitism among African Americans was higher than among other ethnic groups, it was necessary to reach out to them more. The AJC also could not abandon black leaders just because they met with figures like Louis Farrakhan.

The Jewish community had not recognized Yasir Arafat either, he said, but it had still met with foreign leaders and heads of states who had close ties with Arafat and had still used their relationships and contacts as a platform to say why they disagreed with the terrorist policies of the PLO. "When we consider the broad national affairs agenda of the AJC and the Jewish community as a whole, we recognize that *Tikkun Olam,* the quest for social justice, plays a central role," Steinlight declared, using a Hebrew term of questionable significance. "Maintaining the social justice agenda of the American Jewish community is vital to our organization, and black-Jewish relations have always been at the heart of that commitment."[82]

With this commitment in mind AJC pursued a number of projects in an attempt to improve these relations. In April 1996 the agency began in conjunction with Howard University publication of a magazine on black-Jewish relations called *CommonQuest.* The advisory board included Henry Louis Gates, U.S. Representative John Lewis, Kweisi Mfume (head of the NAACP), and Hugh Price (president of the National Urban League). Coeditors were Professors Russell Adams of Howard University and Jonathan Rieder of Barnard College. The magazine published three times yearly until it was discontinued in 2000. The first issue contained essays by prominent blacks and Jews on Louis Farrakhan's "Million Man March" of 1995, as well as an excerpt from a book on the 1958 bombing of an Atlanta synagogue.[83] In 1997, after Hugh Price had addressed the annual meeting, top AJC lay leaders and staff along with their counterparts at the National Urban League held a two-day retreat, where they discussed such themes as "the status and future prospects of black-Jewish relations, the changing racial and ethnic makeup of American society, the role of government in American life, and key public policy issues such as affirmative action, urban public education, and welfare reform." Four cities where AJC had chapters set up cooperative AJC–Urban League projects.[84]

AJC also took note of a wave of burnings of dozens of predominantly black churches, mostly in the South, in 1995–96. National AJC joined an interfaith coalition to provide funds to rebuild the churches, while the Chicago and Atlanta chapters carried on fund-raising drives locally. In December 1996 AJC presented a check for eighty-seven thousand dollars for the rebuilding of Gay's Head Baptist Church in Millen, Georgia, and AJC members were invited to volunteer for a week in the spring to help with the actual construction.[85]

With actions such as these and the improvement of lines of communication in Brooklyn (representatives of the black and Hasidic communities each had one another's cell phone numbers, for example) the Crown Heights riot was not repeated. Outside Brooklyn, blacks and Jews no longer lived in close proximity. Latinos became the largest minority and the focus of AJC's attention. While figures such as Louis Farrakhan continued to be popular and to make antisemitic statements from time to time—including charges in 2005 that American Jews and Israel were solely responsible for getting the United

States into war with Iraq—black-Jewish relations were no longer at the top of the Jewish agenda by the early 2000s.

Amid the whirl of all these activities at the turn of the twenty-first century—social policy, diplomatic negotiations, battling against antisemitism and terrorism, and seeing justice done in the case of the Holocaust—AJC leaders sometimes recalled that first and above all they were a Jewish organization. With all the power they wielded in improving relations with non-Jews, their first responsibility as it had been laid out in their founding statement in 1906 was to save and advance the lives of other Jews. By the 1990s it had been apparent for some time, and the fears were continually being reaffirmed, that perhaps the greatest threat to Jewish existence came not from terrorists or outside forces but from factors that operated within the community itself. Even as the organization strove to bring itself back from its worst financial reverses, AJC president Sholom D. Comay had taken this position. "Our programs contributing to Jewish survival are as important as anything we do," he said to the AJC board in June 1991. "We must meet this challenge so that our grandchildren and great grandchildren will be Jewish."[86]

The tension between AJC's Jewish agenda and general human rights agenda had been constant, and AJC had always found a way of doing both. Now AJC turned more than ever to intensifying the Jewish culture of the organization and applying its skills where they were most badly needed: in improving relations between Jews and other Jews, navigating the delicate area of intermarriage, and addressing the question of whether Jews as a distinct entity in America would survive at all.

The Second Jewish Continuity Crisis, Pluralism, and Jewish Unity

[1990–2006]

Activities and programming in AJC's Jewish Communal Affairs division—renamed Contemporary Jewish Life in 2000—were driven by three notable elements in the 1990s and early 2000s. The first and most important of these were the results of the National Jewish Population Survey of 1990, which ended extensive debate in previous years on whether the new non-Jewish spouses and children of intermarriages actually brought about an increase in the net Jewish population. Much of Jewish communal life in the 1990s and 2000s can be traced to responses to this study. The second was the assassination of Israeli Prime Minister Yitzhak Rabin by an extremist Orthodox Jew in November 1995. The assassination revealed wide religious, denominational, ethnic, and political cleavages within the Jewish people and increased anxieties about maintaining Jewish unity. Most of these divisions were related to differing opinions of the Oslo peace process with the PLO, which lasted from 1993 to 2000. In the wake of the assassination, following a pattern it had established in the 1980s, AJC—which strongly supported the peace process—strove to do what it could to keep opposing groups of Jews together.

In addition to Jewish continuity and unity, a third and related element was Jewish pluralism, meaning full recognition of all the denominations of Judaism. As had been the case for decades, the Israeli Chief Rabbinate, which ruled according to *halacha,* or traditional Jewish law, refused to grant any recognition at all to Reform and Conservative Judaism. There were persistent efforts in the Israeli Knesset and in the courts to amend Israeli law in such a way as to delegitimize non-Orthodox Jewish movements. Such efforts were intensified in the wake of the vast immigration of people from the former Soviet Union. Under the extended Law of Return, as it had been amended in 1970, anyone with a Jewish spouse or even one Jewish grandparent could be admitted automatically to Israel as a citizen. But this citizenship did not give them Jewish religious status for such purposes as birth, marriage, and burial according to the Chief Rabbinate of Israel. It was estimated that among the hundreds of thousands of Jews from the former Soviet Union who came to Israel more than one-third were not Jewish according to Jewish law—meaning their mothers were not Jewish and they had not undergone formal conversion.[1] There was pressure to conduct mass conversions and representatives of Israel's Chief Rabbinate wanted to make sure that Reform and Conservative rabbis had no part in performing them. At the same time there was increasing activism by representatives of the Reform and Conservative movements in Israel to have their movement's activities recognized and funded, to be permitted seats on local religious councils, and to have their conversions ruled valid.

The rift between Orthodoxy from the rest of American Jewry over the peace process, the association in the public mind of the Rabin assassination with right-wing Orthodox extremism, the issue of Jewish pluralism, along with a coincidental wave of blatant Messianism that was sweeping the influential Lubavitch Hasidic community—all poisoned interdenominational relations.[2] Relations were also worsened by triumphalism among some sectors of the Orthodox that at the end of the Jewish continuity battles they would be the only ones left standing. For example, the executive director of the ultra-Orthodox Agudath Israel in 2004 predicted that only 2.5 million Jews would be left in the United States by 2040—and of these, one-half would be Orthodox. He called for his group to be ready to take over the reins of fighting antisemitism, developing political support for Israel, and fighting on public policy issues when the days came that the leadership of the American Jewish Committee and other Jewish mainstream organizations were no longer there.[3]

The issue of Jewish pluralism struck closest to home in the United States and was ultimately far more important to American Jews than disputes over what percentage of the West Bank should be turned over to Palestinian control. The idea that their own brand of Judaism might not be recognized in the alleged Jewish homeland was unacceptable and negated all the activities in support of Israel that had been so much a part of American Jewish communal life. Rage and insult was joined by terror in the hearts of those non-Orthodox Jews who viewed Israel as their insurance policy and as their last refuge on earth if antisemitism overwhelmed the United States. It did not matter how remote this last possibility was. Repeated surveys by the ADL and by AJC's own research department might show that that the actual level of antisemitic activity in the United States was lower than it had ever been. Repeated surveys also showed that hundreds of thousands of American Jews considered antisemitism a serious problem, and they consistently rated it a greater danger to Jewish survival than intermarriage by a ratio of two to one.[4]

Reactions to the 1990 NJPS

The National Jewish Population Survey of 1990, sponsored by the Council of Jewish Federations, was a highly complex and scientifically rigorous study that studied all matters relating to the demography of American Jews, including regional distribution and migration patterns. The statistics it revealed on rates of intermarriage and the status of children reared in mixed-marriage households, however, rapidly passed by word of mouth even before the study was published. Of all born Jews surveyed, 31 percent had married non-Jews; this, as it happened, was about the rate that informed members of the Jewish community assumed that it would reveal.[5] Of all Jews who had gotten married in the previous five years, however—from 1985 to 1990—only 48 percent had married other Jews, leading to an intermarriage rate of more than half or 52 percent. Furthermore, among the children of mixed marriages, only 28 percent of the couples even claimed that they were trying to raise the children as Jews. Of the others, 41 percent were being raised in another religion, and 31 percent were reportedly being raised in no religion at all.[6] The study also showed that only 14 percent of American Jewish households fit the traditional definition of a Jewish family: mother and father, both Jewish, married for the first time, with children. Those who were born Jewish but now considered themselves members of another religion numbered 625,000; many of these were the parents of some 700,000 individuals under the age of eighteen who were of Jewish descent but were being raised in other religions.[7] Brown University sociologist Sidney Goldstein referred to the results of the study as revealing a "silent Holocaust."[8]

After the results of the 1990 study became known, the issue of "Jewish continuity"—which had first been raised in response to the Erich Rosenthal studies of the early 1960s—became the watchword as Jewish institutions and organizations feared that their potential donors, membership, and clientele were literally passing out of existence before their very eyes. Federations questioned their large allocations to Israel, with some thinking that in the short run the funds were more needed at home; only a strengthened American community, they argued, could be of any help to Israel. The *New York Times,* the *Wall Street Journal,* and *Newsweek* ran long, prominent stories on the issues of Jewish continuity and intermarriage. In 1985, author Charles E. Silberman had come out with a famous book titled *A Certain People: American Jews and Their Lives Today* (New York: Simon and Schuster). The book claimed that antisemitism was no longer a serious problem for American Jewry and that the number of Jews was actually rising due to spouses and children gained through intermarriage. Interestingly enough, in the extensive debates on the book scholars disagreed with the idea that the American Jewish population was rising, while laymen disagreed that antisemitism was no longer a threat to

American Jewry. After the release of the 1990 NJPS, a spate of books from American and Israeli scholars came out challenging Silberman's cheerful assessments and projecting a much more pessimistic outlook for American Jewry.[9] Subsequent recalculation—which showed that the 52 percent intermarriage figure was exaggerated and the true rate was closer to 43 percent—did not allay fears that intermarriage was rising precipitously and taking Jewish souls with it. The 2000 National Jewish Population Survey, though regarded as less precise than the 1990 one, also showed an intermarriage rate of less than half: 47 percent.[10]

For some time, however, the fearsome statistic that showed more than half of American Jews intermarrying was accepted as true. Philanthropists and communal leaders, lamenting that current efforts to keep young people Jewish were not working, called for new and innovative approaches. With more than 85 percent of Jewish youth attending college, Hillel: The Foundation for Jewish Campus Life was revitalized and reorganized in 1994 as an independent nonprofit organization.[11] Notable among the philanthropists who spearheaded new programs for Jewish youth were Charles Bronfman and Michael Steinhardt, who along with several millionaire associates established Birthright Israel in late 1998 (known as *Taglit* in Hebrew). Birthright Israel provided free, ten-day educational trips to Israel for young Jewish adults of any affiliation ages eighteen to twenty-six who had never been to Israel before. By 2006 Birthright claimed it had sent its one hundred thousandth participant to Israel; thousands more were on waiting lists because there were not enough funds to accommodate them.[12] Michael Steinhardt also led a consortium of philanthropists and Jewish family foundations in forming the Partnership for Excellence in Jewish Education, an organization dedicated to advancing day schools and day school enrollment in the United States. PEJE offered financial services, coaching in obtaining grants, joint purchasing at bulk discounts, political advocacy both within and outside the Jewish community, and help in establishing new schools.[13]

Michael Steinhardt also reached beyond current programming when at the General Assembly of the UJC in 2003 in Jerusalem he suggested a "Fund for Our Jewish Future" that would be used to give "Newborn Gifts"; that is, a voucher given to all Jewish families upon the birth or adoption of a child to be used toward early childhood education and perhaps a trip to Israel. The community had always been asking Jews to give, he commented, so it would be a revolutionary step to give something to them. Parents who might not have considered raising their child as Jewish might have an additional incentive to do so. Also, he suggested, as community networking would be necessary to identify newborn Jewish children, the program would enhance outreach efforts. He also suggested that the community should seek out the "best and the brightest" to become teachers in Jewish schools and that they should be "paid exorbitantly."[14] Although he received a standing ovation for his remarks, Steinhardt drew sharp criticism from some quarters, especially since he prefaced his remarks by saying that the Jewish denominations other than the Orthodox had failed in their purpose and that identity should be based on Jewish peoplehood, not religion. Some objected that Jewish education should not come at the cost of fighting antisemitism. Others criticized him for not consulting with Federation and other already existing programs and leaders. The president of the Union of Reform Judaism (as the UAHC, Union of American Hebrew Congregations, had been renamed) called his plan "Steinhardt's Folly."[15]

No matter how great the level of philanthropy, it was still not enough to meet all the needs of the community. The high financial cost of living a Jewish life and fear that it was a barrier to affiliation for Jewish individuals and families also became a subject for review. Communal leaders had not been accustomed to thinking that in a modern society Jewish identity was a commodity that could be bought and paid for. In 1992 AJC published the first study on the subject, "The High Cost of Jewish Living," by Aryeh Meir and Lisa Hostein, and followed it up ten years later with "The Cost of Jewish Living" by Gerald B. Bubis. The NJPS of 1990 had revealed that the median income for American Jewish families with children was $75,000–$80,000 dollars, a relatively high figure. However, that statistic still meant that half of American Jewish families earned below that income. Bubis estimated that in 1992 a Jewish family required $25,000–$35,000 of discretionary income for intensive Jewish experiences: synagogue dues, Federation donations, day school and summer camp tuition, and the higher prices for kosher meat. Such a sum was often beyond the reach even of upper-middle-class Jewish homes.[16]

Neither study on the high costs of Jewish living noted an additional factor affecting affiliation: the much-vaunted high level of education, occupation, and income that was necessary to hold up one's head in an American Jewish community. This pressure for accomplishment was particularly true for Jewish men although communal standards were high for women as well. It was an old American Jewish joke—with more than a vestige of truth—that in a Jewish family there were only three acceptable careers: a doctor, a lawyer, or, in the case of one who stuttered and could not stand the sight of blood, a certified public accountant. The alternative was to be a "bum." Jewish singles groups were invariably labeled as "young professionals." Affiliation and marriage within the Jewish community could be more difficult for men who could not or would not fill that mold.[17] At the other end of the economic spectrum, a suitably successful and prosperous Jewish male was all the more attractive as a potential mate to the full range of non-Jewish women.

In the wake of the 1990 NJPS study the debate about day schools and whether to seek government funding for them grew sharper. The Federation world was further convinced to shift its priorities and to give more support to Jewish religious institutions such as synagogues and Jewish schools. "We can rid ourselves of our communal ambivalence about Jewish day schools, the most intensive and most successful means of enhancing Jewish identity," suggested Steve Bayme of Jewish Communal Affairs as the AJC board considered its response to the NJPS study in 1991.[18] The May 1998 annual meeting featured a panel on Jewish continuity with Elliott Abrams, foreign policy adviser to Republican presidents and head of a conservative think tank; under the George W. Bush administration, he was head of the Middle East desk in the National Security Council. Abrams had written *Faith or Fear: How Jews Can Survive in a Christian America*, in which he argued that "civil Judaism"—what he called the focus on Jewish peoplehood, the security of Israel, rescuing endangered Jewish communities, and remembrance of the Holocaust—could no longer instill passionate Jewish identity in the souls of young Jews. Instead, he argued, the new generation was searching for spirituality and would "resonate" to the religious message of Judaism. Otherwise, the continuing secularization of American Jews was a path to assimilation and disappearance. He suggested that Jewish survival in the United States was linked to the continuing strength of religion in American public life. Abrams advised the Jewish community to drop its opposition to government aid for religious schools and to develop a more positive attitude toward the forces of Christian conservatism in the United States.[19]

In 1999 the AJC board debated extensively a new statement on Jewish education, wishing to update the statement it had issued in 1977 that had gone so far as to include support for day schools as a possibility. Even that degree of support from AJC, it will be recalled, was enough for a headline in an Atlanta Jewish newspaper to read that the Messiah had finally come (see chapter 8). The 1999 draft statement put greater emphasis on day schools and included support for a communal fund to help Jewish communal professionals send their children to such schools. As the AJC board of governors considered the statement, there was much negative discussion from the floor. One member said outright that a substantial proportion of the membership was opposed to the statement because supporting or allocating funds for Jewish day schools went against AJC's support for public education; thus, passage would be "unwise." The statement gave "lip service" to other forms of education, but it mainly supported day schools. Joseph Rackman said that a source of opposition to the statement was "fear that our children are going to be 'ghettoized.'" Harold Tanner of New York, who succeeded Bruce M. Ramer as AJC's president in 2001, said that Jewish day schools were the answer "for some people." However, he added, the AJC had been committed to public education for a long time, and had long been opposed to government vouchers as a method of supporting parochial schools. Support of this statement, he suggested, might "diminish AJC's ability to represent the interest of opposing vouchers." Jeffrey Sinensky, AJC's general counsel and director of national affairs, argued in opposition by reminding them of the 1925 U.S. Supreme Court decision in which AJC had supported the right of Catholic parents to send their children to Catholic schools. That, he said, had not adversely affected the agency's position in favor of public education then, "nor should it now."

Mimi Alperin, who was chairing the discussion as head of the Jewish Communal Affairs Commission (and who had been at the AJC in 1977), turned the tide when she declared that she had "heard all these comments before." "But now it is known," she declared, "based on the research of Jewish continuity, that the results from the supplementary schools have been dismal and that from day schools has not." When the statement finally came up for a vote the majority of the board approved it. The Israeli government, on its part, was deciding that assuring Jewish education in the Diaspora was in its own best interest. Starting in 2004, the government through the Jewish Agency began investing $10 million in Jewish education abroad. The sum was to be increased each year until it settled at the rate of $50 million per year from 2008 on. Most of the funds would go to sending Israeli educational emissaries to Diaspora communities around the world.[20]

By 2000 the idea that the U.S. government should play a role in Jewish day school funding was no longer the anathema it had been in the past. The *American Jewish Year Book* for 2001, for example, noted that many had been "shocked" when the JCPA or the Jewish Council for Public Affairs (formerly NJCRAC, the National Jewish Community Relations Council) voted in February 2000 to oppose government aid to private schools.[21] The subject of government aid was seriously discussed at a conference on Jewish education held by the AJC that June. One presenter, a Chicago businessman, brought up the "five percent plan"; that is, the idea of requesting all Jews to leave 5 percent of their estate to Jewish education. However, Jack Wertheimer, provost of the Jewish Theological Seminary of America and a well-known specialist in the study of American Jewish life, insisted that the enormous sums necessary to support Jewish education were not available from Jewish sources and would have to come from the government. Another presenter, John Ruskay, executive director of the New York UJA–Federation, agreed that Federations and family foundations were already too burdened with serving other needs to come up with the billions of dollars that were needed for day schools. The only alternative was to "seriously reconsider the traditional Jewish antipathy to government aid for private education."[22] Still, in the aftermath of the conference, AJC as an organization continued to oppose unambiguously any government support for day schools and periodically reaffirmed that policy.

The concern that American Jewish philanthropy rested on less than firm foundations was confirmed by a study done in 2003. Jews made up 22 percent of all the Americans who gave more than $10 million to charitable causes. But such donors only gave 10 percent of their donation dollars to Jewish institutions, much less than Jewish philanthropists had given in the past.[23] Few non-Jews could be expected to give anything at all. In addition, it had been known for some time that American Jews were increasingly becoming members of professions, and fewer were going into business. While they might earn good incomes, professionals were not inherently wealthy as their income depended on their labor. A professional generally had less money as well as less time to give to philanthropy than the businessman.[24] In time, both the amount and percentages of Jewish charitable giving could be expected to decline. Jewish communal institutions across the board were feeling budgetary strains in the 1990s and 2000s, and the largest umbrella Jewish philanthropy—United Jewish Communities (UJC) created in 1999 out of a merger of the old Council of Jewish Federations (CJF), the United Jewish Appeal (UJA) and the United Israel Appeal (UIA)—was in financial trouble. (The proposed name "United Jewish Federations" was rejected because it was pointed out that to the new generation the only association the word "Federation" evoked was with *Star Trek*).[25] UJC was also adversely affected by the increasing popularity in Jewish philanthropy of family foundations and targeted giving, which bypassed the traditional federation-style or umbrella groups.

The America Jewish-Israel Relationship

The NJPS of 1990 also had an impact on the relationship between the American Jewish community and the State of Israel. Israel was becoming less the poorer object of American Jewish charity. The country had benefited from mass immigration and was growing economically stronger. Most important, in the 1990s Israel appeared to be moving toward the long-awaited peace with the Arab nations and the Palestinians. In the area of demography and intra-Jewish marriage, Israel was obviously in a stronger position than the United States. Israeli Jewish leaders were alarmed that so many supporters and potential citizens in the Diaspora were apparently assimilating and disappearing. At a meeting of AJC's Institute for American Jewish–Israeli Relations (IAJIR) in Jerusalem in March 1994, Israeli President Ezer Weizman stated flatly to his American audience that the only way for American Jews to ensure their Jewish identity was through emigration to Israel, or *aliyah* (literally, "going up" in Hebrew). Equally challenging and provocative was a presentation by Yossi Beilin, the Israeli deputy foreign minister. He said that Israel had achieved such a level of economic development that financial support from American Jews was no longer necessary. He suggested that American Jews use their philanthropic dollars, instead, to give a strong Jewish identity to their children. Young Jews in Israel, even the most secular, according to Beilin, had a strong Jewish consciousness simply by living in a Jewish state and participating in Israeli Jewish culture, while their counterparts in the Diaspora were assimilating at an "alarming" rate.[26]

Ezer Weizman's remarks prompted a public letter from AJC Executive Director David Harris, who took issue with the claim that all American Jews had to make *aliyah*. This 1994 exchange hearkened back to the Blaustein–Ben-Gurion joint statement of 1950, although this time the circumstances were very different. Harris began by admitting that ties between the two communities were growing weaker. The common bonds that had held older generations of Americans and Israeli Jews together, such as the impact of the Holocaust and "shared roots in the towns and villages of Eastern Europe," no longer held the same immediacy for the younger generations of Jews in both countries. Young Israeli Jews were shaped by their unique national experience and culture while American Jews were for the most part far removed from Israeli culture and from the Hebrew language. Because concern for the security of Israel had been such an important part of the relationship on both sides, ties were bound to grow even more tenuous "if, as we all pray, Israel is able to move toward an era of peaceful relations with its immediate neighbors." The problem of weakening Jewish identity was real, but to call for mass *aliyah* from America was not the solution, according to Harris:

For better or worse, the vast majority of American Jews, at least for the foreseeable future, are not prepared to make Aliyah. American Jews have had a love affair with the U.S. and have regarded it as a unique Diaspora experience in which Jews have been able to achieve success in society at large, and simultaneously when they choose, sustain their Jewish identities. I understand that from a Zionist perspective, such thinking may seem unconvincing, but this is nevertheless the prevalent viewpoint among American Jews. If American Jews are not prepared to make Aliyah, and only a minority are studying Hebrew, do we dismiss the majority as inevitable candidates for assimilation? Or, do we recognize that many do want to affirm their Jewishness, however they may define it, and that we must therefore, all of us, strive to emphasize the oneness of the Jewish people and acknowledge diverse expressions of that identity? I subscribe to the latter approach, believing that Israel, over the long run, will gain more adherents, and indeed more candidates for Aliyah, via an admittedly drawn out and incremental approach.[27]

AJC's executive director also pointed out all the political contributions that American Jews had made to Israel without actual emigration, such as "shaping the climate of public opinion in the United States toward Israel and shaping the attitudes of successive Administrations and Congress." These efforts, in turn, had redounded "again and again to Israel's benefit—diplomatically, politically, strategically and economically." Moreover, American Jewish philanthropic generosity to Israel had had a strong impact on Israel's social services, immigrant absorption, health care, education, and culture. Harris ended the letter by expressing the hope that the Israeli president would visit the United States soon.

Weizman replied that as someone born and raised in Israel it had always been "agonizing" for him, as well as for many other fellow Israelis, "to see the majority of the Jewish people choosing to live somewhere else, not in Israel."

He had always felt that if more Jews had chosen to immigrate to Palestine seventy years earlier, "perhaps, just perhaps, our modern history would be different." Those attitudes, however, should not be regarded as "disrespect" for Jewish life elsewhere. With peace about to come to the area, he suggested, both sides had to increase their efforts to remain close. "I believe that the future of peace in the Middle East creates new challenges for Israel and new responsibilities," he wrote. "It is time for us and our partnership with world Jewry to contribute more. . . . I regard this dialogue as the launching pad of continual discussion in efforts to strengthen the relations between Israeli and American Jews as well as Jews throughout the world, and in this way to face the threat of assimilation and the potential loss of another major part of our people in this century. New bridges are needed." He suggested that through educational programs, youth exchanges, courses in Israel, serious study of Hebrew, summer trips to Israel, American investment, and the buying of homes there, "we will be able to bring about a change and prevent ourselves from drifting apart."[28]

In order to prevent that drifting apart AJC had already formed the Institute for American Jewish–Israeli Relations (IAJIR) in 1982, at the time of the Lebanon war. "The relationship between American Jewry and Israel that has existed during the past four decades is not inevitable and cannot be taken for granted," noted institute head Bertram H. Gold, at the time of its founding. Gold personally wondered with some anxiety if his children and grandchildren would have anything in common with Israeli Jews. The relationship as it was then "will not persist in the future without careful and determined attention and cultivation," he wrote. "Among other things, we need to review the history of our relations, to re-articulate them in terms appropriate to our own time and ideals . . . to assess the shortfalls between the dream and the reality, and to identify areas of difficulty and opportunity."[29]

The IAJIR distributed literature on the history of Israel-Diaspora relations, encouraged educational programs about Israel at all levels of education in the United States, encouraged the study of Hebrew, examined the treatment of Israel in American Jewish textbooks and of the United States in Israeli textbooks, and sponsored an extensive exchange program that brought Israeli leaders and educators to the United States. One unusual AJC educational effort to prevent the "drifting apart" of the communities was a three-part, three-hour prime time TV series in Hebrew about American Jews on Israel's major channel, entitled "Distant Relatives." It was produced not long after the Harris-Weizman exchange in cooperation with the Israeli Broadcasting Authority and filmed by an Israeli crew that spent a month in the United States extensively visiting and interviewing American Jewish families. Shula Bahat served as associate producer and the project was made possible by a grant from the Dorothy and Julius Koppelman, after whom the institute was named. Steven Bayme, who had become head of Jewish communal affairs in

1987 after Yehuda Rosenman had passed away from brain cancer at the age of sixty-nine, also took over as director of the institute in 1992. In 2001 the IAJIR shifted its focus from reaching Israelis to enhancing the image of Israel in the United States and internationally. Among its new projects was the Brandeis Summer Institute for Israel Studies, an annual three-week study program for college and university faculty enabling them to introduce or update courses on modern Israel on their campuses.[30]

Jewish Programming

In the post-1990 communal campaign to advance Jewish continuity, AJC's Jewish Communal Affairs Department, later Contemporary Jewish Life, intensified its own efforts toward positive Jewish programming. An additional goal in this effort was to affirm the public identity of the American Jewish Committee as a Jewish organization dedicated to the future of Judaism, and to overcome once and for all the negative stereotypes that still plagued the organization. "Why Be Jewish" was the Committee's own campaign based on showing that joy, gratification, and fulfillment could be had by choosing to live a Jewish life.[31] "The ad series was a very strong statement that the language of Jewish identity needs to be couched much more in language of positive affirmation than a language of terrible things happening to Jews," recalled Steven Bayme. "We always argued that you can't be a defense organization without a critical mass of Jews interested in leading a creative Jewish life."[32] Barry Holtz, a professor of education at the Jewish Theological Seminary, and Bayme prepared a pamphlet that provided ideological justification for such a view, stressing the positive values associated with living Jewishly. It was distributed widely to rabbis, Jewish educators, and communal leaders.[33]

The centerpiece of the campaign was a series of public service advertisements in the *New York Times*, magazines, and college newspapers that featured prominent Jews explaining, as the headline ran, "What Being Jewish Means to Me." The first ad featured a statement by Nobel Peace Prize–winner Elie Wiesel and ran on the op-ed page of the *New York Times* on Sunday, September 27, 1992, the day before the Jewish New Year, and in numerous college papers across the country. The ads featured the name of the American Jewish Committee prominently and encouraged readers to contact the AJC for information about programs and organizations that could provide a connection to Jewish life. Subsequent ads included statements from Senator Joseph I. Lieberman of Connecticut, Nobel Prize–winning scientist Roslyn Yalow, novelist Anne Roiphe, Associate Justice Ruth Bader Ginsburg of the U.S. Supreme Court, actor Leonard Nimoy, prominent executives in the financial and advertising worlds, diplomats, and a professional football player. A Jewish astronaut, pictured in his NASA space suit, described what it was like for a believing Jew to fly in orbit around the earth. A cadet at the U.S. Military Academy at West Point (class of 1996) explained what it meant for an American Jew to prepare himself for a career as a U.S. Army officer. Dr. Ruth Westheimer, the popular sex therapist, author and media personality, who lost her entire family in the Holocaust, stressed that the Nazis "couldn't eradicate my will to live and pass on to my children and grandchildren my love for Judaism, Israel, and the Jewish people."[34]

Response to the ads and to the pamphlet surpassed all expectations, with hundreds of letters and phone calls coming in from those seeking more information about being Jewish. One rabbi of a large congregation in Westchester County wrote that "Why Be Jewish?" was so compelling that he presented a copy to each couple that he married. In the summer of 1994 the Committee did a special mailing to rabbis of copies of the "What Being Jewish Means to Me" ads, along with a packet of AJC publications on Jewish identity, including a pamphlet on Jewish survival authored by AJC President Alfred H. Moses. The packet was supposed to help the rabbis in preparing their High Holidays sermons. More than six hundred rabbis wrote in to express their thanks and to order more copies for their communities.[35] In 1997 to mark the High Holidays season, AJC ran a full-page advertisement in the *New York Times* and other newspapers summing up five years of previous ads in the series, twenty in all.

AJC extended positive Jewish programming to its own leadership as well. Inspiring them with the Jewish tradition's insight into political and social issues of the day was the goal of AJC's Judaic Literacy for Jewish Communal Leaders Institute, held for the first three years at the Brandeis-Bardin Institute in Los Angeles. Scores of AJC members—national and chapter leaders, commission members, regional directors, and alumni of AJC's young leadership program—met for four days of intensive study with AJC staff and such scholars as Dr. Neil Gilman of Jewish Theological Seminary and Dr. Arnold Eisen of Stanford University (in 2006 Eisen was chosen as the chancellor of JTS).

In 1997 Steven Bayme, drawing on his experience in college teaching and adult education, published *Understanding Jewish History: Texts and Commentaries*, which, within one volume, surveyed the range of Jewish history from biblical times to contemporary relations between Israel and world Jewry.[36] Bayme was a graduate of the Maimonides School in Boston, a day school that taught a synthesis of Jewish heritage and Western civilization; he received his B.A. from Yeshiva University and his PhD from Columbia. Over the next five years twenty-two chapters launched in-house study groups for their own membership based on the book.[37] The book was at the center of the December 1997 Judaic Literacy Institute. Fifty AJC leaders from eighteen chapters met for study sessions and practical seminars, topped off with a Shabbat service; by the end of the weekend, they were prepared to begin the local education programs based on *Understanding Jewish History*.[38] Steven Bayme also conducted monthly study sessions in Washington,

D.C., for Jewish government officials, legislators, and congressional staffers on how classical Jewish texts shed light on contemporary public policy issues.[39]

For general adult education AJC also helped implement in 2000 the Meah Program, a one hundred–hour curriculum of Jewish study for lay leaders that was developed by Hebrew College in Boston. For teenagers they developed in 2004 the IKAR program. IKAR stood for Israel Knowledge, Advocacy, and Responsibility; it was an attempt to fill the gap in education about modern Israel found in otherwise committed Jewish youth. The project, which was an interactive course of study boosting connection with Israel and advocacy skills on Israel's behalf, was designed to be used as part of a Solomon Schechter High School curriculum.[40]

Enhancing ties with Israel was also the goal of AJC's "Made in Israel" campaign, begun in 2003 when two years of Palestinian terrorism had taken a severe toll on Israel's economy. More than 10 percent of the population was unemployed. To strengthen the Israeli economy and to express solidarity with Israel's people, the AJC began encouraging American Jewish communities to buy Israeli products whenever and wherever possible. A feature on the wonders of Israeli wine in AJC's magazine encouraged readers to partake of the land's many offerings. To make buying Israeli goods easy and convenient, the AJC assembled on its website a comprehensive list of Israeli products from clothing to crafts to fine art. Items could be purchased by following links to vendors' websites and other "Buy Israel" sites. The article on wine urged every member and their families to buy Israeli products for personal and business use, and also announced that AJC had directed its offices around the world to purchase Israeli goods whenever possible for AJC events. "Supporting Israel," the article read, "is as easy as click and go." In another move to show solidarity with the people of Israel, AJC members and staff joined together on the first-ever American Jewish Committee float in the Salute to Israel Parade down Fifth Avenue in June 2006.

AJC's public image as a self-consciously Jewish, pro-Israel organization was also enhanced when Executive Director David Harris devised a series of four basic tests of Jewish knowledge that were first published as a four-page insert in the New York *Jewish Week*. The test included several questions about Israel. The "Jewish IQ" tests were specifically labeled a part of AJC's "Jewish identity initiative."[41] The tests generated hundreds of calls and requests for more copies to AJC headquarters. They were subsequently reprinted in other Anglo-Jewish papers.

Statements on Intermarriage

By the 1990s within AJC there was nothing controversial about buying Israeli products or supporting educational projects such as the Jewish IQ test. The same was not true of the most delicate and painful ongoing issue the AJC and the general Jewish community faced: how to react to the high rate of intermarriage between Jews and non-Jews that had been revealed in the 1990 NJPS along with the fact that only one-quarter of such families were making any attempt to raise their children as Jewish. The AJC faced the issue again in 1991 when the time came to update its 1977 position statement on intermarriage in light of the NJPS study and the results of its own several research studies. As always, any AJC position statement would set policy and programming for the next several years and would presumably exert a strong influence on other organizations and institutions. Members of the board of governors and individuals in the chapters were deeply divided on how to respond. How far could they go in condemning intermarriage and advocating conversion for non-Jewish spouses without alienating members of their own families? A related question, as it developed within the ranks of AJC and other American Jewish organizations, was the proper allocation of communal resources. Should limited funds best be spent on "outreach" to the periphery, to those who had already chosen to intermarry, or on "inreach"; that is, on supporting and shoring up the already moderately affiliated in the hope that they would lead more intensive Jewish lives?[42] And what about religious life? What role should non-Jewish spouses and relatives play in synagogue for example, during a child's bar mitzvah or wedding?

Charlotte Holstein, who was chair of the Jewish Communal Affairs Commission in 1991, wrote of her divided feelings as a leader in Jewish communal affairs and the parent of an intermarried child. As the commission was in the process of updating its statement on intermarriage, her own daughter was planning her marriage to a longtime boyfriend, who had been born a Catholic. "I love and respect my daughter and I would do anything to protect her happiness and future," she wrote in an essay entitled "When Commitments Clash: One Leader's Personal Dilemma."[43] As the statement was being drafted, she wrote, "I felt that many aspects of it were directed at me personally." The draft statement said that intermarriage ought to be prevented, that most rabbis were prohibited from performing mixed marriages, that in such families there would be difficulties in imparting Jewish knowledge and tradition to the children, and that if intermarriage continued at the current rate it would lead to "an erosion of the size, strength and vitality of the Jewish community."[44] To all of this, she reflected, her own family was contributing. And yet, she wrote, it was necessary for her to "draw the distinction between what I felt emotionally and what rationally was good for the survival of the Jewish community as a whole." She was not alone in her dilemma; it had been true for some time that many AJC leaders had intermarriage in their families or were intermarried themselves. Thus there prevailed among them "a more accepting attitude toward intermarriage" than among more traditional segments of the community, segments AJC had to consider if it was going to assert overall leadership and act in the best interests of preserving Jewish unity.[45]

The actual adoption of the 1991 "Statement on Intermarriage" was as lengthy and complex a process as ever took place within the ranks of AJC. As the chairman of the commission described it, the first draft was composed by the staff and then submitted to the various members of Jewish communal affairs, who came from different parts of the country and followed different denominations of Judaism. Revisions were made, approved, and then it was submitted to the board of governors. After further debate and several changes by the board of governors the statement was distributed to the chapters around the country for their input. Of the twenty chapters consulted, seventeen voted approval, Cleveland abstained, and Minneapolis and St. Louis rejected it.[46] Opinions were made known by letters, phone calls, and, in one instance, a video presentation. Additional concepts were added and a few changes made. Then it came before the board of governors a second time to be debated and discussed. Another addition was made, and then it was finally passed.

The final statement had a strong anti-intermarriage tone and included the sentences "AJC studies as well as other studies show that the rapidly rising number of intermarriages represents a serious risk to the vitality of the Jewish community, Jewish continuity, and identity. Clearly the Jewish community prefers that Jews marry other Jews," along with, "The challenge for the Jewish community is to offer positive communal and personal connection to the intermarried while at the same time to develop and encourage programs that lead to Jews marrying other Jews."[47] The overall thrust of the statement was that endogamy was preferable, that conversion was the best outcome of an intermarriage, and that when there was no conversion any children should still be raised exclusively as Jews. The latter sentence assumed, however, that it was possible to do both "outreach" and "inreach" at the same time.

Similarly controversial was the 1996 "Statement on the Jewish Future," the result of consultations and extensive debates with leading academics, rabbis, and communal professionals affiliated with all the major religious movements in Judaism. The debate had its roots in an article originally published in *Commentary* in which the authors surveyed the Jewish activities of different subjects and classified the subjects as actively engaged, moderately engaged, loosely engaged, and disengaged.[48] The Jewish Communal Affairs Commission took the article, made a programmatic statement out of it, and solicited prominent Jewish thinkers to sign it. Although it did not come to represent official AJC policy, the "Statement on the Jewish Future" was eventually published by AJC as part of a booklet with thirteen essays responding to it—from seven of the thirty communal leaders and scholars who signed the statement, and six who remained critical.[49]

The statement began by noting the rising tide of intermarriage and the community's attempts since 1990 to foster Jewish continuity. "Certain initiatives, however, seem to us more likely to undermine North American Judaism than to strengthen it," the statement declared. "In a well-intentioned effort at inclusiveness, some in the Jewish community seem all too willing to sacrifice distinctive Jewish values and teachings. In response, we call upon American Jews to declare the following five values fundamental to any program of Jewish continuity in North America." Four of the values were "Torah," defined as Jewish learning; *Am Yisrael*, or "Jewish Peoplehood"; *Klal Yisrael*, or "the community of Israel" (which in this sense meant Jewish pluralism; that is, respect for denominations other than the Orthodox); and *Brit*, or "covenant," which "serves to differentiate Jews from non-Jews and insure that the Jews remain a people apart." This section was explicit on what the role of non-Jewish relatives in Jewish ceremonies should be. "Strong, visible boundaries" had to be maintained between Jews and non-Jews, and only Jews should enjoy leadership roles within the Jewish community and within Jewish religious life.

The final value in "Statement on the Jewish Future," and probably the most controversial one, was *keruv* or "outreach," which addressed the question of where community resources should best be allocated: "The moderately affiliated are the most promising candidates for outreach and—given scarce resources—outreach programs are most productively directed toward them." The statement continued, "Outreach directed toward those who have moved furthest from Judaism and toward the non-Jewish marriage partners of Jews may also be valuable and should remain on the Jewish communal agenda. No Jew should be written off." It concluded, however, "Our priority ought to target those in the broad middle of the Jewish population to strengthen their adhesion to the core of Jewish life, in all its manifestations. Outreach to mixed-marrieds should never encourage religious syncretism or ideological neutrality to mixed marriage itself. We part company both with those who believe that any kind of Jewish involvement, no matter how superficial, promotes Jewish continuity, and with those who look upon outreach as a panacea and seek to dilute Judaism to make it more attractive to potential converts. Both of these efforts, while well-meaning, are doomed to fail; they promote not continuity but radical discontinuity and are at variance with our tradition."[50]

The authors of the statement defended themselves for having made hard ideological choices. "The signers of the Statement believe that there is no effective route to Jewish continuity that will not prove offensive, in some measure, to the Jewish communal consensus," declared Steven Bayme. "Some losses are inevitable, and many of these will be personally painful to the leadership of the American Jewish community."[51] Steven M. Cohen, professor of sociology at Hebrew University, argued that the statement's relatively uncompromising stance was necessary both on principle and for strategic considerations. "The moderately affiliated (even if they're intermarried) are much easier to reach than the unaffiliated (especially if they're intermarried)" he wrote. "The same effort, the same dollars, the same rabbis and educators can have a more profound impact on families and individuals who are visible and are already somewhat committed to conventional Jewish life than they can on a population that is remote, uninterested, and invisible."[52]

Jack Wertheimer argued that Jewish institutions such as schools and summer camps were already starved for adequate funds; he recalled some parents who had told him with "tears in their eyes" that they were removing their children from a day school because they could not afford the tuition. "Our present course seems hell-bent on harming that more engaged population," he wrote. "The more we try to make intermarried families feel comfortable in Jewish settings, the further we demolish barriers to intermarriage. Why should young people oppose intermarriage if they see interfaith families treated as equals in the synagogue? How can our youth develop a resistance to interdating and intermarriage when the Jewish community is becoming ever more reluctant to stigmatize intermarriage—and on the contrary, is creating a vast population of lobbyists who favor the elimination of barriers to intermarriage because they themselves are intermarried?"[53]

The six opponents to the statement who submitted essays to the booklet were vehement in their criticism. Some, indeed, were offended. Rabbi Jeffrey K. Salkin, chair of the Reform movement's Outreach Commission, said that the statement was unrealistic and that the community must not choose between but practice outreach to *both* the intermarried and the moderately affiliated. "It is far too late in American Jewish history to turn back the clock," he wrote. "The authors know that only a time-machine–induced trip back to the thirteenth century has any hope of completely ameliorating the threat of mixed marriage. Time and circumstances being what they are, what should the community do? To *not* invest money in interfaith families and their unique needs is tantamount to abandonment."[54] John Ruskay, a vice president of the UJA-Federation, felt that the writers of the statement were unfairly referring to the federations and that their accusations were baseless. The federations, in his view, were already reaching out to the moderately affiliated. He also felt, especially since the writers of the statement were mostly from Conservative and Modern Orthodox backgrounds, that it was unfairly targeting the Reform movement and suggesting that Reform outreach efforts were "beyond the pale." "How the authors could affirm pluralism as a central value while seeking to deny communal funds to the programs of a major religious movement eludes this observer," he wrote.[55] Jonathan Woocher, director of JESNA (Jewish Education Service of North Africa) said he did not sign the statement in part because it was "needlessly strident and confrontational."[56]

Rabbi Eric H. Yoffie, president of the Union of American Hebrew Congregations, was even more specific in his denunciation of the statement; its primary purpose, he insisted, was to "attack the outreach work initiated in the late 1970s by the Reform movement and subsequently emulated by many others in the Jewish community." He accused the authors of engaging in "Jewish Darwinism"; that is, "the belief that only the fittest Jews will survive, and that therefore only they are deserving of our support and attention."[57] In his view the conclusion that Jews on the periphery of the community should be left unattended was "theologically offensive, sociologically blind, and practically disastrous." "Our theological mandate is clear," he declared. "The nature of the covenant forbids the exclusion of any Jew, however wayward, from the people's collective destiny."[58] Like Rabbi Salkin, he expressed the belief that the community was capable of conducting both outreach and programs directed at those already engaged in Jewish life.

Deborah Dash Moore, then a professor at Vassar College and the product of a Reconstructionist family, was also intensely critical of the statement. "Why should we trust these self-appointed gatekeepers with their penchant for drawing boundaries and setting up barriers?" she asked. "They would plan to leverage the future by laying guilt over the survival of the people at the feet of every American Jew and Jewish organization. The new prophets call for errant Jews to come back to the ways of the Torah. . . . Reading this document, I can well understand—and empathize with—many of our forebears who eagerly fled the constraints of the collapsing, corrupt kehillahs of eastern Europe to embrace the freedom and anarchy of American Jewish communal life as a wonderful tonic." She referred to the freedom enjoyed by American women, who had been able to "sacrifice those distinctive Judaic values and teachings" that would have left them as second-class citizens.

Professor Moore also objected to the sentence about the "commanding obligations" of Torah. "Who is commanding?" she asked. "Must all American Jews now believe in God and God's commandments? Are we moving toward requiring a belief in revelation? Will the next step be another thirteen articles of faith as Maimonides constructed them? Here, in late twentieth-century America, Torah is placed in a theological straitjacket that the American Jewish community is urged to adopt to guide its funding priorities." Moore argued that the periphery had always been larger than the center in American Judaism and most Jewish immigrants did not cross the ocean carrying deep knowledge of Jewish rituals and texts. She stated that she "vigorously" objected to placing the Orthodox agenda "at the center of Jewish communal concerns" and echoed the charges of the others that the statement would unfairly deprive the Reform movement of communal funding: "No, American Jews haven't produced a vibrant, powerful, ever-expanding core of committed folk who accept an exclusive covenant and believe God commanded them to fulfill obligations laid down in the Torah, but I suspect that most of them don't want to create such Jews. Or such a core. Most Jews didn't come to America for such a task, and now that they're here, they don't want to take up such a burden of continuity. I agree with them. I might add that restricting Jewish communal funds to the 'moderately affiliated'—that is, largely orthodox and conservative Jews—won't produce such a core either, although it will guarantee that Jewish communal resources are increasingly directed into the hands and pockets of these Jews."

American Jews were already distinctive enough, she stated, in their education, liberalism, secularism, egalitarianism, wealth, civic-mindedness, and tendency to live in metropolitan areas. "We may look like other white Americans," Moore asserted, "But we don't act like them. . . . This statement suggests that we actually become more like other Americans. . . . We are told to become insular, exclusive, and unconcerned with universal values, to withdraw from the public sphere and to commitments to making American society as open and egalitarian and democratic as possible. Implicitly it is suggested that we act more like white Baptists and Methodists and Presbyterians and Episcopalians, not to mention Catholics—all those who have turned their backs on liberal values to cultivate their own narrow garden plots." The writers of the statement, she charged, were "obsessed with excluding Jews, with building ever higher barriers to participation." "Let's keep the Jewish marketplace of ideas and people an open one," she insisted. "Setting boundaries, erecting barriers, excluding people, and choosing gatekeepers is not a promising way to begin to face common problems."⁵⁹

These disagreements were by no means solved when the AJC board of governors met in 1997 to issue a policy statement and action plan on Jewish continuity, which necessarily included discussion of intermarriage. Again a draft statement went back to the chapters for review, and again months went by before a declaration acceptable to everybody could be passed. Mimi Alperin, by then the chair of the Jewish Communal Affairs Commission, noted that people were still having difficulty "separating their own personal choices and experiences from what a Jewish communal agency ought to stand for." AJC's responsibility in 1997, she said, was to reflect what fifteen years of research findings, "much of it our own," had to say about the future of the Jewish community. "It doesn't help to tell people what they want to hear when it isn't the truth," she insisted. "Perhaps the Statement challenges the status quo but that is what AJC has done in the past and must continue to do so."⁶⁰ The final statement, like that on intermarriage in 1991, still affirmed preference for endogamy, conversion, and raising children as Jews—but again it solved the inreach-outreach debate by assuming that it was possible to do both simultaneously. "The Jewish community must develop a multi-track approach to strengthen Jewish identity and positive Jewish experience in both in-marriages and mixed-marriages," it read. "We must reach in and reach out."⁶¹

As the years passed and the population of mixed-marriage couples and their children grew, the old taboos among Jews about intermarriage all but collapsed. Before the 1970s rabbis who performed them had been compared to criminal abortionists. Now it was promoting in-marriage that was becoming taboo, not the other way around. Rabbis risked not having their contracts renewed if they brought up what was now being called "the I word." Jews had been integrated into the Christian mainstream of American life to the point that of four Democratic presidential aspirants in 2004, one was Jewish and four others had Jewish family connections.[62] In its annual survey of American Jewish public opinion done in the fall of 2001, the AJC found that well over half of the sample—56 percent—disagreed with the statement "It would pain me if my child married a Gentile." Most were either positive or neutral toward such a prospect. Only 39 percent agreed and 5 percent were not sure. Seventy-nine percent of the respondents favored a rabbi officiating, and 50 percent said he should do so even if a Gentile clergyman was involved. In answer to the question, "the best response to intermarriage is to encourage the Gentile to convert," 68 percent disagreed, 25 percent agreed, and 7 percent were not sure. Most telling was the response to the statement "It is racist to oppose intermarriage." Exactly half of the respondents agreed with the statement.[63]

As time passed, the boundaries that separated Jewish practice from Christian practice were also eroding. A 2001 study by Sylvia Barack Fishman, "Jewish and Something Else: A Study of Mixed Marriage Families," showed that in mixed-marriage households, even in families where the parents had agreed to raise the children as Jewish, Christian practices tended to creep in over the years, especially if it was the mother who was not Jewish.[64] (For purposes of comparison, the study also examined in-married couples and couples where the non-Jewish partner had converted.) "Historically, American Jews have known they were not Christians," noted Steven Bayme in his introduction to the study. "Even this boundary may today be at risk."[65]

In the sample of "Jewish and Something Else," more than 80 percent of mixed-marriage families reported Christian activities of some sort, with Christmas and Easter celebrations being most common. Two-thirds of them celebrated Christmas at home, and 16 percent actually went to church as well. More than half celebrated Easter at home, and 12 percent also attended church for that holiday.[66] In a finding important for public policy, it was found that parental attitudes regarding intermarriage made a difference. Among mixed-marriage individuals born Jewish, 62 percent said their parents had said nothing to them about being opposed to intermarriage. In comparison, 62 percent of individuals who were in-married and 48 percent of those whose partner had converted indicated that their parents had discouraged mixed marriage and indicated a preference that their children marry other Jews. "A backlash effect of negative reactions to discouragement of mixed marriage," Sylvia Fishman indicated, "was reported in fewer than five percent of cases in any category."[67]

In February 2001, as "Jewish and Something Else" was going to press and in the wake of the annual opinion survey that showed half of American Jews thought it was racist to oppose intermarriage, the Contemporary Jewish Life Department of AJC followed a strategy similar to what it had done in 1996 when it produced the Statement on the Jewish Future. It convened a coalition of approximately twenty-five communal leaders, rabbis, and Judaic scholars, including Sylvia Barack Fishman, who all resolved to "work together to restore the ideals of in-marriage," promote its importance, and encourage Jewish leadership to take responsibility in setting in-marriage as a norm. Absent an in-marriage, the group pledged to advocate forcefully for conversion.[68] "In the face of an American culture that has declared interfaith marriage to be as American as apple pie," the director of the department wrote, "only Jews themselves can articulate the importance of Jewish in-marriage. The question is whether the Jewish leaders have the will do so." [69]

The group, which eventually named itself the Jewish In-marriage Initiative, drew skepticism from some quarters. Sociologist Egon Mayer, who was the founding director of the Jewish Outreach Institute—and had years since parted company with the AJC over his forceful advocacy of far-outreach—called the new endeavor "ludicrous" and "comical." In his view, fighting against intermarriage was like "arguing against the weather." "They're going to make speeches to people who in every other aspect are integrated into American life, and expect those people to listen?" he asked. "It doesn't cost anything to pontificate but the American Jewish Committee could use its collective intelligence in better ways than this."[70] Edgar Bronfman, megaphilanthropist and chairman of the World Jewish Congress, told a London newspaper that opposing intermarriage was "racist and begins to sound a little like Nazism." For him the choice was "an attempt to double the amount of Jews that there are; or we can irritate everybody who's inter-married and lose them all."[71]

As it happened, although the coalition had several important AJC staff and lay leaders in it—including Steven Bayme, Mimi Alperin, Charlotte Holstein, Lynn Korda Kroll, chair of the Contemporary Jewish Life Commission, and Shoshana Cardin, a member of the board of governors—the AJC Executive Committee, a smaller body that met in between meetings of the board of governors, voted not to give it official endorsement. "This particular initiative is not the right fit at this time," Executive Director David Harris told reporters in November 2002. The coalition thus had to disband and reconvene outside the boundaries of the AJC. Mimi Alperin, a member of the coalition, regretted the action. "The Executive Committee didn't want to be front and center on this issue," she said.[72] This was so even though there was nothing in the coalition's platform that directly contradicted any official statement AJC had ever made.

A study commissioned and published by the AJC in 2006 suggested that mixed marriage and children of Jewish descent being raised in other faiths was not the only problem in assuring continuity among non-Orthodox Jews. The survey "Young Jewish Adults in the U.S. Today: Harbingers of the American Jewish Community of Tomorrow?" done by Ukeles Associates, Inc., indicated that the percentage of Jews who were Orthodox in the 18–29 age range was twice that among Jews aged 30–39. It also showed that more than half of all American Jews under the age of forty were not yet married, and that 56 percent

of the American Jewish population consisted of non-Orthodox singles and
married couples without children.[73] The issue of who was marrying whom
and how the children were being raised was now being superseded by the issue
of a generation where many never married or never had any children at all.

The Assassination of Yitzhak Rabin

One reason for AJC as a whole to avoid taking divisive stands on the question
of outreach and intermarriage was its desire to continue a mission it had
begun in the 1980s: to act as a unifying force among different groups of Jews
and to serve as a sort of communal umpire in disputes between the denominations. Aside from intermarriage, conversion, Jewish continuity, and other
subjects that divided the various factions of Judaism, the Oslo peace process—
which began in 1993 and involved the gradual handing over of parts of the
West Bank and the Gaza Strip to Palestinian control—was also highly divisive.
The continued suicide bombings by Hamas that killed and wounded scores of
Israelis, and the possible displacement and endangerment of Jewish settlers in
the territories, caused a shattering along religious and political lines. Organizations such as AIPAC and the Conference of Presidents had increasing difficulty speaking with one voice on the Middle East. A majority of American
Jews when polled showed support for the peace process; when it came to AJC
members, nine out of ten in 1995 supported the peace process and the majority thought there ought to be a Palestinian state.[74] The majority of Orthodox
Jews, however, many of whom considered the territories to be holy and God-
given land, opposed it, and some expressed their opposition in the most vehement and bitter of terms.[75]

In Israel, for example, Orthodox rabbis announced that Israel's peace policies violated Jewish law. In America, Rabbi Abraham Hecht, president of the
Orthodox Rabbinical Alliance of America, stated publicly that Israeli leaders
who gave away land to non-Jews deserved the death penalty. Israeli rabbis
called on Israeli Defense Forces soldiers to refuse to follow orders to hand over
army bases to the PLO. One rabbi compared Rabin to the officers of the Jewish councils during World War II that had supposedly handed fellow Jews over
to the Nazis. When Prime Minister Yitzhak Rabin and PLO Chairman Yasir
Arafat came to the White House to sign an agreement known as Oslo II—
which would hand over even more territory to the Palestinian Authority—the
National Council of Young Israel demonstrated with signs saying that Arafat
was a terrorist, Rabin was a Nazi, and "one Holocaust was enough."[76] The
AJC and other mainstream Jewish organization issued statements deploring
the use of such rhetoric, but it continued nonetheless. Rabin, on his part, in audiences with American Jewish leaders and newspaper reporters denounced
Jewish groups who would "pressure Congress against the policies of the

democratically elected government of Israel" and rejected the idea that American Jews should play any role in Israeli affairs, either for or against his government, other than fund-raising to help pay for immigrant absorption.[77]

On Saturday evening, November 4, 1995, opposition to Rabin culminated in his assassination in Tel Aviv by a right-wing extremist Orthodox Jew, twenty-seven-year-old Yigal Amir. Rabin had been attending a rally held by Peace Now attended by up to 250,000 people. The rally had concluded with the singing of the anthem of the peace movement, "A Song of Peace," and Rabin, holding a copy of the words in his hands, tried to sing along. Afterward, he folded the song sheet and put it in his pocket. As he was preparing to get into his car, he was shot three times at close range in the stomach and chest. He died not long afterward at a Tel Aviv hospital. The now-bloodied sheet of paper was later recovered from his shirt pocket.

His funeral was internationally televised. A delegation of one hundred Americans attended, including former presidents George Bush and Jimmy Carter, secretaries of state from four prior administrations, and dozens of members of Congress. The delegation was led by President Bill Clinton, who was the final speaker at the ceremony. He concluded his address with the words "Shalom Chaver" ("Goodbye, friend," in Hebrew) which quickly became a catchphrase in Israel. Clinton announced a period of national mourning and ordered all American flags on federal buildings to be flown at half-staff. Senator Edward Kennedy (Democrat, from Massacusetts) went to the gravesite after the ceremony to leave earth taken from the graves of his slain brothers, President John F. Kennedy and Senator Robert Kennedy.[78] Yigal Amir, who remained unrepentant to the end, was sentenced to life in prison for the crime, which he claimed he had committed in fulfillment of Jewish law. Rabin, he claimed, fell into the biblical category of a *Rodef* (pursuer) and it was permissible to kill such a person because it would prevent him from killing others. "Everything I did I did for Israel, for the people of Israel, for the land of Israel," he said in his final statement to the court. "The damage that would have been done to Israel had I not done what I did would have been irreversible."[79]

That Rabin should have been the target of an assassination attempt was itself no surprise—he had been surrounded by security guards wherever he went—but there was shock and disbelief around the world that the assassin had been a fellow Jew, and an Orthodox one at that. The event traumatized Israelis and caused bitter hatred against those who had been Rabin's opponents. "Never forget and never forgive" became the motto of some on the Left who saw his death as part of an Israeli right-wing conspiracy. Orthodox Jews in Israel and the United States found themselves in an extremely uncomfortable position as fingers were pointed at them and Orthodoxy was blasted from many a Reform and Conservative pulpit. Yeshiva University was especially perturbed: the previous year it had seen one of its graduates, Baruch Goldstein (also a graduate of the Yeshiva of Flatbush in Brooklyn) kill or wound more than 150 Palestinians by opening fire in a crowded mosque at Friday prayers during Ramadan at the Cave of the Patriarchs in Hebron. Yigal Amir had graduated from the Israeli counterpart to Yeshiva, Bar-Ilan University. Many wondered if there was something in modern Orthodoxy that predisposed these students to violence.[80]

A memorial gathering marking the thirty-day mourning period for Yitzhak Rabin took place in New York on December 10, 1995, after weeks of tension over how prominent talk of the peace process should be in the program and concern that Orthodox Jews would not show up. As it happened, Madison Square Garden was filled with more than fifteen thousand people, including four hundred AJC members and staff. Thousands more were left outside; estimates were that up to 30 percent of the audience was Orthodox.[81] AJC leaders had rushed to do what they could to hold the denominations together and to prevent demonization of Orthodox Jews. The next day, December 11, the AJC hosted a national symposium, "Are We Still One People?" at the Grand Hyatt Hotel. More than two hundred people attended from around the country. Subjects of the addresses included future prospects for a united Jewish community, what divided and what united the different denominations, the difference between free speech and incitement to violence, the nature of democracy in a Jewish state, and how religious leaders and Jewish educators should respond to the assassination. The morning session was chaired by AJC President Robert S. Rifkind and featured presentations by the heads of the three major American rabbinical seminaries: Rabbi Alfred Gottschalk, president of Hebrew Union College (Reform), Rabbi Norman Lamm, president of Yeshiva University (Orthodox), and Rabbi Ismar Schorsch, chancellor of the Jewish Theological Seminary (Conservative).

The first speech was by Israeli Consul General Ambassador Colette Avital, who declared that criticism of Israeli policies should not cross the line into attacking the properly elected democratic government of Israel. Rabbi Lamm spoke about the assassin's Orthodox upbringing and suggested that the Orthodox community should assess its educational system and make changes to assure that such things should never happen again. Rabbi Gottschalk warned against religious "absolutism" that refused to honor other points of view. Rabbi Schorsch faulted Messianism as the root cause of the assassination, and suggested that American donors should scrutinize what exactly Israeli Yeshivot were teaching American students before contributing any money to them. AJC followed up this program in February 1996 with a hundred-page booklet, "Rebuilding Jewish Peoplehood: Where Do We Go From Here?" consisting of responses by thirty-two Israeli and American Jewish leaders and intellectuals from different denominational and political backgrounds on issues of Jewish unity in the wake of the Rabin assassination.[82] With the goal of keeping everyone talking to one another and rallying forces at the center, AJC held a second conference and published a second collection of essays in 1997 entitled "The Condition of Jewish Peoplehood," again soliciting the views of leading American and Israeli thinkers and activists. The conclusion by then was that Jewish unity and the condition of Jewish peoplehood had improved.[83]

Israeli Politics and Jewish Pluralism

After Rabin's death Foreign Minister Shimon Peres, who had been the co-architect of the Oslo Accords, became prime minister of Israel. He quietly implemented Oslo II and handed over further towns to the Palestinians. He set the next election date for May 29, 1996. At that point there was an upsurge in Hamas and Islamic Jihad suicide bombings. All of these incidents took place despite Arafat's public promises to crack down on Hamas. When election day came and Israelis went to the polls to vote directly for prime minister for the first time, Peres lost by barely 1 percent of the vote to Likud opponent Benjamin Netanyahu, who proceeded to build a coalition that gave twenty-three out of one hundred and twenty Knesset seats to the religious parties. Not only was Netanyahu not Labor (and thus not so dedicated to maintaining Oslo as Peres would have been), but the prominence of Orthodox parties in his coalition meant that pressure to amend the Law of Return so that Reform and Conservative conversions would be invalid would be more likely in his government. Indeed, such a bill was soon introduced into the Israeli Knesset.

Once again, American Jews went to the airport to fly the ocean and remonstrate with Israeli officials, warning that American Jews might "disengage" from Israel and cease their philanthropic contributions—which would certainly weaken Israel and possibly weaken the entire Jewish communal infrastructure of the United States.[84] Netanyahu's first answer was that local Israeli coalition politics mandated passage of such a bill and that the state of Jewish pluralism in Israel would change slowly, when more non-Orthodox Jews actually came to live there and became voters.[85]

In reaction, a movement coalesced in the United States to bypass the UJA and donate money directly to Reform and Conservative institutions in Israel instead. Campaign leaders discussed a massive airlift of one thousand American Jewish leaders to Israel to meet with ministers, Knesset members, and the chief rabbis as well as a reverse airlift to the United States of the whole Knesset—at UJA expense—so that they could hear firsthand from American Jews how they felt about the issue.[86] When Netanyahu came to the United States in November 1996 to address the General Assembly of the CJFWF, he received a chilly reception and was greeted by delegates wearing buttons reading "Israel: Don't write off four million Jews."[87] Tensions in the United States over Israel's peacemaking policy and its handling of Jewish pluralism threatened to blight Israel's fiftieth anniversary celebrations in 1998. As the Israeli cabinet was about to vote on the conversion bill, a full-page ad in the *New York Times* mysteriously appeared, suggesting that the "80–90 percent" of American Jews newly disenfranchised might want to find out more about Jews for Jesus.[88] Representatives of the Orthodox religious parties, on their part, were warning Netanyahu that if he wanted to stay in power he had to keep his promises to them, and reminded him that Reform Jews had no voting power in Israel.[89]

Rhetoric in the battle became heated. Representatives of the Israeli Chief Rabbinate refused even to meet with Reform and Conservative representatives. Moshe Gafni, a Knesset member of the ultra-Orthodox United Torah Judaism Party, said that sitting in the same room as Reform Jewish leaders was "like watching a Torah being burned."[90] One of Israel's chief rabbis put responsibility on the Reform movement for the disappearance of more Jews than were killed in the Holocaust.[91] Non-Orthodox leaders, on their part, charged the Israeli Orthodox of living in "hermetically sealed ghettos" and betraying America.[92] Another accused them of being "contemporary cave dwellers."[93] While many non-Orthodox Jews were aware that Orthodoxy was far from monolithic and only a minority of Orthodox rabbis would make such comments, Michael Steinhardt accused Jewish Orthodoxy as a whole of "moral self-centeredness" not only because of their stand on Jewish pluralism but because in his view they stood aloof and did not join in the efforts to ensure Jewish continuity.[94]

The AJC reacted first by debating and passing, based on the consultations it had held after the Rabin assassination, a "Statement on Judaism, Pluralism and Peoplehood."[95] The statement spoke of the dangers of schisms that had occurred in the past when different groups of Jews could not marry one another, and called once again for common conversion procedures that would be acceptable to all the religious streams of Judaism. Ways must be found, it said, to include the Conservative and Reform movements in Israeli life, and Israeli political institutions in Israel "should refrain from action which would result in the delegitimization of the major religious streams within Judaism. Whatever our differences over religion, Jews relate to Israel as a Jewish state and are concerned about the quality of Israel's Jewishness." The statement called for exchange programs and "constructive dialogue" and commented on the need to avoid inflammatory rhetoric. "The assassination of Yitzhak Rabin has taught us that violence and extremist rhetoric have no place in a Jewish civil society and should be condemned by Jews everywhere," the statement concluded. "Our serious differences need to be engaged in ways that build bridges, expand common ground, and deepen understanding. We need dialogue, not diatribe. AJC remains ready to assist in this endeavor."

AJC had been inviting prominent Israelis from different fields to visit and to get to know American Jewish society for many years. Now, having announced that intermovement dialogue was a "national priority," they began exchange programs specifically to target the issue of Jewish pluralism and to bridge internal divisions between the groups. In the fall of 1996 they began to bring Israeli high school principals, especially from the city of Jerusalem, to visit American Jewish schools and to witness firsthand the varieties of Jewish education that flourished in the United States. In 1999 for the first time they hosted a group of Israeli Orthodox, Conservative, Reform, and secular Jewish leaders for a two-week intensive look at "the diversity of American Jewish life." Participants visited three cities, were introduced to the varieties of American Judaism, met with rabbis, saw rabbinical seminaries, and participated in synagogue services and study sessions. Not only did participants get to know American Judaism, they got to know one another. Because they came from such different ideological camps back in Israel, the participants noted, they otherwise would never have had an opportunity to become acquainted.[96] In 1999 AJC once more invited a select group of interdenominational leaders to meet regularly for dialogue in the same manner as had been done to promote dialogue between leaders of different religions. AJC Honorary President Alfred H. Moses chaired the group.

As the conversion bill came closer to being passed under Netanyahu's government, the AJC took more direct and immediate action by taking out a full-page ad, translated into Hebrew, in *Yediot Aharonot*, Israel's largest circulation newspaper, as well as in English in the *Jerusalem Post*, denouncing the damage that would be caused if the bill took effect and the destructive nature of the debate surrounding it:

Acquiescence in the demands of the religious parties to confirm and extend the monopolistic hold of the Orthodox rabbinate on the religious life of Israel, as evidenced most recently by support for the pending conversion bill, is having profound, long-term, adverse affects on the well-being of the Jewish people. So too is intolerant and inflammatory language from extremists on all sides. Measures and rhetoric that deny the legitimacy of the religious life of the overwhelming majority of committed American Jews caused great offense and thereby erode the bonds that have tied the minds and hearts of American Jews to Israel. For the sake of Jewish unity, for the sake of the future of Judaism and the Jewish people, and for the sake of the vital role that Israel must play in the future of world Jewry, we call for a reversal of this trend. We call on the Knesset to refrain from enacting the pending conversion bill. We call on the Government of Israel to consult closely with representatives of all major religious streams of the Diaspora in the interest of protecting the religious pluralism that is essential to a vital and creative Jewish future. We call for an Israel that is hospitable to all expressions of Judaism. That is the Zion of which we have dreamed and for which we have labored.[97]

In the aftermath of this advertisement and all the political activity surrounding it, Netanyahu announced that there would be a moratorium on the conversion bill. Furthermore, he was forming a special interdenominational commission headed by Finance Minister Yaakov Ne'eman to find a solution to the conversion problem that would be acceptable to both the Orthodox and non-Orthodox streams. The AJC came out with a statement strongly supporting the work of the Ne'eman Commission.[98] The commission came out with its recommendations in February 1998. It called for a special institute to be created in Israel to prepare candidates for conversion in which courses would be given by all streams of Judaism, including the Reform and Conservative. The actual final conversion, however, would be done according to *halacha* by an Orthodox rabbinical court acceptable to the Chief Rabbinate. This proposal was accepted by the prime minister's cabinet and by the Knesset. The Chief Rabbinate of the State of Israel, however, withheld its official endorsement, and the proposals were only partially implemented.

It was thought that the "Who is a Jew" issue would recede somewhat when Netanyahu did not win reelection. In May 1999 the majority of votes went to Labor's Ehud Barak, who promised to bring new energy to the lagging peace process. Even in the formation of Barak's government, however, there was fear that he would have to depend on the Orthodox religious parties to form his coalition and the drive for Orthodox hegemony over religious affairs in Israel would continue. At that point AJC ran another piece in an Israeli newspaper, this time in *Ha'aretz*, which was simultaneously published in English in the *Los Angeles Times*, the *Chicago Sun Times*, and excerpted in the *International Herald Tribune*. Entitled "Don't Lose U.S. Jewish Support," it was written by David Harris and was an extensive analysis of what might happen if religious issues came to divide U.S. and Israeli Jews. It also came out forthrightly against what the religious parties in Israel were trying to do. Harris began by asserting that American Jews and Israeli Jews were moving away from one another, and that the consequences over time could be "disastrous for both." "The link between Israel and American Jewry is vital to both sides and cannot be taken for granted," he wrote. "If it begins to fray, it could have catastrophic consequences." Jewish religious issues were once again before the Knesset and this time, he wrote, the risks of such a fraying were real. The identity and continuity of American Jews, he believed, was dependent on a strong link with Israel. "Israel is vital to the Jewish identity of American Jews," Harris wrote. "Israel's miraculous rebirth, remarkable development and sheer survival are sources of immense pride to Jews everywhere. Jewish identity, whether in the Diaspora or Israel, stands on three inter-connective legs: the land, the people and the Book. Removing the land because it is no longer appealing to a growing number of American Jews would be a calamity and only accelerate the worrisome assimilationist trends in the U.S."

In addition to depending on Israel for their own Jewish identity, American Jewry played an "indispensable" role in maintaining the U.S.'s pro-Israel stance, a point that Harris had made many times in communicating with Israelis. "If the American Jewish component is gradually removed from the equation," he predicted, "it will not be long before we witness a more 'even-handed' U.S. approach," he wrote. Quoting AJC research, he pointed out that surveys already showed that support for Israel was weaker among younger

American Jews than among older ones. One factor at work in this weakening here was a sense of "growing religious disenfranchisement, felt most strongly among younger American Jews, overwhelmingly non-Orthodox, who are not as prepared as their elders to 'excuse' Israeli behavior in this arena." American Jews could and would react to battles over Jewish pluralism in Israel by reducing their donations there or becoming less engaged on Israel's behalf. Israeli Jews suffered from those battles too, Harris declared. "For Israelis," he wrote, "it is reflected in a growing cultural divide and the unsettling sense that the State they worked so hard to build is slipping away from them." Harris agreed that no one could expect Israel to have American-style separation of church and state. Nevertheless, some disconnect between the two would be necessary in order to maintain the ties with America as well as the democratic nature of the state:

The entanglement of religion and state in the Israeli political arena is dismaying for most American Jews. Such an unbridled meshing of religion and government is bad for the State, worse for religion. Its effects are corrosive. The Israeli majority needs finally to find the courage to say "enough already" to religious coercion and, while there is still time, define an alternative vision for Israel that maintains democratic values and ensures an enlightened Jewish character of the State. This is not simply a debate about what's good for Jews in America, where the overwhelming majority of Reform and Conservative Jews live. It's every bit as much about what's good for Israel. It is, in fact, a long overdue debate about Israel's soul. I pray that we will see the same courage Israel has demonstrated in diplomacy, rescue and defense applied to preventing some religious dogmatists from hijacking this ever-so-precious country of the Jewish people.

Ehud Barak was able to put together a broad-based coalition that gave him 75 out of 120 Knesset seats; thus he was not overdependent on the religious parties.[99] Barak, however, did not last long. He was brought down in the summer of 2000 by the final breakdown of negotiations when Arafat refused to accept Barak's offer of an agreement and failed to counter with an offer of his own. The second intifada broke out shortly thereafter; during it, the more conservative Likud leader Ariel Sharon became prime minister in March 2001. Yasir Arafat died on November 11, 2004, having voiced worry that the Palestinian movement would splinter upon his death.[100] Ariel Sharon was incapacitated by a stroke on January 4, 2006, and was succeeded by Ehud Olmert. But no matter who the Israeli prime minister was, the dispute over "Who is a Jew" had become almost a permanent part of the Israeli political landscape. The exact status of the Reform and Conservative denominations in Israel and the validity of their conversions remained a source of bitter dispute and litigation in the Israeli courts. Jewish pluralism was not faring much better in the United States, where the three major denominations were increasingly going their separate ways, with Orthodoxy itself torn into factions right, center, and left.

The issue of Jewish continuity had thoroughly permeated Jewish politics. Israel had been born in 1948 with a tiny fraction of the world's Jews in its population, but by 2006 it was well on its way to having the largest Jewish community of any country in the world (already for several years the population of Greater Tel Aviv had by far exceeded the Jewish population of Metropolitan New York).[101] Even in Israel, however, there were hints that demography might be destiny. Even though Jewish fertility in Israel by far exceeded that in the United States (or indeed in any Diaspora community), Arab fertility—both among the Israeli Palestinian Arabs who were citizens of the state and the Palestinians who lived in the West Bank and the Gaza Strip—was three times higher. The leading Jewish demographer in the world, Sergio DellaPergola of the Hebrew University in Jerusalem, wrote that in 2000, in the grand total of the State of Israel and all the Palestinian territories, there was only a slight Jewish majority of 53 percent. At current rates of population growth, by 2050 the percentage of Jews would be down as low as 35 percent—a Jewish-Arab population division not unlike that which had prevailed in the mid-1940s toward the end of the British mandate. Furthermore, the era of mass immigration to Israel (that American Jews had done so much to facilitate) appeared to be at an end. Most of the Soviet Jews had already come to Israel. "The only way this could be reversed," DellaPergola wrote, "would be an unlikely scenario of significant political and economic disruption in the major societies of the West that now host the largest Jewish communities worldwide."[102] Some form of separation from the Palestinians was essential if Israel was to remain a Jewish and a democratic state—and, indeed, by the early twenty-first century Israeli politics was moving in that direction.

Through all this the AJC was putting itself in the forefront of those working to advance Jewish continuity and affirm Jewish identity in the United States. It was working hard, against rising odds, to keep the ties strong between American and Israeli Jews. Indeed, with its exchange programs and partnerships with Diaspora communities it was working to maintain bonds between Jews everywhere. A long road indeed had been traveled since its founding in 1906. At one time the very concept of Jewish peoplehood had been shunned by the leaders of the Committee and the fear of being accused of dual loyalty had colored every pronouncement. The very mention of the possibility of American Jews immigrating to Israel had been enough to cause an international crisis.

In the years since World War II, the AJC and other Jewish organizations had set themselves the goal of helping U.S. Jews integrate into the mainstream, and in large part they had succeeded. A new goal of the late twentieth and early twenty-first century was to help American Jews maintain their distinctiveness as they gathered to fight worldwide some of the greatest threats that Jews and Israel had faced in more than sixty years. The distance the AJC itself had come, along with the continuity with its past, was evident in the organization's mission statement in its one hundredth year: "To safeguard the welfare and security of Jews in the United States, in Israel, and throughout the world; to strengthen the basic principles of pluralism around the world, as the best defense against antisemitism and other forms of bigotry; to enhance the quality of American Jewish life by helping to ensure Jewish continuity and deepen ties between American and Israeli Jews." As it stood on the brink of its second century, proud of its past accomplishments, the main goal was to work toward a future where Jews and Jewish life were safe and flourishing all over the world.

Appendix

American Jewish Committee Presidents, 1906–2006

Mayer Sulzberger	1906–1912
Louis Marshall	1912–1929
Cyrus Adler	1929–1940
Sol M. Stroock	1941
Maurice Wertheim	1941–1943
Joseph M. Proskauer	1943–1949
Jacob Blaustein	1949–1954
Irving M. Engel	1954–1959
Herbert B. Ehrmann	1959–1961
Frederick F. Greenman	1961
Louis Caplan	1961–1962
A. M. Sonnabend	1962–1964
Morris B. Abram	1964–1968
Arthur J. Goldberg	1968–1969
Philip E. Hoffman	1969–1973
Elmer L. Winter	1973–1977
Richard Maass	1977–1980
Maynard I. Wishner	1980–1983
Howard I. Friedman	1983–1986
Theodore Ellenoff	1986–1989
Sholom D. Comay	1989–1991
Alfred H. Moses	1991–1995
Robert S. Rifkind	1995–1998
Bruce M. Ramer	1998–2001
Harold Tanner	2001–2004
E. Robert Goodkind	2004–present

Notes

Preface (pp. xiii–xiv)

1. An earlier volume by the American Jewish historian Naomi W. Cohen, published in 1972, covered the AJC's pre-World War II years.
2. Sergio DellaPergola, "World Jewish Population," in the *American Jewish Year Book* 106 (2006) p. 559.

1. Origins (1903–1948) (pp. 3–27)

1. Monty Noam Penkower, "The Kishinev Pogrom of 1903: A Turning Point in Jewish History," *Modern Judaism* 24, no. 3 (October 2004): 187–88; Nathan Schachner, *The Price of Liberty: A History of the American Jewish Committee* (New York: AJC, 1948), 1–2.
2. Henrietta Szold, "The Year," *AJYB* 4 (1903–1904): 20–21.
3. Howard M. Sachar, *A History of Israel: From the Rise of Zionism to Our Time* (New York: Knopf, 1996), 59–64.
4. Szold, "The Year," 26.
5. Naomi W. Cohen, *Jacob Schiff: A Study in American Jewish Leadership* (Hanover: Brandeis University Press, 1999), 111–112.
6. Naomi W. Cohen, *Not Free to Desist: The American Jewish Committee, 1906–1966* (Philadelphia: JPS, 1972), 5.
7. Schachner, *Price of Liberty*, 10–11.
8. American Jewish Committee minutes, February 3, 1906, vol. 1, Blaustein Library.
9. American Jewish Committee minutes, May 19, 1906, 1:35–36, Blaustein Library.
10. Harry Schneiderman, "The AJC: The Early Years," *AJC Committee Reporter* 17 (March 1960): 30.
11. Cohen, *Not Free to Desist*, 27.
12. Ibid., 20.
13. Ibid., 21.
14. Ibid., 25.
15. Jerome A. Chanes, "A Primer on the American Jewish Community" (New York: AJC, January 2000), 17, Blaustein Library.
16. For more detailed discussion of the founding of the American Jewish Congress and its relations with the American Jewish Committee, see Gerald Sorin, *A Time for Building: The Third Migration, 1880–1920* (Baltimore: Johns Hopkins University Press, 1992), 211–214; and Melvin I. Urofksy, *A Voice That Spoke for Justice: The Life and Times of Stephen S. Wise* (Albany: State University of New York Press, 1982), 134–168.

17. Chanes, "A Primer," 16–17.
18. Harry Schneiderman, "The AJC: The Early Years, Part II," *AJC Committee Reporter*, 17 (May 1960): 26.
19. Cohen, *Not Free to Desist*, 28
20. Howard M. Sachar, *A History of the Jews in America* (New York: Alfred A. Knopf, 1992), 519–521.
21. Arthur M. Schlesinger, Jr., and Roger Bruns, *Congress Investigates: A Documentary History 1792–1974*, vol. 4 (New York: Chelsea House Publishers, 1975), 2735–2767.
22. Cohen, *Not Free to Desist*, 231.
23. On U.S. treatment of Jewish refugees from Europe before and during World War II, see David S. Wyman, *Paper Walls: America and the Refugee Crisis, 1938–1941* (Amherst: University of Massachusetts Press, 1968) and *The Abandonment of the Jews: America and the Holocaust, 1941–1945* (New York: New Press, 1998).
24. Interview with Milton Ellerin, September 1980, AJC Oral History project, p. 21. New York Public Library.
25. Ibid., p. 36.
26. Stuart Svonkin, *Jews Against Prejudice: American Jews and the Fight for Civil Liberties* (New York: Columbia University Press, 1997), 32.
27. Interview by the author with Selma Hirsh, July 10, 2006.
28. For a full description of AJC activities during the 1930s and the years of the Holocaust, see Naomi Cohen, *Not Free to Desist: The American Jewish Committee, 1906–1966*, chaps. 8–10, pp. 154–264.
29. *AJC Committee Reporter* 2, no. 2 (February 1945): 7.
30. Zvi Ganin, *An Uneasy Relationship: American Jewish Leadership and Israel, 1948–1957* (Syracuse, N.Y.: Syracuse University Press, 2005), xvi.
31. When David Ben-Gurion met with representatives of the American Jewish Committee and the Jewish Labor Committee on November 27, 1941, he answered this charge in part; he was reported to have said "as one socialist to another" that he was for the abolition of all states, but if states were to be dissolved, why not start with Russia, England, or the United States? Why did the process have to start with Jews? Cited in Menahem Kaufman. *An Ambiguous Partnership: Non-Zionists and Zionists in America, 1939–1948* (Detroit: Wayne State University Press, 1991), 76.
32. Joseph Proskauer, address to Executive Committee, in the *AJC Committee Reporter* 2 no. 3 (March 1945): 2.
33. Thomas A. Kolsky, *Jews Against Zionism: The American Council for Judaism, 1942–1948* (Philadelphia: Temple University Press, 1992), 40–41.
34. Ibid., 43.
35. Cohen, *Not Free to Desist*, 251.
36. Ibid., 252; Ganin, *Uneasy Relationship*, 91.
37. Kaufman, *Ambiguous Partnership*, 90 and 229.
38. For a memoir of Morris Waldman's life, including descriptions of his term with the AJC, see his autobiography *Nor By Power* (New York: International Universities Press, 1953).
39. Ibid., 240.
40. Minutes, January 1943 AJC annual meeting, p. 39, Blaustein Library.
41. Kolsky, *Jews Against Zionism*, 75–76.
42. Ibid., 76.

43. Ibid.

44. "Statement on Withdrawal from the American Jewish Conference, together with address of Hon. Joseph M. Proskauer" (New York: AJC, 1943), Blaustein Library.

45. Cohen, *Not Free to Desist*, 259.

46. Ibid., 260.

47. See Louis M. Hacker and Mark D. Hirsch, *Proskauer: His Life and Times* (Tuscaloosa: University of Alabama Press, 1978), 150–51; for Proskauer's own account of the change, see his autobiography, *A Segment of My Times* (New York: Farrar, Straus, 1950), 229–61. See also Cohen, *Not Free to Desist*, 298–309.

48. *AJC Committee Reporter* 3 no. 1 (January 1946): 1.

49. *AJC Committee Reporter* 4 no. 10 (October 1947): 1. For a detailed account, see chapter 7 of Kolsky, *Jews Against Zionism*, "The American Jewish Committee Campaign for Partition" (274–311).

50. Evyatar Friesel, "The Holocaust: Factor in the Birth of Israel?" in *Major Changes Within the Jewish People in the Wake of the Holocaust*, ed. Yisrael Gutman (Jerusalem, Yad Vashem, 1996), 540.

51. Memo from Milton Himmelfarb to members of the Staff Committee on Palestine, "AJC Position on the Jewish State," December 31, 1947, cited in Kaufman, *Ambiguous Partnership*, 280. Milton Himmelfarb joined the staff of the AJC in 1943; he had degrees from City College, the Jewish Theological Seminary, and the University of Paris, and had done graduate work in economics and political science at Columbia.

52. For a detailed first-hand account of Israel's War of Independence from the Israeli perspective, see Chaim Herzog, *The Arab-Israeli Wars: War and Peace in the Middle East*. Revised and updated by Shlomo Gazit. (New York: Vintage Books, 2005), 17–108.

53. "AJC Statement on Palestine, March 28, 1948," in *AJC Committee Reporter* (April 1948): 1.

54. This joke was told to the author by American Jewish historian Robert Rockaway of Tel Aviv University, July 2002.

55. Ganin, *Uneasy Relationship*, quoting Jacob Blaustein, untitled address given in Baltimore, February 15, 1948, Jacob Blaustein papers, Baltimore, Md.

56. Ganin, *Uneasy Relationship*, 8

57. Ibid., citing minutes, AJC Executive Committee Meeting, October 16–17, 1948, Blaustein Library.

58. Ibid., 9, citing the *AJYB* 51 (1950): 562.

2. *"With Ever-Increasing Vigor"* (1944–1952) (pp. 28–66)

1. Report, Committee on Reorganization, Minutes, AJC Executive Committee Meeting, May 9, 1944.

2. Naomi W. Cohen, *Not Free to Desist: The American Jewish Committee, 1906–1966* (Philadelphia: Jewish Publication Society, 1972), 261.

3. On the history and development of *Commentary* magazine, see Murray Friedman, ed., *Commentary in American Life* (Philadelphia: Temple University Press, 2005).

4. Address by Norman Rabb, AJC annual meeting transcript, Thursday evening session, May 13, 1971, p. 194.

5. Zvi Ganin, *An Uneasy Relationship: American Jewish Leadership and Israel, 1948–1957* (Syracuse: Syracuse University Press, 2005), 11.

6. Obituary of Jacob Blaustein, Jewish Telegraphic Agency News Bulletin, November 17, 1970, p. 4.

7. Shlomo Shafir, *Ambiguous Relations: The American Jewish Community and Germany Since 1945* (Detroit: Wayne State University Press, 1999), 172.

8. The advent after World War II of the intergroup relations movement among American and particularly Jewish organizations—notably the American Jewish Committee, the American Jewish Congress, and the B'nai B'rith Anti-Defamation League—is examined at length by Stuart Svonkin in his *Jews Against Prejudice: American Jews and the Fight for Civil Liberties* (New York: Columbia University Press, 1997). On the origins of the change, see his introduction (i) and chap. 1, "From Self-Defense to Intergroup Relations" (11–40).

9. Svonkin, *Jews Against Prejudice*, 18, citing John Higham, *Send These to Me: Immigrants in Urban America*, rev. ed. (Baltimore: Johns Hopkins University Press), 155.

10. Svonkin, *Jews Against Prejudice*: "The generation of Jewish leaders who dedicated these agencies [AJC, American Jewish Congress, and ADL] to intergroup relations after World War II made vital contributions to the advancement of political liberalism and civil rights, to the development of strategies for combating prejudice and discrimination, and to the formulation of an ethnic identity for an American Jewish community increasingly distant from its immigrant roots" (2).

11. For an account of the AJC delegation at the United Nations founding conference in San Francisco, see Cohen, *Not Free to Desist*, 270–72. On Proskauer and Blaustein's impact, see also Jerold S. Auerbach, "Human Rights at San Francisco," *American Jewish Archives* 16 (1964): 51f. For Proskauer's own account, see his autobiography, *A Segment of My Times* (New York: Farrar, Straus, 1950), 216–28.

12. Murray Friedman, *What Went Wrong? The Creation and Collapse of the Black-Jewish Alliance* (New York: Free Press, 1995), 147.

13. Naomi W. Cohen, *Not Free to Desist: The American Jewish Committee, 1906–1966* (Philadelphia: JPS, 1972) 385–386.

14. Minutes, AJC Executive Committee meeting, January 25–26, 1947, Blaustein Library.

15. Minutes, AJC Executive Committee meeting, October 1947, Blaustein Library.

16. Robert M. MacIver, "Report on Jewish Community Relations Agencies" (New York: National Community Relations Advisory Council, 1951), Blaustein Library.

17. Letter from Charles W. Morris to Jacob Blaustein, July 11, 1951, in YIVO Archives / JC Record Group 347.17.12/GEN-12/Box 105, folder "MacIver Report, AJC Criticism, 1951–1953."

18. On AJC's withdrawal from NCRAC, see "Statement on the Report on the Jewish Community Relations Agencies by Prof. R.M. MacIver" (New York: AJC, October 25, 1951); "Statement of Withdrawal from the National Community Relations Advisory Council" (New York: AJC, September 22, 1952); "Do you know the whys and wherefores . . . that compelled us to leave the NCRAC?" (New York: AJC, November 1952); and "Questions and Answers on the NCRAC Controversy: Suggested Statements for Use at Meetings and by AJC Speakers" (New York: AJC, December 1952), Blaustein Library.

19. Joseph M. Proskauer. "The Challenges We Face." AJC Annual Meeting summary, January 1953, p. 100, Blaustein Library. On AJC and the MacIver Report, see also Cohen, *Not Free to Desist*, 339.

20. Minutes, AJC Executive Committee / AJC annual meeting, February 4, 1945, Blaustein Library; editorial, *AJC Committee Reporter* 2, no. 7 (July 1945): 4.

21. "Plight of Jews in Conquered Europe Surveyed in *New York Times* Reports, *AJC Committee Reporter* 2, no. 9 (September 1945): 2.

22. "Hungary to Check Antisemitism, Foreign Minister Tells Committee Representatives," *AJC Committee Reporter* 3, no. 7 (July 1946): 3.

23. Minutes, AJC Executive Committee meeting, October 11–12, 1947, Blaustein Library.

24. "From the Paris Observation Post," by Zachariah Shuster, AJC European representative. *AJC Committee Reporter* 6, no. 8 (September 1949): 3.

25. Minutes, AJC Executive Committee meeting (on German reeducation) October 11–12, 1947, Blaustein Library.

26. "In the Wake of the Giesking Case," by S. Andhil Fineberg, *AJC Committee Reporter* 6, no. 4 (April 1949): 3.

27. "Jews in Arab World In Danger of Perishing, AJC Report Says," *AJC Committee Reporter* 5, no. 8 (September 1948): 3.

28. Ibid.

29. Jacob Blaustein, report to AJC Executive Committee meeting, January 21, 1950; Zvi Ganin, *Uneasy Relationship*, 178.

30. "Nuremberg Witness Tells of Propaganda Net in US—Coughlin, Viereck Named in Diplomat's Testimony." *AJC Committee Reporter* 3, no. 5 (May 1946): 1.

31. On Father Coughlin, see Donald Warren, *Radio Priest: Charles Coughlin, the Father of Hate Radio* (New York: Free Press, 1996).

32. "Notes and Quotes," *AJC Committee Reporter* 2, no. 2 (February 1945): 5.

33. "G.L.K. Smith Loses Prestige, Gains Profit: Repudiated by Both Parties, Antisemitic Agitator Remains a Menace," *AJC Committee Reporter* 1, no. 7 (October 1944): 3.

34. Ibid.

35. "Demagogue Testifies on 'Jewish Problem'," *AJC Committee Reporter* 8, no. 3 (November 1944): 3.

36. "Gerald Smith Rants Before House Group," *AJC Committee Reporter* 3, no. 3 (March 1946): 2 and 5.

37. "Ex-Senator Reynolds Leads New Nationalist Movement," *AJC Committee Reporter* 2, no. 5 (May 1945): 3.

38. "Attempt to Revive Christian Front Meetings in N.Y. Fails," *AJC Committee Reporter* 2, no. 11 (November 1945): 8.

39. "AJC Disclosure Results Prompt Action Against Hate Groups," *AJC Committee Reporter* 2, no. 10 (October 1945): 7.

40. Rabbi S. Andhil Fineberg put the principles of his "quarantine" treatment in pamphlet form: "Deflating the Professional Bigot" (New York: AJC, January 1960), Blaustein Library.

41. "Meeting on Antisemitism 'Clinic' Begins Baltimore Membership Drive," *AJC Committee Reporter* 3, no. 10 (October 1946): 7.

42. "Antisemitism Survey Sees Danger Signals," *AJC Committee Reporter* 6, no. 3 (March 1949): 4.

43. "Employment Discrimination Grows Since V-J Day, Survey Discloses," *AJC Committee Reporter* 3, no. 6 (June 1946): 8.

44. "'Christians Only' Barred," *AJC Committee Reporter* 2, no. 5 (May 1945): 6.

45. "Equal Housing Opportunity," *AJC Committee Reporter* 7, no. 1 (January 1950): 5.

46. "N.Y. Mayor's Committee Report Reveals Discrimination in Colleges; Bill Would Establish State University," *AJC Committee Reporter* 3, no. 3 (March 1946): 3.

47. "College Discrimination Widely Scored; Dental School Recommendations Draw Fire from Profession and Public," *AJC Committee Reporter* 2, no. 3 (March 1945): 8.

48. "Proposed Restrictions on Jewish Psychologists Protested by AJC," *AJC Committee Reporter* 2, no. 5 (May 1945): 5.

49. On the alliance of AJC with the Frankfurt School and its adoption of social science as a main research tool, see Svonkin, *Jews Against Prejudice*, 31–40.

50. Ibid., 66–67.

51. The five volumes were *Prophets of Deceit* by Leo Lowenthal and Norbert Guterman, a study of the techniques used by antisemitic rabble-rousers in the United States; *Rehearsal for Destruction* by Paul Massing, which traced the development of antisemitism in Germany from Bismarck to Hitler; *The Dynamics of Prejudice* by Bruno Bettelheim and Morris Janowitz, an investigation into the relationship between veterans' anxieties and their attitudes toward minorities, completed under the auspices of the social science research committee of the University of Chicago; *Anti-Semitism and Emotional Disorder* by Nathan W. Ackerman and Marie Jahoda; and finally *The Authoritarian Personality* by Theodor W. Adorno, Else Frenkel-Brunswik, Daniel J. Levinson, and R. Nevitt Sanford, which reported the findings of psychologists at the University of California who established authoritarianism as a feature of the antisemitic personality.

52. "Roots of Antisemitism Revealed in Study of Psychoanalysts' Cases," *AJC Committee Reporter* 4, no. 5 (May 1947): 5.

53. "Popular Writers Instructed How to Fight Prejudice," *AJC Committee Reporter* 2, no. 8 (August 1945): 6.

54. "Need for Expanded Program Stressed at JDA Executive Meeting," *AJC Committee Reporter* 4, no. 10 (October 1947): 8.

55. Minutes, AJC Executive Committee meeting, September 15, 1946, Blaustein Library.

56. "The Immigrant in Our Textbooks," *AJC Committee Reporter* 7, no. 1 (January 1950): 6.

57. "Laws Limit Entry of Jewish DPs; 3600 Came to U.S. Since Dec. 1945," *AJC Committee Reporter* 3, no. 11 (November 1946): 2.

58. From the *Chicago Sentinel*, quoted in an article by Louis Harap, "Commiphobia and the AJCommittee," in *Jewish Life* (December 1950): 6. Louis Harap was a prominent American Jewish communist and *Jewish Life* was a communist organ.

59. "Many Bills Concerning Minorities Offered at New Congress Session," *AJC Committee Reporter* 2, no. 3 (March 1945): 1 and 5.

60. "AJC Asks DP Law Revision," *AJC Committee Reporter* 5, no. 7 (July–August 1948): 1 and 4.

61. William B. Helmreich, *Against All Odds: Holocaust Survivors and the Successful Lives they Made in America* (New York: Simon and Schuster, 1992), 14.

62. "Exodus of Germany's 150,000 Jews Will be Completed Within Two Years," *AJC Committee Reporter* 5, no. 9 (October 1948): 3.

63. "Haber Says DP Problem Nears Solution in Report to AJC Foreign Affairs Committee," *AJC Committee Reporter* 5, no. 11 (December 1948): 3.

64. Minutes, AJC Executive Committee meeting, May 7–8, 1949, Blaustein Library.

65. On the background of the ACJ and AJC's studies of and reactions toward it, see vertical files, "American Council for Judaism," Blaustein Library.

66. Joseph M. Proskauer, "Restraint and Wisdom," *AJC Committee Reporter* 6, no. 6 (June 1949): 4.

67. *American Jewish Congress Weekly*, 16, no. 24 (September 19, 1949); editorial, "Quislings in Our Midst," citing *Readers' Digest* (September 1949).

68. Conference on Jewish Adjustment in America, summary of discussion, December 26–27, 1945, at the Waldorf-Astoria Hotel (New York: AJC, 1946), 13 pages, Blaustein Library.

69. Material on this program can be found in the AJC Archives, box "Special Project: Education in American Jewish Attitudes, 1941–1952"; also Irving Engel Correspondence, box 1214, folder "Jewish Education, 1947–1950."

70. Minutes, AJC Executive Committee meeting, May 7–8, 1949, Blaustein Library.

71. Jewish Telegraphic Agency News Bulletin, 6, no. 201 (September 1, 1949).

72. Minutes, AJC Executive Committee meeting, October 22–23, 1949, Blaustein Library.

73. "Chronicle of Events," *American Jewish Congress Weekly* 16, no. 34 (December 26, 1949).

74. A detailed account of the meeting as well as the events leading up to it can be found in Ganin, *Uneasy Relationship*, chap. 4, "The Blaustein-Ben Gurion Understanding of 1950," 81–104.

75. Interview with Selma Hirsh, August 19, 2005. "He [Blaustein] was in close touch with Ben Gurion. I was assistant to Dr. Slawson and worked with the president who was then Jacob. Writing it was a long and involved process. Many people drafted it under Blaustein's direction. Ben Gurion had to approve it. There was lots of back and forth, through telegrams. Many drafts went back and forth. We didn't have the kind of communications we have today—no e-mails. There were sticking points. These are all in Blaustein's papers." Jacob Blaustein's papers are now located at Special Collections and Archives, Milton S. Eisenhower Library, Johns Hopkins University, Baltimore, M.D. Online guide is at www.library.jhu.edu/collections/specialcollections/manuscripts/Blaustein/index/.html.

76. The full text of both Ben Gurion's address and Blaustein's reply was published, at Blaustein's insistence, in the 1952 *AJYB* 53:564–68.

77. Interview with Selma Hirsh, August 19, 2005.

78. Ganin, *Uneasy Relationship*, 26.

79. See YIVO Archives/AJC Record Group 347.7.1 Foreign Affairs Department, box 67, folder "Ben Gurion-Blaustein Agreements, 1950–1961," esp. AJC press release, May 1, 1961.

80. "Jews Abroad Criticized," reporting on David Ben-Gurion's speech to the twenty-fifth World Zionist Congress, *New York Times*, December 29, 1960. The full quotation: "The Rabbis taught: a person should dwell in the Land of Israel, even in a city that is principally non-Jewish, rather than dwell outside Israel, even in a city that is principally Jewish, for whoever lives in Israel is like one who has a God, and one who does not live in the Land is like one who has no God, to teach you that whoever lives outside of Israel is like one who worships idols" (*Ketubot* 110b).

81. On the ACJ's attacks against the AJC for their handling of statements by Zionist leaders, see YIVO Archives/AJC Record Group 347.17.10 GEN-10/box 315, folder "Zionism/Ben-Gurion Statement/ACJ-American Jewish Committee (1949–1951, 1957)."

82. Letter from Jacob Blaustein to David Ben Gurion, December 5, 1960, in YIVO Archives/ AJC Record Group 347.7.1 Foreign Affairs Department, box 68 (Israel) folder "Diaspora (Dual Loyalty) 1948, 1950, 1956, 1959–61." See also box 67, folder "Ben-Gurion-Blaustein Agreements, 1950–1961."

83. AJC Press release, December 29, 1960, in YIVO Archives/ AJC Record Group 347.7.1 Foreign Affairs Department, box 68 (Israel) folder "Diaspora (Dual Loyalty) 1948, 1950, 1956, 1959–61."

84. Ibid., AJC press release, May 1, 1961, Foreign Affairs Department (FAD), box 67 (Israel) folder: "Ben-Gurion–Blaustein Agreements, 1950–1961."

85. Address by M. Bernard Resnikoff, director, AJC Israel office, recalling April 1961 memo he had read. AJC annual meeting transcript, Sunday morning session, symposium on "New International Realities and Jewish Concerns," May 7, 1972, 4–15.

86. Cohen, *Free to Desist*, 329.

87. Interview by author with Bertram H. Gold, June 15, 2005.

88. Interview with David Geller (director of European and Latin American Affairs in the Foreign Affairs Department of the AJC), 1981, p. 34, New York Public Library.

3. "This Is Our Home" (1951–1957) (pp. 67–98)

1. Zachariah Shuster, "The European Scene," AJC annual meeting, January 25–27, 1952, p. 108.

2. "AJC Issues Third Report on Neo-Nazism in Germany," *AJC Committee Reporter* 10, no. 7 (Summer 1953): 3.

3. S. Andhil Fineberg, "Germany: A New Nation Arises from the Holocaust of War and Nazism Posing New Problems," *AJC Committee Reporter* 11, no. 5 (September–October 1954): 6.

4. Shlomo Shafir, *Ambiguous Relations: The American Jewish Community and Germany Since 1945* (Detroit: Wayne State University Press, 1999), 172. For the history of the Claims Conference, see also Ronald Zweig, *German Reparations and the Jewish World* (Portland, Ore.: Frank Cass, 2001); and Marilyn Henry, *A History of the Claims Conference* (New York: Vallentine Mitchell, 2006).

5. Irving Engel, "Highlights of 1952," AJC annual meeting, January 25–27, 1952, p. 59, Blaustein Library.

6. Zachariah Shuster, "Survey of European Scene," AJC annual meeting, January 25–27, 1953, p. 122, Blaustein Library.

7. Irving M. Engel, "Testament to Freedom," AJC annual meeting, January 28–30, 1955, p. 20, Blaustein Library.

8. AJC Executive Committee Minutes, October 22, 1955, p. 8, Blaustein Library.

9. These conditions were described in a January 1957 letter to the *New York Times* authored by Irving Engel. See "In Search of Haven," *AJC Committee Reporter* 14, no. 1 (February 1957): 7.

10. John J. McCloy, "Germany and the East-West Conflict," AJC annual meeting, January 1953, p. 87, Blaustein Library.

11. John Slawson, "Problems Facing American Jewry," AJC annual meeting, January 1953, p. 71, Blaustein Library.

12. Ibid.

13. The estimate of twenty million is cited in Robert Conquest, *The Great Terror: A Reassessment* (New York: Oxford University Press, 1991), 486.

14. "Hungarian Deportations," *AJC Annual Report*, January 25–27, 1952, p. 58; *AJC Committee Reporter*, January, April, and November–December issues, 1952, Blaustein Library.

15. "Terror Against Rumanian Jews Spurred by New Trials, Purges," *AJC Committee Reporter* 11, no. 4 (June 1954): 2.

16. "East Germans Revive Nazi Racial Laws," *AJC Committee Reporter* 10, no. 1 (February–March 1953): 7; "East Germans Step Up Anti-Religion Drive," *AJC Committee Reporter* 10, no. 2 (May–June 1953): 2.

17. A translation of the entire *Pravda* article was recently published at www.cyber ussr.com/rus/vrach-ubiica-e.html. It also appears as part of the discussion of the Doctor's Plot, in Alexander N. Yakovlev, *A Century of Violence in Soviet Russia* (New Haven: Yale University Press, 2002), 207.

18. Indications that Stalin planned the mass deportation of Jews appear in AJC as well as several non-AJC sources on the subject of the Doctors' Plot; much of the evidence surfaced only following the fall of the Soviet Union and the mass emigration of its Jews. See, for example, Louis Rapoport, *Stalin's War Against the Jews: The Doctors' Plot and the Soviet Solution* (New York: Free Press, 1990), 176–91; Jonathan Brent and Vladimir P. Nuamov, *Stalin's Last Crime: the Plot Against the Jewish Doctors, 1948–1953* (New York: HarperCollins, 2003), 283–311. Harrison Salisbury, *New York Times* correspondent to Moscow in 1954, observed of the plot: "All informed observers noted that the government-fabricated plot was to initiate a gigantic purge that would probably have claimed millions of victims" (article reprinted in *AJC Committee Reporter* 11, no. 6 [December 1954]: 2); Rabbi Morris Kertzer of the AJC was told of the plan in his interviews with Soviet Jews during a visit in 1956.

19. See "The Jews Under Stalin's Successors: A Fact Sheet" (New York: AJC, 1956), Blaustein Library.

20. Zachariah Shuster (director, AJC European Office), "Survey of the European Scene: Reds Vilify Jews," AJC annual meeting, January 1953, p. 112, Blaustein Library.

21. "Radio Warsaw Blasts AJC," *AJC Committee Reporter* 12, no. 5 (August 1955): 1 and 8.

22. Morris N. Kertzer (director, AJC Department of Jewish Affairs), "Rabbis and Commissars: An Eyewitness Account of Jewish Life in the U.S.S.R. Today," *AJC Committee Reporter* 13, no. 5 (September 1956): 4.

23. Irving M. Engel, "Exposing Communist Tactics," AJC annual meeting, January 29, 1954, p. 40, Blaustein Library. The Jewish communist magazine *Jewish Life* in its September 1953 issue (vol. 7, no. 11) reprinted Harap's testimony before HUAC as an example of "resistance to the pro-fascists" (9–12).

24. On the role of S. Andhil Fineberg in AJC anticommunist efforts and the Rosenberg case, with attention to how AJC tactics compared to those of the American Jewish Congress, see Stuart Svonkin, *Jews Against Prejudice: American Jews and the Fight for Civil Liberties* (New York: Columbia University Press, 1997), 132–34, 143–58; also AJC Records Group 347.17.12 Gen-12, box 139, folders "Rosenberg,

Ethel and Julius 52-55," "Apologia for the Rosenbergs," "Rosenberg Case: Classified Documents 50-55" and Record Group 347.17.10 Gen-12, box 139, folders "Communism: AJC Lay/Staff" (YIVO archives).

25. A series of articles by Louis Harap in *Jewish Life* magazine attacking the AJC used all these terms. These included: "The American Jewish Committee Oligarchy" (April 1948); "The American Jewish Committee "Fights" Antisemitism" (May 1948); "American Jewish Committee and Foreign Policy" (July 1948); "American Jewish Committee as Red-baiter" (June 1948); "'Commiphobia' and the AJCommittee," (December 1950) and "An Open Letter to the Jewish People of the United States," (September 1953), which refers to HUAC as breeding "an American form of Nazism." Victor Navasky, *Naming Names* (New York: Viking Press, 1980) 112–125, includes AJC under the heading of "collaborators."

26. *Time* (April 16, 1951). Stephen J. Whitfield, in *The Culture of the Cold War* (Baltimore: Johns Hopkins University Press, 1996) 31–32, observes that in the heat of the moment Judge Kaufman forgot that the couple was not being charged with treason.

27. Solomon M. Schwarz, *The Jews in the Soviet Union*, with a foreword by Alvin Johnson (Syracuse: Syracuse University Press, 1952); Peter Meyer, Bernard D. Weinryb, Eugene Duschinsky, and Nicolas Sylavain, *The Jews in the Soviet Satellites* (Syracuse: Syracuse University Press, 1953).

28. John Slawson, "Problems Facing American Jewry," AJC annual meeting, January 1953, p. 71, Blaustein Library.

29. Leon Poliakov. *Harvest of Hate: The Nazi Program for the Destruction of the Jews of Europe*, ed. Martin Greenberg, with a foreword by Reinhold Niebuhr (Syracuse: Syracuse University Press, 1954).

30. Zachariah Shuster, "Survey of the European Scene," AJC annual meeting, January 1953, p. 112.

31. Jacob Blaustein, "The Pursuit of Human Equality," AJC annual meeting, January 1956, p. 27, Blaustein Library.

32. "Engel Charges U.S. Immigration Policy 'Loaded' Against Most," *AJC Committee Reporter* 10, no. 2 (May–June 1953): 3.

33. Herbert H. Lehmann, "Our Debt to Jacob Blaustein," AJC annual meeting, January 29, 1954, p. 49, Blaustein Library.

34. "Executive Board Meeting," *AJC Committee Reporter* 12, no. 4 (July 1955): 7.

35. This fact was noted at the AJC annual meeting of January 1953, in an address entitled "Progress Against Prejudice," p. 11.

36. "Challenge in the Streets: What Can Be Done About Youthful Anti-Minority Violence?" *AJC Committee Reporter* 12, no. 3 (May 1955): 5.

37. Ira M. Sheskin, "Dixie Diaspora: The 'Loss' of a Small Southern Jewish Community," in Mark K. Bauman, ed. *Dixie Diaspora: An Anthology of Southern Jewish History* (Tuscaloosa: University of Alabama Press, 2006) 178. See also Melissa Fay Greene, *The Temple Bombing* (Addison-Wesley, 1996).

38. According to Murray Friedman, Kenneth B. Clark, who did his undergraduate work at Howard University and received both his master's and doctoral degrees at Columbia, completed for the AJC in 1950 a six-month study on the impact of discrimination on the personalities of young children. When Chief Justice Earl Warren decided the case on May 17, 1954, he supported his argument in a footnote that included seven works. First on the list was Clark's 1950 AJC study; two others were

prepared by the American Jewish Congress. See *What Went Wrong? The Creation and Collapse of the Black-Jewish Alliance* (New York: Free Press, 1995), 153.

39. Irving M. Engel (president, AJC), AJC annual meeting, January 1956, p. 21, Blaustein Library.

40. Ralph E. Samuel, "Antisemitic Agitation," AJC annual meeting, January 27, 1956, p. 38, Blaustein Library.

41. This fact was noted in a Protestant Sunday School textbook for children. See "Texts for Tomorrow: Protestant, Catholic, and Jewish Educators Appraise Teaching Materials of their Own Faiths," *AJC Committee Reporter* 13, no. 4 (July 1956): 4.

42. AJC Executive Committee Minutes, May 5, 1951, Blaustein Library.

43. Helmut Lowenberg (AJC Israeli correspondent), "Tensions in the Middle East and their Domestic Impact," AJC Executive Committee Minutes, May 7, 1955, p. 7, Blaustein Library; *AJC Committee Reporter* 13, no. 5 (September 1956): 1.

44. Irving Engel, "Arab League Propaganda," AJC Executive Committee Minutes, October 23, 1954, p. 9, Blaustein Library.

45. "Propaganda." *AJC Committee Reporter* 12, no. 7 (December 1955): 4.

46. Ibid.

47. "Assault on American Citizenship Rights," AJC Executive Committee Minutes, May 12, 1956, p. 6, Blaustein Library. Also "Assault on American Citizenship: Arab Discrimination Flaunts American Principles," *AJC Committee Reporter* 13, no. 4 (July 1956): 2.

48. John Slawson, "Arab Discrimination Against American Citizens," AJC annual meeting, April 1957, p. 28, Blaustein Library.

49. "Texts for Tomorrow," 4–5 (see note 41).

50. AJC Executive Committee Minutes, May 2, 1953, p. 18, Blaustein Library.

51. "The Professor and the 'Fossil': An Eminent Historian Presents Some Strange Views of Jews and Judaism," *AJC Committee Reporter* 12, no. 6 (October–November 1955): 1 and 7.

52. Ralph E. Samuel, "Review and Forecast," AJC annual meeting, January 27, 1956, p. 40, Blaustein Library.

53. AJC Executive Committee Minutes, May 7, 1955, p. 11, Blaustein Library.

54. "Resort Bias Subterfuge," *AJC Committee Reporter* 10, no. 3 (September–October 1953).

55. Alfred McClung Lee, "Fraternities: Schools for Prejudice?" *AJC Committee Reporter* 11, no. 5 (September–October 1954), and *AJC Committee Reporter* 12, no. 3 (May 1955): 3.

56. "Who Should be Our Doctors?" *AJC Committee Reporter* 10, no. 4 (November–December 1953): 6.

57. Ibid., 4; AJC annual meeting, January 28, 1955, p. 45, Blaustein Library. On discrimination in undergraduate university admissions, see Edwin J. Lukas and Arnold Forster, "Study of Discrimination at Colleges of New York State" (New York: AJC and Anti-Defamation League of B'nai B'rith, 1950), Blaustein Library.

58. John Slawson, "Church-State Separation," AJC annual meeting, April 1957, p. 36, Blaustein Library.

59. "Christmas in July: AJC Suggests a Community Approach to Christmas in Public Schools," *AJC Committee Reporter* 12, no. 7 (December 1955): 6.

60. "HUAC Reports to Congress and Nation on Neo-Fascist and Hate Groups," *AJC Committee Reporter* 12, no. 1 (January 1955): 4.

61. Ibid, 3.
62. David Sher, "Behind the Soviet 'New Look,'" AJC annual meeting, January 28–30, 1955, p. 93, Blaustein Library.
63. Simon H. Rifkind (chair, administrative committee), "Civil Liberties and National Security," AJC annual meeting, January 29–31, 1954, pp. 96–98, Blaustein Library. At the time there were huge arguments within the committee staff over fighting communism versus preserving civil liberties. According to Morris Fine, who worked at the AJC since 1943, John Slawson commissioned a work that was to "settle the matter once and for all." The result was *American Security and Freedom,* by Maurice J. Goldbloom (Boston: Beacon, 1954), Blaustein Library.
64. John Slawson specifically referred to this when discussing the need of AJC to make its structure and membership more familiar to American Zionists. AJC Executive Committee Minutes, October 26, 1957, p. 12, Blaustein Library.
65. AJC Executive Committee Minutes, October 13, 1951, p. 10, Blaustein Library.
66. AJC Executive Committee Minutes, October 26, 1957, p. 12, Blaustein Library.
67. AJC Executive Committee Minutes, October 13, 1951, p. 19, Blaustein Library.
68. Lawrence Grossman, "Transformation through Crisis: The American Jewish Committee and the Six-Day War," *American Jewish History* 86:1 (March 1998), 37–38.
69. For description of the meeting, which took place in December 1955, see *AJC Committee Reporter* 13, no. 1 (January 1956): 1.
70. AJC Executive Committee Minutes, May 8, 1954, p. 4, Blaustein Library.
71. Ralph E. Samuel, "Review and Forecast: AJC in 1955 and 1956," AJC Annual Meeting, January 27, 1956, p. 55, Blaustein Library.
72. The full text of Dulles's February 11, 1957 address is available at www.us-israel.org/jsource/History/Dulles.html; President Eisenhower's national broadcast of February 20, 1957, condemning Israel has been published at www.us-israel.org/jsource/History/ikewarn1.html.
73. John Slawson, "Challenges and Needs in 1954," AJC annual meeting, January 29, 1954, p. 77, Blaustein Library.
74. Marshall Sklare and Marc Vosk, "The Riverton Study: How Jews Look at Themselves and their Neighbors" (New York: AJC 1957), Blaustein Library.
75. John Slawson, "Current Trends in the American Jewish Community," AJC annual meeting, January 1956, p. 65, Blaustein Library.
76. "Roundtable A: Interreligious Relationships," AJC annual meeting, January 1953, p. 133, Blaustein Library.
77. "Roundtable E: Currents and Conflicts on the American Religious Scene," AJC annual meeting, January 29, 1954, pp. 125–26, Blaustein Library.
78. Discussion on "Jewish Education," AJC Executive Committee Minutes, October 23, 1954, p. 22, Blaustein Library.
79. John Slawson, "Current Trends in the American Jewish Community: Synagogues and Centers," AJC annual meeting, January 27, 1956, p. 67, Blaustein Library.
80. AJC Executive Committee Minutes, May 7, 1955, p. 12, Blaustein Library.
81. "This is Our Home," 50th anniversary edition (New York: AJC, 1957), Blaustein Library. There were fourteen pamphlets in the series.
82. Herbert Ehrmann, "Jewish Attitudes," AJC Annual Report, January 25, 1952, Blaustein Library.

83. "Review of Oscar Handlin, *Adventure in Freedom: Three Hundred Years of Jewish Life in America* (New York: McGraw-Hill, 1954)," *AJC Committee Reporter* 11, no. 6 (December 1954): 6.; On John Higham, see "Social Discrimination," AJC annual meeting, April 1957, p. 34, Blaustein Library.

84. Ralph E. Samuel, "The Tercentenary Celebration: A Progress Report," AJC annual meeting, January 1953, p. 144, Blaustein Library.

85. AJC annual meeting, January 1956, p. 51, Blaustein Library.

86. AJC annual meeting, April 1957, p. 45, Blaustein Library.

87. "Institute of Human Relations." *AJC Committee Reporter* 13, no. 6 (November–December 1956): 4.

4. *The First Jewish Continuity Crisis and the Triumph of Vatican II (1960–1965) (pp. 101–134)*

1. Bertram Gold, interview by author, July 15, 2002.

2. "Amendment of Bylaws," AJC annual meeting proceedings, May 12–15, 1966, p. 159.

3. Michael Anish, interview by author, June 2003.

4. John Slawson, interview, January 12, 1972, AJC Oral History project, New York Public Library.

5. Report, "The Image, Role and Potential of the AJC," by Social Research, Inc., May 1963; in minutes, AJC Executive Committee meeting, November 1–3, 1963, Blaustein Library.

6. Social Research, Inc., "The Image, Role and Potential of AJC" (May 1963), cited in Lawrence Grossman, "Transformation Through Crisis: The American Jewish Committee and the Six-Day War," *American Jewish History* 86, no. 1 (March 1998): 39.

7. Booklet, "The AJC and Israel" (1998; published in honor of Israel's 50th anniversary), p. 6, Blaustein Library.

8. Grossman, "Transformation Through Crisis," 39.

9. John Slawson, keynote address: "AJC at Seventy: A View from the Sixtieth," AJC annual meeting proceedings, May 12–15, 1966, p. 22.

10. "Jews Abroad Criticized," reporting on David Ben-Gurion's speech to the twenty-fifth World Zionist Congress, *New York Times,* December 29, 1960. The full quotation is: The Rabbis taught: a person should dwell in the Land of Israel, even in a city that is principally non-Jewish, rather than dwell outside Israel, even in a city that is principally Jewish, for whoever lives in Israel is like one who has a G-d, and one who does not live in the Land is like one who has no G-d, to teach you that whoever lives outside of Israel is like one who worships idols (Ketubot 110b).

11. Lucy Dawidowicz, "Ben-Gurion, the American Jewish Committee, and American Zionists," *AJYB* 63 (1962): 285.

12. Abram wrote an autobiography, *The Day is Short* (New York: Harcourt, 1982).

13. Morris Abram, interview, April 1976, AJC Oral History project, tape 10, no. 6, p. 362, New York Public Library.

14. Eugene B. Borowitz, "Religion," *AJYB* 62 (1961): 129–52. Borowitz was at the time the director of the Commission on Jewish Education, UAHC and CCAR.

15. Ann G. Wolfe, "Why the Swastika? A Study of Young American Vandals" (New York: Institute of Human Relations Press, January 1962), Blaustein Library.

16. David Danzig and Milton Himmelfarb, "Issues in the Eichmann Trial," in YIVO Archives/AJC Record Group 347.17.12 GEN-12/Box 39, folder "Eichmann Trial 1960–62."

17. Grossman, "Transformation through Crisis," 35.

18. Frederick Greenman, presidential acceptance speech, AJC annual meeting transcript, April 28–30, 1961; AJC brochure, "The Eichmann Case: Moral Questions and Legal Arguments" (April 1961), Blaustein Library.

19. Salo W. Baron, "European Jewry Before and After Hitler," *AJYB* 63 (1962): 3–53. Also "The Eichmann Case in the American Press" (New York: Institute of Human Relations Press, August 1962), Blaustein Library.

20. Perhaps the best-known books using research sponsored by AJC during this period were *The Status Seekers* (1961) by best-selling author and journalist Vance Packard, who had shocked the country with his revelations about the advertising industry in *The Hidden Persuaders* (1957), and *The Protestant Establishment: Aristocracy and Caste in America* (New York: Random House, 1964), by University of Pennsylvania sociologist E. Digby Baltzell. That book is credited for having popularized the word WASP (White Anglo-Saxon Protestant), which, though originating in the 1950s, had not until then been in common usage. Baltzell's book also drew on research directed by Dr. Murray Friedman, who in 1960 was AJC's mid-Atlantic area director.

21. The staff director of AJC's Social Discrimination Division in 1960 was Lawrence J. Bloomgarden.

22. "What's the Point of Grosse Pointe?" *AJC Committee Reporter* 17, no. 3 (May 1960). At the time the case was being investigated by the Michigan attorney general.

23. *AJC Committee Reporter* 16, no. 3 (August 1959).

24. In the "Alton Study," Vance Packard chose a Midwestern city and did forty interviews with non-Jewish leaders in the community including bank presidents, partners in law firms, and Junior League officers. One social leader observed: "A man will be fine but the wife may not get along with other women. Women are more isolated, and there is bound to be some jealousy on the part of our women of all the mink coats the Jewish women have and our women do not have."

25. "Jews in College and University Administration" (New York: AJC, May 1966) Blaustein Library. Also, Melvin N. Jacobs, "What's New and What's Next for AJC in the Community?" Minutes, AJC Executive Committee, October 29, 1966, p. 5, Blaustein Library.

26. In its application to the Large Cities Budgeting Conference (LCBC) in 1968 the AJC noted that "there have been more appointments of Jews to prominent administrative posts during the past year than during the previous ten years," p. 5, Blaustein Library.

27. Irving S. Shapiro, who was the son of Lithuanian immigrants, died in 2001. In an oral history of him done by AJC in the 1990s, he specifically stated his resentment of AJC's tactics and claimed that it had nothing to do with his appointment (see AJC Oral History project, interview, Irving S. Shapiro, New York Public Library). The story of his unusual rise at Du Pont is covered in Edward S. Shapiro's *A Time for Healing: American Jewry Since World War II*, 2d ed. (Baltimore: Johns Hopkins University Press, 1995) in his chapter "A Tale of Two Shapiros."

The chapter also covers the success of Harold T. Shapiro, the first Jew to become president of Princeton University. By that point, the author reported, so many Ivy League colleges had had Jewish presidents that some were joking it ought to be renamed the "oi-vei" league.

28. Minutes, AJC Executive Committee meeting, November 9–11, 1962, Blaustein Library. The speaker was Earl Morse of New York.

29. AJC annual meeting proceedings, April 22–24, 1960. Address, "AJC Responsibility in Jewish Affairs," by Caroline K. Simon, chair, Jewish Communal Affairs Committee: "As adult American Jews begin to understand their own Jewishness better, their problems and confusions in raising their children as secured Jews and Americans will be minimized. Parents will no longer feel so frustrated by the conflicts and difficulties they confront daily. Shall we have a Christmas tree or shall we light Sabbath candles? Many now ask these questions" (100). Among Reform Jews, the custom was that Jewish Christmas trees at least did not have a star on top.

30. Grossman, "Transformation Through Crisis," 40.

31. Staff Advisory Committee Minutes, June 23, 1965, Blaustein Library.

32. Abraham Joshua Heschel, "The Moral Challenge to America," AJC annual meeting proceedings, April 22–24, 1960, p. 95. Commenting on this, Caroline K. Simon, then chair of the Jewish Communal Affairs Committee, said, "We want to plan so that Judaism will not be wasted on us, but will be strengthened by us."

33. Discussion following speech by Dr. Marshall Sklare, AJC annual meeting transcript, May 17–19, 1963, p. 14, Blaustein Library.

34. Irving Greenberg, AJC annual meeting transcript, May 12–16, 1966, p. 130, Blaustein Library.

35. Eric Rosenthal, "Studies of Jewish Intermarriage in the United States," *AJYB* 64 (1963): 3–53.

36. The study revealed intermarriage rates as high as 37 percent in San Francisco and 18 percent in Manhattan.

37. Clippings from JTA: "New York Rabbis, Social Workers Offer Program to Check Intermarriage" (3); "Canadian Rabbis Urge Study on Intermarriage in Small Communities"; and "Minnesota Rabbis Urge Parents to be Firm Against Interfaith Dating" (3). December 14, 1964, Jewish Communal Affairs Department, AJCA box 5, folder "Interoffice Memos from Manheim Shapiro, 1960–1964."

38. Marshall Sklare, AJC annual meeting transcript, May 17–19, 1963, p. 10, Blaustein Library.

39. Charles S. Liebman, "Orthodoxy in American Jewish Life," *AJYB* 66 (1965): 92.

40. Louis Shub, "Zionism," *AJYB* 66 (1965): 311–12.

41. For reports on the Community Service Program, see "Rebuilding a Heritage," *AJC Committee Reporter* 18, no. 1 (March 1961): 6; "Western Europe," *AJC Committee Reporter* 19, no. 1 (March 1962); minutes, AJC Executive Committee meeting, January 19–21, 1962; AJC program and budget, LCBC, 1967.

42. Patricia Blake (*Life* magazine), AJC annual meeting transcript, May 3–6, 1962, p. 445, Blaustein Library.

43. Leon Shapiro, "Soviet Union, Jewish Population: Communal and Religious Life," *AJYB* 63 (1962): 367.

44. Memorandum on the situation of the Jews in the Soviet Union. Submitted to his Excellency Anastas I. Mikoyan, first deputy premier of the Soviet Union, January 22, 1959, Blaustein Library.

45. "Eastern Europe," AJC annual meeting, April 17–19, 1959; *AJYB* 61 (1960): 16.

46. "The Situation of Jews in the Soviet Union," AJC annual meeting transcript, May 3–6, 1962, pp. 442–61, Blaustein Library.

47. Jerry Goodman, interview, May 1979, AJC Oral History project, p. 72, New York Public Library.

48. "The Church Means Business," *AJC Newsletter* 1, no. 6 (November–December 1965): 2.

49. A massive AJC-sponsored study of Protestant textbooks, carried out at the Yale Divinity School by the Rev. Bernhard E. Olson, was published as the book *Faith and Prejudice* in 1963. The first edition sold out within two weeks.

50. Joseph M. Proskauer, *A Segment of My Times* (New York: Farrar, Straus, 1950), 62.

51. On the role of the Vatican II Declaration in hastening the need for Jewish education for AJC members to properly participate in Christian-Jewish dialogue, see Staff Advisory Committee minutes, June 28, 1966 (special meeting with Jewish Communal Affairs and Interreligious Affairs): "Many felt that instead of rushing into dialogues, it might be wiser to concentrate on education of Jews to better equip them for such encounters" (3–4). See also "The Church Means Buisness," *AJC* Newsletter 1, no. 6 (November–December 1965): 3. The article described a recent meeting for members in Chicago who felt unprepared for questions they might be asked on religion, ethics, history, or social problems. The article notes, "Only a year ago, when tentative drafts of the Jewish Declaration were aired, certain Jewish spokesmen predicted that the church's new policy toward the Jews would be an invitation to conversion. Now it looks, on the contrary, as if the Catholic-Jewish rapprochement will spur Jews to seek deeper knowledge of their own heritage. What was conceived as a venture in mutual understanding is also becoming, unexpectedly, an adventure in self-understanding."

52. "Ecumenical Council 1961," 3. Submitted to the Secretariat for Christian Unity, June 22, 1961, Interreligious Affairs, AJCA box 14, folder "Image of the Jews in Catholic Teaching."

53. "The Second Vatican Council's Declaration on the Jews: A Background Report" (marked "private communication not to be published"), November 22, 1965, Interreligious Affairs, AJCA box 43, folder "Ecumenical Council AJC White Papers," p. 8.

54. Rabbi Tanenbaum, who through his efforts in Christian-Jewish relations and decades of radio commentary became one of the best-known rabbis in America, was born in Baltimore (like Jacob Blaustein) and attended the city's Talmudical Academy and public high school before graduating from Yeshiva University. He received rabbinic ordination from the Jewish Theological Seminary, where he became an assistant to Abraham Joshua Heschel (professor of Jewish ethics and mysticism) and he later edited several volumes of Rabbi Heschel's work.

55. Judith Hershcopf, "The Church and the Jews," *AJYB* 66 (1965): 105.

56. Lucy Dawidowicz, "Religion in the 1960 Presidential Campaign," *AJYB* 62 (1961): 111 and 119; the Rev. Robert McAfee Brown, Rabbi Arthur Hertzberg, and Father John LaFarge, "The Presidential Breakthrough: A Symposium," *AJC Committee Reporter* 17, no. 5 (December 1960): 5.

57. Judith Hershcopf, "The Church and the Jews: The Struggle at Vatican Council II," *AJYB* 66 (1965): 105.

58. Egal Feldman, *Catholics and Jews in Twentieth-Century America* (Champaign: University of Illinois Press, 2001), 106.

59. Ibid., 107; letter from Zachariah Shuster to John Slawson, October 28, 1960, Interreligious Affairs / Ecumenical Council, 1960–61, AJCA box 13, folder "Zach Shuster."

60. "Correspondence from August to November 1960," Interreligious Affairs / Ecumenical Council, 1960–61, AJCA box 13, folder "Zach Shuster." On August 10, 1960, John Slawson wrote in reply to Shuster's description of Isaac's visit, "Adopt Jules Isaac!" and suggested that he be made a consultant to the AJC. Isaac remained in close touch with the European office thereafter and the AJC sponsored some of his work, including the translation of his books into English.

61. Morris B. Abram, interview, April 16, 1979, AJC Oral History project, tape 10, p. 6.

62. Eugene J. Fisher, "*Nostra Aetate*, For Our Times and For the Future," in *Twenty Years of Jewish-Catholic Relations*, ed. Eugene Fisher, A. James Rudin, and Marc H. Tanenbaum (New York: Paulist Press, 1986), 1.

63. Hershcopf, "The Church and the Jews," 117; *AJYB* 67 (1966): 63.

64. Marc H. Tanenbaum, "Jewish-Christian Relations in the U.S.," AJC annual meeting proceedings, May 18–21, 1967, pp. 75–76, Blaustein Library.

65. *New York Times*, July 4, 1992, p. 10. The obituary mentioned that Rabbi Tanenbaum kept a copy of the cartoon in his file.

66. See "A Jewish Legal Authority Addresses Jewish-Christian Dialogue: Two Responsa of Rabbi Moshe Feinstein," trans. and annotated by David Ellenson, *American Jewish Archives* 52, nos. 1–2 (2000): 113–28. The article details exchanges between Rabbi Feinstein, who believed that all such contact was forbidden, and Rabbi Joseph Soloveitchik of Yeshiva University, who believed that cooperation was permissible in areas of common social and political concern; indeed, he cooperated with the AJC in its representations to Council officials.

67. Marc Tanenbaum, interview, May 18, 1972, AJC Oral History project, New York Public Library, p. 5.

68. Hershcopf, "The Church and the Jews," 34.

69. Article, "Arabs Keep Pressure Up" *Jewish Chronicle*, January 19, 1965, in Interreligious Affairs / Ecumenical Council, AJCA box 43, folder "Ecumenical Council Clippings."

70. Hershcopf, "The Church and the Jews," 57.

71. Morris Abram, interview, April 16, 1979, AJC Oral History project, pp. 369–86, New York Public Library.

72. Letter from Jacob Blaustein to John Slawson (marked "Personal and Confidential"), September 2, 1965, Interreligious Affairs, AJCA box 90, folder "Blaustein, Jacob and Morton." Rabbi Tanenbaum in his oral history provides vivid details of Blaustein's interventions at this stage.

73. Letter from Marc Tanenbaum to Jacob Blaustein, August 31, 1965, AJCA box 90, folder "Blaustein, Jacob and Morton."

74. Letter from Jacob Blaustein to John Slawson, September 2, 1965, ibid.

75. Marc Tanenbaum, interview, May 18, 1972, AJC Oral History project, p. 9, New York Public Library. Tanenbaum was reporting on a handwritten letter from Cardinal Shehan which he received within the week after Jacob Blaustein's letter.

76. "The Church Means Business," *AJC Newsletter* 1, no. 6 (November–December 1965): 1; Judith Hershcopf, "The Church and the Jews: Fourth Session," *AJYB* 67 (1966): 65. AJC also prepared a pamphlet on its activities during Vatican II for the membership, "The Second Vatican Council's Declaration on the Jews: A

Background Report" (New York: AJC, 1965) labeled "Private communication, not for publication," Blaustein Library.

77. AJC annual meeting proceedings, May 12–15, 1966, p. 13, Blaustein Library.

5. Disaster and Deliverance (1967–1968) (pp. 135–155)

1. Judith Hershcopf, "To Dialogue or Not to Dialogue," *AJYB* 67 (1966): 75; *AJC Newsletter* 1, no. 6 (November–December 1965).

2. This matter had most recently come to the attention of the Jewish world through an article by Robert Gorham Davis, "The Passion of Oberammergau," *Commentary* (March 1960): 198–204.

3. Ibid., 198; "The Stage and the Study," *AJC Newsletter* 4, no. 3 (June–July 1968): 3.

4. AJC Staff Advisory Minutes, January 18, 1967, p. 3, Blaustein Library.

5. Lucy S. Dawidowicz, "The Christian Response," *AJYB* 69 (1968): 220; Judith Hershcopf Banki, "Christian Reactions to the Middle East Crisis: New Agenda for Interreligious Dialogue" (New York: AJC, 1968), 1–20.

6. Howard M. Sachar, *A History of Israel from the Rise of Zionism to Our Time,* 2d ed. (New York: Knopf, 1996), 472.

7. Until 1961 Egypt and Syria were united under the name "United Arab Republic," which Egypt kept after the alliance fell apart; as a counterweight to the UAR, Iraq and Jordan, which had shared the same royal family, were briefly united into a single "Arab Federation," until the Iraqi revolution of July 14, 1958.

8. Annual Meeting Proceedings, May 17–19, 1963, p. 44, Blaustein Library.

9. Booklet, "The AJC and Israel" (AJC, 1998; published for Israel's 50th anniversary), 6, Blaustein Library.

10. George E. Gruen, "Jordan Water Dispute," *AJYB* 68 (1967): 108.

11. Sachar, *History of Israel,* 625.

12. Ibid., 633.

13. Lawrence Grossman, "Transformation through Crisis: The American Jewish Committee and the Six-Day War," *American Jewish History* 86, no. 1 (March 1998): 43.

14. For a comprehensive day-by-day account of the Six-Day War, see Michael Oren, *Six Days of War: June 1967 and the Making of the Modern Middle East* (New York: Random House, 2002). On the American reaction, see Eli Lederhendler, ed. *The Six-Day War and World Jewry* (Bethesda: University of Maryland Press, 2000). For a firsthand account of all Israel's wars from a former president of the country, see Chaim Herzog and Shlomo Gazit, *The Arab-Israeli Wars: War and Peace in the Middle East* (New York: Vintage, 1984; repr. 2005).

15. Sachar, *History of Israel,* 631.

16. Ibid., 635.

17. Misha Louvish, "Reunification of Jerusalem," *AJYB* 69 (1968): 122.

18. John Slawson, interview, January 12, 1972, AJC Oral History project, p. 31, New York Public Library.

19. Irving Engel, interview, June–September 1969, AJC Oral History project, p. 36, New York Public Library.

20. Lucy S. Dawidowicz, "The Jewish Response," *AJYB* 69 (1968): 203–209. For a more recent account of the Jewish response worldwide, see Eli Lederhendler, *The Six-Day War and World Jewry* (Bethesda: University Press of Maryland, 2000).

21. Dawidowicz, "Jewish Response"; Joshua Michael Zeitz, "If I am Not for Myself . . . The American Jewish Establishment and the Six-Day War," *American Jewish History*, 88, no. 2 (June 2000): 259. See also "Blood and Money," *Time* (June 16, 1967): 181; "Give as You Never Gave," *Newsweek* (June 19, 1967): 35.

22. Marshall Sklare, "Memorandum on follow-up study in Lakeville," prepared for the AJC, March 26, 1968, part V: "The Israeli Crisis and the Six-Day War" (21), in Jewish Communal Affairs Department (hereafter JCAD) box, AJC Boards, Committees, and Commissions, 1960s–1970s, folder "Lakeville Follow-up Survey after Six-Day War."

23. Dawidowicz, "Jewish Response," 206.

24. AJC AJC Staff Advisory Minutes, June 6, 1967, p. 2, Blaustein Library; Grossman, "Transformation Through Crisis," 48.

25. Grossman, "Transformation Through Crisis," 50.

26. Ibid., citing Minutes of the Board of Governors, June 20, 1967, pp. 5–6, Blaustein Library.

27. Ibid, 51.

28. April 1961 memo cited by M. Bernard Resnikoff reporting at annual meeting, May 7, 1972, pp. 6–15; George E. Gruen, interview, June 13, 1980, AJC Oral History project, p. 12. Cited in Grossman, "Transformation through Crisis," 53. On the establishment of the Israel office, see also Cohen, *Not Free to Desist*, 329.

29. Grossman, "Transformation Through Crisis," 33.

30. Gary S. Schiff, "American Jews and Israel," *Forum on the Jewish People, Zionism and Israel* 1 (1976): 24–25, cited in Grossman, "Transformation Through Crisis," 54.

31. Norman Podhoretz, "Now, Instant Zionism," *New York Times Magazine* (February 3, 1974): 37, cited in Grossman, "Transformation Through Crisis," 54.

32. "Interreligious Institute," *AJC Newsletter* 4, no. 4 (August–October 1988).

33. Philip E. Hoffman, "Presidential Report," minutes, AJC National Executive Council meeting, December 5, 1970, Blaustein Library.

34. Joshua Michael Zeitz, "'If I am Not For Myself'": The American Jewish Establishment and the Aftermath of the Six-Day War," *American Jewish History* 88, no. 2 (June 2000): 253–86.

35. Minutes, Executive Committee meeting, December 1–3, 1967, p. 14, Blaustein Library.

36. Sklare, "Lakeville Follow-Up Study After Six-Day War," 38.

37. Ibid., 35.

38. Irving Greenberg, "Cloud by Day, Fire by Night—the Future of American Jewry in Light of the Holocaust and Israel," address, AJC annual meeting transcript, May 23–26, 1968, p. 83, Blaustein Library.

39. Lucy S. Dawidowicz, "The Christian Response," *AJYB* 69 (1968): 219, quoting Banki, "Christian Reactions" (see note 5).

40. Lucy S. Dawidowicz, "American Public Opinion: Jewish Disappointment, Christian Resentment," *AJYB* 69 (1968): 221.

41. Ibid., 224.

42. Zeitz, "If I am Not For Myself," 270.

43. "Religion: Jews," *Time* (November 24, 1967): 72.

44. Zeitz, "If I am Not For Myself," 269.

45. Minutes, Executive Committee meeting, December 1–3, 1967, p. 14, Blaustein Library.

46. Eugene DuBow, interview, December 1987, AJC Oral History project, pp. 43–44, New York Public Library.

47. Report of AJC Scope Committee Retreat, summary of discussion, p. 11, "Race Relations—Scope Committee," September 21–24, 1967, Bertram H. Gold Papers (hereafter BHG), box 36, folder "Scope Committee 1967–1968."

48. Bertram H. Gold, interview, December 3, 1991 and March 17, 1992, by AJC Oral History project, p. 3, New York Public Library.

49. Ibid, p. 39.

50. Yehuda Roseman, interview, December 2, 1980, by AJC Oral History project, p. 20, New York Public Library.

51. "Minutes of First Meeting of Professional Advisory Committee," March 31–April 1, 1968, p. 6, 1960s–1970s JCAD box, "Boards, Committees and Commissions."

52. "AJC Memorandum, From Nathan Weisman to AJC Staff Advisory Committee, Re: Expansion and Retention of AJC Membership, Background Paper for 'Scope Committee,' August 7, 1967," BHG, box 36, folder "Scope Committee 1967–1968."

53. The Oral History library had its genesis in June 1968 with an AJC conference, chaired by then director of research Lucy S. Dawidowicz, that brought together thirty scholars and writers who wished to explore ways to preserve the Jewish past. Louis G. Cowan, who had been president of the CBS TV network, served as the first chairman of the organizing committee.

54. Jerry Goodman, interview, May 1979, by AJC Oral History project, p. 77, New York Public Library.

55. AJC Staff Advisory Committee Minutes, December 13, 1967, p. 3, Blaustein Library.

56. Memo: "Summary of Illustrative Jewish Program Activity at AJC Chapters," January 1968, JCAD, box 5, folder Yehuda Rosenman—"JCAD Program Activities: Summaries and Reports, 1968."

57. Irving Greenberg, "Jewish Survival and the College Campus," *Judaism* 17 (Summer 1968): 260–81. Discussion of the college campus as a "disaster area" for commitment to Judaism appears in box AJC: Boards, Committees and Commissions, 1960s–1970s; JCAD, box Meeting of Professional Advisory Committee, January 5–6, 1969.

58. Alfred Jospe, roundtable, "Our Alienated Jewish Youth," annual meeting proceedings, May 23–26, 1968, pp. 137–39, Blaustein Library.

59. Howard Schwartz, "Jewish College Youth Speak Their Minds: A Summary of the Tarrytown Conference," with a foreword by Abraham Joshua Heschel (New York: AJC, 1969), Blaustein Library.

60. Memo to the Scope Committee Retreat prepared by Paul Ritterband, September 13, 1967, for September 21–24, 1967, JCAD box 5, folder "Meeting at Tarrytown." The article he was citing was Seymour Martin Lipset, "The Study of Jewish Communities in a Comparative Context," *Jewish Journal of Sociology* 5 (1963): 157–66.

61. AJC Memo from Samuel Katz (director, community service department) to Participants in Scope Study Group, re: "Aspects of Community Development Affecting AJC's Program Emphasis," September 5, 1967, p. 4, JCAD, box 5.

62. Memo by Yehuda Roseman "New Directions for Jewish Program of AJC: Background Memorandum," April 10, 1968, JCAD, box 5, folder "JCAD Program Activities: Summaries and Reports, 1968."

63. Memo from Milton Himmelfarb to AJC Staff Advisory Committee on Scope, re: "Jewish Identity: A Partial Statement," September 1, 1967, p. 20, JCAD, box 5.
64. Marshall Sklare, Joseph Greenblum, and Benjamin A. Ringer, "Not Quite at Home: How an American Jewish Community Lives with Itself and its Neighbors" (New York: Institute of Human Relations Press, 1969). This material was based on the "Lakeville" studies; see, Marshall Sklare and Joseph Greenblum, *Jewish Identity on the Suburban Frontier: A Study of Group Survival in an Open Society* (New York: Basic Books, 1967).
65. Marshall Sklare (Yeshiva University), "Part IV: The Intermarriage Problem." March 26, 1968, pp. 7–13, JCAD, box AJC Boards, Committees, and Commissions, 1960s–1970s, folder "Lakeville Follow-up Survey after Six-Day War."
66. Memo from Milton Himmelfarb to AJC Staff Advisory Committee on Scope, Re: "Jewish Identity: A Partial Statement," p. 19.
67. Summary of discussion by Bertram H. Gold, p. 8; JCAD, box 5, folder "AJC Scope Committee Retreat September 21–24, 1967."

6. *The Civil Rights Movement and the Great Society (1960–1970)* (pp. 156–196)

1. Selma Hirsh, interview, February–June 1981, by AJC Oral History project, p. 78, New York Public Library.
2. John Slawson, interview, January 12, 1972, AJC Oral History project, p. 37, New York Public Library.
3. Irving Engel, minutes, AJC Executive Committee meeting, October 24–26, 1958, Blaustein Library.
4. Selma Hirsh, interview, February–June 1981, by AJC Oral History project, p. 78, New York Public Library.
5. A. M. Sonnabend, "The Sanctity of the Human Being," *AJC Committee Reporter* 21, no. 1 (February 1964): 12.
6. Philip E. Hoffman, "Civil Rights vs. Jewish Identity," AJC annual meeting transcript, April 29–May 3, 1964, p. 24–26, Blaustein Library.
7. Presentation by the Rev. Martin Luther King Sr. in honor of Morris Abram, AJC Annual Meeting Proceedings, May 23–26, 1968, p. 41, Blaustein Library.
8. Morris B. Abram, "A Southerner Looks at Americus," *AJC Committee Reporter* 21, no. 1 (February 1964): 4.
9. Speech by Robert F. Kennedy (attorney general), AJC annual meeting, May 1962, reported in "Voting Rights," *AJC Committee Reporter* 19, no. 3 (July 1962): 5, Blaustein Library.
10. *Time* (October 4, 1968).
11. Irving Engel, "The Crisis and the Struggle Within," *AJC Committee Reporter* 15, no. 5 (December 1958): 4.
12. Arthur J. Goldberg (AJC president, 1968–69), AJC annual meeting proceedings, May 12–15, 1966, pp. 62–63, Blaustein Library.
13. Theodore Leskes, "Civil Rights," *AJYB* 63 (1962): 155.
14. In a unanimous opinion in *Brown v. Board of Education of Topeka*, the court held that de jure segregation of public education based on race deprived minority children of equal educational opportunities in violation of the Equal Protection Clause of the Fourteenth Amendment.

15. Theodore Leskes, "School Desegregation," *AJYB* 64 (1963): 93.

16. Edwin J. Lukas, "Civil Rights and Race Relations," minutes, AJC Executive Committee meeting, December 4–6, 1964, p. 7, Blaustein Library.

17. Jonathan D. Sarna, *American Judaism: A History* (New Haven: Yale University Press, 2004), 310.

18. Milton Himmelfarb, "Conference on Jewish Identity and Integration Report," 1964, Jewish Communal Affairs Department (hereafter JCAD), box 5, AJC archives; Murray Friedman, "The Jews Who Went South," in *What Went Wrong? The Creation and Collapse of the Black-Jewish Alliance* (New York: Free Press, 1995), 187.

19. John C. Devlin, "Families of Victims Voice Mixed Views on Arrests by F.B.I.," *New York Times*, December 5, 1964.

20. "Statement on AJC and Negro Protest Activities," minutes, AJC Executive Committee meeting, November 1–3, 1963, p. 21, Blaustein Library.

21. "'Focus on Committees,' Report of the Civil Rights and Civil Liberties Committee," *AJC Committee Reporter* 16, no. 2 (June 1959): 3.

22. "Chapters at Work: Cincinnati: The Country Cousins," *AJC Committee Reporter* 17, no. 4 (October 1960): 22.

23. Philip E. Hoffman, "Big City Blues," *AJC Committee Reporter* 16, no. 14 (December 1959): 8.

24. "President Lyndon B. Johnson describes the Great Society: Address at the University of Michigan, May 22, 1964," in *Reading the American Past: Selected Historical Documents*, ed. Michael P. Johnson (New York: Bedford/St. Martin's, 2002), 2:204–207.

25. AJC annual meeting transcript, May 20–23, 1965, p. 89, Blaustein Library.

26. Harry Fleischman, "Review of the Year, US: Civic and Political," *AJYB* 67 (1966): 101.

27. "AJC Report on the Task Force on Civil Rights, Social Action and Urban Affairs," January 1968, p. 5, Bertram H. Gold papers (hereafter BHG), box 36, folder "Scope Committee, 1967–1968," AJC archives.

28. Ibid.

29. Letter from Mr. and Mrs. Joseph Rafton to Philip E. Hoffman (AJC president) on the Forest Hills Controversy, BHG, box 100, folder "Housing, Forest Hills 1971–1974." On the Forest Hills controversy, see also BHG, box 85, folder "Forest Hills Housing, 1972," and "AJC Staff Advisory Committee Summary of Meeting Tuesday September 21, 1971," BHG, folder "AJC Staff Advisory Committee Meeting 1971–1972," AJC archives.

30. Friedman, *What Went Wrong?* 211.

31. Naomi W. Cohen, *Not Free to Desist: The American Jewish Committee, 1906–1966* (Philadelphia: JPS, 1972), 381.

32. Obituary of Barry Goldwater, *Washington Post*, May 30, 1998, p. A1.

33. "Portents for 1968," minutes, AJC Executive Committee meeting, December 1–3, 1967, p. 3, Blaustein Library.

34. Stokley Carmichael, "SNCC Position Paper: The Basis of Black Power," from the Sixties Project, University of Virginia, http://lists.village.virginia.edu/sixties/HTML_docs/Resources/Primary/anifestos/SNCC_black_power.html. See also Kwame Ture and Charles Hamilton, *Black Power: The Politics of Liberation*, with new afterwords by the authors (Vintage, 1967; reissued in paperback 1976 and 1992).

35. Friedman, *What Went Wrong?* 233.

36. "Report of the Task Force on Civil Rights, Social Action and Urban Affairs," BHG, box 36, folder "Scope Committee 1967–1968." AJC archives.

37. AJC program and budget, application to LCBC (Large Cities Budgeting Conference), 1969, p. 2, Blaustein Library.

38. Philip E. Hoffman, "Presidential Report," National AJC Executive Council Dinner Minutes, December 5, 1970, Blaustein Library.

39. Lucy S. Dawidowicz, "Negro Antisemitism," *AJYB* 68 (1967): 77; Friedman, *What Went Wrong?* 227.

40. Minutes, AJC Executive Committee meeting, May 15–17, 1969, p. 2.; "Resolution on IFCO," May 15, 1969, Blaustein Library.

41. Murray Friedman, *What Went Wrong?* 263–64.

42. "John Lindsay's Ten Plagues," *Time* (November 1, 1968).

43. Edward T. Rogowsky, "Intergroup Relations in the United States," *AJYB* 70 (1969): 84.

44. For one journalist's extended account of the 1968 strike, see Tamar Jacoby, *Someone Else's House: America's Unfinished Struggle for Integration* (New York: Basic Books, 2000), 186–226.

45. "AJC Progress Report No. 3: The Kerner Report and AJC: One Year Later," February 15, 1969, pp. 2–6, in BHG, box 41, folder "Urban Affairs: Kerner Commission Report 1968–1969," AJC archives; "School Strike," *AJC Newsletter* 4, no. 4 (August–October 1968): 8; symposium, "Pieties and Realities: Some Constructive Approaches to Negro-Jewish Relations" (chair Maynard Wishner, domestic affairs committee), AJC annual meeting transcript, May 23–26, 1968, p. 126; Edward T. Rogowsky, "The Storm Over Urban Education," *AJYB* 69 (1968): 252.

46. Marc Dollinger, "The Other War: American Jews, Lyndon Johnson, and the Great Society," *American Jewish History*, 89, no. 4 (December 2001): 450; Friedman, *What Went Wrong?* 213–14.

47. Lucy Dawidowicz, "Negro-Jewish Tensions," *AJYB* 66 (1965): 187.

48. Harry Fleischman, "Civil Rights," *AJYB* 67 (1966): 103.

49. *Newsweek* (August 30, 1965).

50. Lucy Dawidowicz, "Antisemitism Among Negroes," *AJYB* 66 (1965): 189, quoting *New York Times*, May 24, 1965.

51. Edward T. Rogowsky, "Negro Antisemitism," *AJYB* 69 (1968): 244.

52. Bayard Rustin, "Address to AJC Annual Meeting," AJC annual meeting transcript, May 23–26, 1968, p. 114, Blaustein Library.

53. Dawidowicz, "Negro Antisemitism," 79.

54. For information on the riots and a history of Newark's Jews, see William B. Helmreich, *The Enduring Community: The Jews of Newark and Metrowest* (New Brunswick, N.J.: Transaction, 1998).

55. Friedman, *What Went Wrong?* 214.

56. Lucy S. Dawidowicz, "AJC Information Service: A Research Report—Supplemental Studies for the 'National Advisory Committee on Civil Disorders,' A Summary and Critique," August 1968, pp. 2 and 19, BHG, box 41, folder "Urban Affairs: Kerner Commission Report 1968–1969," AJC archives.

57. Bertram Gold, "Report of the AJC Executive VP, AJC Executive," AJC Executive Committee Minutes, October 25–27, 1968, Blaustein Library.

58. Joshua Zeitz, "If I am Not For Myself: The American Jewish Establishment and the Aftermath of the Six-Day War," *American Jewish History* 88, no. 2 (June 2000): 265.

59. AJC Staff Advisory Minutes, May 1, 1968, p. 2.

60. Edward T. Rogowsky, "Jewish Response," *AJYB* 69 (1968): 245.

61. *AJC Newsletter* 1, no. 5 (September–October 1965): 1.

62. AJC program and budget, LCBC 1968, p. 7, Blaustein Library.

63. Morris Abram, "Summing Up" (address on civil rights), AJC annual meeting transcript, May 20–23, 1965, Blaustein Library, 99.

64. Morris Abram, "Guest Address," minutes, AJC Executive Committee meeting, October 27, 1968, Blaustein Library.

65. Morris B. Abram, "The Paradoxes of Freedom" (address), AJC annual meeting transcript, May 23–26, 1968, p. 52, Blaustein Library.

66. Morris Abram, "Presidential Address," minutes, AJC Executive Committee meeting, October 28, 1966, Blaustein Library.

67. Arthur J. Goldberg, "Presidential Address," AJC Executive Committee meeting, October 26, 1968, Blaustein Library.

68. "Resolution on Civil Rights," adopted at the AJC Executive Committee meeting, October 28, 1966, Blaustein Library.

69. John Slawson, address on "Internal Organization," AJC annual meeting transcript, May 20–23, 1965, p. 60, Blaustein Library.

70. Rogowsky, "Jewish Response," 245.

71. Zeitz, "If I am Not For Myself," 271.

72. Bayard Rustin, symposium "'Pieties and Realities': Some Constructive Approaches to Negro-Jewish Relations," AJC annual meeting proceedings, May 23–26, 1968, pp. 114–17, Blaustein Library.

73. Kenneth Clark, "Pieties and Realities," AJC annual meeting proceedings, May 23–26, 1968, pp. 119–21, Blaustein Library.

74. Charles E. Silberman, *Crisis in Black and White* (New York: Random House, 1964); *A Certain People: American Jews and Their Lives Today* (New York: Summit Books, 1985).

75. Charles E. Silberman, "Pieties and Realities," AJC annual meeting proceedings, May 23–26, 1968, p. 127, Blaustein Library.

76. Leonard Fein, "Pieties and Realities," AJC annual meeting proceedings, May 23–26, 1968, pp. 105–12, Blaustein Library.

77. Nathan Perlmutter (director of domestic affairs), "Crisis in Our Cities," AJC annual meeting proceedings, May 23–26, 1968, pp. 91–92, Blaustein Library.

78. Nathan Perlmutter, address, AJC annual meeting proceedings, May 18–31, 1967, p. 18, Blaustein Library.

79. Bertram Gold, "Report of AJC Executive VP, minutes, AJC Executive Committee meeting, October 25–27, 1968, p. 1; AJC Scope Committee Retreat, September 21–24, 1967, summary of discussion by Bertram Gold, Blaustein Library.

80. Philip E. Hoffman, "Presidential Report," minutes, National AJC Executive Council dinner, December 5, 1970, Blaustein Library.

81. "Jews and Other Forgotten Men in the War on Poverty," *AJC Newsletter* 4, no. 1 (February–March 1968): 3. The report was released at an AJC press conference on January 31 led by Theodore Ellenoff, president of the New York chapter, and Rabbi Bernard Weinberger, a member of the New York City Council Against Poverty. A larger-scale follow-up study was conducted in 1971.

82. Ibid.

83. Norman Podhoretz, interview, December 2, 1980, by AJC Oral History project, pp. 24–26, New York Public Library.

84. Ibid., 31.

85. Hyman Bookbinder (AJC Washington, D.C., representative), "The Urban Coalition: Best and Possibly Last Hope," *AJC Newsletter* 4, no. 1 (February–March 1968): "AJC Lends a Hand in the Urban Crisis," special supplement (June–July 1968): 4.

86. Marc Dollinger, "The Other War: American Jews, Lyndon Johnson, and the Great Society," in *American Jewish History* 89, no. 4 (December 2001): 448, citing Theodore Ellenoff, "Memo to Members of the AJC Executive Committee in Urban Affairs Committee," AJC New York chapter, March 13, 1968, Blaustein Library.

87. Letter to Otto Kerner (governor of Illinois), April 18, 1968, BHG, box 41, folder "Kerner Commission Report."

88. Memo to Members and Units from Melvan M. Jacobs (chairman, community service committee), "Memo: 'Progress Report: AJC Post-Kerner Commission on Civil Disorders, April 1968,'" March 26, 1968, BHG, box 41, AJC archives.

89. AJC memo to area directors, "Re: Guidelines on Activity in Connection with the National Advisory Committee on Civil Disorders—Top Priority," March 20, 1968, p. 5. BHG, box 41, folder "Kerner Commission Report."

90. "Implementing the Kerner Report: What You Can Do," *AJC Newsletter* 4, no. 2 (April–May 1968): 2.

91. Roundtable summary, "The Urban Revolution: What AJC Can Do," AJC annual meeting transcript, May 23–26, 1968, pp. 131–33, Blaustein Library; "AJC Lends a Hand In the Urban Crisis," *AJC Newsletter*, special supplement (June–July 1968): 1–4; "Memo: 'Progress Report: AJC Post-Kerner Commission Task Forces,' Issued as a Summary of Activities Implementing the Report of the National Advisory Commission on Civil Disorders," BHG, box 41, folder "Urban Affairs: Kerner Commission report 1968–69."

92. "AJC Progress Report No. 3: The Kerner Report and AJC: One Year Later," February 15, 1969, p. 1, BHG, box 41, AJC archives.

93. Hoffman, "Presidential Report."

94. Ethics of the Fathers, Mishnah 14. I am indebted for this formulation and conclusion to Joshua Zeitz, "If I am Not For Myself," 286. At the conclusion of his article, he writes: "Firm in their determination to be for themselves, Jewish leaders in the aftermath of the June 1967 crisis remained acutely aware that they could and must be for others as well."

7. New Challenges (1970–1979) (pp. 199–227)

1. Bertram H. Gold (executive vice president), "Address at Opening Plenary Luncheon," May 4, 1972, AJC annual meeting transcript, pp. 18–22, Blaustein Library. Other references to 1945–67 as the "Golden Age" of American Jewry include Lucy Dawidowicz, *On Equal Terms: Jews in America, 1881–1981* (New York: Henry Holt, 1982), which she first prepared as a study for the 1982 *AJYB* to mark both the 100th anniversary of the Jewish mass migration from Eastern Europe in 1881 and the 75th anniversary of the AJC; (see "A Century of Jewish History, 1881–1981: The View from America," *AJYB* 82 (1982): 3–97. See also Arthur Goren, *The Politics and Public Culture of American Jews* (Bloomington: Indiana University Press, 1999). AJC speechmakers made several references to the "Golden Age" through the 1970s. On both the term and its evaluation, see Hasia

R. Diner, *The Jews of the United States, 1654–2000,* chapter 7, "A Golden Age? 1948–1967." (Berkeley: University of Carlifornia Press, 2004, 259–304.

2. Hirsh Goodman, "What Next," *Present Tense* 8, no. 3 (Spring 1981): 54.

3. Misha Louvish, "Israel," *AJYB* 72 (1971): 429.

4. Misha Louvish, "Israel," *AJYB* 76 (1976): 402.

5. *What's Doing at the Committee* 2, no. 7 (July–August 1972): 2.

6. Louvish, "Israel," 76: 468–473.

7. *What's Doing at the Committee* 3, no. 8 (September–October 1973), 1.

8. Sidney Liskovsky, "The UN Resolution on Zionism," *AJYB* 76 (1976): 105.

9. Broadcast, November 20, 1975, Memo from Israeli Consulate in New York, November 21, 1975, Bertram H. Gold papers (hereafter BHG), box 206, folder "United Nations, Zionism Nov. 1975," AJC archives.

10. On the Yom Kippur War, see Chaim Herzog, *The War of Atonement: The Inside Story of the Yom Kippur War* (London: Greenhill Books, 2006), and *The Arab-Israeli Wars: War and Peace in the Middle East from the War of Independence to the Present,* updated by Shlomo Gazit, with an introduction by Isaac Herzog and Michael Herzog, 2d Vintage Books ed., revised (New York: Vintage Books, 2005), 227–323.

11. See Walter J. Boyne, *The Two O'Clock War: The 1973 Yom Kippur Conflict and the Airlift that Saved Israel* (New York: Thomas Dunne Books, 2002).

12. General Responses—Memo, February 12, 1974, "Interreligious Affairs Department (hereafter IAD), box 145, folder "Israel, Yom Kippur, POWs, 1973–74," AJC archives.

13. Ibid.

14. The members of OPEC were Iran, Iraq, Kuwait, Saudi Arabia, Venezuela, Qatar, Libya, United Arab Emirates, Algeria, Nigeria, and Indonesia.

15. J. J. Goldberg, *Jewish Power: Inside the American Jewish Establishment* (Reading, Mass.: Addison-Wesley, 1996), 268.

16. "A Discussion of the Energy Crisis—with Barbara Walters," *Today Show,* January 25, 1973 (from Radio and TV Reports), BHG, box 74, folder "Energy Crisis December 1972 to July 1974," AJC archives.

17. The IAD reported that in 1974 Saudi Arabia would have $20 billion of excess funds for international investment and Kuwait would have $7–$10 billion.

18. ADL memo, "Target USA: The Arab Propaganda Offensive," November 1975, mimeo. Cited in "Politics and Intergroup Relations: Defeating Arab Propaganda and Arab Investment in Universities and Companies," *AJYB* 76 (1976): 47. The memo also noted that there had been a significant increase in Muslim students on U.S. campuses. Some twenty-five thousand Muslim students were enrolled in the 1974–75 academic year and nearly thirty-five thousand were expected for 1975–76.

19. Marc Tanenbaum, address, "Jewish-Christian Relations: Some International Implications," plenary session, AJC annual meeting transcript, May 18, 1974, pp. 13–45, Blaustein Library.

20. Howard M. Sachar, *A History of the Jews in America* (New York: Knopf, 1992), 878. The sponsors of the bill were Democratic Senators Harrison Williams of New Jersey and William Proxmire of Wisconsin.

21. Letter to Selma Hirsh from Billie Stern, "Subject: Energy Crisis, AJC Annual Meeting and the Houston Chapter," March 19, 1973, BHG, box 74, folder "Energy Crisis December 1972 to July 1973," AJC archives.

22. Memo to Bertram H. Gold from Sonya F. Kaufer, "Subject: Report from Marilyn Schwartz on Reaction of Jews in Dallas," November 30, 1973, BHG, box 74, folder "Energy Crisis, 1972–73," AJC archives.

23. Letter from Guilford Glazer (member of the Los Angeles chapter) to Amnon Barness, December 4, 1973, BHG, box 74, folder "Energy Crisis, 1972–73," AJC archives.

24. Memo, "AJC's Activities in Support of Israel and to Mitigate Backlash from the Energy Crisis," BHG, box 74, folder "Energy Crisis October–December 1973," AJC archives.

25. Minutes, "AJC Operation Emergency Committee Meeting," December 26, 1973, BHG, box 74, folder "Energy Crisis Operation Emergency Committee 1973," AJC archives.

26. "AJC's Activities" (see note 24).

27. Memo, "A Tactical Program Plan to Combat Anticipated Anti-Semitic Fallout from the Energy Crisis. Confidential," December 13, 1973, BHG, folder "Energy Crisis, 1973," also in BHG, box 202, folder "Survey Committee II, 1973–74," p. 4, AJC archives.

28. Ibid., 2, 7–8.

29. Memo from Simon H. Rifkind to List of AJC Executive Committee, May 9, 1974, BHG, box 202, folder "Survey Committee II, 1973–74," AJC archives.

30. Memo on Survey Committee II Dinner Meeting, January 10, 1974, BHG, box 202, folder "Survey Committee II, 1973–74," AJC archives.

31. Elmer L. Winter, letter to the editor, *New York Times*, March 24, 1974.

32. Letter to Isaac L. Auerbach from Simon H. Rifkind, November 11, 1974, BHG, box 202, folder "Survey Committee II, 1973–74,"AJC archives.

33. See "The Oil Squeeze of '79," *Time* (March 12, 1979).

34. AJC annual meeting transcript, Thursday, May 16, 1974, at banquet, AJC archives.

35. Milton Ellerin, interview, September 3, 1980, by AJC Oral History project, 33.

36. Milton Ellerin, "Jewish Concerns About the Watergate Crisis," Trends Analysis Division, Department of Intergroup Relations and Social Action, June 7, 1974, BHG, box 173, folder "Nixon, Richard, 1970–74," AJC archives.

37. Memo to Elmer Winter from Bertram H. Gold, "The Ford Presidency—Confidential," August 9, 1974, BHG, box 82, folder "Ford, Gerald, 1973–76," AJC archives.

38. George E. Gruen, "The United States, Israel and the Middle East," *AJYB* 79 (1979): 120–51.

39. Memo from Bernard Resnikoff, "First Reaction in Israel to the Camp David Agreements," September 18, 1978, BHG, box 124, folder "Monthly Reports Israel," AJC archives.

40. Richard Maass, "Presidential Remarks," AJC annual meeting transcript (dinner), May 10, 1979, p. 1, Blaustein Library.

41. AJC press release, December 14, 1978, BHG, box 62, folder "Carter, James, 1978," AJC archives: "The AJC today urged President Carter to 'continue his efforts toward peace in the Middle East based on the agreements reached at Camp David, and not to superimpose on those agreements the added demands that Egypt has proposed since that conference and that Israel has found it necessary to reject.'" Also, memo to Bertram H. Gold from M. Bernard Resnikoff, BHG, box 121, folder "Israel Government Officials: Begin, Prime Minister, 1978" "There is growing evidence that the US government despite Pres. Carter's disclaimer of two days ago is ultimately planning for a Palestinian state and is promoting the participation of Palestinian people in the peace negotiations on that basis."

42. AJC press release, December 14, 1978, BHG, box 62, folder "Carter, James, 1978," AJC archives. See "Jewish Group Charge Carter Has Abandoned Role of Mediator (On Camp David Summit Meetings)," *New York Times*, December 17, 1978, 3.

43. George E. Gruen, "The US and the Middle East," *AJYB* 80 (1980): 139.

44. Murray Friedman, "Civic and Political: Intergroup Relations: The Andrew Young Affair," *AJYB* 80 (1980): 122–23.

45. Hyman Bookbinder and Morris Amitay, "Noted on Meeting of AJC Officers with Dr. Zbigniew Brzezinski," p. 21 March 1977, BHG, box 60, folder "Brzezinski, Zbigniew, 1977–78," AJC archives.

46. Letter from Morton K. Blaustein to Bertram H. Gold, May 12, 1978, BHG, box 60, folder "Brzezinski, Zbigniew, 1977–78," AJC archives.

47. AJC documentation on the Andrew Young affair is voluminous. See International Affairs Department, box 224, folder "Young, Andrew, 1972–79"; IAD, box 108, folder "Black-Jewish Relations, 1978–79"; BHG, box 160, folders "Middle East, Arab-Israel conflict," "Palestinians," "Young, Andrew Affair August–September 1979 and December 1979," AJC archives.

48. Carl Gershman, "The Andrew Young Affair," *Commentary* 68, no. 5 (November 1979): 27.

49. Memo to Seymour Samet from Haskell L. Lazere, August 15, 1979, "Re: Timothy Mitchell," IAD, box 108, folder "Black-Jewish Relations, 1978–79," AJC archives.

50. Roger Wilkins, "Black Leaders' Meeting: 'Watershed' Effort for Unanimity," *New York Times*, September 24, 1979, p. A11.

51. "Black Group Invites Arafat to US And All Sing 'We Shall Overcome,' *New York Times*, September 22, 1979, 5. The delegation included SCLC head Reverend Joseph E. Lowery and Washington, D.C., Representative Walter Fauntroy.

52. Murray Friedman, "Black Antisemitism on the Rise," *Commentary* (October 1979): 31–35.

53. Murray Friedman, "Review of the Year: US: Intergroup Relations," *AJYB* 80 (1980): 77.

54. Memo from Simon H. Rifkind, summary of meeting October 16, 1979, dated October 22, BHG, box 202, folder "Survey Committee III 1979," AJC archives.

55. George E. Gruen, "The United States, Israel and the Middle East," *AJYB* 79 (1979): 131–32.

56. J. J. Goldberg, *Jewish Power: Inside the American Jewish Establishment* (Reading, Mass.: Addison-Wesley, 1996), 210.

57. Robert Goldman, "A Jew First, an Israeli Second," *Jerusalem Post* (clippings), June 19, 1978, BHG, box 121, folder "Israel Government Officials: Begin, Prime Minister, 1978," AJC archives.

58. AJC press release, June 21, 1978, BHG, box 128, folder "Israel Task Force, Diaspora January–June folder 1978," AJC archives: "Thirty-three prominent American and Israeli Jews, following many months of intensive study of the relationship between Israel and the American Jewish community conclude that in view of the pluralistic nature both of American society and the American Jewish community, 'dissent from majority views' must be permitted—but this should not overshadow the assertion of American Jewish consensus."

59. George E. Gruen, "The United States, Israel, and the Middle East" *AJYB* 82 (1982): 130–32. See also JTA (Jewish Telegraphic Agency News Bulletin), Thursday, February 14, 1980, no. 32, headline "AJCommittee Tells Begin It Will Not

Defend Jewish Resettlement in Hebron," by David Landau. AJC after meetings in Israel and Egypt had spoken its feelings in a "background" interview with the *Jerusalem Post*. The *Jerusalem Post*, which opposed Begin, published the information as part of an antisettlement editorial, and the story was picked up and spread through the United States through the JTA.

60. Milton Ellerin, "Civic and Political Intergroup Relations: Relations with Evangelicals," *AJYB* 79 (1979): 107–19.

61. Memo: "Jews and Christian Evangelism: Questions and Answers," 1972, Jewish Communal Affairs Department (hereafter JCAD), box 10, folder "Jews for Jesus, Key '73, Jewish Messiah, etc. 1972–1973," AJC archives; Murray Friedman, "Politics and Intergroup Relations: The Rise of Evangelical Protestant Movements," *AJYB* 74 (1973): 143–44. The article cites two of several books published that year on the subject: Lowell D. Streiker and Gerald S. Strober's *Religion and the New Majority: Billy Graham, Middle America, and the Politics of the '70s* (New York: Association Press, 1972); and Dean M. Kelley's *Why Conservative Churches are Growing: A Study in Sociology of Religion* (New York: Harper and Row, 1972). Strober was a consultant to the Interreligious Affairs Department.

62. Murray Friedman, "Politics and Intergroup Relations in the US: The Rise of Evangelical Protestant Movements," *AJYB* 74 (1973): 145. The phrase was first used by Republican Senate Minority Leader Hugh Scott.

63. Dawidowicz, "A Century of Jewish History," 20.

64. Philip Perlmutter (director, New England Region of AJC) "Intergroup Relations and Tensions in the US: Conferences with Evangelicals," *AJYB* 72 (1971): 156–57.

65. Milton Ellerin, "Politics and Intergroup Relations: Christian-Jewish Relations," *AJYB* 76 (1976): 54. See also IAD, box 137; this entire box is filled with folders on International Jewish Committee on Interreligious Consultations with the Vatican from 1972 to 1979. Also November 20, 1975, "'Jewish Relations on the Occasion of the Celebration of the Tenth Anniversary of *Nostra Aetate* No. 4,' National Conference of Catholic Bishops, 20 Nov 1975," IA, box 112, folder "Catholic–Jewish Relations, 1971–77."

66. AJC annual meeting transcript, general session, May 15, 1977, p. 3. General session, AJC annual meeting transcript, May 15, 1977, no. 3, Blaustein Library. Marc Tanenbaum was reporting on the incident and read the entire letter aloud.

67. "Carter Denies He Believes Jews are Guilty of the Death of Jesus," *New York Times*, May 14, 1977, p. 48.

68. IAD, box 151, folder "Key '73 June–December 1973." AJC archives.

69. Ellerin, "Civic and Political Intergroup Relations," 107–19. Bright had been the head of Campus Crusade for Christ.

70. Ibid.

71. The Moral Majority dissolved in 1989 but was re-formed under the name "Moral Majority Coalition" in 2004 by televangelist Pat Robertson, whose *700 Club* program was still going strong.

72. Rabbi Balfour Brickner, "America's Religion: What's Right, What's Left," *Present Tense* 8, no. 3 (Spring 1981): 40–43; and Murray Friedman, "Civil and Political Intergroup Relations," *AJYB* 82 (1982): 101–10.

73. Friedman, "Civil," 101–10. On the 1980 elections, see "Baptist Leader Criticized for Statement About Jews: Speech was Recorded," *New York Times*, September 18, 1980, p. A18.

74. Kenneth A. Briggs, "Rabbi Attacks Aims of Moral Majority; Calls for 'Coalitions of Decency' by Jews and Christians to Fight Power of 'Radical Right' Meeting is Requested," *New York Times*, November 23, 1980, p. 29.

75. Brickner, "America's Religion," 42–43.

76. Earl Raab, "Intergroup Relations and Tensions in the US: Evangelicals," *AJYB* 71 (1970): 212.

77. Statement, June 1973, "Key '73: Religious Freedom and Evangelism," IAD, box 101, folder "American Baptist Churches, 1973–74," and letter to Rabbi Marc Tanenbaum, June 11, 1973, from James A. Christison (executive secretary of the American Baptist Churches, USA), referring to the June issue of the magazine *The American Baptist*, which has an article "Religious Freedom and Evangelism," IAD, box 101, folder "American Baptist Churches, 1973–74," AJC archives.

78. Memo, June 15, 1978, IA, box 105, folder "Baptist," AJC archives.

79. Kenneth A. Briggs, "Fundamentalist Asks End to Religious Polarization; Clarification of Attitudes Falwell the Most Prominent," *New York Times*, October 11, 1980, p. 8. See also "Baptists Criticize Remark on Jews," *New York Times*, September 19, 1980, p. A13.

80. Confidential memo, March 26, 1973, to Mr. Melvyn H. Bloom (director of public relations), re: UJA, from Rabbi Marc H. Tanenbaum, IAD, box 129, folder "Graham, Reverend Billy, 1970–74," AJC archives.

81. Letter, October 14, 1977, from Billy Graham to Marc H. Tanenbaum, IA, box 129, folder "Graham, Reverend Billy, 1975–77," AJC archives.

82. Letter from Marc H. Tanenbaum to Billy Graham, January 31, 1973; press release, Billy Graham, March 1973, IAD, box 129, folder "Graham, Reverend Billy, 1970–1974." See also folder "Graham, Reverend Billy, 1975–1977," AJC archives.

83. October 28, 1977, "Address by Billy Graham upon winning AJC National Interreligious Award, Atlanta GA," IAD, box 129, folder "Graham, Reverend Billy, 1975–1977," AJC archives.

84. James Warren, "Nixon and Billy Graham Anti-Semitism Caught on Tape," *Chicago Tribune*, March 1, 2002, http://www.rense.com/general20/billy.htm.

85. G. Shapiro, "History of Jews for Jesus," www.geocities.com/Heartland/Prairie /1551/history/histj4j.htm. See also A. James and Marcia Rudin, "The Jews for Jesus Are Out to Get Your Kids," *Present Tense* (Summer 1977), 17–26; and clipping, *New York Times* May 1977, "Hebrew Christians Disturb Jews" by Kenneth A. Briggs, IAD, box 108, folder "Cults, 1977," AJC archives.

86. "Cult finds Meditation, Mysticism and Yoga Growing in Popularity," *New York Times*, November 18, 1976; see also IAD, box 108, folder "Cults, 1971–1976," AJC archives.

87. Marcia Rudin and Rabbi A. James Rudin, "The Challenge of the Cults," discussion packet. By the Community Services and Membership Department and the Interreligious Affairs Department AJC. IAD, box 108, folder "Cults, 1979," AJC archives. For more on Jews and cults, see Gary D. Eisenberg, *Smashing the Idols: A Jewish Inquiry into the Cult Phenomenon* (Lanham, Md.: Jason Aronson, 1988). See also Murray Friedman, "Religious Cults and Evangelicals," *AJYB* 80 (1980): 121–33.

88. Prof. Leon Jick, dean of Center for Contemporary Jewish Studies at Brandeis University, panel, "What Makes for Jewish Security in America?" AJC annual meeting transcript, Friday, May 18, 1973, pp. 93–96, Blaustein Library. The article was Khushwant Singh's "The Guru Business: Do You Know the Aim of Life?" *New York Times*, April 8, 1973, p. 34. See also Simon Zalkind, "Law on the Guru," business section,

New York Times Magazine, April 29, 1973, p. 81; also Gene Christensen, "Gurus' Disciples Active in Business," *New York Times Magazine,* April 15, 1973, p. 113.

89. Memo, August 12, 1971, to area directors from Milt Ellerin and Steven Windmueller, subject: The "Jesus Freak" movement," JCAD, box 10, folder "Jews for Jesus, Key '73, Jewish Messiah, etc., 1972–1973," AJC archives.

90. For AJC activities on other Passion plays, see IAD boxes 181, 182, 183, and 184, which are almost entirely folders labeled "Passion Play."

91. See memo, Gerald S. Strober to Myron C. Rosenthal, September 5, 1973, and passim, IAD, box 147, folder "Jesus Christ Superstar, Film, July 1973"; (bimonthly folders go through December 1973), AJC archives. Also Murray Friedman, "Jesus Christ Superstar," *AJYB* 3 (1972): 113.

92. *What's Doing at the Committee,* 3, no. 7 (September 1973): 1.

93. Memo: "Jews and Christian Evangelism: Questions and Answers," 1972, JCAD, box 10, folder "Jews for Jesus, Key '73, Jewish Messiah, etc. 1972–1973,"AJC archives. See also Samuel Z. Fishman, B'nai B'rith Hillel Foundations, "Comments from the Campus: The Jesus Freaks" and "Jewish Students and the Jesus Movement: A Follow-Up Report," June 12, 1972, which contradicts the *Newsweek* figures, IAD, box 108, folder "Cults, 1971–1976." The folder also contains samples of cult literature and a pamphlet "Do's and Don'ts: A Guide to the Parents of Children Captured by Unorthodox Religious Cults," AJC archives.

94. Memo to Religious and Communal Leaders, from: Rabbi Marc H. Tanenbaum, re: "Some Issues Raised by Forthcoming Evangelism Campaigns: A Background Memorandum," June 1972, based on research by Gerald Strober (consultant on religious curricula and specialist in Evangelical relations for the AJC), IAD, box 151, folder "Key '73 June–December 1973," AJC archives.

95. Consultation 21, 1972, summary of meeting, JCAD, box 9, folder "Evangelism and the Jewish Community IAD-JCAD Consultation." Rabbis in attendance included Eugene Borowitz, Ira Eisenstein, Judah Nadich, and Emmanuel Rackman; AJC archives.

96. Fishman, "Jewish Students and the Jesus Movement."

97. Mitchell Freedman, "Christian Jews Seek Long Island Converts," *Newsday,* January 2, 1977; clipping in IAD, box 108, folder "Cults, 1977," AJC archives.

98. Meeting on Religious Cults, AJC annual meeting transcript, general session, May 15, 1977, pp. 1–6, Blaustein Library.

99. See clipping, *San Francisco Jewish Bulletin,* June 10, 1977, "AJC Report: Task Forces to Combat Cults," IAD, box 108, folder "Cults, 1977." AJC archives.

100. Press release, December 28, 1976, IAD, box 108, folder "Cults, 1971–1976," AJC archives.

101. David Singer, "The Jewish Messiah: A Contemporary Commentary," *Midstream* 19, no. 5 (May 1973): 57–67.

102. Address by Rabbi A. James Rudin, North Shore Jewish Center, Port Jefferson, New York, June 8, 1978, IAD, box 108, folder "Cults, 1978," AJC archives.

103. Ellerin, "Civic and Political Intergroup Relations," 117.

104. Memo to Jim Rudin, from Shula Bahat, November 28, 1978, Re: discussion packet on "The Challenge of the New Religious Movements or the Cults," and "The Challenge of the Cults." Discussion packet by the Community Services and Membership Department and the IAD of the AJC. Prepared by Marcia Rudin and Rabbi A. James Rudin, IAD, box 108, folder "Cults, 1978," AJC archives.

105. Address by Leon Jick, panel discussion, "What Makes for Jewish Security in America?" AJC annual meeting transcript, May 18, 1973, p. 96, Blaustein Library.
106. AJC annual meeting transcript, general session, May 15, 1977, pp. 6–8, Blaustein Library.

8. *Internal Divisions (1970–1979) (pp. 228–259)*

1. Jonathan D. Sarna and Jonathan J. Golden, "The Twentieth Century through American Jewish Eyes: A History of the American Jewish Year Book, 1899–1999," *AJYB* 100 (2000): 73–75.
2. Victor Levin and Peter Geffen, "Jewish Education, Identity, and Family Life," annual meeting transcript, May 16, 1970, pp. 61–63, Blaustein Library.
3. Yitzhak Rabin is reported to have done so on at least one occasion; in January 1968, according to an anonymous source, President Johnson raised the issue of Jewish opposition to the war in Vietnam in conversations with Israeli Prime Minister Levi Eshkol. He subsequently defended U.S. intervention in Vietnam in meetings with American Jewish leaders. See Charles S. Liebman, *Pressure Without Sanctions: The Influence of World Jewry on Israeli Policy* (Rutherford, N.J.: Fairleigh Dickinson Press, 1977), 27–28.
4. Matthew Brown (of Boston), Saturday afternoon session, annual meeting transcript, May 16, 1970, p. 172, Blaustein Library.
5. The story is told that the Canadian prime minister, Lester Bowles Pearson, made a speech at Temple University in the United States in April 1965 in which he called for a reduction of bombing of North Vietnam. Johnson was furious. When the president next met with Pearson, he grabbed the Canadian by the lapels, lifted him off the rug, and yelled, "You pissed on my rug!" The incident is retold in several books on Canadian-U.S. relations; see Greg Donaghy, *Tolerant Allies: Canada and the United States, 1963–1968* (Montreal: McGill-Queen's University Press, 2002), 130.
6. Lawrence Grossman, "Transformation through Crisis: The American Jewish Committee and the Six-Day War," *American Jewish History* 86, no. 1 (March 1998): 44. For Johnson's feelings, see *New York Times*, "Jewish War Plea Vexes President," September 11, 1966; "Jewish Leaders Deny Johnson Linked Israel and War Support," September 13, 1966; and "Goldberg Sees Jewish Leaders in Effort to Mend Johnson Rift," September 14, 1966.
7. Grossman, "Transformation through Crisis," 44.
8. Lucy S. Dawidowicz, "President Johnson, American Jews, and Vietnam," *AJYB* 68 (1967): 79–81.
9. *Jewish Telegraphic Agency Daily Bulletin*, no. 171 (September 7 1966): 3.
10. "Jewish War Plea Vexes President: Opposition to Vietnam Aims Proves Worry to Johnson," *New York Times*, September 11, 1966, 4.
11. "President Johnson, American Jews, and Vietnam," *AJYB* 68 (1967): 78.
12. Max Frankel, "Jewish Leaders Deny Johnson Linked Israel and War Support," *New York Times*, September 13, 1966, p. 4. The two B'nai B'rith leaders were Dr. William A. Wexler and Rabbi Jay Kaufman.
13. "Goldberg Sees Jewish Leaders in Effort to Mend Johnson Rift," *New York Times*, September 14, 1966, p. 1.
14. John Coogley, "Johnson and the 'Jewish Community'—a Diplomatic Episode," *New York Times*, September 18, 1966, p. 204.

15. "Goldberg Says Role in Talk was His Own," *New York Times*, September 19, 1966, p. 3. For further discussion of Arthur Goldberg's position in the organized Jewish community, see Andrew Kopkin, "The Adventures of Arthur Goldberg," *New Republic* (October 8, 1966): 15–18, cited in *AJYB* 68 (1967): 80.

16. "Goldberg Says Role in Talk," 3.

17. "Goldberg Mollifies Jews in Rift with Johnson on War Criticism," *New York Times*, September 15, 1966, p. 1.

18. Dawidowicz, "President Johnson, American Jews, and Vietnam," 80.

19. Ibid.

20. "An AJC Position on Vietnam?" Summary of National Executive Committee discussion, November 3, 1969 (in a review of past actions since 1966), Blaustein Library.

21. Ibid.

22. Discussion Guide, November 6, 1969, "Should AJC Take a Position on the Vietnam War?" Bertram H. Gold papers (hereafter BHG), box 41, folder "Vietnam," AJC archives.

23. Ad Hoc Committee on Vietnam, "Summary of Discussion Meeting," November 10, 1969 (attached to memo from Philip E. Hoffman), November 14, 1969, BHG, box 41, folder "Vietnam," AJC archives.

24. American Jewish Service Committee for Civilian Relief in Vietnam, minutes of meeting, February 1, 1968, at the Harmonie Club, Morris Abram, chair; Press release, January 12, 1968, AJC archives. *New York Times*, January 12, 1968, BHG, box 41, folder "Vietnam." The other two who traveled with Abram were Jacob Trobe, executive director of the Jewish Child Care Association; and Hyman Wachtel, assistant to the director-general of Malben, the program for rehabilitation of the aged and handicapped immigrants in Israel, conducted by AJC and the Joint.

25. Memo to Bertram Gold from Ann G. Wolfe, May 13, 1970, BHG, box 208, folder "Vietnam and/or Indochina, 1970–75." AJC archives.

26. Letter from Asher J. Fox to Bertram H. Gold, September 8, 1972, BHG, box 108, folder "Vietnam, 1970–75,"AJC archives.

27. The communist forces renewed fighting in 1974, and the United States refused to send any further aid to the South Vietnamese; the entire country fell to the communists in April 1975.

28. There is an extensive literature on the young Americans, both men and women, who went to Canada to avoid serving in the war. These include David Churchill, "When Home Became Away: American Expatriates and New Social Movements in Toronto, 1965–1977" (Ph.D. Diss., University of Chicago 2001), which argues that U.S. expatriates in Canada moved that country farther to the left; John Hagan, *Northern Passage: American Vietnam War Resisters in Canada* (Cambridge, Mass.: Harvard University Press, 2001); Frank Kusch, *All-American Boys: Draft Dodgers in Canada from the Vietnam War* (Westport, Conn.: Praeger, 1999); and Sherry Gottlieb, *Hell No, We Won't Go! Resisting the Draft During the Vietnam War* (New York: Viking, 1991). More works, including films, archives, and oral histories are listed in a bibliography compiled by Joseph Jones at the University of British Columbia in Vancouver: http://www.library.ubc.ca/jones/vwddrbks.html.

29. AJC Intergroup Relations and Social Action Department, minutes of meeting, May 2, 1973, Jewish Communal Affairs Department (hereafter JCAD), box 10, folder "Jewish Women, 1973," AJC archives.

30. Murray Polner, *When Can I Come Home? A Debate on Amnesty for Exiles, Anti-war Prisoners, and Others* (Garden City, N.Y.: Anchor Books, 1972).

31. Memo to Selma Hirsh from Sam Rabinove, January 14, 1975, subject: "Amnesty, AJCongress and AJC, reporting on July 25, 1974 meeting of the Amnesty Sub-committee of the Domestic Affairs Commission," BHG, box 208, folder "Vietnam and/or Indochina, 1970–75," AJC archives.

32. Ibid.

33. Letter, from anonymous to Bert Gold, June 26, 1975, BHG, box 208, folder "Vietnam and/or Indochina, 1970–75," AJC archives.

34. AJC press release, May 3, 1975, BHG, box 208, folder "Vietnam and/or Indochina, 1970–75," AJC archives.

35. National Organization for Women web page, http://www.now.org/nnt/08–95/affirmhs.html.

36. On quotas in academia, see Walter Goodman, "The Return of the Quota System," *New York Times Magazine*, September 10, 1972; Stephen Steinberg, "How Jewish Quotas Began," *Commentary* (September 1971): 67–76; Earl Raab, "Quotas by any other Name," *Commentary* (January 1972): 41–45; and Nathan Glazer, *Affirmative Discrimination: Ethnic Inequality and Public Policy* (Cambridge, Mass.: Harvard University Press, 1987; first ed., 1976).

37. Murray Friedman, "Politics and Intergroup Relations in the US: Affirmative Action and Preferential Treatment," *AJYB* 74 (1973): 172–74.

38. Ibid.; Seymour Martin Lipset and Everett Carll Ladd Jr., "Jewish Academics in the United States: Their Achievements, Culture, and Politics," *AJYB* 72 (1971): 93.

39. Friedman, "Politics and Intergroup Relations," 176.

40. Ibid., citing *Washington Letter*, AJC, October 20, 1972; and Naomi Levine, "Quotas and affirmative action: Where We Stand," *Congress Bi-weekly*, November 10, 1972.

41. "Alliance of Jews and Blacks Urged: Jesse Jackson Bids Leaders 'Reassess Relationship,'" *New York Times*, August 2, 1974, in International Affairs Department, box 108, folder "Black-Jewish Relations 1972–76," AJC archives.

42. Milton Ellerin, "Politics and Intergroup Relations: Affirmative action, quotas, black-Jewish relations," *AJYB* 76 (1976): 131–33.

43. Ibid., 133.

44. "Black-Jewish Consultation at Fisk University," June 9–12, 1974, Nashville, Tennessee, Interreligious Affairs Department (hereafter IAD), box 108, folder "Black-Jewish Relations 1972–76," AJC archives.

45. Document, "Black Americans to Support Israel Committee: Statement of Principles," c. 1975, IAD, box 108, folder "Black-Jewish Relations 1972–76." Also memo from Seymour Samet to Harry Fleischman, March 17, 1975, Re: "Black Americans in Support of Israel Committee, confidential. 1972–76," IAD, box 108, folder "Black-Jewish Relations 1972–76," AJC archives.

46. Howard Ball, *The Bakke Case: Race, Education and Affirmative Action* (Lawrence: University Press of Kansas, 2000), 1.

47. Memo to Bertram H. Gold from Seymour Samet, March 1, 1977, subject: "The Bakke Case, BHG," box 61, folder "California, Bakke Case, 1977," AJC archives.

48. Letter, from Seymour Samet, Director, Domestic Affairs Dept. to Mrs. Jane Wallerstein, July 15, 1977, BHG, box 61, folder "California, Bakke Case, 1977," AJC archives.

49. AJC Memo, "Post Bakke Meeting: Confidential Do Not Reproduce," October 18, 1977, BHG, box 61, folder "California, Bakke Case, 1977," AJC archives.

50. Ibid. On the divisions between Jewish organizations on the case and on the alleged inconsistency in being for civil rights but against affirmative action quotas, see Leonard Fein, "The War Inside the Jews: The Painful Breakdown of the Liberal Consensus," *New Republic* (October 15, 1977), BHG, box 61, folder "California, Bakke Case, 1977," AJC archives.

51. Letter from Charlotte Holstein to Harriet Alpern, November 1, 1977, BHG, box 61, folder "California, Bakke Case, 1977," AJC archives.

52. Press release. August 10, 1977, "Speed Entry of Minorities into Universities on Basis of Disadvantage, not Race, Eight Groups Urge in Brief to Supreme Court in Bakke Case," BHG, box 61, folder "California, Bakke Case, 1977," AJC archives.

53. Murray Friedman, *What Went Wrong? The Creation and Collapse of the Black-Jewish Alliance* (New York: Free Press, 1995), 313.

54. Press release, "Speed Entry of Minorities into Universities."

55. See letter from Jimmy Carter to Richard Maass, October 27, 1977, BHG, box 61, folder "California, Bakke Case, 1977," AJC archives. The information about the library is appended to the letter.

56. Milton Ellerin, "Civic and Political Intergroup Relations: Race and Ethnicity," *AJYB* 79 (1979): 107–108.

57. Ibid.

58. Milton Ellerin, "Civic and Political Intergroup Relations: Affirmative Action and Bakke Case," *AJYB* 79 (1979): 107–108.

59. Friedman, *What Went Wrong?* 313; Ball, *The Bakke Case,* xiii, 135–40.

60. Press release, July 18, 1978, BHG, box 61, folder "California, Bakke Case, 1978," AJC archives.

61. Murray Friedman, *What Went Wrong?* 314.

62. Ibid., 315.

63. Murray Friedman, "Civic and Political: Intergroup Relations," *AJYB* 81 (1980): 121–22. Also Evening Plenary Session, AJC annual meeting transcript, May 11, 1979, pp. 4–5 and 10, Blaustein Library. Weber was a white worker who had been barred from a special training program at his company that reserved half of its places for blacks.

64. Samuel Rabinove, "Affirmative Action for the 1980s: Options for AJC," December 1979, IAD, box 108, folder "Black-Jewish Relations, 1978–79," AJC archives.

65. *Gratz v. Bollinger* and *Grutter v. Bollinger,* decided June 23, 2003.

66. AJC press release, February 17, 2003, "American Jewish Committee Files *Amicus* Brief in Support of University of Michigan."

67. Murray Friedman, "Civic and Political: Intergroup Relations and Tensions in the U.S.," *AJYB* 73 (1972): 97–153. On the Forest Hills Housing Controversy: Samuel Rabinove (director of Legal Services and director of Intergroup Relations and Social Action Department), "Civic and Political: Intergroup Relations and Tensions in the U.S.," *AJYB* 75 (1974–75): 83–132 (on the Forest Hills Controversy, see 106–108).

68. Letter to Philip E. Hoffman (president, AJC), from Mr and Mrs. Joseph Rafton, May 16, 1972, BHG, box 100, folder "Housing, Forest Hills 1971–1974," AJC archives. On general background of the controversy, see Murray Friedman, "Intergroup Relations and Tensions in the US: Forest Hills Housing

Controversy," *AJYB* 73 (1972): 117–19; and Rabinove, "Civic and Political," 106–108. On AJC's activities, see Frances X. Cline, "Lindsay Accepts Compromise Plan for Forest Hills: 'Reluctantly' Backs Program of Cuomo for Reducation in Housing," *New York Times*, August 20, 1972, p. 1; and Walter Goodman, "The Battle of Forest Hills: Who's Ahead?" *New York Times Magazine*, February 20, 1972, 8 pages.

69. AJC Staff Advisory Committee Summary of Meeting, Tuesday, September 21, 1971, BHG, box 199, folder "Staff Advisory Committee Meeting 1971–72," AJC archives.

70. Letter to Bertram H. Gold from Joseph Willen, December 9, 1971, BHG, box 100, folder "Housing, Forest Hills, 1971–1974." See also letter from Bertram Gold to Joseph Willen, October 19, 1972, BHG, box 85, folder "Forest Hills Housing, 1972," AJC archives.

71. Murray Friedman, "Politics and Intergroup Relations in the US: Busing and School Desegregation," *AJYB* 74 (1973): 179.

72. Letter from Bertram H. Gold to Mrs. Richard E. Orgel, November 8, 1972, BHG, box 71, folder "Education, Busing (Integration), 1972–73," AJC archives.

73. "The Great Debate: Challenges to Church-State Separation," May 3, 2000, AJC 94th annual meeting transcript, Washington, D.C., p. 37, Blaustein Library.

74. On this issue see JCAD, box 7, folder "Jewish education /Jewish Day Schools 1971"; BHG, box 71, folders "Education, Aid to Parochial Schools, Committee on Implication of AJC Policy, 1970–71"; IAD, box 114, folder "Church-State, Religion in Public Schools, 1972–76," AJC archives.

75. Report, "Funding the Jewish Day School Movement," September 1971, includes minutes of meeting of Steering Committee of Commission on Church-State and Interreligious Relationships, April 2, 1971. Attendees include Reform and Orthodox rabbis, the ADL, Jewish Labor Committee, the United Synagogue of America, Torah Umesorah, the American Jewish Congress, the Jewish War Veterans, the Council of Jewish Federations and Welfare Funds, two representatives from NJCRAC, and Yehuda Rosenman and Samuel Rabinove of AJC. The dissenter was a Mr. Trubin, JCAD, box 7, folder "Jewish education/ AJC Position Statements, 1970–71," AJC archives.

76. Ibid.

77. Memo from Samuel Rabinove to Morris Fine, May 12, 1971, subject: "Meeting of Synagogue Council of America, May 9–10," IAD, box 114, folder "Church-State Aid to Religious Schools, 1970–77," AJC archives.

78. Jack Wertheimer, "Dollars and Sense in Jewish Education" (New York: Avi Chai Foundation and the AJC, August 2001), 9 and 12.

79. AJC Jewish Communal Affairs Commission Meeting Minutes, October 19, 1971, JCAD, box 7, folder "Jewish Education/Jewish Day Schools 1971," AJC archives.

80. Bert Gold, "Boom in All-Day Schools," address, *AJC Newsletter*, 7, no. 1 (November 1970–January 1971), BHG, box 71, folder "Education, Aid to Private Schools."

81. "AJC Policy Statement on Jewish Education and Jewish Identity," adopted by the NEC in Atlanta, Georgia, October 28, 1977, JCAD, box 14, folder "Jewish Education Re: Policy Statement 1977," AJC archives. The chairman of the Jewish Communal Affairs Commission at the time was E. Robert Goodkind.

82. Clipping from the *Jewish Post*, Atlanta, Georgia, November 4, 1977, JCAD, box 14, folder "Jewish Education Re: Policy Statement 1977," AJC archives.

83. Letter from Philip Siegelman of San Francisco to Reynold H. Colvin, March 17, 1978, forwarded to Yehuda Rosenman, JCAD, box 15, folder "Jewish Education, 1978," AJC archives.

84. Douglas E. Kneeland, "Troubles Multiply for Nazi Leader in Chicago Suburb," *New York Times*, July 22, 1977, 10. Collins denied the charge that his father was Jewish and said it was a lie spread by his enemies. In an interview, he indicated that he became a National Socialist in 1952, while watching a film on TV made by ADL entitled "The Twisted Cross." It was an anti-Nazi film but included much source material. "When they would show a close-up of Hitler's face," he claimed, "I still remember my feeling—that here was a man who was saying something. . . . he was deeply committed to it. He was feeling deeply. And when they showed the crowd, they were deeply moved as if they had just awakened to something. . . . It was like Niagara Falls, and it was something that transcended language and everything else. I've loved Hitler ever since."

85. Eugene DuBow, master's thesis, Hebrew Union College–Jewish Institute of Religion, "The Threatened Nazi March in Skokie and the Jewish Reaction," March 31, 1980, Blaustein Library.

86. Eugene DuBow, interview by AJC Oral History, New York Public Library, p. 83.

87. Letter to S. R. Hirsch from Bertram H. Gold, May 18, 1977. On AJC analysis of the negligibility of these groups, see Milton Ellerin, "American Nazis: Myth or Menace?" report, Trends Analysis Division, Domestic Affairs Dept., AJC, November 22, 1977, BHG, box 170, folder "Skokie," AJC archives.

88. Maynard I. Wishner, "American Nazis and the First Amendment," *Sh'ma*, September 2, 1977; cited in DuBow, "Threatened Nazi March," 57–58.

89. The entire debate on the Skokie resolution is covered in AJC annual meeting transcript, closing plenary session, May 21, 1978, pp. 1–45, Blaustein Library.

90. Whitman was referring to a U.S. Supreme Court obscenity case, *Paris Adult Theatre v. Slaton* (June 1973). The exact quote from Chief Justice Warren E. Burger was "The idea of a 'privacy' right and a place of public accommodation are, in this context, mutually exclusive. Conduct or depictions of conduct that the state police power can prohibit on a public street do not become automatically protected by the Constitution merely because the conduct is moved to a bar or a 'live' theater stage, any more than a 'live' performance of a man and woman locked in a sexual embrace at high noon in Times Square is protected by the Constitution because they simultaneously engage in a valid political dialogue."

91. Maynard I. Wishner, telephone interview by author, January 12, 2006.

92. Memo, Sholom Comay to Chapter and Unit Chairpersons, June 14, 1978 (the memo included a description of the Washington, D.C., chapter and mentioned that copies of the cassette were still available from the national office), BHG, box 170, folder "Skokie," AJC archives.

93. "Nazis Call Off March in Skokie; Leader Says Drive was a Success; Collins Asserts that Plans for Demonstration Were 'Pure Agitation to Restore Free Speech,'" *New York Times*, June 23, 1978, p. A10.

94. Ibid.

95. The Museum of Broadcast Communications, http://www.museum.tv/archives/etv/H/htmlH/holocaust/holocaust.htm.

96. DuBow, "Threatened Nazi March," 81. In the wake of the *Holocaust* miniseries, AJC did a study of its effects on viewers: "Americans Confront the Holocaust: A

Study of Reactions to NBC-TV's Four-Part Drama on the Nazi Era" (New York: AJC, December 1978), Blaustein Library.

9. Jewish Identity (1970–1980) (pp. 260–294)

1. AJC annual meeting transcript, May 17–19, 1963, p. 18. "I asked myself, does this mean extinction? I got up this morning with a start when I thought of this and I called up Dr. Sklare and woke him from his Sabbath slumber and from what I could hear amongst the noise there's about a half dozen babies there, and I found out that there is some hope."
2. Bill Novak (member of the New York *Havurah*), "Jewish Education, Identity and Life," Saturday morning session, AJC annual meeting transcript, May 16, 1970, p. 46, Blaustein Library.
3. Letter from Rabbi Marc H. Wilson to Larry Lowenstein, April 9, 1979, Jewish Communal Affairs Department (hereafter JCAD) box 16, folder "Correspondence, Interoffice, 1979," AJC archives.
4. "Minutes and Reports," Minutes of National Membership Cabinet meeting, May 10, 1979, AJC annual meeting transcript, Blaustein Library.
5. Memo, Bernice Newman to Will Katz, April 30, 1979, JCAD, box 16, folder "Correspondence, Interoffice 1979," AJC archives.
6. Letter to Will Katz from Yehuda Rosenman, May 3, 1979, JCAD, box 16, folder "Correspondence, General, 1979." AJC archives.
7. Letter from Solomon Fisher to Richard Maass, July 17, 1979, JCAD, box 16, folder "Correspondence, General 1979," AJC archives.
8. Jewish Communal Affairs Commission Minutes, July 25, 1979 and September 17, 1979, "Policy Proposal Regarding the Observance of Kashrut and Holidays by AJC," JCAD, box 16, folder "JCAC Minutes 1979," AJC archives.
9. "We have for some years now seen these issues [Jewish poverty] as central to community tensions. As we try to have some influence on the reduction of group tensions and on the development of promising social policy, we discovered that we had a significant problem in the Jewish community with our own poor and that to a very great degree this phenomenon had been all but obscured by the more obvious fact of Jewish affluence." Letter from Bertram Gold to Dr. Arnold Gurin, September 3, 1971, Bertram H. Gold papers (hereafter BHG) 180, folder "Poverty/Welfare/Jewish Poor 1970–71." Dr. Gurin was being invited to AJC's National Consultation on Poverty in the Jewish Community. On the JDL, see also minutes, JCAD Staff Committee on Jewish Defense League, April 4, 1972, JCAD, box 10, folder "Jewish Defense League 1972," AJC archives.
10. Ann G. Wolfe. "The Invisible Jewish Poor," address delivered at the annual meeting of the Chicago chapter of the AJC, June 8, 1971, Blaustein Library. On poor Jews, see also Dorothy Rabinowitz, *The Other Jews: Portraits in Poverty,* with an introduction by Bertram H. Gold (New York: Institute of Human Relations Press, 1972), Blaustein Library.
11. Ann G. Wolfe (social welfare consultant) "The Invisible Jewish Poor," address delivered June 8, 1971, annual meeting, AJC Chicago chapter, Blaustein Library. The estimate of 800,000 poor is on p. 11.

12. Presentation by Bert Gold, AJC National Consultation on Poverty in the Jewish Community, December 1971, BHG, box 180, folder "Poverty/Welfare/Jewish Poor, 1970–71."

13. Memo from Bertram Gold to Ann Wolfe, March 11, 1974, BHG, box 192, folder "Social Program and Policy, Jewish Poor, 1973–79," AJC archives.

14. On the 1977 blackout, see "Night of Terror," *Time* (July 25, 1977): 12–22; Anthony Ramirez, "The Darkest Hours of a Dark Time," *New York Times*, July 13, 1977, p. 3; on the twentieth anniversary, Clyde Haberman, "'77 Blackout: The Heart of Darkness," *New York Times*, July 13, 1997, p. B1.

15. Proposal (prepared by Haskell L. Lazere), "Tentative Plan for Emergency Assistance Centers," July 15, 1977, BHG, box 171, folder "NY Blackout Summer 1977," AJC archives.

16. "Report on Neighborhood Business Assistant Teams Operations" (submitted by Haskell L. Lazere, director, New York chapter), August 1977, BHG, box 171, folder "NY Blackout Summer 1977," AJC archives.

17. Memo to AJC Leaders from Bertram H. Gold, August 22, 1977, BHG, box 171, folder "NY Blackout Summer 1977," AJC archives.

18. Arthur Goren, "Inventing the 'New Pluralism,'" in *The Politics and Public Culture of American Jews* (Bloomington: Indiana University Press, 1999), 205–24.

19. Leonard Dinnerstein, "Remembering the Holocaust: Genocide, Survivors, Commemoration" (New York: Columbia University Press, forthcoming), msp. 246.

20. Jonathan Sarna, *American Judaism: A History* (New Haven: Yale University Press, 2004), 327.

21. Memo from Yehuda Rosenman to area staff, November 19, 1971, subject: "Jewish Student Press Digest," JCAD, box 10, folder "Publications, 1971–72," AJC archives.

22. James A. Sleeper and Alan L. Mintz, *New Jews* (New York: Vintage Books, 1971).

23. Minutes, Jewish Communal Affairs Commission (hereafter JCAC) meeting, February 29, 1972, AJC archives.

24. Memo from David Singer to Eleanor Ashman, subject: "Visits to Chicago and Milwaukee," January 30, 1974, JCAD, box 11, AJC archives.

25. Meeting JCAC minutes, March 1, 1971, JCAD, box 8, folder "Jewish Communal Affairs Commission Minutes of Meetings, 1971," AJC archives.

26. "Jewish Roots" (booklet), JCAD, box 15, folder, "Jewish Roots, 1978," AJC archives.

27. "New Pockets of Jewish Energy: A Study of Adults Who Found Their Way Back to Judaism" (New York: AJC Jewish Communal Affairs Department, November 1982), Blaustein Library.

28. Memo, "Pockets of Religious Rejuvenation: Introduction, Research Focus," JCAD, box 8, folder "New Pockets of Jewish Energy, 1979."

29. Letter from Harold S. Himmelfarb (associate professor of sociology, Ohio State University) to Yehuda Rosenman, January 22, 1979, return letter January 29, 1979; memo from Dr. Carl Sheingold, February 28, 1979, JCAD, box 8, folder "New Pockets of Jewish Energy, 1979."

30. JCAC minutes, May 10, 1979, JCAD, box 16, folder "JCAD Minutes 1979."

31. Letter from Yehuda Rosenman to Rabbi Albert S. Axelrad, August 24, 1978, JCAD, box 16, folder "Correspondence, General, 1979," AJC archives.

32. AJC annual meeting transcript, Sabbath morning program, May 18, 1974, p. 20, Blaustein Library.

33. Sarna, *American Judaism*, 338.

34. "A Tribute to Mrs. Sidney C. Borg (1879–1956) by Judge Joseph M. Proskauer," *Report of the 49th AJC Annual Meeting of the AJC*, January 27–29, 1955, p. 73, Blaustein Library.

35. Interview with Selma Hirsh, February 1978, AJC Oral history project, 31 and 52, New York Public Library.

36. Obituary, "Caroline K. Simon is Dead at 92: Led Fight Against Discrimination," *New York Times*, July 30, 1993. Also Paula E. Hyman and Deborah Dash Moore, eds., *Jewish Women in America: An Historical Encyclopedia* (New York: Routledge, 1997): 2: 1258–1260.

37. Interview of Charlotte Holstein by author, February 6, 2006.

38. Saturday afternoon session, AJC annual meeting transcripts, May 6, 1972, p. 264, Blaustein Library.

39. "National Committee on the Role of Women: A Six-Year Report," "Backgrounder 73rd AJC Annual Meeting," May 10, 1979, AJC annual meeting, AJC archives. The first meeting of AJC's National Committee on the Role of Women was held on January 17, 1974. Those present included Selma Hirsh, Ann G. Wolfe, Ellen Shapiro, Sally Gries, Vivienne Silverstein, and Alice Fisher, BHG, box 212, folder "Women." See also "AJC Statement on the Changing Role of Women," adopted May 17, 1973, AJC archives.

40. Address by A. James Rudin, "Changing Patterns in Jewish Family Life," Panel on Jewish Women, Sabbath morning program, AJC annual meeting transcript, May 18, 1974, p. 36, Blaustein Library.

41. Report, "Consultation on the Portrayal of Women and Girls in Texts and Curricula of Jewish Schools, Summary of Proceedings," February 12, 1978; Gladys Rosen, "The Portrayal of Women and Girls in Jewish Textbooks and Curricula," JCAD, box 15, folder "Consultation on Treatment of Women, 1978," AJC archives. On AJC's publications on Jewish women, see also Rela Geffen Monson, "Jewish Women on the Way Up: the Challenge of Family, Career and Community" (New York: AJC, December 1987); Amy L. Sales, "Women Climb the Corporate Ladder: The Boston Experience," (New York: AJC, May 1988); and Nancy Isserman and Lisa Hostein, "Status of Women in Jewish Organizations," (Philadelphia: AJC Philadelphia chapter, February 1994), Blaustein Library.

42. Anne Lapidus Lerner, "'Who Hast Not Made Me a Man' The Movement for Equal Rights for Women in America," *AJYB* 77 (1977): 3–37.

43. AJC press release on the ERA, June 11, 1982, BHG, box 256, folder "Women," AJC archives.

44. Fred Massaryk and Alvin Chenkin, "US National Jewish Population Survey: A First Report," *AJYB* 74 (1973): 296.

45. Norman Mirsky, "Mixed Marriage and the Reform Rabbinate," *Midstream* (January 1970), 40–46.

46. Massaryk and Chenkin, "US National Jewish Population Survey," 292.

47. U. O. Schmelz, "Jewish Survival: The Demographic Factors," *AJYB* 81 (1981): 85.

48. Arnold Schwartz, "Intermarriage in the United States," *AJYB* 71 (1970): 116.

49. Louis A. Berman, *Jews and Intermarriage: A Study in Personality and Culture* (New York: Thomas Yoseloff, 1968), p. 341; cited in Schwartz, "Intermarriage," 116.

50. Norman Mirsky, "Mixed Marriage and the Reform Rabbinate," *Midstream* (January 1970); cited in Schwartz, "Intermarriage," 120.

51. Samuel Rabinove, "Intergroup Relations and Tensions in the US: Bridget Loves Bernie," *AJYB* 75 (1974–75): 130–32.

52. "Consultation on Intermarriage and Conversion: Summary Report, Jewish Communal Affairs Dept. AJC," February 27, 1975, BHG, box 136, folder "Intermarriage and Conversion, 1975–1977," and JCAD, box 13, folder "Intermarriage, General Materials and Correspondence, 1973–1976," AJC archives.

53. Minutes Informal Rabbinic Consultation on Intermarriage and Conversion, November 3, 1975, section of verbatim transcript—present, Rabbi Max Routtenberg, Rabbi Ludwig Nadelman, Judah Nadich, Emmanual Rackman, Steven Riskin, Saul Roth, Harold Saperstein, JCAD, box 15, folder "Intermarriage/ Rabbinic Consultations/ Max Routtenberg, 1975–76," AJC archives.

54. "Program: National Conference on Mixed Marriage, December 14–15, 1976, Long Branch, NJ," JCAD, box 13, folder "Jews, Judaism and Jewish community: Intermarriage and Conversion, 1976"; letter from Yehuda Rosenman to Rabbi Steven C. Lerner, February 10, 1977, re: "Suggestions of National Institute on Intermarriage," JCAD, box 14, folder "Intermarriage, General, 1975–77," AJC archives.

55. Press release, February 7, 1976, JCAD, box 13, folder "Intermarriage Study of Effects of, Publicity, Articles, etc., 1976," AJC archives.

56. Sidney Goldstein, "Jews in the US: Perspectives from Demography," *AJYB* 81 (1981): 25–26.

57. AJC memo, "Project on the Effects of Intermarriage—Instructions for the Conduct of Telephone Interviews,"; instructions for interviewers, April 27, 1976; form letter by Egon Mayer, sent to 275 people, April 6, 1976; memo: Study on the Impact of Intermarriage: Supplementary Techniques for Obtaining Names," JCAD, box 13, folder "Intermarriage Study, Correspondence, 1976–77," AJC archives.

58. Letter to Dr. Murray Friedman from Seymour Schubin, July 1, 1977, JCAD, box 13, folder "Intermarriage, Study on Effects of, Correspondence, 1976–1977," AJC archives.

59. Egon Mayer, confidential: "Mixed Blessings Under the Canopy"; summary of study and findings of survey on the impact of marriage between Jews and non-Jews on individuals, families, and the Jewish community, memo from Yehuda Rosenman, March 2, 1978, subject: "Reactions to study," BHG, box 135, folder "Jews, Judaism and Jewish Community, Intermarriage and Conversion, 1978," AJC archives.

60. JCAC Minutes, January 18, 1979, JCAD, box 16, folder "Jewish Communal Affairs Commission Minutes, 1979," AJC archives.

61. Memo, confidential: "To Yehuda Rosenman from Carl Sheingold: Subject: Authorship of the Intermarriage Pamphlet," November 30, 1978, BHG, box 135, folder "Jews, Judaism and Jewish community Intermarriage and Conversion, 1978," AJC archives.

62. One summary of Egon Mayer's own interpretations was published in *National Jewish Resource Center* (CLAL) *Policy Studies,* v. 79 (February 15, 1979): "Intermarriage Among American Jews—Consequences, Prospects and Policies," BHG, box 135, folder "Jews, Judaism and Jewish community, Intermarriage and Conversion, 1978," AJC archives.

63. Discussion on Proposed AJC Statement on Intermarriage, Minutes, AJC Board of Governors Meeting, March 21, 1979, JCAD, box 17, folder "Intermarriage Study, 1979," AJC archives.

64. Memo, confidential: "Use of Academy Courses for Soviet Jewry Notes of Meeting," October 26, 1978, attended by Hyman Bookbinder, Morris Fine, David Geller, and Yehuda Rosenman, JCAD, box 17, folder "Soviet Jewry, 1979." Suggested means were cultural exchanges with political support, radio broadcasts, tourist visits, and hand delivery of books and other materials. The program was also discussed in a memo, "For Consideration by the Exec Committee, April 11, 1978, Discussion of Trends, Issues in AJC Policy and Program Implications in Foreign Affairs," BHG, box 183, folder "Program, long-range planning 1977–79," AJC archives.

65. Maurice Friedberg, "Antisemitism as a Policy Tool in the Soviet Bloc," *AJYB* 71 (1970): 139.

66. Abraham J. Bayer, "Response to Soviet Anti-Jewish Policies: Appeals to the World," *AJYB* 74 (1973): 218.

67. Leon Shapiro, "The Soviet Union," *AJYB* 73 (1972): 540–41.

68. William Korey, "The Struggle Over Jackson-Mills-Vanik," *AJYB* 75 (1974–75): 202–203.

69. On AJC policy regarding the tactics of the JDL, see BHG, box 131, folder "Jewish Defense League," AJC archives; and Milton Himmelfarb, "Never Again," *Commentary* (August 1971): 73–76.

70. Abraham J. Bayer, "American Responses to Soviet Jewish Policies," *AJYB* 74 (1973): 211–13.

71. A. James Rudin, "The New York City Chapter of the AJC: Seder for Soviet Jewry," April 19, 1978, IAD, box 184, folder "Passover Haggadah, 1978." AJC archives.

72. Abraham J. Bayer, "American Response to Soviet Jewish Policies," appendix, "Brussels Declaration by the World Conference of Jewish Communities on Soviet Jewry," February 25, 1971, *AJYB* 74 (1973): 224–25.

73. "Europe and the Middle East," Sunday morning session, AJC annual meeting transcript, May 17, 1970, p. 9, Blaustein Library.

74. Ibid.

75. Ibid.

76. Address by Rita Hauser (U.S. Representative to the U.N. Human Rights Commission), session "The State of Jewry Around the World," AJC annual meeting transcript, Sunday, May 16, 1971, pp. 436–44, Blaustein Library.

77. Ibid., 432.

78. The gift was announced by Morton K. Blaustein at the AJC annual meeting, May 13, 1971, six months after Jacob Blaustein had passed away.

79. On Proskauer and Blaustein and human rights in the U.N. Charter, see Jerold Auerbach, "Human Rights at San Francisco," *American Jewish Archives* 16 (1964): 51f; and Joseph Proskauer's account in his autobiography *A Segment of My Times* (New York: Farrar, Straus, 1950), 216–28.

80. Address by Jerome Shestack, symposium on Human Rights, Détente, and American Foreign Policy, AJC annual meeting transcript, May 12, 1977, p. 10, Blaustein Library.

81. I am indebted for these insights on human rights, the Uppsala declaration, and the Helsinki Accords to Dr. Henry Feingold (interview by the author, February 22, 2006).

82. IAD, box 108, folder "Blaustein Institute, Uppsala 1973," AJC archives; Abraham J. Bayer, "American Response to Soviet Policies," *AJYB* 74 (1973): 210–23;

"Appendix, 'The Right to Leave and the Right to Return: A Declaration Adopted by the Uppsala Colloquium, Uppsala, Sweden, June 21, 1972,'" *AJYB* 74 (1973): 241–43.

83. For the reports of Abe Karlikow, AJC representative at Helsinki, see BHG, box 79, folder "Conference on Security and Cooperation in Europe," AJC archives.

84. On the effect of the Sharansky case, see William Korey, "Soviet Jews: American Reaction to the Sharansky Case," *AJYB* 80 (1980): 118–29.

85. Memo to Bertram H. Gold from Rabbi Marc H. Tanenbaum, April 12, 1972, subject: "National Interreligious Consultation on Soviet Jewry," BHG, box 195, folder "Soviet Union Interreligious Consultation on Soviet Jewry, 1972," AJC archives.

86. Memo from Marc H. Tanenbaum to Bertram H. Gold, April 12, 1972, BHG, box 195, folder "Soviet Union Interreligious Consultation on Soviet Jewry, 1972," AJC archives.

87. Letter from Marc H. Tanenbaum to Eleanor Katz, December 29, 1972, subject: "Sister Ann Gillen," BHG, box 195, folder "Soviet Union Interreligious Consultation on Soviet Jewry, 1972," See also IAD, box 127, folder "Gillen, Sister Ann, 1977–78," AJC archives.

88. Rabbi A. James Rudin, "A Rabbi Salutes Five Catholic Nuns," Center for Catholic Jewish Studies, Religion News Service 2005, www.centerforcatholicjewish studies.org.

89. Address by Jerry Goodman on Soviet Jewry, AJC annual meeting transcript, May 17, 1973, p. 21, Blaustein Library.

90. Address by Marc H. Tanenbaum, report on Interreligious Affairs Dept., AJC annual meeting transcript May 17, 1973, p. 21. M. Bernard Resnikoff was the head of the Israel office; the Christian Visitors to Israel program was run at AJC headquarters by Inge Gibel.

91. David Geller, "Second World Conference on Soviet Jewry," *AJYB* 77 (1977): 155–56.

92. Memo by Rabbi A. James Rudin, March 9, 1976, subject: "Brussels II Conference on Soviet Jews," BHG, box 195, folder "Soviet Union Brussels Conference, 1975–1976," AJC archives.

93. See John Lewis Gaddis, *The Cold War: A New History* (New York: Penguin, 2005).

94. Korey, "Struggle Over Jackson-Mills-Vanik," 202–203. See also Fred A. Lazin, *The Struggle for Soviet Jewry in American Politics: Israel versus the American Jewish Establishment* (Lanham, Md.: Lexington Books, 2005), 45–51; and William Korey, "Jackson-Vanik: A 'Policy of Principle,'" in *A Second Exodus: The American Movement to Free Soviet Jews,* ed. Murray Friedman and Albert D. Chernin (Waltham, Mass.: Brandeis University Press, 1999), 97–123.

95. Korey, "Struggle Over Jackson-Mills-Vanik," 224.

96. Richard Maass, interview by AJC Oral History Project, June 6, 1947. Maass called the Jackson-Vanik amendment "the most effective tool in my memory for a single issue in which the Jewish community has been involved."

97. Memo from Richard Maass to Bertram H. Gold, April 26, 1974, subject: Jackson Amendment, BHG, box 195, folder "Soviet Union Jackson-Vanik Amendment, 1973–79," AJC archives.

98. Korey, "Struggle Over Jackson-Mills-Vanick", 217–18.

99. Memo from Richard Maass to Bertram H. Gold (see note 97).

100. See Lazin, *Struggle for Soviet Jewry,* 50.

101. Gold's remarks were later published in a pamphlet titled "New Realities in American Jewish Life—text of keynote address at the Annual Meeting May 15, 1980" (AJC: June 1980); quote on p. 7.

10. A Difficult Decade (1980–1990) (pp. 297–331)

1. Steven M. Cohen, 1984 National Survey of American Jews, Political and Social Outlooks, cited in *AJC Journal* (Summer 1985): 3.
2. Murray Friedman, "Review of the Year: Civic and Political: Intergroup Relations," *American Jewish Year Book* 82 (1982): 105.
3. Minutes, AJC Board of Governors Meeting, December 15, 1980, pp. 4–6, AJC archives.
4. Steven M. Cohen, "AJC National Survey of American Jews 1984 and 1988," Blaustein Library.
5. Details of AJC's role during the AWACS episode can be found in the minutes of the AJC board of governors meetings, September 21, 1981, December 7, 1981, and March 23, 1981, as well as Murray Friedman, "Review of the Year US: Intergroup Relations," *AJYB* 83 (1983): 65–67; and George Gruen, "The US, Israel and the Middle East," *AJYB* 83 (1983): 74, 81–86.
6. George E. Gruen, "US-Israel Relations in the Second Reagan Era," in AJC *News and Views* 7, no. 2 (Winter 1985): 7.
7. "Reagan Presidency," minutes, AJC Board of Governors Meeting, February 5–8, 1981, pp. 7–9.
8. "New York Homeless," AJC *News and Views* 7, no. 2 (Winter 1985): 2.
9. "Combating Hunger," AJC *News and Views* 5, no. 4 (Summer 1983): 1
10. Leonard Fink, "Down on the Farm: Anti-Semites are Active Among Thousands of Troubled Farmers," *AJC Journal* (Winter 1986): 7–8.
11. Evan Bayer, "Jews on the Edge," AJC *News and Views* 5, no. 4 (Summer 1983): 7.
12. Milton Ellerin, "The New Right," AJC *News and Views* 3, no. 3 (December 1980): 3.
13. Cohen, 1984 National Survey, 3. The percentages remained almost identical in a similar poll done in 1988.
14. Minutes, AJC Board of Governors Meeting, March 17, 1986, p. 4, AJC archives.
15. Ibid., 4–6.
16. Letter from Mimi Alperin to Martin I. Bresler, October 19, 1989, Ira Silverman papers, box 3, folder "Reagan, Ronald, 1988–89, American Civil Liberties Medallion Award," AJC archives.
17. Kenneth Jacobson, "The US, Israel and the Middle East," *AJYB* 91 (1991): 140. According to Jacobson, Israel's strategic value was reduced in 1989 with the waning of the cold war, and the Bush administration was more concerned with maintaining close strategic relations with the Arab world than Reagan had been.
18. Letter from Joan G. Schine to Mimi Alperin, chair NEC, October 8, 1989, Ira Silverman papers, box 3, folder "Reagan, Ronald, 1988–89, American Civil Liberties Medallion Award," AJC archives.
19. Letter from Mrs. Victor Shaincock, Houston, to Ira Silverman, executive vice president, October 30, 1989, Ira Silverman papers, box 3, folder "Reagan, Ronald, 1988–89," AJC archives.
20. Letter from Richard Maass of White Plains, New York, to Sholom Comay, president, and Ira Silverman, executive vice president, October 10, 1989, Ira Silverman

papers, box 3, folder "Reagan, Ronald, 1988–89, American Civil Liberties Medallion Award," AJC archives.

21. Deborah E. Lipstadt, "The Bitburg Controversy," *AJYB* 87 (1987): 21.

22. Ibid., 31–32.

23. Article, "Wiesel Asks Reagan Not to Visit Bitburg," *International Herald Tribune*, April 22, 1985; clipping in AJC International Relations Department, box 9, folder "Reagan, Ronald, Presidency," AJC archives.

24. The full text of President Reagan's presentation and Elie Wiesel's acceptance speech, from Reagan's public papers, is available online at a number of sites, including www.pbs.org/eliewiesel/resources/reagan.html.

25. "The Bitburg Affair: An American Jewish Committee Background Memorandum," April 24, 1985, International Relations Department, box 9, folder "Reagan, Ronald, Presidency," AJC archives.

26. Memo from Howard I. Friedman to AJC Leaders, "The AJC Response to Bitburg," May 8, 1985, International Relations Department, box 9, folder "Reagan, Ronald, Presidency," AJC archives.

27. Lipstadt, "Bitburg Controversy," 32.

28. Minutes, AJC Board of Governors Meeting, May 1, 1985, "Reagan Presidency—Bitburg," p. 4, AJC archives.

29. Memo from Howard I. Friedman to AJC Leaders, "The AJC Response to Bitburg," May 9, 1985, International Relations Department, box 9, folder "Reagan, Ronald, Presidency," AJC archives.

30. Minutes, AJC Board of Governors Meeting, May 1, 1985, "Reagan Presidency—Bitburg," p. 4, AJC archives.

31. Memo from Howard I. Friedman to AJC leaders, May 9, 1985, International Relations Department, box 9, folder "Reagan, Ronald, Presidency," AJC archives; also essay by Marc H. Tanenbaum, "The American Jewish Committee at the White House," in *Bitburg and Beyond: Encounters in American, German, and Jewish History* ed. Ilya Levkov (New York: Shapolsky Publishers), 330–34. Ilya Levkov was a consultant to AJC on Soviet and international affairs.

32. Memo, from Marc Tanenbaum to Howard Kohr, May 1, 1985, for Michael Deaver, "(Please forward) White House—Dr. Marshall Breger—*confidential*, International Relations Department, box 9, folder "Reagan, Ronald, Presidency," AJC archives. This memo includes the entire speech, which was a tribute to Konrad Adenauer and a recounting of his apology to the Jewish people and to Israel.

33. William R. Doerner, "Paying Homage to History: Caught in a Storm of Controversy, Reagan Tries to Heal Old Wounds," *Time* (May 13, 1985).

34. Memo, from Tanenbaum to Kohr (see note 32).

35. Memo from Friedman to AJC leaders (see note 31).

36. Gruen, "The US, Israel and the Middle East," 78.

37. Minutes, AJC Board of Governors Meeting, September 21, 1981, report of the Foreign Affairs Commission Steering Committee, Rita E. Hauser, chair, p. 4, AJC archives.

38. Shula Bahat, interview with author, June 25, 2006.

39. George E. Gruen, "The US and Israel: Impact of the Lebanon War," *AJYB* 84 (1984): 79. For an overall in-depth examination of the war, see Richard Gabriel, *Operation Peace for Galilee: The Israeli-PLO War in Lebanon* (New York: Farrar, Straus and Giroux, 1985).

40. Ralph Mandel, "Israel in 1982: The War in Lebanon," *AJYB* 84 (1984): 12; on the different plans for the war in Lebanon and the "divergence" in knowledge between the political and the military leadership, see Gabriel, *Operation Peace for Galilee,* 60–61.

41. Ibid., 55.

42. Ibid., 186; *The Beirut Massacre: The Complete Kahan Commission Report,* with an introduction by Abba Eban (New York: Karz-Cohl, 1983), 21–42, Blaustein Library.

43. Gabriel, *Operation Peace for Galilee,* 186.

44. *Beirut Massacre,* xiii.

45. William E. Smith, "The Verdict is Guilty: An Israeli Commission Apportions the Blame for the Beirut Massacre," *Time* (February 21, 1983); Steven T. Rosenthal, *Irreconcilable Differences: The Waning American Jewish Love Affair With Israel* (Waltham, Mass.: Brandeis University Press, 2001), 70. Ariel Sharon sued *Time* for this article; an account of the legal proceedings was published by Uri Dan in *Blood Libel: The Inside Story of General Ariel Sharon's History-Making Suit Against Time Magazine* (New York: Simon and Schuster, 1987).

46. Rosenthal, *Irreconcilable Differences,* 71.

47. AJC press release, September 20, 1982, International Relations Department, box 6, folder "Lebanon, War in, Sabra and Shatila Massacres, 1982," AJC archives.

48. AJC *News and Views* 5, no. 1 (Autumn 1982): 8.

49. "Reports from the Field by the American Jewish Joint Distribution Committee," December 31, 1982, International Relations Department files, box 6, folder "Lebanon: Repercussions of 1982 War," AJC archives.

50. Kenneth Jacobson, "The US, Israel and the Middle East," *AJYB* 89 (1989): 205.

51. George E. Gruen and Gary Wolf, "The Current Unrest in the West Bank and Gaza: Questions and Answers: An International Relations Department Analysis," January 19, 1988, David Harris, Washington Representative files, box 7, AJC archives.

52. Jacobson, "The US, Israel and the Middle East," 231.

53. Judith Banki, associate director of interreligious affairs, in *AJC Journal* 5, no. 1 (Spring 1989): 13.

54. *AJC Journal* 4, no. 1 (Spring 1988): 16.

55. Letter, from Bertram Gold, "Dear AJC Leader," February 4, 1988, David Harris, Washington Representative files, box 7, AJC archives; *AJC Journal* 4, no. 1 (Spring 1988): 16.

56. Gruen and Wolf, "Current Unrest."

57. Minutes, AJC Staff Advisory Committee Meeting, January 11, 1988, p. 6. David Harris, Washington Representative Files, box 7, AJC archives.

58. Letter, from Bertram Gold, "Dear AJC Leader."

59. Minutes AJC Board of Governors Meeting, January 28–31, p. 9, AJC archives.

60. Special report, "Israel and South Africa: The Mythical Alliance," David Harris, Washington Representative files, box 7, AJC archives.

61. Memo from Charney V. Bromberg, deputy director, international relations, to field staff, January 20, 1988: "Updated and Additional Material on the Current Situation in Israel," David Harris, Washington Representative files, box 7, AJC archives.

62. "Statement by Arafat on Peace in Mideast," *New York Times,* December 15, 1988.

63. Robert Pear, "US Agrees to Talks With PLO, Saying Arafat Accepts Israel and Renounces All Terrorism," *New York Times,* December 15, 1988.

64. Ralph Mandel, "Israel," *AJYB* 86 (1986): 339.

65. Rosenthal, *Irreconcilable Differences,* 144.

66. Text of Joint Statement on Law of Return and Rabbinical Courts Bill Issued by 27 American Jewish Organizations, November 14, 1988, International Relations Department, box 11, folder "Israel, 'Who is a Jew?' 1988," AJC archives.

67. Minutes, AJC Board of Governors Meeting, March 20, 1989, appendix B: "AJC Report on Dialogue With Haredi Leadership, February 1–9, 1989" prepared by Steven Bayme, AJC archives.

68. Jack Wertheimer, *A People Divided: Judaism in Contemporary America* (New York: Basic Books, 1993), 114–18, 125–32.

69. Irving Greenberg, "Will There be One Jewish People by the Year 2000?" *Perspectives,* newsletter of the National Jewish Resource Center for Learning and Leadership—CLAL (June 1985): 8 pages, ed. Nina Beth Cardin, Blaustein Library. For discussion of the article and the debate surrounding it, see also Samuel G. Freedman, *Jew vs. Jew: The Struggle for the Soul of American Jewry* (New York: Simon and Schuster, 2000), 26–27.

70. Harold Schulweis, "Jewish Apartheid: Terrifying Examples of Intra-Jewish Separatism—And an Urgent Call for the Courage to Break Down Barriers," *Moment* (December 1985): 23–25.

71. Steven Bayme, "Jewish Religious Dialogue, an Interim Report," Jewish Communal Affairs, box 29, folder "JCAC Correspondence, 1988," AJC archives.

72. Memo by David Gordis, "American Jews and the Pollard Case," March 1987, David Gordis files, box 13, folder "Pollard, Jonathan, Affair," AJC archives.

73. Ibid., 216.

74. Excerpts from AJC "Talking Points," on the Pollard Affair, December 4, 1985, International Relations Department files, box 8, folder "Pollard Affair," AJC archives.

75. Memo from Mort Yarmon to David Gordis, June 5, 1986, David Gordis files, box 13, folder "Pollard, Jonathan: Affair," AJC archives.

76. Memo from Shimon Samuels to George E. Gruen, March 9, 1987, "Pollard Affair," David Gordis files, box 13, folder "Pollard, Jonathan: Affair," AJC archives.

77. Lawrence Grossman, "Jewish Communal Affairs," *AJYB* 89 (1989): 212–13.

78. David Gordis, "American Jews and the Pollard Case," March 1987, David Gordis files, box 13, folder "Pollard, Jonathan: Affair," AJC archives.

79. David M. Gordis, "Israel Can't Ignore Bond between Jews, America," originally titled, "The Anguish of American Jews," *Los Angeles Times* March 12, 1987, p. 1, David Gordis files, box 13, folder "Pollard, Jonathan: Affair," AJC archives.

80. Charles Krauthammer, column in the *Washington Post,* March 20, 1987.

81. Cover letter from George E. Gruen to Ari Rath, editor and managing director of the *Jerusalem Post,* to article "Back to Basic Principles," March 30, 1987, International Relations Department files, box 8, folder "Pollard Affair, 1987," AJC archives.

82. Grossman, "Jewish Communal Affairs," 215.

83. Dan Fisher, "Spy Case Strains Alliance Between Israel, US Jews," in the *Los Angeles Times,* David Gordis files, box 13, folder "Pollard, Jonathan and Anne Affair," AJC archives.

84. "The Impact of the Pollard Affair on American Jewry, A Review of Recent Comment and Discussion Paper for AJC, *confidential,* March 1987, David Gordis files, box 13, folder "Pollard, Jonathan and Anne Affair," AJC archives.

85. Minutes, AJC Board of Governors Meeting, March 23, 1987, "Pollard Affair," p. 2, AJC archives.

86. Mimi Alperin, "New Rules," *AJC Journal* 3, no. 3 (Autumn 1987): 12.

87. Jerome Chanes, "Review of the Year, US: Intergroup Relations," *AJYB* 92 (1992): 208.

88. Letter from Jack Berger to David Harris, June 23, 1992, David Harris 1992–1993 files, box 7, folder "Pollard, Jonathan," AJC archives.

89. Letter Alfred H. Moses to President Bill Clinton, March 23, 1993, David Harris 1992–1993 files, box 7, folder "Pollard, Jonathan," AJC archives.

90. James B. Stewart, Pulitzer Prize winner and journalist for the *Wall Street Journal*, covered the details of the insider-trading scandals of the 1980s in his bestselling book, *Den of Thieves* (New York: Simon and Schuster, 1992).

91. Grossman, "Jewish Communal Affairs," 200.

92. Memo from George E. Gruen to Hyman Bookbinder, *confidential,* "Iran-Iraq," December 3, 1986, David Gordis files, box 13, folder "Iran-Contra Affair," AJC archives.

93. Memo to regional and area directors from David Gordis, December 8, 1986, "Iran Crisis: Chapter Activity and Reactions," David Gordis files, box 13, folder "Iran-Contra Affair," AJC archives.

94. For an account of this conflict between the United States and Israel between 1967 and 1989, see Fred A. Lazin, *The Struggle for Soviet Jewry in American Politics: Israel versus the American Jewish Establishment* (Lanham, Md.: Lexington Books, 2005), 79–178; Also Steven F. Windmueller, "The 'Noshrim' War: Dropping Out," *A Second Exodus: The American Movement to Free Soviet Jews,* ed. Murray Friedman and Albert D. Chernin (Waltham, Mass.: Brandeis University Press, 1999) 161–72.

95. Minutes, AJC Board of Governors Meeting, September 22, 1980, President's report by Maynard Wishner, pp. 5–6, AJC archives.

96. Donald Feldstein, AJC executive vice president, "The Noshrim—again?" April 8, 1983, Donald Feldstein files, box 4, folder "Yordim-Noshrim, Soviet Union, 1983." The piece appeared in the JTA. AJC archives.

97. Minutes, AJC Board of Governors Meeting, December 7, 1987, "Assessing the Impact of Freedom Sunday," report by David Harris, p. 5, AJC archives.

98. *AJC Journal* 3, no. 4 (Winter 1988): 16.

99. Grossman, "Jewish Communal Affairs," 221; Minutes, AJC Board of Governors Meeting, March 23, 1987, AJC archives.

100. Grossman, "Jewish Communal Affairs," 220–21.

101. "Jewish Emigration from the Former Soviet Union to Israel and the United States," by year at NCSJ (formed as the National Council for Soviet Jewry) at www.ncsj.org/stats.shtml#PAST.

102. Grossman, "Jewish Communal Affairs," 90 *AJYB* (1990): 271.

103. Minutes, AJC Board of Governors Meeting, November 1, 1987, financial report, AJC archives.

104. Interview with Philip Hoffman, July 1983, AJC Oral history project, p. 69, New York Public Library.

105. Interview with E. Robert Goodkind, September 14, 2006.

106. Minutes, AJC Board of Governors Meeting, November 9, 1985. The speaker was Rita Hauser. AJC archives.

107. Interview, Milton Himmelfarb, July 1981, AJC Oral history project, p. 40, New York Public Library.

108. Minutes, AJC Board of Governors Meeting, June 27, 1988, AJC archives.

109. Andrew Willow Carroll, "Perestroika at AJCommittee," *Washington Jewish Week* (February 15, 1990); Elana Neuman, "How AJCommittee Fell in Need of Perestroika," *Forward* (April 17, 1991), in subject folder "American Jewish Committee," Blaustein Library, AJC. This folder contains the extensive press coverage of the AJC's restructuring, including articles in the *New York Times*.

110. Minutes, AJC Board of Governors Institute, St. Petersburg Beach, Florida, February 1–4, 1990, p. 2, AJC archives.

111. The figure of sixty people is mentioned in the minutes of the AJC Board of Governors meeting, June 25, 1990, AJC archives.

112. "David A. Harris: The AJC Chooses One of Its Own for its New Executive VP," *AJC Journal* 6, no. 1 (Winter 1991): 2.

11. *"The Global Jewish Committee" (pp. 332–366)*

1. For voluminous documents related to the first merger attempt in the 1970s, see Bertram Gold collection, boxes 43–45, subject: "The American Jewish Congress," AJC archives. For the second merger see Leadership and Board Services, box 6, folder "American Jewish Congress," AJC archives.

2. Minutes, AJC Board of Governors Institute, February 4–7, 1993, Palm Springs, California, p. 5,. AJC archives.

3. For a description of the proposed AJC-AJCongress merger and the reasons it did not work, see Lawrence Grossman, "Jewish Communal Affairs," *AJYB* 95 (1995): 175; Also, Elena Neuman, "AJCommittee Spurned Link with AJCongress," *Forward*, March 22, 1991, clipping in subject folder "AJC," Blaustein Library.

4. Minutes, AJC Board of Governors meeting, March 11, 1991, p. 7, AJC archives.

5. Menachem Shalev, "Israel," *AJYB* 93 (1993): 343.

6. *AJC Journal* (March 1991), special edition, Gulf War, p. 1

7. Memo from David Harris to Shula Bahat, January 30, 1990, subject: "Zionism is Racism," describing talks at the Israeli embassy, International Relations Department, box 13, folder "'Zionism Equals Racism' campaign, 1990," AJC archives.

8. "The Efforts to Repeal Resolution 3379. An American Jewish Committee conference Nov. 9, 1990 at the US Mission to the UN" (New York, April 1991), 43 pp., Blaustein Library.

9. For a partial description of AJC's Pacific Rim program, which began in response to manifestations of antisemitism in Japan, see David G. Goodman and Masanori Miyazawa, *The Jew in the Japanese Mind* (New York: Free Press, 1995), 236, 258–59.

10. *AJC Journal* (February 1992): p. 1.

11. Kenneth Jacobson, "The United States, Israel and the Middle East" *AJYB* 93 (1993): 167.

12. "AJC Merges with UN Watch," *AJC Journal* (September 1999): 5.

13. Menachem Shalev, "Israel," *AJYB* 92 (1992): 477.

14. Letter from David A. Harris to James A. Baker III, Secretary of State, May 24, 1991, David A. Harris Executive Director Files (hereafter DAH/EXD), box 1, folder "Baker, James, 1987–1992." Also AJC Board of Governors, "AJC Statement of Principles on the Middle East," June 24, 1991, AJC archives.

15. Interview with Steven Bayme, June 13, 2006.

16. Shalev, "Israel," 440.

17. The first report of this remark came in a *New York Post* article on March 6, 1992, by former New York mayor Ed Koch, who did not name his source. The story was corroborated by columnist William Safire in the *New York Times* on March 19. Safire, who like Koch did not reveal his sources, said that Baker had actually made the remark on two separate occasions, but "it was agreed that everybody would deny that it was ever said."

18. "Second Report Says Baker Cursed Out US Jews," *New York Post*, March 20, 1992. See also JTA, "Baker Denial about Remark on Jews Does Not Entirely Eliminate Doubts." March 9, 1992: clippings found in DAH/EXD, box 1, folder "Baker, James, 1987–1992," AJC archives.

19. Jacobson, "US, Israel, and the Middle East," 164.

20. Letter from David Harris and Alfred H. Moses to George Bush, President of the U.S., September 13, 1991, DAH/EXD, box 1, folder "Baker, James, 1987–1992," AJC archives.

21. Memo, from Jason Isaacson to file, May 12, 1992, "AJC Meeting with Secretary of State James Baker, State Department, Washington, DC, May 8, 1992." DAH/EXD, box 1, folder "Baker, James, 1987–1992," AJC archives. On the State Department side the meeting was attended by Secretary James Baker, Assistant Secretary Margaret Tutweiler, and Dennis Ross. The AJC delegation consisted of Alfred Moses, David Harris, Bob Goodkind, Morton Kornreich, Abe Pollin, Sy Lazarus, Michael Gross, and Jason Isaacson.

22. Mnutes, NEC/AJC Board of Governors Meeting, September 13, 1993, "Reports on the Israel-PLO Recognition Agreement," AJC archives.

23. "AJC Diplomacy," *AJC Journal* (December 1998): 2.

24. Minutes, AJC Board of Governors Meeting, December 6, 1993, "Project Ukraine," p. 1, AJC archives.

25. "AJC Holds Consultations in Eight Countries," *AJC Journal* (May 1995): 2.

26. "Promoting Pluralism in Europe," *AJC Journal* (November 1996): 3.

27. "AJC Brings Asian Americans to Israel," *AJC Journal* (May 1994): 3.

28. "AJC's First Coordinator of Russian-Jewish Affairs," *AJC Journal* (July 2003): 10; AJC annual report, 2004, "Jewish Community," p. 26. See also "Russian Jewish Immigrants in New York City: Status, Identity, and Integration" (Study conducted for the AJC by the Research Institute for New Americans) (New York: AJC, April 2000), which covers interviews with more than one thousand Jewish immigrants from the former Soviet Union, Blaustein Library.

29. Document: Reunification of Germany, February 26, 1990. "Israeli press highlights, a weekly review of the Israeli press by the Israel office of the AJC," in Ira Silverman files (ISX), box 7, folder "Germany West-East unification, etcetera, 1990–1991," AJC archives.

30. Jerome A. Chanes, "Review of the Year, United States," *AJYB* 92 (1992): 208.

31. The American Jewish Committee statement on German Unification, May 17, 1990, AJC annual meeting, AJC archives.

32. Donna Greene, "Germans and Jews Look to the Future," *New York Times*, November 7, 1999.

33. "A Berlin Office," *AJC Journal* (April 1998): 2.

34. "AJC's Role in Eastern Europe," minutes, NEC/AJC Board of Governors Meeting, September 13, 1993, p. 4, AJC archives. In the 1990s AJC had a full-time consultant in Poland named Stanislaw Krajewski.

35. *AJC Journal* (May 1991): 3.

36. "Poland and Polish Americans," *AJC Journal* (February 1997): 4.

37. Lawrence Grossman, "Jewish Communal Affairs," *AJYB* 95 (1995): 165.

38. "Holocaust Reverberations," in AJC annual meeting session, ("Legacy of the Holocaust," reported in *AJC Journal* (July 1999): 2.

39. Address by Robert S. Rifkind, "Remembering the Past, Assessing the Present, Influencing the Future," minutes, NEC/AJC Board of Governors Meeting, Washington, D.C., May 8, 1996, AJC archives.

40. "AJC on Vatican Document," *AJC Journal* (April 1998): 2.

41. "Vatican Statement," *AJC Journal* (June 1998): 3–4.

42. Richard T. Foltin, "Review of the Year: US—Catholics," *AJYB* 101 (2001): 181.

43. Ibid.

44. "AJC Exposes Holocaust Deniers and Falsifiers,"*AJC Journal* (June 1993): 2.

45. "New Manifestations of Antisemitism: Holocaust Denial," report by Mimi Alperin, Minutes, NEC/AJC Board of Governors Meeting, September 13, 1993, p. 4, AJC archives. Also of concern were scholars who did not deny the reality of the Holocaust, but strongly criticized its role in Jewish life and what they saw as the exploitation of it for questionable social and political ends. One of the most notable of such books was *The Holocaust in American Life* by Peter Novick (New York: Houghton Mifflin, 1999). Novick argued that since the 1970s Jewish leaders had been invoking the Holocaust both to deflect criticism of Israeli policies and to construct Jewish identity for young people. See also Alvin H. Rosenfeld, "The Assault on Holocaust Memory," *AJYB* 101 (2001): 3–20.

46. Minutes, NEC/AJC Board of Governors Meeting, September 14, 1998; "The lawsuit of a Holocaust denier," p. 3, AJC archives.

47. Minutes, NEC/AJC Board of Governors meeting, September 14, 1998; "Comments by Deborah Lipstadt," p. 4, AJC archives.

48. Deborah E. Lipstadt, professor of modern Jewish and Holocaust studies at Emory University and director of the Jewish studies program there, also wrote *Beyond Belief: The American Press and the Coming of the Holocaust, 1933–1945* (New York: Free Press, 1986). She recounted her six-year battle with Irving in *History on Trial: My Day In Court With David Irving* (New York: Ecco, 2005).

49. Jerome A. Chanes, "Antisemitism," *AJYB* 105 (2005): 172.

50. "Germany to Compensate Double Victims," *AJC Journal* (April 1998): 3.

51. "AJC Turns Up the Heat on German Industry," *AJC Journal* (February 2000): 1; Richard T. Foltin, "Review of the Year: US," *AJYB* 100 (2000): 184.

52. Alvin H. Rosenfeld, "Anti-Americanism and Anti-Semitism: A New Frontier of Bigotry" (New York: AJC, 2003), 9, Blaustein Library.

53. AJC has published a series of pamphlets on terrorism. These include Yehudit Barsky, "Al-Qa'ida, Iran and Hezbollah: A Continuing Symbiosis," (New York: AJC, January 2004); "Hizballah, a Mega-Terrorist Organization" (New York: AJC, 2005) and "Hezbollah: The Face of Global Terror" (New York: AJC, July 2006). AJC also publishes a regular bulletin, "Counterterrorism Watch."

54. Edward S. Shapiro, *Crown Heights: Blacks, Jews, and the 1991 Brooklyn Riot* (Waltham, Mass.: Brandeis University Press, 2006), xi.

55. Ibid., 4.

56. Ibid., 3–4. A minute-by-minute account of the first night of the riot is available in Richard H. Girgenti, *A Report to the Governor on the Disturbances in Crown Heights* (Albany, N.Y.: New York State Division of Criminal Justice Services, 1993), 1:57–66.

57. Shapiro, *Crown Heights,* 5, citing Guy Trebay, "Mean Streets: Death and Hatred at the Corner of Utica and President," *Village Voice* 36 (September 3, 1991): 32–33; Jerome A. Chanes, "Review of the Year: Intergroup Relations," *AJYB* 83 (1993): 92.

58. Shapiro, *Crown Heights,* 38–40.

59. Ibid., 6.

60. Ibid., 15. The speakers were Al Sharpton and the Reverend Herbert D. Daughtry Sr., pastor of the House of the Lord Pentecostal Church in Brooklyn.

61. Shapiro, *Crown Heights,* 21, citing Frances McMorris, "Summons for the Rebbe?" *Daily News,* September 21, 1991; Clyde Haberman, "Sharpton Tries to Serve Summons in Israel but Doesn't Find His Man," *New York Times,* September 18, 1991.

62. Shapiro, *Crown Heights,* 40; Girgenti, *Report to the Governor.*

63. Jerome A. Chanes "Review of the Year: Intergroup Relations," *AJYB* 94 (1994): 123.

64. Richard T. Foltin, "Review of the Year: National Affairs," *AJYB* 99 (1999): 132–33; Joseph P. Fried, "Mayor Apologizes for City Response to Crown Heights," *New York Times,* April 3, 1998.

65. Zachary Sholem Berger, "New Play About Crown Heights Blames Jews for Deadly Riots," *Forward,* January 30, 2004; Jerome A. Chanes, "Review of the Year: Blacks and Jews," *AJYB* 105 (2005): 165–66.

66. Jerome A. Chanes, "Review of the Year: Intergroup Relations," *AJYB* 93 (1993): 92.

67. A. M. Rosenthal, "On My Mind: Pogrom in Brooklyn," *New York Times,* September 3, 1991.

68. Shapiro, *Crown Heights,* 60.

69. Sidney Zion, "First Cut," *New York Observer,* September 16, 1991; "Crown Heights and the Failure of Jewish Leaders," *New York Post* , July 30, 1993; cited in Shapiro, *Crown Heights,* 59.

70. David A. Harris, letter to the *New York Post,* August 13, 1993, cited in Shapiro, *Crown Heights,* 59.

71. Address, "Race in America: A Challenge for American Jews," Stephen Solender, executive vice president of the New York–UJA Federation, reprinted in *AJC Journal* (December 1991): 1 and 5.

72. "Crown Heights Controversy," *AJC Journal* (February 1993): 2.

73. *AJC Journal* (November 1991), excerpt from "Crown Heights: A Case Study in Antisemitism and Community Relations," by Kenneth S. Stern. The full study is available in the Blaustein Library.

74. Jerome A. Chanes, "Review of the Year: Intergroup Relations: Antisemitism in the Black Community," *AJYB* 91 (1991): 90–91.

75. Address by Gary Rubin on Crown Heights and Leonard Jeffries, minutes, AJC Board of Governors Meeting, September 16, 1991, p. 5, AJC archives.

76. Jacques Steinberg, "CUNY Professor Criticizes Jews," *New York Times,* August 6, 1991. The entire text of the speech, entitled "Our Sacred Mission," is available on Jeffries' personal web page at www.africawithin.com/jeffries/our_sacred_mission.htm.

77. Chanes, "Review of the Year: Intergroup Relations," *AJYB* 94 (1994): 125.

78. "Schooled in Hate: Anti-Semitism on Campus," (New York: Anti-Defamation League, 1997), Blaustein Library.

79. Refutations include Harold Brackman, *Farrakhan's Reign of Historical Error: The Secret Relationship Between Blacks and Jews* (Los Angeles: Simon Wiesenthal Center, 1992); Marc Caplan, *Jew-hatred as History: An Analysis of the Nation of Islam's "The Secret Relationship Between Blacks and Jews"* (New York: Anti-Defamation League, 1994); Nat Trager, *An Empire of Hate: A Refutation of the Nation of Islam's "The Secret Relationship Between Blacks and Jews,"* (Fort Lauderdale, Fla.: Coral Reef Books, 1995); Eli Faber, *Jews, Slaves, and the Slave Trade: Setting the Record Straight* (New York: New York University Press, 1998) and Saul Friedman, *Jews and the American Slave Trade* (New Brunswick, N.J.: Transaction Publishers, 1999). On the Jewish role in the slave trade, see also Seymour Drescher, "Jews and New Christians in the Atlantic Slave Trade," in *The Jews and the Expansion of Europe to the West,* ed. Paolo Bernardini and Norman Fiering (New York: Berghahn, 2001), 439–70; and David Brion Davis, "The Slave Trade and the Jews," *New York Review of Books,* December 22, 1994, pp. 14–17.

80. Minutes, AJC Board of Governors Institute, January 29, 1994, p. 7, AJC archives. See also Kenneth S. Stern, "Dr. Jeffries and the Anti-Semitic Branch of the Afrocentrism Movement" (New York: AJC, August 1991), Blaustein Library.

81. "What to Do on Campus?" *AJC Journal* (December 2002): 2–5.

82. Minutes, NEC/AJC Board of Governors Meeting, "Black-Jewish Relations," September 12, 1994, p. 4, AJC archives. The term *tikkun olam* as a religious obligation of Jews to work for social justice is of "dubious Judaic authenticity." The term appears nowhere in the Hebrew Bible and appears in standard Jewish encyclopedias solely as a concept of Kabbalah, or Jewish mysticism related to the end of days; in the *Zohar* the phrase relates to prayer, not social justice. On "tikkun olam," see Mordecai Lee, "Organization Theory and the Future of Jewish Community Relations Councils," *Jewish Political Studies Review* 12, nos. 1–2 (Spring 2000), published by the Jerusalem Center for Public Affairs.

83. *AJC Journal* (February 1996); Richard T. Foltin, "Review of the Year, US: National Affairs," *AJYB* 97 (1997): 163–64.

84. "Black-Jewish Relations: Across the Racial Divide," *AJC Journal* (September 1997): 2.

85. "Rebuilding a Burned Church," *AJC Journal* (February 1997): 6.

86. Speech by Sholom D. Comay at AJC Board of Governors Institute, January 31, 1991, *AJC Journal* (June 1991): 4.

12. The Second Jewish Continuity Crisis, Pluralism, and Jewish Unity (1990–2006) (pp. 367–397)

1. David Horowitz, "Israel," *AJYB* 96 (1996): 426.

2. Lawrence Grossman, "Jewish Communal Affairs: Religious Affairs," *AJYB* 97 (1997): 194. On divisions between U.S. Jews, particularly those between Orthodox and non-Orthodox movements, see Jack Wertheimer, *A People Divided: Judaism in Contemporary America* (New York: Basic Books, 1993; Waltham, Mass.: Brandeis University Press, 1997); and Samuel G. Freedman, *Jew vs. Jew: The Struggle for the Soul of American Jewry* (New York: Simon and Schuster, 2000). See also most recently, Jack Wertheimer, "All Quiet on the Religious Front? Jewish Unity, Denominationalism, and Postdenominationalism in the United States" (New York: AJC, April 2005).

3. Text of speech by Agudath Israel Executive Director Shmuel Bloom, at eighty-second national convention, November 25, 2004. Rabbi Bloom cited research by Richard Horowitz and Chanan Gordon of Los Angeles that by 2040 there would be approximately 2.5 million Jews left in the United States and one million of them would be Orthodox. Others, he said, were "poised to fall off the demographic cliff." "Who will replace . . . the leaders of the American Jewish Congress and the American Jewish Committee, and B'nai B'rith and the Anti-Defamation League when the non-Orthodox Jewish community's withering to less than one million will take its inevitable toll on those groups?" See also Lawrence Grossman, "Jewish Communal Affairs," *AJYB* 105 (2005): 201.

4. For example, in AJC's 1997 annual survey of American Jewish opinion, 40 percent of those polled considered antisemitism "a very serious problem." Asked whether antisemitism or intermarriage is the greater threat to American Jewish life, 61 percent said antisemitism and 32 percent said intermarriage. In 1998, some 62 percent deemed antisemitism a greater threat than intermarriage. In 2003, some 97 percent of American Jews polled said antisemitism was a problem and 37 percent considered the problem serious.

5. Interview with Steven Bayme, May 25, 2006.

6. The CJF released the study in the spring of 1991. The complete study is available online from the North American Jewish Data Bank (based in Storrs, Connecticut), a collaborative project between the United Jewish Communities and the University of Connecticut's Center for Judaic Studies and Contemporary Jewish Life and Roper Center for Public Opinion Research, at www.jewishdatabank.org/NJPS1990.asp. See also Barry Kosmin and Jeffrey Scheckner, "Jewish Population in the US," *AJYB* 91 (1991): 206; and Sidney Goldstein, "Profile of American Jewry: Highlights from the 1990 National Jewish Population Survey," *AJYB* 92 (1992): 126–27.

7. Grossman, "Jewish Communal Affairs," *AJYB* 93 (1993): 178.

8. Goldstein, "Profile of American Jewry," 77.

9. Among these were American Jewish history surveys by Arthur Hertzberg, *The Jews in America: Four Centuries of an Uneasy Encounter* (New York: Columbia University Press, 1998); and Samuel C. Heilman, *Portrait of American Jews: the Last Half of the Twentieth Century* (Seattle: University of Washington Press, 1995).

10. National Jewish Population Survey, 2000–2001, at North American Jewish Data Bank, http://www.jewishdatabank.org/NJPS2000.asp.

11. For a brief history of Hillel, see Jeff Rubin, "The Road to Renaissance, 1923–2003: Hillel," 20 pages at www. Hillel.org.

12. See www.birthrightisrael.com.

13. See www.peje.org. Partners in the Partnership for Excellence in Jewish Education include the Abramson Family Foundation, the Baker Foundation, the Andrea and Charles Bronfman Philanthropies, Edgar M. Bronfman, the Gottesman Fund, the Harold Grinspoon Foundation, the Jesselson Family, the Jim Joseph Foundation, Robin and Brad Klatt, Fran and Bobby Lent, Charles and Lynn Schusterman, Sheila Schwartz and Family, Michael H. Steinhardt/ Jewish Life Network, Jeffrey and Deborah Swartz, UJA–Federation of New York, Harry and Jeanette Weinberg Foundation, and Leslie H. and Abigail S. Wexner.

14. Address by Michael H. Steinhardt at the general assembly of the United Jewish Communities, Jerusalem, November 19, 2003, www.peje.org/docs/GA03.pdf (6 pages).

15. Lawrence Grossman, "Jewish Communal Affairs," *AJYB* 104 (2004): 111.

16. Gerald B. Bubis, "The Costs of Jewish Living: Revisiting Jewish Involvements and Barriers" (New York: William Petschek National Jewish Family Center, AJC, February 2002), Blaustein Library.

17. While this factor has not been a subject of scientific research, there is much anecdotal evidence to support this thesis. For example, Hank Greenberg once told interviewers that his decision to make baseball a career was a disappointment to his father and a disgrace to his mother. His parents wished him to go to college and become a professional man: "a doctor, a lawyer, or a teacher." In 1935 he told the *Detroit News* "Jewish women on my block . . . would point me out as a good-for-nothing, a loafer, and a bum who always wanted to play baseball rather than go to school. Friends and relatives sympathized with my mother because she was the parent of a big gawk who cared more for baseball . . . than school books. I was Mrs. Greenberg's disgrace." (article by Laurie J. Marzejka, "The Tigers' 'Hammerin' Hank' Greenberg" *Detroit News*, at information.detnews.com/history /story). Greenberg's son, Steve, was raised and identified as a Christian and at Greenberg's funeral there were no Jewish ceremonies at all. On Hank Greenberg, see Edward S. Shapiro, *A Time for Healing: American Jewry since World War II* (Baltimore: Johns Hopkins University Press, 1992), 14.

   David Paymer, a well-known supporting actor in Hollywood who has been nominated for an Academy Award, spoke in 2001 at his guilt in seeking his career. "In my neighborhood, you were expected to become a Jewish doctor or lawyer. . . . I didn't want to let my parents down. I didn't want to be a 'bum.'" Quote is from Naomi Pfefferman, "'State and Main' Actor Plays Jewish Producer," *Jewish Journal of Greater Los Angeles* (January 5, 2001).

18. Address by Steven Bayme, "Enhancing Jewish Identity: Form and Content," *AJC Journal* (September 1991): 4.

19. "Jewish Continuity," account of May 1998 AJC annual meeting, *AJC Journal* (June 1998): 4.

20. Yair Sheleg, "A Diplomatic Campaign Not to Insult Those Married to Non-Jews," *Ha'aretz* (November 11, 2003).

21. Lawrence Grossman, "Jewish Communal Affairs," *AJYB* 101 (2001): 230.

22. Ibid.

23. Lawrence Grossman, "Jewish Communal Affairs," *AJYB* 104 (2004): 95. The article also referred, especially in the New York area, to hardship suffered by Jewish communal institutions in the wake of the attacks of September 11. See Gary A. Tobin, Jeffrey R. Solomon, and Alexander C. Karp, *Mega-Gifts in American Philanthropy: General and Jewish Giving Patterns Between 1995–2000* (San Francisco, Calif.: Institute for Jewish and Community Research, 2003).

24. "The High Cost of Jewish Living," *AJC Journal* (February 1992): 5.

25. Lawrence Grossman, "Jewish Communal Affairs," *AJYB* 104 (2004): 95; *AJYB* 100 (2000): 241.

26. "American Jewish-Israeli Relations Board Meeting," *AJC Journal* (May 1994): 2. Yossi Beilin wrote at length on this philosophy of Diaspora-Israel relations in *His Brother's Keeper: Israel and Diaspora Jewry in the Twenty-First Century* (New York: Schocken, 2000).

27. Letter from David Harris to Israeli President Ezer Weizman, March 21, 1994, *AJC Journal* (May 1994): 3–4.

28. Letter from Ezer Weizman to David Harris, April 6, 1994, *AJC Journal* (May 1994): 3–4.

29. Report on Israeli-American Jewry Relations, Jewish Communal Affairs Commission, December 9, 1982, Jewish Communal Affairs Department, box 22, folder "Israel-American Jewry Relations," p. 2, AJC archives.

30. "AJC Co-Produces Israeli TV Series on American Jewry," *AJC Journal* (November 1995): 4

31. "Why Be Jewish?" and "Jewish Identity Ad Campaign," in *AJC Journal* (December 1992): 6; (February 1993) 5.

32. Interview with Steven Bayme, June 14, 2006.

33. Barry W. Holtz and Steven Bayme, "Why Be Jewish?" (AJC, 1993), Blaustein Library.

34. "Enhancing Jewish Identity," *AJC Journal* (April 1997): 6.

35. "Rabbis Laud AJC on Jewish Continuity," *AJC Journal* (October 1994): 3.

36. Steven Bayme, ed., *Understanding Jewish History: Texts and Commentaries* (Hoboken, N.J.: KTAV Publishing House, 1997).

37. "Report of Agency Activities," by Robert Rifkind, minutes, AJC Board of Governors Meeting, June 23, 1997, AJC archives.

38. "Training Program for Jewish Literacy," *AJC Journal* (February 1998): 6.

39. "Jewish Study," *AJC Journal* (February 1995): 3.

40. AJC annual report, 2004, p. 20, Blaustein Library.

41. "Enhancing Jewish Identity," 6.

42. For a discussion of this debate, and a suggestion that in 1998 the proponents of "outreach" appeared to be winning, see Lawrence Grossman, "Jewish Communal Affairs," *AJYB* 99 (1999): 191. For an overview of AJC's approach to the debate and advocacy of inreach, see Steven Bayme, "Intermarriage and Jewish Leadership in the US" (Jerusalem Center for Public Affairs, April 16, 2006), based on a lecture presented at the Jerusalem Center for Public Affairs, January 9, 2006.

43. Charlotte Holstein, "When Commitments Clash: One Leader's Personal Dilemma," in *The Intermarriage Crisis* (New York: AJC, 1991), 36–37; Elliott Abrams, *Faith or Fear: How Jews Can Survive in a Christian America* (New York: Free Press, 1997), 106–107.

44. Holstein, "When Commitments Clash," 35.

45. Ibid.

46. Minutes, AJC Board of Governors Meeting, May 2, 1991, AJC archives.

47. AJC 1991 Statement on Intermarriage at www.ajc.org under Jewish living: "Jewish continuity and intermarriage."

48. Jack Wertheimer, Charles S. Liebman, and Steven M. Cohen, "How to Save American Jews," *Commentary* 101, no. 1 (January 1996): 47–51.

49. "Statement on the Jewish Future: Texts and Responses," (New York: AJC 1996), at www.ajc.org.

50. Ibid., 7.

51. Ibid., 8.

52. Ibid., 14–15.

53. Ibid., 41. For Wertheimer's views against outreach, see "Surrendering to Intermarriage," *Commentary* 111, no. 3 (March 2001): 25–32.

54. "Statement on the Jewish Future: Texts and Responses" (New York: AJC 1996), 34, at www.ajc.org.

55. Ibid., 31–32.

56. Ibid., 42

57. Ibid., 45. The comment on "Jewish Darwinism" had first been made by Rabbi Jonathan Sacks of Great Britain.

58. Ibid., 45.

59. Ibid., 24–27.

60. Minutes, AJC Board of Governors Meeting, December 8, 1997, "Statement on Jewish continuity," p. 5, AJC archives.

61. AJC, "Jewish Continuity: Policy Statement and Action Plan," adopted by the board of governors, December 8, 1997, at www.ajc.org.

62. Lawrence Grossman, "Jewish Communal Affairs," AJYB 104 (2004): 111.

63. "Widespread Acceptance of Intermarriage," AJC Journal (December 2000): 10.

64. Sylvia Barack Fishman, "Jewish and Something Else: A Study of Mixed Married Families" (William Petschek National Jewish Family Center, AJC, 2001), at www.ajc.org. On the role of gender in determining the dynamics of a mixed-marriage household, see pages 2 and 31–33.

65. Ibid., v.

66. Ibid., 6–7.

67. Ibid., 7–8.

68. AJC press release, "AJC Convenes Communal Leaders, Rabbis, Judaic Scholars to Explore Strategies to Address Intermarriage," February 27, 2001, at www.ajc.org.

69. Fishman, "Jewish and Something Else," vi. See also Steven Bayme, "Intermarriage and Jewish Leadership in the US," Jerusalem Center for Public Affairs, no. 7 (April 16, 2006): 16 pages, at www.jcpa.org.

70. Debra Nussbaum, "Coalition to Fight Intermarriage," Jewish Telegraphic Agency News Bulletin (March 9, 2001).

71. Lawrence Grossman, "Jewish Communal Affairs," AJYB 105 (2005): 207.

72. Joe Berkofsky, "Influential Coalition Wants to End Taboo Against Promoting Inmarriage," Jewish Telegraphic Agency News Bulletin (November 5, 2002).

73. AJC press release, "AJC Study: Young Adults to Reshape US Jewry," April 27, 2006, citing "Young Jewish Adults in the US Today: Harbingers of the American Jewish Community of Tomorrow?" prepared for the AJC by Ukeles Associates, Inc., at www.ajc.org. The results of the study were presented to the centennial annual meeting in May 2006.

74. "AJC Surveys American Jews and the Peace Process," AJC Journal (November 1995): 2–3.

75. Lawrence Grossman, "Jewish Communal Affairs: Prelude to Assassination," AJYB 97 (1997): 176–81.

76. Ibid., 180.

77. Ibid.

78. Richard T. Foltin, "Review of the Year, US, National Affairs," AJYB 97 (1997): 145.

79. David Horowitz and Peter Hirschberg, "Israel," AJYB 97 (1997): 447.

80. Grossman, "Jewish Communal Affairs," "Prelude to Assassination," 183.

81. J. J. Goldberg, Jewish Power: Inside the American Jewish Establishment (Reading, Mass.: Addison-Wesley, 1996), 372–74.

82. "AJC Responds to Rabin Assassination," AJC Journal (February 1996): 3–4.

83. "AJC Publications," AJC Journal (April 1997): 4.

84. Lawrence Grossman, "Jewish Communal Affairs: Conversion Bill Proposed," AJYB 98 (1998): 119–21.

85. Lawrence Grossman, "Jewish Communal Affairs: Israeli Elections," *AJYB* 98 (1998): 192.

86. Peter Hirschberg, "Israel: Israel and American Jews," *AJYB* 98 (1998): 444.

87. Grossman, "Jewish Communal Affairs: Conversion Bill Proposed," 119–21.

88. Ibid., 121.

89. Peter Hirschberg, "Israel: The Conversion Battle," *AJYB* 98 (1998): 458.

90. Ibid., 459.

91. Peter Hirschberg, "Israel," *AJYB* 100 (2000): 472.

92. Lawrence Grossman, "Jewish Communal Affairs: Denominational Developments," *AJYB* 99 (1999): 180.

93. Lawrence Grossman, "Jewish Communal Affairs: The Pluralism Battle," *AJYB* 100 (2000): 229.

94. Grossman, "Jewish Communal Affairs: Denominational Developments," 180.

95. AJC Statement on Judaism, Pluralism and Peoplehood, approved by the AJC National Council/Board of Governors, September 9, 1996, at www.ajc.org.

96. "Jewish Identity Exchange," *AJC Journal* (February 1999): 4.

97. "Religious Pluralism," *AJC Journal* (June 1997): 1, from AJC board of governors resolution, passed May 7, 1997. The ad appeared on May 30.

98. "Statement on the Ne'eman Comission," adopted by the AJC board of governors, December 8, 1997, AJC archives.

99. George E. Gruen, "The US, Israel and the Middle East," *AJYB* 100 (2000): 200–201.

100. Ibid., 190–91: "A realization of his own mortality and fear that the Palestinian movement would splinter after his death added a sense of urgency to Arafat's repeated vow to proclaim an independent Palestinian state with Jerusalem as its capital."

101. Sergio DellaPergola, "World Jewish Population 2005," *AJYB* 105 (2005): 122.

102. Sergio DellaPergola, "Demographic Trends in Israel and Palestine: Prospects and Policy Implications," *AJYB* 103 (2003): 43 and 66.

Selected Bibliography

Abram, Morris B. *The Day is Short: An Autobiography.* New York: Harcourt, Brace Jovanovich, 1982.

Ball, Howard. *The Bakke Case: Race, Education, and Affirmative Action.* Lawrence: University Press of Kansas, 2000.

Bauman, Mark K. *Dixie Diaspora: An Anthology of Southern Jewish History.* Tuscaloosa: University of Alabama Press, 2006.

Cohen, Naomi W. *Encounter with Emancipation: The German Jews in the United States, 1830–1914.* Philadelphia: Jewish Publication Society of America, 1984.

———. *Jacob H. Schiff: A Study in American Jewish Leadership.* Waltham, Mass: Brandeis University Press, 1999.

———. *Not Free to Desist: The American Jewish Committee, 1906–1966.* Philadelphia: Jewish Publication Society of America, 1972.

Dawidowicz, Lucy S. *On Equal Terms: Jews in America, 1881–1981.* New York: Holt, Rinehart and Winston, 1982.

Diner, Hasia R. *The Jews of the United States, 1654–2000.* Berkeley and Los Angeles: University of California Press, 2004.

Dinnerstein, Leonard. *America and the Survivors of the Holocaust.* New York: Columbia University Press, 1986.

———. *Antisemitism in America.* New York: Oxford University Press, 1994.

Dobkowski, Michael N., ed. *Jewish American Voluntary Organizations.* Westport, Conn.: Greenwood, 1986.

Dollinger, Marc. *Quest for Inclusion: Jews and Liberalism in Modern America.* Princeton, New Jersey: Princeton University Press, 2000.

Eban, Abba. Introduction to *The Beirut Massacre: The Complete Kahan Commission Report.* Princeton, N.J.: Karz-Cohl, 1983.

Elazar, Daniel. *Community and Polity: The Organizational Dynamics of American Jewry.* Revised and updated edition. Philadelphia: Jewish Publication Society of America, 1995.

Feingold, Henry L. *A Time for Searching: Entering the Mainstream, 1920–1945.* Baltimore: Johns Hopkins University Press, 1992.

Freedman, Samuel G. *Jew vs. Jew: The Struggle for the Soul of American Jewry.* New York: Simon and Schuster, 2000.

Friedman, Murray. *What Went Wrong? The Creation and Collapse of the Black-Jewish Alliance.* New York: Free Press, 1995.

———, ed. *Commentary in American Life.* Philadelphia: Temple University Press, 2005.

Friedman, Murray, and Albert D. Chernin, eds. *A Second Exodus: The American Movement to Free Soviet Jews.* Waltham, Mass.: Brandeis University Press, 1999.

Gabriel, Richard A. *Operation Peace for Galilee: The Israeli-PLO War in Lebanon.* New York: Hill and Wang, 1984.

Ganin, Zvi. *An Uneasy Relationship: American Jewish Leadership and Israel, 1948–1957.* Syracuse: Syracuse University Press, 2005.

Goldberg, J. J. *Jewish Power: Inside the American Jewish Establishment.* Reading, Mass.: Addison-Wesley, 1996.

Goodman, David G., and Masanori Miyazawa. *Jews in the Japanese Mind: The History and Use of Cultural Stereotype.* New York: Simon and Schuster, 1994.

Goren, Arthur A. *The Politics and Public Culture of American Jews.* Bloomington: Indiana University Press, 1999.

Hacker, Louis M., and Mark D. Hirsch. *Proskauer: His Life and Times.* Tuscaloosa: University of Alabama Press, 1978.

Harris, David A. *In the Trenches: Selected Speeches and Writings of an American Jewish Activist.* 4 vols. Hoboken, N.J.: KTAV Publishing House, 2000.

Helmreich, William B. *Against All Odds: Holocaust Survivors and the Successful Lives they Made in America.* New York: Simon and Schuster, 1992. Reprint, with a new introduction by the author; New Brunswick, N.J.: Transaction Publishers, 1997.

Herzog, Chaim. *The Arab-Israeli Wars: War and Peace in the Middle East.* New York: Vintage, 1984.

Ivers, Gregg. *To Build a Wall: American Jews and the Separation of Church and State.* Charlottesville: University Press of Virginia, 1995.

Jacoby, Tamar. *Someone Else's House: America's Unfinished Struggle for Integration.* New York: Basic Books, 2000.

Kaufman, Menachem. *An Ambiguous Partnership: Non-Zionists and Zionists in America, 1939–1948.* Detroit: Wayne State University Press, 1991.

Kolsky, Thomas A. *Jews Against Zionism: The American Council for Judaism, 1942–1948.* Philadelphia: Temple University Press, 1992.

Kranzler, George. *Hassidic Williamsburg: A Contemporary American Hasidic Community.* Northvale, N.J.: Jason Aronson, 1995.

Lazin, Fred A. *The Struggle for Soviet Jewry in American Politics: Israel versus the American Jewish Establishment.* Lanham, Md.; Lexington Books, 2005.

Lederhendler, Eli, ed. *The Six-Day War and World Jewry.* Bethesda: University Press of Maryland, 2000.

Levkov, Ilya, ed. *Bitburg and Beyond: Encounters in American, German, and Jewish History.* New York: Shapolsky Publishers, 1987.

Liebman, Charles S. *Pressure Without Sanctions: The Influence of World Jewry on Israel Policy.* Rutherford, N.J.: Fairleigh Dickinson University Press, 1977.

Navasky, Victor. *Naming Names.* New York: Viking Press, 1980.

Patterson, James T. *Grand Expectations: The United States, 1945–1974.* New York: Oxford University Press, 1996.

———. *Restless Giant: The United States from Watergate to Bush vs. Gore.* New York: Oxford University Press, 2005.

Proskauer, Joseph Meyer. *A Segment of My Times.* New York: Farrar, Straus, 1950.

Rosenthal, Steven T. *Irreconcilable Differences? The Waning of the American Jewish Love Affair with Israel.* Waltham, Mass.: Brandeis University Press, 2001.

Sachar, Howard M. *A History of Israel: From the Rise of Zionism to Our Time.* 2nd ed. New York: Knopf, 1996.

———. *A History of the Jews in America.* New York: Knopf, 1992.

Sarna, Jonathan D., and David G. Dalin. *Religion and State in the American Jewish Experience*. Notre Dame: University of Notre Dame Press, 1997.

Sarna, Jonathan D., and Jonathan J. Golden. "The Twentieth Century Through American Jewish Eyes: A History of the *American Jewish Yearbook*, 1899–1999." *American Jewish Yearbook* 100 (2000): 3–102.

Schachner, Nathan. *The Price of Liberty: A History of the American Jewish Committee*. New York: American Jewish Committee, 1948.

Shafir, Shlomo. *Ambiguous Relations: The American Jewish Community and Germany Since 1945*. Detroit: Wayne State University Press, 1999.

Shapiro, Edward S. *Crown Heights: Blacks, Jews, and the 1991 Brooklyn Riot*. Waltham, Mass.: Brandeis University Press, 2006.

——. *A Time for Healing: American Jewry since World War II*. Baltimore: Johns Hopkins University Press, 1992.

Silberman, Charles. *A Certain People: American Jews and Their Lives Today*. New York: Summit Books, 1985.

Sklare, Marshall, and Mark Vosk. *The Riverton Study: How Jews Look at Themselves and Their Neighbors*. New York: American Jewish Committee, 1957.

Sorin, Gerald. *A Time for Building: The Third Migration, 1880–1929*. Baltimore: Johns Hopkins University Press, 1992.

Svonkin, Stuart. *Jews Against Prejudice: American Jews and the Fight for Civil Liberties*. New York: Columbia University Press, 1997.

Waldman, Morris D. *Nor By Power*. New York: International University Press, 1953.

Wertheimer, Jack. *A People Divided: Judaism in Contemporary America*. New York: Basic Books, 1993. Pbk. ed., Waltham, Mass.: Brandeis University Press, 1997.

Whitfield, Stephen J. *The Culture of the Cold War*. Baltimore: Johns Hopkins University Press, 1996.

Yakolev, Alexander N. *A Century of Violence in Soviet Russia*. Translated from the Russian by Anthony Austin. With a Foreword by Paul Hollander. New Haven: Yale University Press, 2002.

Index